THE VOYAGES
OF
CAPTAIN WILLIAM DAMPIER

DAMPIER'S VOYAGES

Consisting of a New Voyage Round the World, a Supplement to the Voyage Round the World, Two Voyages to Campeachy, a Discourse of Winds, a Voyage to New Holland, and a Vindication, in answer to the Chimerical Relation of William Funnell

BY

CAPTAIN WILLIAM DAMPIER

EDITED BY

JOHN MASEFIELD

IN TWO VOLUMES

II

LONDON

E. GRANT RICHARDS

7 CARLTON STREET

1906

Printed by Ballantyne, Hanson & Co.
At the Ballantyne Press, Edinburgh

CONTENTS OF VOL. II

PART I

Supplement of the Voyage round the World, continued from Vol. I.

PART II

The Campeachy Voyages

CONTENTS OF VOL. II

PART III

A Discourse of Winds, Storms, Seasons, Tides, and Currents in the Torrid Zone

PART IV

A Voyage to New Holland

PART V

LIST OF MAPS AND ILLUSTRATIONS

VOYAGES AND DESCRIPTIONS

CHAP. IV

Of the Government of Tonquin. The two Kings Boua and Choua; the Revolt of the Cochinchinese, and Original of the present Constitution at Tonquin. Of the Boua's Confinement, and the Choua's or ruling King's Person and Government; and the Treasure, Elephants and Artillery. Their manner of making Gun-powder. Of the Soldiers, their Arms, Employment, &c. Of the Naval Force, their fine Gallies and Management of them. The Watch kept in their Towns, their Justice and punishing of Debtors, and Criminals of all sorts. Of the Eunuch Mandarins: Their Promotion and Dispositions. Of their swearing upon a draught of Hens Blood: and the Trial by bitter Waters in Guinea. Of the Mandarins Entertainments. The Chop-sticks used at Meals; and their kindness to Strangers.

THIS Kingdom is an absolute Monarchy, but of such a kind as is not in the World again; for it has two Kings, and each supreme in his particular way: The one is called Boua, the other Choua; which last Name I have been told signifies Master. The Boua and his Ancestors were the sole Monarchs of Tonquin; tho' I know not whether as independent Sovereigns, or as Tributaries to China, of which they have been thought to have been a Frontier Province, if not a Colony: for there is a great Affinity between them in their Language, Religion, and Customs. These two Kings they have at present, are not any way related in their Descent or Families: nor could I learn how long their Government has continued in the present Form; but it appears to have been for some Successions. The occasion is variously reported; but some give this account of it.

AN. 1688

AN. The Boua's or antient King's of Tonquin, were formerly
1688 Masters of Cochinchina, and kept that Nation in subjection by an Army of Tonquinese constantly kept there, under a General or Deputy, who ruled them. When Cochinchina threw off the Tonquinese Yoak, the King had two great Generals, one in Cochinchina, and another in Tonquin it self. These two Generals differing, he who was in Cochinchina revolted from his Sovereign of Tonquin, and by his Power over the Army there, made himself King of Cochinchina: since which these two Nations have always been at Wars; yet each Nation of late is rather on the defensive part than on the offensive. But when the General who commanded in Cochinchina had been thus successful in his Revolt from under the Boua, the Tonquinese General took the Courage to do so too; and having gained the Affections of his Army, deprived the King his Master of all the Regal Power, and kept it with all the Revenues of the Crown in his own Hands: yet leaving the other the Title of King; probably, because of the great Zeal the People had for that Family. And thus the Kingdom came wholly into the Power of this Tonquinese General, and his Heirs, who carry the Title of Choua; the Boua's of the Ancient Family having only the shadow of that Authority they were formerly Masters of. The Boua lives the Life of a kind of a Prisoner of State, within the old Palace, with his Women and Children; and diverts himself in Boats among his Fish-ponds within the Palace Walls, but never stirs without those Bounds. He is held in great Veneration by all the Tonquinese, and seemingly by the Choua also; who never offers any violence to him, but treats him with all imaginable respect. The People say they have no King but Boua; and seem to have sad Apprehensions of the Loss they should have, if he should dye without an Heir: and whenever the Choua comes into his presence, which is 2 or 3 times in the Year, he useth abundance of Compliments to him, and tells him, that his very Life is at his Service, and that he governs and rules wholly to do him a Kindness: and always gives him the upper Hand.

So also when any Ambassadors are sent from the Emperour of China, they will deliver their Message to none but the Boua, and have their Audience of him. Yet after all this Pageantry, the Boua has only a few Servants to attend him, none of the Mandarins make their Court to him, nor is he allowed any Guards: All the Magistracy and Soldiery, Treasure, and the ordering of all Matters of Peace or War, are entirely at the Choua's disposal; all Preferment is from him, and the very Servants who attend the Boua, are such only as the Choua places about him. Besides these Servants, none are ever suffered to see the Boua, much less Strangers: So that I could learn nothing as to his Person. But as to the Choua, I have been informed that he is an angry, ill-natured, leprous Person. He lives in the second Palace, where he has ten or twelve Wives; but what Children I know not. He governs with absolute Authority over the Subjects, and with great Tyranny: for their Lives, Goods, and Estates are at his Command. The Province of Tenehoa is said to have belonged properly to his Ancestors, who were great Mandarins before the Usurpation. So that he now seems to have a particular value for it, and keeps his Treasure there, which by report, is very great. This Treasure is buried in great Cisterns full of Water, made purposely for that use: and to secure it, he keeps a great many Soldiers there; and commits the charge, both of them and the Treasure, to the Governour of the Province, who is one of his principal Eunuchs.

The Choua has always a strong Guard of Soldiers about his Palace, and many large Stables for his Horses and Elephants. The Horses are about 13 or 14 Hands high, and are kept very fat: there are 2 or 300 of them. The Elephants are kept in long Stables by themselves, each having a peculiar Room or Partition, with a Keeper to dress and feed him. The number of the King's Elephants are about 150 or 200. They are watered and washed every day in the River.

Some of the Elephants are very gentle and governable, others are more indocil and unruly. When these rude ones are to pass through the Streets, though only to be

AN. 1688 watered, the Rider or Dresser orders a Gong or Drum to be beaten before him, to warn People that an unruly Elephant is coming; and they presently clear the Streets and give a passage for the Beast; who will do Mischief to any that are in the way, and their Riders or Keepers cannot restrain him.

Before the Choua's Palace, there is a large Parade, or square place for the Soldiers to be drawn up. On one side there is a place for the Mandarins to sit, and see the Soldiers exercise, on the other side there is a Shed, wherein all the Cannon and heavy Guns are lodged. There be 50 or 60 Iron Guns from Falcon[1] to Demy-Culverin,[2] 2 or 3 whole Culverin[3] or Demi-Cannon,[4] and some old Iron Mortars lying on Logs. The Guns are mounted on their Carriages, but the Carriages of these Guns are old and very ill made. There is one great Brass Gun, much bigger than the rest, supposed to be 8 or 9000 pound weight. It is of a taper bore;[5] of a foot diameter at the Mouth, but much smaller at the Britch. It is an ill-shaped thing, yet much esteemed by them, probably because it was cast here, and the biggest that ever they made. It was cast about 12 or 13 Years ago, and it being so heavy, they could not contrive to mount it, but were beholding to the English, to put it

[1] The falcon was an M.L. iron gun of 2½-inch bore, and flung a 3 lb. ball to a distance of 1500 yards when fired with a full charge (3 lbs. of powder) and elevated 10°. The gun weighed about 6 cwt., and measured about 7 feet in length.

[2] The demi-culverin corresponded roughly to the 9-pounder of the Napoleonic wars. It was a 4-inch M.L. gun, throwing a ball of 9½ lbs. for about a mile and a half, at extreme range (200 yards point blank). It took a charge of 8 lbs., weighed about a ton and a half, and measured 11 feet in length.

[3] The culverin was the forerunner of the Napoleonic 18-pounder. It was a 5 or 5½-inch M.L. gun with a ball of 17½ lbs. and a range of 2500 paces. It weighed rather more than 2 tons, and took a charge of 12 lbs. of powder.

[4] The demi-cannon corresponded to the 32-pounder, the heavy gun with which Trafalgar was fought. The ball was 33½ lbs., the range about a mile, the charge 18 lbs., and the weight rather more than 2 tons. There were "intermediate" guns between the falcon and the demi-culverin. The minion and saker have been described in a previous note. There was also the bastard culverin.

[5] With a bore rather larger at the base or breech than at the muzzle, or, *vice versâ*, as in the present instance.

into the Carriage; where it now stands more for a show then service. But though this is but an ordinary piece of Workmanship, yet the Tonquinese understand how to run Metals, and are very expert in tempering the Earth, wherewith they make their Mould. AN. 1688

These are all the great Guns, that I saw or heard of in this Kingdom, neither are here any Forts, yet the King keeps always a great many Soldiers. 'Tis said that he has always 70 or 80000 constantly in pay. These are most Foot, they are arm'd with Curtans or Swords, and Hand-Guns of 3 foot and an half or 4 foot in the Barrel. The Bore is about the bigness of our Horse Pistols, they are all Match-locks,[1] and they are very thick and heavy. The Soldiers do all make their own Powder. They have little Engines for mixing the Ingredients, and make as small a Quantity as they please. They know not how to corn it, and therefore it is in unequal lumps, some as big as the top of a Man's Thumb, and some no bigger than a white Pea: neither have I seen any Powder well corn'd, that has been made in any of these Eastern Nations.

The Soldiers have each a Cartage Box covered with Leather, after the manner of the West-Indian Privateers; but instead of Paper Cartages, these are filled with small hollow Canes, each containing a load or charge of Powder; which they empty out of the Cane into the Gun; so that each Box has in it, as it were, so many Bandoleers. Their Arms are kept very bright and clean: for which purpose every one of them has a hollow Bambo to lay over the Barrel of his Gun; and to keep the Dust from it as it lies over the wrack in his House. When they march also in rainy Weather, they have another Bambo to cover their Guns. This is large enough to cover the whole Barrel, and very well lackered; so that it is not only handsome, but also preserves the Gun dry.

The Soldiers when they march are led by an Officer, who is Leader of the File; and every File consists of 10 Men: but as I have been informed by one who has

[1] Fired by a match, instead of by percussion.

AN. 1688 seen them march, they don't keep their Ranks in marching. The Soldiers are most of them lusty strong well-made Men: for 'tis that chiefly recommends them to the King's Service. They must also have good Stomachs, for that is a greater recommendation than the former; neither can any Man be entertained as a Soldier, that has not a greater stroke than ordinary at eating: for by this they judge of his Strength and Constitution. For which Reason, when a Soldier comes to be listed, his Stomach is first proved with Rice, the common Subsistence of the ordinary People in this Kingdom: and according as he acquits himself in this first Tryal of his Manhood, so he is either discharged or entertained in the Service. 'Tis reported, that at these Tryals they commonly eat 8 or 9 Cups of Rice, each containing a pint, and they are ever afterwards esteemed and advanced, according to the first Day's Service: and the greatest eaters are chiefly employed as Guards to the King, and commonly attend on his Person. The Province of Ngean breeds the lustiest Men, and the best eaters: for that reason those of that Province are generally imployed as Soldiers. After 30 Years Service a Soldier may petition to be disbanded; and then the Village where he was born must send another Man to serve in his room.

The Horsemen are but few, and armed with Bows, and long Spears or Lances, like the Moors and Turks. Both these and the Foot Soldiers are very dexterous in using their Weapons, and shoot very well either with Gun or Bow; for they are often exercised by shooting at Marks. The King orders a shooting Match once a Year, and rewards the best Marks-man with a fine Coat, or about 1000 Cash, as 'tis called, which is a Summ about the value of a Dollar. The Mark is a white earthen Cup, placed against a Bank. The distance they stand to fire at it is about 80 Yards. He who breaks the first Cup has the finest Coat; for there are others also of less worth and finery for the rest, that have the good Fortune to break the other Cups, or Cash in lieu of them. This is all at the King's Charge, who incourages this exercise very much, as a means to make them good Marks-men; and they generally prove such. They will load and fire the quickest of any People. They draw the Rammer at one Motion,[1] and pouring down the Powder and Bullet, they ram all down at one Motion more. Then they withdraw the Rammer, and put it into its place at 2 Motions more. All the 4 Motions are performed very dexterously and quick: and when they shoot at a Mark, they level, and fire at first Sight, yet very successfully. AN 1688

Though the King of Tonquin has no Forts, yet he keeps always a great many Soldiers on the Frontier Towns of his Kingdom; especially on the S. W. part thereof, to check the Cochinchinese, his implacable Enemies: and though there seldom happens a pitch'd Battle between them, yet there are often Skirmishings, which keep the Soldiers on each side upon their Guards: and sometime there are considerable Excursions made by one or other Party into the Enemies Territories, where they kill, spoil, and bring away what Booty they can find. The King also has always about 30000 near his Person, and quarter'd in or about Cachao, ready on all Occasions. The dry Season is the time for his Armies to take the Field, or go against an Enemy: for in these Countries there is no marching in the Wet Season. When he sends an Army by Land on any Expedition, the General, and other great Officers are mounted on Elephants. These have neat little boarded Houses or Castles fastned on their backs, where the great Men sit in State, secur'd from the Sun or Rain. They have no Field-pieces in their Armies, but instead thereof they carry on Mens Backs Guns that will carry a four ounce Shot. The Barrels of these Guns are about 6 or 7 foot long: but though one Man carries one of them on his Back, yet he cannot hold it out to fire, like small Guns, but rests it on its Carriage, which is another Man's Burden, and they two manage it between them.

[1] The English seem to have "drawn" their rammers in three motions, "shortened" them (or prepared to ram with them) in another three, and "rammed" in from four to seven more. To withdraw and return the rammer the English musketeer needed eleven motions; the whole operation thus requiring more than twenty separate movements.

AN. 1688 The Carriage is only a round piece of Wood, about 4 Inches thick, and 6 or 7 foot long. One end of the Carriage is supported with two Legs, or a Fork of three Foot high, the other rests on the Ground. The Gun is placed on the top, where there is an Iron Socket for the Gun to rest in, and a Swivel to turn the Muzzel any way. From the Britch of the Gun there is a short stock for the Man who fires the Gun to traverse it[1] withal, and to rest it against his Shoulder. The use of these Guns is to clear a Pass, or to fire over the Rivers, when the Enemy is so commodiously placed, that there is no other way to move him; and they are carried by these two Men almost with as much ease as Muskets. In these Land-Expeditions they carry but little Baggage, besides their necessary Arms, Ammunition, and Provender; so that if they are routed they lightly scamper away; and generally in these Countries the Dispute is soon over, for they will not long sustain a smart Onset.

Besides the Soldiers on the Frontiers; and those who attend the King about Cachao, he has many others that keep Guards in several parts of his Kingdom, especially in the great Roads, and on the Rivers. These search all exported Goods, to see that no prohibited Goods are sent out of the Kingdom, especially Arms: and no prohibited Goods brought in. They also look after the Customs, and see that all Goods have paid, before they may pass further. All Travellers are also search'd by them, and strictly examined; and if any Persons are taken only on Suspicion, they are used very severely, till they can clear themselves: so that no disaffected or rebellious Person can stir; without being presently known; and this renders the King very safe in his Government.

The King's Naval-force consists only in a sort of flat-bottom Gallies, and these seemingly designed more for State than Service, except to transport Soldiers from one Place to another. These Vessels are 50, 60, or 70 foot long, and about 10 or 12 foot broad in the waste; and the

[1] To turn it to the right or left in taking aim.

2 ends near as many foot high out of the Water, especially the hinder part or Stern: but the waste or middle of the Vessel is not above 2 foot and an half from the Water, that being the place, by which all the Men go in and out, from thence towards each end, it is gently and very artificially raised to a considerable heighth, so that the whole Fabrick appears very graceful and pleasant, as it moves on the Water. The Head or forepart is not altogether so high as the Stern, neither is there so much cost bestowed on it for Ornament: for though it wants neither carv'd-work or painting, yet 'tis not comparable to that of the Stern, which has great variety of carving, and is curiously lackered and gilded. The Place where the Captain sits in is the Stern, and is neatly covered to keep off the Sun or the Rain, and it being higher than any other part of the Vessel, appears like a little Throne, especially that of the General's Galley. This is more magnificent than the rest, tho' all are built much of one form. From the Stern to the waste, it is covered over with a slight covering, to shelter the Men and their Arms from the Rain in the wet Season, and the scorching Sun in the dry. Before the waste there are places for the Oars on each side, and a plain even Deck for the Rowers to stand by their Tackling. Each Galley carries a small Brass Gun, either Minion or Saker, which is planted afore, and looks out through a Port in the Bow. They have a small Mast[1] and Matt Sail, and they are rowed with from 16 or 20 to 24 Oars.

The Soldiers are always the Men that row, and they are all naked, except that they have a narrow piece of black Cloath like a Sash about their Wastes, which is brought between their Thighs, and tuckt again under their Waste. Every one stands upright behind his Oar, which lies in its notch on the Gunnal, and he thrusts or pushes it forward with a great Strength; and they plunge their Oars all at one instant into the Water, keeping exact Time with each other: and that they may the better do this, there is one that strikes on a small Gong, or a wooden Instrument,

[1] "They have no Masts," according to Baron.

An. 1688 before every stroke of the Oar. Then the Rowers all at once answer with a sort of a hollow noise, through the Throat, and a stamp on the Deck with one Foot, and immediately plunge their Oars into the Water. Thus the Gong and the Rowers alternately answer each other, making a sound that seems very pleasant and warlike to those who are at a small distance on the Water or Shoar.

These Boats draw about 2 Foot and a half Water. They are only serviceable in Rivers, or at Sea near the Shoar, and that in very fair Weather too. They are best in the broad Rivers near the Sea, where they may take the Advantage of the Tides to help them: for though they row pretty swift when they are light, yet when they have 60, 80, or 100 Men on a Board, as sometimes they have, they are heavy and row slowly against the Stream. Nevertheless when there is occasion they must go against the Stream a great way, tho' they perform it with great labour.

The Soldiers in these Vessels are equipt with Bows, Swords, and Lances, and when many of them are sent on any Expedition, they are divided into Squadrons. They are distinguished by their several Flags of different Colours; as appeared by an Expedition they made up the River, against some of their Northern Neighbours, while we were there. There were then about 60 of these Galleys sent out up the River; and they had from 16 to 40 Soldiers in each, all well armed. Their General was called Ungee Comei, who was a great Mandarin, and was the Person appointed by the King to inspect into our English Traffick; being made Director or Protector of the English Factory, who used to speak of him as a generous Man. There were two more great Officers under him, each in a Vessel by himself. These three had Flags of Distinction: the first was yellow, the second blue, the third red or green. They went away from Cachao towards the Mountains, but did not return while we were there: but since we came from thence, I have been informed that the Expedition prov'd fruitless, and that the General Ungee Comei was much disgraced.

When the Galleys are not in Service, they are dragged ashore, and placed in Houses built for that purpose; where they are set upright on their bottoms, made very clean, and kept neat and dry. These Galley-Houses are 50 or 60 paces from the River side; and when they bring the Galleys into them, there is a strong Rope brought round the stern of the Vessel, and both ends stretched along, one on each side: then 3 or 400 Men standing ready with the Rope in their Hands, wait for the signal; which being given by the beat of a Gong, they begin to draw with all their Strength; and making a great shrieking noise, they run her up in a trice into her place. This also is their Soldiers work, who having thus housed all their Galleys, return to their Land-Service.

AN. 1688

Some of the Soldiers are employed also in keeping Watch and Ward, for the Security of private Men, as well as in the King's Business: and the Tonquinese are observed to keep good order in the Night in all Towns and Villages: but more particularly in the great Cities, and especially at Cachao. There every Street is guarded with a strong Watch, as well to keep Silence, as to hinder any disorder. The Watch-men are armed with Staves, and stand in the Street by the Watch-Houses, to examine every one that passeth by. There is also a Rope stretched cross the Street Breast high, and no Man may pass this place till he is examined, unless he will venture to be soundly bang'd by the Watch. These Men can handle their Weapons so well, that if they design Mischief, they will dextrously break a Leg or Thigh-bone, that being the place which they commonly strike at. There is a pair of Stocks by every Watch-House, to secure Night Ramblers in: but for a small piece of Money a Man may pass quiet enough, and for the most part only the poor are taken up. These Watch-men are Soldiers, but belong to the Governour or some other Men of great Power, who will hear no Complaints against them, though never so justly made: and therefore they often put Men in the Stocks at their pleasure, and in the Morning carry them before a Magistrate; who commonly fines the Prisoners to pay somewhat, and be it more or less, it falls part to the

AN. 1688 Magistrate. Neither dares any Man complain of Injustice upon such usage, in this case especially; though his Cause be never so just: and therefore Patience is in this Country as necessary for poor People, as in any part of the World.

But notwithstanding these Abuses, they have one Custom in the administring Justice that is pleasing enough. For if a difference or quarrel at any Time happens between two mean Men, and they are not to be reconciled without going before a Magistrate, he usually considering their Poverty, lays no heavy Mulct on the Offender, but enjoins him this as his Penalty, that he shall treat the injur'd Person with a Jarr of Arack and a Fowl, or a small Porker, that so feasting together, they may both drown all Animosity in good Liquor, and renew their Friendship.

But if it be a Controversy about a Debt, they take a very different Method. For the Debtors are many times order'd to be Prisoners in their Creditor's Houses, where they are beaten, or kept with a Log of Wood made fast to their Legs, to hinder them from running away. These poor Prisoners eat nothing but Rice, and drink Water, and are tyrannically insulted over by their rigid Creditors, till the Debt is satisfied. Their Corporal Punishments upon Malefactors, and sometimes upon others are very severe. Some are loaden with Iron Chains fastened to their Legs, with Logs also like the Debtors but now mentioned. Others have their Necks inclosed between two great heavy Planks made like a Pillory, but moveable, for they carry it about with them where-ever they go, and even when they go to rest they are forced to lye down and sleep in it as they can.

There is another sort of punishing Instrument not unlike this, called a Gongo.[1] This also is made to wear about the Neck, but is shaped like a Ladder. The sides of it are 2 large Bamboes, of about 10 or 12 foot long, with several such rounds or sticks as Ladders have to keep the sides asunder; but much shorter: for the 2 side Bamboes are

[1] The Cangue.

no farther asunder, than to admit of a narrow Room for the Neck; and the 2 rounds in the middle are much at the same distance from each other, on each side the Neck, forming a little Square: through which the Man looks as if he were carrying a Ladder on his Shoulders, with his Head through the rounds. If either of these Yokes were to be taken off in a short time, as in 6, 9, or 12 Hours, it would be no great matter: but to wear one of them a Month, 2, 3, or longer, as I have been informed they sometimes do, seems to be a very severe Punishment. Yet 'tis some Comfort to some, that they have the Liberty to walk abroad where they will: but others are both yoked and imprison'd: and the Prisoners in publick Prisons are used worse than a Man would use a Dog, they being half starved, and soundly beaten to boot.

AN. 1688

They have a particular Punishment for such as are suspected to fire Houses, or who are thought to have occasioned the Fire through their neglect. The Master of the House, where the Fire first breaks out, will hardly clear himself from Suspicion, and the Severity of the Law. The Punishment in this Case is to sit in a Chair of 12 or 14 foot high, bare-headed 3 whole Days successively in the hot scorching Sun: this Chair is set, for his greater disgrace, before the place where his House stood.

Other smaller Crimes are punished with Blows; which we call Bambooing. The Criminal is laid flat on his Belly on the Ground, with his Breeches pluckt down over his Hams: in which Posture a lusty Fellow bangs his bare Breech with a split Bambo, about 4 Fingers broad, and 5 foot long. The number of his Blows are more or less, according to the nature of the Crime, or the pleasure of the Magistrate; yet Money will buy favour of the Executioner, who knows how to moderate his Strokes for a Fee beforehand. Otherwise his Blows usually fall so heavy, that the poor Offender may be lamed a Month or two. After a Man has suffered any of these Punishments, he can never obtain any publick Favour or Employment.

They have no Courts of Judicature, but any single Magistrate issues out his Warrants for the apprehending

AN. 1688 of Malefactors, and upon taking them immediately tries them: and as the Sentence is final, and without appeal, so 'tis no sooner past, but 'tis executed also without more ado. Their Punishment in capital Crimes is usually beheading. The Criminal is carried immediately from the Magistrate's House to his own: for there is no common place of Execution, but the Malefactor suffers near his own House, or where the Fact was committed. There he is placed sitting on the Ground, with his Body upright, and his Legs stretched out: and the Executioner being provided with a large Curtane or Back-Sword, and striking a full Back-Blow on the Neck, at one stroke he severs the Head from the Body; the Head commonly tumbling down into the Owner's Lap, and the Trunk falling backward on the Ground.

Theft is not thought worthy of Death, but is punished with cutting off some Member, or part of a Member, according to the degree of the Offence. For sometimes only one Joint of a Finger is chopt off, for other Crimes a whole Finger, or more, and for some the whole Hand.

The Magistrates and other great Men of this Kingdom are called Mandarins. Most of them in Office about the King are Eunuchs, and not only gelded, but also their Members cut off quite flat to their Bellies. These, as I have been informed, are all very learned Men after their way, especially in the Laws of the Country. They rise gradually by their Merit or Favour, from one Degree to another, as well they who are employed in Civil as in Military affairs: And scarce a Place of Trust or Profit goes beside them. No Man is permitted to walk familiarly about the King's Palace without the Leave of the Eunuch Mandarins; and for this Reason having such free Access to the King themselves, and excluding whom they will, they engross his Favour. This is taken so much to Heart by some, that through Envy and Discontent, they often pine away, as is commonly said, even to Death: And I heard of such an one, who was called Ungee Thuan Ding: Ungee seems a Title of Honour among them. He was a Man of great Learning in the Laws, extremely Politick, and mighty high Spirited. This Man sought all the means imaginable to be preferred, but could not for want of being an Eunuch. He fretted to see his Inferiors raised: but plainly seeing that there was no rising without removing that Objection, he one Day in a Rage took up a sharp Knife, and qualify'd himself effectually. He had a Wife and 6 or 8 Children, who were all in great Fear of his Life: but he was not at all dismayed, tho' in that Condition; and the King advanced him. He was living when I was there, and was a great Mandarin. He had the care of the Armory and Artillery, being great Master of the King's Ordnance. AN. 1688

There was another Mandarin also, one Ungee Hane, who finding himself baffled by the Eunuchs, was forced to make himself one to be upon the level with them. This Gentleman, it seems, was Lord of a Village or two, where both he and his Tenants were often plagued with the domineering Eunuchs; and having born their Malice for some time, and seeing no end of it, he agreed with an expert Gelder to castrate him: For here are many in this Country, who profess this Art, and are so expert at it, that they will undertake to cut a Man of any Age, for so many thousand Cash as the Man is Years old. 'Tis reported, that they first put the Patient into a Sleep: But how long they are curing him after the Operation is over, I know not. I heard of but three Mandarins of any grandeur in the Government, who were not Eunuchs. One was the Governor of the East Province, whose Daughter was married to a Prince of the Royal Family. The other two, who were Governors of Cachao, were also married Men, and had Children, and one of these married the King's Daughter. All the Mandarins rule with absolute Power and Authority in their several Precincts, yet in great Obedience to the King; who is as absolute over them, as they are over the common People.

These Eunuch Mandarins especially live in great State. Many of these have command of the Soldiery, and have Guards attending them at their own Houses: There being a certain number of Soldiers allowed to attend on each

i. 8 Mandarin according to his Quality. They are generally
1688 covetous beyond measure, and very malicious. Some of them are Governours of Provinces, but all are raised to Places of trust and profit.

Once every Year the Mandarins receive an Oath of Allegiance to the King, from all the principal Officers under them. This is done with great Ceremony: they cut the Throat of a Hen, and let the Blood fall into a Bason of Arack. Of this Arack every Man has a small draught given him to drink, after he has publickly declared his sincerity and readiness to serve his Prince. 'Tis esteemed the solemnest tye by which any Man can ingage himself. This way of giving solemn potions to drink, is used also in other Countries, on different occasions. As particularly on the Gold Coast of Guinea; where when Men or Women are taxed for a Crime, be it of what Nature it will, but especially Adultery, and the matter cannot be proved by Evidence, the Fetissero or Priest decides the difference, by giving a potion of bitter Water to the Person accused: which if they refuse to take, they are supposed to be guilty without farther proof: but if they drink it off, the event is said to be, that if the Persons be guilty, this Water immediately swells their bodies till they burst; but if innocent, they are not hurt thereby. What tricks the Fetissero's may play in compounding this Water, I know not; but this kind of Tryal is frequent among them, and seems to be a remainder of the old Jewish Tryal[1] by the Waters of jealousy, spoken of in the 5th Chapter of Numbers. I am not sufficiently inform'd whether the Event of the Tryal be such as it was among the Jews; but it seems they have a strong perswasion of it: and a guilty Person does ordinarily so dread the being brought to this Trial, that for the most part he or she choose rather to suffer the punishment of the Country, which is to be sold to Europeans as Slaves. This potion is called Bitter-water, and 'tis given by way of Trial upon any light suspicion even of a small injury. This account I have

[1] The biblical rite is rather too long for quotation.

had from several who have been in Guinea,[1] but especially from Mr. Canby. AN. 1688

But to return to the Eunuch Mandarins, tho' they are bitter Enemies to those whom they take aversion against, yet on the other Hand, they are as kind to their Favourites, and as complacent to their Visitants, whether Foreigners or others, feasting them often. They love mightily to be visited, esteeming themselves highly honoured thereby. When they treat any, they are best pleased with those who eat and drink heartily; for this they suppose proceeds from their Love and hearty Affection to them: And indeed the Tonquineers in general are very free to their Visitants, treating them with the best Cheer they are able to procure.

In their Entertainments, and at their ordinary Eating, instead of Forks and Spoons, they use two small round Sticks about the Length and Bigness of a Tobacco Pipe. They hold them both in the right Hand, one between the Fore-Finger and Thumb; the other between the Middle-Finger and the Fore-Finger, as our Boys do their Snappers. They use them very dextrously, taking up the smallest Grain of Rice with them; nor is it accounted mannerly to touch the Food after it is drest, with their Hands: And tho' it be difficult for Strangers to use them, being unaccustom'd to them, yet a little use will overcome that Difficulty; and Persons that reside here ought to learn this, as well as other Customs of the Country, that are innocent, that so their Company may be more acceptable. All the Tonquineses keep many of these Sticks in their Houses, as well for their own use, as to entertain Strangers at Meals: They are as ordinarily placed at the Table here, as Knives, Forks, and Spoons are in England: And a Man that cannot dextrously handle these instruments, makes but an odd Figure at their Tables. The richer sort of People, especially the Mandarins, have them tipt with

[1] *Cf.* Richard Jobson's "Description and historicall Declaration of the golden Kingdom of Guinea," in Purchas (ed. Mac Lehose, vol. vi. pp. 315, 316). "This Drinke among them is as much as an Oath, and is called Enchionkenou; which they make of the same greene Herbs whereof they make their Fetissos; and as they say, it hath such a force, that if a Man drinketh it falsely, their Fetisso causeth him to die."

AN. 1688 Silver. In China also these things are constantly used: they are called by the English Seamen Chopsticks. When the Eunuch Mandarins dye, all their Riches fall to the King, who as Heir presently seizeth on their Estates, and by it gets vast Riches: For there is but little Money in the Kingdom, but what falls into the Clutches of these Birds of Prey. This probably may be one Reason why the King is for preferring none but them; for they are excellent Spunges for him: and whatever some have said of their Love to Justice, I could never learn that they deserve that Character: But through their Oppression, and injurious Dealings, trading is discouraged, and the Country is kept Poor, which otherwise might be a flourishing Kingdom. After all, as very Eunuchs as these Mandarins are, yet they are as great Admirers of the Female Sex as any Men, and not satisfied without them, but they all keep several handsome young Wenches to dally and spend their time withal. They also love to be courted by Strangers to favour them with a Miss of their procuring. Nothing will engage them more than to petition them on this account; and the Person thus sollicited will not fail to procure a young Damsel for his Friend, be it but for a Night or two, or for 4 or 5 Months. Ever afterwards he will take a more than ordinary Care of the Persons he has thus brought together, and their Affairs; and this base sort of Office is here accounted very decent and honourable. Yet the common Baudy-houses, tho' extreamly rife here, are by all of them accounted hateful and scandalous.

CHAP. V

Some Vessels sent from Cachao to Tenan to fetch Rice. A Rencounter with some suppos'd Robbers. Cash, a sort of Coin, and Pearl-Oysters. The Author's second Journey up to Cachao: Of the Pagoda's and Funeral Tower and Feast he met by the way. The French Bishops and Missionaries at Hean, their House, the Author's entertainment there, and discourse with one of their Priests. The state of their Mission, and of Christianity, in these Idolatrous Countries. His making of Gun-Powder. He goes on from Hean to Cachao, and after a short stay there, back again to the Ships. Of the Improvements that might be made of our English Factory here. The Author's departure from Tonquin.

AN. 1688

I HAVE already spoken of my first going up the River to Cachao, and my returning back again to our Ships after a few days. There I lay on board for a great while, and sickly for the most part; yet not so, but that I took a boat and went ashore one where or other almost every day: and by this means I took as particular notice as I could of the Country, and have supplied my own observations with those of our Merchants residing there, and other Persons of Judgment, and Integrity.

During this interval, Rice being dear at Cachao, as it had been for some time, both our Merchants and Natives were for making up a Fleet of small Vessels, to fetch Rice from the Neighbouring Provinces, both for their own use and to supply the Markets: and they never go in single Vessels, for fear of Pirates, who infest the Coast with their Canoas, and shelter themselves among several little Islands, lying at the edge of the East Province, and bordering upon the Province of Tenan, whither these Merchants were bound.

Captain Weldon was one who concerned himself in this

An. 1688 expedition, hiring a Vessel and Seamen of the Tonquinese, and sending some of his own Men with them as a Guard, among whom I would very fain have gone, had I not been indisposed. Mr. Ludford, who had liv'd sometime at Cachao before our arrival, was another Undertaker, and went himself on board the Bark he had hired; but Captain Weldon staid behind at the City, yet took care to get a Commission from the Governour of the East-Province for his Vessel. In the Commission 'twas exprest, that his Boat should be armed with Guns, or other Weapons, and that his Men should resist any that came to oppose them, or any Vessels in their Company; and that they might kill and destroy any Robbers that they met with. The Passage to Tenan lay most within Land, thro' Creeks and narrow Channels, among the Islands before-mentioned, which are so many, and lye on the East-side of the Bay so thick together, and so nigh the shoar, that at a small distance off at Sea they appear to be part of the Main. This little Archipelago lies within the precincts of the Governour of the East-Province, from whom Captain Weldon had his Commission, and who was a very great Man in the Court of Tonquin. When the Fleet came to this place, some who lay here came forth; and they concluded they must be the Pirates, come to seize their Prey as at other times. These always choose rather to take the outward-bound Vessels, because then they have all of them Cash or Money aboard to purchase their Ladings; but in their Returns they would have only Rice, which these People do not so much regard. At this time Captain Weldon's Dutch Pilot, the chief Man whom he sent in his Bark, was aboard Mr. Ludford's: And when the supposed Pirates came up, Mr. Ludford and he made the Seamen row the Bark to meet them, and in a short time got so near, that they fired at them. These Men not expecting to have met such a Reception, for the Tonquinese have no Guns, but in the King's Gallies, thought to save themselves by Flight: but were so eagerly pursued by Mr. Ludford, that at last they yielded to his Mercy, after they had lost one Man in Fight. He, joyful of this Success, secured the Prisoners, and made the best of his Course to the next Town on the Coast in his way; there delivering up his Prisoners to the Magistrates, and giving a full Relation of the Action. He expected a Reward for his Pains, or at least to be highly applauded for it; but found himself mistaken. For the Prisoners obstinately denying what was alledged against them by Mr. Ludford, saying they were poor Fishermen, they were immediately acquitted as very honest Persons, and Mr. Ludford was accused for committing a Riot on Men who were about their lawful Occasions. Mr. Ludford brought many of the Natives, that were in his Company, to justify what he had done, but to no Purpose; for he was fined 100000 Cash, as our Merchants call it, for the Man that was killed. Cash are a small kind of Copper-Money: and 'tis the only Coin they have of their own, if it be their own, and not rather brought them from China. They rise and fall in value according to the Want or Plenty of them, or as the Women-exchangers can manage them: But at this Time they were at the Rate of a Dollar a thousand; so that his Fine was 100 Dollars. When Mr. Ludford saw how hard it was like to go with him, he thought to clear himself, or lessen his fine, by bringing Captain Weldon into the Snare; saying that he had no Guns in his Bark, but made use of Captain Weldon's, and that Captain Weldon's Pilot was aboard his Vessel, and assisted in the Action. But neither did this help him: for upon trying the matter at Cachao, whither 'twas carried by Appeal, Captain Weldon's Commission saved him: so that Mr. Ludford was forced to pay the Money, which was more than he got by the Voyage. This might be a warning to him, how he meddled with Tonquin Pirates again; for it was not enough for him to plead that they came with an Intent to rob him. Indeed if he had been robbed, he might have been pitied by the Magistrates on Complaint of his Misfortune: But yet it is very probable, that if he should have taken them in the very Fact, possest of his Goods, those Vermin would have had one Hole or another to creep out at; so corrupt are the great Men of this Kingdom. And indeed 'tis not improbable that these Fellows were Fisher-

AN. 1688

AN. 1688 men, and going about their Business: For there is good Fishing in all the Bay of Tonquin clear round it, and there are many Boats that go out a Fishing, and the Fishermen are generally very honest and harmless Men; except now and then, they attempt to make a Prize of some poor Vessel they meet, and can overcome by their Numbers without Fighting; for such an one they board, and strip all the Men naked even to their Skin. Among these Islands also, by report, there are Plenty of Pearl Oysters, that have good Pearls in them; but the Seamen are discouraged from fishing for them by the King, for he seizeth on all he finds. But this by the way; nor was any thing else observable in this Voyage to Tenan.

These vessels were 5 or 6 weeks in their Voyage to and from Tenan: And at their return Captain Weldon's Bark went not up to Cachao with the Rice, but unladed it into our Ship to supply us. Soon after this I went a second time up to Cachao, not in a Boat as before, but on Foot along the Country, being desirous to see as much of it as I could: and I hired a Tonquinese for about a Dollar to be my Guide. This, tho' but a small matter, was a great deal out of my Pocket, who had not above 2 Dollars in all, which I had gotten on board, by teaching some of our young Seamen Plain Sailing.[1]

This was all I had to bear my own charges and my Guides; and 'twas the worse with me, because I was forced to make short Journeys every Day by Reason of my Weakness: It was about the latter end of November 1688, when we set out. We kept on the East-side of the River, where we found the Roads pretty dry, yet in some places dirty enough. We ferryed over several Creeks and Brooks running into the great River, where are Ferry-Boats always plying, which have a few Cash for their Fare. The Fever and Ague which I brought with me from Achin was gone; yet the Fruits I eat here, especially the small Oranges, brought me into a Flux. However though I was but weak, yet I was not discouraged from this Journey, being

[1] One of the simplest calculations by which a ship's position may be determined.

weary of lying still, and impatient of seeing somewhat that might further gratify my curiosity. AN. 1688

We found no Houses of Entertainment on the Road, yet at every Village we came to we got House-room, and a Barbecue of split Bamboes to sleep on. The People were very civil, lending us an earthen Pot to dress Rice, or any thing else. Usually after Supper, if the Day was not shut in, I took a ramble about the Village, to see what was worth taking notice of, especially the Pagoda of the place. These had the Image of either an Horse, an Elephant, or both, standing with the Head looking out of the Doors: The Pagodas themselves were but small and low. I still made it dark Night before I returned to my Lodging, and then I laid me down to sleep. My Guide carried my Sea-Gown, which was my covering in the night, and my Pillow was a Log of Wood: But I slept very well, tho' the weakness of my Body did now require better accommodation.

The third day after my setting out, about 3 a Clock in the afternoon, I saw before me a small Tower; such as I mentioned before, as erected for a time in honour of some great Person deceased. But I knew not then the meaning of it, for I had not seen the like before in the Country. As I came nearer to it, I saw a Multitude of People, most of them Men and Boys; and coming nearer still, I saw a great deal of Meat on the Stalls, that were plac'd at a small distance from the Tower. This made me conclude that it was some great Market, and that the Flesh I saw was for sale: Therefore I went in among the Crowd, as well to see the Tower as to buy some of the Meat for my Supper, it being now between 4 and 5 a Clock in the Afternoon. My Guide could not speak English, neither could I speak the Tonquinese Language: So I asked him no questions about it; and he too went readily in with me; it may be not knowing my intent was to buy. First I went round the Tower and viewed it: It was four-square, each side about 8 foot broad: at the Ground the heighth of it was about 26 foot, but at the top somewhat narrower than at the bottom. I saw no door to enter into

An. 1688 it: it seemed to be very slightly built, as least covered with thin boards, which were all joyned close together, and painted of a dark reddish colour. I then went on to the Stalls, which had Sheds built over them: And there I viewed the Fruits and Flesh, each of which was ranged in order apart. I past by Abundance of Oranges packt up in Baskets, which I think were the fairest I ever saw, and for Quantity more than I had seen gathered all the Time I was at Tonquin. I past by these, and seeing no other Fruit, I came to the Flesh-Stalls, where was nothing but Pork, and this also was all cut into Quarters and Sides of Pork: I thought there might be fifty or sixty Hogs cut up thus, and all seemed to be very good Meat. When I saw that there was none of it in small pieces, fit for my use, I, as was customary in the Markets took hold of a Quarter, and made Signs to the Master of it, as I thought, to cut me a Piece of two or three Pound. I was ignorant of any Ceremony they were about, but the superstitious People soon made me sensible of my Errour: For they assaulted me on all Sides, buffeting me and renting my Cloaths, and one of them snatched away my Hat. My Guide did all he could to appease them, and dragg'd me out of the Crowd: Yet some surly Fellows followed us, and seemed by their Countenance and Gestures to threaten me; but my Guide at last pacifyed them and fetched my Hat, and we marched away as fast as we could. I could not be informed of my Guide what this meant; but sometime after, when I was return'd to our Ship, the Guide's Brother, who spoke English, told me, it was a Funeral Feast, and that the Tower was the Tomb which was to be burned; and some English Men who lived there told me the same. This was the only Funeral Feast that ever I was at among them, and they gave me cause to remember it: but this was the worst Usage I received from any of them all the time I was in the Country. When I was out of this trouble, my Guide and I marched forwards. I was both weary and hungry, and I think my appetite was raised by seeing so much Food: For indeed at first sight of it I concluded to have had a good Supper; but now I was likely to sup only on Rice, or a Yam roasted, and two Eggs, as I us'd to do. For tho' there were Fowls to be bought at every House where I lay, yet my Pocket would not reach them; and for other Flesh, there was none to be had, unless my way had lain thro' the Town when it was Market-day with them. AN. 1688

Two Days after this I got with much ado to Hean, for my Flux encreased, and my strength decreased. I presently made towards the French Bishops, as the likeliest Place for me both to rest at, and get larger Informations of the Country, from the European Missionaries, whose Seat it is. The Bishop's Palace is a pretty neat low House, standing at the North-end of the Town, by the side of the River. 'Tis encompassed with a pretty high Wall, and has a large Gate to enter at. The Gate stands fronting to the Street, and runs up with Houses on both sides, and ends at the Palace. Within the Wall there is a small Yard, that goes round the Palace; and at the farther End of the Yard there are small lodging-rooms for the Servants, and other necessary Offices. The House it self is not very large nor high; it stands not in the middle of the Yard, but rather nearest the Gate, which Gate is open all day, but shut in the Night. That part that fronts the Gate, has a pretty neat Room, which seems to be designed for the reception of Strangers: for it has no communication with any other Room in the House, tho' joyned to it as one building: the Door by which you enter it, fronts to the Gate, and this Door also stands open all the day.

When I came hither I entred the Gate, and seeing no Body in the Yard, I went into that Room. At the Door thereof, I found a small Line hanging down, which I pulled; and a Bell ringing within, gave notice of my being there: yet no Body appearing presently, I went in and sate down. There was a Table in the middle of the Room, and handsome Chairs, and several European Pictures hung upon the Walls.

It was not long before one of the Priests came into the Room to me, and received me very civilly. With him I had a great deal of Discourse: He was a French Man by

AN. 1686 Nation, but spoke Spanish and Portuguese very well. It was chiefly in Spanish that we entertained each other, which I understood much better than I could speak: yet I ask'd him Questions, and made a shift to answer him to such Questions as he asked me; and when I was at a loss in my Spanish, I had recourse to Latin, having still some smatterings of what I learnt of it at School in my youth. He was very free to talk with me, and first asked me my business thither? I told him that my business was to Cachao, where I had been once before; that then I went by Water, but now I was moved by my curiosity to travel by Land, and that I could not pass by any Europeans without a Visit, especially such a famous place as this. He asked me many other Questions, and particularly if I was a Roman Catholick? I told him no; but falling then into a Discourse about Religion, he told me what Progress the Gospel was like to make in these Eastern Nations. First he began with the Nicobar Islands, and told me what I have related of that matter, in the 17 Chapter of my "Voyage round the World," page 464, for this was the Person I there quoted, and from whom I had that Relation; as he told me he had it from the Friar, who wrote to him from Fort St. George. But that Friar having been a Passenger in Captain Weldon's Ship, from one of the Nicobar Islands to Fort St. George, I askt the Captain's Opinion of that relation since my writing that Book, and he gave me a quite contrary account of the People of Nicobar; that they were a very perverse, false and thievish People, and did not deserve the good Character the Friar gave of them.

But to proceed with the discourse I had with the French Priest at Hean. He told me, that in Siam the Gospel was in a very fair way to receive incouragement by the means of a French Bishop there, and several Ecclesiasticks he had with him there to assist him: That the great Minister of State, Constant Falcon, had embraced the Romish Faith; and that the King was very much inclined to it, the Courtiers also seeming well enough pleased with it. Insomuch that 'twas hop'd that in a short Time the whole Nation would be converted: And that though the Country People in general were against it, yet by the example of the King and his Court, the rest might come over by degrees; especially because the Priests had free Toleration to use their endeavours. As for Tonquin, he told me that the People in general were inclined to embrace the Christian Faith, but that the Government was wholly averse to it: that the Missionaries who lived here did not openly profess to be Teachers of their Doctrine, but that they lived here under the notion of Merchants, and not as Clergy-Men; that this was a great Obstacle to Christianity, yet nevertheless they found ways to draw the People from their Ignorance: that at present they had about 14000 Converts, and more coming in daily. He told me, that here were two Bishops, I think both French Men; one of them was entitled the Bishop of Ascalon, the other of Auran; and that here were ten Priests of Europe, and three more of the Natives of Tonquin, who had been ordained Popish Priests. But since I have been informed, that these French Bishops were not suffered to live at Cachao; neither may they at any time go thither without a Licence from the Governour; and such a Licence also must be procured by the Favour of some Mandarin who lives at Cachao, for whom the Bishop or other Missionary is to perform some trivial Work or other. For the Missioners living here are purposely skilled in mending Clocks, Watches, or some Mathematical Instruments, of which the Country People are ignorant; and this gives them the opportunity of being often sent for to Cachao by the Mandarins: And when they are there, a small Job that would not require above 5 or 6 Hours to perform, they will be twice as many days about, pretending great difficulty in the work; by which means they take their liberty privately to teach their Disciples that live there; and then also they enjoy themselves with the English and Dutch Merchants, to whom they are always welcome.

AN. 1688

As to the Converts these People have made, I have been credibly informed that they are chiefly of the very

poor People: and that at the same time their Alms of
1688. Rice have converted more than their preaching: and as to those also, who have been converted, as they call it, that is, baptized and wear Images and believe in the Pope, they have fallen off again as fast as they grew numerous, and would no longer be Christians than while the Priests administred Food to them. Yet I cannot think but that these People, who have such Notions of a supreme Deity, might by the industry and example of good Men be brought to embrace the Christian Faith. But as things stand at present, it seems very improbable that Christianity should fructify there: For as the English and Dutch in these Parts of the World are not zealous Lovers to gain Reputation to their Religion, so are the other Europeans, I mean the Missionary Priests, especially the Portuguese, but very blind Teachers. But indeed as the Romanists are the only Men who compass Sea and Land to gain Proselytes, so they may seem to have one Advantage over Protestant Ministers in these Idolatrous Countries, that they present them with such kind of Objects for Religious Worship as they have been used to already: For the exchange is not great from Pagan Idols to Images of Saints, which may serve altogether as well for the poor Souls they convert, who are guided only by Sense. But then even here also, these People having been bred up in the Belief of the Goodness of their own Gods or Heroes, they will more hardly be brought over to change their own Idols for new ones, without some better Arguments to prove these to be more valuable, than the Missionaries ordinarily are able to afford them: And if I may freely speak my Opinion, I am apt to think, that the gross Idolatry of the Papists is rather a Prejudice, than Advantage to their Missions, and that their first care should be to bring the People to be virtuous and considerate, and their next, to give them a plain History and Scheme of the Fundamental Truths of Christianity, and shew them how agreeable they are to natural Light, and how worthy of God.

But to return to the French Priest; he at length asked me if any of our English Ships brought Powder to sell?

I told him, I thought not. Then he asked me if I knew the Composition of Powder? I answered that I had Receipts how to make either Cannon or fine Powder,[1] and told him the manner of the Composition. Said he, I have the same Receipts from France, and have tryed to make Powder, but could not; and therefore I think the fault is in our Coals. Then he asked me many Questions about the Coals, what were proper to be used, but that I could not satisfie him in. He desired me to try to make a Pound, and withal told me, that he had all the Ingredients, and an Engine to mix them. I was equally persuaded to try my Skill, which I had never yet tried, not knowing what I might be put to before I got to England; and having drank a Glass or two of Wine with him, I went to work; and it succeeded so well, that I pleased him extremely, and satisfied my own desire of trying the Receipt, and the Reader shall have the History of the Operation, if he pleases. He brought me Sulphur and Salt-petre, and I weighed a Portion of each of these, and of Coals I gathered up in the Hearth, and beat to Powder. While his Man mixed these in a little Engine, I made a small Sieve of Parchment, which I pricked full of Holes, with a small Iron made hot, and this was to corn it. I had two large Coco-nuts to roul in the Sieve, and work it thro' the Holes to corn it. When it was dry we proved it, and it answer'd our Expectation. The Receipt I had out of Captain Sturmey's *Magazin*[2] of Arts.

AN. 1688

The being so successful in this put me afterwards on the renewing of Powder at Bencouli, when I was there Gunner of that Fort. There being then about 30 Barrels

[1] Cannon, ordnance, or corn powder was generally made as follows: To five or six parts of refined saltpetre, one part of good alder charcoal, and the same quantity of fine yellow sulphur. The ingredients were braised together in a mortar which was kept wet with brandy. When the mixture was complete the stuff was dried and sifted. Fine powder, for priming or for small-arms, needed a larger proportion of saltpetre.

[2] Captain Samuel Sturmey, author of "The Mariner's Magazine." The third edition of this work (the only edition I have handled) was published in 1684, with amendments by J. Colson. It is an instructive and entertaining work, containing a number of receipts and "wrinkles in navigation." Sturmey was something of a poet. His portrait is that of a handsome, melancholy gentleman. It is marked with a curious mystical symbol.

AN. 1688 damnified, which was like mud, they took it out of the Cask, and put it into earthen Jars, that held about 8 Barrels a piece. These they call Montaban Jars, from a Town of that name in Pegu, whence they are brought and carried all over India. In these 'twas intended to send the Powder to Fort St. George, to be renewed there: But I desired the Governour to let me first try my skill on it, because we had but little Powder in the Fort, and might have wanted before any returns could be expected from thence. The Salt-petre[1] was sunk to the bottom of the Jars, but I mixt it and beat it all together, and corned it with Sieves which I made of my own old Parchment Draughts. I made thus 8 Barrels full of very good Powder before I went from thence. The French Priest told me in conclusion, that the Grandees make all their own Powder; and since I have been informed, that the Soldiers make Powder, as I have already said.

I spent the remainder of the Day in the Palace with the Priest. He told me that the Bishop was not well, otherwise I should have seen him: And that because it was a Fish-day, I could not expect such Entertainment, as I might have had on another Day; yet he ordered a Fowl to be broiled for my Dinner, and I dined by my self. In the Evening he sent me out of the Palace, desiring to be excused, that he could not entertain me all Night: yet he ordered his Man to lodge me in a Tonquinese Christian House not far from thence. The People were civil, but very poor, and my Lodging such as I had met with on the Road. I have since been told, that the new Christians come to do their Devotion in the Palace at Night, and for that Reason probably, I was so soon dismist.

I was now again pretty well refreshed, and might have gone to Cachao City a foot: but fearing my strength, I chose to go by Water. Therefore I sent back my Guide: yet before he departed back to our Ships, he bargained with a Tonquinese Waterman for my Passage to Cachao.

The Tide not serving presently to imbark, I walked

[1] It had this property. Aboard ships of war the powder-casks had to be turned at least once a month in order that the nitre should not separate.

about the Town, and spent the Day in viewing it: in the Evening I embarked, and they choose an Evening for coolness, rowing all Night. The boat was about the bigness of a Gravesend Wherry, and was used purposely to carry Passengers, having a small covering over-head to keep them dry when it rained. There were 4 or 5 more of these Boats, that went up this Tide full of Passengers. In our Boat were about 20 Men and Women, besides 4 or 6 that rowed us. The Women chose their Places and sat by themselves, and they had much respect shewed them: But the Men stowed close together, without shewing any respect more to one than to another, yet all very Civil. I thrust in among the thickest of them at first, but my Flux would not suffer me to rest long in a Place. About Midnight we were set ashore to refresh ourselves at a Baiting-Place, where there were a few Houses close by the Rivers Side, and the People up, with Candles lighted, Arack and Tea, and little Spits of Meat, and other Provisions ready drest, to receive us. For these were all Houses of Entertainment, and probably got their living by entertaining Passengers. We stayed here about an Hour, and then entered again on our Boat, and rowed forwards. The Passengers spent the Time in merry Discourse, or Singing, after their Way, tho' to us it seems like crying; but I was mute for want of a Person I could converse with. About 8 or 9 a Clock the next Day I was set ashore: the rest of the Passengers remained in the Boat, but whither they were bound I know not, nor whether the Boat went quite up to Cachao. I was now 5 or 6 Miles short of the City, but in a good Path: for the Land here was pretty high, level and sandy, and the Road plain and dry, and I reached Cachao by Noon. I presently went to one Mr. Bowyers House, who was a free Merchant, with whom Captain Weldon lodged, and staid with them a few Days; but so weak with my Flux, which daily encreased, that I was scarce able to go about, and so was forced to learn by others, in a great Measure, several particulars relating to this Place. This my weakness, joined with my disappointment, for I found that I was not like to be employed in any Voyage to the Neighbouring

AN. 1688

AN. 1688 Countries, as it had been proposed to me, made me very desirous of returning back again, as soon as might be: and it happened opportunely, that Captain Weldon had by this time done his Business, and was preparing for his Departure.

I went therefore down the River again to our Ships, in a Vessel our Merchants had hired, to carry their Goods aboard from Cachao. Among other freight, there were 2 Bells of about 500 weight each, which had been cast at Cachao by the Tonquinese, for my Lord Falcon, the King of Siam's chief Minister of State, and for the use of some of the Christian Churches in Siam. The Person who bespoke them, and was to carry them, was Captain Brewster, who had not very long before come from Siam in a Ship of that King's, and had been cast away on the Coast of Tonquin, but had saved most of his Goods. With these he traded at Cachao, and among other Goods he had purchased to return with to Siam, were these 2 Bells, all which he sent down to be put on Board Captain Weldon's Ship. But the Bark was no sooner come to Hean, in going down the River, but the Governor of Hean's Officers came on Board the Bark and seized the 2 Bells in Behalf of the chief of the English Factory; who understanding they were designed for the King of Siam, which they were not so sure of as to the rest of the Goods, and the English being then at War with the Siamers, he made this his pretence for seizing them, and got the Governor to assist him with his Authority: and the Bells were accordingly carried ashore, and kept at Hean. This was thought a very strange Action of the chief of the Factory to seize Goods as belonging to the King of Siam, while they were in a River of Tonquin: but he was a Person but meanly qualified for the Station he was in. Indeed had he been a Man of Spirit, he might have been serviceable in getting a Trade with Japan, which is a very rich one, and much coveted by the Eastern People themselves as well as Europeans. For while I was there, there were Merchants came every Year from Japan to Tonquin; and by some of these our English Factory might probably have settled a Corespondence and Traffick, but he who was little qualified for the Station he was in, was less fit for any new Undertaking: and tho' Men ought not to run inconsiderately into new Discoveries or Undertakings, yet where there is a prospect of Profit, I think it not amiss for Merchants to try for a Trade, for if our Ancestors had been as dull as we have been of late, 'tis probable we had never known the way so much as to the East-Indies, but must have been beholden to our Neighbours for all the product of those Eastern Nations. What care was formerly taken to get us a Trade into the East-Indies, and other Countries? What Pains particularly did some take to find out the Muscovites by doubling the North Cape, and away thence by land Trade into Persia? but now, as if we were cloy'd with Trade, we sit still contented, saying with Cato, *Non minor est virtus quam quærere parta tueri.* This was the Saying of an eminent Merchant of the East-India Company to me: but by his leave, our Neighbours have encroached on us, and that in our times too. However, 'tis certainly for the Interest of our Merchants to employ fit Men in their Factories, since the Reputation of the Company riseth or falls by the discreet Management, or the ill Conduct of the Agents. Nor is it enough for the chief of a Factory to be a good Merchant, and an honest Man: For tho' these are necessary Qualifications, yet the Governour, or chief of the Factory ought to know more than barely how to buy, sell, and keep Accompts: Especially where other European Merchants reside among them, or trade to the same Places; for they keep a diligent Eye on the Management of our Affairs, and are always ready to take all Advantages of our Mis-improvements. Neither ought this Care to be neglected where we have the Trade to our selves, for there ought to be a fair Understanding between us and the Natives, and care taken that they should have no reason to complain of unjust dealings, as I could shew where there has been; but 'tis an invidious Subject, and all that I aim at is to give a caution. But to the Matter in Hand, it seemed to me that our Factory at Tonquin might have got a Trade with Japan: and to China as much as they pleased. I confess the continual Wars between Tonquin and Cochinchina, were enough to obstruct

AN. 1688

AN. 1688 the Designs of making a Voyage to this last: and those other Places of Champa and Cambodia as they are less known, so was it more unlikely still to make thither any profitable Voyages: yet possibly the Difficulties here also is not so great, but Resolution and Industry would overcome them; and the Profit would abundantly compensate the Trouble.

But to proceed, we found there was no recovering the Bells: so we fell down from Hean to our Ships: and Captain Weldon coming to us in a few Days, and Captain Brewster with him, to go as a Passenger in his Ship, together with one or two more; and 2 Ships who came with us being also ready for their Departure, we all weighed Anchor, and took leave of Tonquin.

CHAP. VI

They set sail out of the Bay of Tonquin. Of the R. and Country of Cambodia: Of Chinese Pirates settled there, and the Buggasses, a sort of Soldiers under the King of Siam, both routed by the English in his service. They pass by Pulo Condore, are in fear of the King of Siam, and enter the Streights of Malacca by Brewer's Streights. They arrive at Malacca. The Story of Captain Johnson: his buying a Vessel at Malacca, and going over to Bancalis, a Town on the opposite Coast of Sumatra, to buy Pepper. His Murder by the Malayans there, and the narrow escape of his Men and Vessel. The State of Trade in those Parts, and the Restraint put upon it. Captain Johnson's Vessel brought to Malacca by Mr. Wells. The Author's Departure from Malacca, and arrival at Achin.

IT was the beginning of February 168$\frac{8}{9}$ when we left AN.
this Country. We went over the Bar 3 Ships in 1689
Company, the *Rainbow* Captain Pool Commander, bound for London, and Captain Lacy in the *Saphire*, bound for Fort St. George, and I was in Captain Weldon's Ship the *Curtane*, bound thither also. We kept Company some time after our departure from Tonquin, and having an Easterly Wind we kept more to the middle of the Bay of Tonquin, or towards the Eastern Side, than when we entered: by which means we had the Opportunity of sounding as well in the middle of the Bay now, as we had on the West side of it, at our coming into the Bay.

Coming out of the Bay of Tonquin, we stood away Southward, having the Sholes of Pracel on our Larboard, and the Coasts of Cochinchina, Champa, and Cambodia on our Starboard. I have just mentioned these Kingdoms in my former Volume; and here I have but little to say of them, having only sail'd by them. But not altogether to fail the Readers Expectation, I shall give a brief Account

AN. 1689 of one or two Particulars relating to Cambodia: for as to Champa I have nothing material to speak; and Cochinchina, I have already spoken of in this Volume, as I went to Tonquin.

The Kingdom of Cambodia seems to be much such a kind of Country within Land as the lower Parts of Tonquin: low Land, very woody, and little inhabited, lying on each Side a great River that comes from the North a great way, and falls into the Sea over against Pulo Condore. I know not the particular Product of Cambodia, but in the Vessels mentioned in my former Vol. p. 396. as taken at Pulo Ubi, and which came thither from Cambodia; there were besides Rice, Dragons Blood, Lack, in great Jars, but it looked blackish and thick; and the yellow purging Gum, which we from thence call Cambodia, in great Cakes, but I know not whence they get it. This River and Kingdom (if it be one) is but little known to our Nation, yet some Englishmen have been there; particularly Captain Williams and Captain Howel, the last of whom I came acquainted with some time after this at Fort St. George, and I had of him the following Account, the Particulars of which I have also had confirmed by the Seamen who were with them.

These two Captains, with many more Englishmen, had been for some time in the Service of the King of Siam, and each of them commanded a stout Frigat of his, mann'd chiefly with English and some Portuguese born at Siam. These the King of Siam sent against some Pyrates, who made spoil of his Subjects trading in these Seas, and nested themselves in an Island up the River of Cambodia, Captain Howel told me, that they found this River very large, especially at its Mouth; that 'tis deep and navigable for very great Vessels, 60 or 70 Leagues up, and that its depth and wideness extended much further up, for ought we knew: but so far they went up at this time with their Ships. The Course of the River is generally from North to South: and they found the Land low on each side, with many large Creeks and Branches, and in some Places considerable Islands. They bended their Course up that

Branch which seemed most considerable, having the Tide of Flood with them, and the River commonly so wide, as to give them room to turn or make Angles where the bending of the River was such as to receive a contrary East, or South-East Sea-Wind. These Reaches or Bendings of the River East and West were very rare; at least so as to make their Course be against the Sea-wind, which commonly blew in their Stern, and so fresh, that with it they could stem the Tide of Ebb. But in the Night when the Land-winds came, they anchored, and lay still till about 10 or 11 a-Clock the next Day, at which time the Sea-breezes usually sprang up again, and enabled them to continue their Course, till they came to the Island, where the Pirates inhabited. They presently began to fire at them, and landing their Men routed them, and burnt their Houses and Fortifications; and taking many Prisoners, returned again.

AN. 1689

These Piratical People were by Nation Chinese, who when the Tartars conquered their Country, fled from thence in their own Ships: as chosing rather to live any where free, than to submit to the Tartars. These it seems in their flight bent their Course towards this Country, and finding the River of Cambodia open before them, they made bold to enter, and settle on the Island before mentioned. There they built a Town, and fenced it round about with a kind of Wood pile, or Wall of great Timber Trees laid along, of the Thickness of 3 or 4 of these Trees, and of about as many in heighth. They were provided with all sorts of Planters Instruments, and the Land hereabouts was excellent good, as our Englishmen told me, so that it is like they might have lived here happily enough, had their Inclinations led them to a quiet Life: but they brought Arms along with them, and chose to use them, rather than their Instruments of Husbandry: and they lived therefore mostly by rapin, pillaging their Neighbours, who were more addicted to traffick than fighting. But the King of Siam's Subjects having been long harrassed by them at Sea, he first sent some Forces by Land to drive them out of their Fort: till not succeeding that way, he entirely

AN. routed them by sending these 2 Ships up the River. The
1689 2 English Captains having thus effected their Business, returned out of the River with many Prisoners: but the South-West Monsoon being already set in, they could not presently return to Siam, and therefore went to Macao in China; as well to wait for the N. East Monsoon, as to ingratiate themselves with the Tartars, who they thought would be pleased with the Conquest, which they had made over these Chinese Pyrates. They were well entertained there by the Tartarian Governor, and gave him their Prisoners; and upon the shifting of the Monsoon, they returned to Siam. There they were received with great Applause. Nor was this the first successful Expedition the English have made in the King of Siam's Service. They once saved the Country, by suppressing an Insurrection made by the Buggasses. The Buggasses are a sort of war-like trading Malayans, and mercenary Soldiers of India: I know not well whence they come, unless from Macasser in the Island Celebes. Many of them had been entertained at Siam in the King's Service: but at last being disgusted at some ill Usage, they stood up in their own Defence. Some Hundreds of them got together, all well armed: and these struck a Dread into the Hearts of the Siamites, none of whom were able to stand before them; till Constant Falcon the chief Minister, commanded the English that were then in the King's Service to march against them, which they did with Success, though with some considerable loss. For these Services the King gave every Year to each of them a great Silk Coat, on which were just 13 Buttons. Those of the chief Commanders were of Massy Gold, and those of the inferior Officers were of Silver Plate. This Expedition against the Chinese Pyrates was about the Year 1687: the other Broil with the Buggasses was, as I take it, some time before.

But to proceed with our Voyage, we still kept our way Southward, and in Company together, till we came about Pulo Condore; but then Captain Pool parted from us, standing more directly South for the Streights of Sundy: and we steered more to the Westward, to go through the

Streights of Malacca, through which we came before. AN. 1689
Captain Brewster and another of our Passengers began now to be in fear that the King of Siam would send Ships to lie at the Mouth of the Streights of Malacca, and intercept our Passage, because there was a war broke out between the English East-India Company and that Prince. This seemed the more likely, because the French at this time were employed in that King's Service, by the Means of a French Bishop and other Ecclesiasticks, who were striving to convert the King and People to Christianity, through the Interest they had got in Constant Falcon. Particularly they were afraid that the King of Siam would send the 2 Ships before-mentioned, which Captain Williams, and Captain Howel had commanded a little before, to lie at the West-End of the Streights Mouth; but probably manned with Frenchmen and French Commanders to take us. Now though this made but little Impression on the Minds of our Commanders and Officers, yet it so hapned, that we had such thick dark Weather when we came near the first Entrance of the Streights of Malacca, which was that we came by, and by which we meant to return, that we thought it not safe to stand in at Night, and so lay by till Morning. The next Day we saw a Jonk to the Southward, and chased her; and having spoke with her we made Sail, and stood to the Westward to pass the Streights, and making the Land, we found we were to the Southward of the Streights first Mouth, and were gotten to the Southermost Entrance,[1] near the Sumatra Shore: but Captain Lacy, who chose to go the old Way, made sail again to the Northward, and so passed nearer the Malacca Shore by the Sincapore, the way we went before. His was also the best and nearest way: But Captain Weldon was willing to satisfy his Curiosity, and try a new Passage: which we got through, though we had but little Depth of Water: and this Entrance we past is called Brewer's Streights.

Brewer's Streights are sometimes passed by small Ships, that sail from Batavia to Malacca, because for them it is

[1] Through the Lingga and Rhio Archipelagoes.

An. 1689 a nearer Cut, than to run so far as Pulo Timaon, or the Streights of Sincapore. In this Channel, though in some Places we found but 14 or 15 Foot Water, yet the Bottom was soft Oaze: and it lies so among Islands, that there cannot go a great Sea. Captain Weldon had also a Dutchman aboard who had been this way, and he professing to know the Channel, encouraged our Captain to try it, which we effected very well, though sometimes we had but little more Water than we drew. This made us make but an easy Sail, and therefore we were 7 or 8 Days before we arrived at Malacca; but Captain Lacy was there 2 or 3 Days before us.

Here we first heard of the Death of Constant Falcon, for whom Captain Brewster seemed to be much concerned. There also we found, besides several Dutch Sloops, and our Companion Captain Lacy, an English Vessel of 35 or 40 Tuns. This Vessel was bought by one Captain Johnson, who was sent by the Governor of Bencouli, in a small Sloop, to trade about the Island of Sumatra for Pepper, but Captain Johnson being killed, the Sloop was brought hither by one Mr. Wells.

Being thus insensibly fallen into the mention of this Captain Johnson; and intending to defer what little I have to say of Malacca, till my coming thither again from Achin, I shall bestow the rest of this Chapter in speaking of this Man's Tragedy, and other Occurrences relating to it, which though of no great Moment in themselves, yet the Circumstances I shall have occasion to relate with them may be of use to the giving some small light into the State of the opposite Coast of Sumatra, which was the Scene of what I am going to speak of: for though I shall have other occasion to speak of Achin and Bencouli, yet I shall not have Opportunity to say any thing of this Part of that Island, opposite to Malacca, unless I do it here. To go on therefore with his Story, it seems Captain Johnson was part Owner of the small Bencouli Sloop: but thinking it too small for his turn, he came to Malacca, intending to buy a larger Sloop of the Dutch, if he could light of a Bargain. He had the best Part of a Thousand

Dollars in Spanish Money aboard, for which one may purchase a good Sloop here: for the Dutch, as I have before observed, do often buy Proe-bottoms for a small Matter, of the Malayans, especially of the People of Jihore, and convert them into Sloops, either for their own use, or to sell. Of these sort of Vessels therefore the Dutchmen of Malacca have plenty, and can afford good Penny-worths; and doubtless it was for this Reason that Captain Johnson came hither to purchase a Sloop. Here he met with a Bargain, not such a Proe-bottom reformed, but an old ill-shaped thing, yet such a one as pleased him. The Dutchman who sold him this Vessel, told him withal, that the Government did not allow any such Dealings with the English, though they might wink at it: and that therefore the safest Way for them both to keep out of trouble, would be to run over to the other Side of the Streights, to a Town called Bencalis, on Sumatra; where they might safely buy and sell, or exchange without any Notice taken of them. Captain Johnson accepting the Offer, they sailed both together over to Bencalis,[1] a Malayan Town on that Coast, commanding the Country about it. There they came to an Anchor, and Captain Johnson paying the Price agreed on for the Vessel, he had her delivered to him. The Dutchman immediately returned over to Malacca again, leaving Captain Johnson with 2 Vessels under his Command, viz. the Sloop that he brought from Bencouli, and this new-bought Vessel. The Bencouli Sloop he sent into a large River hard by, to trade with the Malayans for Pepper, under the Command of Mr. Wells. He was no Seaman; but a pretty intelligent Person, that came first out of England as a Soldier, to serve the East-India Company in the Island Santa Helena. He liv'd sometime very meanly in that Island, but having an aspiring Mind, he left that poor, but healthy Place, to serve the Company at Bencouli; which though it is accounted the most unhealthy Place of any that we trade to, yet the hopes of Preferment

AN. 1689

[1] Bangkali, on the eastern shore. It must not be confused with Bencouli (Benkulen) on the west coast, where Dampier served as gunner.

An. 1689 engaged him to remove thither. After some stay there, he was sent with Captain Johnson to assist him in this Pepper Expedition; more because he could use his Pen than his Hands in Sea Service. He had 3 or 4 raw Seamen with him to work the Sloop up into the River. Captain Johnson stayed near Bencalis to fit his new Vessel: for with other Necessaries she wanted a new Boltsprit, which he intended to cut here, having a Carpenter with him for that purpose; as also to repair and fit her to his Mind. He had also a few other raw Seamen, but such as would have made better Landmen, they having served the King of Siam as Soldiers: and they were but lately come from thence with the French, who were forced to leave that Country. But here in the Indies our English are forced for want of better, to make use of any Seamen such as they can get, and indeed our Merchants are often put hard to it for want of Seamen. Here are indeed Lascars or Indian Seamen enough to be hired; and these they often make use of: yet they always covet an Englishman or 2 in a Vessel to assist them. Not but that these Lascars are some of them indifferent good Sailors, and might do well enough: but an Englishman will be accounted more faithful, to be employed on matters of Moment; beside the more free Conversation that may be expected from them, during the Term of the Voyage. So that though oft-times their Englishmen are but ordinary Sailors, yet they are promoted to some Charge of which they could not be so capable any where but in the East-Indies. These Seamen would be in a manner wholly useless in Europe, where we meet with more frequent and hard Storms, but here they serve indifferent well, especially to go and come with the Monsoons; but enough of that.

Mr. Wells being gone to purchase Pepper, Capt. Johnson went ashore about 5 or 6 Leagues from Bencalis Town with his Carpenter, to cut a Boltsprit; there being there Plenty of Timber Trees fit for his purpose. He soon chose one to his Mind, and cut it down. He and his Carpenter wrought on it the first and second Days without

Molestation. The third Day they were both set upon by a Band of armed Malayans, who killed them both. In the Evening the Sailors who were left aboard, lookt out for their Commander to come off: but Night approached without seeing or hearing from him. This put them in some doubt of his Safety; for they were sensible enough, that the Malayans that inhabited thereabouts were very treacherous: as indeed all of them are, especially those who have but little Commerce with Strangers: and therefore all People ought to be very careful in dealing with them, so as to give them no Advantage; and then they may trade safe enough.

AN. 1689

There were but 4 Seamen on board Captain Johnson's Sloop. These being terrified by the absence of their Commander, and suspecting the Truth, were now very apprehensive of their own Safeties. They charged their Guns, and kept themselves on their Guard, expecting to be assaulted by the Malayans. They had 2 Blunderbusses, and 5 or 6 Muskets: each Man took one in his Hand, with a Caduce[1]-box at his Waste, and looked out sharp for fear of any Enemy. While they were thus on their Guard, the Malayans in 6 or 8 Canoas came very silent to attack the Sloop. They were about 40 or 50 Men, armed with Lances and Cressets. The darkness of the Night favoured their Designs, and they were even aboard before the Seamen perceived them. Then these began to fire, and the Enemy darted their Lances aboard, and boarding the Vessel, they entered her over the Prow. The Seamen resolutely defended her, and drove them over-board again. Of the 4 Seamen 2 were desperately wounded in the first attack. The Malayans took fresh Courage and entered again; and the 2 Seamen who were not wounded, betook themselves to close Quarters[2] in the Steerage; and there being Loop-holes to fire out at, they repulsed the Malayans again, forcing them into their Canoas. Their Bellies being now

[1] Cartouche.

[2] Under the poop. The forward bulkhead of the cabin was generally pierced for muskets, so that a few men standing within might clear the upper deck in circumstances similar to that described.

AN. 1689 pretty full, they returned ashore without hopes of conquering the Sloop. The poor Seamen were still in fear, and kept watch all Night; intending to sell their Lives as dear as they could, if they had been attacked again. For they might not, neither did they expect Quarter from the Salvage Malayans: but they were no more assaulted. These two that were wounded dyed in a short Time.

The next Day the 2 Seamen got up their Anchor, and run as nigh the Town of Bencalis as they could, it may be within half a Mile. There they anchor'd again, and made Signs for the People to come on Board. It was not long before the Shabander or chief Magistrate of the Town came off: to him they told all their Misfortunes, and desired him to protect them, because they were not of sufficient Strength to hold out against another Attack. The Shabander seemed very sorry for what had happened, and told them withal, that he could not help what was past, for that the People that did it were wild unruly Men, not subject to Government, and that it was not in his Power to suppress them: but as long as they lay there some of his Men should lye aboard to secure the Ship; and he in the mean time would send a Canoa to their Consort Mr. Wells, to give him an account how Things went. Accordingly he left 10 or 12 of his own Malayans aboard the Bark, and sent a Letter written by the Seamen to Mr. Wells; who was, as I have said, dealing with the Natives for Pepper, in a River at some distance.

It was 2 or 3 Days before Mr. Wells came to them. He had not then received the Letter, and therefore they suspected the Shabander of falsehood; though his Men were yet very kind, and serviceable to the 2 Seamen. Mr. Wells had heard nothing of their Disasters, but returned for want of Trade; at least such a full Trade as he expected. For tho' here is Pepper growing, yet not so much as might allure any one to seek after it: for the Dutch are so near, that none can come to trade among them but by their Permission. And though the Natives themselves were never so willing to trade with any Nation, as indeed they are, yet the Dutch could soon hinder it, even by destroying them, if in order to it they should set themselves to produce such Pepper. Such small quantities as they do at present raise up, or procure from other parts of the Island, is lickt by the Dutch, or by their Friends of Bencalis for them: for the Town of Bencalis being the principal of these Parts, and so nigh Malacca, as only parted by the narrow Sea or Streights, 'tis visited by the Dutch in their small Vessels, and seems wholly to depend on a Trade with that Nation, not daring to Trade with any besides: and I judge it is by the Friendship of the Town, that the Dutch drive a small Trade for Pepper in these parts, and by it also vend any of their own Commodities: and these also trading with their Neighbours into the Country, do bring their Commodities hither, where the Dutch come for them. The People of Bencalis therefore, though they are Malayans, as the rest of the Country, yet they are civil enough, engaged thereto by Trade: for the more Trade, the more Civility; and on the contrary, the less Trade the more Barbarity and Inhumanity. For Trade has a strong Influence upon all People, who have found the sweet of it, bringing with it so many of the Conveniencies of Life as it does. And I believe that even the poor Americans, who have not yet tasted the Sweetness of it, might be allured to it by an honest and just Commerce: even such of them as do yet seem to covet no more than a bare Subsistence of meat and drink, and a clout to cover their Nakedness. That large Continent hath yet Millions of Inhabitants, both on the Mexican and Peruvian parts, who are still ignorant of Trade: and they would be fond of it, did they once Experience it; though at the present they live happy enough, by enjoying such Fruits of the Earth as Nature hath bestowed on those Places, where their Lot is fallen: and it may be they are happier now, than they may hereafter be, when more known to the Avaritious World. For with Trade they will be in danger of meeting with Oppression: Men not being content with a free Traffick, and a just and reasonable Gain, especially in these remote Countries: but they must have the Current run altogether in their own Channel, though to the depriv-

AN. 1689

AN. 1689 ing the poor Natives they deal with, of their natural Liberty: as if all Mankind were to be ruled by their Laws. The Islands of Sumatra and Java can sufficiently witness this: the Dutch having in a manner ingrost all the Trade of those, and several of the neighbouring Countries to themselves: not that they are able to supply the Natives with a quarter of what they want, but because they would have all the produce of them at their own disposal: Yet even in this they are short, and may be still more disappointed of the Pepper Trade if other People would seek for it. For the greatest part of the Island of Sumatra propagates this Plant, and the Natives would readily comply with any who would come to trade with them, notwithstanding the great Endeavours the Dutch make against it: for this Island is so large, populous, and productive of Pepper, that the Dutch are not able to draw all to themselves. Indeed this place about Bencalis, is in a manner at their Devotion; and for ought I know, it was through a Design of being revenged on the Dutch that Captain Johnson lost his Life. I find the Malayans in general are implacable Enemies to the Dutch; and all seems to spring from an earnest desire they have of a free Trade, which is restrained by them, not only here, but in the Spice-Islands, and in all other places where they have any Power. But 'tis freedom only must be the means to incourage any of these remote People to Trade; especially such of them as are industrious, and whose Inclinations are bent this way; as most of the Malayans are, and the major-part of the People of the East-Indies, even from the Cape of Good Hope Eastward to Japan, both Continent and Islands. For though in many places they are limited by the Dutch, English, Danes, &c. and restrained from a free Trade with other Nations, yet have they continually shewn what an uneasiness that is to them. And how dear has this Restraint cost the Dutch? when yet neither can they with all their Forts and Guard-Ships secure the Trade wholly to themselves, any more than the Barlaventa Fleet can secure the Trade of the West-Indies to the Spaniards: but enough of this matter.

You have heard before that Mr. Wells came with his Sloop to Bencalis, to the great Joy of the two Men that were yet alive in Captain Johnson's Vessel. These two Seamen were so just, that they put all Captain Johnson's Papers and Money into one Chest, then lockt it and put the Key of it into another Chest; and locking that, flung the Key of it into the Sea: and when Mr. Wells came aboard, they offered him the Command of both Vessels. He seemingly refused it, saying, that he was no Seaman, and could not manage either of them: yet by much importunity he accepted the Command of them, or at least undertook the account of what was in the Sloop, engaging to give a faithful account of it to Governour Bloom.

AN 1689

They were all now so weakened, that they were but just enough to sail one of the Vessels. Therefore they sent to the Shabander of Bencalis, to desire some of his Men, to help sail the Sloops over to Malacca, but he refused it. Then they offered to sell one of them for a small Matter, but neither would he buy. Then they offered to give him the smallest: To that he answered, that he did not dare to accept of her, for fear of the Dutch. Then Mr. Wells and his Crew concluded to take the Pepper and all the Stores out of the small Vessel, and burn her, and go away with the other to Malacca. This they put in Execution, and presently went away, and opening Captain Johnson's Chest they found 2 or 300 Dollars in Money. This with all his Writings, and what else they found of value, Mr. Wells took in his Possession. In a very short Time they got over to Malacca. There they stayed expecting the coming of some English Ship, to get a Pilot to navigate the Sloop: for neither of them would undertake to navigate her further. Captain Lacy coming thither first, he spared Mr. Wells his chief Mate to navigate her to Achin: When we came thither they were ready to Sail, and went away two or three Days before us.

To return therefore to our own Voyage, Captain Weldon having finished his Business at Malacca, we sailed again, steering towards Achin, where he designed to touch in his way to Fort St. George. We overtook Mr. Wells

AN. 1689 about 35 Leagues short of Achin against the River Pass Jonca: and shortly after we both arrived at Achin, anchored in the Road, about the beginning of March 1 Here I took my leave of Captain Weldon, and of Friend Mr. Hall, who went with us to Tonquin, an went ashore, being very weak with my Flux, as I had all the Voyage. Captain Weldon offered me any Kind that lay in his Power at Fort St. George, if I would with him thither: but I chose rather to stay here, ha some small Acquaintance, than to go in that weak Con tion, to a Place where I was wholly unknown. But Hall went with Captain Weldon to Fort St. George, from thence in a short Time returned to England in *Williamson* of London.

CHAP. VII

The Country of Achin described: its Situation and Extent. Golden Mount, and the neighbouring Isles of Way and Gomez, &c. making several Channels and the Road of Achin. The Soil of the Continent; Trees and Fruits; particularly the Mangastan and Pumple-nose. Their Roots, Herbs, and Drugs, the Herb Ganga or Bang, and Camphire: the Pepper of Sumatra, and Gold of Achin. The Beasts, Fowl and Fish. The People, their Temper, Habits, Buildings. City of Achin, and Trades. The Husbandry, Fishery, Carpenters and Flying Proes. The Money Changers, Coin and Weights. Of the Gold-Mines. The Merchants who come to Achin: and of the Chinese Camp or Fair. The washing used at Achin. A Chinese Renegado. Punishments for Theft and other Crimes. The Government of Achin; of the Queen, Oronkeys or Nobles; and of the Slavery of the People. The State kept by the Eastern Princes. A Civil War here upon the choice of a new Queen. The A. and the other English in a fright, upon a seizure made of a Moor's Ship by an English Captain. The Weather, Floods, and Heat at Achin.

BEING now arrived at Achin again, I think it not amiss to give the Reader some short account of what Observation I made of that City and Country. AN. 1689
This Kingdom is the largest and best peopled of many small ones that are up and down the Isle of Sumatra; and it makes the North West end of that Island. It reaches Eastward from that N. W. point of the Island, a great way along the Shore, towards the Streights of Malacca, for about 50 or 60 Leagues. But from Diamond point, which is about 40 Leagues from Achin, towards the Borders of the Kingdom, the Inhabitants, though belonging to Achin are in less Subjection to it. Of these I can say but little; neither do I know the Bounds of this Kingdom, either

AN. 1689 within Land, or along the West Coast. That West Side of the Kingdom is high and mountainous: as is generally the rest of the West Coast of the whole Island. The Point also of Achin, or extremity of the Island, is high Land: but Achin, it self, and the Country to the Eastward, is lower, not altogether destitute of small Hills, and every where of a moderate Heighth, and a Champion Country, naturally very fit for Cultivation.

There is one Hill more remarkable than ordinary, especially to Seamen. The English call it, the Golden[1] Mount: but whether this Name is given it by the Natives, or only by the English, I know not. 'Tis near the N. W. end of the Island; and Achin stands but 5 or 6 Mile from the Bottom of it. 'Tis very large at the Foot, and runs up smaller towards the Head; which is raised so high, as to be seen at Sea 30 or 40 Leagues. This was the first Land that we saw coming in our Proe from the Nicobar Islands, mentioned in my former Voyage. The rest of the Land, though of a good Heighth, was then undiscerned by us, so that this Mountain appeared like an Island in the Sea; which was the Reason why our Achin Malayans took it for Pulo Way. But that Island, though pretty high Champion Land, was invisible, when this Golden Mount appeared so plain, though as far distant as that Island.

Besides what belong to Achin upon the Continent, there are also several Islands under its Jurisdiction, most of them uninhabited; and these make the Road of Achin. Among them is this Pulo Way, which is the Eastermost of a Range of Islands, that lye off the N. W. end of Sumatra. It is also the largest of them, and is inhabited by Malefactors, who are banisht thither from Achin. This with the other Islands of this Range, lye in a semi-circular Form, of about 7 Leagues Diameter. Pulo Gomez is another large Island about 20 Mile West from Pulo Way, and about 3 Leagues from the N. W. point of Sumatra. Between Pulo Gomez and the Main are 3 or 4 other small Islands; yet with Channels of a sufficient breadth between them, for Ships to

[1] The Queen's Peak.

pass through; and they have very deep Water. All Ships bound from Achin to the Westward, or coming from thence to Achin, go in or out through one or other of these Channels: and because Shipping comes hither from the Coast of Surrat, one of these Channels which is deeper than the rest, is called the Surrat Channel. Between Pulo Gomez and Pulo Way, in the bending of the Circle, there are other small Islands, the chief of which is called Pulo Rondo. This is a small round high Island, not above 2 or 3 Mile in Circumference. It lies almost in the extremity of the bending on the N. E. part of the Circle, but nearer Pulo Way than Pulo Gomez. There are large deep Channels on either side, but the most frequented is the Channel on the West side. Which is called the Bengal Channel, because it looks towards that Bay; and Ships coming from thence, from the Coast of Coromandel, pass in and out this way. Between Pulo Way and the main of Sumatra, is another Channel of 3 or 4 Leagues wide: which is the Channel for Ships that go from Achin to the Streights of Malacca, or any Country to the East of those Streights, and *vice versa.* There is good riding in all this Semi-circular Bay between the Islands and Sumatra: but the Road for all Ships that come to Achin is near the Sumatra Shore, within all the Islands. There they anchor at what distances they please, according to the Monsoons or Seasons of the Year. There is a small navigable River comes out into the Sea, by which Ships transport their Commodities in smaller Vessels up to the City. The Mouth of this River is 6 or 7 leagues from Pulo Rondo, and 3 or 4 from Pulo Way, and near as many from Pulo Gomez. The Islands are pretty high Champion Land, the Mold black or yellow, the Soil deep and fat, producing large tall Trees, fit for many uses. There are Brooks of Water on the two great Islands of Way and Gomez, and several sorts of wild Animals; especially wild Hogs in abundance.

AN. 1689

The Mold of this Continent is different according to the natural position of it. The Mountains are rocky, especially those towards the West Coast, yet most that I have seen seems to have a superficial covering of Earth, naturally producing

AN. 1689 Shrubs, small Trees, or pretty good Grass. The small Hills are most of them cloathed with Woods; the Trees whereof seem by their growth to spring from a fruitful Soil: The Champion Land, such as I have seen, is some black, some grey, some reddish, and all of a deep Mold. But to be very particular in these Things, especially in all my Travels, is more than I can pretend to: though it may be I took as much notice of the difference of Soil as I met with it, as most Travellers have done, having been bred in my Youth in Somersetshire, at a place called East Coker [1] near Yeovil or Evil: in which Parish there is as great Variety of Soil, as I have ordinarily met with any where, viz. black, red, yellow, sandy, stony, clay, morass or swampy, &c. I had the more reason to take notice of this, because this Village in great measure is let out in small Leases for Lives of 20, 30, 40, or 50 Pound per An. under Coll. Helliar [2] the Lord of the Mannor: and most, if not all these Tenants, had their own Land scattering in small pieces, up and down several sorts of Land in the Parish: so that every one had some piece of every sort of Land, his black Ground, his Sandy, Clay, &c. some of 20, 30, or 40 Shillings an Acre, for some uses, and others not worth 10 Groats an Acre. My Mother being possest of one of these Leases, and having of all these sorts of Land, I came acquainted with them all, and knew what each sort would produce, (viz.) Wheat, Barley, Maslin,[3] Rice, Beans, Peas, Oats, Fetches,[4] Flax, or Hemp: in all which I had a more than usual Knowledge for one so young; taking a particular delight in observing it: but enough of this Matter.

The Kingdom of Achin has in general a deep Mold: It is very well watered with Brooks and small Rivers, but none navigable for Ships of Burden. This of Achin admits not of any but small Vessels. The Land is some part very Woody, in other Places Savannah; the Trees are of divers sorts, most unknown to me by Name. The Cotton and

[1] East Coker: Dampier's native village.

[2] Colonel Helliar, or Hellier, or Helyar, was the head of a wealthy Somersetshire family then resident at East Coker.

[3] Maslin, a mixture of wheat and rye. Rice must be a slip for Rye.

[4] Vetches.

Cabbage-Trees grow here, but not in such plenty as in some part of America. These Trees commonly grow here, as indeed usually where-ever they grow, in a Champion dry Ground, such at least as is not drowned or morassy; for here is some such Land as that by the Rivers; and there grow Mangrove Trees, and other Trees of that kind. Neither is this Kingdom destitute of Timber-Trees fit for building. AN. 1689

The Fruits of this Country are Plantains, Bonanoes, Guava's, Oranges, Limes, Jacks, Durians, Coco-nuts, Pumple-noses,[1] Pomgranates, Mangoes, Mangastans,[2] Citrons, Water-melons, Musk-melons, Pine Apples, &c. Of all these sorts of Fruits, I think the Mangastan is without compare the most delicate. This Fruit is in shape much like the Pomgranate, but a great deal less. The outside rind or shell is a little thicker than that of the Pomgranate, but softer, yet more brittle; and is of a dark red. The inside of the shell is of a deep Crimson Colour. Within this shell the Fruit appears in 3 or 4 Cloves, about the bigness of the top of a Man's Thumb. These will easily separate each from the other; they are as white as Milk, very soft and juicy, inclosing a small black stone or Kernel. The outside rind is said to be binding, and therefore many when they eat the Fruit, which is very delicious, do save the rind or shell, drying it and preserving it, to give to such as have Fluxes. In a small Book,[3] entituled, "A new Voyage to the East-Indies," there is mention made of Mangastans, among the Fruits of Java: but the Author is mistaken, in that he compares it to a Sloe, in shape and taste: Yet I remember there is such a sort of Fruit at Achin; and believe by the description he gives of it, it may probably be the same that he calls the Mangastan, tho' nothing like the true Mangastan.

The Pumple-nose is a large Fruit like a Citron, with a very thin tender uneven rind. The inside is full of Fruit: It grows all in Cloves as big as a small Barley Corn,

[1] *C. Pepo* (?). [2] Mangosteens: *Garcinia mangostana*.
[3] By Monsieur Du Quesne. The English translation was first published in 1696.

and these are as full of Juice as an Orange or a Lemon, though not growing in such Partitions. 'Tis of a pleasant Taste, and tho' there are of them in other parts of the East-Indies, yet these at Achin are accounted the best. They are ripe commonly about Christmas, and they are so much esteemed that English Men carry them from hence to Fort St. George, and make Presents of them to their Friends there. The other Fruits mentioned here, are most of them described by me in my first Volume.

The eatable Roots of this Country are Yams and Potatoes, &c. but their chiefest bread-kind is Rice. The Natives have lately planted some Quantities of this Grain, and might produce much more were they so disposed, the Land being so fruitful. They have here a sort of Herb or Plant called Ganga, or Bang.[1] I never saw any but once, and that was at some distance from me. It appeared to me like Hemp, and I thought it had been Hemp, till I was told to the contrary. It is reported of this Plant, that if it is infused in any Liquor, it will stupify the Brains of any Person that drinks thereof; but it operates diversly, according to the Constitution of the Person. Some it keeps sleepy, some merry, putting them into a Laughing-fit, and others it makes mad: but after 2 or 3 Hours they come to themselves again. I never saw the Effects of it on any Person, but have heard much Discourse of it. What other use this Plant may serve for I know not: but I know it is much esteemed here, and in other Places too whither it is transported.

This Country abounds also with Medicinal Drugs and Herbs, and with variety of Herbs for the Pot. The chief of their Drugs is Camphire, of which there are Quantities found on this Island, but most of it either on the Borders of this Kingdom to the Southward, or more remote still, without the Precincts of it. This that is found on the Island Sumatra is commonly sent to Japan to be refined, and then brought from thence pure, and transported whither the Merchants please afterwards. I know that

[1] Bhang: Hemp. Its exhibition is very various. As a rule it induces violent laughter.

here are several sorts of Medicinal Herbs made use of by AN.
the Natives, who go often a simpling, seeming to under- 1689
stand their Virtues much, and making great use of them: but this being wholly out of my Sphere, I can give no account of them; and though here are plenty of Pot-Herbs, yet I know the Names of none, but Onions, of which they have great abundance, and of a very good sort, but small.

There are many other very profitable Commodities on this Island: but some of them are more peculiar to other parts of it than Achin, especially Pepper. All the Island abounds with that Spice, except only this North West-end; at least so much of it, as is comprehended within the Kingdom of Achin. Whether this defect is through the negligence or laziness of these People, I know not.

Gold also is found, by report, in many parts of this Island: but the Kingdom of Achin is at present most plentifully stored with it. Neither does any place in the East-Indies, that I know of, yield such Quantities of it as this Kingdom. I have never been at Japan, and therefore can make no Estimate of the great Riches of that Kingdom; but here I am certain there is abundance of it.

The Land Animals of this Country are Deer, Hogs, Elephants, Goats, Bullocks, Buffaloes, Horses, Porcupines, Monkeys, Squirrils, Guanoes, Lizards, Snakes, &c. Here are also abundance of Ants of several sorts, and Wood-lice, called by the English in the East-Indies White Ants. The Elephants that I saw here were all tame: yet 'tis reported there are some wild; but I judge not many, if any at all. In some places there are plenty of Hogs; they are all wild, and commonly very poor. At some times of the Year, when the wild Fruits fall from the Trees, they are indifferent fat, or at least fleshy: and then they are sweet and good: they are very numerous; and whether for that reason, or scarcity of Food, it is very rare to find them fat. The Goats are not very many, neither are there many Bullocks: but the Savannahs swarm with Buffaloes, belonging to some or other of the Inhabitants, who milk them and eat them; but don't work them, so far as I saw.

An. 1689 The Horses of this Country are but small, yet sprightly; and sometimes they are transported hence to the Coast of Coromandel. The Porcupines and Squirrels are accounted good Food by the English; but how they are esteemed by the Natives I know not.

The Fowls of this Country are Dunghil Fowls and Ducks; but I know of no other tame Fowls they have. In the Woods there are many sorts of wild Fowls, viz. Maccaws, Parrots, Parakites, Pigeons and Doves of 3 or 4 sorts. There are plenty of other small Birds; but I can say nothing of them.

The Rivers of this Country afford plenty of Fish. The Sea also supplies divers sorts of very good Fish, (viz.) Snooks, Mullets, Mudfish, Eels, Stingrays, which I shall describe in the Bay of Campeachy, Ten-pounders, Old Wives, Cavallies, Crawfish, Shrimps, &c.

The Natives of this Country are Malayans. They are much the same People with those of Queda, Jihore, and other Places on the Continent of Malacca, speaking the same Malayan Language, with very little difference: and they are of the same Mahometan Religion, and alike in their haughty Humour and manner of living: so that they seem to have been originally the same People. They are People of a middle Stature, straight, and well shaped, and of a dark Indian Copper-Colour. Their Hair is black and lank, their Faces generally pretty long, yet graceful enough. They have black Eyes, middling Noses, thin Lips, and black Teeth, by the frequent use of Betle. They are very lazy, and care not to work or take pains. The poorer sort are addicted to Theft, and are often punished severely for it. They are otherwise good-natured in general, and kind enough to Strangers.

The better Sort of them wear Caps fitted to their Heads, of red or other coloured Woollen Cloath, like the Crown of a Hat without any Brims; for none of the Eastern People use the Complement of uncovering their Heads when they meet, as we do. But the general Wear for all Sorts of People is a small Turban, such as the Mindanaians wear, described in the 12th Chapter of my former Volume, page 334. They have small Breeches, and the better Sort will have a Piece of Silk thrown loosely over their Shoulders; but the Poor go naked from the Waste upwards. Neither have they the use of Stockings and Shoes, but a sort of Sandals are worn by the better Sort. AN. 1689

Their Houses are built on Posts, as those of Mindanao, and they live much after the same Fashion: but by Reason of their Gold Mines, and the frequent Resort of Strangers, they are richer, and live in greater Plenty. Their common Food is Rice, and the better Sort have Fowls and Fish, with which the Markets are plentifully stored, and sometimes Buffaloes Flesh, all which is drest very savourly with Pepper and Garlick, and tinctured yellow with Turmerick, to make it pleasant to the Eye, as the East-Indians generally love to have their Food look yellow: neither do they want good Achars or Sauces to give it a Relish.

The City of Achin is the chief in all this Kingdom. It is seated on the Banks of a River, near the N. W. end of the Island, and about two Miles from the Sea. This Town consists of 7 or 8000 Houses, and in it there are always a great many Merchant-strangers, viz. English, Dutch, Danes, Portuguese, Chinese, Guzarats, &c. The Houses of this City are generally larger than those I saw at Mindanao, and better furnished with Household Goods. The City has no Walls, nor so much as a Ditch about it. It has a great Number of Mosques, generally square built, and covered with Pantile, but neither high nor large. Every Morning a Man made a great Noise from thence: but I saw no Turrets or Steeples, for them to climb up into for that Purpose, as they have generally in Turky. The Queen has a large Palace here, built handsomely with Stone: but I could not get into the Inside of it. 'Tis said there are some great Guns about it, four of which are of Brass, and are said to have been sent hither as a Present by our K. James the first.

The chief Trades at Achin are Carpenters, Blacksmiths, Goldsmiths, Fishermen, and Money-changers: but the Country-people live either on Breeding Heads of Cattle,

An. 1689 but most for their own Use, or Fowls, especially they who live near the City, which they send weekly thither to sell: others plant Roots, Fruits, &c. and of late they have sown pretty large Fields of Rice. This thrives here well enough; but they are so proud, that it is against their Stomach to work: neither do they themselves much trouble their Heads about it, but leave it to be managed by their Slaves; and they were the Slaves brought lately by the English and Danes from the Coast of Coromandel, in the Time of a Famine there, I spoke of before, who first brought this Sort of Husbandry into such Request among the Achinese. Yet neither does the Rice they have this way supply one Quarter of their Occasions, but they have it brought to them from their Neighbouring Countries.

The Fishermen are the richest working People: I mean such of them as can purchase a Net: for thereby they get great Profit; and this Sort of Imployment is managed also by their Slaves. In fair Weather you shall have eight or ten great Boats, each with a Sain or haling Net: and when they see a Shole of Fish, they strive to encompass them with these Nets, and all the Boats that are near assist each other to drag them ashore. Sometimes they draw ashore this way 50, 60, or 100 large Fish, as big as a Man's Leg, and as long: and then they rejoyce mightily, and scamper about, making a great Shout. The Fish is presently sent to the Market in one of their Boats, the rest looking out again for more. Those who fish with Hook and Line, go out in small Proes, with about one or two Slaves in each Proe. These also get good Fish of other Sorts, which they carry Home to their Masters.

The Carpenters use such Hatchets as they have at Mindanao. They build good Houses after their Fashion: and they are also ingenious enough in building Proes, making very pretty ones, especially of that Sort which are Flying-Proes; which are built long, deep, narrow, and sharp, with both Sides alike, and Outlagers on each Side, the Head and Stern like other Boats. They carry a great Sail, and when the Wind blows hard, they send a Man or two to sit at the Extremity of the Windward Outlager, to poise the Vessel. They build also some Vessels of 10 or 20 Tuns Burthen, to trade from one Place to another: but I think their greatest Ingenuity is in building their Flying-Proes; which are made very smooth, kept neat and clean, and will sail very well: for which Reason they had that Name given them by the English. AN. 1689

There are but few Blacksmiths in this Town, neither are they very skilful at their Trade. The Goldsmiths are commonly Strangers, yet some of the Achinese themselves know how to work Metals, tho' not very well. The Money-changers are here, as at Tonquin, most Women. These sit in the Markets and at Corners of the Streets, with leaden Money called Cash, which is a Name that is generally given to small Money in all these Countries: but the Cash here is neither of the same Metal, nor Value with that at Tonquin; for that is Copper, and this is Lead, or Block-Tin, such as will bend about the Finger. They have but two sorts of Coin of their own; the least sort is this Leaden Money call'd Cash, and 'tis the same with what they called Petties at Bantam. Of these, 1500 make a Mess, which is their other sort of Coin, and is a small thin Piece of Gold, stampt with Malayan Letters on each Side. It is in Value 15 Pence English, 16 Mess make a Tale, which here is 20 Shillings English, 5 Tale make a Bancal, a Weight so called, and 20 Bancal make a Catty, another Weight. But the Gold Coin seldom holds Weight, for you shall sometimes have 5 Tale and 8 Mess over, go to make a Pecul, and tho' 1500 Cash is the Value of a Mess, yet these rise and fall at the Discretion of the Money-changers: for sometimes you shall have 1000 Cash for a Mess: but they are kept usually between these two Numbers; seldom less than 1000, and never more than 1500. But to proceed with these Weights, which they use either for Money or Goods, 100 Catty make a Pecul, which is 132 Pound English Weight. Three hundred Catty is a Bahar, which is 396 Pound English Weight; but in some Places, as at Bencouli, a Bahar is near 500 English Weight. Spanish Pieces of Eight go here also, and they are valued according to the Plenty or Scarcity of them. Sometimes a

AN. 1689 Piece of Eight goes but for 4 Mess, sometimes for 4 and a half, sometimes 5 Mess.

They coin but a small Quantity of their Gold; so much as may serve for their ordinary Occasions in their Traffick one with another. But as the Merchant, when he receives large Summs, always takes it by Weight, so they usually pay him unwrought Gold, and Quantity for Quantity: the Merchants chuse rather to receive this, than the coined Gold; and before their leaving the Country will change their Messes for uncoined Gold: perhaps because of some Deceits used by the Natives in their Coining.

This Gold they have from some Mountain a pretty way within Land from Achin, but within their Dominions, and rather near to the West Coast than the Streights of Malacca. I take Golden Mount, which I spoke of before, to lye at no great Distance from that of the Mines; for there is very high Land all thereabouts. To go thither they set out Eastward, towards Passange Jonca, and thence strike up into the Heart of the Country. I made some Inquiry concerning their getting Gold, and was told, that none but Mahometans were permitted to go to the Mines: That it was both troublesome and dangerous to pass the Mountains, before they came thither; there being but one way, and that over such steep Mountains, that in some Places they were forced to make use of Ropes, to climb up and down the Hills. That at the Foot of these Precipices there was a Guard of Soldiers, to see that no uncircumcised Person should pursue that Design, and also to receive Custom of those that past either forward or backward. That at the Mines it was so sickly that not the half of those that went thither did ever return again; tho' they went thither only to traffick with the Miners, who live there, being seasoned: that these who go thither from the City stayed not usually above 4 Months at the Mines, and were back again in about 6 Months from their going out. That some there made it their constant Imployment to visit the Miners once every Year: for after they are once seasoned, and have found the Profit of that Trade, no Thoughts of Danger can deter them from it: for I was credibly told, that these made 2000 per cent. of whatever they carryed with them, to sell to the Miners: but they could not carry much by Reason of the Badness of the ways. The rich Men never go thither themselves, but send their Slaves: and if 3 out of 6 return, they think they make a very profitable Journey for their Master, for these three are able to bring Home as much Gold as the Goods which all six carried out could purchase. The Goods that they carry thither are some Sort of Cloathing, and Liquor. They carry their Goods from the City by Sea, part of the way: Then they land somewhere about Passange Jonca, and get Horses to carry their Cargo to the Foot of the Mountains. There they draw it up with Ropes, and if they have much Goods, one stays there with them, while the rest march to the Mines with their Load; and return again for the rest. I had this Relation from Captain Tyler, who lived at Achin, and spoke the Language of the Country very well. There was an English Renegado that used that Trade, but was always at the Mines when I was here. At his Return to Achin he constantly frequented an English Punch-house, spending his Gold very freely, as I was told by the Master of the House. I was told also by all that I discoursed with about the Gold, that here they dig it out of the Ground; and that sometimes they find pretty large Lumps.

AN. 1689

It is the Product of these Mines that draws so many Merchants hither, for the Road is seldom without 10 or 15 Sail of Ships of several Nations. These bring all sort of vendible Commodities, as Silks, Chints, Muzlins, Callicoes, Rice, &c. and as to this last, a Man would admire to see what great Quantities of Rice are brought hither by the English, Dutch, Danes and Chinese: when any arrives, the Commanders hire each a House to put their Goods in. The Silks, Muzlins, Callicoes, Opium, and such like rich Goods, they sell to the Guzurats, who are the chief Men that keep Shops here; but the Rice, which is the Bulk of the Cargo, they usually retail. I have heard a Merchant say, he has received 60, 70, and 80 *l.* a Day for Rice, when it has been scarce; but when there are many Sellers, then 40 or 50 Shillings worth in a Day is a good Sale: for then

AN. 1689 a Mess will buy 14 or 15 Bamboes of it: whereas when Rice is scarce, you will not have above 3 or 4 Bamboes for a Mess. A Bamboe is a small seal'd Measure, containing, to the best of my Remembrance, not much above half a Gallon. Thus it rises and falls as Ships come hither. Those who sell Rice keep one constantly attending to measure it out; and the very Grandees themselves never keep a Stock before hand, but depend on the Market, and buy just when they have Occasion. They send their Slaves for what they want, and the poorer Sort, who have not a Slave of their own, will yet hire one to carry a Mess worth of Rice for them, though not one hundred Paces from their own Homes, scorning to do it themselves. Besides one to measure the Rice, the Merchants hire a Man to take the Money; for here is some false Money, as Silver and Copper Mess gilt over: Besides, here are some true Mess much worn, and therefore not worth near their Value in Tale. The Merchants may also have occasion to receive 10 or 20 *l.* at a Time for other Commodities; and this too besides those little Summs for Rice, he must receive by his Broker, if he will not be cheated; for 'tis work enough to examine every Piece: and in receiving the Value of 10 *l.* in Mess, they will ordinarily be forc'd to return half or more to be chang'd; for the Natives are for putting off bad Money, if possibly they can. But if the Broker takes any bad Money, 'tis to his own Loss. These Sort of Brokers are commonly Guzurats, and 'tis very necessary for a Merchant that comes hither, especially if he is a Stranger, to have one of them, for fear of taking bad or light Money.

The English Merchants are very welcome here, and I have heard that they do not pay so much Custom as other Nations. The Dutch Free-men may trade hither, but the Company's Servants are deny'd that Privilege. But of all the Merchants that trade to this City, the Chinese are the most remarkable. There are some of them live here all the Year long; but others only make annual Voyages hither from China. These latter come hither some time in June, about 10 or 12 Sail, and bring Abundance of Rice, and several other Commodities. They take up Houses all by one another, at the end of the Town, next the Sea: and that end of the City is call'd the China Camp, because there they always quarter, and bring their Goods ashore thither to sell. In this Fleet come several Mechanicks, (viz.) Carpenters, Joyners, Painters, &c. These set themselves immediately to work, making of Chests, Drawers, Cabinets, and all sorts of Chinese Toys: which are no sooner finish'd in their Working-houses, but they are presently set up in Shops and at the Doors to sale. So that for two Months or ten Weeks this Place is like a Fair, full of Shops stuft with all sort of vendible Commodities, and People resorting hither to buy: and as their Goods sell off, so they contract themselves into less Compass, and make use of fewer Houses. But as their Business decreases, their Gaming among themselves increases; for a Chinese, if he is not at work, had as lieve be without Victuals as without Gaming; and they are very dexterous at it. If before their Goods are all sold, they can light of Chapmen to buy their Ships, they will gladly sell them also, at least some of them, if any Merchant will buy; for a Chinese is for selling every thing: and they who are so happy as to get Chapmen for their own Ships, will return as Passengers with their Neighbours, leaving their Camp, as 'tis call'd, poor and naked, like other Parts of the City, till the next Year. They commonly go away about the latter end of September, and never fail to return again at the Season: and while they are here, they are so much followed, that there is but little Business stirring for the Merchants of any other Nations; all the Discourse then being of going down to the China Camp. Even the Europeans go thither for their Diversion: the English, Dutch, and Danes, will go to drink their Hoc-ciu, at some China Merchants House who sells it; for they have no tippling Houses. The European Seamen return thence into the City drunk enough, but the Chinese are very sober themselves.

AN. 1689

The Achinese seem not to be extraordinary good at Accounts, as the Banians or Guzurats are. They instruct their Youth in the knowledge of Letters, Malayan prin-

AN. 1689 cipally, and I suppose in somewhat of Arabick, being all Mahometans. They are here, as at Mindanao, very superstitious in washing and cleansing themselves from Defilements: and for that Reason they delight to live near the Rivers or Streams of Water. The River of Achin near the City is always full of People of both Sexes and all Ages. Some come on Purpose to wash themselves, for the Pleasure of being in the Water: which they so much delight in, that they can scarce leave the River without going first into it, if they have any Business brings them near. Even the Sick are brought to the River to wash. I know not whether it is accounted good to wash in all Distempers, but I am certain from my own Experience, it is good for those that have Flux, especially Mornings and Evenings, for which Reason you shall then see the Rivers fullest, and more especially in the Morning. But the most do it upon a Religious Account: for therein consists the chief Part of their Religion.

There are but few of them resort daily to their Mosques; yet they are all stiff in their Religion, and so zealous for it, that they greatly rejoyce in making a Proselyte. I was told, that while I was at Tonquin, a Chinese inhabiting here turn'd from his Paganism to Mahometanism, and being circumcised, he was thereupon carry'd in great State through the City on an Elephant, with one crying before him, that he was turn'd Believer. This Man was call'd the Captain of the China Camp; for, as I was informed, he was placed there by his Country-men as the chief Factor or Agent, to negotiate their Affairs with the People of the Country. Whether he had dealt falsly, or was only envied by others, I know not: but his Country-men had so entangled him in Law, that he had been ruin'd, if he had not made use of this way to disingage himself; and then his Religion protected him, and they could not meddle with him. On what Score the two English Runagadoes turn'd here, I know not.

The Laws of this Country are very strict, and Offenders are punished with great Severity. Neither are there any Delays of Justice here; for as soon as the offender is taken, he is immediately brought before the Magistrate, who presently hears the Matter, and according as he finds it, so he either acquits, or orders Punishment to be inflicted on the Party immediately. Small offenders are only whipt on the Back, which sort of Punishment they call Chaubuck. A Thief for his first offence, has his right Hand chopt off at the Wrist: for the second Offence off goes the other; and sometimes instead of one of their Hands, one or both their Feet are cut off; and sometimes (tho' very rarely) both Hands and Feet. If after the Loss of one or both Hands or Feet, they still prove incorrigible, for they are many of them such very Rogues, and so arch, that they will steal with their Toes, then they are banish'd to Pulo Way, during their Lives: and if they get thence to the City, as sometimes they do, they are commonly sent back again; tho' sometimes they get a License to stay. AN. 1689

On Pulo Way there are none but this sort of Cattle: and tho' they all of them want one or both hands, yet they so order Matters, that they can row very well, and do many things to admiration, whereby they are able to get a livelihood: for if they have no hands, they will get somebody or other to fasten Ropes or Withes about their Oars, so as to leave Loops wherein they may put the stumps of their Arms; and therewith they will pull an Oar lustily. They that have one hand can do well enough: and of these you shall see a great many even in the City. This sort of punishment is inflicted for greater Robberies; but for small pilfering the first time Thieves are only whipt; but after this a Petty Larceny is looked on as a great crime. Neither is this sort of punishment peculiar to the Achinese Government, but probably, used by the other Princes of this Island, and on the Island Java also, especially at Bantam. They formerly, when the King of Bantam was in his prosperity, depriv'd Men of the right hand for Theft, and may still for ought I know. I knew a Dutch-man so serv'd: he was a Seaman belonging to one of the King of Bantam's Ships. Being thus punished, he was dismist from his service, and when I was this time at Achin he lived there. Here at Achin, when a member is thus cut off,

AN. 1689 they have a broad piece of Leather or Bladder ready to clap on the Wound. This is presently applyed, and bound on so fast, that the Blood cannot issue forth. By this means the great Flux of Blood is stop'd, which would else ensue; and I never heard of any one who died of it. How long this Leather is kept on the Wound I know not: but it is so long, till the Blood is perfectly stanched; and when it is taken off, the clods of Blood which were prest in the Wound by the Leather, peel all off with it, leaving the Wound clean. Then, I judge, they use cleansing or healing Plaisters, as they see convenient, and cure the Wound with a great deal of ease.

I never heard of any that suffered Death for Theft. Criminals, who deserve Death, are executed divers ways, according to the Nature of the Offence, or the Quality of the Offender. One way is by Impaling on a sharp Stake, which passeth up right from the Fundament through the Bowels, and comes out at the Neck. The Stake is about the Bigness of a Man's Thigh, placed upright, one End in the Ground very firm; the upper sharp End is about 12 or 14 Foot high. I saw one Man spitted in this manner, and there he remain'd two or three Days: but I could not learn his Offence.

Noblemen have a more honourable Death; they are allowed to fight for their Lives: but the Numbers of those with whom they are to engage, soon put a Period to the Combat, by the Death of the Malefactor. The manner of it is thus; the Person condemned is brought bound to the Place of Execution. This is a large plain Field, spacious enough to contain Thousands of People. Thither the Achinese, armed as they usually go, with their Cresset, but then more especially, resort in Troops, as well to be Spectators, as Actors in the Tragedy. These make a very large Ring, and in the midst of the Multitude the Criminall is placed, and by him such Arms as are allowed on such Occasions: which are, a Sword, a Cresset, and a Lance. When the Time is come to Act, he is unbound, and left at his Liberty to take up his fighting Weapons. The Spectators being all ready, with each Man his Arms in his Hand, stand still in their Places, till the Malefactor advances. He commonly sets out with a Shriek, and daringly faces the Multitude: but he is soon brought to the Ground, first by Lances thrown at him, and afterwards by their Swords and Cressets. One was thus executed while I was there: I had not the fortune to hear of it till it was ended: but had this relation the same evening it was done, from Mr. Dennis Driscal, who was then one of the Spectators.

AN. 1689

This Country is governed by a Queen, under whom there are 12 Oronkeys, or great Lords. These act in their several Precincts with great Power and Authority. Under these there are other inferiour Officers, to keep the Peace in the several parts of the Queens Dominions. The present Shabander of Achin is one of the Oronkeys. He is a Man of greater knowledge than any of the rest, and supposed to be very rich. I have heard say, he had not less than 1000 Slaves, some of whom were topping Merchants, and had many Slaves under them. And even these, tho' they are Slaves to Slaves, yet have their Slaves also; neither can a stranger easily know who is a Slave and who not among them: for they are all, in a manner, Slaves to one another: and all in general to the Queen and Oronkeys; for their Government is very Arbitrary. Yet there is nothing of rigour used by the Master to his Slave, except it be the very meanest, such as do all sorts of servile Work: but those who can turn their hands to any thing besides Drudgery, live well enough by their industry. Nay, they are encouraged by their Masters, who often lend them Money to begin some trade or business withal: Whereby the Servant lives easie, and with great content follows what his Inclination or Capacity fits him for; and the Master also, who has a share in the gains, reaps the more profit, yet without trouble. When one of these Slaves dies, his Master is Heir to what he leaves; and his Children, if he has any, become his Slaves also: unless the Father out of his own clear gains has in his life time had wherewithal to purchase their Freedom. The Markets are kept by these People, and you scarce trade with any other. The Money-

An. 1689 changers also are Slaves, and in general all the Women that you see in the streets; not one of them being free. So are the Fisher-men, and others who fetch Firewood in Canoas from Pulo Gomez, for thence those of this City fetch most of their Wood, tho' there is scarce anything to be seen but Woods about the City. Yet tho' all these are Slaves, they have habitations or houses to themselves in several parts of the City, far from their Masters Houses, as if they were free People. But to return to the Shabander I was speaking of, all Merchant Strangers, at their first arrival, make their Entries with him, which is always done with a good Present: and from him they take all their dispatches when they depart; and all Matters of Importance in General between Merchants are determined by him. It seems to have been by his Conversion and Acquaintance with Strangers, that he became so knowing, beyond the rest of the Great men: and he is also said to be himself a great Merchant.

The Queen of Achin, as 'tis said, is always an old Maid, chosen out of the Royal Family. What Ceremonies are used at the chusing her I know not: Nor who are the Electors; but I suppose they are the Oronkeys. After she is chosen, she is in a manner confined to her Palace; for by report she seldom goes abroad, neither is she seen by any People of inferiour rank and quality; but only by some of her Domesticks: except that once a Year she is drest all in white, and placed on an Elephant, and so rides to the River in state to wash herself: but whether any of the meaner sort of People may see her in that Progress I know not: for it is the custom of most Eastern Princes to skreen themselves from the sight of their Subjects: Or if they sometimes go abroad for their pleasure, yet the People are then ordered either to turn their backs towards them while they pass by, as formerly at Bantam, or to hold their Hands before their Eyes, as at Siam. At Mindanao, they may look on their Prince: but from the highest to the lowest they approach him with the greatest respect and veneration, creeping very low, and oft-times on their Knees, with their Eyes fixed on him: and when they withdraw, they return in the same manner, creeping backwards, and still keeping their Eyes on him, till they are out of his sight. AN. 1689

But to return to the Queen of Achin, I think Mr. Hackluit or Purchas, makes mention of a King[1] here in our King James I. time. But at least of later Years there has always been a Queen only, and the English who reside there, have been of the Opinion that these People have been governed by a Queen *ab Origine;* and from the antiquity of the present Constitution, have formed Notions, that the Queen of Sheba who came to Solomon was the Queen of this Country; and the Author of an old Map of the World, which I have seen, was, it seems, of this Opinion, when writing the old Hebrew names of Nations, up and down the several Parts anciently known of Europe, Asia, and Africa, he puts no other name in the Isle of Sumatra, but that of Sheba. But, be that as it will, 'tis at present part of it under a Queen, tho' she has little Power or Authority: for tho' there is seemingly abundance of respect and reverence shewn Her, yet she has little more than the Title of a Sovereign, all the Government being wholly in the hands of the Oronkeys.

While I was on my Voyage to Tonquin, the old Queen died, and there was another Queen chosen in her room, but all the Oronkeys were not for that Election; many of them were for chusing a King. Four of the Oronkeys who lived more remote from the Court, took up Arms to oppose the new Queen and the rest of the Oronkeys, and brought 5 or 6000 Men against the City: and thus stood the State of Affairs, even when we arrived here, and a good while after. This Army was on the East-side of the River, and had all the Country on that side, and so much of the City also, as is on that side the River, under their Power: But the Queen's Palace and the main part of the City,

[1] Purchas, "Captaine Best, his entertainment at Achen" (ed. Mac Lehose, vol. iv. p. 137, *et seq.*): "the custome is, at landing, to present the King with some small thing, and he requiteth it by severall dishes of meate," A-, &c. This particular king sent a gift to James I., viz., "a Cryse or Dagger, an Hasegu (spear ?), foure pieces of fine Callicut lawne, and eight Camphire dishes."

AN. 1689 which stands on the West side, held out stoutly. The River is wider, shallower, and more sandy at the City, than any where else near it: yet not fordable at low Water. Therefore for the better communication from one side to the other, there are Ferry-boats to carry Passengers to and fro. In other places the Banks are steep, the River more rapid, and in most places very muddy: so that this place, just at the City itself, is the most convenient to transport Men or Goods from one side to the other.

It was not far from this place the Army lay, as if they designed to force their passage here. The Queens party, to oppose them, kept a small Guard of Soldiers just at the Landing-place. The Shabander of Achin had a Tent set up there, he being the chief manager of her Affairs: and for the more security, he had 2 or 3 small brass Guns of a Minion Bore planted by his Tent all the day, with their Muzzels against the River. In the Evening there were 2 or 3 great Trees drawn by an Elephant, and placed by the side of the River, for a Barricado against the Enemy: and then the Brass Guns were drawn from the Shabander's Tent, which stood not far from it, and planted just behind the Trees, on the rising Bank: So that they looked over the Trees, and they might fire over, or into the River, if the Enemy approached. When the Barricado was thus made and the Guns planted, the Ferry-boats passed no more from side to side, till the next Morning. Then you should hear the Soldiers calling to each other, not in menacing Language, but as those who desired Peace and Quietness, asking why they would not agree, why they could not be of one Mind, and why they should desire to kill one another. This was the Tone all Night long; in the Morning as soon as Sun was risen, the Guns were drawn again to the Shabander's Tent, and the Trees were drawn aside, to open the Passage from one Side to the other: and every Man then went freely about his Business, as if all had been as quiet as ever, only the Shabander and his Guard staid still in their Stations: So that there was not any Sign of Wars, but in the Night only, when all stood to their Arms: and then the Towns-people seemed to be in fear, and sometimes we should have a Rumour, that the Enemy would certainly make an Attempt to come over. AN. 1689

While these Stirs lasted, the Shabander sent to all the Foreigners, and desired them to keep in their own houses in the Night, and told them, that whatever might happen in the City by their own civil Broils, yet no harm should come to them. Yet some of the Portuguese, fearing the worst, would every Night put their richest Goods into a Boat, ready to take their Flight on the first Alarm. There were at this Time not above 2 or 3 English Families in the Town, and 2 English Ships, and one Dutch Ship, besides 2 or 3 Moors Ships of the Moguls Subjects, in the Road. One of the English Ships was called the *Nellegree;* the Name taken from Nellegree Hills in Bengal, as I have heard. She came from the Bay of Bengal, laden with Rice, Cotton, &c. the other was the *Dorothy* of London, Captain Thwait Commander, who came from Fort St. George, and was bound to Bencouli with Soldiers, but touched here, as well to sell some Goods, as to bring a Present to the Queen from our East-India Company. Captain Thwait, according to custom went with his Present to the Queen, which she accepted; and complemented him with the usual Civilities of the Country; for to honour him he was set upon an Elephant of the Queen's to ride to his Lodgings, dressed in a Malayan Habit, which she gave him; and she sent also two Dancing Girls to shew him some Pastime there: and I saw them at his Lodgings that Evening, dancing the greatest Part of the Night much after the same Manner of the Dancing-women of Mindanao, rather writhing their Hands and Bodies with several Antick Gestures, than moving much out of the Place they were in. He had at this Time about twenty great Jars of Bengal Butter, made of Buffaloes Milk; and this Butter is said also to have Lard or Hog's Fat mixt with it, and rank enough in these hot Countries, tho' much esteemed by all the Achinese, who give a good Price for it; and our English also use it. Each of the Jars this came in contained 20 or 30 Gallons; and they were set in Mr. Driscal's Yard at Achin: What other Goods the Captain brought I know not.

But not long after this he being informed that the Moors Merchants residing here had carried off a great Treasure aboard their Ships, in Order to return with it to Surrat, and our Company having now Wars with the great Mogul, Captain Tiwait in the Evening drew off all his Seamen, and sent them on board of the Moors Ships, where he thought the Treasure was. The biggest he let alone: She was a Ship that the Captain Constant took in the Road sometime before, and having plundered her, he gave her to the Queen, of whom the Moors bought her again. The Moors Merchants had speedy Notice of this Action of Captain Tiwait, and they presently made their Application to the Queen for Satisfaction. But her Affairs at this Time being in such a Posture as I mentioned, by Reason of their intestine Broils, she said she could do nothing for them.

It was 10 or 11 a Clock the next Day, before we who lived ashore heard of Captain Tiwaits Proceedings: but seeing the Moors flock to Court, and not knowing what Answer they had from the Queen, we posted off to the Ships for fear of being imprisoned, as some English Men had been while I was at Tonquin, on the like Score. Indeed I had at this Time great Cause to be afraid of a Prison, being sick of a Flux, so that a Prison would have gone near to have killed me: yet I think it fared not much better with me, for the Ships I fled to afforded me but little Comfort. For I knew no Man aboard the *Dorothy*, and could expect no Comfort there. So I and the rest went aboard the *Nellegree*, where we could more reasonably expect Relief, than in a Ship that came from England: For these which come so long a Voyage, are just victualled for the Service, and the Seamen have every one their stinted Allowance, out of which they have little enough to spare to Strangers.

But tho' there were Victuals enough aboard the *Nellegree*, yet so weak as I then was, I had more mind to rest my self than to eat: and the Ship was so pestered with Goods, that I could not find a Place to hang up my Hammock in. Therefore it being fair Weather, I made a Shift to lye in the Boat that I came aboard in. My Flux was violent, and I slept but little; so I had the Opportunity of observing the Moon totally Eclipsed, had I been in a Condition to observe any Thing. As soon as I perceived the Moon to be eclipsed, I gazed at it indeed, as I lay, till it was totally obscured, which was a pretty while: but I was so little curious, that I remembred not so much as what Day of the Month it was; and I kept no Journal of this Voyage, as I did of my other, but only kept an Account of several particular Remarks and Observations as they occurred to me. I lay three or four Days thus in this Boat, and the People of the Ship were so kind as to provide me with Necessaries: and by this Time the Moors had got a Pass from the Dutch Captain then in the Road, for 4 or 500 Dollars, as I was then told, and Captain Thwait delivered them their Ship again, but what Terms he made with them, I know not. Thus that Fray was over, and we came ashore again, recovered of the Fright we had been in. In a short Time also after this, the Achinese all agreed to own the new Queen, and so the War ended without any Bloodshed.

I was perswaded to wash in the River, Mornings and Evenings, for the Recovery of my Health: and tho' it seemed strange to me before I tried it, yet I found so much Comfort in the first Trial, that I constantly applied my self to it. I went into the River till the Water was as high as my Waste, and then I stooped down and found the Water so cool and refreshing to my Body, that I was always loth to go out again. Then I was sensible that my Bowels were very hot, for I felt a great Heat within me, which I found refresht by the cool Water. My Food was Salt-fish broyled, and boiled Rice mixt with Tire. Tire is sold about the Streets there: 'tis thick sower Milk. It is very cooling, and the Salt-fish and Rice is binding: therefore this is thought there the proper Food for the common People, when they have Fluxes. But the richer Sort will have Sago, which is brought to Achin from other Countries, and Milk of Almonds.

But to return to the State of Achin: before I go off from it I shall add this short Account of the Seasons of Year there, that their Weather is much the same as in other

AN. 1689 Countries North of the Line, and their dry Seasons, Rains, and Land-floods come much at the same Time, as at Tonquin and other Places of North Latitude. Only as Achin lies within a few Degrees of the Line, so upon the Sun's crossing the Line in March, the Rains begin a little sooner there than in Countries nearer the Tropick of Cancer: and when they are once set in, they are as violent there as any where. I have seen it rain there for 2 or 3 Days without Intermission; and the River running but a short Course, its Head not lying very far within Land, it soon overflows, and a great part of the Street of the City, shall on a sudden be all under Water; at which Time People row up and down the Streets in Canoas. That Side of the City towards the River especially, where the Foreign Merchants live, and which is lower Ground, is frequently under Water in the wet Season: a Ship's Long-boat has come up to the very Gate of our English Factory laden with Goods; which at other Times is Ground dry enough, at a good Distance from the River, and moderately raised above it. I did not find the Heat there any Thing different from other Places in that Latitude; tho' I was there both in the wet and dry Season. 'Tis more supportable than at Tonquin; and they have constantly the Refreshment of Sea and Land-Breezes every 24 Hours.

CHAP. VIII

The Author prepares to go for Pegu. Among others a Ship arrives here from Merga in Siam. Of the Massacre of the English there. His intended Cargo for Pegu. The arrival of other English Men from the City of Siam. The Author sets out for Malacca instead of Pegu. They are becalmed, and soon after in great Danger of running aground. The Coast of Sumatra from Diamond Point to the River Dilly. They water there and at Pulo Verero; where they meet a Ship of Danes and Moors from Trangambar. Pulo Arii, and Pulo Parselore, a useful Sea-mark to avoid Sholes near Malacca Shore. The Author arrives at Malacca Town. The Town and its Forts described: the Conquest of it by the Dutch, from the Portuguese. Chinese and other Merchants residing here. The Sale of Flesh and Fish; the Fruits and Animals. The Shabander, State of the Trade, and Guard-Ships. Opium, a good Commodity among the Malayans. Rattan Cables. They prepare for their return back to Achin.

AS soon as I was pretty well recovered, I was shipt AN.
Mate of the Sloop that came from Malacca 1689
with us, which Mr. Wells had sold to Captain Tyler, who lately came from Siam: and I was sent aboard to take Possession of her, about the Beginning of May, 1689. He who was designed to command her came to Achin Mate of the *Nellegree;* and we were now to go to Pegu, but before the Middle of June he left the Employ, being sick, and loth to go at this dead Time of the Year to Pegu, because the Westerly Wind was set in strong, and the Coast of Pegu is low Land, and we were both unacquainted on the Coast. I was then made Commander, and took in Goods in order to depart for that Coast. In the mean time Mr. Coventry arrived in his Ship from the Coast of Coromandel laden with Rice, and a

AN. 1689 small Vessel belonging to Capt. Tyler came also from Merga much about the same Time.

This last Ship had been at Merga[1] a considerable time, having been seized on by the Siamites, and all the Men imprisoned, for some difference that happened between the English and them. Neither was a Prison then thought hard Usage by them, for during the Havock was made of the English there, many of those who lived at Merga were massacred. Those who were imprisoned, were kept there till all the English who lived at the City of Siam, on the other Side of the Kingdom, withdrew from thence: and then these Men had their Liberty restored also, and their Ship given them, but no Goods, nor Satisfaction for their Losses, nor so much as a Compass to bring with them, and but little Provision. Yet here they safely arrived. This being a better Ship than I was gone aboard of, Captain Tyler immediately fitted her up for the Sea, in order to send her to Pegu.

By this Time my Vessel was loaden, and my Cargo was eleven thousand Coco-nuts, five or six hundred Weight of Sugar, and half a dozen Chests of Drawers of Japan work, two were very large, designed for a Present to the King. Besides this, Capt. Tyler, for so we used to call him, tho' he was only a Merchant, said he intended to send a good Quantity of Gold thither, by which he expected to gain 60 or 70 per Cent; for by Report the King of Pegu had lately built a very magnificent Pagoda, and was gilding it very richly with Gold: besides he was making a large Image of Massy Gold for the chief Pagod of this Temple. By this Means Gold was risen in its Value here: and Achin being a place abounding in that Metal, much of it had already been sent thither from hence, and more was going in other Vessels, belonging to the Moors of Achin, beside what Captain Tyler designed to send.

It was now about the Middle of August; and tho' I was ready to sail, yet I was ordered to stay for Captain

[1] Mergui.

Tyler's other Vessel, till she had taken in her Lading, which was daily sent off. Her Cargo also was Coco-nuts, and she had about 8 or 9000 already aboard: when I received an Order from Captain Tyler to hale aboard of her, and put all my Cargo into her; as also all my Water-cask, and whatever else I could spare that they wanted; but withal he desired me to be satisfied, and told me I should in a short Time be sent to Sea: but that Ship being the biggest, he thought it more convenient to dispatch her first. I presently did as I was ordered; and finding that I should not go this Voyage, I sold also my small Cargo, which consisted only of some Coco-nuts and about 100 Nutmegs, which had the shells on as they grew on the Trees. I bought all that I could meet with in the Town, and paid about 3 d a piece, and expected to have had 12 d. a Piece for them at Pegu, where they are much esteemed if the Shells be on, for else they don't value them.

AN. 1689

About this Time the *George*, a great English Ship belonging to one Mr. Dalton, arrived here from the City of Siam, coming thro' the Streights of Malacca. He had been there some Years trading to and fro, and had made very profitable Voyages: but the late Revolution that hapned there by the Death of the King, and the unhappy fate of my Lord Falcon, caused the English to withdraw from thence. The French were all sent away some Months before, being not suffered to stay in the Kingdom: but before this Ship came from thence, the Broils of State were over; for the new King being settled, all Tumults which commonly arise in these Countries at the Death of the King, were appeased. The English were then desired to stay there, and those who had yielded up their Places and Offices, were even intreated to accept them again, for they owned that they had all served the Nation faithfully. But not long before the Revolution, the Governor of Fort St. George sent for all the English from thence particularly, and from the Service of all other Indian Princes, to come and serve the East-India Company at the Fort, or where else they should send them. For that Reason they all came away with Mr. Dalton, and he, in kindness to his

AN. 1689 Country-men, refused to take in Goods or Freight, because he would have room enough for their Passage, and their Household Goods: for here were some Families of Men, Women and Children.

They were a long time coming from Siam to Achin, because they came against the Monsoon; and in their Passage they touch'd at Malacca, and when they arrived at Achin, Mr. Dalton went ashore and hired an House, as did also most of his Passengers: and among the rest Captain Minchin, who had formerly served the East-India Company at Surrat, but on some disgust left that Place and came to Siam. There he was made Gunner of a Fort, and maintained his Wife and Family very well in that Employ, till the Revolution there, and the Companies orders came and called him from thence. He being now destitute of Employment, the Merchants there thought of making him Commander of the Vessel that I was in, because Captain Tyler was minded to sell part of Her. Accordingly they met about it, and the Vessel was divided into four Parts, three of which were purchased by Mr. Dalton, Mr. Coventry, and Capt. Minchin, and Captain Tyler kept the 4th. The next Day Capt. Minchin came off with an order to me to deliver him the possession of the Ship, and told me, that if I liked to go his Mate, I might still keep aboard till they had agreed on a Voyage. I was forced to submit, and accepted a Mate's Employ under Captain Minchin. It was not long before we were ordered for Malacca to buy Goods there. We carried no Goods with us, besides 3 or 400 pound of Opium.

It was about the middle of September, 1689, when we sailed from Achin. We were four white Men in the Vessel, the Captain, and Mr. Coventry, who went Supercargo, myself and the Boatswain. For common Seamen we had 7 or 8 Moors: and generally in these Country Ships the White-men are all Officers. Two Days after we left Achin, being becalmed under the Shore, we came to an Anchor. Not long after a Ship coming in from the Seaward, came to an Anchor about 2 Mile a-head of us. Mr. Coventry knew her to be a Danish Ship belonging to Trangambar; and therefore we hoisted out our Boat, and thought to have spoken with her: but a small Breeze springing up, they weighed their Anchors and went away; neither would they speak with us, tho' we made signs for them to stay. We weighed also and jogg'd on after them, but they sailed better than we. We met little Winds and Calms, so that it was seven or eight Days before we got as far as Diamond-point, which is about forty leagues from Achin. AN. 1689

Being about four leagues short of that Point, Captain Minchin desired me to set the Land, and withal prick the Card, and see what Course we ought to keep all Night; for it was now about 6 a-Clock, and we had a fine gale at W. S. W. our course yet being E. S. E.

After I had set the Land, I went into the Cabbin to look over the Draught to see what course we must steer after we came about the Point. Mr. Coventry followed me, and when I had satisfied my self, he asked me what course we must steer? I told him E. S. E. till 12 a-Clock, if the gale stood, and then we might hale more Southerly. He seemed to be startled at it, and told me, that the Captain and he had been pricking the Card, and thought that S. E. or S. E. by S. course would do well at 8 a-Clock. I said it was a good course to run ashore; he argued a long time with me, but I persisted in my Opinion, and when I told Captain Minchin of my Opinion, he was well satisfied. Presently after this we had a pretty strong Tornado out of the S. W. which obliged us to hand our Top-sail. When the stress of the weather was over, we set our sails again, and went in to Supper, and ordered the Man at Helm not to come to the Southward of the E. S. E. We stayed in the Cabbin till about 8 a-Clock, and then we came out to set the Watch. It was now very dark, by reason of a Thunder-Cloud that hung rumbling over the Land: yet by the flashes of lightning we plainly saw the Land, right a-head of us. I was much surprised, and ran into the Steeridge to look on the Compass, and found that we were steering S. S. E. instead of E. S. E. I clapt the Helm a Starboard, and brought her to N. E. by E. and N. E. and we very narrowly escap'd being cast away.

AN. 1689 When we first went to Supper we were 3 leagues off Land, and then E. S. E. was a good course, the Land lying E. S. E. parallel with our course.

But then the Man at Helm mistaking his Compass steer'd S. S. E. which runs right in upon the Shore. I believe we had also some counter-current or Tide that help'd us in, for we were quickly got into a Bay within the points of Land. So that 'twas now absolutely necessary to steer Northerly to get out of the Bay; and by this time Mr. Coventry was satisfied with what I told him in the Evening, and was convinced of his Error. I undertook to direct the Man at Helm, and the Wind continuing, I kept off till ten a-Clock: then I steered E. S. E. till 12, and then haled up S. S. E. and in the Morning we were about 4 leagues S. E. from Diamond-point, and about 3 leagues to the North of an Island.

The Land from hence lying S. S. E. we steered so; but meeting with calms again, we anchored several times before we came to the River of Dilly, which is 28 leagues from Diamond-point. The Land between seems to be uneven, most of it pretty high, and very woody: and 'tis said that all this Country, as far as the River Dilly, is under the Queen of Achin.

About a League before we came to that River, being within 2 Mile of the Shore, we saw the Water of a muddy grey Colour, and tasting it, found it to be sweet. Therefore we presently filled some of our Water Cask; and 'tis an ordinary thing in several places to take up fresh Water at Sea, against the mouth of some River where it floats above the Salt-water: but we must dip but a little way down; for sometimes if the Bucket goes but a foot deep it takes up Salt-water with the fresh.

In the Evening we had a fine Land Breeze, with which we ran along the Shore, keeping on a wind, and sounding every now and then. At last we were got among the Sholes, at the mouth of that River, and puzzled to get out again. The River is in Lat. 3 d. 50 m. N. It seems to be very large, but it is not well known, but only to the Natives who inhabit it; and they are not very sociable;

but are, by Report, a Sort of Pirates living on Rapine. AN. 1689 In the Morning we saw a Sail standing off to an Island called Pulo Verero, lying in Lat. 3 d. 30 m. N. seven Leagues from the Mouth of the River Dilly. We having a fair Wind, stood after them, intending there to wood and water at Pulo Verero. For though we took no fresh Water the Evening before out of the Sea, yet at the River of Dilly it was brackish: for tho' the fresh Water is born up by the Salt, and might be intire without Mixture, yet by plunging of the Bucket somewhat too low, we might probably take up some of the Salt water with it. They came to an Anchor about two or three a-Clock in the Afternoon: but the Wind slacken'd, and it was eight a-Clock at Night before we came thither. We anchored about a Mile from them, and presently hoysed out our Boat to go aboard: for we judged that this was the Danish Ship, that we saw when we came first from Achin. I went in the Boat, because Mr. Coventry told me, that Mr. Coppinger was Surgeon of her, the same Person who was with me in the Boat when I was set ashore at the Nicobar Isles, but was not suffered to stay with me. Mr. Coventry was now in the Boat with me, and we went and haled the Ship, asking whence she came? and who was Commander? They answered, they were Danes from Trangambar, for 'twas the Ship we took it to be. Then they askt who we were? I answered English from Achin, and that Mr. Coventry was in the Boat, but they would not believe it till Mr. Coventry spoke and the Captain knew his Voice: neither did they till then believe we were Friends; for they had every Man his Gun in his Hand, ready to fire on us, if we had gone aboard without haling, as Mr. Coventry would have done, in Confidence that they knew him, had not I disswaded him. For it seems they were extreamly afraid of us, insomuch that the Commander, seeing us follow them in the Morning, would not have touched at these Islands, though he was in great want of Water; and had not his Black Merchants fallen before him on their Knees, and even prayed him to take Pity on them, they had not anchored here. These Merchants were Inhabitants of Trangambar on the Coast

AN. 1689 of Coromandel. They having no Ships of their own, when the Danes fit out a Ship, on any Voyage that they are inclined to, these Moors are obliged to joyn Stock with them, and they first make an Offer of it to them as a Kindness: and the Moors being generally desirous to trade, frequently accept of it almost on any Terms: but should they be unwilling, yet dare they not refuse, for fear of disobliging the Danes, who are Lords of the Place. In this Ship I found Mr. Coppinger: and he was the first that I had seen of all the Company that left me at the Nicobar Islands. The next Morning we filled our Water and weigh'd again; the Dane being gone a little before. He was bound to Jihore, to load Pepper, but intended to touch at Malacca, as most Ships do that pass these Streights. He also sailed better than we, and therefore left us to follow him.

We stood on yet nearest to the Sumatra Shore, till we came in Sight of Pulo Arii, in Lat. 3 d. 2 m. N. These are several Islands lying S. E. by E. Easterly from Pulo Verero about 32 Leagues distant. These Islands are good Marks for Ships bound thro' the Streights: for when they bear S. E. at 3 or 4 Leagues Distance, you may steer away E. by S. for the Malacca Shore, from whence you then may be about 20 Leagues. The first Land you will see is Pulo Parselore, which is a high peeked Hill in the Country, on the Malacca Coast: which standing by it self amidst a low Country, it appears like an Island though I know not whether it is really one; for it stands some Miles within the Shoar of the Continent of Malacca. It is a very remarkable Hill, and the only Sea-mark for Seamen to guide themselves through certain Sands that lye near the Main; and if it is thick hazy Weather, and the Hill is obscur'd, Pilots, unless they are very knowing in the Soundings, will hardly venture in: for the Channel is not above a League wide, and there are large Shoals on each Side. These Shoals lye ten Leagues from Pulo Arii, and continue till within 2 or 3 of the Malacca Shoar. In the Channel there is 12 or 14 Fathom Water, but you may keep 7 or 8 Fathom on either Side; and sounding all the Way, you may pass on without Danger.

We had a good Gale at West, which brought us in Sight of Pulo Parselore: and so we kept sounding till we came within the Shoar, and then we had the Town of Malacca about 18 Leagues distant from us, to the S. E. and by E. Being shot over to the Malacca Shore, there is a good wide Channel to sail in, you having the Shoals on one Side, and the Land on the other; to which last you may come as nigh as you see convenient, for there is Water enough, and good anchoring. The Tide runs pretty strong here; the Flood sets to the Eastward, and the Ebb to the West: and therefore when there is little Wind, and Ships cannot stem the Tide, they commonly anchor. But we being in with the Malacca Shoar, had a westerly Wind, which brought us before Malacca Town, about the Middle of October; and here I first heard that King William and Queen Mary were crowned King and Queen of England. The Dane that left us at Pulo Verero was not yet arrived: for, as we afterwards understood, they could not find the way thro' the Sands, but were forced to keep along without them, and fetch a great Compass about, which retarded their Passage.

AN. 1689

Malacca is a pretty large Town, of about 2 or 300 Families of Dutch and Portuguese, many of which are a mixt Breed between those Nations. There are also many of the Native Malayans inhabiting in small Cottages on the Skirts of the Town. The Dutch Houses are built with Stone, and the Streets are wide and straight, but not paved. At the North West of the Town there is a Wall and Gate to pass in and out: and a small Fort always guarded with Soldiers. The Town stands on a level low Ground, close by the Sea. The Land on the Backside of the Town seems to be morassy, and on the West-side, without the Wall, there are Gardens of Fruits and Herbs, and some fair Dutch Houses: but that Quarter is chiefly the Habitation of the Malayans. On the East-side of the Town, there is a small River which at a Spring-Tide will admit small Barks to enter. About 100 Paces from the Sea there is a Draw-bridge, which leads from the midst of the Town to a strong Fort, built on the East-side of the River.

AN. This is the chief Fort, and is built on a low level
1689 Ground, close by the Sea, at the Foot of a little steep Hill. Its Form is semicircular, according to the natural Position of the adjacent Hill. It fronts chiefly to the Sea, and having its Foundation on firm Rocks, the Walls are carried up to a good Height, and of a considerable Thickness. The lower Part of it is washed by the Sea every Tide. On the Back of the Hill, the Land being naturally low, there is a very large Moat cut from the Sea to the River, which makes the whole an Island; and that back Part is stockadoed round with great Trees, set up an end: so that there is no entring when once the Draw-bridge is haled up. On the Hill, within this Fort stands a small Church big enough to receive all the Towns-people, who come hither on Sundays to hear Divine Service: and on the Main, beyond the Fort, the Malayans are also seated close by the Sea.

The first Europeans who settled here were the Portuguese; They also built the great Fort: but whether they moted round the Hill, and made an Island of that Spot of Ground, I know not, nor what Charges have been bestowed on it since to make it defenceable; nor what other Alterations have been made; but the whole Building seems to be pretty ancient, and that Part of it which fronts to the Sea, was in all Probability, built by the Portuguese; for there are still the Marks of the Conquerours shot in the Walls. It is a Place so naturally strong, that I even wonder how they could be beaten out: but when I consider what other Places they then lost, and their Mismanagements, I am the less surprized at it. The Portuguese were the first Discoverers by Sea of the East-Indies, and had thereby the Advantage of Trade with these rich Eastern People, as also an Opportunity, thro' their Weakness, to settle themselves where they pleased. Therefore they made Settlements and Forts among them in divers Places of India, as here for one: and presuming upon the Strength of their Forts, they insulted over the Natives; and being grown rich with Trade, they fell into all Manner of Looseness and Debauchery; the usual Concomitant of Wealth, and as commonly the Fore-runner of Ruin. The Portuguese, at this Place, by Report, made use of the Native Women at their Pleasure, whether Virgins or married Women; such as they liked they took without Controul; and it is probable, they as little restrained their Lust in other Places; for the Breed of them is scattered all over India; neither are there any People of more different Complexions than of that Race, even from the Coal-black to a light Tawney. These Injuries exasperated the Native Malayans here who joyning with the Dutch, as I have been informed, found Means to betray to them their insolent Masters the Portuguese: than whom there are not a more despicable People now in all the Eastern Nations: and of all they once possest, they have now only Goa left, of any Place of Consequence. The Dutch are now Masters of most of the Places they were once possest of; and particularly this of Malacca.

AN. 1689

Malacca is a Place of no great Trade, yet there are several Moors Merchants always residing here. These have Shops of Wares, such as come from Surrat, and the Coast of Coromandel and Bengal. The Chinese also are seated here, who bring the Commodities of their Country hither, especially Tea, Sugar-candy, and other Sweet-meats. Some of them keep Tea-houses, where for a Stiver, a Man has near a Pint of Tea, and a little Porrenger of Sugar-candy, or other Sweet-meats, if he pleases. Others of them are Butchers: their chief Flesh is Pork, which you may have very reasonably, either fresh or salted: Neither are you desired to take any particular Piece, but they will cut a Piece at one Place, and the like at another, either fat or lean, as you would have it. Others among these Chinese are Trades-people; and they are all in general very industrious, but withal extraordinary Gamesters: and if they can get any to play with them, all Business must submit to that.

This Town is plentifully stored with Fish also. When the Fishermen come in, they all resort to a Place built purposely for the Sale of them. There are Soldiers waiting, who take the best for the Officers of the Fort; whether they pay for it, or that 'tis a Toll of Custom

AN. 1689 belonging to the Governor I know not; but after they are served, the rest are sold to any who will buy. The manner of selling is thus: The Fish which every Man brings in is sorted, yet all sold by the Lump at once, in the manner of an Outcry or Auction, but not by raising, but lowering the Price: for there is one appointed for this Sale, who sets the first Price higher than the Value of the Fish, and falls by Degrees, till the Price seems reasonable: then one or other buys. But these first Bargains are commonly bought by the Fish-wives, who retail them out again. Oysters are in great Plenty here, and very good when they are salt; but sometimes they are fresh and unsavory.

As for other Provisions, their Rice is brought to them from abroad. Such Fruits as they have are much the same as I have already described and are proper to the Climate, as Plantains, Bonanoes, Pine-apples, Oranges, Water-melons, Pumple-noses, Mango's, &c. but these are only in their Gardens, in no great Plenty; and the Country is all covered with Wood, like one Forest: and most of our Walking-Canes used in England, are brought from thence. They have also a few Cattle, Bullocks, and Horses, &c. having but little Pasturage, but good Store of tame Fowl, Ducks, and Poultry. The principal Person in the Town is the Shabander, a Dutch man, next in Power to the Governour, who lives in the Fort, and meddles not with Trade, which is the Shabander's Province, who seems to be chiefly concerned about the Customs of Goods.

This Town has no great Trade, by what I could see, but it seems to be designedly built to command the Passage of Shipping, going this way to the more Eastern Nations. Not but that Ships may pass far enough out of reach of their Cannon; but Guard-Ships belonging to the Town, and lying in the Road, may hinder others from passing. How the Portuguese managed their Affairs I know not: but the Dutch commonly keep a Guard-ship here; and I have been told they require a certain Duty of all Vessels that pass this way, the English only excepted: for all Ships touch at this Place, especially for Wood, Water, and Refreshment.

Two days after our Arrival here, the Danish Ship came also to an Anchor; but reporting that they were bound to Jihore, to lade Pepper, the Dutch told them it was but in vain for them to seek a Trade there; for that the King of Jihore, had agreed with the Dutch to trade only with them; and that to secure that Trade, they had a Guard-ship lying there. I had this Account from the Surgeon, Mr. Coppinger, who seemed a little concerned at it: because when he told me this, he could not tell whether they should proceed thither or no; but they did go thither, and found all this a Sham, and traded there to their own and the Natives Satisfaction, as he told me the next time I met him. This of Jihore being but a small Kingdom on the same Malacca Coast, 'tis not of Strength sufficient to resist the Power of the Dutch: neither could it benefit the Dutch to take it, should they attempt it; for the People would probably forsake it, and it would be too great a Charge for the Dutch to settle it themselves. And therefore they only endeavour to ingross the Pepper Trade; and it is probable enough that the Dutch might sometimes keep a Guard-ship there, as they do at other Places, particularly at Queda, Pulo Dinding, &c. For where there is any Trade to be had, yet not sufficient to maintain a Factory; for where there may not be a convenient Place to build a Fort, so as to secure the whole Trade to themselves, they send their Guard-ships, which lying at the Mouth of the Rivers, deter Strangers from coming thither, and keep the petty Princes in awe of them. They commonly make a Shew as if they did this out of Kindness to those People; yet most of them know otherwise, but dare not openly resent it. This probably causes so many petty Robberies and Piracies as are committed by the Malayans on this Coast. The Malayans, who inhabit on both sides the Streights of Malacca, are in general a bold People, and yet I do not find any of them addicted to Robbery, but only the pilfering poorer Sort, and even these severely punished among the trading Malayans, who love Trade and Property. But being thus provoked by the Dutch, and hindred of a free Trade by their Guard-ships,

AN. 1689

AN. 1689 it is probable, they therefore commit Piracies themselves, or connive at and incourage those who do. So that the Pirates who lurk on this Coast, seem to do it as much to revenge themselves on the Dutch, for restraining their Trade, as to gain this way what they cannot obtain in way of Traffick.

But to return to our Concerns here. I have said already, that we had only three or four hundred Pound of Opium in Goods, the rest was in Money to the Value of 2000 Dollars in the whole: but we did not pretend that we came hither purposely to trade, but that finding our Vessel unfit for the Sea, we put in here to mend and repair her. Leave was granted us for this; and I prepared to hale our Vessel ashore, at the West-end of the Town, not far from the small Fort. It is there soft Oazy Ground, near a Mile off Shore, and it deepens very leisurely, being Shole Water just by the Shore; and when the Tide goes out, it leaves the Oaz dry a Quarter of a Mile from the Shore: but a Mile from Shore, you have clean Sand, and about four Fathom at Low Water. Our Vessel floated in close to the Fort, and lay not twenty Yards from it, and at low Water it sunk down into the Mud: that we could not fit the After-part, as I would have done. Opium, which is much used by the Malayans in most Places, was a great Commodity here at this Time: but it is prohibited Goods, and therefore tho' many asked for it, we were shy of having it too openly known that we had any. But in short Mr. Coventry found a Customer, and they found means to get it ashore, while the Soldiers of the Fort were at Dinner. The Customer was a Dutch Man; and the Price he was to pay for it was as much as he was worth: and finding it to be naught, he would have been off his Bargain; and when Mr. Coventry would not release him, he absconded. But Mr. Coventry having an Interest in the Shabander, he compell'd the Man's Wife to pay for the Opium, under the Name of Gold; for so Mr. Coventry call'd it. The Shabander chid Mr. Coventry for smuggling with an Inferiour, when he might have done it better with him; but stood his Friend in compelling the Woman, though unjustly, to pay for the Opium. I saw this Dutch-man on board his own Vessel, when he had bought the Opium, and he was very pensive and sad. He had a pretty fine House without the Gates, and a Garden which maintained his Family with Pot-Herbs, Sallading, and Fruits, besides some for the Market. This was managed by his Wife, and he himself had two Sloops, and either imployed them in Trading among the Malayans for Pepper, carrying them such Commodities as they wanted, especially Opium, or by hiring himself and Sloop to the Dutch East-India Company, to go whither they would send him. It was not long since he had been at the Spice Islands with Rice, which he sold at a profitable Rate: but he told me he was not suffered to bring any Spice from thence, except eight or ten Pound for his own spending: neither was there so much Profit that way for him, as by trading at Home among the Malayans, either on the Coast of Malacca or Sumatra. For though he and other free Men are not suffered to trade for themselves to any Places where the Company have Factories, or Guard-ships, yet they could find Trade enough nearer Home, and by this Trade the Freemen of Malacca pick up a good Livelihood. It was on this Home Trade that he was now bound, and the Opium had been very beneficial to him, had it been good: but he went away and ordered his Wife not to pay for it, but left Mr. Coventry to take it again; and upon the Shabander's compelling her to take it and pay for it, she complained they were utterly undone, for the Opium, when it came to be examined was really very bad, and worth little or nothing.

AN. 1689

Here Mr. Coventry bought Iron-Bars, Arack, Canes, and Rattans, wherewith we loaded our Vessel, which was now set afloat again. The Dutch brought most of our Goods aboard, and were more kind than I expected, for they had not used to trade with us, and I believe the News of our Revolution in England had sweetened them; for they often drank the Konings Health with us very heartily. While we were here we made two new Cables of Rattans, each of them four Inches about. Our Captain

AN. 1689 bought the Rattans, and hired a Chinese to work them, who was very expert at making such wooden Cables. These Cables I found serviceable enough after, in mooring the Vessel with either of them; for when I carried out the Anchor, the Cable being thrown out after me, swam like Cork in the Sea; so that I could see when it was tight, which we cannot so well discern in our Hemp Cables, whose Weight sinks them down: nor can we carry them out but by placing two or three Boats at some Distance asunder, to buoy up the Cable, while the Long-Boat rows out the Anchor. To conclude with Malacca, our Goods being all aboard, we fill'd our Water; and got all in a Readiness for our Departure back again.

CHAP. IX

The Author departs from Malacca. They lose a Yard, and return to refit. They set out again, and run on a Shole, but get off with the Flood. Pulo Sambilong. They lose their Mizen-yard, and put into Pulo Dinding. The Island and Fort described; The opposite Coast. Tutaneg, a Sort of Tin. The Enmity between the Dutch here, and the Malayans on the Coast. A Rencounter with them. They leave Pulo Dinding and arrive at Achin. The Escape of some English Prisoners out of Bengal. The Author sets out again from Achin, and arrives at Fort St. George. Its pleasant Prospect. He goes thence to Bencouli in Sumatra. Its sight at Sea. Point of Sillabar. The Situation of Bencouli, Houses, Weather, Soil, Fruits, Animals, and Inhabitants. The Pepper Trade here and elsewhere. The first Settlement of the English here. The Fort, and Usage of the Natives. The Conclusion of the Supplement.

WE departed from Malacca towards Achin about the Middle of November 1689. Mr. Coventry being weary of Captain Minchin's Company, had bought a small Vessel of 7 or 8 Tuns, and laded her also with the same Kind of Goods. This he commanded himself, having a Portuguese Pilot, and 3 or 4 Mariners under him, and we set out both Ships in Company together. We had now in Captain Minchin's Ship but 2 white Men, the Captain and I, the Boatswain being gone with Mr. Coventry; but we took in as a Passenger one Mr. Richards an Englishman, who having lately married a Dutch Woman at Malacca, came aboard us with her, to go as Passengers to Achin with us. AN. 1689

We had a Land-Wind in the Morning and about eleven a Clock had the Wind at N. W. a pretty strong Gale: and at twelve our Fore-yard broke in the Middle. We made signs to Mr. Coventry to bear down to us; who

AN. weighing before was a Mile to Windward of us; but he
1689 kept on, fearing to return, as having bought his Ship there by Stealth: and we therefore returned alone into Malacca Road. As soon as we anchored, Mr. Richards was sent ashore to buy a new Yard; I gave him the Length and Bigness. It was Evening before he came aboard again, and he brought aboard an old Yard much too big and too long for us. This Piece I shortned and shaped to my Mind, and by twelve a Clock at Night, had it fixed and slung, rigg'd and the Sail bent to it.

Then we weighed again having a small Land Wind; but the Tide of Flood was against us, and drove us to the Eastward. When the Ebb came we jogg'd on, and got about three Leagues, anchoring when the Flood came, because the Winds were against us. Thus we continued plying with the Ebb, and anchoring every Flood, till we came to Pulo Parselore, where the Captain told me he would not go out the same way we came in, as I would have persuaded him, but kept the Malacca Shore aboard, and past within the Sholes. But in a few Hours after we ran upon a Shole, driven on it by the Tide of Flood, which here set to the Eastward, tho' by our reckoning it should have been half Ebb, and the Flood should have set Westward, as we had it all the rest of the way from Malacca: but the Sholes probably caused some whirling about of the Tide. However, the Sand we were stuck upon was not above 100 Yards in Circumference, and the Flood being rising we waited the Time of high Water, and then drove over it, having sent our Boat to discover how the Sholes lay, while our Ship was a-ground: Mr. Richards all the while being in great Fear, lest the Malayans should come off in their Boats and attack the Vessel.

We were now afloat again, and soon got without all the Sholes: yet we did not stand over towards Sumatra, but coasted along nearest the Malacca Shore, it being now most proper for us so to do; yet for having the Winds westerly, we could not have beat under the other Shore. 2 or 3 Days after this we had sight of some Islands called Pulo Sambilong, which in the Malayan Language signifies

nine Islands, there being so many of them, lying scattering AN.
at unequal Distances from each other. It was near one of 1689
these Islands, that Captain Minchin in a former Voyage was like to lose his Hand by a Prick with a Cat-fishes Fin, as I have said in my former Vol. p. 172, and tho' his Hand was cured, yet he has lost the use of it ever since; and is never likely to regain it more.

We stood in pretty near the Shore, in Hopes to gain a fresh Land Wind. About ten a Clock the Land Wind came off, a gentle Breeze, and we coasted along the Shore. But a small Tornado coming off from the Shore about Midnight, we broke our Mizen Yard, and being near a Dutch Island called Pulo Dinding, we made in for it, and anchored there the Night ensuing, and found there a Dutch Sloop, mann'd with about thirty Soldiers, at an anchor.

This is a small Island lying so nigh the Main, that Ships passing by cannot know it to be an Island. It is pretty high Land and well watered with Brooks. The Mould is blackish, deep and fat in the lower Ground: but the Hills are somewhat rocky, yet in general very woody. The Trees are of divers Sorts, many of which are good Timber, and large enough for any Use. Here are also some good for Masts and Yards; they being naturally light, yet tough and serviceable. There is good Riding on the East-side, between the Island and the Main. You may come in with the Sea Breeze, and go out with a Land Wind, there is Water enough, and a secure Harbour.

The Dutch, who are the only Inhabitants, have a Fort on the East-side, close by the Sea, in a Bending of the Island, which makes a small Cove for Ships to anchor in. The Fort is built 4 square, without Flankers or Bastions, like a House: every Square is about ten or twelve Yards. The Walls are of a good Thickness, made of Stone, and carried up to a good Heighth, of about thirty Foot, and covered over Head like a dwelling House. There may be about twelve or fourteen Guns in it, some looking out at every Square. These Guns are mounted on a strong Platform, made within the Walls, about sixteen Foot high;

AN. 1689 and there are Steps on the Outside to ascend to the Door that opens to the Platform, there being no other way into the Fort. Here is a Governour and about twenty or thirty Soldiers, who all lodge in the Fort. The Soldiers have their Lodging in the Platform among the Guns, but the Governour has a fair Chamber above it, where he lies with some of the Officers. About a hundred Yards from the Fort on the Bay by the Sea, there is a low timbered House, where the Governour abides all the Day Time. In this House there were two or three Rooms for their Use, but the chiefest was the Governour's Dining-Room. This fronted to the Sea, and the End of it looked towards the Fort. There were two large Windows of about seven or eight Foot square; the lower part of them about four or five Foot from the Ground. These Windows were wont to be left open all the Day, to let in the refreshing Breeze; but in the Night, when the Governour withdrew to the Fort, they were closed with strong Shutters, and the Doors made fast till the next day. The Continent of Malacca opposite to the Island, is pretty low champion Land, cloathed with lofty Woods; and right against the Bay where the Dutch Fort stands, there is a navigable River for small Craft.

The product of the Country thereabouts, besides Rice and other Eatables, is Tutaneg, a sort of Tin; I think courser than ours. The Natives are Malayans, who, as I have always observed, are bold and Treacherous: yet the Trading People are affable and courteous to Merchants.

These are in all respects, as to their Religion, Custom, and manner of Living, like other Malayans. Whether they are governed by a King or Raja, or what other manner of Government they live under, I know not. They have Canoas and Boats of their own, and with these they fish and traffick among themselves: but the Tin Trade is that which has formerly drawn Merchant Strangers thither. But tho' the Country might probably yield great quantities of this Metal, and the Natives are not only inclinable, but very desirous to trade with Strangers, yet are they now restrained by the Dutch, who have monopoliz'd that Trade to themselves. It was probably for the lucre of this Trade that the Dutch built the Fort on the Island; but this not wholly answering their ends, by reason of the distance between it and the Rivers mouth, which is about 4 or 5 Miles, they have also a Guard-ship commonly lying here, and a Sloop with 20 or 30 armed Men, to hinder other Nations from this Trade. For this Tutaneg or Tin is a valuable Commodity in the Bay of Bengal, and here purchased reasonably, by giving other Commodities in exchange: neither is this Commodity peculiarly found hereabouts, but farther Northerly also on the Coast; and particularly in the Kingdom of Queda there is much of it: The Dutch also commonly keep a Guard-ship, and have made some fruitless Essays to bring that Prince and his Subjects to trade only with them; but here over against P. Dinding, no Strangers dare approach to Trade; neither may any Ship come in hither but with consent of the Dutch. Therefore as soon as we came to an Anchor at the East-end of the Island, we sent our Boat a-shore to the Governour, to desire leave to wood, water, and cut a new Mizen-yard. He granted our request, and the Boat returned again aboard, and brought word also that Mr. Coventry touched here to water, and went out that Morning. The next Morning betimes Captain Minchin sent me a-shore to cut a Yard. I applyed my self to the Governour, and desired one of his Soldiers might go with me, and shew me the best Timber for that use; but he excused himself, saying, that his Soldiers were all busie at present, but that I might go and cut any Tree that I lik'd. So I went into the Woods, where I saw abundance of very fine strait Trees, and cut down such a one as I thought fit for my Turn: and cutting it of a just length, and stripping off the Bark, I left it ready to be fetcht away, and returned to the Fort, where I dined with the Governour. Presently after Dinner, our Captain, with Mr. Richards and his Wife came a-shore, and I went aboard. The Governour met them at Landing, and conducted them into the Dining-Room I spoke of, where they treated the Governour with Punch, made of Brandy, Sugar,

AN. 1689

AN. and Lime-juice, which they brought with them from aboard:
1689 for here is nothing, not so much as the Governour's Drink, but what is brought from Malacca: no Herbs or Fruit growing here: but all is either fetch'd from Malacca, or is brought by the Malayans from the Main. It is not through any sterility in the Soil, for that is very fat and fruitful: neither is it through laziness of the Dutch, for that is a Vice they are not guilty of: but it is from a continual fear of the Malayans, with whom tho' they have a Commerce, yet dare they not trust them so far, as to be ranging about the Island in any work of Husbandry, or indeed to go far from the Fort, for there only they are safe. But to return to the Governour, he, to retalliate the Captains and Mr. Richard's kindness, sent a Boat a fishing, to get some better Entertainment for his Guests, than the Fort yielded at present. About four or five a-Clock the Boat returned with a good Dish of Fish. These were immediately drest for Supper, and the Boat was sent out again to get more, for Mr. Richards and his Lady to carry aboard with them. In the mean time the Food was brought into the Dining-Room, and placed on the Table. The Dishes and Plates were of Silver, and there was a Silver Punch-Bowl full of Liquor. The Governour, his Guests, and some of his Officers were seated, but just as they began to fall to, one of the Soldiers cried out, Malayans, and spoil'd the Entertainment; for immediately the Governour, without speaking one word, leapt out of one of the Windows, to get as soon as he could to the Fort. His Officers followed, and all the Servants that attended were soon in Motion. Every one of them took the nearest way, some out of the Windows, others out of the Doors, leaving the 3 Guests by themselves, who soon followed with all the haste they could make, without knowing the meaning of this sudden Consternation of the Governour and his People. But by that time the Captain and Mr. Richards and his Wife were got to the Fort, the Governour, who was arrived before, stood at the door to receive them. As soon as they were entred the Fort, the Door was shut, all the Soldiers and Servants being within

already: nor was any Man suffered to fetch away the Victuals, or any of the Plate: but they fired several Guns to give notice to the Malayans that they were ready for them; but none of them came on. For this Uproar was occasioned by a Malayan Canoa full of armed Men that lay skulking under the Island, close by the Shore: and when the Dutch Boat went out the second time to fish, the Malayans set on them suddenly, and unexpected, with their Cressets and Lances, and killing one or two, the rest leapt overboard, and got away, for they were close by the Shore; and they having no Arms were not able to have made any resistance. It was about a Mile from the Fort: and being landed, every one of them made what haste he could to the Fort, and the first that arrived was he who cried in that manner, and frighted the Governour from Supper. Our Boat was at this time a-shore for water, and was filling it in a small Brook by the Banquetting-house. I know not whether our Boats Crew took notice of the Alarm, but the Dutch call'd to them; and bid them make haste aboard, which they did; and this made us keep good watch all Night, having all our Guns loaden and primed for Service. But it rained so hard all the night, that I did not much fear being attack'd by any Malayan; being inform'd by one of our Sea-men, whom we took in at Malacca, that the Malayans seldom or never make any attack when it rains. It is what I had before observed of other Indians, both East and West: and tho' then they might make their Attacks with the greatest advantage on Men arm'd with Hand-guns, yet I never knew it practised; at which I have wondered; for it is then we most fear them, and they might then be most successful, because their Arms, which are usually Lances and Cressets, which these Malayans had, could not be damaged by the Rain, as our Guns would be. But they cannot endure to be in the Rain: and it was in the Evening, before the Rain fell, that they assaulted the Dutch Boat. The next Morning the Dutch Sloop weighed, and went to look after the Malayans; but having sailed about the Island, and seeing no Enemies, they anchored again. I also sent Men ashore in our Boat to bring off the

AN. 1689

AN. 1689 Mizen-yard that I had cut the Day before: But it was so heavy a kind of Timber, that they could not bring it out of the Woods. Captain Minchin was still ashore, and he being acquainted with it, desired the Governour to send a Soldier, to shew our Men what Trees were best for our use: Which he did, and they presently cut a small Tree, about the bigness and length of that which I cut, and brought it aboard. I immediately went to work, and having fitted it for use, bent my Sail, and hoised it up in its place. In the Evening Captain Minchin and Mr. Richards and his Wife came aboard, having staid one Night at the Fort; and told me all that hapned to them ashore.

We now waited only for a Land Wind to carry us out. The former part of the Night we had much Rain, with Thunder and Lightning; but no Wind. At one a-Clock we had a small Land Wind, and got up our Anchors. We got out before Day clear of the Island, and we steered along shore to the Northward, intending to keep this shore aboard for 20 or 30 Leagues farther, if the Winds did not favour us; for the Sea Winds were now at N. W. This Day we kept near the shore, and the Night ensuing; but the next Day the Wind coming at N. and N. N. E. we stood over for Sumatra, and the next Evening we past by Diamond Point: And the Wind coming at E. N. E. we got, in about 2 Days more to Achin, about the end of November 1689.

Here we found Mr. Coventry, who had got hither 2 or 3 Days before us. Captain Minchin went ashore with his Passengers, and was discharged of his Command. I kept aboard till all the Goods were unladen, and then lay ashore, and was very sick for a Fortnight of a kind of Fever. But after Christmas I was sent aboard again, by order of Mr. Coventry, who had then bought out Mr. Dalton's and Capt. Tiler's Shares, to take the Charge of the Vessel, which he had then laded with Pepper, Cubebs (which I think grow somewhere in Sumatra) and Tutanegg, which he bought of an English Vessel that came from Queda to Achin; and with these he had also some of our Malacca Cargo, which we kept on board, viz. Rattans and Walking-Canes. With this Cargo we were bound for Fort St. George. We took in also 2 English Passengers, who had escaped out of Prison in the Mogul's Country. The one belong'd to the *Defence*, Capt. Heath's Ship, which I came home to England in afterwards; he was Purser of it: the other was a Midshipman in the *Princess Ann*, which return'd to England at the same Time. But during our War with the Mogul these Ships had been in the Bay of Bengal, to fetch away our Effects from the R. of Hugly. These 2 Men, with 2 or 3 others, went ashore upon some Occasion, and were taken Prisoners by the Mogul's Subjects; who sent them a great way up into the Country, where they were kept in close Custody, and often threatned with Death. The old Anabob, or Governour of the Province, being remov'd, and a new one coming thither, he released these Men, and gave them leave to go to the Sea-side, where finding a Dutch Ship bound to Batavia, these 2 and one more, went aboard her, the rest getting other Passage: But she meeting with that English Ship coming from Queda, which brought the Tutanegg I but now mentioned to Achin, they left the Dutch Ship, and went to Achin with the other English Vessel; and those 2 were now for going with us to Fort St. George.

AN. 1690

'Twas about New-years Day, 1690, that we set out from Achin again: We steered away toward the Nicobar Islands, and came in sight of that, which I had been formerly set ashore upon. But leaving it on our Starboard, we stood more Northerly up into the Bay; for by Mr. Coventry I had learnt there were Northerly and North Easterly Winds in the Bay at this time of Year. We stood over therefore as high as Pallacat; and having then a fair N. E. Wind, we run along the Coast till we came before Fort St. George, which was about the middle of January.

I was much pleased with the beautiful prospect this Place makes off at Sea. For it stands in a plain Sandy spot of Ground, close by the shore, the Sea sometimes washing its Walls, which are of Stone and high, with

An. 1690 Half-Moons and Flankers, and a great many Guns mounted on the Battlements: so that what with the Walls and fine Buildings within the Fort, the large Town of Maderas without it, the Pyramids of the English Tombs, Houses, and Gardens adjacent, and the variety of fine Trees scatter'd up and down, it makes as agreeable a Landskip as I have any where seen.

But 'tis not my design to enter into a Description of a place so well known to my Country-men as this is. It may suffice to have mentioned it; and that after some Months stay here, and meeting with Mr. Moody and Jeoly the Painted Prince, I prepared to go for Sumatra again; to Bencouli, as I have said in my former Vol. p. 495. I set out from Fort St. George with Captain Howel in July 1690, we steered a pretty way along the Coast of Coromandel, before we stood over for Sumatra; and then made the best of our way for Bencouli. I have in that Volume spoken of my Arrival there; but having given no account of the place, I shall do it briefly now, and so shut up this Supplement.

Bencouli lies on the West Coast of the Island of Sumatra, in about 4 d. S. Lat. It is a place noted enough at Sea; by Reason of a high slender Hill in the Country. It has a small Island before it within which Ships ride. The Point of Sillabar lies 2 or 3 Leagues to the Southward of it, and runs out farther than any part of the Shore, making a small Bay within it. Besides these marks, when you come within 2 or 3 Leagues of the Shore, you'll see the English Fort fronting to the Sea, which makes a fine show: On the N. W. of the Fort is a small River, at the Mouth of which is a large Store-house to put Pepper in. About a quarter of a Mile from the Sea stands a small Indian Village, close by the River, on the same side that the Fort is on, and but a small distance from it. The Houses are small and low, all built on Posts, after the Malayan manner, as at Mindanao and Achin; for 'tis a Swamp that the Town stands on: But the Malayans usually choose to build in such low places near Rivers, for the convenience of washing themselves, which they greatly delight in; as 'tis indeed a part of their Religion as Mahometans: And if they can, they will have their Houses stand on Posts over the River. AN. 1690

The Weather here is none of the pleasantest. There are great Rains chiefly in September, October, and November, and pretty great Heats. But when the Wind blew hard, which 'twould often do, the Air would be chill: And the Sea-breezes in fair Weather were generally pretty fresh and comfortable. The Land-winds coming over Swamps, usually brought a Stink with them. 'Tis in general an unhealthy Place; and the Soldiers of the Fort were sickly and died very fast. On the South side of the Fort is a fair champion Savannah, of a Mile or 2 Square, called Greenhil. It produces long thick Grass: The N. W. part of it fronts the Sea, and the S. E. is bounded with lofty Woods.

The Soil of this Country is very different, according to its different position: For within Land 'tis hilly, yet those Hills are clothed with Trees; which shews it to be fruitful enough. The low Land, near the River, especially near the Sea, is swampy, producing nothing but Reeds, or Bamboes: But the higher Ground, which is of a reasonable heighth, is very fruitful. The Mould is deep, and is either black or yellow; and in some places Clay; or such Mould as is very proper for making Bricks.

The Trees in the Woods are mostly large bodied, straight and tall: They are of divers sorts, some or other of them fit for any uses. The Fruits of the Country are much the same as at Achin and Malacca, viz. Limes, Oranges, Guava's, Plantains, Bonanoes, Coco-Nuts, Jacks, Durians, Mangoes, Mangastans; Pomkins, Pine-apples, and Pepper. The Roots are Yams, and Potatoes: Rice grows here pretty well also; but whether the Natives sow enough for their own spending or no, I know not. The Land Animals are Buffaloes, Bullocks, Deer, Wild Hogs, Porcupines, Guanoes, Lizards, &c. The tame Fowls are Ducks and Dunghil Fowls, both in great plenty. The wild Fowl are Parrots, Parakites, Pidgeons, Turtle-Doves, and many sort of smaller Birds.

AN. The Natives also are swarthy Indians, like their Neighbours of Achin. They are slender, straight, active, and industrious. They are sociable and desirous of Trade; but if they are affronted, they are treacherous and revengeful. They live together in Towns, and speak the Malayan Language: Conforming themselves in their Habit, Food, and Customs to other Malayans; who are all, so far as I learnt, of the Mahometan Religion. There are some Mechanicks among them; a few Smiths: But most of them are Carpenters, and let themselves out to hire to the English at the Fort. The Hatchets they work with are such as they use at Mindanao, so contrived as to serve also for an Adds. Here are also Fishermen, who get a livelihood by Fishing; and there are several sorts of Fish on the Coast, besides plenty of Green Turtle: Such of the Malayans as live near the English Fort are usually employed in the East-India Companies Service, to work for them: but the Country People are most Husbandmen. They plant Roots, Rice, Pepper-bushes, &c.

1690

Pepper is the chief vendible Commodity in this Country, it thrives very well on all the Coast; but the greatest quantity of what is exported from hence, is either brought down this River out of the Country, or fetched from Sillabar, or other places bordering on the Sea in small Vessels. Pepper grows plenty in other places of this Island; as at Indrapore, Pangasanam, Jamby, Bancalis, &c. It grows also on the Island Java, on the Coast of Malacca, Malabar, Cochinchina, &c. The Coast of Malabar is said to produce the best; or at least there the Natives take most care to have the best, by letting it grow till it is full ripe; for which reason it is larger and fairer than here where they gather it too soon, to avoid losing any: for as soon as it grows ripe 'tis apt to shed, and fall in waste to the ground.

It was the Pepper Trade that drew our English Merchants to settle here. For after Bantam[1] was lost, our English, who were wont to trade thither for this Spice,

[1] In 1683; but for some years before, the Dutch had hindered our merchants in the English factory there.

were at a great loss to regain the Pepper Trade, which now AN. 1690 was in a manner fallen with the other sorts of Spice into the hands of the Dutch: tho' the Pepper which we were wont to fetch from Bantam did not all grow on this Island Java, nor perhaps the tenth part of it; for as I have been informed it came most from Sumatra, particularly from Bencooly, and the adjacent parts. For this Reason it behoved our Merchants to get an Interest here to prop up their declining Trade. Yet, as I have been told, the success was more owing to the Natives of this place than themselves; for that some of the Raja's of the Country sent Ambassadors to Fort St. George to invite the English hither to take possession, before the Dutch should get it; who are never slack to promote their Interest, and were now setting out on the same design. But however that were, the English had the good fortune to get hither first: though so narrowly, that the Dutch were within an ace of preventing them, their Ships being in sight before our Men got ashore. But the Dutch coming thus too late, were put by their designs; for the English immediately got ashore some Guns, and stood ready to defend their interest. This might happen about the Year 1685, as I was informed; for they told me it was 5 or 6 Years before I came hither: and the English immediately fortified themselves. The Fort[1] as I said before, fronts to the Sea, and stands about 100 paces from the River. There has been a great deal of cost bestowed on it, but to little purpose; for 'tis the most irregular piece I ever saw. I told the Governour the best way was to new-model it, and face it with Stone or Brick, either of which might be easily had. He said he liked my Council, but being saving for the Company, he rather chose to repair it, by the making some Alterations:

[1] Alexander Hamilton says that it was called York Fort; and that "Brick and Stone Walls in that Country cannot long continue firm, because Concussions of the Earth are so frequent." The East India Company paid for its construction. The Governor, who managed the fort so "sorrily" during Dampier's stay, was "one Mr. Sowdon," who was "not very fit for that Charge, because of his intemperate drinking." He was recalled according to Hamilton and "either dyed or was killed" according to Dampier's Malayan Merchant. Hamilton adds that "another" was "sent in his place less sanguin."

AN. 1690 but still to as little purpose, for 'twas all made ground, and having no facing to keep it up, 'twould moulder away every wet Season, and the Guns often fall down into the Ditches.

What was possible to be done I endeavoured to do while I was there. I made the Bastions as regular as I could upon the Model they were made by: And whereas the Fort was designed to be a Pentagone, and there were but 4 of the Bastions made, I staked out ground for a 5th, and drew a Plan of it, which I gave the Government; and had I staid longer I should have made up the other Bastion: but the whole Plan is too big by half for so sorry a Garrison: and the best way of mending it, is to demolish all of it, and make a new one.

The Fort was but sorrily governed when I was there; nor was there that care taken to keep a fair Correspondence with the Natives in the Neighbourhood as I think ought to be, in all Trading places especially. When I came thither there were 2 Neighbouring Raja's in the Stocks, for no other Reason, but because they had not brought down to the Fort such a quantity of Pepper as the Governour had sent for. Yet these Raja's rule in the Country, and have a considerable number of Subjects; who were so exasperated at these Insolencies, that, as I have since been informed, they came down and assaulted the Fort, under the Conduct of one of these Raja's. But the Fort, as bad as it is, is Guard enough against such indifferent Soldiers as they are: who tho' they have Courage enough, yet scarce any Arms besides Back-swords, Cressets, and Lances, nor Skill to use Artillery, if they had it. At another time they made an Attempt to surprize the Fort, under pretence of a Cock-match; to which they hoped the Garrison would come out to share in the Sport, and so the Fort left with small Defence. For the Malayans here are great lovers of Cock-fighting, and there were about 1000 of them got together about this Match, while their armed Men lay in ambush. But it so hapned, that none of the Garrison went out to the Cock-match, but one John Necklin, a Dane, who was a great Gamester himself: And he discovering the Ambush, gave notice of it to the Governour, who was in disorder enough upon their Approach: But a few of the great Guns drove them away. AN. 1690

I have nothing more to add but what concerns my self; which is not so material, that I should need to trouble the Reader with it. I have said in my former Volume, p. 503, upon what Motives I left Bencouli: And the particulars of my Voyage thence to England are also in that Volume: So that I may here conclude this Supplement to my Voyage round the World.

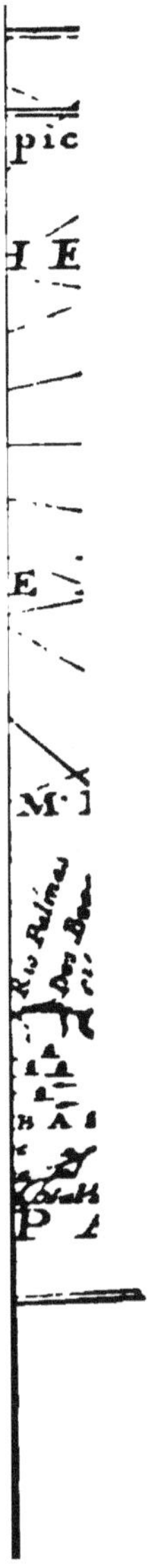

pic

H E

E

M·

Rio Palmas

Dos Bor

P A

MR. DAMPIER'S VOYAGES

TO THE

BAY OF CAMPEACHY

VOL. II. PART II

CONTAINING AN ACCOUNT OF THE BAY OF CAMPEACHY IN THE WEST-INDIES, AND PARTS ADJACENT.

CHAP. I

The Author's first going to Sea, to France, to Newfoundland, and after to the East-Indies. His setting out for the West-Indies. Of St. Lucia, the Caribbe-Indians, and Captain Warner. He arrives at Jamaica; His Abode and Travels there, and first Voyage to Campeachy. The East and North of Jucatan described. Key-Mugere, Cape-Catoch, and its Logwood-cutting. The Mount and its Salt-petre Earth. The Indian Towns, the Tarpom-Fish, Fishermen, and Lookouts. Rio de la Gartos, Salt-Ponds, Selam, Sisal, and Cape Condecedo. His first Arrival at Island Trist, in the Bay of Campeachy. His anchoring at One-Bush-Key, and Entertainment among the Logwood-cutters. The escape of four English Prisoners from Mexico, and Campeachy. He returns for Jamaica, and is chased by two Spanish Vessels. The difficulty of their Passage back, and his falling foul of the Alcranes Isles. The Boobies and Egg-Birds there, &c. Sword-Fish, Nurses, Seals, &c. Of Captain Long and others Ship-wrack'd here. The Soundings hereabout: He passeth through the Colorado Shoals, and anchors near Cape St. Antonio in Cuba; and standing to the Island of Pines, anchors at the Island of Grand Caymanes. He goes back and anchors at Island Pines, its Product, Racoons, Land-Crabs, fierce Crocodiles, Cattle, &c. He stands off to Sea again, and with the help of a seasonable North Wind, after much difficulty, arrives at Jamaica.

An. 1673 AMONG other Things referred to in my former Volume, I mentioned an Account I intended to give of the Bay of Campeachy, where I lived first and last about 3 Years. I shall now discharge my self of that Promise; and because my Campeachy Voyages were in order of Time, before that Round the World, I shall upon this occasion go so far back as to speak briefly of my first going to Sea, and the Rambles I made till my setting out for Campeachy.

My Friends did not originally design me for the Sea, but bred me at School till I came to Years fit for a Trade. But upon the Death of my Father and Mother, they who had the disposal of me, took other Measures; and having removed me from the Latin School to learn Writing and Arithmetick, they soon after placed me with a Master of a Ship at Weymouth, complying with the Inclinations I had very early of seeing the World: With him I made a short Voyage to France: and returning thence, went to Newfoundland, being then about eighteen Years of Age. In this Voyage I spent one Summer; but so pinched with the rigour of that cold Climate, that upon my return I was absolutely against going to those parts of the World, but went home again to my Friends. Yet going up a while after to London, the offer of a warm Voyage and a long one, both which I always desired, soon carried me to Sea again. For hearing of an outward-bound East-India Man, the *John and Martha* of London, Captain Earning Commander, I entered my self aboard, and was employed before the Mast, for which my two former Voyages had some way qualified me. We went directly for Bantam in the Isle of Java, and staying there about two Months, came home again in little more than a Year; touching at

St. Jago of the Cape Verd Islands at our going out, and at Ascension in our return. In this Voyage I gained more Experience in Navigation, but kept no Journal. We arrived at Plymouth about two Months before Sir Robert Holmes[1] went out to fall upon the Dutch Smyrna Fleet: and the second Dutch Wars[2] breaking out upon this, I forbore going to Sea that Summer, retiring to my Brother in Somersetshire. But growing weary of staying ashore, I listed my self on board the *Royal Prince*, commanded by Sir Edward Sprague,[3] and served under him in the Year 1673, being the last of the Dutch War. We had three Engagements that Summer; I was in two of them, but falling very sick, I was put aboard an Hospital Ship a Day or two before the third Engagement, seeing it at a distance only; and in this Sir Edward Sprague was killed. Soon after I was sent to Harwich with the rest of the Sick and Wounded: And having languished a great while, I went home to my Brother to recover my Health.

AN. 1673

By this time the War with the Dutch was concluded; and with my Health, I recovered my old Inclination for the Sea. A neighbouring Gentleman, Colonel Hellier of East-Cocker in Somersetshire, my Native Parish, made me a seasonable Offer to go and manage a Plantation of his in Jamaica, under one Mr. Whalley: for which Place I set out with Capt. Kent in the *Content* of London.

I was then about 22 Years old, and had never been in the West-Indies; and therefore, lest I might be trepann'd[4] and sold as a Servant after my Arrival in Jamaica, I agreed with Captain Kent to work as a Seaman for my Passage, and had it under his Hand to be cleared at our first Arrival. We sailed out of the River Thames in the Beginning of the Year 1674, and meeting with favourable

[1] Sir Robert Holmes (1622-1692) attacked the "Dutch Smyrna Fleet" on the 12th of March 1671-2; and continued the action the day following.

[2] The first "Dutch Wars" lasted from 1664-5 until 1667.

[3] Sir Edward Spragge. The three engagements were fought on May 28, June 4, and August 11. In the last of the three, Sir Edward Spragge was killed as he rowed from the *Royal Prince* to the *St. George*.

[4] Many immigrants suffered this fate.

AN. 1674 Winds, in a short Time got into the Trade-wind, and went merrily along, steering for the Island Barbadoes. When we came in sight of it Captain Kent told his Passengers, if they would pay his Port-Charges he would anchor in the Road, and stop whilst they got Refreshment: But the Merchants not caring to part with their Money, he bore away, directing his Course towards Jamaica.

The next Island that appeared in our view was St. Lucia. 'Tis distant from Barbadoes about 30 Leagues, and very wealthy in large Timber Trees fit for all uses. For this Reason 'tis often visited by the English, who stock themselves here with Rollers, &c. They have endeavoured to settle an English Colony there, but hitherto unsuccessfully, because of the Caribbe-Indians.

The Caribbees are a sort of Warlike Indians, delighting to rove on the Sea in Periagoes or large Canoas. Their chiefest Habitations are on the Main; but at certain Seasons of the Year they visit the Islands for their Pleasure. Barbadoes was formerly much frequented by them; but since the English settled there they have been forced to abandon it, and content themselves in their Sea-Voyages, or with such Islands only as are not possessed by the Europeans; except where they have hopes of conquering; as they have done at St. Lucia.

Near the Main where these Indians live, lies Tabago, which, when it was first settled by the Dutch, was much infested by them. These Indians, as I have heard, had formerly Plantations on most of the Caribbe-Islands; and in their Sea-Voyages did use to remain three Weeks or a Month at a Time on an Island, and then remove to another; and so visit most of them before their return to the Main.

St. Vincent is another of these Islands lying near St. Lucia: We passed between them; and seeing a Smoke on St. Lucia, we sent our Boat ashore there. Our Men found some of the Caribbe-Indians, and bought of them Plantains, Bonanoes, Pine-Apples, and Sugar-Canes; and returning aboard again, there came with them a Canoa with 3 or 4 of the Indians. These often repeated the Word Captain

Warner, and seemed to be in some disquiet about him. We did not then understand the meaning of it; but since I have been informed that this Captain Warner, whom they mentioned, was born at Antego,[1] one of our English Islands, and the Son of Governour Warner,[2] by an Indian Woman, and bred up by his Father after the English manner; he learned the Indian Language also of his Mother; but being grown up, and finding himself despised by his English Kindred, he forsook his Father's House, got away to St. Lucia, and there lived among the Caribbe-Indians, his Relations by the Mother side. Where conforming himself to their Customs he became one of their Captains, and roved from one Island to another, as they did. About this Time the Caribbees had done some spoil on our English Plantations at Antego: and therefore Governour Warner's Son by his Wife took a Party of Men and went to suppress those Indians, and came to the Place where his Brother the Indian-Warner lived. Great seeming Joy there was at their Meeting; but how far it was real the Event shewed; for the English-Warner providing plenty of Liquor, and inviting his half-Brother to be merry with him, in the midst of his Entertainment ordered his Men upon a Signal given to murder him and all his Indians: which was accordingly performed.[3] The Reason of this inhumane Action is diversly reported; some say that this Indian-Warner committed all the Spoil that was done to the English; and therefore for that Reason his

AN. 1674

[1] Antigua.

[2] "Old Sir Th. Warner," the Governor of the Caribbee Islands.

[3] "Governor Warner's son by his wife" was Colonel Philip Warner, Deputy-Governor of Antigua. "After the dispute was over, Colonel Warner invited Thomas Warner and his Indians, to the number of sixty or seventy men, women and children to an entertainment of thanks, and having made them very drunk with rum, gave a signal, and some of the English fell upon and destroyed them" (*Deposition of William Hamlyn*). Colonel Warner was sent to England to stand his trial, and remained a year in the Tower, after his dismissal from the king's service. At his trial it appeared that the Indian Warner was not his half-brother; that the Indians slain at the massacre "were always confederates with those that attacked us;" that they were "treacherous and bloody malefactors," and that they were killed in fair fight. He was acquitted, and William Hamlyn was punished for perjury; but many held that Warner was guilty, and that the trial was not rightly conducted.

AN. 1674 Brother kill'd him and his Men. Others that he was a great Friend to the English, and would not suffer his Men to hurt them, but did all that lay in his power to draw them to an amicable Commerce; and that his Brother killed him, for that he was ashamed to be related to an Indian. But be it how it will, he was called in Question for the Murder, and forced to come Home to take his Tryal in England. Such perfidious Doings as these, besides the Baseness of them, are great hindrances of our gaining an Interest among the Indians.

Putting from these Islands we steered away further West, and falling in with the East-end of Hispaniola, we ranged down along on the South Side even to Cape Tiburon, which is the West-end of the Island. There we lay by and sent our Boat ashore; for Captain Kent had been informed that there were great Groves of Orange-Trees near this Cape; but our Men not finding any, he then concluded there were none: But I have been since informed my self by several that have been there, that there are enough of them thereabouts.[1] From hence we steered away for Jamaica, where we arrived in a short Time, bringing with us the first News they had of the Peace with the Dutch.

Here, according to my Contract, I was immediately discharged; and the next Day I went to the Spanish Town, called Sant' Jago de la Vega;[2] where meeting with Mr. Whalley, we went together to Colonel Hellier's Plantation in 16 Mile-Walk. In our way thither we past through Sir Thomas Muddiford's Plantation, at the Angells, where at that Time were Otta and Cacao Trees growing; and fording a pretty large River, we past by the side of it 2 or 3 Miles up the Stream,[3] there being high Mountains on each

[1] Henry Morgan gathered great numbers here (as anti-scorbutics for his fleet) a few days before he sailed to take Old Providence.

[2] Sir Hans Sloane makes this note :—" St. Jago de la Vega, or St. James of the Plain, a Town improving every day, 'tis the place where the Governor usually resides, and where the Courts of Justice and Records of the Island are Kept. It was very great in the Spaniard's time."

[3] "The Road thither (to Sixteen Mile Walk) is by the Water-side or along the banks of the Rio Cobre, where there is a Stone under which one passes, as under an Arch" (Sir Hans Sloane, *Voyage*, vol. i.).

side. The way to 16 Mile-walk was formerly a great AN.
deal about, round a large Mountain; till Mr. Cary Hellier 1674
the Colonel's Brother, found out this way. For being desirous of making out a shorter Cut, he and some others coasted along the River, till they found it run between a Rock that stood up perpendicularly steep on each side, and with much difficulty they climbed over it. But a Dog that belonged to them, finding a hole to creep through the Rock, suggested to them that there was a hollow Passage; and he cleared it by blowing up the Rock with Gun-powder, till he had made a way through it broad enough for a Horse with a Pack, and high enough for a Man to ride through. This is called the Hollow Rock. Some other Places he levelled, and made it an indifferent good Passage.

He was a very ingenious Gentleman, and doubtless had he lived, he might have propagated some advantagious Arts on that Island. He was once endeavouring to make Salt-Petre at the Angells, but did not bring it to Perfection. Whether the Earth there was not right, I know not; but probably there may be Salt-petre Earth in other Places, especially about Passage-Fort, where, as I have been informed, the Canes will not make good Sugar, by Reason of the Saltness of the Soil.

I liv'd with Mr. Whalley at 16 Mile-Walk for almost six Months, and then enter'd my self into the Service of one Captain Heming, to manage his Plantation at St. Anns, on the North-side of the Island, and accordingly rode from St. Jago de la Vega toward St. Anns.

This Road has but sorry Accommodations for Travellers. The first Night I lay at a poor Hunter's Hut, at the Foot of Mount Diabolo[1] on the South-side of it, where for want of Clothes to cover me in the Night I was very cold when the Land-wind sprang up.

This Mountain is part of the great Ridge that runs the length of the Island from East to West; to the East 'tis called the Blew Mountain, which is higher than this.

[1] It seems to have been the custom to sleep at the foot of Mt. Diavolo, when crossing the Island. A rest-house, or hunter's hut, provided shelter, with beds, or shakedowns, of "plantain and palm-leaves."

An. The next Day crossing Mount Diabolo, I got a hard
1675 Lodging at the Foot of it on the North-side; and the third Day after arrived at Captain Heming's Plantation.

I was clearly out of my Element there, and therefore as soon as Captain Heming[1] came thither I disingaged my self from him, and took my Passage on Board a Sloop to Port-Royal, with one Mr. Statham, who used to trade round the Island, and touched there at that Time.

From Port-Royal I sailed with one Mr. Fishook, who traded to the North-side of the Island, and sometimes round it: and by these coasting Voyages I came acquainted with all the Ports and Bays about Jamaica, and with all their Manufactures; as also with the Benefit of the Land and Sea-winds. For our Business was to bring Goods to, or carry them from Planters to Port-Royal; and we were always entertained civilly by them, both in their Houses and Plantations, having Liberty to walk about and view them. They gave us also Plantains, Yams, Potatoes, &c. to carry aboard with us; on which we fed commonly all our Voyage.

But after six or seven Months, I left that Employ also, and shipt my self aboard one Captain Hudsel, who was bound to the Bay of Campeachy to load Logwood.

We sailed from Port-Royal about the beginning of August, 1675, in Company with Captain Wren in a small Jamaica Bark, and Captain Johnson Commander of a Ketch belonging to New-England.

This Voyage is all the way before the Wind, and therefore Ships commonly sail it in twelve or fourteen Days; neither were we longer in our Passage; for we had very fair Weather, and touched no where till we came to Trist Island in the Bay of Campeachy, which is the only place they go to. In our way thither we first sailed by little Caimanes, leaving it on our Larboard-side, and Key Monbrack,[2] which are two small Islands, lying South of Cuba. The next Land we saw was the Isle of Pines: and

[1] Captain Hemings, or Hemmings, owned the ruins of "the town called Sevilla," a fine brick and stone built Spanish city.

[2] Cayman Brac.

steering still Westerly, we made Cape Corientes:[1] and sailing on the South-side of Cuba, till we came to Cape Antonio, which is the West-end of it, we stretched over towards the Peninsula of Jucatan, and fell in with Cape Catoch, which is in the extream part of that Promontory towards the East.

AN. 1675

The Land trends from this Cape one way South about forty Leagues till you come to the Island Cozumel,[2] and from thence it runs S. W. down into the Bay of Honduras. About ten Leagues from Cape Catoch, between it and Cozumel, lies a small Island called by the Spaniards, Key-Muger,[3] or Womens-Island; because 'tis reported that when they went first to settle in these parts they left their Wives there, while they went over on the Main to find some better Habitation: Though now they have no Settlement near it, whatever they have had formerly.

About three Leagues from Cape Catoch, and just against it is a small Island called [4] Loggerhead Key; probably because it is frequently visited by a sort of Turtle so called: near this Island we always find a great Ripling, which Seamen call the Rip-raps. This Cape, though it appears to be part of the Main, yet is divided from it by a small Creek, scarce wide enough for a Canoa to pass through, though by it 'tis made an Island. This I have been credibly informed of by some, who yet told me that they made a shift to pass it in a Canoa.

The Cape is very low Land by the Sea, but somewhat higher as you go further from the shore. It is all overgrown with Trees of divers sorts, especially Logwood; and therefore was formerly much frequented by the Jamaica Men, who came thither in Sloops to load with it, till all the Logwood-Trees near the Sea were cut down; but now 'tis wholly abandoned, because the Carriage of it to the shore requires more Labour, than the cutting, logging, and chipping. Besides they find better Wood now in the Bays of Campeachy and Honduras, and have but a little way to carry it; not above 300 Paces, when I was there; whereas

[1] The S.W. end of Cuba.
[2] Cozumel retains its ancient name.
[3] Mugeres Island.
[4] Perhaps Contoy Island.

An. 1675 at Cape Catoch they were forc'd to carry it 1500 Paces before they left that Place.

From Cape Catoch we coasted along by the shore, on the North-side of Jucatan towards Cape Condecedo.[1] The Coast lies nearest West. The distance between these two Capes is about 80 Leagues. The shore lies pretty level without any visible Points or Bendings in the Land. It is woody by the shore, and full of sandy Bays and lofty Mangroves.

The first place of note to the West of Cape Catoch, is a small Hill by the Sea, call'd the Mount;[2] and is distant from it about 14 Leagues. It is very remarkable, because there is no other High-Land on all this Coast. I was never ashore here, but have met with some well acquainted with the Place, who are all of Opinion that this Mount was not natural, but the Work of Men: And indeed it is very probable this Place has been inhabited; for here are a great many large Cisterns, supposed to have been made for the receiving of Rain-water, for there are no fresh Springs to be found here, the Soil being all sandy and very salt. So that, as I have been credibly informed by an intelligent Person, the Spaniards do fetch of it to make Salt-Petre. He also told me, that being once there in a Privateer, and landing some Men on the Bay, they found about 100 Packs of this Earth bound up in Palmeto Leaves; and a Spanish Mulatto to guard it. The Privateers at first sight of the Packs were in hopes there had been Maiz or Indian-Corn in them, which they then wanted; but opening them they found nothing but Earth; and examining the Mulatto for what use it was, he said to make Powder, and that he expected a Bark from Campeachy to fetch it away. He further told me, that tasting of it he found it very salt; as all the Earth thereabouts was. So that it is not improbable that those Cisterns were made for the carrying on of Salt-Petre Work. But whatever was the design at first, it is now wholly laid aside: for there is no use made of them; neither are there any Inhabitants near this Place.

[1] Pt. Piedras. [2] Monte de Cuyo.

Between the Mount and Cape Condecedo, close by the Sea, are many little Spots of Mangrove Trees, which at a distance appear like Islands: but coming nearer, when other lower Trees appear, it shows like ragged and broken Ground; but at last all the Land presents it self to your view very even. AN. 1675

The next place of note on this Coast is Rio de la Gartos,[1] almost in the mid-way between Cape Catoch and Cape Condecedo. This also is a very remarkable Place; for here are two Groves of high Mangroves, one on each side the River, by which it may be known very well. The River is but small, yet deep enough for Canoas. The Water is good, and I know not any other Brook or fresh River on all the Coast from Cape Catoch till within three or four Leagues of Campeachy Town.

A little to the East of the River is a Fish-Range, and a small Indian Hutt or two within the Woods; where the Indian Fishers who are subject to the Spaniards, lye in the Fishing-Seasons, their Habitations and Families being farther up in the Country. Here are Poles to hang their Nets on, and Barbecues to dry their Fish. When they go off to Sea, they fish with Hook and Line about four or five Leagues from the Shore, for Snappers and Gropers, which I have already described in my Voyage round the World. Chap. iv. page 118.

Since the Privateers and Logwood-ships have sailed this way, these Fisher-men are very shy, having been often snapp'd by them. So that now when they are out at Sea, if they see a Sail, they presently sink their Canoas even with the edge of the Water; for the Canoas when they are full of Water, will sink no lower, and they themselves lye fast with their heads above Water, till the Ship which they saw is pass'd by or comes nigh. I have seen them under Sail, and they have thus vanished on a sudden. The Fish which they take near the Shore with their Nets, are Snooks, Dog-Fish, and sometimes Tarpoms.

The Tarpom is a large scaly Fish, shaped much like a

[1] Laguna de Lagartos.

Salmon, but somewhat flatter. 'Tis of a dark Silver Colour, with Scales as big as a Half Crown. A large Tarpom will weigh [illegible] or [illegible] Pound. 'Tis good sweet wholesome Meat, and the Flesh solid and firm. In its Belly you shall find two large Bladders of Fat, weighing two or three Pound each. I never knew any taken with Hook and Line; but are either with Nets, or by striking them with Harpoons, at which the Moskito-Men are very expert. The Nets for this Purpose are made with strong double Twine, the Meshes five or six Inches square. For if they are too small, so that the Fish be not entangled therein, he presently draws himself a little backward, and then springs over the Net: Yet I have seen them taken in a Sain made with small Meshes in this manner. After we have inclosed a great Number, whilst the two ends of the Net were drawing ashore, ten or twelve naked Men have followed; when a Fish struck against the Net, the next Man to it grasped both Net and Fish in his Arms, and held all fast till others came to his Assistance. Besides these we had three Men in a Canoa, in which they mov'd side-ways after the Net; and many of the Fish in springing over the Net, would fall into the Canoa: And by these means we should take two or three at every draught. These Fish are found plentifully all along that shore from Cape Catoch to Trist, especially in clear Water, near sandy Bays; but no where in muddy or rocky Ground. They are also about Jamaica, and all the Coast of the Main; especially near Carthagena.

West from Rio de la Gartos, there is a Look-out or Watch-tower, called Selam. This is a Place close by the shore, contrived by the Spaniards for their Indians to watch in. There are many of them on this Coast: Some built from the Ground with Timber, others only little Cages placed on a Tree, big enough for one or two Men to sit in, with a Ladder to go up and down. These Watch-towers are never without an Indian or two all the Day long; the Indians who live near any of them being obliged to take their turns.

About three or four Leagues Westward of[1] Selam, is

[1] Silan. There is a good spring at this place.

another Watch-box on a high Tree, called Linchanchee Lookout, from a large Indian Town of that Name, four Leagues up in the Country; and two Leagues farther within Land is another Town called Chinchanchee. I have been ashore at these Lookouts, and have been either rowing in a Canoa, or walking ashore on all this Coast, even from Rio de la Gartos to Cape Condecedo: but did never see any Town by the Shore, nor any Houses besides Fishing-Hutts on all the Coast, except only at Sisal. Between Selam and Linchanchee are many small regular Salt Ponds, divided from each other by little Banks; the biggest Pond not above ten Yards long and six broad.

AN. 1675

The Inhabitants of these two Towns attend these Ponds in the Months of May, June, and July to gather the Salt, which supplies all the Inland Towns of these Parts; and there is a skirt of Wood between the Sea and the Ponds, that you can neither see them nor the People at work till you come ashore.

From these Salt Ponds further West, about three or four Leagues, is the Lookout called Sisal.[1] This is the highest and most remarkable on all the Coast; it stands close by the Sea, and it is built with Timber. This is the first Object that we make off at Sea; and sometimes we take it for a Sail, till running nearer we discover the high Mangrove-Trees appearing in small Tufts at several distances from it.

Not far from hence there is a Fort with forty or fifty Soldiers to guard the Coast; and from this place there is a Road through the Country to the City of Merida. This is the chiefest City in all the Province of Jucatan, it being inhabited mostly with Spaniards: Yet there are many Indian Families among them, who live in great Subjection, as do the rest of the Indians of this Country. The Province of Jucatan, especially this Northern and the most Easterly part of it is but indifferently fruitful, in comparison of that rich Soil farther to the West: Yet is it pretty populous of Indians, who all live together in Towns; but none within

[1] Sisal. There is a lighthouse here.

An. five or six Miles of the Sea, except (as I said) at two or 1675 three Fishing places; and even there the Indians resort to fish but at certain Seasons of the Year. Therefore when Privateers come on this Coast, they fear not to land and ramble about, as if they were in their own Country, seeking for Game of any sort, either Fowl or Deer; of both of which there are great plenty, especially of the latter, though sometimes they pay dear for it: A small Jamaica Privateer once landed six or seven Men at this Lookout of Sisal; who not suspecting any Danger, ordered the Canoa with three or four Men to row along by the shore, to take them in upon their giving a sign or firing a Gun: But within half an Hour they were attack'd by about forty Spanish Soldiers, who had cut them off from the shore, to whom they surrendered themselves Prisoners. The Spaniards carried them in Triumph to the Fort, and then demanded which was the Captain. Upon this they all stood mute, for the Captain was not among them; and they were afraid to tell the Spaniards so, for fear of being all hanged for Straglers; neither did any one of them dare to assume that Title, because they had no Commission with them, nor the Copy of it; for the Captains don't usually go ashore without a Copy at least of their Commission, which is wont to secure both themselves and their Men.——At last one John Hullock cock'd up his little cropt Hat, and told them he was the Captain; and the Spaniards demanding his Commission, he said it was aboard; for that he came ashore only to hunt, not thinking to have met any Enemy. The Spaniards were well satisfied with this Answer, and afterwards respected him as the Captain, and served him with better Provision and Lodging than the rest; and the next day when they were sent to the City of Merida about twelve or thirteen Leagues from thence, Capt. Hullock had a Horse to ride on, while the rest went on Foot: And though they were all kept in close Prison, yet Hullock had the Honour to be often sent for to be examined at the Governour's House, and was frequently Regal'd with Chocolate, &c. From thence they were carried to Campeachy Town, where still Captain Hullock was better served than his Comrades: At last, I know not how, they all got their Liberties, and Hullock was ever after called Captain Jack. AN. 1675

It is about eight Leagues from Sisal to Cape Condecedo; twenty Leagues North of which lies a small Island, call'd by the Spaniards, Isles des Arenas,[1] but the English Seamen, as is usual with them, corrupt the Name strangely; and some call it the Desarts, others the Desarcusses;[2] but of this Island, having never seen it, I can give no account.

All this Coast from Cape Catoch to Cape Condecedo, is low Land, the Mount only excepted. It is most sandy Bay by the Sea; yet some of it is Mangrovy Land; within which you have some Spots of dry Savannah, and small scrubbed Trees, with short thick Bushes among them. The Sea deepens gradually from the shore, and Ships may anchor in sandy Ground in any depth from seven or eight Foot to ten or twelve Fathom Water.

In some Places on this Coast we reckon our distance from the Shore by the depth of the Sea, allowing four Fathom for the first League, and for every Fathom afterwards a League more.

But having got thus to Cape Condecedo, I shall defer the further description of these Parts from this Cape Southward and Westward to the High-Land of St. Martin,[3] which is properly the Bay of Campeachy: and from thence also further Westward, till my second coming on this Coast, when I made so long a stay here. To proceed therefore with my present Voyage; having past Cape Catoch, the Mount, Rio de la Gartos, Sisal, and Cape Condecedo, we stood Southward directly for Trist, the Haven of our Logwood-Cutters; at which Place being not above 60 Leagues distant, we soon arrived.

Trist is the Road only for big Ships, smaller Vessels that draw but a little Water run 3 Leagues farther, by crossing over a great Lagune that runs from the Island up

[1] Cay Arenas; a stony, sandy islet some ninety miles to the N.W. of Pt. Piedras.

[2] "The English Seamen" were confounding it with the Arcas, and the Desertas Cays, which are similar islets to the south of Cay Arenas.

[3] The Volcano de Tuxtla.

AN. 1675 by the Spaniards, was sent to the City of Mexico, where they remained Prisoners six or eight Months, but at last were remanded to La Vera Cruz, and from thence by Sea to Campeachy: They were not imprisoned, but only kept to work on Board the Ship that brought them, and soon found an Opportunity of making their Escapes in this manner. They had been employed ashore all the Day, and being sent aboard at Night they fell to contrive how to run away with the Boat; but considering that they wanted Necessaries for their Voyage, they resolved first to go back and supply themselves, which they might then do the better, because they knew there were none but a few Indians on Board. Accordingly having seized and bound the Indians, taking with them a Compass, with some Bread and Water, they put off to Sea, and arriv'd at Trist a Week before our Departure: And this Will. Wooders was the means under God of the Preservation of our Ship.

The third Day, after we left Trist, about eight in the Morning, near twelve or fourteen Leagues W. S. W. from Campeachy, we saw two Sail about three Leagues to Windward coming directly towards us, the Captain supposing that they had been Jamaica Vessels, would have lain by to hear some News, and to get some Liquor from them; for we had now none on Board but a few Bottles in a small Case, that the Captain reserved for his own Drinking. But Wooders withstood the Captain's Proposal, and told him, that when he came from Campeachy there were two small Vessels ready to sail for Tobasco River, which is not above 11 or 12 Leagues Leeward of Trist, and that it was more probable these were those two Vessels than any from Jamaica. Upon this we edged off more to Sea, and they also altered their Course steering away still directly with us; so that we were now assured they were Spaniards; and therefore we put away; quartering, and steering N. W. and though they still fetched on us a-pace, yet to make the more Speed they turned a Boat loose that was in Tow at one of their Sterns, and She being a good Sailer came within Gun-shot of us; when, as it pleased God, the

Land-wind dyed away of a sudden, and the Sea Breeze did not yet spring up. AN. 1675

While the Wind lasted we thought our selves but a Degree from Prisoners; neither had we yet great Hopes of escaping; for our Ketch, even when light, was but a dull Sailer, worse being deep loaden. However, we had now time to unbend the Foresail, and make a studding Sail of it, to put right before the Sea-Breeze when it should spring up. This was accordingly done in a Trice, and in less than an Hour after the Breeze sprung up fresh, and we put right before the Wind. We had this Advantage in it, that all the Sail we had did us Service; while on the contrary, those who chased us, being three Mast Vessels, could not bring all theirs to draw; their After-sails becalmed their Head-sails, and we held them tack for two or three Hours, neither gaining nor losing Ground. At last the Wind freshing on by the coming of a Tornado, we gained considerably of them; so they fired a Gun and left their Chase, but we kept on crouding till Night; and then clapp'd on a Wind again and saw no more of them.

In about a Fortnight after this, we were got as far to the East as Rio de la Gartos, and there overtook us a small Barmudoes Boat belonging to Jamaica which had not been above ten Days come from Trist, but sailed much better than we did. Therefore our Merchant went on board of her, for he saw we were like to have a long Passage; and Provision began to be scarce already, which he could not so well brook as we. Our Course lay all along against the Trade-wind.

All the Hopes that we had was a good North, this being the only Time of the Year for it: and soon after we saw a black Cloud in the N. W. (which is a Sign of a North, but of this more in my Discourse of Winds) for two Days, Morning and Evening. The third Day it rose apace and came away very swiftly. We presently provided to receive it by furling all but our Main-sail; intending with that to take the Advantage of it. Yet this did us but little Service; for after an Hour's time, in which it blew fresh at N. W. the Cloud went away, and the Wind came about again at E. N. E. the usual Trade in these Parts. We therefore made use of the Sea and Land-Breezes, as we had done before: and being now as high as the beforemention'd Fishing Banks on the North of Jucatan, we so ordered our Business, that with the Land-winds we run over to the Banks: and while it was calm between the Land-winds and Sea-Breeze, we put out our Hooks and Lines and fished, and got Plenty every Morning: One Time our Captain after he had haled in a good Fish, being eager at his Sport, and throwing out his Line too hastily, the Hook hitched in the Palm of his Hand, and the Weight of the Lead that was thrown with a Jerk, and hung about six Foot from the Hook, forced the Beard quite through, that it appeared at the Back of his Hand.

Soon after this we got as high as the Mount, and then stood off about 30 Leagues from Land, in hopes to get better to Windward there, than near the Shore; because the Wind was at E. S. E. and S. E. by E. a fresh Gale: continuing so 2 or 3 Days. We steered off to the North, expecting a Sea-Breeze at E. N. E. and the third Day had our Desire. Then we tack'd and steered in again S. E. for the Shore of Jucatan. Our Ketch, as I said, was a heavy Sailer, especially on a Wind: for she was very short; and having great round Bows, when we met a Head-Sea, as now, she plunged and laboured, not going a-head, but tumbling like an Egg-shell in the Sea. It was my Fortune to be at the Helm from 6 a Clock in the Evening till 8. The first 2 Glasses she steered very ill; for every Sea would strike her dead like a Log; then she would fall off 2 or 3 Points from the Wind, though the Helm was a Lee;[1] and, as she recovered, and made a little way, she would come again to the Wind, till another Sea struck her off again. By that Time 3 Glasses were out the Sea became more smooth; and then she steered very well, and made pretty fresh way through the Water. I was somewhat surprized at the sudden Change, from a rough Sea

[1] It may be necessary to point out that when the helm is put down, or to leeward, the ship comes up into the wind. When it is put up, or to windward, the ship "falls off" from the wind.

to a smooth; and therefore looked over-board 2 or 3 AN.
Times; for she steered open on the Deck,[1] and it being 1675
very fair Weather, all our Men were lain down on the Deck and fallen asleep. My Captain was just behind me on the Quarter Deck fast asleep too, for neither he nor they dreaded any Danger, we being about 30 Leagues from the Main-Land, at Noon, and as we thought, not near any Island.

But while I was musing on the sudden Alteration of the Sea, our Vessel struck on a Rock, with such Force that the Whipstaff[2] threw me down on my Back: This frighted me so much that I cried out, and bad them all turn out, for the Ship struck. The Surge that the Ship made on the Rock, awakened most of our Men, and made them ask, What the matter was? But her striking a second Time, soon answered the Question, and set us all to work for our Lives. By good Fortune she did not stick, but kept on her way still, and to our great Comfort, the Water was very smooth, otherwise we must certainly have been lost; for we very plainly saw the Ground under us: so we let go our Anchor, in 2 Fathom Water, clean white Sand: When our Sails were furled, and a sufficient Scope of Cable veered out, our Captain, being yet in amaze, went into his Cabin, and most of us with him to view his Draught, and we soon found we were fallen foul of the Alcranes.[3]

The Alcranes are 5 or 6 low sandy Islands, lying in the Lat. of about 23 d. North, and distant from the Coast of Jucatan about 25 Leagues: the biggest is not above a Mile or two in Circuit. They are distant from one another 2 or 3 Miles, not lying in a Line, but scattering here and there, with good Channels of 20 or 30 Fathom Water,[4] for a Ship to pass between. All of them have good Anchoring on the West-sides, where you may ride in what Depths you please, from 10 to 2 Fathom Water, clean sandy

[1] *I.e.*, the wheel was not under a poop or half deck.

[2] The whipstaff was a bar of iron or wood used as a tiller aboard small ships.

[3] The Alacran Reefs.

[4] The channels are rather shallower than Dampier states. "20 or 30 feet" would be more accurate.

AN. 1675 Ground. On some there are a few low Bushes of Burton-wood, but they are mostly barren and sandy, bearing nothing but only a little Chicken-Weed; neither have they any fresh Water. Their Land-Animals are only large Rats, which are in great Plenty; and of Fowls, Boobies in vast Abundance, with Men of War and Egg-Birds. These inhabit only some of the Northermost of them, not promiscuously one among another, but each sort within their own Precincts, (viz.) the Boobies and the other two sorts each a-part by themselves; and thus two or three of the Islands are wholly taken up. The Boobies being most numerous, have the greatest Portion of Land. The Egg-Birds,[1] tho' they are many, yet being but small, take up little room to the rest: Yet in that little part which they inhabit, they are sole Masters, and not disturbed by their Neighbours. All three Sorts are very tame, especially the Boobies, and so thick settled, that a Man cannot pass through their Quarters, without coming within Reach of their Bills, with which they continually peckt at us. I took notice that they sat in Pairs; and therefore at first thought them to be Cock and Hen; but upon striking at them, one flew away from each Place, and that which was left behind seemed as malicious as the other that was gone. I admired at the Boldness of those that did not fly away, and used some sort of Violence to force them, but in vain; for indeed these were young Ones, and had not yet learned the use of their Wings, tho' they were as big and as well feathered as their Dams, only their Feathers were something whiter and fresher. I took notice that an old one, either the Cock or Hen, always sat with the Young to secure them; for otherwise these Fowls would prey on each other, the Strong on the weak, at least those of a different Kind would make bold with their Neighbours: the Men-of-War-Birds as well as the Boobies left Guardians to the Young, when they went off to Sea, lest they should be starved by their Neighbours; for there were a great many old and lame Men-of-War-Birds that could not fly off to Sea to

[1] A sort of tern common throughout the West Indies (*Hydrochelidon fuliginosum*).

seek their own Food. These did not inhabit among their Consorts, but were either expelled the Community, or else chose to lye out at some Distance from the rest, and that not altogether; but scattering here and there, where they could rob securest: I saw near 20 of them on one of the Islands, which sometimes would sally into the Camp to seek for Booty, but presently retreated again, whether they got any thing or nothing. If one of these lame Birds found a young Booby not guarded, it presently gave him a good Poult[1] on the Back with his Bill to make him disgorge, which they will do with one Stroak, and it may be cast up a Fish or two as big as a Man's Wrist; this they swallow in a Trice, and march off, and look out for another Prize. The sound Men-of-War will sometimes serve the old Boobies so off at Sea. I have seen a Man-of-War fly directly at a Booby, and give it one blow, which has caused it to cast up a large Fish, and the Man-of-War flying directly down after it, has taken it in the Air, before it reach'd the Water.

AN. 1675

There are Abundance of Fish at some Distance from these Islands, by which the Fowls inhabiting here, are daily supplied.

The Fish near the Island, are Sharks, Sword-Fishes, and Nurses; all three sorts delighting to be near sandy Bays; those that I saw here were but of a small Size, the Sword-fish not above a Foot and a half, or two Foot long; neither were the Sharks much longer, and the Nurses about the same Length. The Nurse is just like a Shark, only its Skin is rougher, and is used for making the finest Rasps. Here are many Seals: they come up to sun themselves only on two or three of the Islands, I don't know whether exactly of the same kind with those in colder Climates, but, as I have noted in my former Book, they always live where there is Plenty of Fish.

[1] An excellent old word which deserves to be retained. *Cf.* Purchas, [illegible] I. Book 6, Chap. 6, concerning another Somersetshire sailor. "John [illegible] . . . tooke off the Pumpe brake or handle, and cast it to William [illegible] . . . bidding him knocke him (a Turkish pirate) downe, which he was not [illegible] in doing, but lifting up the wooden weapon he gave him such a palt [illegible] the pate as made his braines forsake the possession of his head."

An. 1675 To the North of these Islands lyes a long Ledge of Rocks bending like a Bow; it seems to be 10 or 12 Yards wide, and about 4 Leagues long, and 3 Leagues distant from the Island. They are above Water, all joining very close to one another, except at one or two Places, where are small Passages about 9 or 10 Yards wide; 'twas through one of these that Providence directed us in the Night; for the next Morning we saw the Riff about half a Mile to the North of us, and right against us was a small Gap, by which we came in hither, but coming to view it more nearly with our Boat, we did not dare to venture out that way again. One Reason why we would have gone out to the Northward, was, because from our Main-top we saw the Islands to the Southward[1] of us, and being unacquainted, knew not whether we might find among them a Channel to pass through; our second Reason was the Hopes of making a better Slant in for the Shore, if we could weather the East end of the Riff. In order to this we weighed Anchor, keeping down by the Side of the Riff till we were at the West end of it, which was about a League from where we anchored: then we stood off to the North, and there kept plying off and on to weather the East end of the Riff, three Days; but not being able to effect it, by Reason of a strong Current setting to the N. W. we ran back again to the West end of the Riff, and steered away for the Islands. There we anchored and lay three or four Days, and visited most of them, and found Plenty of such Creatures, as I have already described.

Though here was great Store of such good Food and we like to want, yet we did neither salt any, nor spend of it fresh to save our Stock. I found them all but one Man averse to it, but I did heartily wish them of another Mind, because I dreaded wanting before the end of the Voyage; a Hazard which we needed not to run, there being here such Plenty of Fowls and Seals, (especially of the latter) that the Spaniards do often come hither to make Oyl of their Fat; upon which Account it has been visited by

[1] They must have run aground a little to the north of the Isla Desterrada, the most northerly of the group.

English-men from Jamaica, particularly by Capt. Long: AN.
who having the Command of a small Bark, came hither 1675
purposely to make Seal-Oyl, and anchored on the North side of one of the sandy Islands, the most convenient Place, for his Design:——Having got ashore his Cask to put his Oyl in, and set up a Tent for lodging himself and his Goods, he began to kill the Seal, and had not wrought above three or four Days before a fierce North-wind blew his Bark ashore. By good Fortune she was not damnified: but his Company being but small, and so despairing of setting her afloat again, they fell to contriving how to get away; a very difficult Task to accomplish, for it was 24 or 25 Leagues to the nearest Place of the Main, and above 100 Leagues to Trist, which was the next English Settlement. But contrary to their Expectation, instead of that, Capt. Long bid them follow their Work of Seal-killing and making Oyl; assuring them that he would undertake at his own Peril to carry them safe to Trist. This though it went much against the Grain, yet at last he so far prevailed by fair Words, that they were contented to go on with their Seal-killing, till they had filled all their Cask. But their greatest Work was yet to do, viz. how they should get over to the Main, and then coast down before the Wind to Trist. Their Boat was not big enough to transport them, so they concluded to cut down the Barks Masts and rip up her Deck to make a Float for that Purpose.

This being agreed on, the next Morning betimes, pursuant to their Resolution, they were going to break up their Vessel; but it happened that very Night, that two New-England Ketches going down to Trist, ran on the Backside of the Riff, where they struck on the Rocks, and were bulged; and Captain Long and his Crew seeing them in Distress, presently took their Boat, and went off to help them unlade their Goods, and bring them ashore: and in Requital they furnished the Captain with such Tackle and other Necessaries as he wanted, and assisted him in the launching his Vessel, and lading his Oyl, and so they went merrily away for Trist. This lucky Accident

AN. 1675 into the Main-Land, where they anchor at a Place called One-Bush-Key. We stayed at Trist three Days to fill our Water, and then with our two Consorts sailed thence with the Tide of Flood; and the same Tide arrived there. This Key is not above forty Paces long, and five or six broad, having only a little crooked Tree growing on it, and for that Reason it is called One-Bush-Key. It seems to be only a Heap of Shells, for the Island is covered with them. The greatest Part are Oyster-shells. There are a great many Oyster-banks in this Lagune, and the adjacent Creeks, but none afford better, either for Largeness or Taste, than the Bank about this Island. In the wet Season the Oysters as well of One-Bush-Key as other Places here, are made fresh by the Freshes running out of the Country: But in the dry Time they are salt enough. In the Creeks they are smaller, but more numerous; and the Mangrove-Roots that grow by the Sides of the Creeks are loaden with them; and so are all the Branches that hang in the Water.

One-Bush-Key is about a Mile from the Shore; and just against the Island is a small Creek that runs a Mile farther, and then opens into another wide Lagune; and through this Creek the Logwood is brought to the Ships riding at the Key. Between the Oyster-Banks that lye about the Island and the Main, there is good Riding in about 12 Foot Water. The bottom is very soft Oaz, insomuch that we are forced to shooe our Anchors to make them hold. The Main by it is all low Mangrovy-Land, which is overflow'd every Tide; and in the wet Season is covered with Water. Here we lay to take in our Lading.

Our Cargo to purchase Log-wood was Rum and Sugar; a very good Commodity for the Log-wood-cutters, who were then about 250 Men, most English, that had settled themselves in several Places hereabouts: Neither was it long before we had these Merchants come aboard to visit us; we were but 6 Men and a Boy in the Ship, and all little enough to entertain them: for besides what Rum we sold by the Gallon or Firkin, we sold it made into Punch, wherewith they grew Frolicksome. We had none but small Arms[1] to fire at their drinking Healths, and therefore the Noise was not very great at a Distance; but on Board the Vessels we were loud enough till all our Liquor was spent: We took no Money for it, nor expected any; for Log-wood was what we came hither for, and we had of that in lieu of our Commodities after the Rate of five Pound per Ton, to be paid at the Place where they cut it: and we went with our Long-boat to fetch small Quantities. But because it would have taken up a long time to load our Vessel with our own Boat only, we hired a Periago of the Logwood-Cutters to bring it on Board; and by that means made the quicker Dispatch. I made two or three Trips to their Huts, where I and those with me were always very kindly entertain'd with Pig and Pork, and Pease, or Beef and Dough-Boys. Their Beef they got by hunting in the Savannahs. As long as the Liquor lasted, which they bought of us, we were treated with it, either in Drams or Punch. But for a more particular Account of the Logwood-Cutters I shall refer the Reader to my second Voyage hither, which I made shortly after my Return to Jamaica, because I saw a great Prospect of getting Money here, if Men would be but diligent and frugal.

AN. 1675

But let's proceed with our Voyage. It was the latter end of September, 1675, when we sailed from One-Bush-Key with the Tide of Ebb; and anchored again at Trist that same Tide; where we watered our Vessel in order to sail. This we accomplished in two Days, and the third Day sailed from Trist toward Jamaica. A Voyage which proved very tedious and hazardous to us, by Reason of our Ships being so sluggish a Sailer that She would not ply to Windward, whereby we were necessarily driven upon several Shoals that otherwise we might have avoided, and forced to spend thirteen Weeks in our Passage, which is usually accomplished in half that Time.

We had now a Passenger with us, one Will. Wooders a Jamaica Seaman, that with three others that were taken

[1] It was then the sea-custom to fire a gun when drinking a health. The custom led to great waste of powder.

AN 1675 found no Water nor any Provision, but saw many Crocodiles on the Bay, some of which would scarce stir out of the way for us. We kill'd none of them (which we might easily have done) though Food began to be short with us; indeed had it been in the Months of June or July we might probably have gotten Turtle, for they frequent this Island some Years as much as they do little Caymanes. We stayed here but 3 or 4 Hours, and steered back for Pines, intending there to hunt for Beef or Hog, of both which there is in great plenty. The second day in the Morning we fell in with the West-end of Pines, and running about 4 or 5 Miles Northward, we anchored in 4 fathom Water clean Sand, about 2 Mile from the Shore, and right against a small Creek through the Mangroves into a wide Lagune.

The Isle of Pines lies on the South-side, towards the West-end of Cuba, and is distant from it 3 or 4 Leagues. Cape Corientes on Cuba is five or six Leagues to the Westward of the Isle of Pines. Between Pines and Cuba are many small woody Islands scattered here and there, with Channels for Ships to pass between; and by report there is good anchoring near any of them. Jamaica Sloops do sometimes pass through between Cuba and Pines, when they are bound to Windward, because there the Sea is always smooth: They are also certain to meet good Land-winds; besides they can anchor when they please, and thereby take the benefit of the Tides; and when they are got past the East-end of Pines, they may either stand out to Sea again, or if they are acquainted among the small Islands to the East of it, (which are called the South Keys of Cuba) they may range amongst them to the Eastward, still taking the greater benefit of the Land-winds and Anchoring; besides, if Provision is scarce they will meet Jamaica Turtlers, or else may get Turtle themselves, at which many of them are expert. There is also plenty of Fish of many Sorts, but if they are not provided with Hooks, Lines, or Harpoons, or any other Fishing-Craft, nor meet with any Turtles, Cuba will afford them Sustenance of Hog or Beef. The great inconvenience of going

in the inside of Pines between it and Cuba, proceeds from AN.
a Spanish Garrison of about 40 Soldiers at Cape Corientes, 1675
who have a large Periago, well fitted with Oars and Sails, and are ready to launch out, and seize any small Vessel, and seldom spare the Lives as well as the Goods of those that fall into their Hands for fear of telling Tales. Such Villanies are frequently practised not only here, but also in several other places of the West-Indies, and that too with such as come to trade with their Country-men. The Merchants and Gentry indeed are no way guilty of such Actions, only the Soldiers and Rascality of the People; and these do commonly consist of Mulatoes or some other sort of Copper-colour'd Indians, who are accounted very barbarous and cruel.

The Isle of Pines is about 11 or 12 Leagues long, and 3 or 4 broad. The West-end of it is low Mangrovy-Land; and within, which is a Lagune of about 3 or 4 Miles wide, running to the Eastward, but how far I know not, with a small Creek of 2 or 3 Foot Water, reaching to the Sea. The Lagune it self is so shallow, especially near the Island, that you cannot bring a Canoa within 20 or 30 Paces of the shore. The South-side of the Island is low, flat, and rocky; the Rocks are perpendicularly steep towards the Sea, so that there is no Anchoring on that side; but the West-end very good in Sandy Ground. The Body of the Island is high Land, with many little Hills incompassing a high Pike or Mountain standing in the middle. The Trees that grow here are of divers sorts, most of them unknown to me. Red Mangroves grow in the low swampy Land against the Sea, but on the firm hilly part Pine-Trees are most plentiful. Of these here are great groves of a good height and bigness, streight and large enough to make Top-masts, or standing Masts for small Vessels; at the West-end there is a pretty big River of fresh Water, but no coming at it near the Sea for Red Mangroves, which grow so thick on both sides of it, that there is no getting in among them.

The Land-Animals are Bullocks, Hogs, Deer, &c. Here are small Savannahs for the Bullocks and Deer to feed in, as well as Fruit in the Woods for the Hogs:

AN. Here are also a sort of Racoons or Indian Conies, and in
1675 some places plenty of Land-Turtle, and Land-Crabs of two sorts, white and black: Both of them make holes in the Ground like Conies, where they shelter themselves all Day, and in the Night come out to feed; they will eat Grass, Herbs, or such Fruit as they find under the Trees: The Manchaniel Fruit, which neither Bird nor Beast will taste, is greedily devoured by them, without doing them any harm. Yet these very Crabs that feed on Manchaniel, are venomous both to Man and Beast that feeds on them, though the others are very good Meat; the white Crabs are the largest sort; some of them are as big as a Mans two Fists joyned together; they are shaped like Sea-Crabs, having one large Claw, wherewith they will pinch very hard, neither will they let go their Hold, though you bruise them in Pieces, unless you break the Claw too; but if they chance to catch your Fingers, the way is to lay your Hand, Crab and all, flat on the Ground, and he will immediately loose his Hold and scamper away. These white-ones build in wet swampy dirty Ground near the Sea, so that the Tide washes into their Holes; but the black Crab is more cleanly, delighting to live in dry Places, and makes its House in sandy Earth: black Crabs are commonly fat and full of Eggs; they are also accounted the better Meat, tho' both sorts are very good.

Here are also a great many Alligators and Crocodiles that haunt about this Island, and are said to be the most daring in all the West-Indies. I have heard of many of their Tricks; as that they have followed a Canoa, and put their Noses in over the Gunnal, with their Jaws wide open, as if ready to devour the Men in it: and that when they have been ashore in the Night near the Sea, the Crocodiles have boldly come in among them, and made them run from their Fire, and taken away their Meat from them. Therefore when Privateers are hunting on this Island, they always keep Centinels out to watch for these ravenous Creatures, as duly as they do in other Places for fear of Enemies, especially in the Night, for fear of being devoured in their Sleep.

The Spaniards of Cuba have here some Craules, *i.e.* Herds of Hogs, with a few Indians or Mulatoes to look after them: Here are also Hunters that gain a Livelihood by killing wild Hog and Beef. AN. 1675

This Island is reported to be very wet. I have heard many say, that it rains here more or less every Day in the Year; but this I suppose is a Mistake, for there fell no Rain about us, so long as we staid here, neither did I see any Appearance of it in other Places of the Island.

We were no sooner at an Anchor, but five of us went ashore, leaving only the Cook and Cabbin-Boy aboard: We had but two bad Fowling-Pieces in the Ship; those we took with us, with a Design to kill Beef and Hog. We went into the Lagune, where we found Water enough for our Canoa, and in some Places not much to spare; when we were got almost over it, we saw eight or ten Bulls and Cows feeding on the Shore close by the Sea. This gave us great Hopes of good Success. We therefore rowed away aside of the Cattle, and landed on a sandy Bay, about half a Mile from them: there we saw much Footing of Men and Boys; the Impressions seemed to be about eight or ten Days old, we supposed them to be the Track of Spanish Hunters. This troubled us a little, but it being now their Christmas, we concluded that they were gone over to Cuba to keep it there, so we went after our Game; the Boatswain and our Passenger Will. Wooders having one Gun, and presuming on their Skill in Shooting, were permitted to try their Fortune with the Cattle that we saw before we landed, while the Captain and my self with our own Gun struck up directly into the Woods. The fifth Man, whose Genius led him rather to fish than hunt, stayed in the Canoa: and had he been furnished with a Harpoon, he might have gotten more Fish than we did Flesh, for the Cattle smelling our two Men before they came nigh them, ran away; after that our Men rambled up into the Country to seek for some other Game.

The Captain and I had not gone half a Mile before we came among a Drove of near 40 great and small wild Hogs. The Captain firing, wounded one of them, but

AN. 1675 they all ran away; and though we followed the Blood a good way, yet did not come up with him, nor with any other to get a second Shot; however, because there was such a great Track of Hogs in the Woods, we kept beating about, being still in hopes to meet with more Game before Night, but to no Purpose, for we saw not one more that Day. In the Evening we returned to our Boat weary and vext at our ill Success. The Boatswain and his Consort were not yet returned, therefore we stayed 'till 'twas dark, and then went aboard without them: the next Morning betimes we went ashore again, as well to try our Fortune at Hunting, as to recover our two Men which we thought might now be returned to the Place where they landed; but not seeing them, the Captain and I went again out to hunt, but came back at Night with no better Success than before; neither did we see one Beef or Hog, though much Track all the Day. This Day he that look'd to the Boat kill'd a young Sword-fish with the Boat-hook; there were a great many of them, as also Nurses and Dog-fish, playing in shole Water; he had also discover'd a Stream of fresh Water, but so inclosed with thick red Mangroves, that 'twas impossible to fill any in Cask; we could scarce get a little to drink. Our two Men that went out the Day before, were not yet returned; therefore when 'twas dark we went aboard again, being much perplex'd for fear of their falling into the Hands of the Spanish Hunters; if we had been certain of it, we would have sailed presently, for we could not expect to redeem them again, but might have been taken our selves, either by them, or by the Cape Soldiers before mentioned. Indeed these Thoughts about their Danger and our own, kept me waking all Night. However the next Morning betimes we went ashore again, and before we got into the Lagune we heard a Gun fired, by which we knew that our Men were arrived; so we fired another in Answer and rowed away as fast as we could to fetch them, designing to sail as soon as we came aboard; for by the flattering South and S. W. Winds together with the Clearness of the Sky, we supposed we should have a North; the Land intercepted our Prospect near the Horizon in the N. W. therefore we did not see the black Cloud there, which is a pure Prognostic of a North; when we came ashore we found our two Men. They killed a Hog the first Day, but losing their way, were forced to march like Tigres all the next Day to get to us, and threw away most of their Meat to lighten themselves, yet 'twas Night before they got to the Side of the Lagune; and then being three or four Miles still from us, they made a Fire and roasted their Meat, and having fill'd their Bellies, lay down to sleep, yet had still a small Pittance left for us. We presently returned aboard, and feasted on the Remains of the Roast-meat, and being now pretty full, got up our Anchor and stood away to the South, coasting along by the Island; and doubling the S. W. Point, we steered away E. S. E. We had the Wind when we weighed at West a moderate Gale, but veering about to the North, got at N. W. By that Time we got to the South West Point of Pines, and it now blew a fierce Gale, and held thus two Days, and then came to the N. N. W. blowing hard still, and from thence to the North: then we edged away S. E. for it blew hard, and we could not bring her nearer the Wind. From the N. it came about to the N. N. E. then we knew that the Heart of it was broke, however it blew hard still: then it came about to the N. E. and blew about four Hours, and so by Degrees dyed away and edged more Easterly, till it came to the E. by N. and there it stood. We were in good Hopes while the North continued, to have gotten to Jamaica before it ceased, and were sorry to find our selves thus disappointed; for we could not see the Island, though we judged we could not be far from it; at Noon we had a good Observation, and found ourselves in the Latitude of the Island.

AN. 1675

We now had not one Bit of any Kind of Food aboard; therefore the Captain desired to know our Opinions what to do, and which way we might soonest get to some Shore, either to beat for Jamaica, or to bear away before the Wind, for the South Keys. All the Seamen but myself, were for going to the South Keys, alledging that our Ship being such a dull Sailer would never go to Wind-ward without

AN. 1675 the Help of Sea and Land Breezes, which we could not expect at such a Distance as we were, being out of the Sight of any Land: and that it was probable that in three or four Days Time we might be among the South Keys, if we would put for it; and there we should find Provision enough, either Fish or Flesh. I told them that the Craft was in catching it, and it was as probable that we might get as little Food in the South Keys, as we did at Pines, where, though there was Plenty of Beefs and Hogs, yet we could not tell how to get any: besides we might be six or seven Days in getting to the Keys; all which Time we must of Necessity fast, which if 'twere but two or three Days, would bring us so low, that we should be in a weak Condition to hunt. On the contrary, if they would agree to beat a Day or two longer for the Island Jamaica, we might in all Probability see, and come so near it, that we might send in our Boat and get Provision from thence, though we could not get in to anchor: for by all Likelihood we were not so far from the Island, but that we might have seen it, had it been clear; and that the hanging of the Clouds seemed to indicate to us, that the Land was obscured by them. Some of them did acquiesce with me in my Opinion; however, 'twas agreed to put away for the South Keys, and accordingly we veered out our Sheets, trimm'd our Sails, and steered away N. N. W. I was so much dissatisfied, that I turned into my Cabbin, and told them we should be all starved.

I could not sleep, tho' I lay down; for I was very much troubled to think of fasting 3 or 4 Days, or a Week; having fared very hard already. Indeed 'twas by meer Accident that our Food lasted so long; for we carried two Barrels of Beef out with us to sell, but 'twas so bad that none would buy it; which proved well for us: for after our own Stock was spent, this supplied us. We boiled every Day two Pieces[1] of it; and because our Peas were all eaten, and our Flour almost spent, we cut our Beef in

[1] In seaman's measure the "piece" of beef weighed four pounds; the "piece" of pork two pounds. In practice, the pieces weighed rather less than this; the beef about $3\frac{1}{2}$ lbs. and the pork $1\frac{1}{2}$ lbs.

small Bits after 'twas boiled, and boiled it again in Water, thicken'd with a little Flour, and so eat it altogether with Spoons. The little Pieces of Beef were like Plumbs in our Hodge-Podge. Indeed 'twas not fit to be eaten any other way; for though it did not stink, yet it was very unsavoury and black, without the least sign of Fat in it: Bread[1] and Flour being scarce with us, we could not make Dough-boys[2] to eat with it. But to proceed, I had not lain in my Cabbin above three Glasses, before one on the Deck cryed out, *Land! Land!* I was very glad at the News, and we all immediately discerned it very plain. The first that we saw was High-land, which we knew to be Blewfields-Hill.[3] by a Bending or Saddle on the Top, with two small Heads on each Side. It bore N. E. by E. and we had the Wind at E. therefore we presently clapp'd on a Wind, and steered on N. N. E. and soon after we saw all the Coast, being not above 5 or 6 Leagues from it. We kept jogging on all the Afternoon, not striving to get into any particular Place; but where we could fetch, there we were resolved to Anchor: The next Day being pretty near the Shore, between Blewfields Point, and Point-Nigrill, and having the Wind large enough to fetch the latter, we steered away directly thither; and seeing a small Vessel about two Leagues N. W. of us, making Signs to speak with us by hoising and lowring her Topsails, we were afraid of her, and edged in nearer the Shore; and about three a Clock in the Afternoon, to our great Joy, we anchored at Nigrill, having been thirteen Weeks on our Passage. I think never any Vessel before nor since, made such Traverses in coming out of the Bay as we did, having first blunder'd over the Alcrany Riff, and then visited those Islands; from thence fell in among the Colorado Shoals, afterward made a Trip to Grand Caymanes; and lastly, visited Pines, tho' to no Purpose. In all these Rambles we got as much Experience as if we had been sent out on a Design. AN. 1675

As soon as we came to anchor, we sent our Boat ashore

[1] By "bread" a sailor means biscuit.
[2] A dough-boy is a sort of sodden dumpling.
[3] On the S.W. coast.

AN. 1675 to buy Provisions to regale our selves, after our long Fatigue and Fasting, and were very busie going to drink a Bowl of Punch: When unexpectedly Capt. Rawlins, Commander of a small New-England Vessel, that we left at Trist; and one Mr. John Hooker, who had been in the Bay a Twelve-month cutting Logwood, and was now coming up to Jamaica to sell it, came aboard, and were invited into the Cabbin to drink with us; the Bowl had not yet been touch'd, (I think there might be six Quarts in it) but Mr. Hooker being drunk to by Capt. Rawlins, who pledg'd Capt. Hudswel, and having the Bowl in his Hand, said, That he was under an Oath to drink but three Draughts of strong Liquor a Day, and putting the Bowl to his Head, turn'd it off at one Draught, and so making himself drunk, disappointed us of our Expectations, till we made another Bowl. The next Day having a brisk N. W. Wind, which was a kind of Chocolatto North,[1] we arrived at Port-Royal; and so ended this troublesome Voyage.

[1] A brisk north-westerly gale was known as a Chocolatto North.

CHAP. II

The Author's second Voyage to the Bay of Campeachy. His arrival at the Isle of Trist, and settling with the Logwood-Cutters. A Description of the Coast from Cape Condecedo to Trist. Salinas or Salt Ponds. Salt gathered for the Spaniards by the Indians. Hina, a remarkable Hill. Horse-hoof-fish. The Triangle Islands. Campeachy Town twice taken. Its chief Trade, Cotton. Champeton River; and its Logwood, a rich Commodity. Port-Royal Harbour and Island. Prickly-Grass. Sapadillo Trees. Trist Island describ'd. Coco-Plumb-bushes. The Grape-Tree. Its Animals, Lizards. Laguna Termina and its strong Tides. Summasenta-River, and Chucquebull Town. Serles his Key. Captain Serles his Adventure. The East and West Lagunes, with their Branches inhabited by Logwood-Cutters. Oaks growing there, and no where else within the Tropicks. The Original of the Logwood-Trade. The Rainy Season, and great Floods occasioned by Norths. The dry Season. Wild Pine-plant. The Logwood-Tree. Blood-Wood, Stock-fish Wood and Camwood. A Description of some Animals, Squashes, large long-tail'd Monkeys, Ant-bears, Sloths, Armadillos, Tigre-Cats, Snakes of three sorts, Galliwasps, Huge Spiders, Great Ants and their Nests. Rambling Ants, Humming Birds, Black-Birds, Turtle-Doves, Quams, Corresos, Carrion Crows, Subtle Jacks, Bill-birds, Cockrecos, Ducks of several sorts, Curlews, Herons, Crabcatchers, Pelicans, Cormorants, Fishing Hawks. Several sorts of Fish. Ten-pounders, Paricootas, Garr-fish, Spanish Mackril: The Ray, Alligators. Crocodiles, how they differ from Alligators. A narrow Escape of an Irish-man from an Alligator.

IT was not long after our Arrival at Port-Royal, before we were paid off, and discharged. Now Captain Johnson of New-England, being bound again into the Bay of Campeachy, I took the Opportunity of going a Passenger with him, being resolved to spend some Time at the Logwood Trade; and accordingly provided such AN. 1675

AN. 1675 Necessaries as were required about it (viz.) Hatchets, Axes, Macheats, (*i.e.* Long Knives) Saws, Wedges, &c. a Pavillion to sleep in, a Gun with Powder and Shot, &c. and leaving a Letter of Attorney with Mr. Fleming, a Merchant of Port-Royal, as well to dispose of any thing that I should send up to him, as to remit to me what I should order, I took leave of my Friends and imbarked.

About the Middle of Feb. 75–6, we sailed from Jamaica, and with a fair Wind and Weather, soon got as far as Cape Catoch; and there met a pretty strong North, which lasted two Days. After that the Trade settled again at E. N. E. which speedily carried us to Trist Island. In a little time I settled my self in the West Creek of the West Lagune with some old Logwood-Cutters, to follow the Employment with them. But I shall proceed no farther with the Relation of my own Affairs, till I have given a Description of the Country, and its Product, with some Particulars of the Logwood-Cutters; their hunting for Beef, and making Hides, &c.

I have in my former Voyage described the Coast from Cape Catoch to Cape Condecedo. Therefore I shall now begin where I then left off, and following the same Method, proceed to give some Account of the Sea-coast of the Bay of Campeachy; being competently qualified for it by many little Excursions that I made from Trist during my Abode in these Parts.

The Bay of Campeachy is a deep bending of the Land, contained between Cape Condecedo on the East, and a Point shooting forth from the High-Land of St. Martins on the West. The Distance between these two Places is about 120 Leagues, in which are many large and navigable Rivers, wide Lagunes, &c. Of all which I shall treat in their Order, as also of the Land on the Coast; its Soil, Product, &c. Together with some Observations concerning the Trees, Plants, Vegetables, Animals, and Natives of the Country.

From Cape Condecedo to the Salinas[1] is 14 or 15

[1] Real de las Salinas.

Leagues; the Coast runs in South: It is all a sandy Bay between, and the Land also within is dry and sandy, producing only some scrubbed Trees. Half-way between these two Places you may dig in the Sand above High-water Mark, and find very good fresh Water. AN. 1675

The Salina is a fine small Harbour for Barks: but there is not above 6 or 7 Foot Water; and close by the Sea, a little within the Land, there is a large Salt Pond, belonging to Campeachy Town, which yields Abundance of Salt. At the Time when the Salt kerns, which is in May or June, the Indians of the Country are ordered by the Spaniards, to give their Attendance, to rake it ashore, and gather into a great Pyramidal Heap, broad below and sharp at the Top, like the Ridge of a House; then covering it all over with dry Grass and Reeds, they set Fire to it; and this burns the out-side Salt to a hard black Crust: The hard Crust is afterwards a Defence against the Rains that are now settled in, and preserves the Heap dry even in the wettest Season. The Indians, whose Business I have told you, is to gather the Salt thus into Heaps, wait here by Turns all the Kerning Season, not less than forty or fifty Families at a Time; yet here are no Houses for them to lie in, neither do they at all regard it; for they are relieved by a fresh Supply of Indians every Week: and they all sleep in the open Air, some on the Ground, but most in very poor Hammocks fastened to Trees or Posts, stuck into the Ground for that Purpose. Their Fare is no better than their Lodging; for they have no other Food while they are here but Tartilloes and Posole. Tartilloes are small Cakes made of the Flour of Indian Corn; and Posole is also Indian Corn boiled, of which they make their Drink. But of this more hereafter, when I treat of the Natives and their manner of Living. When the Kerning Season is over, the Indians march Home to their settled Habitations, taking no more Care of the Salt. But the Spaniards of the Campeachy, who are Owners of the Ponds, do frequently send their Barks hither for Salt, to load Ships that lye in Campeachy Road; and afterwards transport it to all the Ports in the Bay of Mexico, especially

AN. 1675 to Alvarado and Tompeck,[1] two great Fishing Towns: and I think that all the Inland Towns thereabouts, are supplied with it; for I know of no other Salt Ponds on all the Coast, besides this and those before mentioned. This Salina Harbour was often visited by the English Logwood-Cutters in their way from Jamaica to Trist. And if they found any Barks here, either light or laden, they made bold to take and sell both the Ships and the Indian Sailors that belonged to them. This they would tell you was by way of Reprizal, for some former Injuries received of the Spaniards; though indeed 'twas but a Pretence: for the Governours of Jamaica knew nothing of it, neither durst the Spaniards complain; for at that Time they used to take all the English Ships they met with in these Parts, not sparing even such as came laden with Sugar from Jamaica, and were bound for England; especially if they had Logwood aboard. This was done openly, for the Ships were carried into the Havana, there sold, and the Men imprisoned without any Redress.

From the Salinas to Campeachy Town, is about 20 Leagues; the Coast runs S. by W. The first 4 Leagues of it, along the Coast is drowned Mangrove-Land, yet about two Mile South of the Salina, about 200 Yards from the Sea, there is a fresh Spring, which is visited by all the Indians that pass this way either in Bark or Canoa; there being no Water besides near it; and there is a small dirty Path leads to it thro' the Mangroves; after you are past these Mangroves, the Coast riseth higher with many sandy Bays, where Boats may conveniently land, but no fresh Water till you come to a River near Campeachy Town. The Land further along the Coast is partly Mangrovy, but most of it dry Ground, and not very fruitful; producing only a few scrubbed Bushes: and there is no Logwood growing on all this Coast, even from Cape Catoch to Campeachy Town.

About six Leagues before you come to Campeachy, there is a small Hill called Hina, where Privateers do

[1] Tampico.

AN. summoned the Governour, and afterwards stayed 3 Days
1675 for an Answer before he landed his Men, yet then took it by Storm, and that only with small Arms. I have been told that when he was advised by the Jamaica Privateers, to take it by Stratagem in the Night, he replied, that he scorned to steal a Victory; therefore when he went against it, he gave them warning of his Approach, by his Drums and Trumpets; yet he took the Fort at the first Onset, and immediately became Master of the Place.

It was taken a second time by English and French Privateers, about the Year 1678,[1] by surprise. They landed in the Night about two Leagues from the Town, and marching into the Country, lighted on a Path that brought them thither. The next Morning near Sun-rising, they entered the Town, when many of the Inhabitants were now stirring in their Houses; who hearing a noise in the Street, looked out to know the Occasion; and seeing armed Men marching towards the Fort, supposed them to be some Soldiers of their own Garrison, that were returned out of the Country; for about a Fortnight or 3 Weeks before, they had sent out a Party to suppress some Indians, then in Rebellion; a thing very common in this Country. Under favour of this Supposition, the Privateers marched through the Streets, even to the Fort, without the least Opposition. Nay, the Towns-People bad them Good Morrow; and congratulated their safe return; not discovering them to be Enemies, till they fired at the Centinels on the Fort-wall, and presently after began a furious Attack; and turning two small Guns, which they found in the Parade, against the Gates of the Fort, they soon made themselves Masters of it. The Town is not very rich, though as I said before, the only Sea-port on all this Coast. The chiefest Manufacture

[1] By a strong company of several hundreds of men with French commissions. "In revenge for Spanish injuries they took Campeachy and kept it several days" in the summer of 1678. The French buccaneer de Grammont captured it again in July 1686, and made it his base for two months, while he pillaged the district for *dix ou douze lieues à la ronde*. Before he left the place *il fit sauter la Forteresse* and *brula généralement toute la Ville*.

of the Country is Cotton-Cloth; this serves for cloathing the Indians, and even the poorer sort of Spaniards wear nothing else. It is used also for making Sails for Ships, and remitted to other parts for the same purpose. AN. 1675

Beside, Cotton-Cloth, and Salt fetched from the Salinas, I know of no other vendible Commodity exported hence. Indeed formerly this place was the Scale of the whole Logwood-Trade; which is therefore still called Palo (*i.e.* Wood) de Campeachy; tho' it did not grow nearer than at 12 or 14 Leagues distance from the Town.

The place where the Spaniards did then cut it, was at a River called Champeton,[1] about 10 or 12 Leagues to Leeward of Campeachy Town; the Coast from thence South, the Land pretty high and rocky. The Native Indians that lived hereabouts, were hired to cut it for a Ryal a Day, it being then worth 90, 100 or 110*l.* per Tun.

After the English had taken Jamaica, and began to cruise in this Bay, they found many Barks laden with it, but not knowing its value then, they either set them adrift or burned them, saving only the Nails and Iron work; a thing now usual among the Privateers, taking no notice at all of the Cargo, till Capt. James, having taken a great Ship laden with it, and brought her home to England, to fit her for a Privateer, beyond his Expectation, sold his Wood at a great rate; tho' before he valued it so little that he burned of it all his Passage home. After his return to Jamaica, the English visiting this Bay, found out the place where it grew, and if they met no Prize at Sea, they would go to Champeton River, where they were certain to find large Piles cut to their Hand, and brought to the Sea-side ready to be shipp'd off. This was their Common Practice; till at last the Spaniards sent Soldiers thither to prevent their Depredations.

But by this time the English knew the Trees, as growing; and understanding their value, began to rummage other Coasts of the Main, in search of it, till, according to

[1] Champoton. To leeward is here to the south and west.

An. their desire, they found large Groves of it, first at Cape
1675 Catoch; (which, as I have said before, was the first Place where they settled to Logwood-cutting) and loaded many Vessels from thence to Jamaica, and other Places. But it growing scarce there, they found out the Lagune of Trist in the Bay of Campeachy; where they followed the same Trade, and have ever since continued it, even to the time of my being here: But to proceed.

From the River Champeton to Port-Royal,[1] is about 18 Leagues; the Coast S. S. W. or S. W. by S. Low-land with a sandy Bay against the Sea, and some Trees by the shore, with small Savannahs, mixt with small shrubby Woods within Land all the way. There is only one River between Champeton and Port-Royal, called Port Escondedo.

Port-Royal is a broad entrance into a Salt Lagune, of 9 or 10 Leagues long, and 3 or 4 wide, with 2 Mouths, one at each end. This Mouth of Port-Royal hath a Barr, whereon there is 9 or 10 Foot Water. Within the Barr it is deep enough, and there is good Anchoring on either side. The entrance is about a Mile over, and two Miles in length; it hath fair sandy Bays on each side, with smooth Landing.

Ships commonly anchor on the Weather or East-side next Champeton, both for the convenience of some Wells there dug on the Bays by the Privateers and Logwood-Cutters, as also to ride more out of the Tide, which here runs very strong. This Place is remarkable enough, because from hence the Land trends away West, and runs so for about 65 or 70 Leagues farther.

On the West-side of this Harbour is a low Island, call'd by Us Port-Royal-Island;[2] which makes one side of the Mouth, as the Main does the other: It is about 2 Miles wide and 3 Leagues long, running East and West.

[1] Port Royal, or Puerto Real, the entrance to the Laguna de Terminos. The bar is of hard sand and sandstone, with much such a depth as Dampier gives. Within the bar there is good anchorage in from 9 to 1 fathoms, with hard sand, and ooze. The tide runs E.S.E. and W.N.W., from 3 to 1½ knots.

[2] Puerto Real Island.

The East-end of this Island is sandy and pretty clear of Woods, with some Grass, bearing a small prickly Bur, no bigger than a Grey Pea, which renders it very troublesome to those that walk bare-foot, as the Bay-Men often do. There are some Bushes of Burton-wood: and a little further to the West grow large Sapadillo-Trees, whose Fruit is long and very pleasant. The rest of the Island is more woody, especially the North-side, which is full of white Mangrove close to the shore. AN. 1676

On the West-side of this Island, is another small low Island, called Trist, separated from the former by a small Salt-Creek, scarce broad enough for a Canoa to paddle through.

The Island Trist is in some Places three Miles wide, and about four Leagues in length; running E. and W. The East-end is swampy and full of white Mangroves; and the South-side much the same: The West-part is dry and sandy, bearing a sort of long Grass, growing on Tufts very thin. This is a sort of Savannah, with some large Palmeto-Trees growing in it. The North-side of the West-end is full of Coco-Plum Bushes, and some Grapes.

The Coco-Plum Bush[1] is about eight or nine Foot high, spreading out into many Branches. Its Rhind black and smooth, the Leaves oval and pretty large, and of a dark Green. The Fruit is about the bigness of a Horse-Plum, but round; some are black, some white, others reddish: The Skin of the Plum is very thin and smooth; the inside white, soft and woolly, rather fit to suck than bite, inclosing in the Middle a large soft Stone. This Fruit grows commonly in the Sand near the Sea; and I have tasted some that have been saltish; but they are commonly sweet and pleasant enough, and accounted very wholesome.

The Body of the Grape-Tree[2] is about two or three Foot in Circumference, growing seven or eight Foot high, then sends forth many Branches, whose Twigs are thick and gross; the Leaves are shaped much like an Ivy-Leaf,

[1] The coco-plum (*Chrysobalanus Icaco*).
[2] The grape tree, a shrub of the genus Coccolobo.

but smaller and more tart. The Fruit is as big as an ordinary Grape, growing in Bunches or Clusters among the Twigs all over the Tree: it is black when ripe, and the inside reddish, with a large hard Stone in the middle. This Fruit is very pleasant and wholesome, but of little substance, the Stones being so large. The Body and Limbs of the Tree are good Fewel, making a clear strong Fire, therefore often used by the Privateers to harden the Steels of their Guns when faulty.

The Animals of this Island are, Lizards, Guanoes, Snakes and Deer: Beside the common small Lizard, there is another sort of a large kind, call'd a Lyon-Lizard: This Creature is shap'd much like the other, but almost as big as a Man's Arm, and it has a large Comb on its Head; when it is assaulted it sets its Comb up an end; but otherwise it lies down flat: Here are two or three sorts of Snakes: some very large, as I have been told.

At the West-end of the Island close by the Sea, you may dig in the Sand five or six foot deep, and find good fresh Water: There are commonly Wells ready made by Seamen to water their Ships; but they soon fill up, if not clear'd; and if you dig too deep, your Water will be salt. This Island was seldom clear of inhabitants when the English visited the Bay for Logwood; for the biggest Ships did always ride here in six or seven Fathom Water close by the shore; but smaller Vessels ran up three Leagues farther to One-Bush Key, of which in my former Chapter.

The Second Mouth or Entrance into the Lagune is between Trist, and Beef-Island,[1] and is about three Mile wide. It is shoal without, and only two Channels to come in: The deepest Channel on the Spring-Tide, has twelve Foot Water. It lies near the middle of the Mouth; hard Sand on the Bar; the West Channel is about ten Foot Water, and lies pretty near Beef-Island: you run in with the Sea-Breeze, and sound all the way; taking your sounding from Beef-Island shore. The bottom is soft Oaz, and it shoals gradually. Being shot in within Beef-

[1] Carmen Island.

Island Point, you will have three Fathom; then you may stand over towards Trist, till you come near the shore, and there anchor as you please: There is good anchoring any where within the Bar between Trist and Beef-Island, but the Tide is much stronger than at Port-Royal. This is the other Mouth or Opening to the Salt Lagune before mentioned. This Lagune is call'd by the Spaniards, Laguna Termina, or the Lagune of Tides, because they run very strong here. Small Vessels, as Barks, Periagoes, or Canoas, may sail through this Lagune, from one Mouth to the other, or into such Creeks, Rivers, or smaller Lagunes, as empty themselves into this, of which here are many: The first of note on the East-part of this Lagune, as you come in at Port-Royal, is the River Summasenta. AN. 1676

This River, though but small, yet is big enough for Periagoes to enter. It disembogues on the South-side near the middle of the Lagune.[1] There was formerly an Indian Village named Summasenta, near the Mouth of the River; and another large Indian Town call'd Chucquebul, seven or eight Leagues up in the Country. This latter was once taken by the Privateers; by whom I have been informed, that there were about two thousand Families of Indians in it, and two or three Churches, and as many Spanish Friars, though no white Men beside. The land near this River yields plenty of Logwood.

From Summasenta River to One-Bush-Key[2] is four or five Leagues, the shore running West. I have described One-Bush-Key, and the Creek against it, which, as I said, is very narrow, and not above a Mile long before it opens into another wide Lake, lying nearest N. and S. called the East Lagune. It is about a League and a half wide, and three Leagues long, encompassed with Mangrove-Trees. At the S. E. Corner of it there is another Creek about a Mile wide at the Mouth, running six or seven Miles into the Country; on both sides of it grows plenty of Logwood;

[1] The Usumasinta has so many mouths that this mouth cannot be identified. That called Rio Balchaco appears to be the one meant here.

[2] One-Bush Key, and the logwood lagoons, are situated at the mouth of the Rio Palizada, to the S.W. of the Laguna de Terminos.

AN. 1676 therefore it was inhabited by Englishmen who lived in small Companies from three to ten in a Company; and settled themselves at their best convenience for cutting. At the head of the Creek they made a Path, leading into a large Savannah full of black Cattle, Horses, and Deer; which was often visited by them upon occasion.

At the North-end, and about the middle of the East Lagune, there is another small Creek like that which comes out against One-Bush-Key, but less and shallower, which dischargeth it self into Laguna Termina, against a small sandy Key, called by the English Serles's Key, from one Captain Serles,[1] who first careen'd his Vessel here, and was afterwards killed in the Western Lagune, by one of his Company as they were cutting Logwood together. This Captain Serles was one of Sir Henry Morgan's Commanders, at the sacking of Panama; who being sent out to cruise in a small Vessel in the South-Seas, happened to surprize at Taboca, the Boatswain and most of the Crew belonging to the *Trinity*, a Spanish Ship, on board which were the Friars and Nuns, with all the old Gentlemen and Matrons of the Town, to the number of 1500 Souls, besides an immense Treasure in Silver and Gold, as I was informed by Captain Peralta,[2] who then commanded her,

[1] Captain Serles or Searles. Panama was sacked in January 1671. After the city had been won, Henry Morgan despatched Captain Searles to cruise for the *Trinity*, a galleon "very richly laden with all the King's plate and great quantity of riches of gold, pearl, jewels, and other most precious goods, of all the best and richest merchants of Panama. On board of this galleon were also the religious women, belonging to the nunnery of the said city, who had embarked with them all the ornaments of their church, consisting in great quantity of gold, plate, and other things of great value." This golden galleon had "only seven guns and ten or twelve muskets" for her defence. She had little food aboard her, and "no more sails than the uppermost sails of the main mast." Her "Boatswain and most of the Crew" were taken at Taboga, where they were trying to get water. Unfortunately for the buccaneers, Taboga was stored with "several sorts of rich wines" with which Searles' men "plentifully debauched themselves." By the time they had recovered their wits the galleon had been brought to some safe harbour.

[2] Don Francisco de Peralta, "an old and stout Spaniard, a native of Andalusia in Spain." He became a prisoner to the buccaneers at the bloody battle of Perico. His ship the *Trinity* became the buccaneer's cruiser, and as such she roved the South Seas under Bartholomew Sharp. Peralta was released at Coquimbo, December 6, 1680. He had become "very frantic through too much hardship and melancholy," and the buccaneers were afraid to keep him longer.

as he did afterwards, when she was taken by Captain Sharp;[1] all which he might have taken in the Ship had he pursued her. AN. 1676

On the West-side of the East-Lagune, there is a small Skirt of Mangroves, that separates it from another running parallel with it, called the East-Lagune, which is about the bigness of the former.

Towards the North-end of this Lagune runs a small Creek, coming out of the East-Lagune, deep enough for small Barks to pass through.

At the South-end of this Lagune, there is a Creek about a Mile wide at its Mouth; and half a Mile from thence it divides into two Branches; one called the East, the other the West Branch, both deep enough for small Barks seven or eight Miles up. The Water is fresh ten Months; but in the midst of the dry Season 'tis brackish. Four Miles from the Mouth, the Land on both sides these two Branches is wet and swampy, affording only Mangroves by the Creek's sides; only at the Heads of them, there are many large Oaks, besides which I did never see any growing within the Tropicks: but 20 Paces within that grows plenty of Logwood, therefore the Cutters settled themselves here also.

On the West-side of the West-Branch lyes a large Pasture for Cattle about three Miles from the Creek, to which the Logwood-Cutters had made Paths from their Huts to hunt Cattle, which are always there in great numbers, and commonly fatter than those in the neighbouring Savannahs; and therefore was called the fat Savannah; and this West-Creek was always most inhabited by Logwood-Cutters.

The Logwood-Trade was grown very common before I came hither, here being, as I said before, about 260 or 2[illegible]0 Men living in all the Lagune and at Beef-Island, of which Isle I shall speak hereafter: This Trade had its Rise from the decay of Privateering; for after Jamaica was well settled by the English, and a Peace established with Spain,

[1] She was taken by Sawkins. Sharp was not engaged at Perico.

AN. 1676 the Privateers who had hitherto lived upon plundering the Spaniards, were put to their shifts[1]; for they had prodigally spent whatever they got, and now wanting Subsistence, were forced either to go to Petit Guavas, where the Privateer-Trade still continued, or into the Bay for Logwood.——————The more Industrious sort of them came hither, yet even these, though they could work well enough if they pleased; yet thought it a dry Business to toil at Cutting Wood. They were good Marks-Men, and so took more delight in Hunting; but neither of those Employments affected them so much as Privateering; therefore they often made Sallies out in small Parties among the nearest Indian Towns; where they plundered and brought away the Indian Women to serve them at their Huts, and sent their Husbands to be sold at Jamaica; besides they had not forgot their old Drinking-bouts, and would still spend 30 or 40*l.* at a sitting aboard the Ships that came hither from Jamaica; carousing and firing of Guns three or four Days together. And though afterwards many sober Men came into the Bay to cut Wood, yet by degrees the old Standards so debauched them that they could never settle themselves under any Civil Government, but continued in their Wickedness, till the Spaniards, encouraged by their careless Rioting, fell upon them, and took most of them singly at their own Huts; and carried them away Prisoners to Campeachy or La Vera Cruz; from whence they were sent to Mexico, and sold to several Tradesmen in that City; and from thence, after two or three Years, when they could speak Spanish, many of them made their Escapes, and marched in by-Paths, back to La Vera Cruz, and by the *Flota* conveyed to Spain, and so to England. I have spoke with many of them since, who told me that none of them were sent to the Silver Mines to work, but kept in or near the City, and never suffered to go with their Caravans to New Mexico, or that way. I relate this, because it is generally suggested that the Spaniards commonly send their Prisoners thither, and

[1] In 1672, when Lord John Vaughan became Governor of Jamaica, "with orders to enforce the late treaty with Spain."

use them very barbarously; but I could never learn that any European has been thus served; whether for fear of discovering their Weakness, or for any other Reason, I know not. But to proceed. It is most certain that the Logwood-Cutters, that were in the Bay when I was there, were all routed or taken; a thing I ever feared, and that was the reason that moved me at last to come away, although a Place where a Man might have gotten an Estate. AN. 1676

Having thus given an Account of the first setling of this Place by my Country-men, I shall next say something concerning the Seasons of the Year, some particulars of the Country, its Animals, of the Logwood-Trade, and their manner of Hunting, and several remarkable Passages that happened during my stay there.

This part of the Bay of Campeachy lies in about 18 d. of North Lat. The Sea-Breezes here in fair Weather, are at N. N. E. or N. The Land-winds are at S. S. E. and S. but in bad Weather at E. S. E. a hard gale for two or three Days together. The dry Season begins in September, and holds till April or May; then comes in the wet Season, which begins with Tornadoes; first one in a Day, and by degrees increasing till June; and then you have set Rains till the latter end of August. This swells the Rivers so that they overflow, and the Savannahs begin to be covered with Water; and although there may be some intermission of dry Weather, yet there are still plentiful showers of Rain: so that as the Water does not increase, neither does it decrease, but continues thus till the North Winds are set in strong, and then all the Savannahs for many Miles, seem to be but part of the Sea. The Norths do commonly set in about the beginning of October, and continue by intervals till March. But of these I shall speak more in my Chapter of Winds. These Winds blowing right in on the Land, drive in the Sea, and keep the Tides from their constant Course as long as they last, which is sometimes two or three Days; by this means the Freshes are pent up, and overflow much more than before, though there be less Rain. They blow most fiercely in December and January;

AN. 1676 but afterwards they decrease in Strength; and are neither so frequent nor lasting, and then the Freshes begin to drain from off the low Ground. By the middle of February the Land is all dry; and in the next Month perhaps you will scarce get Water to drink, even in those Savannahs that but six Weeks before were like a Sea. By the beginning of April, the Ponds also in the Savannahs are all dryed up, and one that knows not how to get Water otherways may perish for Thirst; but those that are acquainted here, in their Necessity make to the Woods, and refresh themselves with Water that they find in wild Pines.

The wild Pine is a Plant so called, because it somewhat resembles the Bush that bears the Pine: they are commonly supported, or grow from some Bunch, Knot or Excrescence of the Tree, where they take root, and grow upright. The Root is short and thick, from whence the Leaves rise up in Folds one within another, spreading off at the top: They are of a good thick substance, and about ten or twelve Inches long. The out-side Leaves are so compact as to contain the Rain-water as it falls. They will hold a Pint and a half, or a Quart; and this Water refreshes the Leaves and nourishes the Root. When we find these Pines, we stick our Knives into the Leaves just above the Root, and that lets out the Water, which we catch in our Hats, as I have done many times to my great Relief.

The Land near the Sea or the Lagunes is Mangrovy, and always wet, but at a little distance from it, it is fast and firm, and never overflow'd but in the wet Season. The Soil is a strong yellowish Clay: But yet the upper Coat or Surface is a Black Mold, though not deep. Here grow divers sorts of Trees of no great bulk or height. Among these the Logwood-Trees thrive best, and are very plentiful; this being the most proper Soil for them: for they do not thrive in dry Ground, neither shall you see any growing in rich black Mold. They are much like our White-Thorns in England; but generally a great deal bigger: the Rind of the young growing Branches is white and smooth; with some Prickles shooting forth here and there: So that an Englishman not knowing the difference, would take them for White-Thorns; but the Body and old Branches are blackish; the Rind rougher, with few or no Prickles. The Leaves are small and shaped like the Common White-Thorn-Leaf, of a palish Green. We always chuse to cut the old black-rinded Trees; for these have less Sap, and require but little pains to chip or cut it. The Sap is white, and the Heart red: The Heart is used much for dyeing; therefore we chip off all the white Sap, till we come to the Heart; and then it is fit to be transported to Europe. After it has been chip'd a little while, it turns black; and if it lyes in the Water it dyes it like Ink; and sometimes it has been used to write with. Some Trees are five or six Foot in circumference: and these we can scarce cut into Logs small enough for a Man's Burthen, without great Labour; and therefore are forced to blow them up. It is a very ponderous sort of Wood, and burns very well, making a clear strong fire, and very lasting. We always harden the Steels of our Fire-Arms, when they are faulty, in a Log-wood fire, if we can get it, but otherways, as I said before, with Burton-wood or the Grape-Tree. The true Logwood I think grows only in the Country of Jucatan; and even there but only in some Places near the Sea. The chiefest places for it are either here or at Cape Catoch, and on the South-side of Jucatan in the Bay of Honduras. There are other sorts of Wood much like it in Colour, and used for dyeing also; some more esteemed, others of lesser value. Of these sorts Blood-wood and Stock-fish-wood are of the natural growth of America. AN. 1676

The Gulph of Nicaragua, which opens against the Isle of Providence, is the only Place that I know in the North-Seas, that produces the Blood-wood. And the Land on the other side of the Country against it in the South-Seas, produceth the same sorts.

This Wood is of a brighter red than the Log-wood. It was sold for 30*l.* per Tun, when Log-wood was but at 14 or 15; and at the same time Stock-fish-wood went at 7 or 8. This last sort grows in the Country near Rio la Hacha, to the East of St. Martha, by the sides of Rivers in

AN. 1676 the Low-Land. It is a smaller sort of Wood than the former. I have seen a Tree much like the Logwood, in the River of Conception in the Samballoes; and I know it will dye; but whether it be either of these two sorts, I know not: Besides here and in the places before-mentioned, I have not met with any such Wood in America.

At Cherburg near Sierra-Leone in Africa, there is Camwood, which is much like Blood-wood, if not the same. And at Tunqueen, in the East-Indies, there is also such another sort: I have not heard of any more in any part of the World. But to proceed.

The Land as you go farther from the Sea riseth still somewhat higher; and becomes of a more plantable Mould: There the Trees are generally of another sort; growing higher and taller than the Logwood-Trees or any near them: Beyond this, you still enter into large Savannahs of long Grass, two or three Miles wide; in some Places much more.

The Mould of the Savannahs is generally black and deep, producing a coarse sort of sedgy Grass: In the latter end of the dry Time, we set fire to it, which runs like Wild-fire, and keeps burning as long as there is any Fewel; unless some good shower of Rain put it out: Then presently springs up a new green Crop, which thrives beyond all belief. The Savannahs are bounded on each side with Ridges of higher Land, of a light-brown Colour; deep and very fruitful: producing extraordinary great high Trees. The Land for ten or twenty Miles from the Sea, is generally compos'd of many Ridges of delicate Woodland, and large Furrows of pleasant grassy Savannahs, alternately intermix'd with each other.

The Animals of this Country are, Horses, Bullocks, Deer, Waree, Pecary, Squashes, Possums, Monkeys, Ant-Bears, Sloths, Armadilloes, Porcupines, Land-turtle, Guanoes, and Lizards of all kinds.

The Squash is a four-footed Beast, bigger than a Cat: Its Head is much like a Foxes, with short Ears and a long Nose. It has pretty short Legs, and sharp Claws, by which it will run up Trees like a Cat. The Skin is covered with

short fine yellowish Hair. The Flesh of it is good, sweet, AN.
wholesome Meat. We commonly skin and roast it; and 1676
then we call it Pig; and I think it eats as well. It feeds on nothing but good Fruit; therefore we find them most among the Sapadillo-Trees; This Creature never rambles very far: and being taken young, will become as tame as a Dog, and be as roguish as a Monkey.

The Monkeys that are in these Parts are the ugliest I ever saw. They are much bigger than a Hare, and have great Tails about two Foot and a half long. The under-side of their Tails is all bare, with a black hard Skin; but the upper-side, and all the Body, is covered with coarse, long, black, staring Hair. These Creatures keep together 20 or 30 in a Company, and ramble over the Woods; leaping from Tree to Tree. If they meet with a single Person they will threaten to devour him. When I have been alone I have been afraid to shoot them, especially the first Time I met them. They were a great Company dancing from Tree to Tree, over my Head; chattering and making a terrible Noise; and a great many grim Faces, and shewing antick Gestures. Some broke down dry Sticks and threw at me; others scattered their Urine and Dung about my Ears; at last one bigger than the rest, came to a small Limb just over my Head; and leaping directly at me, made me start back; but the Monkey caught hold of the Bough with the tip of his Tail; and there continued swinging to fro, and making Mouths at me.——At last I past on, they still keeping me Company, with the like menacing Postures, till I came to our Huts. The Tails of these Monkeys are as good to them as one of their Hands; and they will hold as fast by them. If two or more of us were together they would hasten from us. The Females with their young ones are much troubled to leap after the Males; for they have commonly two: one she carries under one of her Arms; the other sits on her Back, and clasps her two Fore-Paws about her Neck. These Monkeys are the most sullen I ever met with; for all the Art we could use, would never tame them. It is a hard matter to shoot one of them, so as to take it; for if it gets hold with

AN. 1676 its Claws or Tail, it will not fall as long as one breath of Life remains. After I have shot at one and broke a Leg or an Arm, I have pitied the poor Creature to see it look and handle the wounded Limb, and turn it about from side to side. These Monkeys are very rarely, or (as some say) never on the Ground.

The Ant-Bear is a four-footed Beast, as big as a pretty large Dog; with rough black-brown Hair: It has short Legs; a long Nose and little Eyes; a very little Mouth, and a slender Tongue like an Earth-worm about five or six Inches long. This Creature feeds on Ants; therefore you always find them near an Ants Nest or Path. It takes its Food thus. It lays its Nose down flat on the Ground, close by the Path that the Ants travel in, (whereof here are many in this Country) and then puts out his Tongue athwart the Path: the Ants passing forwards and backwards continually, when they come to the Tongue make a stop, and in two or three Minutes time it will be covered all over with Ants; which she perceiving draws in her Tongue, and then eats them; and after puts it out again to trapan more. They smell very strong of Ants, and taste much stronger; for I have eaten of them. I have met with these Creatures in several places of America, as well as here; (*i.e.* in the Samballoes and in the South-Seas, on the Mexican Continent).

The Sloth is a four-footed, hairy, sad-coloured Animal; somewhat less than the Ant-Bear, and not so rough: Its Head is round, its Eyes small; it has a short Nose, and very sharp Teeth; short Legs, but extraordinary long sharp Claws. This Creature feeds on Leaves, whether indifferently of all sorts, or only on some particular kinds, I know not. They are very mischievous to the Trees where they come, and are so slow in Motion, that when they have eaten all the Leaves on one Tree, before they can get down from that and climb another, and settle themselves to their fresh Banquet (which takes them up five or six Days, though the Trees stand near,) they are nothing but Skin and Bones, although they came down plump and fat from the last Tree. They never descend till they have stript every

Limb and Bough, and made them as bare as Winter. It takes them up eight or nine Minutes to move one of their Feet three Inches forward; and they move all their four Feet one after another, at the same slow rate; neither will stripes make them mend their pace; which I have tried to do, by whipping them; but they seem insensible, and can neither be frighted, or provoked to move faster. AN. 1676

The Armadillo (so called from its Suit of Armour) is as big as a small sucking Pig: The Body of it pretty long. This Creature is inclosed in a thick Shell, which guards all its Back, and comes down on both Sides, and meets under the Belly, leaving room for the four Legs; the Head is small, with a Nose like a Pig, a pretty long Neck, and can put out its Head before its Body when it walks; but on any danger she puts it in under the Shell; and drawing in her Feet, she lies stock-still like a Land-Turtle: And though you toss her about she will not move herself. The Shell is jointed in the Middle of the Back; so that she can turn the Fore-part of her Body about which way she pleases. The Feet are like those of a Land-Turtle, and it has strong Claws wherewith it digs holes in the Ground like a Coney. The flesh is very sweet, and tastes much like a Land-Turtle.

The Porcupine being a Creature well known, I'll pass it in silence.

The Beasts of Prey that are bred in this Country are Tigre-Cats, and (as is reported by our Men) Lions. The Tigre-Cat is about the Bigness of a Bull-Dog, with short Legs, and a truss Body shaped much like a Mastiff, but in all things else, (viz.) its Head, the colour of its Hair, and the manner of its Preying, much resembling the Tigre, only somewhat less. Here are great Numbers of them. They prey on young Calves or other Game; whereof here is plenty. And because they do not want Food, they are the less to be feared. But I have wisht them farther off, when I have met them in the Woods; because their Aspect appears so very stately and fierce. I never did see any Lion in this Country; but I have been informed by two or three Persons that they did see Lions here: But I am assured that they are not numerous.

AN. 1676 Here are a great many poisonous Creatures in this Country; more particularly Snakes of divers sorts, some yellow, some green, and others of a dun Colour, with black and yellowish Spots. The yellow Snake is commonly as big as the Small of a Man's Leg; and six or seven Foot long. These are a lazy sort of Creatures, for they lie still and prey on Lizards, Guanoes, or other small Animals that come in their way.

It is reported that sometimes they lirk in Trees: and that they are so mighty in strength, as to hold a Bullock fast by one of his Horns, when they happen to come so near that she can twist her self about the Limb of the Tree, and the Horn at once. These are accounted very good Meat by some, and are eaten frequently: I my self have tried it for curiosity, but cannot commend it. I have heard some Bay-men report, that they have seen some of this kind here as big as an ordinary Man's Waste; but I never saw any such.

The green Snakes are no bigger about than a Mans Thumb, yet four or five Foot long: The Backs are of a very lively green Colour, but their Bellies inclining to yellow. These are commonly in Bushes among the green Leaves, and prey upon small Birds. This I have often seen, and was once in danger to be bit by one before I saw it: For I was going to take hold of a Bird that fluttered and cried out just by me, yet did not fly away, neither could I imagine the Reason, till reaching out my Hand, I perceived the Head of a Snake close by it; and looking more narrowly, I saw the upper Part of the Snake, about two or three Inches from his Head, twisted about the poor Bird.

What they feed on besides Birds I know not, but they are said to be very venomous.

The dun-coloured Snake is a little bigger than the green Snake, but not above a Foot and a half, or two Foot long; these we should often see in and about our Huts; but did not kill them, because they destroyed the Mice, and are very nimble in chacing those Creatures. Besides Snakes, here are Scorpions and Centapees in abundance. Here are also Gally-wasps. These are Creatures somewhat resembling Lizards, but larger; their Bodies about the thickness of a Man's Arm, having four short Legs, and small short Tails; their colour a dark brown. These Creatures live in old hollow Trunks of Trees, and are commonly found in wet swampy Ground, and are said to be very poisonous. AN. 1676

Here are also a sort of Spiders of a prodigious Size, some near as big as a Man's Fist, with long small Legs like the Spiders in England: they have two Teeth, or rather Horns an Inch and a half, or two Inches long, and of a proportionable Bigness, which are black as Jett, smooth as Glass, and their small End sharp as a Thorn; they are not strait but bending. These Teeth we often preserve. Some wear them in their Tobacco-pouches to pick their Pipes. Others preserve them for Tooth-Pickers, especially such as were troubled with the Tooth-ach; for by report they will expel that Pain, though I cannot justify it of my own Knowledge. The Backs of these Spiders are covered with a dark yellowish Down, as soft as Velvet. Some say these Spiders are venomous, others not; whether is true I cannot determine.

Though this Country be so often over-flown with Water, yet it swarms with Ants, of several sorts, viz. great, small, black, yellow, &c. The great black Ant stings or bites almost as bad as a Scorpion; and next to this the small yellow Ant's Bite is most painful; for their Sting is like a Spark of Fire; and they are so thick among the Boughs in some Places, that one shall be covered with them before he is aware. These Creatures have Nests on great Trees, placed on the Body between the Limbs: some of their Nests are as big as a Hogshead; this is their Winter Habitation; for in the wet Season they all repair to these their Cities: Here they preserve their Eggs. Ants-Eggs are as much esteemed by the Planters in the West-Indies for feeding their Chickens, as Great Oat-meal with us in England. In the dry Season when they leave their Nests, they swarm over all the Woodland; for they never trouble the Savannahs: You may then see great

AN. 1676 Paths made by them in the Woods of three or four Inches broad beaten as plain as the Roads in England. They go out light, but bring home heavy Loads on their Backs, all of the same Substance, and equal in Bigness: I never observed any thing besides pieces of green Leaves, so big that I could scarce see the Insect for his Burthen; yet they would march stoutly, and so many still pressing after, that it was a very pretty Sight, for the Path lookt perfectly green with them. There was one sort of Ants of a black Colour, pretty large, with long Legs; these would march in Troops, as if they were busie in seeking somewhat; they were always in haste, and followed their Leaders exactly, let them go whither they would; these had no beaten Paths to walk in, but rambled about like Hunters: Sometimes a Band of these Ants would happen to march through our Huts, over our Beds, or into our Pavilions, nay sometimes into our Chests, and there ransack every part; and where-ever the foremost went, the rest all came after: We never disturbed them, but gave them free Liberty to search where they pleased; and they would all march off before night. These Companies were so great, that they would be two or three Hours in passing by, though they went very fast.

The Fowls of this Country are Humming-Birds, Black-Birds, Turtle-Doves, Pigeons, Parrots, Parakites, Quams, Corresoes, Turkies, Carrion-Crows, Subtle-Jacks, Bill-Birds, Cockrecoes, &c. The Humming-Bird is a pretty little feather'd Creature, no bigger than a great over-grown Wasp, with a black Bill no bigger than a small Needle, and his Legs and Feet in Proportion to his Body. This Creature does not wave his Wings like other Birds when it flies, but keeps them in a continued quick Motion like Bees or other Insects, and like them makes a continual humming Noise as it flies. It is very quick in Motion, and haunts about Flowers and Fruit, like a Bee gathering Honey, making many near Addresses to its delightful Objects, by visiting them on all Sides, and yet still keeps in Motion, sometimes on one Side, sometimes on the other; as often rebounding a Foot or two back on a sudden, and as quickly returns again, keeping thus about one Flower five or six Minutes, or more. There are two or three sorts of them, some bigger than others, but all very small, neither are they coloured alike; the largest are of a blackish Colour.

The Black-Bird is somewhat bigger than ours in England; it has a longer Tail, but like them in Colour: They are sometimes called Chattering Crows, because they chatter like a Magpy.

There are three Sorts of Turtle-Doves (viz.) white-breasted Doves, dun-coloured Doves, and Ground-Doves. The white Breasts are the biggest; they are of a blewish grey Colour with white Breasts; these are fine, round and plump, and almost as big as a Pigeon. The next sort are all over of a dun, lesser than the former, and not so round. The Ground-Dove is much bigger than a Sky-Lark, of a dull grey, very round and plump, and commonly runs in Pairs on the Ground, and probably thence have their Name. The other two sorts fly in Pairs, and feed on Berries, which they commonly gather themselves from the Trees where they grow; and all three sorts are very good Meat.

Pigeons are not very common here; they are less than our Wood-Quests,[1] and as good Food.

The Quam[2] is as big as an ordinary Hen Turkey, of a blackish dun Colour; its Bill like a Turkeys; it flies about among the Woods; feeds on Berries, and is very good Meat.

The Correso[3] is a larger Fowl than the Quam: The Cock is black, the Hen is of a dark brown. The Cock has a Crown of black Feathers on his Head, and appears very stately. These live also on Berries, and are very good to eat; but their Bones are said to be poisonous; therefore we do either burn or bury them, or throw them into the Water for fear our Dogs should eat them.

[1] The name "quest" or "wood-quest" (for the wild pigeon) is still in use in dialect.

[2] The quam is a guan. There are some sixty varieties.

[3] Another form of the word curassow (curaçao), or wild turkey.

AN. 1676 Carrion-Crows are blackish Fowls about the Bigness of Ravens; they have bald Heads, and reddish bald Necks like Turkeys, and therefore by Strangers that come newly from Europe, are often mistaken for such. These live wholly on Flesh, (and are therefore called Carrion-Crows:) There are great numbers of them: They are heavy, dull Creatures, and by their perching long at one place they seem to be very lazy: yet they are quick enough to find out their Prey; for when we hunt in the Woods or Savannahs, as soon as we have killed a Beast, they will immediately flock about us from all Parts, and in less than an Hour's Time there will be two or three hundred, though at first there was not one to be seen. I have sometimes admired from whence so many came so suddenly; for we never see above two or three at a place, before they come to feast on a Carkass.

Some of the Carrion-Crows are all over white, but their Feathers look as if they were sullied: They have bald Heads and Necks like the rest; they are of the same Bigness and Make; without any Difference but in Colour; and we never see above one or two of these white ones at a time; and 'tis seldom also that we see a great Number of the black ones, but we see one white one amongst them.

The Logwood-Cutters call the white ones King Carrion-Crows, and say, that they are much bigger than the others; and that when a great Number are assembled about a Carcass, if a King Carrion-Crow be among them, he falls on first, and none of the others will taste the least Morsel, till he has filled his Belly and is withdrawn; nay, they will sit perching on the Trees about him, without approaching the Carcass, till he flies away; and then in an instant they fall on all together. I have seen of the King Carrion-Crows, but could not perceive them to be bigger than the rest; neither were the black ones, their Companions, so unmannerly as to let them eat without Company; they are very voracious, and will dispatch a Carcass in a Trice: For that Reason the Spaniards never kill them, but fine any one that shall: And I think there is also an Act in Jamaica that prohibits their Destruction; and the Logwood-Cutters, tho' under no such Obligation, yet are so zealously superstitious, that none will hurt them, for fear of receiving some Damage afterwards. AN. 1676

Subtle-Jacks[1] are Birds as big as Pigeons; they are mostly blackish; the Tips of their Wing-Feathers are yellowish, as are also their Bills. They have a peculiar and wonderful cunning way of building different from any others: Their Nests hang down from the Boughs of lofty Trees, whose Bodies are clean without Limbs for a considerable Height: The Branches to which they fasten them, are those that spread farthest out from the Body; and the very Extremities of those Boughs are only used by them. On Trees that grow single by themselves at some distance from others, they build clear round; but if they joyn to others, they make Choice of such only as are bordering upon a Savannah, Pond or Creek, and hang down their Nests from those Limbs that spread over those Savannahs, &c. neglecting such as are near other Trees: Their Nests hang down two or three Foot from the Twigs to which they are fastned, and look just like Cabbage-Nets stuft with Hay. The Thread that fastens the Nest to the Twig is made of long Grass (as is also the Nest it self) very ingeniously twisted together: It is but small at the Twig; but near the Nest grows thicker. The Nest has a Hole in the Side for the Bird to enter at, and 'tis very pretty to see twenty or thirty of them hanging round a Tree. They are all called by the English, Subtle-Jacks, because of this uncommon way of Building.

There are two or three sorts of Bill-Birds,[2] so called by the English, because their Bills are almost as big as themselves. The largest I ever saw are about the Size of English Wood-peckers, and much like them: There are others of a smaller sort; but they are not often met with, and I never saw many of them.

Cockrecoes are short-winged Birds, coloured like Partridge, but somewhat lesser; neither are they so plump and round. They have long Legs, delighting to run on

[1] Subtle-jacks, hangnests. Orioles of the genus Icterus.
[2] Toucans.

AN. 1676 the Ground among Woods in swampy Places or near Creeks. They make a loud Noise Mornings and Evenings, and answer one another very prettily; and they are extraordinary sweet Meat.

The Water-Fowls are Duck and Mallard; Curlews, Herons, Crabcatchers,[1] Pelicans, Cormorants, Fishing-Hawks, Men-of-War-Birds, Boobies, &c.

There are three sorts of Ducks, viz. The Muscovy, the Whistling and the common Duck. Muscovy-Ducks are less than ours, but otherwise exactly alike. They perch on old dry Trees, or such as have no Leaves on them, and seldom light on the Ground but to feed. Whistling-Ducks are somewhat less than our common Duck, but not differing from them in Shape or Colour: In flying, their Wings make a pretty sort of whistling Noise. These also perch on Trees as the former. The other sort are like our Common Ducks, both in Bigness and Colour, and I have never observed them to pitch upon Trees. All three sorts are very good Meat.

Here are two sorts of Curlews different in Bigness and Colour; the greater are as big as Turkeys, with long Legs and long crooked Bills, like a Snipe's, in Length and Bigness proportionable to the Bulk of their Bodies: They are of a dark Colour; their Wings black and white; their Flesh black, but very sweet and wholesome: They are call'd by the English double Curlews, because they are twice as big as the other sort.

The small Curlews are of a dusky brown, with long Legs and Bills like the former: their Flesh is most esteemed as being the sweetest.

Herons are like ours in England in Bigness, Shape and Colour.

Crabcatchers are shaped and coloured like Herons, but they are smaller: They feed on small Crabs no bigger than one's Thumb, of which there is great Plenty.

Pelicans are large flat-footed Fowls, almost as big as Geese, and their Feathers in Colour like them: they have

[1] The crab-eating American herons (*Butorides virescens*).

short Legs, long Necks, and their Bills are about two AN.
Inches broad and seventeen or eighteen long; the fore-part 1676
of their Necks or Breasts is bare, and covered with a soft, smooth, yet loose Skin, like that about the Necks of Turkies: This Skin is of the Colour of their Feathers, mixt with a dark and light grey, so exactly interwoven that it appears very beautiful. They are a very heavy Bird, and seldom fly far, or very high from the Water: They commonly sit on Rocks at some Distance from the Shore, where they may look about them. They seem to be very melancholy Fowls, by their perching all alone: they sit as if they were sleeping, holding their Heads upright, and resting the ends of their Bills on their Breast; they are better Meat than Boobies or Men-of-War-Birds.

Cormorants are just like young Ducks in Shape, having such Feet and Bills: They are black with white Breasts, and live on small Fish which they take near the Shore, or on Worms which they get out of the Mud at low Water. They taste very fishy, yet are indifferent good Meat, they being very fat.

Fishing-Hawks are like our smallest sort of Hawks in Colour and Shape, with such Bills and Talons; They perch upon Stumps of Trees or dry Limbs that hang over the Water about Creeks, Rivers or against the Sea: and upon Sight of any small Fish near them, they skim along just over them, and snatching up the Prey with their Talons, presently rise again without touching the Water with their Wings. They don't swallow the Fish whole as all other Fishing Fowls, that ever I saw do, but tear it with their Bills and eat it Piece-Meal.

The Lagunes, Creeks and Rivers are plentifully stored with great Variety of Fish (viz.) Mullets, Snooks, Tenpounders,[1] Tarpoms, Cavallies, Parricootas, Gar-fish, Sting-rays, Spanish Mackril, with many others.

Tenpounders are shaped like Mullets, but are so full of

[1] The tenpounder is *Elops saurus*; the cavally is the horse mackerel or *Caranx caballus*; the parricoota is the *Sphryænia barracuda*, a swift, gluttonous fish, sometimes poisonous.

AN. 1676 very small stiff Bones, intermixt with the Flesh, that you can hardly eat them.

Parricootas are long Fish, with round Bodies like Mackril: They have very long Mouths and sharp Teeth; they are about eight or ten Inches round, and three Foot and half long. They commonly haunt in Lagunes among Islands, or in the Sea near the Shore. They are a floating Fish, and greedily take the Hook, and will snap at Men too in the Water. We commonly take them when we are under Sail, with a Hook towing after our Stern. They are firm well-tasted Fish; but 'tis dangerous eating them, for some Men have been poisoned with them.

Divers Persons are of Opinion that these Creatures are poysonous in some Places only, and that but at some Times of the Year. I know that in many parts of the West-Indies, some have been injured by eating them, and that at different Seasons of the Year; therefore Seamen commonly taste the Liver before they venture any further; and if that has a biting Taste like Pepper, they esteem the Fish unwholsome, but if not, they eat it: and yet I have found even this Rule fail too. I judge the Head and the Parts near it, to be chiefly venomous.

Gar-fish[1] are round, but neither so big nor long as the former; but what is more peculiar, they have long bony Snouts, like the Sword-fish, only as the Sword-fish's Snout is flat, and indented like a Saw on each side; so on the contrary these have their Snouts like a Spear, round, smooth and sharp at the end, and about a Foot long. These are a sort of floaty or flying Fish: for they skip along a Foot or two above the Water, for the length of twenty or thirty Yards: then they just touch the Edge of the Water, and spring forward so much farther, and then touch the Water, and spring forward again, a great many times before they cease. They dart themselves with such a Force that they strike their Snout through the sides of a Cotton-Tree Canoa; and we often fear that they will strike quite through our very Bodies.——They are extraordinary sweet Fish.

[1] The common hornbeak.

Spanish Mackril are in Shape and Colour like our Mackril, but larger: They are three Foot or three and half long, and nine or ten Inches about, and they also are generally esteemed very excellent Fish. AN. 1676

The Ray is a flat Fish, like Skate, and I have seen three sorts of them; viz. the Stingray, the Raspray and the Whipray. The Stingray and Raspray are much alike in shape; but the former has three or four strong sharp Prickles, near two Inches long, at the Root of its Tail, which are said to be very venomous, but the rest of his Skin is smooth. The Raspray has a rough knotty Skin wherewith Rasps are made: the Skins of the largest are so rough, that the Spaniards in some Places grate their Cassavy with them, which is a Root very common all over the West-Indies; and of which the Spaniards and English frequently make their Bread; but the fairest Skins are used to cover Surgeons Instrument Cases, and other such fine Things; but of late they are counterfeited. I have been told that in Turkey Asses Skins are stamped with small hard Seeds, which gives them Impressions like Raspray.

The Whipray differs from the other two sorts, having a small, but longer Tail, and ending with a Knob, shaped like a Harpoon. All these three sorts are much about a Foot and half broad. There is yet another sort of these flat Fish of the Whipray kind, but of a prodigious bigness; viz. three or four Yards square, and their Tails as long: these we call Sea-Devils; they are very strong Fish, and are sometimes Gamesom; but they make an odd Figure when they leap out of the Water, tumbling over and over.

Neither are Turtle and Manatee wanting in this Lagune. Here are some Hawks-bill-Turtle, but the green Turtle is most plentiful. They are of a middle size; yet here was once a very large one taken, as I have mentioned in my Voyages round the World.

Here are abundance of Manatee, which are both large and sweet.

Alligators are also in great numbers in all the Creeks, Rivers and Lagunes in the Bay of Campeachy; and I

AN. 1676 think that no part of the Universe is better stock'd with them.

The Alligator is a Creature so well known every where, that I should not describe it, were it not to give an Account of the difference between it and the Crocodile; for they resemble each other so nearly in their shape and bulk, as also in their Natures, that they are generally mistaken for the same Species; only the one supposed to be the Male, the other the Female: Whether they are so or not, the World may judge by the following Observations. As to their Bulk and length, I never saw any so large as some I have heard and read of; but according to my best Judgment, though I have seen Thousands, I never met with any above sixteen or seventeen Foot long, and as thick as a large Colt. He is shaped like a Lizard, of a dark brown Colour, with a large Head and very long Jaws, with great strong Teeth, especially two of a remarkable Length, that grow out of, and at the very end of the under Jaw in the smallest part, on each side one; there are two holes in the upper Jaw to receive these, otherways he could not shut his Mouth. It has 4 short Legs and Broad Claws, with a long Tail. The Head, Back and Tail is fenced with pretty hard Scales, joyned together with a very thick tough Skin: Over its Eyes there are two hard scaly Knobs, as big as a Mans Fist, and from the Head to the Tail, along the Ridge of his Back 'tis full of such knotty hard Scales, not like Fish-Scales, which are loose, but so united to the Skin, that it is all one with it, and can't be taken asunder, but with a sharp Knife. From the Ridge of the Back down on the Ribs towards the Belly, (which is of a dusky yellow colour like a Frog) there are many of these Scales, but not so substantial nor so thick placed as the other. These Scales are no hindrance to him in turning; for he will turn very quick, considering his length. When he goes on Land his Tail drags on the Ground.

The Flesh smells very strong of Musk; especially four Kernels or Cods that are always found about them, two of which grow in the Groin, near each Thigh; the other two at the Breast, one under each Fore-leg, and about the bigness of a Pullets Egg; therefore when we kill an Alligator, we take out these, and having dried them wear them in our Hats for a perfume. The Flesh is seldom eaten but in case of Necessity, because of its strong scent. AN. 1676

Now the Crocodile hath none of these Kernels, neither doth his Flesh taste at all Musky, therefore esteemed better Food. He is of a yellow Colour, neither hath he such long Teeth in his under Jaw. The Crocodile's Legs also are longer, and when it runs on Land, it bears its Tail above the Ground, and turns up the tip of it in a round Bow, and the Knots on the Back are much thicker, higher and firmer than those of the Alligator; and differ also as to the Places where they are found. For in some Parts, as here in the Bay of Campeachy, are abundance of Alligators, where yet I never saw nor heard of any Crocodiles. At the Isle Grand Caymanes, there are Crocodiles, but no Alligators. At Pines by Cuba, there are abundance of Crocodiles, but I cannot say there are no Alligators, tho' I never saw any there. Both Kinds are called Caymanes by the Spaniards; therefore probably they may reckon them for the same. And I know of no other difference, for they both lay Eggs alike, which are not distinguishable to the Eye: They are as big as a Goose-Egg, but much longer, and good Meat; yet the Alligators Eggs taste very Musky: They prey both alike in either Element, for they love Flesh as well as Fish, and will live in either fresh or salt Water. Beside these Creatures, I know none that can live any where, or upon any sort of Food, like them. 'Tis reported, that they love Dog's-Flesh better than any other Flesh whatsoever. This I have seen with my own Eyes, that our Dogs were so much afraid of them, that they would not very willingly drink at any great River or Creek where those Creatures might lurk and hide themselves, unless they were (through Necessity) constrained to it; and then they would stand five or six Foot from the brink of the Creek or River, and bark a considerable time before they would Adventure nearer; and then even at the sight of their own Shadows in the Water, they would again retire to the Place

AN. from whence they came, and bark vehemently a long time;
1676 so that in the dry Season, when there was no fresh Water but in Ponds and Creeks, we used to fetch it our selves and give it our Dogs; and many times in our Hunting, when we came to a large Creek that we were to pass through, our Dogs would not follow us; so that we often took them in our Arms, and carried them over.

Besides the fore-mentioned difference between the Alligator and Crocodile; the latter is accounted more fierce and daring than the Alligator: Therefore when we go to the Isles of Pines or Grand Caymanes to hunt, we are often molested by them, especially in the Night. But in the Bay of Campeachy, where there are only Alligators, I did never know any Mischief done by them, except by accident Men run themselves into their Jaws. I remember one Instance of this Nature, which is as follows.

In the very height of the dry time seven or eight Men (English and Irish) went to a place called Pies Pond, on Beef-Island, to hunt. This Pond was never dry, so that the Cattle drew hither in swarms, but after two or three days Hunting they were shy, and would not come to the Pond till Night, and then if an Army of Men had lain to oppose them, they would not have been debarr'd of Water. The Hunters knowing their Custom, lay still all Day, and in the Night visited this Pond, and killed as many Beefs as they could. This Trade they had driven a Week, and made great profit. At length an Irish-man going to the Pond in the Night, stumbled over an Alligator that lay in the Path: The Alligator seized him by the Knee; at which the Man cries out, Help! help! His Consorts not knowing what the matter was, ran all away from their Huts, supposing that he was fallen into the Clutches of some Spaniards, of whom they were afraid every dry Season. But poor Daniel not finding any Assistance, waited till the Beast opened his Jaw to take better hold; because it is usual for the Alligator to do so; and then snatch'd away his Knee, and slipt the But-end of his Gun in the room of it, which the Alligator griped so hard, that he pull'd it out of his Hand and so went away. The Man being near a small Tree climb'd up out of his reach; and then cried out to his Consorts to come and assist him; who being still within Call, and watching to hear the Issue of the Alarm, made haste to him with Fire-brands in their Hands, and brought him away in their Arms to his Hut; for he was in a deplorable Condition, and not able to stand on his Feet, his Knee was so torn with the Alligator's Teeth. AN. 1676

His Gun was found the next Day ten or twelve Paces from the place where he was seized, with two large Holes made in the But-end of it, one on each side, near an Inch deep; for I saw the Gun afterwards. This spoiled their sport for a time, they being forced to carry the Man to the Island Trist, where their Ships were, which was six or seven Leagues distant.

This Irish-Man went afterwards to New-England to be cured, in a Ship belonging to Boston, and nine or ten Months after returned to the Bay again, being recovered of his Wound, but went limping ever after.

This was all the mischief that ever I heard was done in the Bay of Campeachy, by the Creatures call'd Alligators.

CHAP. III

Logwood Mens way of Living. Their Hunting for Beefs in Canoas. Alligators. The Author's setling with Logwood-Men. He is lost in Hunting. Captain Hall and his Mens disaster. The way of preserving Bullocks Hides. Two hairy Worms growing in the Author's Leg. Dangerous Leg-worms in the West-Indies. The Author strangely cured of one. A violent Storm. A Description of Beef-Island: its Fruits and Animals. The Spaniards way of hocksing Cattle. Their care of preserving their Cattle. The wasteful destruction made of them by the English and French Privateers. The Author's narrow Escape from an Alligator.

AN. 1676 THE Logwood-Cutters (as I said before) inhabit the Creeks of the East and West Lagunes, in small Companies, building their Huts close by the Creeks sides for the benefit of the Sea-Breezes, as near the Logwood Groves as they can, removing often to be near their Business: yet when they are settled in a good open Place, they chuse rather to go half a Mile in their Canoas to work, than lose that convenience. Tho' they build their Huts but slightly, yet they take care to thatch them very well with Palm or Palmeto Leaves, to prevent the Rains, which are there very violent, from soaking in.

For their Bedding they raise a Barbecue, or wooden Frame 3 Foot and a half above Ground on one side of the House; and stick up four Stakes, at each corner one, to fasten their Pavilions; out of which here is no sleeping for Moskitoes.

Another Frame they raise covered with Earth for a Hearth to dress their Victuals: and a third to sit at when they eat it.

During the wet Season, the Land where the Logwood

grows is so overflowed, that they step from their Beds into the Water perhaps two Foot deep, and continue standing in the wet all Day, till they go to bed again; but nevertheless account it the best Season in the Year for doing a good Day's Labour in. AN. 1676

Some fell the Trees, others saw and cut them into convenient Logs, and one chips off the Sap, and he is commonly the principal Man; and when a Tree is so thick, that after it is logg'd, it remains still too great a Burthen for one Man, we blow it up with Gun-powder.

The Logwood-Cutters are generally sturdy strong Fellows, and will carry Burthens of three or four hundred Weight; but every Man is left to his choice to carry what he pleaseth, and commonly they agree very well about it: For they are contented to labour very hard.

But when Ships come from Jamaica with Rum and Sugar, they are too apt to mispend both their Time and Money. If the Commanders of these Ships are Free, and treat all that come the first Day with Punch, they will be much respected, and every Man will pay honestly for what he drinks afterwards; but if he be niggardly, they will pay him with their worst Wood, and commonly they have a stock of such laid by for that purpose; nay, they will cheat them with hollow Wood filled with dirt in the middle and both ends plugg'd up with a piece of the same drove in hard, and then sawed off so neatly, that it's hard to find out the Deceit; but if any Man come to purchase with Bills payable at Jamaica, they will be sure to give him the best Wood.

In some places, especially in the West Creek of the West Lagune, they go a Hunting every Saturday to provide themselves with Beef for the Week following.

The Cattle in this Country are large and fat in February, March and April: At other times of the Year they are fleshy, but not fat, yet sweet enough. When they have kill'd a Beef, they cut it into four Quarters, and taking out all the Bones, each Man makes a hole in the middle of his Quarter, just big enough for his Head to go thro', then puts it on like a Frock, and trudgeth home; and

AN. 1676 if he chances to tire, he cuts off some of it, and flings it away.

It is a Diversion pleasant enough, though not without some danger, to hunt in a Canoa; for then the Cattle having no other feeding Places than the Sides of the Savannahs, which are somewhat higher Ground than the middle, they are forced sometimes to swim; so that we may easily come to shoot them, when they are thus in the Water.

The Beast, when she is so hard pursued that she cannot escape, turns about and comes full tilt at the Canoa, and striking her Head against the Prow, drives her back twenty or thirty Paces; then she scampers away again: But if she has received a Wound, she commonly pursues us till she is knock'd down. Our chiefest Care is to keep the Head of the Canoa towards her; for if she should strike against the Broad-side, it would endanger over-setting it, and consequently wetting our Arms and Ammunition. Besides, the Savannahs at this time swarm with Alligators, and therefore are the more dangerous on that account.

These Creatures in the wet Season forsake the Rivers, and inhabit the Drowned-Savannahs to meet with Purchase, and no Flesh comes amiss to them, whether alive or dead. Their chief Subsistence then is on young Cattle, or such Carkasses as we leave behind us, which in the dry Season feed the Carrion-Crows, but now are a Prey to the Alligators. They remain here till the Water drains off from the Land; and then confine themselves to the stagnant Ponds; and when they are dry, they ramble away to some Creek or River.

The Alligators in this Bay are not so fierce as they are reported to be in other Places; for I never knew them pursue any Man, although we do frequently meet them, nay, they will flee from us: and I have drank out of a Pond in the dry Time that hath been full of them, and the Water not deep enough to cover their Backs, and the compass of the Pond so small, that I could get no Water but by coming within two Yards of the Alligator's

Nose; they lying with their Heads towards mine as I was drinking, and looking on me all the while. Neither did I ever hear of any bit in the Water by them, tho' probably should a Man happen in their way, they would seize upon him. AN. 1676

Having thus given some Description of the Country, I shall next give an Account of my living with the Logwood Men, and of several Occurrences that happened during my Stay here.

Tho' I was a Stranger to their Employment and Manner of living, as being known but to those few only of whom we bought our Wood, in my former Voyage hither; yet that little Acquaintance I then got, encouraged me to visit them after my second arrival here; being in hopes to strike in to work with them. There were six in Company, who had a Hundred Tuns ready cut, logg'd and chipp'd, but not brought to the Creek-side, and they expected a Ship from New-England in a Month or two, to fetch it away.

When I came hither, they were beginning to bring it to the Creek: And because the Carriage is the hardest Work, they hired me to help them at the rate of a Ton of Wood per Month; promising me that after this Carriage was over, I should strike in to work with them, for they were all obliged in Bonds to procure this 100 Tuns jointly together, but for no more.

This Wood lay all in the Circumference of 5 or 600 Yards, and about 300 from the Creek-side in the middle of a very thick Wood, unpassable with Burthens. The first Thing we did was to bring it all to one Place in the middle, and from thence we cut a very large Path to carry it to the Creek-side. We laboured hard at this Work five Days in the Week; and on Saturdays went to the Savannahs and killed Beeves.

When we killed a Beef, if there were more than four of us, the Overplus went to seek fresh Game, whilst the rest dress'd it.

I went out the first Sunday and complied very well with my Master's Orders, which was only to help drive

AN. 1676 the Cattle out of the Savannahs into the Woods, where two or three Men lay to shoot them: And having kill'd our Game, we marched Home with our Burthens. The next Saturday after I went with a Design to kill a Beef my self, thinking it more Honour to try my own skill in Shooting, than only to drive the Game for others to shoot at. We went now to a Place called the Upper-Savannah, going four Miles in our Canoas, and then landing, walked one Mile through the Woods, before we came into the Savannah, and marched about two Miles in it, before we came up with any Game. Here I gave my Companions the slip, and wandered so far into the Woods that I lost my self; neither could I find the way into the open Savannah, but instead of that ran directly from it, through small spots of Savannahs and Skirts of Woods. This was sometime in May, and it was between ten a Clock and one when I began to find that I was (as we called it, I suppose from the Spaniards) Morooned, or lost, and quite out of the Hearing of my Comrade's Guns. I was somewhat surprised at this; but however, I knew I should find my way out, as soon as the Sun was a little lower. So I sat down to rest myself; resolving however to run no farther out of my way; for the Sun being so near the Zenith, I could not distinguish how to direct my Course. Being weary and almost faint for want of Water, I was forced to have recourse to the Wild-Pines, and was by them supplied, or else I must have perished with Thirst. About three a clock I went due North, as near as I could judge, for the Savannah lay East and West, and I was on the South-side of it.

At Sun-set I got into the clear open Savannah, being about two Leagues wide in most Places, but how long I know not. It is well stored with Bullocks, but by frequent hunting they grow shy, and remove farther up into the Country. Here I found my self four or five Miles to the West of the Place where I stragled from my Companions. I made homewards with all the speed I could, but being overtaken by the Night, I lay down on the Grass a good distance from the Woods, for the benefit of the Wind, to keep the Muskitoes from me, but in vain: for in less than an Hours Time I was so persecuted, that though I endeavoured to keep them off by fanning my self with Boughs and shifting my Quarters three or four Times; yet still they haunted me so that I could get no sleep. At Day-break I got up and directed my Course to the Creek where we landed, from which I was then about two Leagues. I did not see one Beast of any sort whatever in all the way; though the Day before I saw several young Calves that could not follow their Dams, but even these were now gone away, to my great Vexation and Disappointment, for I was very hungry. But about a Mile farther, I spied ten or twelve Quams perching upon the Boughs of a Cotton-Tree. These were not shy, therefore I got well enough under them; and having a single Bullet (but no shot) about me, fired at one of them, but miss'd it, though I had before often killed them so. Then I came up with, and fired at five or six Turkeys, but with no better Success. So that I was forced to march forward still in the Savannah, toward the Creek; and when I came to the Path that led to it through the Woods, I found (to my great Joy) a Hat stuck upon a Pole: and when I came to the Creek I found another. These were set up by my Consorts, who were gone home in the Evening, as Signals that they would come and fetch me. Therefore I sat down and waited for them; for although I had not then above three Leagues home by Water, yet it would have been very difficult, if not impossible for me to have got thither over Land, by reason of those vast unpassable Thickets abounding every where along the Creek side; wherein I have known some puzzled for two or three Days, and have not advanced half a Mile, though they laboured extreamly every Day. Neither was I disappointed of my hopes; for within half an Hour after my Arrival at the Creek, my Consorts came, bringing every Man his Bottle of Water, and his Gun, both to hunt for Game, and to give me notice by firing, that I might hear them; for I have known several Men lost in like manner, and never heard of afterwards.

AN. 1676

Such an Accident befel one Captain Hall of New-England, who came hither in a Boston Ship, to take in

AN. 1676 Logwood, and was fraighted by two Scotchmen, and one Mr. W. Cane, an Irish-man who designing to go with Goods from Jamaica to New-England; for that reason when his Logwood was aboard, tarried at Trist with the Ship, and hunted once in two or three Days for Beef to lengthen out his Salt Provision. One Morning the Captain designing to hunt, took five of his Men, with his Mate, as also his Merchant Mr. Cane along with him. They landed at the East-end of the Island, which is low Mangrove-Land; the Savannah is a considerable distance from the Sea, and therefore troublesome to get to it. However, unless they would row four or five Leagues farther, they could not find a more convenient place; beside, they doubted not of Mr. Cane's skill to conduct them. After they had followed him a Mile or two into the Woods, the Captain seeing him to make a Halt (as being in some doubt) to consider of the way, told him in derision, that he was but a sorry Woodsman, and that he would swing him but twice round, and he should not guess the way out again; and saying no more to him went forwards, and bid his Seamen follow him, which they did accordingly. Mr. Cane, after he had recollected himself, struck off another way, and desired them to go with him: But instead of that, they were all for following the Captain. In a short time Mr. Cane got out of the Woods into the Savannah, and there killed a good fat Cow, and quartering it, made it fit for Carriage, supposing the Captain and Crew would soon be with him. But after waiting three or four Hours, and firing his Gun several Times, without hearing any Answer, took up his Burden and returned towards the Sea-side; and upon giving a signal a Boat came and brought him aboard. In the mean Time the Captain and his Men after four or five Hours ranging the Woods, began to grow tired, and then his Mate happily trusting more to his own Judgment, left him and the four Seamen, and about four or five a Clock, being almost spent with Thirst, got out of the Woods to the Sea-shore, and as weak as he was, fired his Gun for the Boat to fetch him, which was immediately done.

When he came aboard he gave an Account whereabout, and in what a Condition he left the Captain and his Men; but it being then too late to seek him, the next Morning very early Mr. Cane and two Seamen taking Directions from the Mate (who was so fatigued that he could not stir) where he had left the Captain, went ashore, and at length came within call of him, and at last found him laid down in a Thicket, having just sense to call out sometimes, but not Strength enough to stand; so they were forced to carry him to the Sea-side. When they had a little refreshed him with Brandy and Water, he told them how his Company had fainted for Thirst, and drop'd down one after another, though he still encouraged them to be chearful and rest themselves a while, till he got some supplies of Water for them; that they were very patient, and that two of his Men held out till five a Clock in the Afternoon, and then they fainted also; but he himself proceeded in quest of his way till Night; and then fell down in the place where they then found him. AN. 1676

The two Seamen carried the Captain aboard, while Mr. Cane searched about for the rest, but to no purpose; for he returned without them, and could never hear of them afterwards.

This was a warning to me never to straggle from my Consorts in our Hunting. But to proceed.

When my Month's Service was up, in which time we brought down all the Wood to the Creek-side, I was presently pay'd my Tun of Logwood; with which, and some more that I borrowed, I bought a little Provision, and was afterwards entertained as a Companion at Work with some of my former Masters; for they presently broke up Consortship, letting the Wood lye till either Mr. West came to fetch it, according to his Contract, or else till they should otherwise dispose of it. Some of them immediately went to Beef-Island to kill Bullocks for their Hides, which they preserve by pegging them out very tite on the Ground. First they turn the fleshy-side, and after the Hair upwards, letting them lye so till they are very dry. Thirty-two strong Pegs as big as a Man's Arm, are re-

AN. 1676 quired to stretch the Hide as it ought to be. Whey they are dry they fold them in the middle from Head to Tail, with the Hair outward; and then hang them cross a strong Pole, so high that the ends may not touch the Ground, 40 or 50 one upon another, and once in three Weeks or a Month they beat them with great Sticks, to strike off the Worms that breed in the Hair, and eat it off, which spoils the Hide. When they are to be ship'd off, they soak them in salt Water to kill the remaining Worms; and while they are yet wet they fold them in four folds, and afterwards spread them abroad again to dry. When they are fully dry, they fold them up again, and so send them aboard. I was yet a Stranger to this Work, therefore remained with three of the old Crew to cut more Logwood. My Consorts were all three Scotch-Men; one of them named Price Morrice had lived there some Years, and was Master of a pretty large Periago; for without some sort of Boat, here is no stirring from one place to another. The other two were young Men that had been bred Merchants, viz. Mr. Duncan Campbell; and Mr. George ——These two not liking either the Place or Employment, waited an Opportunity of going away by the first Ship that came hither to take in Logwood. Accordingly not long after the above-mentioned Capt. Hall of Boston, came hither on that design, and was fraighted by them with 40 Tun. It was agreed that George should stay behind to cut Logwood; but Campbell should go to New-England to sell this Cargo, and bring back Flour, and such other Commodities that were proper to purchase Hides and Logwood in the Bay. This retarded our Business; for I did not find Price Morrice very intent at Work: for 'tis like he thought he had Logwood enough. And I have particularly observed there, and in other Places, that such as had been well-bred, were generally most careful to improve their Time, and would be very industrious and frugal, when there was any probability of considerable Gain. But on the contrary, such as had been inur'd to hard Labour, and got their Living by the sweat of their Brows, when they came to a Plenty, would extravagantly squander away their Time and Money in Drinking and making a Bluster. AN. 1676

To be short, I kept to my Work by my self, till I was hindered by a hard, red, and angry Swelling like a Boyl, in my right Leg; so painful that I was scarce able to stand on it: but I was directed to roast and apply the Roots of White Lillies (of which here is great plenty growing by the Creek-sides) to draw it to a Head. This I did three or four Days, without any Benefit. At last I perceived two white Specks in the middle of the Boil; and squeezing it, two small white Worms spurted out: I took them both up in my Hand, and perceived each of them to be invested with three Rows of black, short, stiff Hair, running clear round them; one Row near each end; the other in the middle; each Row distinct from other; and all very regular and uniform. The Worms were about the bigness of a Hen's Quill, and about three fourths of an Inch long.

I never saw Worms of this sort breed in any Man's Flesh. Indeed Guinea Worms[1] are very frequent in some Places of the West-Indies, especially at Curasao; They breed as well in Whites as Negroes: And because that Island was formerly a Magazin of Negroes, while the Dutch drove that Trade with the Spaniards, and the Negroes were most subject to them; 'twas therefore believed that other People took them by Infection from them. I rather judge that they are generated by drinking bad Water; and 'tis as likely that the Water of the other Island of Aruba and Bonairy may produce the same Effects; for many of those that went with me from thence to Virginia (mentioned in my former Volume) were troubled with them after our Arrival there: particularly I my self had one broke out in my Ancle, after I had been there five or six Months.

These Worms are no bigger than a large brown Thread, but (as I have heard) five or six Yards long, and if it breaks in drawing out, that part which remains in the Flesh will putrifie, and be very painful, and indanger the Patient's

[1] The guinea-worm (*Filaria medinensis*) is a whitish threadlike parasite, which thrives in human skin, particularly in the skin of the feet and ankles.

An. Life; or at least the use of that Limb: and I have known 1676 some that have been scarified and cut strangely, to take out the Worm. I was in great Torment before it came out: my Leg and Ancle swell'd and look'd very red and angry; and I kept a Plaister to it to bring it to a Head. At last drawing off my Plaister out came about three Inches of the Worm; and my Pain abated presently. Till then I was ignorant of my Malady; and the Gentlewoman, at whose House I was, took it for a Nerve; but I knew well enough what it was, and presently roll'd it up on a small Stick. After that I opened it every Morning and Evening, and strained it out gently, about two Inches at a time, not without some pain, till at length I had got out about two Foot.

Riding with one Mr. Richardson, who was going to a Negro to have his Horse cured of a gall'd Back, I asked the Negro if he could undertake my Leg: which he did very readily; and in the mean time I observed his Method in curing the Horse; which was this. First he strok'd the sore Place, then applying to it a little rough Powder, which looked like Tobacco-Leaves dryed and crumbled small, and mumbling some Words to himself, he blew upon the part three times, and waving his Hands as often over it, said, it would be well speedily. His Fee for the Cure was a white Cock.

Then coming to me, and looking on the Worm in my Ancle, he promised to cure it in three Days, demanding also a white Cock for his Pains, and using exactly the same Method with me, as he did with the Horse. He bad me not open it in three Days; but I did not stay so long; for the next Morning the Cloath being rubb'd off, I unbound it, and found the Worm broken off, and the hole quite healed up. I was afraid the remaining Part would have given some Trouble, but have not felt any Pain there from that Day to this.

To return. I told you how I was interrupted in following my Work, by the Worm's breeding in my Leg. And to compleat my Misfortune, presently after we had the most violent Storm for above 24 Hours, that ever was known in these Parts. An Account of which I shall give more particularly in my Discourse of Winds, and shall now only mention some Passages. AN. 1676

I have already said, we were four of us in Company at this Place cutting Logwood: and by this Storm were reduced to great Inconveniences; for while that lasted we could dress no Victuals, nor even now it was over, unless we had done it in the Canoa; for the highest Land near us was almost three Foot under Water: besides our Provision too was most of it spoiled, except the Beef and Pork, which was but little the worse.

We had a good Canoa large enough to carry us all; and seeing it in vain to stay here any longer, we all embarked and rowed away to One-Bush-Key, about four Leagues from our Huts. There were four Ships riding here, when the Storm began: but at our Arrival we found only one, and hoped to have got some Refreshment from it, but found very cold Entertainment: For we could neither get Bread nor Punch, nor so much as a Dram of Rum, though we offered them Money for it. The Reason was, they were already over-charged with such as being distressed by the Storm, had been forced to take Sanctuary with them. Seeing we could not be supplied here, we asked which way the other three Ships were driven? they told us that Captain Prout of New-England was driven towards Trist, and 'twas probable he was carried out to Sea, unless he struck on a Sand, called the Middle-Ground; that Captain Skinner of New-England was driven towards Beef-Island; and Captain Chandler of London, drove away towards Man-of-War Lagune.

Beef-Island lies North from One-Bush-Key; but the other two Places lie a little on each side: One to the East; the other to the West. So away we went for Beef-Island: and coming within a League of it, we saw a Flag in the Woods, made fast to a Pole, and placed on the top of a high Tree. And coming still nearer, we at last saw a Ship in the Woods, about 200 Yards from the Sea. We rowed directly towards her; and when we came to the Woods side, found a pretty clear Passage made by the Ship thro'

AN. the Woods, the Trees being all broke down; and about
1676 three Foot Water Home to the Ship. We rowed in with our Canoa, and went aboard, and were kindly entertained by the Seamen: but the Captain was gone aboard Captain Prout, who stuck fast on the middle Ground before-mentioned. Captain Prout's Ship was afterwards got off again; but the Stumps of the Trees ran clear through the bottom of Captain Skinners, therefore there was no hope of saving her. Here we got Victuals and Punch, and stayed about two Hours, in which Time the Captain came aboard and invited us to stay all Night. But hearing some Guns fired in Man-of-War Lagune, we concluded that Captain Chandler was there, and wanted Assistance. Therefore we presently rowed away thither, for we could do no Service here; and before Night found him also stuck fast on a Point of Sand. The Head of his Ketch was dry, and at the Stern there was above four Foot Water. Our coming was very seasonable to Captain Chandler, with whom we stayed two Days: in which Time we got out all his Goods, carried off his Anchor, &c. and so not being able as yet to do him more Service, we left him for the present, and went away to hunt at Beef-Island.

At Trist were four Vessels riding before this Storm; one of them was driven off to Sea, and never heard of afterwards. Another was cast dry upon the shore, where she lay and was never got off again: But the third rode it out. Another was riding without the Bar of Trist, and she put to Sea, and got to New-England; but much shattered. About three Days before this Storm began, a small Vessel, commanded by Captain Vally, went hence, bound to Jamaica. This Vessel was given for lost by all the Logwood-Cutters; but about four Months after she returned thither again; and the Captain said he felt nothing of the Storm, but when he was about 30 Leagues to Windward of Trist, he had a fresh Summasenta Wind that carried him as high as Cape Condecedo; but all the Time he saw very black Clouds to the Westward.

Beef-Island is about seven Leagues long, and three or four broad. It lies in length East and West. The East-end looks towards the Island Trist; and is low drowned Land: and near the Sea produceth nothing but white and black Mangrove-Trees. The North-side lies open to the Main Sea, running straight from East to West. The Eastermost part for about three Leagues from Trist is Low and Mangrovy; at the end of which there is a small salt creek, deep enough at high Water for Boats to pass. AN. 1676

From this Creek to the West-end, is four Leagues all sandy Bay, closed on the back-side with a low Sand-bank, abounding with thick prickly Bushes, like a White-thorn; bearing a whitish hard shell-Fruit, as big as a Sloe, much like a Callabash. The West-end is washed with the River St. Peter St. Paul.[1] This end is over-grown with red Mangroves. About three Leagues up from the Mouth of this River shoots forth a small Branch, running to the Eastward, and dividing Beef-Island from the Main on the South, and afterwards makes a great Lake of fresh Water, called Fresh-Water Lagune. This afterwards falls into a salt Lake, called Man-of-War Lagune; which empties it self into Laguna Termina, about two Leagues from the South-East Point of the Island.

The inside or middle of this Island is a Savannah, bordered all round with Trees, most Mangrovy; either black, white or red, with some Logwood.

The South-side, between the Savannahs and the Mangroves is very rich. Some of this Land lyes in Ridges higher than the Savannahs.

The Savannahs produce plenty of long Grass, and the Ridges curious high flourishing Trees of divers sorts.

The Fruits of this Island are Penguins, both red and yellow, Guavers, Sapadilloes, Limes, Oranges, &c. These last but lately planted here by a Colony of Indians; who revolted from the Spaniards and settled here.

It is no new Thing for the Indians in these woody Parts of America, to fly away whole Towns at once, and settle themselves in the unfrequented Woods to enjoy their

[1] San Pedro.

AN. Freedom; and if they are accidentally discovered, they will
1676 remove again; which they easily do; their Houshold-Goods being little else but their Cotton Hammocks, and their Callabashes. They build every Man his own House, and tye up their Hammocks between two Trees; wherein they sleep till their Houses are made. The Woods afford them some Subsistence, as Pecary and Warree, but they that are thus stroling (or morooning, as the Spaniards call it) have Plantain-Walks that no Man knows but themselves, and from thence they have their Food, till they have raised Plantation Provision near their new built Town. They clear no more Ground than what they actually employ for their Subsistence. They make no Paths: but when they go far from Home, they break now and then a Bough, letting it hang down, which serves as a Mark to guide them in their return. If they happen to be discovered by other Indians, inhabiting still among the Spaniards, or do but mistrust it, they immediately shift their Quarters to another Place. This large Country affording them good fat Land enough, and very Woody, and therefore a proper Sanctuary for them.

It was some of these fugitive Indians that came to live at Beef-Island; where, besides gaining their Freedom from the Spaniards, they might see their Friends and Acquaintance, that had been taken some Time before by the Privateers, and sold to the Logwood-Cutters, with whom some of the Women lived still, tho' others of them had been conducted by them to their own Habitations.——————It was these Women after their return made known the kind Entertainment that they met with from the English; and perswaded their Friends to leave their Dwellings near the Spaniards, and settle on this Island; and they had been here almost a Year before they were discovered by the English: and even then were accidentally found out by the Hunters, as they followed their Game. They were not very shy all the time I lived there; but I know that upon the least disgust they would have been gone.

The Animals of this Island are, Squashes in abundance,

Porcupines, Guanoes, Possomes, Pecary, Deer, Horses, and Horn-Cattle. AN. 1676

This Island does properly belong to John d' Acosta a Spaniard of Campeachy Town, who possessed it when the English first came hither to cut Logwood. His Habitation was then at the Town of Campeachy; but in the dry Season he used to come hither in a Bark, with six or seven Servants, and spend two or three Months in hocksing and killing Cattle, only for their Hides and Tallow.

The English Logwood-Cutters happened once to come hither, whilst John d' Acosta was there; and he hearing their Guns, made towards them, and desired them to forbear firing; because it would make the Cattle wild; but told them that any Time when they wanted Beef, if they sent to him he would hox as many as they pleased, and bring the Meat to their Canoas. The English thankfully accepted his Offer; and did never after shoot his Cattle; but sent to him when they wanted; and he (according to his Promise) supplied them. This created him so much Friendship, that they intended when they returned to Jamaica to bring him a Present, and Goods also to Trade with him; which would have been very Advantagious to both Parties: but some of his Servants acquainted the Townsmen of it, at his return to Campeachy. And they being Jealous of the English, and envying him, complained to the Governour; who presently cast him into Prison, where he remained many Years: This happened about the Year 71 or 72. Thus the Project of Trading with the English miscarried here, and John d' Acosta was forced to relinquish his Right of this pleasant and profitable Island, leaving it wholly to the English; for neither he nor any other Spaniard ever came hither afterward to hocks Cattle.

This way of Hocksing Bullocks seems peculiar to the Spaniards; especially to those that live hereabouts, who are very dextrous at it. For this Reason some of them are constantly employed in it all the Year; and so become very expert. The Hockser is mounted on a good Horse,

AN. 1676 bred up to the Sport; who knows so well when to advance or retreat upon Occasion, that the Rider has no trouble to manage him. His Arms is a Hocksing Iron, which is made in the Shape of a Half-Moon, and from one Corner to the other is about six or seven Inches; with a very sharp Edge.

This Iron is fastned by a Socket to a Pole about fourteen or fifteen Foot long. When the Hockser is mounted, he lays the Pole over the Head of his Horse, with the Iron forward, and then rides after his Game; and having overtaken it, strikes his Iron just above the Hock, and hamstrings it. The Horse presently wheels off to the left; for the wounded Beast makes at him presently with all his Force; but he scampers away a good Distance before he comes about again. If the Hamstring is not quite cut asunder with the Stroke, yet the Bullock by continual springing out his Leg, certainly breaks it: and then can go but on three Legs, yet still limps forward to be revenged on his Enemy. Then the Hockser rides up softly to him and strikes his Iron into the Knee of one of his fore-Legs; and then he immediately tumbles down. He gets off his Horse, and taking a sharp-pointed strong Knife, strikes it into his Pole, a little behind the Horns, so dextrously that at one Blow he cuts the String of his Neck; and down falls his Head. This they call Poling. Then the Hockser immediately mounts, and rides after more Game, leaving the other to the Skinners, who are at hand, and ready to take off his Hide.

The right Ear of the Hocksing-Horse by the Weight of the Pole laid constantly over it when on Duty, hangs down always, by which you may know it from other Horses.

The Spaniards pick and chuse only the Bulls and old Cows, and leave the young Cattle to breed; by which means they always preserve their Stock entire. On the contrary, the English and French kill without Distinction; yea, the Young rather than the Old; without regard of keeping up their Stock. Jamaica is a remarkable Instance of this our Folly in this Particular. For when it was first taken by the English, the Savannahs were well stockt with AN. 1676 Cattle; but were soon all destroyed by our Soldiers, who suffered great Hardships afterwards for it: and it was never stock'd again till Sir Thomas Linch[1] was Governour. He sent to Cuba for a Supply of Cattle, which are now grown very plentiful, because every Man knows his own proper Goods. Whereas before, when there was no Property, each Man destroyed as fast as he could. The French (I think) are greater Destroyers than the English.

Had it not been for the great care of the Spaniards in stocking the West-Indies with Hogs and Bullocks, the Privateers must have starved. But now the Main, as well as the Island, is plentifully provided; particularly the Bay of Campeachy, the Islands of Cuba, Pines, Hispaniola, Portarica, &c. Where, besides wild Hogs, there are Abundance of Crawls or Hog-farms; in some of which, I have heard, there are no less than 1500. This was the main Subsistence of the Privateers.

But to return again to Beef-Island. Our English Hunters have much lessened the numbers of the Cattle there. And those that are left, by constant shooting now are grown so wild and desperate, that it is dangerous for a single Man to fire at them, or to venture through the Savannahs. For the old Bulls that have been formerly shot, will make at him: and they will all draw up in Battalia to defend themselves upon our Approach; the old Bulls in the Front; behind them the Cows, in the same manner; and behind them the young Cattle. And if we strive to wheel about to get in the Reer, the Bulls will certainly face about that way, and still present a Front to us. Therefore we seldom strive to shoot any out of a great Herd; but walk about in the Woods, close by the Savannah; and there we light of our Game. The Beast makes directly at the Hunter, if it be desperately

[1] Sir Thomas Lynch, "a pretty understanding gentleman, and very useful," was born in Kent *circa* 1630. He was Lieutenant-Governor of [illegible] from 1670–1676, and again from 1682 till 1684, in which year he [illegible] He restocked the island during his first governorship.

AN. 1676 wounded (as I have experienced my self) but if but slightly, they commonly run away. The old Hunters tell us, that a Cow is more dangerous of the two; because they say, she runs at her Enemy with her Eyes open; but the Bull shuts his, so that you may easily avoid him. But this I cannot affirm upon my own Knowledge, and rather doubt the Truth of it; for I knew one shrewdly gor'd by a Bull. He was a Consort with Mr. Baker, in the West Lagune; where having tir'd themselves with cutting of Logwood, they took an Occasion to go in their Canoa to Beef-Island, to refresh themselves there a Fortnight or three Weeks; because here were several sorts of Fruits, and Plenty of Cabbage to eat with their fresh Beef, which they could not fail to meet with. They came to a Place call'd the Salt-Creek; and there built them a Hut. About four a Clock, while Mr. Baker lay down to sleep, his Consort march'd out into the Savannah, about a Mile from their Huts; and there coming within Shot of a Bull, wounded him desperately; but yet the Bull had still so much Strength left as to pursue and overtake his Adversary, trampling on him; and goring his Thigh, so that he was not able to rise. The Bull by this Time was spent, and fell down dead by him: And there the Man had also perished, if Mr. Baker had not come the next morning to seek him; who finding him by the dead Beast, took him on his Back, and lugg'd him home to their Hut. The next Day he put him in his Canoa, and delivered him aboard a Ship, into the Hands of a Surgeon, who cured him in a little time.

I told you we left Capt. Chandler, with a Design of going to Beef-Island, to spend some time in Hunting at Pies Pond, before mentioned. But before we came thither we went ashore to kill a Beef for Supper; where I was surprized with an odd Accident. Passing through a small Savannah, about two or three Foot deep, we smelt a strong Scent of an Alligator; and presently after I stumbled over one, and fell down immediately. I cry'd out for Help; but my Consorts, instead of assisting me, ran away towards the Wood. I had no sooner got up to follow them, but I

stumbled on him a second time; and a third time also; AN.
expecting still when I fell down to be devoured. Yet 1676
at last I got out safe; but so frighted that I never cared for going through the Water again as long as I was in the Bay.

CHAP. IV

The River St. Peter St. Paul. The Mountain-Cow and Hippopotamus. Tobasco Island. Guavers. Tobasco River. Manatee. Villa de Mosa. Estapo. Halapo. Tacatalpo de Sierra. Small Bees. Indians. Tartillos. Posole. Cotton Garments. Early Marriages. Towns. Festivals. Shape and Features.

AN. 1676 THE River St. Peter St. Paul[1] springs from the high Mountains of Chiapo, about 20 Leagues within the Country, which are so called from a City not far distant. Its first Course is Easterly for a considerable Length, till it meets with Mountains on that Side: then it turns short about Northward, till within twelve Leagues of the Sea. And lastly, it divides its self into two Branches. The Western Branch falls into the River Tobasco; the other keeps its Course till within four Leagues of the Sea; then divides it self again. The Eastermost of these Branches separates Beef-Island from the Main; and falls into Man-of-War-Lagune, as is before related. The other keeps its Course and Name till it falls into the Sea, between Beef-Island and Tobasco-Island; where it is no broader than the Thames at Gravesend. There is a Bar at its Entrance, but of what Depth I know not; over which small Vessels may pass well enough by the Benefit of the Tide. It is both deeper and broader after you are in; for there it is fifteen or sixteen Foot Water, and very good Riding. By Report of the Privateers who have been up this River, it is very broad before it parts; and beyond that farther in the Country, has divers large Indian Towns built on its Banks: the chief of which is called Summasenta;[2] and many large

[1] San Pedro. [2] Usumasinta.

Cacao and Plantain-walks: the Soil on each Side being very fruitful. The unmanur'd Land is overgrown with lofty Trees of many sorts, especially the Cotton or Cabbage; of the latter there are whole Groves; and in some Places (especially a little way from the River's side) great Savannahs full of Bullocks, Horses, and other Animals; amongst which the Mountain Cow [1] (called by the Spaniards Ante) is most remarkable.

AN. 1676

This Beast is as big as a Bullock of two Years old. It is shaped like a Cow in Body; but her Head much bigger. Her Nose is short, and the Head more compact and round. She has no Horns. Her Eyes are round, full, and of a prodigious Size. She has great Lips, but not so thick as the Cows Lips. Her Ears are in Proportion to the Head, rather broader than those of the Common Cow. Her Neck is thick and short. Her Legs also shorter than ordinary. She has a pretty long Tail; thin of Hairs, and no Bob at the end. She has coarse thin Hair all over her Body. Her Hide is near two Inches thick. Her Flesh is red; the Grain of it very fine. The Fat is white, and altogether it is sweet wholsome Meat. One of them will weigh 5 or 600 Weight.

This Creature is always found in the Woods near some large River; and feeds on a sort of long thin Grass, or Moss, which grows plentifully on the Banks of Rivers; but never feeds in Savannahs, or Pastures of good Grass, as all other Bullocks do. When her Belly is full, she lies down to sleep by the Brink of the River; and at the least Noise slips into the Water: where sinking down to the Bottom, tho' very deep, she walks as on dry Ground. She cannot run fast, therefore never rambles far from the River; for there she always takes Sanctuary, in case of danger. There is no shooting of her, but when she is asleep.

They are found, besides this Place, in the Rivers in the

[1] The tapir. Probably the mountain tapir, *Tapirus Roulini*; perhaps *T. Bairdi*. "M. W.", in his "Familiar description of the Mosqueto Kingdom," describes it as being "of the bigness of an *English* calf of a year old, having a snout like an elephant, and not horned; they hide all day in muddy plashes to escape the tigers, and in the night swim across the river to get food; they are very good meat, but scarce or hard to find."

AN. 1676 Bay of Honduras; and on all the Main from thence as high as the River of Darien. Several of my Consorts have kill'd them there, and knew their Track, which I my self saw in the Isthmus of Darien; but should not have known it, but as I was told by them. For I never did see one, nor the Track of any but once. The Impression in the Sand, seemed much like the Track of a Cow, but I was well assured that none of our common Cows could live in that Place, neither are there any near it by many Miles.

My Consorts then gave me this Relation, and since I have had the same from other English-men as well as Spaniards.

Having shew'd the foregoing Description to a Person of Honour, he was pleased to send it to a learned Friend in Holland; from whom he received this answer.

SIR,

THE Account I have of this Paper from the English Minister at Leyden is this. The Description of your Sea-Cow, agrees with the Hippopotamus kept here so exactly, that I take them to be Creatures of the same kind. Only this here at Leyden is bigger than any Ox. For the Eyes, Ears and Hair, nothing can be said, seeing this Skin wants all these. The Teeth are worth noticing, which are very large, and firm, and fine as any Ivory.

I have spoke with a very Intelligent Person, Kinsman to the Burgomaster of Leyden, who having had that Hippopotamus (as they call it) presented to him, made a Present thereof to the University; who having viewed that Skin very well, saith, It's much bigger than you make yours, and cannot weigh less than one Thousand Weight.

Let me add of mine own, that perhaps they are greater, about the Cape of Good Hope; whence that of Leyden came. And seeing there are no horns, perhaps it may as well be called a River-Horse as a River-Cow: But for that, it must bear the Denomination given it by the People of the Place where they are; which may be different in Africa and America.

But what he says of her sinking to the Bottom in deep Rivers, and walking there, if he adds, what I think he supposes, that she rises again, and comes on the Land; I much question. For that such a huge Body should raise it self up again (though I know Whales and great Fishes can and do) transcends the Faith of I. H. AN. 1676

I readily acknowledge, there is some resemblance between this Mountain-Cow of America, and the African Hippopotamus; but yet am of Opinion that they must needs be of a different Species; for the Mountain-Cow is never known to swim out to Sea, nor to be found near it; and is not above half so big, and has no long Teeth. But for further Satisfaction, I have here inserted two Accounts of the African Hippopotamus, as they were sent; the one to the Honourable Person before-mentioned, from Captain Covent of Porbury, near Bristol, a Gentleman of great Ability and Experience, as well as known Integrity, who used to trade to Angola: The other to my self, from my worthy Friend Captain Rogers,[1] as he has seen them in the River Natal, in the Latitude of thirty, on the East side of the Cape of Good Hope.

The Sea-Horse's Head, Ears and Nostrils are like our Horses; with a short Tail and Legs. And his Footsteps in the Sand like a Horse's; but the Body above twice as big. He grazes on the Shore, and dungs like a Horse. Is of a dark-brown, but glistering in the Water. His Pace is but slow on the Shore; in the Water more swift. He there feeds on small Fish and what he can get; and will go down to the Bottom in three Fathom Water. For I have watch'd him; and he hath staid above half an Hour before he arose. He is very mischievous to white Men. I have known him open his Mouth and set one Tooth on the Gunnel of a Boat, and another on the second Strake from the Keel (which was more than four Foot distant) and there bit a Hole through the Plank, and sunk the Boat; and after he had done, he went away shaking his Ears. His Strength is

[1] Captain Rogers: perhaps Captain Woodes-Rogers, afterwards the commander of the *Duke and Duchess* in the voyage to the South Seas.

AN. 1676 incredibly great; for I have seen him in the Wash of the Shore, when the Sea has tossed in a Dutch-man's Boat, with fourteen Hogsheads of Water in her, upon the said Beast; and left it dry on his Back; and another Sea came and fetch'd the Boat off, and the Beast was not hurt, as far as I could perceive. How his Teeth grow in his Mouth I could not see; only that they were round like a Bow, and about sixteen Inches long; and in the biggest part more than six Inches about. We made several Shot at him; but to no Purpose, for they would glance from him as from a Wall. The Natives call him a Kittimpungo, and say he is Fetisso, which is a kind of a God; for nothing, they say, can kill him: And if they should do to him, as the white Men do, he would soon destroy their Canoas and Fishing-Nets. Their Custom is when he comes near their Canoas, to throw him Fish; and then he passeth away, and will not meddle with their Fishing-Craft. He doth most Mischief when he can stand on the Ground; but when afloat, hath only Power to bite. As our Boat once lay near the Shore, I saw him go under her, and with his Back lift her out of the Water; and overset her with six Men aboard, but, as it happened, did them no harm. Whilst we lay in the Road we had three of them, which did trouble this Bay every Full and Change, and two or three Days after: the Natives say, they go together, two Males and one Female. Their Noise is much like the Bellowing of a large Calf.

This past Remark was made of a Sea-Horse at Loango, in the Year 1695.

Captain ROGER's Letter.

SIR,

THE Hippopotamus or Sea-Horse, lives as well on the Land as in the Sea or in the Rivers. It is shaped much like an Ox, but bigger; weighing 1500 or, 1600 Pound. This Creature is very full-bodied, and covered with Hair of a Mouse-Colour; thick, short and of a very beautiful Sleekness, when he first comes out of the Water. The Head is flattish on the Top.

It has no Horns: but large Lips, a wide Mouth, and strong Teeth; four of which are longer than the rest, (viz.) two in the upper Jaw; one on each side, and two more in the under: These last are four or five Inches long; the other two are shorter. It has large broad Ears; great goggle Eyes; and is very quick-sighted. It has a thick Neck, and Strong Legs, but weak Footlocks. The Hoofs of his Feet are Cloven in the Middle: And it has two small Hoofs above the Footlock, which bending to the Ground when it goes, make an Impression on the Sand like four Claws. His Tail is short and tapering like a Swines; without any Bob at the end. This Beast is commonly fat and very good Meat. It grazeth ashore in wet swampy Ground near Rivers or Ponds; but retires to the Water, if pursued. When they are in the Water, they will sink down to the Bottom; and there walk as on dry Ground. They will run almost as fast as a man; but if chased hard, they will turn about and look very fierce, like a Boar; and fight if put to it. The Natives of the Country, have no Wars with these Creatures; but we had many Conflicts with them, both on Shore and in the Rivers: and though we commonly got the better by killing some, and routing the rest; yet in the Water we durst not molest them, after one Bout; which had like to have proved fatal to 3 Men that went in a small Canoa to kill a single Sea-Horse, in a River where was 8 or 10 Foot Water. The Horse, according to his Custom, was marching in the bottom of the River; and being spied by these Men, they wounded him with a long Lance; which so enraged the Beast, that he rose up immediately, and giving a fierce look he opened his Jaws and bit a great piece of the Gunnal or upper edge of the Canoa, and was like to over-set it, but presently sunk down again to the bottom: and the Men made away as fast as they could, for fear he should come again.

AN. 1676

The West branch of the River St. Peter St. Paul, after it has run 8 or 9 Leagues N. W. loseth it self in Tobasco River about 4 Leagues from the Sea, and so makes the Island Tobasco, which is 12 Leagues long, and 4 Broad at

AN. the North-end: for from the River St. Peter St. Paul, to 1676 the Mouth of Tobasco River, is accounted 4 Leagues; and the Shore lies East and West.

The first League on the East is Mangrove Land, with some sandy Bay, where Turtle come ashore to lay their Eggs.

The West-part of it is sandy Bay quite to the River Tobasco. But because here is constantly a great Sea, you have no good Landing till within the River. The N. W. part of it is full of Guaver Trees, of the greatest variety, and their Fruit the largest and best tasted I have met with; and 'tis really a very delicious Place. There are also some Coco-Plums and Grapes, but not many. The Savannahs here are naturally fenced with Groves of Guavers, and produce good Grass for Pasture, and are pretty well stock'd with fat Bullocks: and I do believe it is from their eating the Guaver Fruit that these Trees are so thick. For this Fruit is full of small Seeds; which being swallowed whole by the Cattle, are voided whole by them again; and then taking root in their Dung, spring up abundantly.

Here are also Deer in great numbers; these we constantly find feeding in the Savannahs Mornings and Evenings. And I remember an unlucky Accident whilst I was there. Two or three Men went out one Evening purposely to hunt; when they were in the spots of Savannahs, they separated to find their Game, and at last it so happened, that one of them fired at a Deer and killed it, and while he was skinning it, he was shot stark dead by one of his Consorts, who fired at him, mistaking him for a Deer. The poor Man was very sorry for so sad a mischance; and for fear of the dead Man's Friends, durst never go back again to Jamaica.

The River of Tobasco is the most noted in all the Bay of Campeachy, and springs also from the high Mountains of Chiapo; but much more to the Westward than that of St. Peter St. Paul. From thence it runs N. E. till within 4 Leagues of the Sea, where it receives the fore-mentioned Branch of St. Peter St. Paul, and then runs North till it falls into the Sea. Its Mouth is about two Miles wide, and there is a Bar of Sand lying off it, with not above 11 or 12 foot Water; but a Mile or two within the Mouth, at a nook or bending of the River on the East-side there is three Fathom, and good Riding, without any danger from the strength of the Current. The Tide flows up about four Leagues in the dry Season, but in the Rains not so far; for then the Freshes make the Ebb run very strong.

AN. 1676

During the Norths it overflows all the low Land for 14 or 15 Leagues up the River, and you may then take up fresh Water without the Bar.

This River, near its Mouth, abounds with Catfish, with some Snooks, and Manatee in great plenty; there being good feeding for them in many of its Creeks, especially in one place on the Starboard-side about 2 Leagues from the Sea, which runs into the Land 2 or 300 paces, and then opens very wide, and is so shoal that you may see their backs above Water as they feed; a thing so rare, that I have heard our Musketo-Men say, they never saw it any where else; on the least noise they will all scamper out into the River: yet the Musketo-men seldom miss of striking them. There are a sort of Fresh-water Manatee, not altogether so big as the Sea-kind, but otherwise exactly alike in shape and taste, and I think rather fatter. The Land by the Rivers, especially on the Starboard side, is swampy, and overgrown with Trees.

Here are also abundance of Trees, (the largest that I ever saw, till I came to the Gallapagoes Islands in the S. Seas) viz. Mangroves, Macaws, and other sorts that I know not. In some places near the River-side, further up the Country, are Ridges of dry Land, full of lofty Cabbage and Cotton Trees, which make a very pleasant Landskip. There is no Settlement within 8 Leagues of the River's Mouth, and then you come to a small Breast-work, where there is commonly a Spaniard with 8 or 9 Indians posted on each side the River, to watch for Boats coming that way: And because there are divers Creeks running in from the Savannahs, some of these Centinels are so placed in the

AN. 1676 Woods, that they may look into the Savannahs, for fear of being surprized on the back side: Yet for all their caution, these Centinels were snap'd by Captain Nevil,[1] Commander of a small Brigantine, in a second Expedition that he made to take the Town called Villa de Mosa. His first attempt miscarried by his being discovered. But the second time he got into a Creek, a League below these Centinels, and there dragging his Canoas over some Trees that were laid cross it, purposely to hinder his Passage, he came in the Night upon their Backs in their several Posts; so that the Town, having no notice of his coming by their firing as they should have done, was taken without any resistance.

Villa de Mosa is a small Town standing on the Starboard side of the River, 4 Leagues beyond this Breast-work. 'Tis inhabited chiefly by Indians, with some Spaniards: There is a Church in the middle, and a Fort at the West-end, which commands the River. Thus far Ships come to bring Goods, especially European Commodities; viz. Broad-cloth, Serges, Perpetuana's,[2] Kersies, Thread-Stockings, Hats, Osnabrugs white and blew, Kentins, Platilloes, Britannia's, Hollandilloes, Iron-work, &c. They arrive here in November or December, and stay till June or July, selling their Commodities, and then load chiefly with Cacao, and some Sylvester. All the Merchants and petty Traders of the Country Towns come hither about Christmas to Traffick, which makes this town the chiefest in all these parts, Campeachy excepted; yet there are but few Rich Men that live here. Sometimes Ships that come hither load Hides and Tallow, if they cannot fraight with Cacao. But the chiefest place for Hides is a Town lying on a Branch of this River, that comes out a League below the Breast-work, where Spanish Barks usually lade once a

[1] Mentioned in Calendar of State Papers, West Indian and Colonial Series, Addenda, p. 490, Sir H. Morgan to various privateers under French commissions, telling them that they are welcome to Jamaica, and that Port Royal is free to them. He does not appear again.

[2] *Perpetuanas*, or coarse woollens; woven chiefly at Sudbury. *Kerseys*, a ribbed coarse woollen cloth. *Osnaburgs*, or *Osnaburgh*, a rough linen. *Kentin*, fine linen, gauze or muslin. *Britannias*, linen of medium quality. *Hollandilloes*, fabrics of unbleached linen. *Platilloes* I cannot identify.

Year; but I can give no further account of it. Four AN.
Leagues beyond Villa de Mosa further up the River lies 1676
Estapo, inhabited partly with Spaniards, but most Indians, as generally the Towns in this Country are: It's said to be pretty rich; stands close by the River, on the South-side, and is so built between two Creeks, that there is but one Avenue leading to it; and so well guarded with a Breast-work, that Captain Hewet[1] a Privateer, who had under him near 200 Men, was there repulsed, losing many of them, and himself wounded in the Leg. In his way thither he took Villa de Mosa, and left a Party there to secure his Retreat. If he had taken Estapo, he designed to pass on to Halpo, a Rich Town, three Leagues farther up the River, and from thence to visit Tacatalpo, lying 3 or 4 Leagues beyond, which is accounted the wealthiest of the three: the Spaniards call it Tacatalpo de Sierra: whether to distinguish it from another Town of that Name, or to denote its nearness to the Mountains, I know not. 'Tis the best Town on this River, having three Churches, and several rich Merchants; and between it and Villa de Mosa are many large Cacao Walks on each side the River.

I have seen a sort of white Cacao brought from hence, which I never met with any where else. It is of the same bigness and colour on the outside, and with such a thin husky Coat as the other; but the inner Substance is white, like fine Flower; and when the outward Coat is broken, it crumbles as a lump of Flower doth. Those that frequent the Bay call it Spuma, and affirm that it is much used by the Spaniards of those Parts, to make their Chocolate froth, who therefore set a great value on it. But I never yet met with any in England that knew it, except the Right Honourable the Earl of Carbery,[2] who was pleased to tell me he had seen of it.

[1] Captain Hewet: he is mentioned here, and in two other passages a little further on. I can learn no more of him than that he took part in the attack mentioned above, that he lost some hands at Dos Boccas, and that his intended raid with Captain Rives was made impossible by the rains.

[2] John Vaughan, 3rd Earl of Carbery, born 1640. Governor of Jamaica in 1674-5, recalled in 1678. He was President of the Royal Society from 1686-9. He died in 1713.

AN. 1676 The Land on the South-side of the River is low Savannahs or Pasture: The side where the Town of Villa de Mosa stands, is a sort of gray sandy Earth; and the whole Country, the Up-land I mean, seems to be much the same: But the Low-land is of a black deep Mold, and in some places very strong Clay; and there is not a Stone to be found in all the Country. The healthy dry Land is very woody, except where inhabited or planted. It is pretty thick settled with Indian Towns, who have all a Padre or two among them, and a Cacique or Governour to keep the Peace. The Cacao Tree thrives here very well; but the Nuts are smaller than the Caraccas Nuts; yet Oyly and Fat whilst new. They are not planted near the Sea, as they are on the Coast of Caraccas, but at least 8 or 10 Miles up in the Country. The Cacao-walks belong chiefly to the Spaniards; and are only planted and dress'd by Indians, hired for that purpose; yet the Indians have of their own, Plantain-walks, Plantations of Maiz, and some small Cacao-walks; about which they spend the chiefest of their time. Some employ themselves to search in the Woods for Bees that build in hollow Trees; and get a good livelihood by the Honey and Wax. These are of two sorts: One pretty large; the other no bigger, but longer, than an ordinary black Fly: in other respects, just like our common Bees; only of a darker Colour. Their Stings are not strong enough to enter a Man's Skin; but if disturbed, they will fly at one as furiously as the great Bees; and will tickle, but cannot hurt you. Their Honey is white and clear; and they make a great deal of it. The Indians keep of them tame, and cut hollow Trunks for them to make their Combs in. They place one end of the Log (which is saw'd very even) on a Board, leaving a hole for the Bees to creep in at: and the upper end is covered with a Board, put close over it. The young and lusty Indians (such as want Employment) hire themselves to the Spaniards. They Work cheap, and are commonly paid in such Goods as the Spaniards do not value. And I have been told that they are obliged to work for their Masters, one Day in a Week, gratis: But whether this Priviledge belongs only to the Padres, or to the Laity also, I know not. The Indians inhabiting these Villages, live like Gentlemen in Comparison of those that are near any great Town, such as Campeachy or Merida: for there even the poorer and rascally Sort of People, that are not able to hire one of these poor Creatures, will by violence drag them to do their drudgery for nothing, after they have work'd all Day for their Masters: nay, they often take them out of the Market from their Business; or at least enjoyn them to come to their Houses when their Market is ended: and they dare not refuse to do it.

AN. 1676

This Country is very fruitful; yielding plentiful Crops of Maiz, which is their chiefest Subsistence. After it is boiled they bruise it on such a Rubbing-Stone as Chocolate is ground on. Some of it they make into small thin Cakes, called Tartilloes. The rest is put into a Jar till it grows sowr; and when they are thirsty, mix a handful of it in a Callabash of Water, which gives it a sharp pleasant Taste, then straining it through a large Callabash prick'd full of small Holes to keep out the Husks, they drink it off. If they treat a Friend with this Drink, they mix a little Honey with it; for their Ability reaches no higher: And this is as acceptable to them as a Glass of Wine to us. If they travel for two or three Days from home, they carry some of this ground Maiz in a Plantain Leaf, and Callabash at their Girdles to make their Drink, and take no farther care for Victuals, till they come home again. This is called Posole: And by the English Poorsoul. It is so much esteemed by the Indians, that they are never without some of it in their Houses.

Another Way of preparing their Drink, is to parch the Maiz, and then grind it to Powder on the Rubbing-stone, putting a little Anatta[1] to it; which grows in their Plantations, and is used by them for no other purpose. They mix it all with Water, and presently drink it off without straining.

In long Journeys they prefer this drink before Posole.

[1] *Bixa orellana*, a reddish dye.

AN. 1676 They feed abundance of Turkies, Ducks and Dunghill Fowls, of which the Padre has an exact Account; and is very strict in gathering his Tithe: and they dare not kill any except they have his Leave for it.

They plant Cotton also for their Cloathing. The Men wear only a short Jacket and Breeches. These with a Palmeto-Leaf Hat is their Sundays Dress; for they have neither Stockings nor Shoes; neither do they wear these Jackets on Week Days. The Women have a Cotton-Petticoat, and a large Frock down to their Knees; the Sleeves to their Wrists, but not gathered. The Bosom is open to the Breast, and Imbroidered with black or red Silk, or Grogram Yarn, two Inches broad on each side the Breast, and clear round the Neck. In this Garb, with their Hair ty'd up in a Knot behind, they think themselves extreme fine.

The Men are obliged by the Padres (as I have been informed) to marry when they are Fourteen Years old, and the Women when Twelve: And if at that Age they are not provided, the Priest will chuse a Virgin for the Man (or a Man for the Virgin) of equal Birth and Fortune; and join them together.

The Spaniards give several Reasons for this Imposition, viz. That it preserves them from Debauchery, and makes them Industrious.—That it brings them to pay Taxes both to the King and Church; for as soon as they are married they pay to both.—And that it keeps them from rambling out of their own Parish, and settling in another, which would by so much lessen the Padre's Profit. They love each other very well; and live comfortably by the Sweat of their Brows: They build good large Houses, and inhabit altogether in Towns. The side Walls are Mud or Watling, plaister'd on the Inside, and thatch'd with Palm or Palmeto Leaves.

The Churches are large, built much higher than the Common Houses, and covered with Pantile; and within adorned with coarse Pictures and Images of Saints; which are all painted tawny like the Indians themselves. Besides these Ornaments, there are kept in the Churches Pipes,

Hautboys, Drums, Vizars [1] and Perruques [2] for their Recreation at solemn Times; for they have little or no Sport or Pastime but in common, and that only upon Saints Days, and the Nights ensuing. AN. 1676

The Padres that serve here, must learn the Indian Language before they can have a Benefice. As for their Tithes and other Incomes, Mr. Gage, (an Englishman) hath given a large Account of them in his "Survey of the West-Indies." But however, this I will add of my own Knowledge, that they are very dutiful to their Priests, observing punctually their Orders, and behave themselves very circumspectly and reverently in their Presence.

They are generally well-shaped, of a middle Size; streight and clean Limbed. The Men more spare, the Women plump and fat, their Faces are round and flat, their Foreheads low, their Eyes little, their Noses of a middle Size, somewhat flattish; full Lips; pretty full but little Mouths; white Teeth, and their Colour of a dark tawny, like other Indians. They sleep in Hammocks made with small Cords like a Net, fastned at each End to a Post. Their Furniture is but mean, viz. Earthen Pots to boil their Maiz in, and abundance of Callabashes. They are a very harmless Sort of People; kind to any Strangers; and even to the Spaniards, by whom they are so much kept under, that they are worse than Slaves: nay, the very Negroes will domineer over them; and are countenanced to do so by the Spaniards. This makes them very melancholly and thoughtful: however they are very quiet, and seem contented with their Condition, if they can tolerably subsist: But sometimes when they are imposed on beyond their Ability, they will march off whole Towns, Men, Women, and Children together, as is before related.

[1] Vizards or masks.

[2] "A counterfeit cap of false haire."

CHAP. V

The River of Checapeque. The River of Dos Bocas. The Towns up the Country. Halpo. Their Trade. Old Hats, a good Commodity. A Sad Accident in Hunting. Tondelo River. Musketoes troublesom on this Coast. Guasickwalp River. Teguantapeque River. Few Gold Mines on all this part of the Sea-coast. Teguantapeque Town. Keyhooca and its Canoa-Trade. Vinellos. Alvarado River, and its Branches. Its Forts, Town and Trade. Cod-Pepper. La Vera Cruz. The Fort of St. John d' Ulloa. The Barra la Venta Fleet; and their Navigation about the West-India Coast. The Town of Tispo. Paunuk River and Town. Lagune and Town of Tompeque. Huniago Island. Its Trade in Shrimps. The Author's Return to Logwood-cutting at Trist. Captain Gibbs killed there by some Indians he brought from New-England. The Author's setting out to Jamaica and return for England.

AN. 1676 HAVING given the Reader an account of the Indians inhabiting about the River of Tobasco; I come next to describe the Western-Coast of this Bay, with its Rivers and other most remarkable Particulars. From Tobasco River to the River Checapeque[1] is seven Leagues. The Coast lies East and West; all woody low Ground, sandy Bay, and good Anchoring; but there falls in a pretty high Sea on the shore, therefore but bad landing; yet Canoas may with care run in, if the Men are ready to leap out, as soon as she touches the Ground; and then she must immediately be dragg'd up out of the Surf. And the same caution and dexterity is to be used when they go off again. There is no fresh Water between Tobasco River and Checapeque. This latter is rather a salt Creek than a River; for the

[1] Chiltepec.

Mouth of it is not above 20 Paces wide, and about 8 or 9 Foot Water on the Bar; but within there is 12 or 13 Foot at low Water, and good riding for Barks, half a Mile within the Mouth. AN. 1676

This Creek runs in E. S. E. about two Miles, and then strikes away South up into the Country. At its Mouth between it and the Sea is a bare sandy Point of Land: Where on the side next the River, close by the Brink of it (and no where else) you may scrape up the Sand (which is coarse and brown) with your Hands, and get fresh Water; but if you dig lower the Water will be salt. Half a Mile within the Mouth, when you are past the sandy Point, the Land is wet and swampy, bearing only Mangroves on each side for four or five Leagues up; and after that firm Land; where you will find a run of fresh Water, it being all Salt till you come hither. A League beyond that is a Beef Estantion or Farm of Cattle, belonging to an Indian Village. In the Woods on each side this River there are plenty of Guanoes, Land Turtle, and abundance of Quams and Corresos, with some Parrots; and there is no Settlement nearer than the Beef Estantion; nor any Thing else remarkable in this River that I know.

A League West from Checapeque there is another small River called Dos Boccas, 'tis only fit for Canoas to enter: It has a Bar at its Mouth, and therefore is somewhat dangerous. Yet the Privateers made light of it; for they will govern a Canoa very ingeniously. However Captain Rives and Captain Hewet, two Privateers,[1] lost several Men here in coming out; for there had been a North, which had raised the Bar, and in going out most of their Canoas were overset, and some Men drowned.

This River will not float a Canoa above a League within its Mouth, and so far is Salt: but there you meet with a fine clear Stream of fresh Water, about a League up in the Country: and beyond this are fair Savannahs of long Grass, fenced in with Ridges of as rich Land as any in

[1] Of Captain Rives I can learn nothing more than Dampier tells us. He is again mentioned on p. 217. His associate, Captain Hewet, is mentioned on p. 207.

AN. 1676 the World. The Mold such as is formerly described; all plain and level, even to the Hills of Chiapo.

There are no Indian Towns within four or five Leagues of the Sea; but further off they are pretty thick; lying within a League, two or three one after another: Halpo[1] is the chiefest.

The Indians make use of no more Land than serves to maintain their Families in Maiz; and to pay their Taxes: And therefore between the Towns it lies uncultivated.

In all this Country they rear abundance of Poultry, viz. Turkeys, Ducks and Dunghil Fowls: but some of them have Cacao-Walks. The Cacao of these Parts is most of it sent to Villa de Mose, and ship'd off there. Some of it is sold to Carriers that travel with Mules, coming hither commonly in November or December, and staying till February or March. They lye a Fortnight at a time in a Village to dispose of their Goods; which are commonly Hatchets, Macheats, Axes, Hoes, Knives, Cizars, Needles, Thread, Silk for sowing, Women's Frocks; small Looking-glasses, Beads, Silver or Copper-Rings wash'd with Gold, set with Glass instead of Stones, small Pictures of Saints, and such like Toys for the Indians. And for the Spaniards, Linnen and Woollen Cloaths, Silk-Stockings, and old Hats new dress'd, which are here very valuable, and worn by those of the best Quality; so that an old English Beaver thus ordered, would be worth 20 Dollars; so much is Trade wanted here in this Country. When he has sold off his Goods, he is generally paid in Cacao, which he carries to La Vera Cruz.

From Dos Boccas to the River Palmas is four Leagues, low Land and sandy Bay between.

From Palmas[2] to the Halover is two Leagues.

The Halover[3] is a small Neck of Land, parting the Sea from a large Lagune. It is so called by the Privateers, because they use to drag their Canoas in and out there.

From the Halover to St. Anns is six leagues.

[1] Now Jalpa. [2] Palmas would seem to be Tupilco.
[3] The Halover is a bar of land shutting the Laguna de Santa Anna from the sea.

St. Anns[1] is a Mouth that opens the Lagune before- AN.
mention'd: there is not above six or seven Foot Water, 1676
yet Barks often go in there to Careen.

From St. Anns to Tondelo[2] is five Leagues. The Coast still West; the Land low, and sandy Bay against the Sea: a little within which are pretty high Sand-Banks, cloathed with prickly-Bushes, such as I have already described at Beef-Island.

Against the Sea near the West-end, within the Sand-Bank, the Land is lower again; the Woods not very high, and some spots of Savannahs, with plenty of fat Bullocks; In hunting of which a Frenchman unhappily lost his Life. For his Company being stragled from him to find Game, he unluckily met a Drove of Cattle flying from them in the Woods, which were so thick that there was no passing but in these very narrow Paths that the Cattle themselves had made; so that not being able to get out of their way, the foremost of the Drove thrust his Horns into his Back and carried him 100 Paces into the Savannah, where he fell down with his Guts trailing on the Ground.

The River Tondelo is but narrow, yet capable to receive Barks of 50 or 60 Tuns: There is a Bar at the Entrance, and the Channel crooked. On the West-side of the Bar there is a spit of Sand shoots out; therefore to avoid it at your coming in, you must keep the East-side aboard; but when once entered, you may run up for two or three Leagues; on the East-side a quarter of a Mile within the Mouth, you may lye secure: but all this Coast, and especially this River, intolerably swarms with Musketoes, that there is no sleeping for them.

About four or five Leagues from the Mouth this River is fordable, and there the Road crosses it; where two French Canoas that lay in this River intercepted the Caravan of Mules laden with Cacao,[3] that was returning to La Vera Cruz, taking away as much as they could carry with them.

[1] The Laguna de Santa Anna. [2] Tonala.

[3] This raid does not appear to have been chronicled elsewhere.

AN. 1676 From Tondelo River, to the River of Guasickwalp,[1] is eight Leagues more, the Coast still West; all along sandy Bay and sand Hills, as between St. Anns and Tondelo; only towards the West-part the Bank is lower, and the Trees higher. This is one of the principal Rivers of this Coast; 'tis not half the Breadth of the Tobasco River, but deeper. Its Bar is less dangerous than any on this Coast, having 14 foot Water on it, and but little Sea. Within the Bar there is much more, and soft Oasie Ground. The Banks on both sides are low. The East-side is woody, and the West-side Savannah. Here are some Cattle; but since it has been frequented by Privateers, the Spaniards have driven most of their Bullocks from hence farther into the Country. This River hath its rise near the South-Sea, and is navigable a great way into Land; especially with Boats or small Barks.

The River Teguantepeque, that falls into the South-Seas, has its Origine near the Head of Guasickwalp; and it is reported that the first Naval Stores for the Manila Ships were sent through the Country from the North to the South-Seas, by the conveniency of these two Rivers, whose Heads are not above ten or twelve Leagues asunder, I heard this discoursed by the Privateers long before I visited the South-Seas; and they seemed sometimes minded to try their Fortunes this way: supposing (as many do still) that the South-Sea shore is nothing but Gold and Silver. But how grosly they are mistaken, I have satisfied the World already. And for this part of the Country, though it is rich in Land, yet it has not the least Appearance of any Mine, neither is it thick inhabited with Spaniards: And if I am not deceived, the very Indians in the Heart of the Country are scarce their Friends.

The Town of note on the South-Sea, is Teguantapeque; and on the North-Seas Keyhooca[2] is the chiefest near this River. Besides these two, the Country is only inhabited by Indians; therefore it is wholly unfrequented by Shipping.

Keyhooca is a large rich Town of good Trade, about

[1] Coatzocoalcos.

[2] Acayuca.

four Leagues from the River Guasickwalp, on the West-side. It is inhabited with some few Spaniards and abundance of Mulatoes. These keep many Mules, they being most Carriers, and frequently visit the Cacao Coast for Nuts; and travel the Country between Villa de Mose and La Vera Cruz.

This Country is pleasant enough in the dry Season; but when the furious North Winds rage on the Coast, and violently drive in the Sea, it suffers extremely, being so much overflown, that there is no travelling. It was in the wet Season when Captain Rives and Captain Hewet made an Expedition in Canoas from the Island Trist to the River Guasickwalp, and there landed their Men, designing to attack Keyhooca; but the Country was so wet that there was no marching; neither was the Water high enough for a Canoa. Here are great plenty of Vinelles.

From the River Guasickwalp the Land runs West two or three Leagues, all low Land with sandy Bay to the Sea, and very woody in the Country. About three Leagues to the West of it the Land trends away to the North for about 16 Leagues; rising higher also even from the very Shore, as you go up within Land, making a very high Promontory called St. Martins Land; but ending in a pretty bluff point;[1] which is the West Bounds of the Bay of Campeachy.

From this bluff Point to Alvarado is about twenty Leagues; the first four of it a high rocky shore, with steep Cliffs to the Sea; and the Land somewhat woody. Afterwards you pass by very high Sand-Hills by the Sea, and an extraordinary great Sea falls in on the shore, which hinders any Boats from Landing. Within the Sand-hills again the Land is lower, pretty plain and fruitful enough in large Trees.

The River of Alvarado is above a Mile over at the Mouth, yet the entrance is but shole, there being Sands for near two Mile off the Shore, clear from side to side,

[1] Punta Morillo.

AN. 1676 nevertheless there are two Channels through these Sands. The best, which is in the middle, has twelve or fourteen Foot Water. The Land on each side of the Mouth is high Sand-banks, above 200 Foot high.

This River comes out of the Country in three Branches, meeting altogether just within the Mouth, where it is very wide and deep. One of these Branches comes from the Eastward; another from the Westward; and the third, which is the true River of Alvarado and the biggest, comes directly out of the Country, opposite to the Sand-hills, about a Mile West of the River's Mouth. This last Springs a great way from the Sea, passing through a very fertile Country, thick setled with Towns of Spaniards and Indians. On the West-side, and just against the Mouth of the River, the Spaniards have a small Fort of six Guns, on the declivity of the Sand-bank, a great height above the River; which commands a small Spanish Town on the back of it, built in a Plain close by the River. It is a great Fishery, chiefly for Snooks, which they catch in the Lake; and when they are salted and dryed, drive a great Trade in Exchanging them for Salt and other Commodities. Besides salt Fish, they export from hence abundance of dry Cod-Pepper, and some pickled and put in Jars. This Pepper is known by the Name of Guinea-Pepper.[1] Yet for all this Trade, 'tis but a poor Place, and has been often taken by the Privateers,[2] chiefly to secure their Ships while they should go up in their Canoas to the rich Towns within Land, which notwithstanding they never yet attempted, by reason that La Vera Cruz bordering so near, they were still afraid of being attacked both by Sea and Land from thence, and so never durst prosecute their Designs on the Country Towns.

Six Leagues West from Alvarado there is another large Opening out into the Sea; and it is reported to have a Communication by a small Creek with this River of Alvarado; and that Canoas may pass through it from one

[1] Cayenne pepper.

[2] I can trace no record of any other capture than that in which Dampier took part.

River to the other. And at this Opening is a small Fishing Village. The Land by the Sea is a continued high Sand-bank, and so violent a Sea, that it is impossible to land with Boat or Canoa. AN. 1676

From this River to La Vera Cruz is six Leagues more, the Coast still West. There is a Riff of Rocks[1] runs along the shore from Alvarado to Vera Cruz, yet a good Channel for small Vessels to pass between it and the Shore. And about two Leagues to the East of Vera Cruz are two Islands called Sacrifice Islands.[2] I have set down the distance between Alvarado and La Vera Cruz, according to the common Account of twelve Leagues, which I take to be truer, but our Draughts make it 24. The Land by the Sea is much the same.

La Vera Cruz is a fair Town seated in the very bottom of the Bay of Mexico, at the S. W. Point or Corner of the Bay; for so far the Land runs West; and there it turns about to the North. There is a good Harbour before it, made by a small Island,[3] or Rock rather, just in its Mouth; which makes it very commodious. Here the Spaniards have built a strong Fort, which commands the Harbour; and there are great Iron Rings fix'd in the Fort-Wall against the Harbour for Ships to fasten their Cables. For the North Winds blow so violently here in their Seasons, that Ships are not safe at Anchors.

This Fort is called St. John d'Ulloa; and the Spaniards do frequently call the Town of Vera Cruz by this Name.

The Town is a Place of great Trade; being the Sea-Port to the City of Mexico, and most of the great Towns and Cities in this Kingdom. So that all the European Commodities, spent in these Parts, are landed here, and

[1] The Cabeza, and other reefs.

[2] Islas Sacrificios, the Pajaros Reef, and others.

[3] "This Port is a little Island of stones not three foot above the water in the hiest place, and but a bow-shoote of length any way. This Island standeth from the maine land two bow-shootes or more (600 yards), also, it is to be understood that there is not in all this coaste any other place for shippes to arrive in safetie, because the north wind hath there such violence that unles the shippes be very safely mored with their ancres fastned upon the Island, there is no remedie for these North windes but death" (John Hawkins, his *Third Voyage*).

An. their Goods brought hither and exported from hence.
1676 Add to this, that all the Treasure brought from Manila, in the East-Indies comes hither through the Country from Acapulca.

The Flota comes hither every three Years from Old Spain; and besides Goods of the Product of the Country, and what is brought from the East-Indies and ship'd aboard them: The King's Plate that is gathered in this Kingdom, together with what belongs to the Merchants, amounts to a vast Summ. Here also comes every Year the Barralavanta Fleet in October and November, and stays till March. This is a small Squadron, consisting of six or seven sail of stout Ships, from 20 to 50 Guns. These are ordered to visit all the Spanish Sea-Port Towns once every Year; chiefly to hinder Foreigners from Trading; and to suppress Privateers. From this Port they go to the Havana on the North-side of Cuba to sell their Commodities——From hence they pass through the Gulph of Florida; standing so far to the North as to be out of the Trade-Winds, which are commonly between 30d. and 40d. of Lat. and being in a variable Winds way they stretch away to the Eastward till they may fetch Portarica, if they have Business there; if not, they keep still to the Eastward till they come to Trinidado, an Island near the Main, inhabited by the Spaniards, and the most Eastern-part of any Consequence in the North-Seas. The Barralaventa Fleet touches there first, and from thence sails to the Margarita, a considerable Spanish-Island near the Main. From thence they Coast down to Comana and La Guiary, and passing by the Coast of Carraccas, they sail towards the Gulph of Mericaia,[1] from thence they double Cape La Vell,[2] and so down to Rio la Hacha, St. Martha and Carthagena. If they meet with any English or Dutch Trading Sloops, they chace and take them, if they are not too nimble for them: The Privateers keep out of their way, having always Intelligence where they are.

From Carthagena they sail to Portobello; and from

[1] Maracaibo.

[2] Cape de Vela.

thence to Campeachy: and lastly, to La Vera Cruz: And this is their Annual Navagation about the West-Indian Coast. AN. 1676

La Vera Cruz was taken by the Privateers, about the Year 85 under the Conduct of one John Russel an old Logwood-Cutter that had formerly been taken by the Spaniards and sent to Mexico; where learning Spanish, he by that means escaped to La Vera Cruz; and being released from thence, he afterwards managed this Expedition.

From hence to Old Vera Cruz is five Leagues. This was the first Town of that Name; but wanting a good Harbour there, it was removed to the Place where it now stands.

From Old Vera Cruz to Tispo[1] is about fifteen Leagues; the Coast lies N. and S. Tispo is a pretty handsome small Town, built close by the Sea, and watered with a little Rivulet; but wanting a Harbour, 'tis destitute of any Maritime-Trade.

From Tispo to the River Panuk[2] is about twenty Leagues: The Coast lies N. and S. nearest, it is a large River, descending out of the very Bowels of the Country, and running East, falls into the Gulph of Mexico, in Lat. about 21–50 Minutes. It has ten or eleven Foot Water on the Bar, and is often visited with Barks that sail up it, as far as the City Panuk, lying distant from the Sea about twenty Leagues, and is the principal of this Country, being a Bishop's See. There are two Churches, one Convent, and a Chapel; and about five Hundred Families of Spaniards, Mulatoes and Indians. The Houses are large and strong; with Stone Walls; and they are thatched with Palmeto Leaves.

One Branch of this River comes out of the Lagune of Tompeque,[3] and mixes with this, three Leagues before it falls into the Sea. Therefore it is sometimes called the River of Tompeque. The Lagune of Tompeque lies on

[1] Probably Tuxpan. Dampier's distances are misleading in this instance.

[2] Panuco.

[3] Tampico.

AN. 1676 the South Side of the River; and breeds abundance of Fish, especially Shrimps. There is a Town of the same Name, built on its Banks, whose Inhabitants are most Fishermen. Beyond this Lagune there is another large one, wherein is an Island and Town named Haniago; its Inhabitants most Fishermen, whose chief Employment is to take Shrimps. These they boil with Water and Salt, in great Coppers, for the purpose; and having dried them afterwards in the Sun, they are made up in Packs, and sent to all the chief Towns in the Country, especially to Mexico, where, tho' but a hungry Sort of Food, they are mightily esteemed.

The Account I have given of the Campeachy Rivers, &c. was the Result of the particular Observations I made in cruising about that Coast, in which I spent eleven or twelve Months. For when the violent Storm before-mentioned took us, I was but just settling to Work, and not having a Stock of Wood to purchase such Provision as was sent from Jamaica, as the old Standards had; I, with many more in my Circumstances, was forced to range about to seek a Subsistence in Company of some Privateers then in the Bay. In which Rambles we visited all the Rivers from Trist to Alvarado; and made many Descents into the Country among the Villages there, where we got Indian Corn to eat with the Beef, and other Flesh that we got by the way, or Manatee and Turtle, which was also a great Support to us.

Alvarado was the Westermost Place I was at. Thither we went in two Barks with thirty Men in each, and had ten or eleven kill'd and desperately wounded in taking the Fort; being four or five Hours engag'd in that Service, in which time the Inhabitants having plenty of Boats and Canoas, carried all their Riches and best Moveables away. It was after Sunset before the Fort yielded; and growing dark, we could not pursue them, but rested quietly that Night; the next Day we killed, salted and sent aboard twenty or thirty Beefs, and a good Quantity of Salt-fish, and Indian Corn, as much as we could stow away. Here were but few Hogs, and those eat very fishy; therefore we did not much esteem them: but of Cocks, Hens and Ducks were sent aboard in abundance. The tame Parrots we found here were the largest and fairest Birds of their Kind that I ever saw in the West-Indies. Their colour was yellow and red, very coarsely mixt; and they would prate very prettily; and there was scarce a Man but what sent aboard one or two of them. So that with Provision, Chests, Hen-Coops and Parrot-Cages, our Ships were full of Lumber, with which we intended to sail: But the second Day after we took the Fort, having had a Westerly Wind all the Morning, with Rain, seven Armadilloes that were sent from La Vera Cruz appeared in Sight, within a Mile of the Bars, coming in with full Sail; but they could scarce stem the Current of the River; which was very well for us; for we were not a little surprized. Yet we got under Sail, in order to meet them; and clearing our Decks by heaving all the Lumber overboard, we drove out over the Bar, before they reached it: But they being to Wind-ward, forced us to exchange a few Shot with them. Their Admiral was called the *Toro*. She had 10 Guns and 100 Men; another had 4 Guns and 80 Men: The rest having no great Guns, had only 60 or 70 Men apiece, armed with Muskets, and the Vessels barricadoed round with Bull-hides Breast high. We had not above 50 Men in both Ships, 6 Guns in one and two in the other. As soon as we were over the Bar, we got our Larboard-Tacks aboard and stood to the Eastward, as nigh the Wind as we could lye. The Spaniards came away quartering on us; and our Ship being the Head-most, the *Toro* came directly towards us, designing to board us. We kept firing at her, in hopes to have lamed either Mast or Yard; but failing, just as she was shearing aboard, we gave her a good Volley, and presently clapp'd the Helm a Weather, wore our Ship, and got our Starboard Tacks aboard, and stood to the Westward: and so left the *Toro*, but were saluted by all the small Craft as we past by them, who stood to the Eastward after the *Toro*, that was now in Pursuit and close by our Consort. We stood to the Westward till we were against the River's Mouth; then we tackt, and by the help

AN. 1676

AN. 1676 of the Current that came out of the River, we were near a Mile to Windward of them all. Then we made sail to assist our Consort, who was hard put to it; but on our Approach the *Toro* edged away towards the Shore, as did all the rest, and stood away for Alvarado: And we, glad of the Deliverance, went away to the Eastward, and visited all the Rivers in our Return again to Trist; and searched the Bays for Munjack to carry with us for the Ship's use, as we had done before for the use both of Ships and Canoas.

Munjack is a sort of Pitch or Bitumen, which we find in Lumps, from three or four Pounds to thirty Pounds in a Lump; washed up by the Sea, and left dry on all the Sandy-Bays on all this Coast: It is in Substance like Pitch, but blacker; it melts by the Heat of the Sun, and runs abroad as Pitch would do if exposed, as this is, on the Bays: The smell of it is not so pleasant as Pitch, neither does it stick so firmly as Pitch, but it is apt to peel off from the Seams of Ships Bottoms; however we find it very useful here where we want Pitch; and because it is commonly mixed with Sand by lying on the Bays, we melt it and refine it very well before we use it; and commonly temper it with Oyl or Tallow to correct it; for though it melts by the Heat of the Sun, yet it is of a harsher Nature than Pitch. I did never find the like in any other Part of the World, neither can I tell from whence it comes.

And now the Effects of the late Storm being almost forgot, the Lagune Men settled again to their Imployments; and I among the rest fell to work in the East Lagune, where I remained till my Departure for Jamaica.

I will only add as to this Logwood-Trade in general, that I take it to be one of the most profitable to England, and it nearest resembles that of Newfoundland; since what arises from both, is the Product of bare Labour; and that the Persons imployed herein are supported by the Produce of their Native Country.

It is not my Business to determine how far we might have a right of cutting Wood there, but this I can say, that the Spaniards never receive less Damage from the Persons who generally follow that Trade, than when they are employed upon that Work. AN. 1676

While I was here the last time, Capt. Gibbs arriv'd in a Ship of about 100 Tons, and brought with him 20 stout New-England Indians that were taken in the Wars there, designing to have sold them at Jamaica, but not finding a good Market, brought them hither to cut Logwood, and hired one Mr. Richard Dawkins to be their Overseer, who carried them to work at Summasenta; But it so happened that about a Week after, the Captain came thither in his Boat from One-Bush-Key where his Ship lay, and the Overseer having some Business, desired leave to be absent for two or three Days: But as soon as he and the Seamen were gone, the Indians taking their Opportunity killed the Captain and marched off, designing to return to their own Country by Land: They were seen about a Month afterward, and one of them was taken near the River Tondelo.

After I had spent about ten or twelve Months at the Logwood-Trade, and was grown pretty well acquainted with the way of Traffick here, I left the Imployment, yet with a design to return hither after I had been in England; and accordingly went from hence with Captain Chambers of London, bound to Jamaica. We sailed from Trist the Beginning of April, 1678, and arrived at Jamaica in May, where I remained a small Time, and then return'd for England with Captain Loader of London. I arriv'd there the beginning of August the same Year: and at the Beginning of the following Year I set out again for Jamaica, in order to have gone thence to Campeachy; but it proved to be a Voyage round the World; of which the Publick has already had an Account in my former Volume, and the First Part of This.

CAP. DAMPIER

HIS

DISCOURSE

OF THE

TRADE-WINDS, BREEZES, STORMS, SEASONS OF THE YEAR, TIDES AND CURRENTS OF THE TORRID ZONE THROUGHOUT THE WORLD

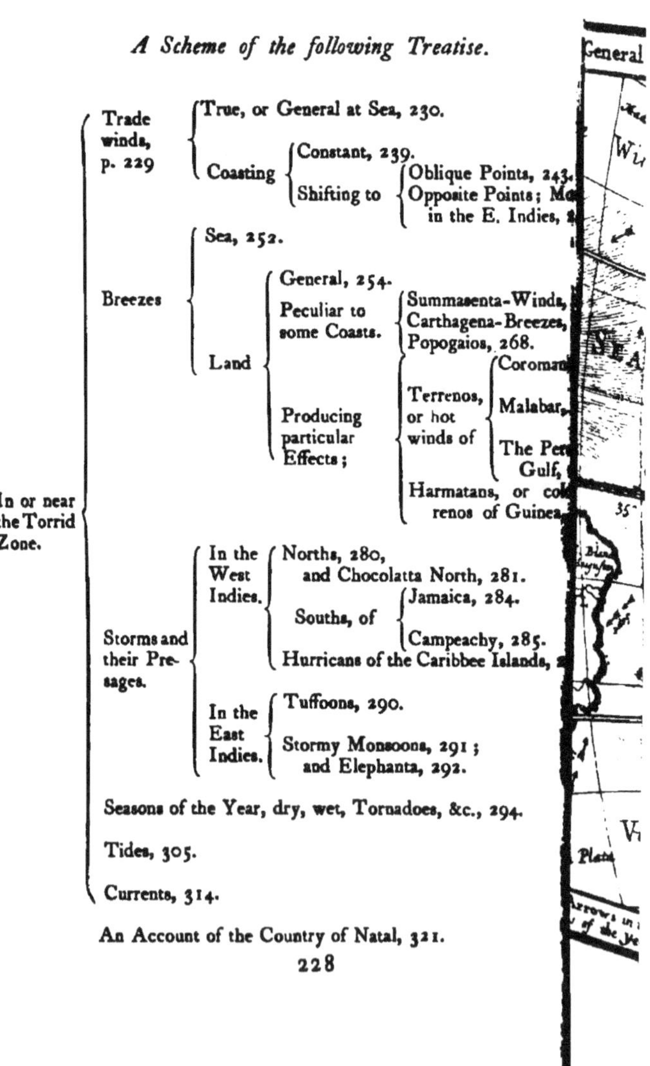

A Scheme of the following Treatise.

- In or near the Torrid Zone.
  - Trade winds, p. 229
    - True, or General at Sea, 230.
    - Coasting
      - Constant, 239.
      - Shifting to
        - Oblique Points, 243.
        - Opposite Points; Mo in the E. Indies, 2
  - Breezes
    - Sea, 252.
    - Land
      - General, 254.
      - Peculiar to some Coasts.
        - Summasenta-Winds,
        - Carthagena-Breezes,
        - Popogaios, 268.
      - Producing particular Effects;
        - Terrenos, or hot winds of
          - Coroma
          - Malabar,
          - The Pe Gulf,
        - Harmatans, or co renos of Guinea,
  - Storms and their Presages.
    - In the West Indies.
      - Norths, 280, and Chocolatta North, 281.
      - Souths, of
        - Jamaica, 284.
        - Campeachy, 285.
      - Hurricans of the Caribbee Islands,
    - In the East Indies.
      - Tuffoons, 290.
      - Stormy Monsoons, 291; and Elephanta, 292.
  - Seasons of the Year, dry, wet, Tornadoes, &c., 294.
  - Tides, 305.
  - Currents, 314.

An Account of the Country of Natal, 321.

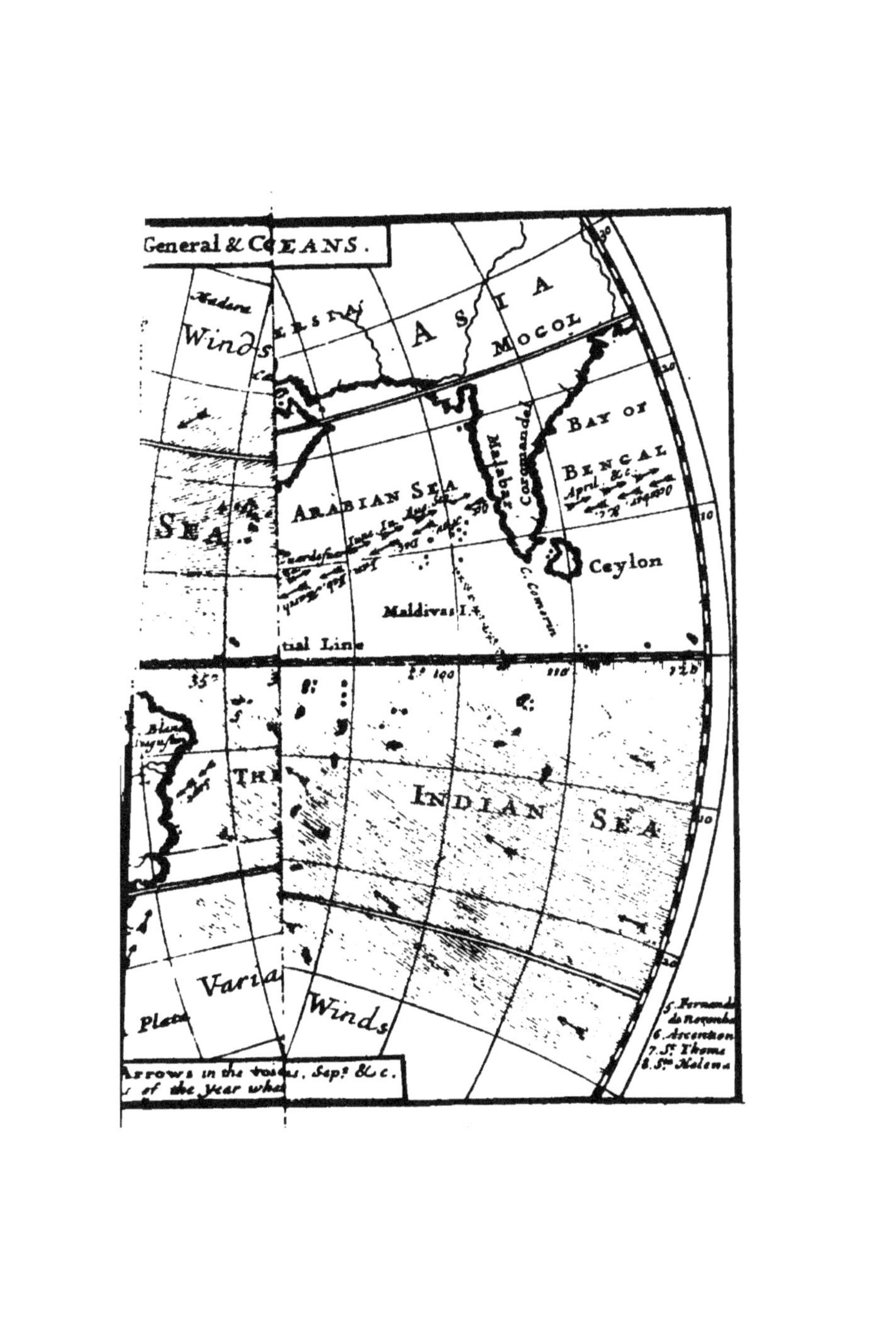

General & OCEANS.
ASIA
MOCOL
Winds
ARABIAN SEA
BAY OF
BENGAL
Malabar
Coromandel
Ceylon
Maldivas I.
C. Comorin
INDIAN SEA
Winds
5. Fernando de Noronha
6. Ascention
7. St. Thome
8. St. Helena

MR. DAMPIER'S VOYAGES

VOL. II. PART III

A DISCOURSE OF WINDS, BREEZES, STORMS, TIDES, AND CURRENTS

CHAP. I

Of the General Trade-Wind

THE INTRODUCTION

Of the General Trade-Wind at Sea. Of the best Time of the Year to cross the Equinoctial. The Winds near the Line commonly uncertain, and attended with Calms and Tornadoes. A Reason of the Winds blowing South near the Line, in the Atlantick Sea. How Ships homeward-bound from the Bite of Guinea, should cross the Line. Of the Trade-Wind in the South-Sea, and in the East-Indian Ocean.

I SHALL reduce what I have to say on this Subject to some General Heads; beginning with the Trade-winds, as being the most remarkable.

Trade-winds are such as do blow constantly from one Point or Quarter of the Compass, and the Region of the World most peculiar to them, is from about 30 d. North, to 30 d. South of the Equator.

There are divers sorts of these Winds; some blowing from East to West, some from South to North, others from West to East, &c. Some are constant in one Quarter all the Year; some blow one half the Year one way, and the other six Months quite contrary; and others blow six Months one way, and then shifting only eight or ten

Points, continue six Months more, and then return again to their former Stations, as all these shifting Trade-winds do; and so as the Year comes about, they alternately succeed each other in their proper Seasons.

There are other sorts, called Sea-Winds and Land-winds, differing much from any of the former, the one blowing by Day, the other by Night, constantly and regularly succeeding each other.

Within the Torrid Zone also are violent Storms, as fierce, if not fiercer, than any are in other Parts of the World. And as to the Seasons of the Year, I can distinguish them there, no other way than by Wet and Dry; and these wet and dry Seasons do as successively follow each other, as Winter and Summer do with us.

Here are also strong Currents, sometimes setting one way, sometimes another; which though it is hard to describe, with that Accuracy which is desirable, yet I shall give as particular an Account of them, as also of the several sorts of Winds, as my own Observations, and the judicious Informations from others, will afford me Matter to do.

Of the General Trade-Wind.

Of all Winds before-mentioned, I shall endeavour to treat distinctly; beginning with the True Trade-Wind first, which I call the General Trade-Wind at Sea; because all other Trade-Winds, whether constant or shifting, seem to have their Dependance on some accidental Cause; whereas the Cause of these, be it what it will, seems uniform and constant.

These General Trade-Winds are only in the Atlantick Ocean which parts Africa from America, in the East-Indian Ocean, and in the Great South-Sea.

In all these Seas, except just under or near the Line, they constantly blow without Intermission, as well to the South, as to the North of the Equator, but not with equal Force at all Times, nor in all Latitudes; Neither do these constant Trade-Winds usually blow near the

Shore, but only in the Ocean, at least 30 or 40 Leagues off at Sea, clear from any Land; especially on the West Coast, or Side of any Continent: For indeed on the East-side, the Easterly Wind being the true Trade-Wind, blows almost home to the Shore; so near as to receive a Check from the Land-Wind, and oft-times to admit of the Sea-Breeze, by which it is drawn from its Course frequently four or five Points of the Compass: But of the Sea-Breeze I shall speak in its Place. In some Places, and particularly the South Seas, in South Lat. the true Eastern Trade is not found to blow within 150 or near 200 Leagues of the Coast, but in North Lat. in those Seas, it comes within 30 or 40 Leagues distance of the Shore: And this I shall give as a general Rule, that in North Lat. these Winds are commonly at E. N. E. in South Lat. at E. S. E.

When we go from England, and are bound to the East or West-Indies, or to Guinea, we commonly find these Winds in the Lat. of 30 d. sometimes sooner, as in the Latitudes of 32 or 35. And it may so happen that we may meet with an Easterly Wind in 40 d. or go out of our Channel with a North-East Wind, which sometimes also fails us not till we come into a true Trade-Wind; but this is only accidental, therefore is not the Wind that I speak of; but between 32 and 28 I did never know nor hear, that the true Trade-Wind failed.

If in coming from England, we have a North-Easterly Wind that brings us hither, (*i.e.* into the true Trade-wind) it sometimes stays at North-East, especially if we keep near the African Shore, as Guinea Ships do, till we are near the Tropick of Cancer, and then comes to the E. N. E. where it settles; but commonly it settles there in 28 d. if we are so far off Shore as to receive the true Trade. When the Wind is thus settled, we have commonly fair Weather, and a clear Sky, especially if the Sun is in any Southern Sign; but if in a Northern Sign, the Weather is usually cloudy.

On the contrary, when we are in South Lat. in the Atlantick, if the Sun is in Northern Signs, the Sky is clear, but if in Southern Signs, the Sky is cloudy. This I once experienced to my Sorrow, in my return from Bantam, in the Year 1671. We had cloudy Weather and brisk Winds, while we were crossing the East-India Ocean, and had a very good Passage also about the Cape of Good Hope; where we had fair clear Weather; And steering from thence, for the Island of St. Hellena, where we thought to water and refresh, as all our English East-India Ships do, we mist it for want of an Observation. For before we came to the Tropick of Capricorn, the Sky was again clouded, so that we seldom saw the Sun or Stars, till we were quite past the Island. However we found the Isle of Ascention, where we struck two Turtle, (for this was not the laying Time, but the beginning of the Cooting or Ingendring Season; therefore some few only were drawn hither.) This was the latter-end of November. From the time that we thought our selves to the West of St. Hellena, we had our Water measured out to us, two Pints a Man per Day, till we came into our Channel. This was the first time that I began to know the Value of fresh Water; for we took in none in all our Way home from Bantam. But so much for this Digression.

The Winds, as I said before, as we run to the Southward from England, do first settle in the E. N. E. about the Lat. of 28 d. or be sure between that and 24 d. especially when the Sun is to the Southward of the Line; but in May, June, and July you will find the Winds at E. by S. or E. S. E.

These Winds, whether we meet them to the North of the East, or to the South of it, we find blowing a moderate Gale from our first meeting them in 30 or 28 d. till we come to the Tropick, there we find the Trade stronger: It commonly blows a good Top-sail Gale, as we sail large: And if we were to sail on a Wind, our lower Sails would be enough.

These brisk Gales blow in the Atlantick Ocean, and North of the Equator, from the Lat. of 23 to 12 or 14 constantly, between the E. N. E. and the E. but between 10 to 12 degrees and the Line, they are not so fresh nor constant, to that Point; for in the Months of July and August, the South-Winds do oft-times blow even to 11 d. or 12 d. of North Lat. keeping between the S. S. E. and the S. S. W. or S. W. but in December and January the true Trade blows between 3 d. or 4 d. of the Equator. And as the Sun returns again to the Northward, so the Southerly Winds do increase and draw more to the Northward of the Line, till July, and then gradually withdraw back again towards the Line: When the Sun is in Southern Signs, 'tis the best time of the Year to cross the Line, if bound to the Southward; for besides the Benefit of the true Trade, to bring a Ship near the Line, the Wind is then more constant and fresh, the Weather clearer, and the Winds which at other Times are between the S. S. E. and S. S. W. are now at S. E. or S. E. and by E. but in our Summer Months we find nothing but Calms and Tornadoes; and tho' Tornadoes do usually rise against the settled Wind; yet but few Commanders will endeavour to take the Advantage of the Winds that come from them, but rather furl their Top-sails, haul up their Corses,[1] and lye still till the Gust of Wind is past, except Necessity requires haste; for the sudden Tornadoes do not continue long; and besides often very violent and fierce, so that a Ship with her Sails loose, would be in danger to be over-set by them, or at least lose Masts or Yards, or have the Sails split; besides the Consternation that all Men must needs be in at such a Time, especially if the Ship, by any unforeseen Accident, should prove unruly, as by the Mistake of the Man at Helm, or he that Conns,[2] or by her broaching to[3] against all Endeavours, which often happens when a fierce Gust comes; which tho' it does not last long, yet would do much Damage in a short Time; and tho' all things should fall out well, yet the Benefit of it would not compensate the Danger: For 'tis much if a Ship sails a Mile before either the Wind dyes wholly away, or at least shifts about again to the

[1] The lowest sails on the fore and main masts of square-rigged ships are known as courses.

[2] Or directs the helmsman.

[3] To broach-to is to fly up into the wind.

South. Nor are we sure that these Winds will continue three Minutes before they shift; and sometimes they fly round faster than the Ship will, tho' the Helm lies for it; and all Seamen know the Danger of being taken a-back[1] in such Weather.

But what has been spoken of the Southerly Winds, Calms, and Tornadoes is to be understood of the East-side of the Atlantick to as far West as the Longitude of 359 d. or thereabouts; for farther Westerly we find the Winds commonly at S. E. even in crossing the Line, and a very brisk Gale; 'tis for that Reason our experienced Guinea Commanders do keep to the Southward of the Line, till they are about that Longitude. Some run over nearer the American Shore before they cross the Line; Our East-India Commanders do also cross the Line, coming from India near the American Coast, and find brisk Gales at S. E. all the times of the Year; but going to the Indies, they steer away South, from the Island St. Jago, where they commonly water, and meet the Winds in that Longitude. But of this enough.

The Winds near the Line in the Indian Ocean and South-Sea are different from this, yet there the Winds are also Southerly, and therefore different from what they are farther off; for 2 d. or 3 d. on each side the Line, the Winds are commonly very uncertain, and oftentimes there are perfect Calms, or at least very small Winds and some Tornadoes in the East-Indian Sea. In the South-Seas, near and under the Line, the Winds are at South 130 Leagues off from the Shore, but how farther off I know not; there the Winds are but small, yet constant, and the Weather clear from March till September; but about Christmas there are Tornadoes; yet in both the East-Indian Sea, and the South Sea, the Winds near or under the Line, are often at South; yet these Winds do not blow above 2 or 3 d. to the North or South of the Line, except near some Land; but in the Atlantick Sea, as I have said before, the South and South-West Winds do sometimes blow even to 10 or

[1] So that the wind presses the sails against the masts and rigging.

12 d. North of the Line. And for the South Winds to blow constantly near the Line in the Atlantick, between Cape Verd in Africa, and C. Blanco in Brazil, is no wonderful thing, if a Man will but consider those Promontories that shoot out from the Continents on each side the Sea; one on the North, the other on the South-side of the Equator, leaving but a small space clear for the Winds to blow in; where there is always a pretty brisk Gale, especially on the American side. And as within 2 or 3 d. of the Equator, it is most subject to Calms and Tornadoes, and small faint Breezes in other Seas not pent up as this is. So this Sea, except just in the very Opening between both Promontories, is much more subject to it than any other, especially on the East-side; that is, from the Bite or the Inland Corner of the Coast of Guinea to 28 or 30 d. distance West: But this seems not to be altogether the Effects of the Line, but owing partly to the nearness of the Land to the Line, which shoots out from the Bite of Guinea, even to Cape St. Anns, almost in a Parallel with the Equator (allowing for the Bays and Bendings) and this is 23 or 24 d. of Longitude, and not above 80 Leagues from the Line in some Places: So that this part of the Sea between the Coast of Guinea, and the Line or 2 d. South of it, lying, as it were, between the Land and the Line, is seldom free from bad Weather; especially from April to September; but when the Sun is withdrawn towards the Tropick of Capricorn, then there is something better Weather there.

And in the Sea under the Line between the African Promontory and the American, it is free from Tornadoes and Calms, and more subject to fair Weather and fresh Breezes. Therefore both our English and Dutch East-India Ships, when outward-bound, endeavour to cross the Line as near as they can in the mid-Channel, between both Promontories; and although they meet the Winds sometimes at S. S. E. or at S. S. W. or farther Easterly or Westerly; yet will they not run above a degree to the East, or a degree to the West of the mid-Channel, before they tack again, for fear of meeting with the soaking

Current on the West,[1] or Calms on the East-side; either of which would be alike prejudicial to their Course.

The Portuguese in their Voyages to Brazil, take the same method, and get to the South of the Line before they fall in with the Land, for fear of falling to leeward of Cape St. Augustine,[2] for there are so many things which make that a difficult Cape to pass, that hardly any Man would try to do it, but at a distance.

But our Guinea Ships do generally pass on to their Ports on the Coast of Guinea, at any time of the Year, without using such Methods; because their Business lies mostly on the North of the Line, where they always find a fair Westerly Wind. But in their returns from thence, they cross the Line, and run 3 or 4 d. to the Southward of it, where they meet the Wind between the S. S. E. and the S. S. W. and a brisk gale: with this Wind, they run away in the same parallel 35 or 36 d. before they cross the Line again to the Northward, which is about mid-way between the Extreams of both Promontories, there they find a brisk gale, which carries them to the West-Indies, or where they please. Some run West 40 d. before they cross the Line, and find strong Gales; whereas should they come from Old Callabar, or any other Place in the Bite,[3] on the North of the Line, and steer away West, thinking to gain their Passage the sooner because it is the nearest way, they would doubtless be mistaken, as many Men have been: For if they keep near the Line, they meet with great Calms; and if they keep near the Land, they meet with Westerly Winds; and if they keep in the middle between both, they must of necessity meet with both Inconveniencies, as also with Tornadoes, especially in May, June, July and August.

By which means some Ships, if they go any of these three ways now cautioned against, spend more time in going from the Bite to Cape Verd, than another Ship will

[1] The Brazil current, setting to the SW. at the rate of nearly one sea mile an hour.

[2] Santo Agostinho, near Pernambuco.

[3] The Bight, or loop, of Benin.

do if it cross the Line in the right Places, before-mentioned, in going to the Barbadoes.

Sometimes unexperienced Guinea Masters in their return from thence, after they have cross'd the Line from N. to S. and are in a fair way to gain a speedy Passage, will be so obstinate in their Opinions, after they have run 26, 28 or 30 d. West from Old Callabar (with a fair Wind) to steer away W. by N. or W. N. W. it being the directest Course they can steer for Barbadoes, then they must of Necessity keep within a Degree of the Line, while they are running 2 or 300 Leagues, which may prove to be a long time in doing, because of the Uncertainty of the Winds near the Equator; therefore they that cross it near the Middle, between both Promontories, or near the American Coast, when they are minded to fall away to the Northward, steer away N. W. or N. W. by N. and so depress or raise a degree in running 28 Leagues at most; therefore (which is best) they are but a short time near the Equator: And besides, in thus crossing it in the middle between both Promontories, they seldom miss of a Wind: for the Wind in these Seas has no other Passage, but between these two Promontories.

What I have said already on this Head, has been chiefly of the Atlantick, and of that too mostly about the Line, because it is the most difficult Place to pass in going to the Southward. In other Seas, as in the East-India Sea, and the Great South-Sea there is no such Difficulty to pass any way, because there is Sea-room enough, without coming into such Inconveniences as we meet with in the Atlantick; and as to the Winds between the Line and the Tropicks, in the East-Indian Sea and the South-Sea, they are in their Latitudes, as I said before, viz. in South Latitude, at E. S. E. and in North Lat. at E. N. E. blowing constantly fresh Breezes, especially in the South-Seas, even from within a Degree or two of the Line, on each side to the Tropick, or to 30 Degrees of Lat. And this I may truly say, that neither the Atlantick nor the East-Indian Seas have the true Trade-Winds so constant nor brisk at all times of the Year, and in all Latitudes, as they are here.

For being once got in the Trade, I mean without the Verge of the coasting Trade-Wind, it blows a very brisk Gale all over the Ocean. Capt. Eaton experienced this in sailing from the Gallapagos Islands to the Ladrones, in the latter end of the Year 1685. We had the like Experience, sailing from Cape Corientes to Guam the Year after (as appears by my Journal of that Run, in my "Voyage round the World," Chap. 10. Pag. 297.) And as for the Wind to the Southward of the Line, I had great Experience of it in my Ramble there with Captain Sharp; and since that Capt. Davis, in his Return out of the South-Sea, had greater Experience, because he took his Departure from the Gallapagos Islands also, and steering W. S. W. from thence till he met the true Trade at E. S. E. he steered directly South, clear from the Line, till he got to the Southward of the Tropick of Capricorn, and so quite without the Trade.

In the East-Indian Sea, between the Lat. of 30 d. and 4 degrees South of the Equator, the true Breeze is at E. S. E. or S. E. by E. yet not so constant nor brisk as in the South-Seas; besides that part of it which lyes to the Northward of the Line, has not such a constant steady Breeze, but is more subject to Calms, and near the Shore to shifting Winds, according to the Seasons of the Year.

CHAP. II

Of the constant coasting Trade-Winds

A Parallel of the South-Part of Africa and Peru. The Trade-Winds blow with an acute Angle an any Coast. The Winds about Angola and in the South-Seas alike; as also at Mexico and Guinea. The Winds shift not in some Places. Sand blown from the Shore about Cape Blanco in Guinea. An Account of the Trade-Winds from thence to Cape Logos.

THE Trade-winds which blow on any Coast, are either Constant or Shifting.

The Coasts that are subject to Constant Trade-winds, are the South-Coast of Africa and Peru, and Part of the Coast of Mexico, and Part of Guinea.

The South-part of Africa and Peru, are in one Lat. both Coasts trending North and South; both on the West-side of their Continents; both in South Lat. and tho' they do not lye exactly parallel, by Reason of some Capes or Bendings in the Land, yet are the Winds much alike on both Coasts, all the Year long.

On the Coast of Angola the Winds are between the S. W. and S. And on the Coast of Peru, we reckon them between the S. S. W. and S. S. E. But this the Reader must take notice of: That the Trade-Winds that blow on any Coast, except the North Coast of Africa, whether they are constant, and blow all the Year, or whether they are shifting Winds, do never blow right in on the Shore, nor right along Shore; but go slanting, making an acute Angle of about 22 degrees. Therefore as the Land trends more Easterly or Westerly from the North or South on these Coasts, so the Winds do alter accordingly; as for example, where the Land lies N. and S. the Wind would be at

S. S. W. but where the Land lies S. S. W. the Trade would be at S. W. But if the Land lies S. S. E. then the Wind would be at South. This is supposed of Coasts lying on the West-side of any Continent, and on the South-side of the Equator, as the two Coasts of Africa and Peru are; but the North part of Africa has the Trade blowing off from the Shore, two or three Points.

These Southerly Winds do blow constantly all the Year long, on both the Coasts of Peru and Africa; they are brisk, and blow farther off from the Coasts than any shifting Winds.

On the Coast of Peru, these Winds blow 140 or 150 Leagues off Shore, before you can perceive them to alter: But then as you run farther off, so the Wind will come about more Easterly, and at about 200 Leagues distance it settles at E. S. E. which is the true Trade.

Between Angola and Brazil the Winds are much as they are in the South-Seas, on the West-side of the Peruvian Coast; only near the Line, within 4 degrees of it, in South Lat. the Wind holds in the S. S. W. or S. W. for 28 or 30 d. of Longitude, and so it may in the same Lat. in the South-Seas, for ought I know; for it was at South, as far as any of us were, which was 200 Leagues.

As the Coasts of Peru and Angola have their constant Trade-winds, so has the Coast of Mexico and Guinea. And as the Coast of Peru lies North and South, so those lye nearer East and West. Accordingly to the Course of the General Trade, the Winds should be Easterly on these Coasts; but here we meet with the quite contrary; for from the Lat. of 10 d. North to 20 d. North on the Coast of Mexico, the Winds are constantly near the West on all the Coast, except check'd sometimes with Tornadoes, which do commonly rise against the Wind; the same is observed on the Coast of Angola, where there are Tornadoes also: But the Coast of Peru is not subject to any, yet on that Coast there are sometimes Calms two or three Days together off of the Bay of Arica, between the Lat. of 16 and 23. In the Lat. of 19 you shall have Calms 30 or 40 Leagues off Shore, but not so far on either side the Bay, neither are such Calms usual on the Coasts of Angola and Mexico only after a Tornado, as is common in other Places.

As the Coasts of Angola and Peru, do in most things run parallel each with other; so do the Coasts of Mexico and Guinea: And if I am not mistaken, the Winds on both these Coasts are much alike; Both these Coasts do begin at the Bite or Bending of the Land, where the other two parallel Lands do end; for as the Mexican Continent begins at or near Panama, which is eight or nine degrees North of the Equator; so that part of Guinea, which I speak of, begins about Old Callabar, in about four or five Degrees of North Lat.

The Land trends away Westerly from both these Places some hundreds of Leagues; and tho' not on one Point of the Compass, because of the small Points, Bays and Bending in the Land, yet the Winds that on more regular Shores, keep their constant Course, and blow in upon the Shore, about two Points from the Sea, do also here on the Guinea Coast, blow on the Shore from the West Quarter, and as the Land lies pointing in on the Shore, even from Cape Mount to Old Callabar, which is above 400 Leagues; and that with such Constancy that the East-part of that Coast is called the Leeward Coast; and the West-part the Windward Coast; And yet this is so contrary to the general Opinion of Seamen, concerning the Course of the Winds, that nothing but their own Experience will convince them of the Truth of it; for thus they generally reason; Barbadoes is the Easter-most of the Caribbe-Islands, therefore the rest are said to be Leeward of it, and so of any other Island; as indeed it usually holds true, because the Winds there are commonly at East; but this Counter-Wind on the Coast of Guinea astonishes most Seamen that have seen nothing like what they meet with here. There are other Coasts where the Winds shift very little, as on the Coast of Carraccos, and the South-side of the Bay of Mexico, *i.e.* in the Bay of Campeachy, and all the Caribbe Islands. Indeed there may be sometimes some small Flurts of a Westerly Wind on these Coasts, but neither constant, certain, or lasting.

And indeed this was the great Stumbling-Block tha met with in running from the Gallapagos Islands for Island Cocos, mention'd in my former Book, Chap Pag. 136.

But that part of Africa, which lies between Cape in 14 d. North, and Cape Bayedore[1] in 27, has comm Northerly Winds; or between the N. and N. E. very Gales; therefore our Guinea Ships bound to Guinea s to keep near that Shore, and oft-times make the C And being to the Southward of Cape Blanco, which ly Lat. about 21, they are sometimes so troubled with which the Wind brings off Shore, that they are scarce to see one another: Their Decks are also strewed wi and their Sails all red, as if they were tanned with the that sticks to them, it being of a reddish Colour.

From Cape Verd to Cape St. Anns, which is ab degrees North, the Trade is between the E. and S. E. Cape St. Anns, to Cape Palmas, in about 4 d. North Trade is at S. W. from Cape Palmas to the Bite of G which is at the bending of the Coast, the Wind is at W. From this Bending the Land begins to turn ab the South; and from thence to Cape Logos,[2] which the South of the Line, the Trade is at S. W. as it is that Coast, even to 30 degrees South.

This last Account I had from Mr. Canby, wh made many Voyages to Guinea.

[1] Bojadore. [2] Cape Lopez.

CHAP. III

Of the Coasting Trade-Winds that shift

The Coast where the Winds shift. Of the Winds between Gratia de Dios, and Cape La Vela. Of those on the Coast of Brazil: At Panama: About Natal: And Cape Corientes; And the Red-Sea: From the Gulph of Persia to Cape Comorin. Of the Monsoons in India: Their Benefit for sailing from Place to Place. Sea and Land Breezes serviceable for the same purpose. By what helps long Voyages are made in an open Sea.

THE Coast where the Winds do usually shift, are some in the West-Indies, as that part of the Coast between Cape Gratia de Dios, and Cape La Vela chiefly: The Coast of Brazil; the Bay of Panama in the South-Seas, and all the Coast of the East-Indies, even from the River Natal, which is in the Lat. of 30 d. South, on the East-side of Africa, beyond the Cape of good Hope, to the North-East Parts of China, comprehending all the Bays between. The Islands also have their Annual Changes; Of all these I shall treat in their order, beginning first with that Coast which lyes between Cape Gratia de Dios and Cape La Vela: And I the rather begin with this part first, because this part of the West-Indies is all that is subject to change; neither is the change altogether so orderly, or certain as the Monsoons in the East-Indies, or the shifting Winds on the Coast of Brazil.

The Common Trade-Wind on this Coast is between the N. E. and the East: This Trade blows constantly from March till November, but is often check'd with Tornadoes in the Months of May, June, July, and August, especially between the River of Darien and Costarica; but to Windward there is a more serene Air, and a brisker Wind: From October till March there are Westerly Winds, not constant, nor violent, but blowing moderately, sometimes two or three Days or a Week; and then the Breeze may blow again as long. These Winds are most in December and January; before and after these two Months the Trade-Wind is only checked a Day or two near the full or change of the Moon; and when the Westerly Winds blow longest and strongest on the Coast, the Easterly Trade-Wind blows off at Sea, as at other Times. Near Cape La Vela, the true Trade blows within eight or ten Leagues off the Shore, when the Westerly Winds blow on the Coast, except in a strong North, which turns the Trade-Wind back, and on the Costarica, and between it and the River Darien, the Westerly Winds, as they are more frequent and lasting than towards Cape La Vela, so also they blow farther off at Sea, sometimes as far as to twenty or thirty Leagues from the Shore.

Therefore Ships bound to Windward, if they have far to go, either take the Opportunity of the Westerly Wind-Season, or else go through the Gulph of Florida, and stretch away to the North, till they get into a variable Wind's way, and then run to the Eastward as far as they think convenient before they stretch to the Southward again. All that are bound from the West-Indies to Guinea must take this Course, if they sail from Jamaica (because they must pass through the Gulph of Florida) but from other Islands they may stretch away directly to the North, and use the same Method.

But if Ships have only a small way to sail to Windward, they make use of the Sea and Land-Breezes, making no account of the Time of the Year.

The Winds on the Coast of Brazil, are from September till March at E. N. E. and from March till September again they are at South.

The Winds in the Bay of Panama are from September till March Easterly, and from March till September again they are at South and S. S. W.

From the Cape of good Hope Eastwards, as far as the

River Natal, which lies in 30 d. South Latitude, and Cape Corientes in Lat. of 24 degrees South, the Winds from May to October are constantly from the West to the North West, within thirty Leagues of the Shore: They blow hardest at North West. When the Wind comes to North West, it is commonly stormy and tempestuous Weather, attended with much Rain, and then the Weather is cold and chilly. From October till March the Winds are Easterly from the E. N. E. to the E. S. E. you have then very fair Weather: The E. N. E. Winds are pretty fresh, but the Winds at E. S. E. are small and faint, sometimes affording some drops of Rain.

From Cape Corientes to the Red-Sea, from October till the middle of January the Winds are variable, but most times Northerly, and oft shifting round the Compass: The strongest Winds are at North; these are often very violent and stormy, and accompanied with much Rain, and thus it blows about the Island of Madagascar and the adjacent Islands.

These Storms are commonly preceeded by a great Sea out of the North. From January till May the Winds are at N. E. or N. N. E. fine fresh Gales and fair Weather. From May till October the Winds are Southerly, in July, August, and September, there are great Calms in the Bay of Pate and Melende, and a strong Current setting into the Bay: Therefore Ships that have occasion to pass this way in those three Months, ought to keep at least a hundred Leagues from the Coast to avoid being driven by the Current into the Bay; for these Calms do sometimes last six Weeks, yet off at Sea, at the distance of a hundred Leagues the Winds are fresh at South. At the entrance into the Red-Sea near Cape Guardefuer there are commonly very hard Gales and turbulent Weather, even when the Calms are so great in the Bay of Melende, and not above ten or twelve Leagues at Sea from the said Cape, there is also very fair Weather, and pretty fresh Gales.

In the Red-Sea from May till October, the Winds are strong at S. W. and the Current setting out strong, so that there is no entering into that Sea in those Months, except you keep close to the South-shore, there you have Land-Winds, and an eddy Current. In the Months of September or October, the Wind shuffles about to the North, and at last settles at N. E. then comes fair Weather on this Coast; and so continues till the Monsoon shifts, which is in April or May; then it first takes one flurry at North, and from thence it veers to the East, and so about to the South, and there it settles.

The Account of this Coast from the Cape of good Hope hither, I had from Captain Rogers.

And as this hither-most part of the East-Indies, even from the Cape of good Hope to the Red-Sea, which Coast lies nearest N. E. and S. W. hath its shifting Seasons, so the other parts of India, from the Gulph of Persia to Cape Comorin, has its constant Annual change, and from Comorin, clear round the Bay of Bengal, the change is no less; and even from thence, through the Streights of Malacca, and Eastwards as far as Japan, the shifting Trade-Winds do alternately succeed each other as duly as the Year comes about.

It cannot be supposed that the Trade Wind in all these Places, should be exactly on one Point of the Compass: For I have already shown, that these Trade-Winds on any Coast do commonly blow slanting in on the Shore about two or three Points; therefore in Bays where the Land lies on several Rombs, the Winds must alter accordingly. Though that Rule does not hold altogether true in Bays that are deep, but is chiefly meant for a pretty streight Coast, which lies near alike; allowing for Points of Land and small Coves, which make no alteration: But on the sides and in the bottom of large Bays, such as the Bay of Bengal, the Bay of Siam, &c. the Wind differs much on one side of the Bay from what it does on the other; and both sides differ from the constant Trade on the open Coast: yet all shift in the shifting Seasons, which are April and September, at one and the same Time, to their opposite Points: I mean on the open Coast, for in some Bays there is a little alteration from that general Rule.

These shifting Winds in the East-Indies, are called

Monsoons; one is called the East-Monsoon, the other the West-Monsoon. The East-Monsoon sets in about September, and blows till April; then ceaseth, and the West-Monsoon takes place and blows till September again.

And both the East and West-Monsoons blow in their Seasons slanting in on the Coast, as is before described: The East-Monsoon brings fair Weather; the West brings Tornadoes and Rain. For (as I said before in the first Chap. of the General Trade-Wind at Sea) when the Sun comes to the North of the Line then all Places North of the Equator, within the Tropicks, are troubled with Clouds and Rain, but when the Sun is in Southern Signs then the Sky is clear. And as most of the Trading-Countries in the East-Indies, especially those on the Main Continent, do lye between the Line and the Tropick of Cancer: So these Countries are all subject to the Changes and Seasons already described. But the Islands lying under the Line, and to the South between the Line and the Tropick of Capricorn, have contrary Seasons to these. Yet do they change at the self-same Time.

The difference between the Monsoons on the North of the Line, and the Monsoons on the South of the Line is that in April, when the West-Monsoon sets in to the North of the Line, the S. S. W. Wind sets into the South of the Lat. and is called the S. S. W. Monsoon. And in September when the East Monsoon sets into the North of the Line, the N. N. E. Wind blows in South Lat. and is called the N. N. E. Monsoon. And whereas the West-Monsoon is accompanied with Tornadoes and Rain in North Lat. the S. S. W. Monsoon, which blows at the same Time in South Lat. is accompanied with fair Weather. And as the East-Monsoon is attended with fair Weather in North Lat. the N. N. E. Monsoon, which blows at the same Time in South Lat. is attended with Tornadoes and very bad Weather. And though these Winds do not shift exactly at one Time in all Years; yet September and April are always accounted the turning Months, and do commonly participate of both sorts of Winds. For these Monsoons do as constantly shift by turns, as the Year comes about.

And by means of this change of Wind, Ships have the benefit to sail from one part of India, with one Wind, and return with the contrary: So that most of the Navigation in India depends on the Monsoons. And Ships do constantly wait for these Changes; and the Merchants fit out to any Place according as the Season of the Year draws on: And wheresoever they go they certainly dispatch their Business so as to return back again with next or contrary Monsoon: For here is no sailing to and from any Place, but with the Monsoon: One carries them out, the other brings them back. Neither do I know how it were possible for Merchants in these Parts to trade by Sea from one Country to another, were it not for these shifting Monsoons. For as I have said before, most of the trading Kingdoms in India do lye between the Line, and the Tropick of Cancer. And the Land lies so to the North, that Ships cannot go to the North of the Tropick, and by that means get into variable Winds way, as they may and do in the West-Indies, when they are bound far to the Eastward. Neither could it be any Advantage to stand off to Sea, as they may in the South-Sea; for that would be of little Moment, because they would then come so near the Line, that they would be always lyable to Tornadoes and Calms; and should they cross the Line and run to the Southward of it, thinking that way to gain their Passage, it is likely they might succeed no better there: For that part of the Sea which lies to the Southward of the Line is open and free to the true Trade, which seldom fails: But indeed that Wind would carry them to the Southward quite beyond the Trade into a variable Winds-way. But the Sea is not open there, for Ships to pass so far to the Eastward as to gain their Ports.

For our East-India Ships that are bound to Siam, Tunqueen, China, &c. cannot get thither but in the Season of the West-Monsoon, though they go directly from England; and though, after they are past the Cape, they have the convenience to stretch to the Eastward, as far as the Land will permit, yet they cannot go so far as is convenient before they will be obliged to steer down within the Course of the Trade-Winds, which would obstruct their Passage, if they were as constant here as in other Places. And therefore if these Anniversary Monsoons did not constantly succeed each other, Ships could not pass but one way; they might sail to the Westward, but there they must lye up, or be three or four Years in their return from a place which may be sailed in six Weeks, yet I say that to Places near each other, Ships may and do very often sail against the Monsoon, and that with success: For here are Sea and Land-Breezes under the shore, and in many Places good Anchoring, by which means Ships may stop when they find the Current against them: But Voyages of a great distance cannot be made only with Land and Sea-Winds without some other helps.

In the West-Indies we have these helps of Land-winds and Sea-Breezes by which we sail from one Place to another, provided they are no great distance asunder, and perform our Voyages well enough; but when we are to sail a great way to the Eastward against the Trade-wind, then we are forced, as is said before, either to pass thro' the Gulph of Florida, if we are far to Leeward, or else to pass between the Islands, and so stretch away to the Northward, till we are clear out of the Trade, and so get our Longitude that way. So in the South-Seas also, and on the Coast of Guinea, the Coast of Brazil, and the Coast of Africa, between the Cape of good Hope and the Red-Sea, there are Sea and Land-Breezes, which may be made use of to sail against the Trade, if the Voyages be short: But when we are to sail a great way against the Trade-wind, we must not wholly depend on the Sea and Land-Breezes; for then we should be a long Time in accomplishing such Voyages. In such Cases we have recourse to other helps, such as Providence has supplied these Seas with, which seems to be wanting in the East-Indies: as for example, in the South-Seas and on the Coast of Peru where the Southerly Winds blow constantly all the Year, there Ships that are bound to the Southward stretch off to the Westward till they are out of the Coasting Trade-Wind, and there meet with the true Trade at E. S. E. with which they sail as far as they please to the Southward, and then steer in for their Port. So on the Coast of Mexico, where the Coasting Trade is westerly, there they run off to Sea, till they meet the true E. N. E. Trade; and then stretch away to the Northward, as far as their Port; and Ships that come from the Philipines, bound for the Coast of Mexico, stretch away to the North, as far as 40 Degrees, to get a Wind to bring them on the Coast.

Thus also all Ships bound to the East-Indies after they have past the Line in the Atlantick Ocean, stretch away to the Southward beyond the Trade, and then stand over to the Eastward, towards the Cape; so in returning home, after they have crost the Line to the Northward, they steer away North, with the Wind at E. N. E. till they are to the Northward of the Trade-Wind, and then direct their Course Easterly. All Guinea Ships and West-India Ships do the same in their Returns: And this is the Benefit of an open Sea. But to return.

The Monsoons among the East-India Islands that lie to the Southward of the Line, as I said before, are either at N. N. E. or S. S. W. These also keep time, and shift, as the Monsoons do, to the North of the Line, in the Months of April and September, but near the Line, as a Degree or two or each side, the Winds are not so constant. Indeed there they are so very uncertain, that I cannot be particular so as to give any true Account of them: Only this I know, that Calms are very frequent there, as also Tornadoes and sudden Gusts; in which the Winds fly in a Moment quite round the Compass.

CHAP. IV

Of Sea and Land-Breezes

How Sea-Breezes differ from common Trade-Winds. The Time and Manner of their Rise; And particularly at Jamaica. Of the Land-Breezes. The Time and Manner of their Rise: As on the Isthmus of Darien and at Jamaica. The places where these Winds blow strongest or slackest; as at Capes and Head-Lands, deep Bays, Lagunes and Islands. Seal-Skin Bladders used instead of Bark-Loggs.

SEA-Breezes, generally speaking, are no other than the Common Trade-Wind of the Coasts on which they blow, with this difference, that whereas all Trade-Winds, whether they are those that I call the general Trade-Winds at Sea, or coasting Trade-Winds, either constant or shifting, do blow as well by Night as by Day, with an equal briskness, except when Tornadoes happen; so contrarily Sea-Winds are only in the Day, and cease in the Night; and as all Trade-Winds blow constantly near to one Point of the Compass, both where the constant Trade-Winds are, or where they shift; on the contrary, these Sea-Winds do differ from them in this, that in the Morning when they first spring up, they blow commonly as the Trade-Winds on the Coast do, at or near the same Point of Compass; but about Mid-day they fly off two, three or four Points further from the Land, and so blow almost right in on the Coast, especially in fair Weather; for then the Sea-Breezes are truest; as for Instance, on the Coast of Angola the Land lies almost North and South, there the Trade-Wind is from the S. S. W. to the S. W. the true Sea-Breezes near the Shore are at W. by S. or W. S. W. and so of any other Coast.

These Sea-Breezes do commonly rise in the Morning about Nine a-Clock, sometimes sooner, sometimes later: they first approach the Shore so gently, as if they were afraid to come near it, and oft-times they make some faint Breathings, and as if not willing to offend, they make a halt, and seem ready to retire. I have waited many a time both Ashore to receive the Pleasure, and at Sea to take the Benefit of it.

It comes in a fine, small, black Curle upon the Water, when as all the Sea between it and the Shore not yet reach'd by it, is as smooth and even as Glass in comparison; in half an Hour's time after it has reached the Shore it fans pretty briskly, and so increaseth gradually till Twelve a-Clock, then it is commonly strongest, and lasts so till Two or Three a very brisk Gale; about Twelve at Noon it also veers off to Sea two or three Points, or more in very fair Weather. After Three a-Clock it begins to die away again, and gradually withdraws its force till all is spent, and about Five a-Clock, sooner or later, according as the Weather is, it is lull'd asleep, and comes no more till the next Morning.

These Winds are as constantly expected as the Day in their proper Latitudes, and seldom fail but in the wet Season. On all Coasts of the Main, whether in the East or West-Indies, or Guinea, they rise in the Morning, and withdraw towards the Evening, yet Capes and Head-Lands have the greatest Benefit of them, where they are highest, rise earlier, and blow later.

Bays contrarily have the Disadvantage, for there they blow but faintly at best, and their continuance is but short. Islands that lie nearest East and West, have the Benefit of these Winds on both sides equally; for if the Wind is at S. W. or S. W. and by S. on the South-side of any Island, then on the North-side it would be at N. W. or N. W. by N. *i.e.* in fair Weather; but if turbulent Weather, it would be E. S. E. on the South-side, and E. N. E. on the other: But this true Sea-Breeze does not veer so far out, except only near the Shore, as about three or four Leagues distant; for farther than that, you will find only the right Coasting Trade-Wind. This I have experienced in several Parts of the World, particularly at Jamaica; about which I have made many Voyages, both on the North and the South-side, where I have experienced the Sea-Breezes very much to differ; for on the South-side I have found the true Sea-Wind after Twelve a-Clock, and in very fair Weather at S. or S. S. E. though it sprung up in the Morning at E. S. E. or S. E. And on the North-side I have found the Sea-Breeze at N. or N. N. E. though it rose in the Morning at E. N. E. but whether there may be the like difference about smaller Islands, as at Barbadoes, &c. I cannot determine, though I am apt to believe there is not. So much for the Sea-Winds, next of the Land-Breezes.

Land-Breezes are as remarkable as any Winds that I have yet treated of; they are quite contrary to the Sea-Breezes; for those blow right from the shore, but the Sea-Breeze right in upon the shore; and as the Sea-Breezes do blow in the Day and rest in the Night; so on the contrary, these do blow in the Night and rest in the Day, and so they do alternately succeed each other. For when the Sea-Breezes have performed their Offices of the Day, by breathing on their respective Coasts, they in the Evening do either withdraw from the Coast, or lie down to rest: Then the Land-Winds, whose Office is to breathe in the Night, moved by the same Order of divine Impulse, do rouze out of their private Recesses, and gently fan the Air till the next Morning; and then their Task ends, and they leave the Stage.

There can be no proper time set when they do begin in the Evening, or when they retire in the Morning, for they do not keep to an Hour; but they commonly spring up between six and twelve in the Evening, and last till six, eight or ten in the Morning. They both come and go away again earlier or later, according to the Weather, the Season of the Year, or some accidental Cause from the Land: For on some Coasts they do rise earlier, blow fresher, and remain later than on other Coasts, as I shall shew hereafter.

They are called Land-Winds, because they blow off shore contrary to the Sea-Breeze, which way soever the Coast lies: Yet I would not so be understood, as if these Winds are only found to breathe near the Shores of any Land, and not in the Inland Parts of such Countries remote from the Sea; for in my Travels I have found them in the very Heart of the Countries that I have passed through; as particularly on the Isthmus of Darien, and the Island of Jamaica: Both which Places I have travelled over from Sea to Sea; yet because these are but small Tracts of Land in comparison with the two main Bodies of Land of Mexico and Peru, and those vast Regions in Asia and Africa lying within the Tropicks, I cannot determine whether the Land-Winds are there, as I have found them in my small Travels: therefore I shall only confine this particular Discourse to these and other Places within my own Observations. I shall begin first with the Isthmus of Darien; there I have found the Land-Winds in the middle of the Country blowing all Night, and till ten or eleven a-Clock in the Morning, before I could perceive the Sea-Breeze to arise, and that not discernable many times, but by the flying of the Clouds, especially if I was in a Valley; and it was in Vallies that I did chiefly perceive the Land-Winds, which blew in some Places one way, in others contrary, or side-ways to that according as the Vallies lay pent up between the Mountains; and that without any respect to either the North or the South-Seas, but indeed near either side of the Land, they always bent their Course towards the nearest Sea, unless there was any Hill between them and the Sea, and then they took their Course along in the Vallies; but from both Shores, as well from the North as the South, they blow right-forth into the Sea.

In the Island of Jamaica these Land-Winds are in the middle of the Country; also I have found them so, as I travelled from one side of the Island to the other, having lain two Nights by the way, as I had before observed them, when I liv'd at sixteen Miles walk, where I continued about six Months; but there and in other Islands the

Land-winds do blow towards the nearest Shores, and so from thence off to Sea, whether the Shores lie East, West, North or South.

These Winds blow off to Sea, a greater or less Distance, according as the Coast lies more or less exposed to the Sea-winds: For in some Places we find them brisk three or four Leagues off shore; in other Places not so many Miles; and in some Places they scarce peep without the Rocks, or if they do sometimes in very fair Weather make a sally out a Mile or two, they are not lasting, but suddenly vanish away, though yet there are every Night as fresh Land-winds ashore at those Places as in any other Part of the World.

Places most remarkable for the fewest or faintest Land-winds, are those that lie most open to the Common Trade-winds, as the East-ends of any Islands where the Trade-winds do blow in upon the Shore, or the Head-Lands on Islands or Continents that are open to the Sea-Breeze, especially where the Trade-wind blows down side-ways by the Coast; for there such Head-Lands as stretch farthest out to Sea are most exposed to Winds from the Sea; and have the less Benefit of the Land-Breezes.

I shall give a few Instances of either. And first of all begin with the N. E. and S. E. Points of the Island of Jamaica: These Points are at the East-end of the Island, one is at the very Extreme of the North-side towards the East, the other on the South Extreme towards the same Point; at these two Places we seldom light of a Land-wind; nor very often at the End of the Island between them, except near the Shore. For that reason the Sloop-men of Jamaica that Trade round the Island are commonly put to their Trumps, when they come there in their Voyages: For if they meet no Land-wind, they are obliged to beat about by turning to Windward against the Sea-Breeze in the Day time; they then curse these Points of Land, and are foolishly apt to believe that some Dæmon haunts there.

And if they are two or three Days in beating about (as sometimes they are) when they return to Port-Royal, they will talk as much of their Fatigues, as if they had been beating a Month to double the Cape of Good Hope, though indeed the Men are brisk enough, and manage their Sloops very well; which also are generally very good Boats to sail on a Wind. I think they are the best small Trading-Boats in the King's Dominions.

Point Pedro on the South-side of the Island, is another very bad Point to double, if a Ship come from the West-end of the Island; This Point runs out far into the Sea, and is not only destitute of the Common Land-winds: But if there is any Current setting to Leeward, here the Sloop-men meet it. Therefore they are many times longer beating about it, than about the two former Points of the South-East and the North-East, and not without bestowing some Curses upon it. Nay some Captains of Privateers, when they have been beating about it, have stood close into the Point, and fired their Guns to kill the old Dæmon that they say inhabits there to disturb poor Seamen. I have related these odd Passages to shew how ignorant Men are that cannot see the Reason of it. And because I am not willing to leave my Reader in the dark, I shall give a few Instances more on this Subject. The North-side of Jucatan, at the Entrance into the Bay of Campeachy, gives us another Instance of bad Land-winds; and commonly where the Land-winds are scanty, the Sea-Breezes are but indifferent neither. This will partly appear by what I have observed of them on this Coast, between Cape Catoch, and Cape Condecedo, at the Entrance of the Bay of Campeachy, which two Places are about eighty Leagues distant; for there the Land trends East and West. It is a streight Coast, and lies all of it equally exposed to the Trade-wind, which is commonly there at E. N. E. To the W. of these Places the Sea and Land-winds do as duly succeed each other, as on any other Coast, but here they are each of them of a Bastard Kind; for the Sea-Breezes are at N. E. by E. which is no better than a Coast Trade-wind, and the Land-Wind is at E. S. E. or S. E. by E. whereas if the Winds were as true there as on other Coasts, the Sea-Breeze would be at N. N. E. sometimes at N. and the

Land-Winds would be at S. S. E. and S. as they are indeed close under the Shore; which if they do at any time come off from, they are very faint.[1] The Land on this Coast is low and even, and the Land-Winds ashore are pretty brisk.

The Capes on the Peruvian Coast in the South-Seas, will more fully make it appear, that Head-Lands do seldom afford any Land-Winds. I shall only Instance in Cape Passao, in Lat. 8 Minutes South, Cape St. Laurence, in Lat. 1 d.——South, and Cape Blanco, in 3 d.——South. I have pass'd by them all several Times and at different Seasons; yet did never find any Land-winds there, though between these Places there are very good Land-winds. Therefore Ships that sail to the Southward against the Breeze, must beat it about by hard Labour, especially about Cape Blanco, for that lies more exposed than the other two: and if there is any Current, as commonly, the Spaniards are a long Time getting about, sometimes a Fortnight or three Weeks; and when they have split their Sails, which are seldom very good, they run back to Guiaquill to mend them again. We found it hard getting about, tho' our Sails were good; and I think we could work our Ships better than the Spaniards are ever able to do in those Seas.

I have already given several Instances of such Places, as have no Land-winds, or at least but very ordinary ones; I shall next proceed in order to shew where the strongest or best Land-winds are met with; and then I shall speak of those Places where there blows a moderate and indifferent Gale between both Extremes: That so any one may judge by the Lying of the Land, whether it may afford a good Land-wind or no.

The briskest Land-winds are commonly in deep Bays, in great Lakes within Land, and among great Ranges of Islands or small Keys that lye near the Shore: I shall give Instances of all these. And as for Bays, I shall first pitch on the Bay of Campeachy, which lies between Cape Con-

[1] No land-wind has much force unless the land from which it blows is mountainous some miles from the sea.

decedo and the High-Land of St. Martin; between both these Places the Land-winds are as brisk two or three Leagues off at Sea, as in any Place that I know. In the Cod or Middle of the Bay, the Land trends from East to West, there the Sea-breezes are at North, and the Land-winds at South; they commonly begin to blow at seven or eight a Clock in the Evening, and continue till eight or nine the next Morning, in the dry Season especially. In that Bay there is an Island, call'd by the English Beef-Island from the Multitude of Bulls and Cows that inhabit it. The Smell of these wild Cattle is driven off to Sea, by the Land-winds so fresh, that by it Masters of Ships sailing in the Night on this Coast have known where they were, and have presently anchored that Night, and come into the Island of Trist the next Day; whereas they would otherwise have past farther to the Westward quite out of their way, if they had not smell'd the strong Scent of these Cattle.

So all the Bottom of the Bay of Mexico, even from the High-Land of St. Martin down to La Vera Cruz, and from thence Northerly towards the River Meschasipi[1] affords good Land-winds and Sea-breezes. The Bay of Honduras also, and almost all the Coast between it and Cape La Vela, affords the like, allowing for the Capes and Points of Land, which lye between; where it fails more or less, as the Points do lye more or less exposed to the Sea-Breezes.

So in the South-Seas, the Bays of Panama, Guiaquil, Paita, &c. have their fresh Land-winds and Sea-breezes. But in some Places, as particularly at Paita, the Land-winds do not spring up till twelve a Clock in the Night, but then are always very fresh, and last till seven or eight the next Morning; and they are constant all the Year long; Whereas in the Bay of Panama, and also in all the Bays and Coasts of the other, or North-side of America already described, they are not so constant in the wet Season as they are in the dry.

The Bay of Campeachy will also afford us Instances of

[1] Mississipi.

the Land-winds that blow in Lagunes: As for Instance, the Lagune of Trist, which is about nine or ten Leagues long and three broad, is barricadoed from the Sea by the Island of Trist. There the Land-winds blow in the dry Season from five or six a Clock in the Evening, till nine or ten in the Morning. There are two other Lagunes lying within that, and parted from it by low Mangrove-Land: there the Land-winds are fresher and the Sea-Breeze duller, and of a less Continuance, than in the Lagune of Trist. Nay, sometimes the Land-wind blows all Day; so in the Lagune of Maracabo to Windward of Cape Alta Vela, the Land-winds are very fresh and lasting. The like may be said of the Lagune of Venizuella or Comana.

Sometimes in the fore-mentioned Lagunes, the Land-winds do blow for three or four Days and Nights together, scarce suffering the Sea-Breeze to breathe there; though at the same time the Sea-Breeze may blow fresh out at Sea: and if the Sea-Breeze at such times should make a bold Sally into these Lagunes, it would be but of a Short Continuance. On the other Hand at Capes and Head-Lands more exposed to Sea-Breezes, the Land-winds are shyer of coming there, than the Sea-winds are into Lagunes. Neither may we forget the Harbour of Jamaica, for there are very good Land-winds. It is compassed in on one side with a long Neck of Sand, and many small Islands at the Mouth of it, and within there is a pretty deep Lake, in which are constant Sea and Land-winds, by which the Wherry-men run with full sail, both to Legany[1] or Passage Fort,[2] from the Town and back again. They go away with the Sea-Breeze, and return with the Land-wind. Therefore Passengers that have occasion to go either way, wait for the coming of these Winds, except their Business requires haste: for then they are rowed against the Breeze; and tho' the Land-winds do sometimes fail or come very late, yet the Wherries seldom stay beyond their constant Hours of seven or eight a Clock, and sometimes the Land-winds do come by three or four, but when they come so

[1] Liguanea.
[2] To the west of the harbour, on the western side of Hunt Bay.

early it is commonly after a Tornado from the Land. This may suffice as to the Land-winds in Lakes or Bays.

As to what may be spoken concerning the Land-winds among Islands, I shall only mention two Places, both of them in the West-Indies; the first are the Keys of Cuba, which are Abundance of small Islands bordering on the South-side of Cuba, reaching in length from East to West, or near those Points as the Island lies, about seventy Leagues; and in some Places reaching near twenty Leagues from the said Island. Among these Islands, even from the outermost of them, quite home to Cuba, there are very brisk Land-winds. They spring up early in the Evening, and blow late in the Morning. The Jamaica Turtlers visit these Keys with good Success for Turtle all the Year long, and from thence bring most of their Turtle wherewith the Market of Port-Royal is served. The other Islands I shall mention are the Sambaloe Islands betwixt Cape Samblass[1] and Golden Island, tho' they are not so large a Range as the Keys of Cuba, yet do they afford very good Land-winds; near as good as the Keys of Cuba do. And thus much for the Places where the best as well as where the scantiest or faintest Land-winds are found. I shall next give some Instances of the Medium between both Extremes.

I have already shown that Capes and such Head-Lands as lye out farthest from the rest of the Shore, are thereby most exposed to the Sea-Winds, and consequently the Land-winds are there much fainter than in other Places, especially in deep Bays or Lagunes within Land, or among Islands and small Keys near the Land: All which is no more than my own Experience has taught me. I shall now shew how the Land-winds blow on Coasts that do lye more level. As all Coasts have their Points and Bendings, so accordingly the Land-winds are fresher or fainter, as you come either towards these Bendings or towards intermitting Points or Head-Lands.

I shall give an Instance of this by shewing how the Winds are on the Coast of Curaccos. It is as streight a

[1] San Blas.

Shore as I can pitch on, yet full of small Bays, divided from each other by a like number of Ridges of High-Land, that shoot forth their Heads a little way without the Bays on each side. There in the Night or Morning, while the Land-wind blows, we find fresh Gales out of the Bays: but when we come abreast of the Head-Lands, we find it calm; yet see the Breeze curling on the Water on both sides of us, and sometimes get a Spurt of it to help us forward; and having recovered the Wind out of the next Bay, we pass by the Mouth of it presently, till we come to the next Head; and there we lye becalmed as before.

These Bays are not above half a Mile or a Mile wide; neither are the Heads much wider; but these Heads of the Ridges lying in between the Bays, have steep Cliffs against the Sea; and where-ever I have met the like steep Cliffs against the Sea, I have seldom found any Land-winds. But in all other Places where the Bays strike deeper into the Land, there we find the Land-winds more lasting and strong; and where the Points are farther out, there are still the less Land-winds, and the Brisker Sea-Breezes. For the Capes and smaller Points on all Shores seem to be so many Barricadoes to break off the Violence of the Sea-Breezes; for this we always find when we are turning to Windward being to Leeward of a Cape, that the Breeze is moderate, especially if we keep very near the Shore; but when once we come within a Mile, more or less of the Cape and stand off to Sea, as soon as we get without it, we find such a huffing Breeze, that sometimes we are not able to ply against it, but in the Night we find a fresh Land-wind to Leeward; tho' when we come to the Cape we find it calm; or perhaps sometimes meet with a Sea-wind. The Land-Breezes on the Coast of Guinea between Cape St. Anns and Cape Palmas, (mentioned in the second Chapter of this Discourse), are at E. blowing brisk four Leagues off Shore: the Sea-winds there are at S. W. The Land-winds on the Coast of Angola are at E. N. E. the Sea-winds at W. S. W. these are very true Winds of both kinds.

The Land-winds on the Coast of Peru and Mexico in the South-Seas, are in most Places right off from the Shore, else the Fisher-men could never go out to Sea, as they do, on Bark-Loggs. And as the Land-winds are true there, so are the Sea-Breezes also; for with the Land-wind they go out to fish, and return in again with the Sea-winds. In some Places they use Seals-Skins instead of Bark-Loggs; they are made so tight that no Bladder is tighter. To these they have long Necks like the Neck of a Bladder, into which they put a Pipe and blow them up as we do Bladders; two of these being fastned together, a Man sets a-stride them, having one before and the other behind him; and so sits firmer than in a Trooper's Saddle. His Paddle is like a Quarter-staff, with a broad Blade at each end; with this he strikes the Sea back, first on one side and then on the other, with each end of his Paddle, and so gives himself fresh way through the Water.

In the East-Indies also there are true Sea-Breezes, as well on the Islands, as on the Main. On Islands, as at Bantam in the Island Java, and at Achin in the Island Sumatra, and in many Places on the Island Mindanao: And on the Main also, as particularly at Fort St. George on the Coast Coromandel. There the Land-winds blow right off from the Shore, and the Sea-winds right in; but sometimes they come slanting in; and about Christmas they blow from the N. E. or N. N. E. I found them so when I came on the Coast, and being advised of it by Mr. Coventry, in whose Sloop I then was, I fell in with the Land ten or twelve Leagues to the Northward of the Fort, and had a brisk Northerly Sea-wind to bring me into the Road.

I think these Instances are enough to shew how these Land-winds do usually blow in most parts of the World; should I be very particular, 'tis not a larger Treatise than I intend this to be, would hold a quarter-part of it. But I have been more particular in the West-Indies and South-Seas, because these Land-winds are of more use there than in the East-Indies: For though sometimes Men in the East-Indies do turn against the Monsoons, yet they do generally tarry for them before they budge.

Indeed these Winds are an extraordinary Blessing to

those that use the Sea in any part of the World, within the Tropicks; for as the constant Trade-winds do blow, there could be no sailing in these Seas: But by the Help of the Sea and Land-Breezes, Ships will sail 2 or 300 Leagues; as particularly from Jamaica, to the Lagune of Trist, in the Bay of Campeachy; and then back again, all against the Trade-wind; And I think this is one of the longest Voyages that is used of this kind. If any of our Jamaica Sloops do go to Trist, and design to carry their Wood to Curasao, then they put through the Gulph of Florida.

The Spaniards also that come from any part of the Bay of Mexico, and are bound to any Place to Windward of the Island Cuba, are wont to put through the Gulph, and so stretch away to the Northward, till they come clear of the Trade, and then stand away as far as they please to the East-ward; This is also the usual way from Jamaica to Barbadoes, though sometimes they turn up by the Caribbee Islands, only taking the Benefit of these Sea and Land-winds. So also Ships may and do pass from Portobello to Carthagena, or to St. Martha, or to any other Place, by the help of these Breezes, if the distance is not too far. So by taking the Advantage of these Winds, Sloops in the West-Indies sail clear round the Islands, or to any part of them, in a short time.

In the South Seas also the Spaniards in their Voyages from Panama to Lima, by taking the Advantage of these Winds, do sail as high as Cape Blanco; but in all their Voyages to the Southward of that Cape, they stand quite off to Sea into the Trade. Thus you see the Use and Advantage of them.

The Seamen that sail in Sloops or other small Vessels in the West-Indies, do know very well when they shall meet a brisk Land-wind, by the Fogs that hang over the Land before Night; for it is a certain sign of a good Land-wind, to see a thick Fog lye still and quiet, like Smoak over the Land, not stirring any way; and we look out for such Signs when we are plying to Windward. For if we see no Fog over the Land, the Land-wind will be but faint and short that Night. These Signs are to be observed chiefly in fair Weather: for in the wet Season Fogs do hang over the Land all the Day, and it may be neither Land-wind nor Sea-Breeze stirring. If in the Afternoon also in fair Weather, we see a Tornado over the Land, it commonly sends us forth a fresh Land-wind.

These Land-winds are very cold, and though the Sea-Breezes are always much stronger, yet these are colder by far. The Sea-Breezes indeed are very comfortable and refreshing; for the hottest Time in all the Day is about nine, ten or eleven a Clock in the Morning, in the Interval between both Breezes: For then it is commonly calm, and then People pant for Breath, especially if it is late before the Sea-Breeze comes, but afterwards the Breeze allays the Heat. However, in the Evening again after the Sea-Breeze is spent, it is very hot till the Land-wind springs up, which is sometimes not till twelve a Clock or after.

For this Reason Men when they go to Bed uncloath themselves and lye without any thing over them: Nay, the ordinary sort of People spread Mats at their Doors, or else in their Yards, in Jamaica, and lye down to sleep in the open Air.

In the East-Indies at Fort St. George, also Men take their Cotts or little Field-Beds, and put them into the Yards, and go to sleep in the Air: And Seamen aboard Ships in these hot Countries lye on the Deck, till the Land-wind comes.

The Inhabitants of Jamaica or Fort St. George, have somewhat to cover themselves when the Land-Wind comes, beside a Pillow on their Breast, or between their Arms. But Seamen who have wrought hard all Day lye naked and exposed to the Air, it may be all Night long, before they awake, without any Covering, especially if they have had their Dose of Punch. But next Morning they are scarce able to budge, being stiff with cold, that brings them to Fluxes, and that to their Graves; and this is the Fate of many stout and brave Seamen: and it is a great Pity that Masters of Ships have so little Regard for their Men, as not by some good Orders, to prohibit this dangerous Custom of lying abroad and naked in the Nights.

CHAP. V

Of Land-winds and Sea-Breezes, peculiar to some Coasts at some particular Seasons of the Year; as also of some Winds that produce strange Effects

Of the Summasenta-Winds in the Bay of Campeachy. Of the Winds peculiar to the Coasts of Carthagena. Winds on the Mexican Coasts, call'd Popogaios. Others on the Coast of Coromandel, call'd Terrenos: The same about Malabar, but at a different Season: As also in the Persian Gulph. And of the Hermatans on the Coast of Guinea.

I SHALL begin with the Summasenta-Winds, as they are called, which blow in the Bay of Campeachy. These are Winds that come in the Months of February, March and April, and they blow only in that Bay between the High-Land of St. Martin and Cape Condecedo; which Places are about 120 Leagues asunder. They are, properly speaking, neither Sea-Breezes nor true Land-winds, yet in Respect of their blowing in some Measure from the Shore, they are in that somewhat of kin to the Land-winds. These Winds are commonly at E. S. E. in the Cod or Middle of the Bay where the Land lies E. and W. and the true Land-winds there are at S. S. E. but from thence towards Cape Condecedo, the Land trends away N. E. and N. N. E. and N. So that they become Land-winds there respecting the Land from whence they blow; but then they differ both from Sea and Land-Breezes in Respect to their Duration: For these Summasenta-Winds blow three or four Days, sometimes a Week, both Night and Day before they cease. They are commonly dry Winds and blow very fresh, and Ships that go from Trist with Logwood at the Time when these Winds blow, will be at

Cape Condecedo in three or four Days; whereas if they go at any other Time, it will take up eight or ten Days, tho' seldom more than that: For here are good Land-winds and Sea-Breezes at other times.

These Winds are commonly colder than the Sea-winds, though not so cold as the Land-winds, yet stronger than either. I never could perceive that these Winds did make any Alteration on our Bodies different from other Winds. But the Tides when these Winds blow on that Coast, are very small especially in the Lagunes of Trist: so that the Logwood-Barks that bring the Wood aboard of the Ships, are then forced to lye still for want of Water to float them over some Flats in the Lagunes.

On the Coast of Carthagena there are a peculiar sort of Winds that blow in the Months of April, May and June so very fierce, that Ships are not able to ply to Windward on that Coast while these Winds last. These Winds blow about forty or fifty Leagues to Windward of Carthagena Town, and about ten to Leeward of it. They are very fierce from the Middle of the Channel between it and Hispaniola, and so continue almost to the Coast of Carthagena. Tho' they are sometimes a little fainter within two or three Leagues of the Shore, especially Mornings and Evenings. They commonly rise in the Morning before Day, sometimes at 3 or 4 a Clock, and so continue till 9, 10 or 11 at Night, and thus they will blow 10 or 11 Days together very fiercely. At this time the Land-winds besides their short Continuance are very faint and blow but a little way off Shore: So that from 10 or 11 at Night till 3 in the Morning 'tis quite calm and not one Breath of Wind from a League distant off the Shore; tho' 3 or 4 further off you'll find the Breeze, and nearer a small Land-wind. These Winds are at E. N. E. as the common Trade is; whereas the Sea-Breezes are at N. E. by N. or N. N. E.

While these fierce Winds stay, the Sky is commonly clear without any Cloud to be seen; tho' doubtless 'tis imperceptibly hazy, for then the Sun does not give a true black Shade on the Ground, but very faint and dusky. The Horizon too looks very dusky, thick and hazy, and while the Sun is near the Horizon, either in the Morning or Evening, it looks very red. Sometimes, tho' but seldom, when these Winds blow the Sky is over-cast with small Clouds, which afford some drizling small Rain. But though these Winds are so fierce on the Coast of Carthagena, yet both to Windward and to Leeward at the distances before-mentioned, the Breezes blow moderate as at other Times. For the Sea and Land-winds do there keep their constant and regular Courses. Neither are the Coasts of Hispaniola or Jamaica troubled with these fierce Winds, any nearer than half Channel over as was said before.

It has not been my Fortune to have been on this Coast when these Winds have blown, yet I have had the Relation of it so often, and from so many Persons, that I am very well satisfied of the Truth of it: Nay, it is so generally known among the Jamaica Seamen and Privateers that they call a Talkative Person in Derision, a Carthagene-Breeze. I remember two or three Men that went by that Name, and I knew them by no other, tho' I was in the same Ship with them several Months.

Some of our English Frigots that have been sent to Jamaica have experienced these Breezes when the Governour has sent them upon Business to that Coast: For plying between Portobello and Carthagena, when they have been within 10 Leagues of Carthagena, they have met with the Sea-Breeze so strong that they have been forced to riff their Topsail, which even then they could not maintain, but have been obliged to furl it quite up; and so with only their lower Sails, which sometimes they have been forced to riff too, have been beating eight or ten Days, to get only so many Leagues; which tho' at last they have done, yet has it been with much Trouble, and not without Damage to their Sails and Rigging. Neither can I forget a Squadron of French Frigots, commanded by the Count de Estrees, that came to Jamaica, and demanded leave of the Governour to wood and water there; which because it seemed strange that they should want in coming only from Petit Guavas; it was demanded of them why they came from thence so ill provided? They said they went from Petit Guavas over to the Coast of Carthagena, with a Design to have plyed to Wind-ward under that Shore, but met the Breezes so hard on the Coast, that they were not able to hold up their sides against it, and for that Reason stood back again towards Petit Guavas; but not being able to fetch it, therefore they came to wood and water at Jamaica, designing to go from thence thro' the Gulph: And tho' the Pilots of Jamaica did all conclude that the Breeze-time was past by more than a Month, yet the Governour gave them leave to wood and water at Blewfields Bay, and sent one Mr. Stone to be their Pilot thither. This was in 1679 and in one of our Summer Months, but I can't tell which, tho' I was there.

In the South-Seas on the Mexican Coast, between Cape Blanco in the Lat. of 9 D. 56 M. North and Realeja, in Lat. 11 North, which two Places are about 80 Leagues Distance, there are Winds which blow only in the Months of May, June, and July, call'd by the Spaniards Popogaios. They blow Night and Day without Intermission, sometimes 3 or 4 Days or a Week together. They are very brisk Winds, but not violent: I have been in one of them when we went from Caldera Bay, bound to Realeja mentioned in my "Voyage round the World," Chap. 5, Pag. 144, which blew at North.

In the East-Indies on the Coast of Coromandel, there are Winds call'd by the Portuguese Terrenos, because they blow from the Land. These are not those Land-Winds that I have already treated of; for these blow only in June, July and August, and are in several respects quite contrary to them. For whereas the true Land-Winds blow only in the Night, including Evenings and Mornings; on the contrary, these blow 3 or 4 Days without intermission; nay sometimes a Week or 10 Days together: and as the true Nocturnal Land-Winds are very cold, on the contrary these are the hottest of all Winds I ever heard of: They come with hot Blooms, such as I have mentioned in my "Voyage round the World," Chap. 20, Pag. 511. These Winds are at West, and they blow only in the Months of June, July and August, which is the West Monsoon-Season, tho' the proper Monsoon then on this Coast is S. W. When these hot Winds come, the better sort of People at Fort St. George keep close: They also shut up their Windows and Doors to keep them out; and I have heard Gentlemen that lived there say, that when they have been thus shut up within Doors, they have been sensible when the Wind shifted by the Change they have felt in their Bodies. And notwithstanding that these Winds are so hot, yet the Inhabitants don't sweat while they last, for their Skins are hard and rough, as if they had been parched by the Fire, especially their Faces and Hands, yet does it not make them sick. The Sands which are raised by these Winds are a great annoyance to those whose business lyes abroad, and who can't keep their Houses. For many times they wheel about and raise the Sands so thick, that it flies like smoak in Peoples Eyes; and the Ships also that lye in the road at that time have their Decks covered with this Sand.

On the Coast of Malabar they have of these sorts of Winds also, but not at the same time of the Year. For as these on the Coast of Coromandel blow in the months of June, July and August, when the West Monsoon reigns; on the contrary on the Malabar Coast they blow in the Months of December, January and February, when the East or North-East Monsoon blows: for then the Easterly Wind, which is then the true Monsoon, comes from over the Land of this Coast; This being the West-side, as the Coast of Coromandel is the East-side of this long East-Indian Promontory.

The Persian Gulph is as remarkable for these hot Winds as either of the former; they come there in the Months of June, July and August in the West Monsoon time; and the heat there by all Accounts does by far exceed that on the other two Coasts.

The European Merchants that are imployed in the Ports within the King of Persia's Dominions, do leave their Coast, Habitations and Business there, during these hot Months, and spend their time at Ispahan till the Air is more agreeable to their Bodies; but their Servants must indure it. And if any Ships are there, then the Seamen also must do as well as they can. 'Tis reported the Commanders do keep Bathing-Troughs full of Water to lye and wallow in, and hide their Bodies from the noisom hot Blooms. I was never in any of these hot Winds, for I went from Fort St. George before they came on the Coast.

On the Coast of Guinea there are a particular Sort of Land-winds, which are very remarkable; not for their Heat, as those last-mentioned, but for their exceeding Cold and searching Nature. They are called Harmatans. I have had an Account of them from several who have traded to Guinea; but more especially from a very sensible and experienced Gentleman, Mr. Greenhill, Commissioner of His Majesty's Navy at Portsmouth; who upon my Request, was pleased to send me the following Account: which the Reader cannot have better than in his own Words. Where together with the Harmatans, he gives an Account also of all the Winds on that Coast.

Mr. Greenhill's Letter.

Sir,

I HAVE been very ill since my return Home with the Gout; so that I have not been capable of answering your Expectation: But being a little better recovered, I shall make as good a Return to your Enquiry of the Harmatans on the Coast of Guinea, as my Circumstances will permit. The usual time of their blowing is between the latter part of December, and the beginning of February; before and beyond which Seasons, they never exceed. They are of so very cold, sharp and piercing a Nature, that the Seams of the Floors of our Chambers and the Sides and Decks of our Ships (as far as they are above Water) will open so wide, as that with Facility you may put a Caulking-Iron a considerable way into them; in which Condition they continue so long as the Harmatan blows, (which is sometimes two or three, and very rarely five Days, which is the very utmost I ever observed or heard of) and when they are gone, they close again and are as tight as if it never had been. The Natives themselves and all Persons who inhabit those parts (during that short Season) to prevent their pernicious Effects, are obliged to confine themselves within Doors; where they endeavour their own security, by rendering their Habitations as close and impenetrable as possible: Neither will they once stir abroad, unless induced thereto by a more than ordinary Occasion. It is as destructive to the Cattle also; whose safe Guard consists in their Proprietors Care, who against this Season ought to provide some such like place for them: Otherwise they must expect but a pitiful Account when the Season is over; for it most certainly destroys them, and that in a very short time.

This I accidentally experimented by exposing a couple of Goats to the Asperity thereof; which in four Hours Space or thereabouts, were depriv'd of Life. Nay we our selves (unless assisted by the like Conveniency and the benefit of some sweet Oyls to correct the Air) cannot fetch our Breath so freely as at other times; but are almost suffocated with too frequent and Acid Respirations. They generally blow between the E. and E. N. E. to the Northward of which they never exceed, being the most settled and steddy (but fresh) Gales I ever observed; coming without Thunder, Lightning or Rain; but close gloomy Weather; the Sun not shining all the time: And when they expire, the Trade-wind (which constantly blows on that Coast at W. S. W. and S. W.) returns with the accustomary seasonableness of Weather.

The Coast of Africa from Cape Palmas to Cape Formosa, lies E. and E. by N. and near those Points the Land Breezes blow on that Coast, which commonly begin about seven in the Evening, and continue all Night, till near that time the next Morning: During which interval, we are troubled with stinking Fogs and Mists off Shore, which by return of the Sea-Breezes upon the opposite Points are all driven away; and we have the benefit of them, in a curious fresh Gale, till about 5 in the Afternoon.

And here let me note it for a general Observation, That in these and all other Places within the Tropicks (as far as ever I took Notice) the Wind is drawn by the Land. For if an Island or Head-Land, were inclining to a circular Form, the Sea and Land-Breezes fall in diametrically opposite to that part where you are. So that if you are on the South-side, the Sea-Breeze shall be at South, and the Land-Breeze (when it comes in its Season) at North.

In getting on the Coast, we indeavour to fall in with Cape Mount or Cape Miserada, which is about 18 Leagues to the E. S. Eastward thereof; and after that we double Cape Palmas (whence as aforesaid, the Land trends away E. by N.) the Current near the shore sets upon that Point down into the Bite. But in getting off, we as much attempt (if possible) to lay hold of St. Thomas; and thence to run to the Southward of the Line, perhaps 3 or 4 Degrees; for the further Southerly we go, the stronger we find the Gales, and more beneficial for getting off the African Coast; but those who keep to the Northward thereof, generally meet with more Calms; and consequently longer Voyages ensue. In or about those Latitudes we continue, till we are got between 25 and 30 Degrees to the Westward of Cape Lopez de Gonsalvo, and then we cross again to go either for England or the West-Indies. But by the way let me observe to you, that when once we are to the Westward of the said Cape, and in South Latitude, the Current sets Northerly, and the Wind to 20 Degrees of Latitude, is at E. S. E. as (to the like number of Degrees) on the North-side of the Line it blows at E. N. E. Neither did I ever observe any Mutation of the Currents, unless in the Tornado-Season, when during their blowing, they commonly set to Wind-ward; tho' perhaps the Moon upon Full and Change, may have the like Influence there, as in other Places; but I never took any particular notice thereof.

The said Tornadoes usually come in the Beginning of April, and seldom relinquish the Gold Coast till July commences, and with frequent Visits make us sensible of their Qualities. We have sometimes three or four in a day; but then their Continuance is but short; perhaps not above two Hours, and the Strength or Fury (it may be) about a quarter or half an Hour; but accompanied with prodigious Thunder, Lightning and Rain; and the Violence of the Wind so extraordinary, as that it has sometimes rolled up the Lead wherewith the Houses are cover'd, as close and compactly, as possible it could be done by the Art of Man. The Name implies a Variety of Winds: But the Strength of them is generally at S. E. and by Ships that are bound off the Coast, they are made use of to get to Windward.

I shall conclude with that most worthy Observation of the Season wherein the Rains begin; which on the Gold Coast is about the 10th of April and this may be generally remarked, from 13 d. N. to 15 d. South Latitude, that they follow the Sun within 5 or 6 d. And so proceed with him till he has touched the Tropick, and returns to the like Station again. This I shall illustrate by the following Example, viz. Cape Corso Castle lies in 4 d. 55 North. About the 10th of April the Sun has near 12 degrees N. Declination. At that Time the Rains begin, and continue with the Inhabitants of that Place, untill he has performed his Course to the greatest Obliquity from off the Equator, and returned to the like Position South. The same I suppose may be observed, and understood of other Places within the Tropicks.

The Variation (of which in the Year 1680, I made frequent Observations) was 2 d. 14 m. Westerly: And it generally flows at the aforesaid place S. S. E. and N. N. W. upon the Full and Change. The Water rising upon Spring Tides about six or seven Foot up and down. I remain.

SIR,

Your Humble Servant,

HENRY GREENHILL.

From his Majesty's Yard, near Portsmouth,
June the 5th, 1698.

Upon the Receipt of this from the Gentleman aforesaid, I wrote to him again, to have his Opinion about what I have said concerning the particular Longitude, in which 'tis best to cross the Line, in going from Guinea to the

West-Indies: And so much of his Answer as concerns this Matter was in these Words.

Mr. Greenhill's second Letter.

Sir,

I DO not dissent from Crossing the Line at 35 or 36 d. Longitude, Westward of Cape Lopes, and it may as well be done at 30 provided the Breezes continue fresh. But if we have but little Winds, we generally run on the South-side of the Line, till we reach the distance West: And then crossing we steer away West North West, and West by North for Barbadoes.

And this you may observe, (as I have already hinted to you,) that the further we keep to the Southward of the Line, the fresher, and consequently more advantageous the Breezes are.

I remain Sir,

Your obliged Friend,

And most humble Servant,

Henry Greenhill.

And here I judge it will not be unacceptable to the Reader to insert two other Letters from an Experienced Captain of a Ship, because they have a general Relation to the Subject I am now upon, as well as to the Coast of Guinea in particular.

Part of two Letters from Captain John Covant *of Portbury, to a Gentleman in London.*

LETTER I

Honoured Sir,

I HAVE sent Mr. Dampier's Book, which you were pleased to send me, to Captain S——— I have gone through it, and find it very well worth my time, being very delightsome, and I believe true.

I have made some Remarks on it, as having found the like of what he asserts, in other places. At p. 94, mention is made of the Sucking-Fish, or Remora (as Mr. Dampier calls it). These are mighty plenty on the Coast of Angola and at Madagascar, and between Cape Lopes de Gonsalvas and the River Gabon. They are shaped as he describes them.

As to what he saith, p. 101, I have found the Indians in the Gulph of Florida, offering false Ambergreece to sale, and particularly in Lat. 25 d. where in the Year 1693, several of our Men were cheated with it.

What Mr. Dampier saith of the Laziness of the People of Mindanao, p. 333, the very same may be said of the People of Loango on the Coast of Guinea exactly.

Their manner of Worship, mentioned p. 345, is the very same with what I have seen at Algier, on the Coast of Barbary.

The Nocturnal Dancings used by the Hottantotts at the Cape of good Hopè every Full and New Moon, p. 521, are also practised by the Inhabitants of Loango, Molinbo and Cabendo.

I shall give you the trouble of a small Relation of a Passage to Loango in the Year 1693. When we came so far to the Southward as 2 d. 40 m. N. Lat. and 8 d. 25 m. Long. Westward from the Meridian of Lundy, it being 31st of March, we had small Wind at S. S. W. and S. W. with showers of Rain. There we met with prodigious shoals of Fish, consisting chiefly of Albicores and Bonetoes. There were also great numbers of Sharks; some 10 or 12 foot long. For diversion we catched above 100 of them at times. The other Fish we took as we had Occasion, fresh and fresh: and one day we caught a Barrel of them with empty Hooks. These shoals of Fish kept us Company till we were under the Equator in Long. 4 d. 3 m. Eastward of the Meridian of Lundy. This was April 27. We had the Winds at S. E. and S. E. by E. fresh Gales and clear Weather, but a mighty Leeward Current. At the Fishes parting with us that Day, I caught an Albicore that weighed 75 *l.* It is a mighty strong Fish, so that the Fishing-Craft must be very strong to take them.

The City of Loango I find to lye in Lat. 4 d. 30 m. S. and Longi. 18 d. 8 m. Eastward from the Meridian of Lundy: from whence I took my departure, bound for Jamaica, Oct. 7, 1693.

When we find the Winds South, S. by W. and S. S. W. fresh Gales; veerable to S. W. and back to South, we stand off to the Westward with Larboard Tacks on Board, till we get 14 d. Long. to the Westward of Loango. And there we find the Winds veerable from S. S. E. to S. E. fresh Gales. When we get 34 d. to the Westward of Loango, we are then 16 d. Westward from the Meridian of Lundy: and there we find the Winds veerable from S. E. by E. to E. by S. and East: and so they continue blowing fresh as we will still run to the Westward between the Lat. of 3 and 4 d. South, till we make the Island Fernande Noronho, which I find to lye in Lat. 3 d. 54 m. 30 s. South. And by the Experience of two Voyages have found its Long. 40 d. 59 m. Westward from Loango, and 22 d. 51 m. from the Meridian of Lundy. This Island appears with a very high Pyramid. And when we come close to it, the Pyramid looks like a large Cathedral. On the N. W. side is a small Bay to anchor in. But Ships must come pretty near the Shore, because it is deep Water. Here is Plenty of Fish. And on the Island is some fresh Water, and low Shrubs of Trees. We could see no living Creature on it but Dogs. It was formerly inhabited by the Portuguese, but the Dutch having then War with them, took it, and carried the Portuguese all away. The Body of the Island I judge to be about 4 Miles long, lying N. E. and S. W. near on the North-side are some Rocks, pretty high above Water; and many Birds, as Sea-Gulls and Man-of-War-Birds (which are something like our Kites in England). I find the Current sets strong to the N. W. The Variation very little. From thence I steered N. W. with fresh Gales S. E. and at E. S. E. in order to cross the Equator, and designing to make the Island Tobago: which by my Run from the aforesaid Island, I find to lye in Lat. 11 d. 33 m. North Long. Westward of Fernando, 28 d. 19 m. $\frac{2}{10}$. The Meridian distance from Fernando 1721 Miles $\frac{6}{10}$. And by my Reckoning or Journal Tobago is West from the Meridian of the Isle of Lundy 51 d. 10 m. $\frac{2}{10}$. In this Passage between the said Islands we find strange Ripling and Cockling Seas, ready to leap in upon the Ship's Deck; which makes us think the Current to be strong: And it seems to be occasioned by the great River on the main Land; which is not far from us in this Passage. Tobago is an high Island with a brave sandy Bay on the S. W. side, where the Dutch had formerly a great Fort, till molested by the English in the last Dutch War. From this Island I shaped my Course for Jamaica, and found the N. E. Corner to lye in Lat. 18 d. North; and in Long. West from Tobago 13 d. The Meridian distance from Tobago is 749 Miles West. In our Passage we saw no Land or Island, till we made the N. E. end of Jamaica: which lyeth in Long. West from the Meridian of Lundy 64 d. 10 m. and West from the City of Loango 82 d. 18 m. I shall only add that I am of Opinion that the Gallopagos Islands do lye a great deal farther to the Westward than our Hydrographers do place them, according as Mr. Dampier hints, p. 127 of his "Voyage round the World."

I am,

Sir,

Your most humble Servant,

JOHN COVANT.

Portbury, *Octob.* 20. 1698.

Part of a second Letter from Captain COVANT; *dated from Bristol, Decemb.* 10. 1697.

LETTER II

SIR,

YOURS of the 6th Instant came to my Hands, with the inclosed Queries, which I shall endeavour to answer in part, as far as my memory will assist me, being now from home, and at a distance from my Journals, &c.

A DISCOURSE OF WINDS

ANSWERS TO THE QUERIES

1. The common Trade-Winds on the Coast of Angola, blow from the S. W. to South, till about 12 d. Long. from the Meridian of the Isle of Lundy.

2. I have found them always in the same Quarter, and not subject to shift in all the Time I have used this Coast, except that at a small Distance off the Shore, they are sometimes a Point more to the Westward.

3. The Dry Season on this Coast I observed to be from the latter end of April to September; tho' sometimes intermix'd with some pleasant Showers of Rain. I cannot be so punctual as to the Time of the Wet Seasons.

4. The true Sea-Breeze I have commonly found here to be from W. S. W. to W. by S. if it be fair Weather: and the Land-Breeze is at E. by N. But if a Tornado happens, it causes the Winds to shift all round the Compass, and at last it settles at S. W. which is the former true Trade-Wind.

I am yours

JOHN COVANT.

CHAP. VI

Of Storms

Storms less frequent, but more fierce between the Tropicks. Presages of the coming of Norths, the Times and Places where they blow: Signs of their Approach: N. Banks. A Chocolatta North. A North beneficial to Ships going from Campeachy to Jamaica. A very uncommon way of wearing a Ship in a North. Of Souths, the Times and Places where they blow. A Description of a South at Jamaica, and at the Bay of Campeachy: Much Fish kill'd by that Storm. Of Hurricanes. A Description of a terrible one at Antegoa, where Abundance of Fish and Sea-Fowls were destroyed by it. The difference between North-Banks, and the Clouds before an Hurricane: the latter adorned with radiant Colours. Tuffoons in the East-Indies the same with Hurricanes in the West. Of Monsoons in the East-Indies. A Storm called by the Portuguese, the Elephanta, which is the violentest Monsoon of that Season.

STORMS within the Tropicks are generally known to us by some Name or other, to distinguish them from other common Winds: and though Storms are not so frequent there, as they are in Latitudes nearer the Poles; yet are they nevertheless expected yearly in their proper Months; and when they do come, they blow exceeding fierce, though indeed some years they do not come at all, or at least do not blow with that Fierceness as at other times. And as these Winds are commonly very fierce, so are they but of a short Continuance, in Comparison with Storms that we meet with in higher Latitudes.

In the West-Indies there are three sorts, viz. Norths, Souths, and Hurricanes: In the East-Indies there are only two sorts, viz. Monsoons and Tuffoons.

All these sorts of violent Storms, except the Norths, are expected near one time of the Year: and this is taken notice of by those that have been in any of them; that they give certain Presages of their being at hand, several Hours before they come. Norths are violent Winds, that frequently blow in the Bay of Mexico from October till March: They are chiefly expected near the Full or Change of the Moon, all that Time of the Year, but they are most violent in December and January. These Winds are not confined to the Bay of Mexico only, but there they are most frequent, and Rage with the greatest Violence. They blow on the North-side of Cuba very fierce too, and in the Gulph of Florida: as also about Hispaniola, Jamaica, &c. and in the Channel between Jamaica and Portabel; and in all the West-Indian Sea between the Islands and the Main as high as the Island Trinidado. But from Jamaica Eastward, except on the North-side of the Island Hispaniola, they blow no harder than a pretty brisk Sea Wind. They are here at W. N. W. or N. W. though in the Bay of Mexico they blow strongest at N. N. W. and this is the Season of Westerly Winds in these East-parts of the West-Indies, as I have before noted in the third Chapter of this Discourse. I shall be most particular of them that blow in the Bay of Mexico, and what Signs they give us beforehand.

Commonly before a North the Weather is very serene and fair, the Sky clear, and but little Wind, and that too veering from its proper Point, or the common Trade-Wind of the Coast; and breathing gently at S. at S. W. and West a Day or two before the North comes. The Sea also gives notice of a Storm, by an extraordinary and long Ebb. For a Day or two before a North, there will be hardly any discernable Flood, but a constant ebbing of the Sea. And the Sea-Fowls also before a Storm, do commonly hover over the Land, which they do not at other times use to do, in such great Flights and Numbers. All these Signs concurring, may give any Man notice of an approaching Storm, but the greatest and most remarkable Sign of a North, is a very black Cloud in the N. W. rising above the Horizon to about 10 or 12 degrees: the upper Edge of the Cloud appears very even and smooth, and when once the upper part of the Cloud is 6, 8, 10 or 12 degrees high, there it remains in that even form parallel to the Horizon without any Motion; and this sometimes 2 or 3 Days before the Storm comes: At other times not above 12 or 14 Hours, but never less.

This Cloud lying so near the Horizon, is not seen but in the Mornings or Evenings, at least it does not appear so black as then; this is called by English Seamen a North Bank, and whenever we see such a Cloud in that part of the World, and in the Months before-mentioned, we certainly provide for a Storm; and tho' sometimes it may happen that such a Cloud may appear several Mornings and Evenings, and we may not feel the Effects of it, or but very little; yet we always provide against it; for a North never comes without such a foreboding Cloud. But if the Winds also whiffle about to the South, with fair flattering Weather, it never fails. While the Wind remains at S. S. W. or any thing to the South of the West, it blows very faint; but when once it comes to the North of the West, it begins to be brisk and veers about presently to the North-West, where it blows hard; yet does it not stay there long before it veers to the N. N. W. and there it blows strongest and longest. Sometimes it continues 24 or even 48 Hours, and sometimes longer. When the Wind first comes to the N. W. if the black Cloud rises and comes away, it may chance to give but one Flurry, like that of a Tornado; and then the Sky grows clear again; and either the Wind continues at N. W. blowing only a brisk Gale, which the Jamaica Seamen call a Chocolatta North, or else it veers about again to the East, and settles there. But if when the Wind comes to the N. W. the Cloud still remains settled, the Wind then continues blowing very fierce even so long as the black Bank continues near the Horizon. It is commonly pretty dry and clear, but sometimes much Rain falls with a North: and tho' the Clouds which bring Rain, come from the N. W. and N. N. W. yet the black Bank near the Horizon seems not to move till the Heart of the Storm is broke. When the Wind starts from the N. N. W. to the N. 'tis a sign that the Violence of the Storm is past, especially if it veers to the East of the North; for then it soon flies about to the East, and there settles at its usual Point and brings fair Weather: But if it goes back from the N. to the N. W. it will last a day or two longer, as fierce as before; and not without a great deal of Rain.

When our Jamaica Logwood-ships are coming loaden out of the Bay of Campeachy in the North-Season, they are glad to have a North. For a good North will bring them almost to Jamaica; neither have any of our Vessels miscarried in one of these Storms that I did ever hear of, though sometimes much shattered; but the Spaniards do commonly suffer by them, and there is seldom a Year but one or more of them are cast away in the Bay of Campeachy in this Season: for they don't work their Ships as we do ours. They always bring their Ships too under a Fore-sail and Mizen, but never under a Main-sail and Mizen, nor yet under the Mizen alone; but we generally bring too under Main-sail and Mizen; and if the Wind grows too fierce we bring her under a Mizen only; and if we cannot maintain that, then we balast our Mizen: which is by riffing and taking up great Part of the Sail. If after all this, the Winds and Seas are too high for us, then we put before it, but not before we have tryed our utmost, especially if we are near a Lee-Shore. On the contrary, the Spaniards in the West-Indies, (as I said before) lye under a Fore-sail and Mizen: But this must needs be an extraordinary Strain to a Ship, especially if she be long. Indeed there is this Convenience in it, when they are minded to put away before it, 'tis but halling up the Mizen, and the Fore-Sail veers the Ship presently: and I judge it is for that Reason they do it. For when the Wind comes on so fierce that they can no longer keep on a Wind, they put right afore it, and so continue till the Storm ceaseth, or the Land takes them up (*i. e.* till they are run a-shore). I knew two Spaniards did so, while I was in the Bay. One was a King's Ship, called the

Piscadore. She run ashore on a sandy Bay, a Mile to the Westward of the River Tobasco. The other was come within four or five Leagues of the Shore, and the Storm ceasing, she escaped Shipwreck, but was taken by Captain Hewet, Commander of a Privateer, who was then in the Bay. Her Main-mast and Mizen were cut down in the Storm. Both these ships came from La Vera Cruz, and were in the North-side of the Bay when first the Storms took them. And tho' we don't use this Method, yet we find means to wear our Ships as well as they; for if after the Mizen is hall'd up and furled, if then the Ship will not wear, we must do it with some Head-sail, which yet sometimes puts us to our Shifts. As I was once in a very violent Storm, sailing from Virginia, mentioned in my "Voyage round the World," we scudded before the Wind and Sea some time, with only our bare Poles; and the Ship by the mistake of him that con'd, broched too, and lay in the Trough of the Sea; which then went so high that every Wave threatned to overwhelm us. And indeed if any one of them had broke in upon our Deck, it might have foundred us. The Master,[1] whose Fault this was, rav'd like a mad Man, and called for an Axe to cut the Mizen Shrouds, and turn the Mizen Mast over Board: which indeed might have been an Expedient to bring her to her Course again. Captain Davis was then Quarter-master, and a more experienced Seaman than the Master. He bid him hold his Hand a little, in hopes to bring her some other way to her Course: The Captain also was of his Mind. Now our Main-yard and Fore-yard were lowered down a Port last, as we call it, that is, down pretty nigh the Deck, and the Wind blew so fierce that we did not dare to loose any Head-sail, for they must have blown away if we had, neither could all the Men in the Ship have furled them again; therefore we had no hopes of doing it that way. I was at this time on the Deck with some others of our Men; and among the rest one Mr. John Smallbone, who was the main Instrument at that Time of

[1] The master ("whose Fault this was") was Ambrose Cowley. The captain was John Cook.

saving us all. Come! said he to me, let us go a little way up the Fore-shrouds, it may be that may make the Ship wear; for I have been doing it before now. He never tarried for an Answer, but run forward presently, and I followed him. We went up the Shrouds Half-mast up, and there we spread abroad the Flaps of our Coats, and presently the Ship wore.[1] I think we did not stay there above three minutes before we gain'd our Point and came down again, but in this time the Wind was got into our Main-sail, and had blown it loose; and tho' the Main-yard was down a Port-last and our Men were got on the Yard as many as could lye one by another, besides the Deck full of Men, and all striving to furl that Sail, yet could we not do it, but were forced to cut it all along by the Head-rope, and so let it fall down on the Deck.

Having largely treated of Norths, I shall next give some Account of Souths.

South Winds are also very violent Winds. I have not heard any thing of these sorts of Storms, but at Jamaica or by Jamaica Sailors. The Time when they blow at Jamaica is about June, July or August, Months that Norths never blow in. The greatest Stress of Wind in these Storms is at South, from whence it's probable they are named Souths. In what they differ from the Hurricanes that rage among the Caribbee Islands, I know not, unless in this, that they are more constant to one Point of the Compass, or that they come sooner in the Year than Hurricanes do, but those Storms call'd Hurricanes, had never been known at Jamaica when I was there. Yet since I have heard that they have felt the Fury of them several Times. But I was at Jamaica when there happened a violent South. It made great Havock in the Woods; and blew down many great Trees; but there was no great Damage done by it. Port Royal was in great Danger then of being washed away, for the Sea made a Breach clear through the Town; and if the Violence of Weather had continued but a few Hours

[1] *Cf.* Anson's voyage: "As we dared not venture any sail abroad, we were obliged to make use of an expedient which answered our purpose; this was putting the helm a-weather, and manning the fore-shrouds."

longer, many of the Houses had been washed away: For the Point of Land on which that Town stands, is Sand; which began to wash away apace: but the Storm ceasing, there was no further Damage. This was in July or August in the Year 1674.

I was afterwards in the Bay of Campeachy, when we had a much more violent Storm than this, called also by the Logwood-cutters a South. It happened some time in June 1676.

I was then cutting Logwood in the Western Creek of the West Lagune. Two days before this Storm began, the Wind whiffled about to the South, and back again to the East, and blew very faintly. The Weather also was very fair, and the Men-of-War-Birds came hovering over the Land in great Numbers; which is very unusual for them to do. This made some of our Logwood-Cutters say, that we should have some Ships come hither in a short Time; for they believed it was a certain Token of the Arrival of Ships, when these Birds came thus hovering over the Land. And some of them said they had lived at Barbadoes, where it was generally taken Notice of: and that as many of these Birds as they saw hovering over the Town, so many Ships there were coming thither. And according to that Rule they foolishly guess'd that here were a great many Ships coming hither at that Time; tho' 'tis impossible that they could imagine there could be the hundredth part of the Ships arrive, that they saw Birds fly over their Heads. But that which I did most admire was, to see the Water keep ebbing for two Days together, without any Flood, till the Creek, where we lived, was almost dry. There was commonly at low Water seven or eight Foot Water; but now not above 3, even in the middle of the Creek.

About 4 a Clock the 2d Day after this unusual Ebb, the Sky looked very black, and the Wind sprung up fresh at S. E. and increasing. In less than two Hours time it blew down all our Huts, but one; and that with much Labour we propt up with Posts, and with Ropes cast over the Ridge, and fastning both ends to stumps of Trees, we secured the Roof from flying away. In it we huddled all together till the Storm ceased. It rained very hard the greatest part of the Storm, and about two Hours after the Wind first sprang up, the Waters flowed very fast in. The next Morning it was as high as the Banks of the Creek: which was higher than I had ever seen it before.

The Flood still increased, and run faster up the Creek than ever I saw it do in the greatest Spring-Tide; which was somewhat strange, because the Wind was at South, which is right off the Shore on this Coast. Neither did the Rain any thing abate, and by ten a Clock in the Morning the Banks of the Creek were all overflown. About twelve at Noon we brought our Canoa to the side of our Hut, and fastned it to the Stump of a Tree that stood by it; that being the only Refuge that we could now expect; for the Land a little way within the Banks of the Creek is much lower than where we were: So that there was no walking through the Woods because of the Water. Besides, the Trees were torn up by the Roots, and tumbled down so strangely a-cross each other, that it was almost impossible to pass through them.

The Storm continued all this Day and the Night following till ten a Clock: then it began to abate, and by two in the Morning it was quite calm.

This Storm made very strange work in the Woods by tearing up the Trees by the Roots: The Ships also riding at Trist and at One-Bush-Key, felt the Fury of it to their Sorrow; for of four that were riding at One-Bush-Key, three were driven away from their Anchors, one of which was blown into the Woods of Beef-Island. And of the four Ships that were at Trist, three also were driven from their Anchors, one of which was cast up about twenty Paces beyond High-Water-Mark on the Island of Trist. The other two were driven off to Sea; and one of them was never heard of since.

The poor Fish also suffered extremely by this Storm, for we saw Multitudes of them either cast on the Shore, or floating dead on the Lagunes. Yet this Storm did not reach 30 Leagues to Wind-ward of Trist, for Captain Vally of Jamaica, went hence but three Days before the

Storm began, and was not past 30 Leagues off when we had it so fierce, yet he felt none of it; but only saw very black dismal Clouds to the Westward, as he reported at his Return from Jamaica to Trist four Months after.

I shall speak next of Hurricanes.

These are violent Storms, raging chiefly among the Caribbee Islands; though, by Relation, Jamaica has of late been much annoyed by them; but it has been since the Time of my being there. They are expected in July, August or September.

These Storms also as well as the Norths or Souths, give some Signs of their Approach before they come on. I have not been in any one of them my self, but have made Enquiry of many Men that have, and they all agree that either they are preceded by flattering unusual small Winds and very fair Weather, or by a great Glut of Rain, or else by both Rains and Calms together.

I shall give an Instance of one that gave such Warning. It happened at Antegoa in August 1681. I had the Relation of it from Mr. John Smallbone,[1] before-mentioned, who was Gunner of a Ship of 120 Tons and 10 Guns, commanded by Capt. Gadbury.

Before this Storm it rained two Days excessively, then it held up two or three Days more: but the Sky was clouded and appear'd to be much troubled, yet but little Wind. The Planters by this were certain of a Hurricane, and warned the Ship-Commanders to provide for it, especially Capt. Gadbury; who had careen'd his Ship in Muskito Cove in St. John's Harbour but a little before, and by this Warning given him by the Planters, had gotten his Goods on Board again, which though all he had, yet was but about half his lading of Sugar, Molosses and Rum. He also moored his Ship as secure as he could, with all his Cables and Anchors, besides some Cables which he had made fast ashore to great Trees. And about 7 a Clock that Evening that the Storm came, he dreading it, went ashore with all his Men, and retired into a poor Planter's

[1] This John Smallbone afterwards accompanied Dampier on his voyage with Funnell to the South Seas.

House about half a Mile from the Shore. By that Time he and his Men were arriv'd at the House, which was before 8 a Clock; the Wind came on very fierce at N. E. and veering about to the N. and N. W. settled there, bringing with it very violent Rains. Thus it continued about four Hours, and then fell flat calm, and the Rain ceased.

In this Calm he sent 3 or 4 of his Men down to the Cove to see what Condition the Ship was in, and they found her driven ashore dry on the Sand, lying on one side, with the Head of her Mast sticking into the Sand; after they had walk'd round her and view'd her a-while, they return'd again to the Capt. to give him an Account of the Disaster, and made as much haste as they could, because the Wind began to blow hard at S. W. and it blew so violently before they recover'd the House, that the Boughs of the Trees whipt them sufficiently before they got thither; and it rained as hard as before. The little House could scarce shelter them from the wet; for there was little beside the Walls standing: For the 1st Northerly Gust blew away great part of the Ridge and most of the Thatch. Yet there they staid till the next Morning, and then coming to the Ship found her almost upright; but all the Goods that were in the Hold were wash'd out, and the Sugar was wash'd out of the Cask. Some of the Rum they found; a Cask in one place and a Cask in another: some on the Shore, and some half a Mile in the Woods; and some stav'd against the Trees and leek'd out; for it seems there had been a violent Motion in the Sea, as well as in the Air. For in the Beginning of the Night when the N. E. Gust raged, the Sea ebb'd so prodigiously, or else was driven off the Shore by the Violence of the Wind so far, that some Ships riding in the Harbour in 3 or 4 Fathom Water, were a-ground, and lay so till the S. W. Gust came, and then the Sea came rowling in again with such prodigious Fury, that it not only set them a-float, but dash'd many of them on the Shore. One of them was carried up a great way into the Woods: another was strangely hurl'd on two Rocks that stood close by one another; with her

Head resting on one Rock, and her Stern on the other: And thus she lay like a Bridge between the two Rocks, about ten or eleven Foot above the Sea, even in the highest Tides; for the Tides do usually rise here but little, not above two or three Foot, but in these Hurricanes it always ebbs and flows again prodigiously.

It was not the Ships only that felt the Fury of this Storm, but the whole Island suffered by it; for the Houses were blown down, the Trees tore up by the Roots, or had their Heads and Limbs sadly shattered, neither was there any Leaves, Herbs or green Thing left on the Island, but all look'd like Winter. Insomuch that a Ship coming thither a little after, that used that Trade, could scarce believe it to be the same Island. Neither did the Fury of this Storm light only here, for Nevis and St. Christopher's had their Shares also; but Mountsurat felt little of it, tho' not above a Fortnight after there happened another Storm, as violent as this, and raged extremely there, but did little Damage at Nevis and St. Christophers. Antegoa had a great Share of this too. Capt. Gadbury's Ship, that lay a-ground before it came, was by it hurled over to the opposite part of the Harbour, and there thrown dry on the Sand.

The Day after the Storm, the Shore was strew'd with Fish of divers sorts, as well great as small; such as Porpoises, Sharks, &c. and Abundance of Sea-Fowls also were destroyed by it.

I would not have any Man think that these Hurricanes, or any other Storms, do always give warning of their coming exactly alike: For there may be some Difference in those Signs, tho' all of them be plain enough if well observed. Besides sometimes they are duplicated, sometimes only single Signs, and sometimes the Signs may be more visible and plain than at other Times: when by some accidental Cause those Signs may be less visible by Reason of some high Hill or Mountain that may be interpos'd between you and the Horizon, especially if any Hill lies N. E. from you, which is the Quarter that Hurricanes do commonly rise in.

The Clouds that precede a Hurricane are different from the North-Banks, in this, that whereas the Clouds preceding Norths are uniform and regular; of an exact Blackness even from the Horizon to the upper Edge of it, and that as streight and even as a Line stretched out. On the contrary, the Hurricane-Clouds tower up their Heads, pressing forwards as if they all strove for Precedency; yet so linked one within another, that all move alike. Besides, the Edges of these Clouds are gilded with various and afrighting Colours, the very Edge of all seems to be of a pale fire-colour, next that of a dull yellow, and nearer the Body of the Cloud of a Copper-Colour, and the Body of the Cloud which is very thick appears extraordinary black: and altogether it looks very terrible and amazing even beyond Expression. Tho' I have never been in any Hurricane in the West-Indies, yet I have seen the very Image of them in the East-Indies, and the Effects have been the very same; and for my part I know no Difference between a Hurricane among the Caribbee-Islands in the West-Indies, and a Tuffoon on the Coast of China in the East-Indies, but only the Name: And I am apt to believe that both Words have one Signification, which is, a violent Storm.

I have given a large Account of one of these in my "Voyage round the World," Chapter XV, Page 409. That gave warning by flattering Weather beforehand, and a very dismal Cloud, set out with such Colours as I have before described, rising in the N. E. from whence the Violence of the first Gust came, which was wonderful fierce and accompanied with extraordinary hard Rain; then it afterwards fell calm about an Hour, and then the Wind came about at S. W. and blew as fierce as it did before at N. E. which is much like the Hurricane before-mentioned at Antegoa, but of a longer Continuance than that: Besides, in both places they blow at one time of the Year, which is in July, August or September; and commonly near the Full or Change of the Moon.

Another thing that we must also take notice of, is,

that both Places are North of the Equator, though not exactly in one Latitude.

But of these Tuffoons I shall say no more now, having described them particularly in my Voyage to Tonquin, Chap. II. Pag. 586.

The Monsoons in the East-Indies are the next to be treated of; by which I do not mean the Coasting Trade-wind, so called, which I have already described in Page 243 of this Discourse; for though Monsoon is a general Word for the Wind there, distinguished by East or West, according to the Points from whence they blow; yet it sometimes also signifies a Storm, as I now take it. And it is easie to be understood, when it is used in Reference to the Trade-wind, or when spoken of a Storm; for if applied to a Storm, 'tis express'd by some Epithet going before: As Violent, Terrible, &c. without any Distinction of East or West, which is commonly used in speaking of the Trade-Wind.

These Monsoons or Storms on the Coast of Coromandel are expected either about April or September, which are accounted the two shifting Months. For in these two Months the Winds begin to shift and turn from that Point, on which they have blown several Months before to the contrary Points of the Compass; as from East to West, or the contrary: but commonly this Shift is attended with a turbulent Sky, which ends in a violent Storm of Wind, or excessive Rains, or both: And this is called also the breaking up of the Monsoon. It was in one of these that I past from Nicobar to Sumatra, mentioned in my "Voyage round the World," Chap. XVIII. Page 479. This was the April Monsoon.

The September Monsoons are generally more violent than these last: yet by the Account I have lately had from Fort St. George, they have suffered very much by one of the April Monsoons (if it may be so called) for it came before its usual time, even before it could be expected.

As for the September Monsoons, tho' the time of the Year is so well known, and the Warnings of their Approach almost certain; yet our East-India Merchants have had very considerable Losses there; for the Stress of the Winds blows right in upon the Shore, and often hurries the Ships from their Anchors, and tosses them in a Moment on the sandy Bay.

Indeed the want of a secure Place to ride in, is the greatest Inconvenience of that Factory, a Place doubtless designed by the English from its Original to be the Center of the Trade of these Parts. For all our Factories, and the Trade in general, East from Cape Comorin, are now subordinate to this.

The Dutch had once a place of Consequence, called Pallacat, on this Coast, about twenty Leagues to the North of it; but they withdrew most of their Families and Effects from thence in the Year 1691, mentioned in my "Voyage round the World," Chap. XX. Page 505. And it is very probable that these rageing Winds might be one Cause of this their deserting it, whatever was the Motive of settling here; for they have secure Harbours, and Roads enough in India, which we to our great Disadvantage very much want.

But to return to the Monsoons.

These (as I have told you) blow fiercest in September, and, as I have been informed, blow on several Points of the Compass.

The stormy Monsoons on the Mallabar Coast differ from these on the Coast of Coromandel, in that they are more common, and last even from April to September, which is as long as the common West-Monsoon lasts, though not so frequent and lasting in the Beginning of the Monsoon, as towards the latter end.

The Months of July and August afford very bad Weather, for then there is hardly any Intermission, but a continued troubled Sky full of black Clouds which pour down excessive Rains, and often very fierce Winds. But towards the breaking up of the Monsoon, they have one very terrible Storm called by the Portuguese the Eliphanta, which concludes the bad Weather. For after that they put to Sea without fear of any more Storms that Season.

These violent Winds blow directly in upon the Shore;

and they dam up the Harbours on this Coast, especially that of Goa, so that no Ships can go in or come out then; but after the violent Winds are past, the Channel opens again, and so continues till the next Season.

This Relation I had from a very ingenious Gentleman who was at Goa during the bad Weather.

I shall only take notice that these Storms are also at the same Time of the Year, when the Hurricanes and Souths are in the West-Indies, and the Tuffoons on the Coasts of China, Tunqueen, Cochinchina and Cambodia in the Eastern Parts of the East-Indies, and that all these Places are to the North of the Equator.

CHAP. VII

Of the Seasons of the Year

The Wet and Dry Seasons on the North-side of the Equator; and on the South of it. Places famous for much dry Weather; as part of Peru, and Africa. A Comparison between those Coasts. Of raining Coasts; as Guinea. Why Guinea more subject to Rains than the opposite Coast of Brazil. The time of Sugar-making. Of the Seasons at Suranam. Bays more subject to Rain than Head-Lands. Several Instances of this, as at Campeachy, Panama, Tunqueen, Bengala, &c. Mountains more subject to Rains than Low Land: An Instance of this at Jamaica. The Isle of Pines near Cuba, a wet Place. So is also Gorgonia in the South-Seas. The manner how Tornadoes arise.

AS Summer and Winter are the two most different Seasons in our Climate; so the Dry and the Wet are within the Torrid Zone; and are always opposite to each other. They are often called by Europeans Winter and Summer, but more generally, Dry and Wet.

The Seasons on each side of the Equator, are as different as the Seasons of Summer and Winter are in temperate Climates, or near each Pole. For as 'tis Summer near the North-Pole, when 'tis Winter near the South-Pole, and the contrary; so when 'tis fair and dry Weather North of the Equator, 'tis blustering and rainy Weather South of it; and the contrary, except within a few degrees of the Line, and that in some places only.

There is also this difference between the Torrid and Temperate Zones, either North or South of the Equator; that when it is fair and dry Weather in the one, it is Winter in the other: and when it is wet in the one, it is

Summer in the other. I speak now of Places lying on the same side of the Equator: For as the Sun when it passes the Equinox, and draws towards either of the Tropicks, begins to warm their respective Poles, and by how much the nearer he approaches, by so much is the Air without the Tropicks clear, dry and hot; on the contrary, within the Torrid Zone (though on the same side of the Line) the farther the Sun is off, the dryer is the Weather. And as the Sun comes nearer, the Sky grows more cloudy and the Weather more moist: for the Rains follow the Sun, and begin on either side of the Equator, within a little while after the Sun has crost the Equinox, and so continue till after his return back again.

The wet Season on the North side of the Equator in the Torrid Zone, begins in April or May, and so continues till September or October.

The dry Weather comes in November or December, and continues till April or May.

In South Latitudes the Weather changes at the same times, but with this difference, that the dry Months in South Latitude, are wet Months in North Latitude, and the contrary, as I have said before. Yet neither do the wet or dry Seasons set in or go out exactly at one time, in all Years; neither are all places subject to wet or dry Weather alike. For in some places it rains less than in others; and consequently there is more dry Weather. But generally Places that lye under the Line, or near it, have their greatest Rains in March and September.

Head-Lands or Coasts that lye most exposed to the Trade-winds have commonly the best share of dry Weather. On the contrary, deep Bays or Bendings of the Land, especially such as lye near the Line, are most subject to Rains. Yet even among Bays or Bendings, there is a great deal of difference in the Weather as to dry or wet; for the Weather, as well as the Winds seem to be much influenced by accidental Causes; and those Causes themselves, whatever they are, seem to be subject to great variation.

But to proceed with Matter of Fact; I shall begin with the driest Coasts; and first with that of Peru, from

3 d. South to 30 d. South. There it never Rains, neither at Sea for a good distance off shore, as for 250 or 300 Leagues; no nor on the shore for a considerable way within Land; though exactly how far I know not; yet there are small Mists sometimes in a Morning for two or three Hours, but seldom continuing after 10 a-Clock; and there are Dews also in the Night.

This Coast lies N. and S. it has the Sea open to the West, and a Chain of very high Mountains running along shore on the East, and the Winds constantly Southerly, as I said before in the second Chapter of Winds.

In which Head I have made a Comparison as well of the Winds on the Coast of Africa in the same Latitude, as of the lying of the Coasts. Only there is this difference, that the coasting Trade-winds on the American side do blow further from the Land than those on the African side. Which difference may probably arise from the disproportion of the Mountains that are in the two Continents; for 'tis known that the Andes in America are some of the highest Mountains in the World, but whether there are any on the Continent of Africa in those Latitudes so high, I know not. I have not heard of any, at least none such are visible to Seamen.

I come now to speak of the Weather on the African Coast, which though 'tis not so dry as the Coast of Peru, yet is it the next to it. The Weather there is very dry from March till October, which is the dry Season.

The rainy Season, which is from October till March, is moderate, without that excess that is in most other Places in those Latitudes; so that the wettest Season can only be called so from some gentle showers of Rain.

There are some Tornadoes, but not so many as are in many other Places, both of the East or West Indies, the Peruvian Coast excepted. And if the height of the Andes are the cause that the true East-Breeze does not take place in the Pacifick-Sea, within 200 Leagues distance from the shore, when yet the Trade blows within 40 Leagues of the African Coast; that Coast may perhaps be supposed to want such high Mountains. And if those American

Mountains do stop the Winds from their Career, why may they not as well break the Clouds before they reach near the shore, and be the cause of the dry Weather there? And seeing both Coasts do lye alike, and the Wind is alike; why should not the Weather be the same; were it not for the disproportion between the Mountains of these Coasts? For the East-side of those Mountains are supplied with Rain enough, as may be known by the great Rivers that disembogue from thence into the Atlantick Sea; whereas the Rivers on the South-Sea Coast are but very few and small; some of which do wholly dry away for a good part of the Year; but yet they constantly break out again in their Seasons, when the Rains in the Country do come, which always fall on the West-side of those Mountains, and this is about February.

As I have spoken before of dry Coasts, so now I shall speak of rainy ones. I shall begin with the Coast of Guinea, from Cape Lopes, which lies one degree South, taking in the Bite or Bending of the Land, and all the Coast West from thence, as far as Cape Palmas.

This is a very wet Coast, subject to violent Tornadoes and excessive Rains, especially in July and August: In those Months there is scarce any fair Day. This Coast lies all of it very near the Equator, and no where above 6 or 7 degrees Distance; so that from its nearness to the Equator only, we might probably conjecture that it is a rainy Coast; for most places lying near the Line are very subject to Rains: yet some more than others; and Guinea may be reckoned among the wettest Places in the World. There may be Places where the Rains continue longer, but none are more violent while they last.

And as its nearness to the Line may be a great cause of its Moisture; so by its situation also one would guess that it should be subject to a great deal of Rain; because there is a great Bite or Bending in of the Land, a little to the North of the Line; and from thence the Land stretcheth West parallel with the Line. And these circumstances singly taken, according to my Observations do seldom fail, but more especially where they both meet. Yet there may be other causes that may hinder those Effects, or at least serve to allay the violence of them, as they do on some other Coasts. I shall only instance in the opposite Coast of America between the North Cape, which lies North of the Equator, and Cape Blanco on Brazil, in South Latitude. Now this Land lies much after the Form of the Coast of Guinea, with this difference, that one Coast lies in South Lat. the other lies North of the Equator, both of these Promontories lay parallel with the Equator, and there's not much difference in their distance from it; but that which makes the difference is, that one juts out Westward, the other Eastward; and so one is the very Westermost Land of the Continent of Africa, the other is the Eastermost Land of the Continent of America: The one has only an eddy Wind, which seems to me to be the Effect of two contrary Winds: The other Coast lies open to the Trade, and never wants a Breeze. And the former is troubled with Tornadoes and violent Rains during the wet Season, which is May, June, July, August and September: But the extremest wet Months are July and August; when it rains in a manner continually. April and October also sometimes are wet Months.

The other Coast on the American Continent, which lies open to the E. and N. E. or S. E. and which enjoys the freer Trade-Wind, is less subject to Rain; only as it lies near the Line, it has its part, but not to Excess, nor in any Comparison with Guinea. And as the Line is to the N. of it, so its wet Months are from October till April, and the dry Season from April to October. And these Seasons reach even to six or seven Degrees North of the Line: Which I do not know to be so in any other part of the World again. Indeed Cape Lopes in Guinea, is in one degree South, yet participates of the same Weather that the rest of Guinea has, which lies to the North of the Line.

Now the Reason why Europeans do account the dry Season Summer, and the wet Season Winter; is because the dry Season is their Harvest time, especially in our Plantations, where we chiefly make Sugar; for then the Canes are as yellow as Gold. They have then indeed less Juice, but that little there is, is very sweet. Whereas in the wet Season, tho' the Canes are ripe, and come to their Maturity; yet do they not yield such Quantities of Sugar, neither is it so good, tho' the Pains in boiling it be also greater. Therefore in Northern Climates, as all our Plantations are in, they commonly begin to work about making of Sugar at Christmas; after the dry Season has brought the Canes to a good Perfection. But in South Climates, as on the Coast of Brazil, they begin to work in July. Some Places there are in the North Latitudes also near the Line, where the Weather bears Time with the Seasons in South Lat. as at Suranam, which though it is in North Lat. yet are the Seasons there the same as in South Latitudes; but I know not such another Instance any where. And tho' the dry Season is the Time to gather in the Canes, and the wet Season to plant; yet are they not so limited as to make use only of these Seasons for either; but do it chiefly for their best Convenience; for they may plant at any Time of the Year, and that with good Success: especially after a moderate Shower of Rain, which often happens even in the dry Seasons.

But I must proceed.

I have said before that Bays have greater Quantities of Rain than Head-Lands.

The Bay of Campeachy is a good Instance of this; for the Rains are very great there, especially in the Months of July and August. On the contrary, the Coast from Cape Catoch to Cape Condecedo, which lies more exposed to the Trade, has not near the Rains as the Bay of Campeachy hath.

The Bay of Honduras also is very wet, and all that bending Coast from Cape Gratia de Dios, even to Carthagena. But on the Coast of Caraccos, and about Cape La Vela, where the Breezes are more brisk, the Weather is more moderate. Whereas in those little Bays between, there is still a Difference: For in the Bay of Mericaya, which lies a little to the East of Cape La Vela, there is much more Rain than at or near the Cape.

The Bay of Panama also will furnish us with a Proof

of this, by its immoderate Rains; especially the South-side of it, even from the Gulph of St. Michael, to Cape St. Francis; the Rains there are from April till November; but in June, July, and August, they are most violent.

There are many small Bays also West from the Bay of Panama, which have their Shares of these wet Seasons, as the Gulph of Dulce, Caldera Bay, Amapalla, &c. but to the West of that, where the Coast runs more plain and even, there are not such wet Seasons; yet many times very violent Tornadoes.

The East-Indies also has many Bays that are subject to very violent Rains, as the Bay of Tonqueen, that of Siam, the Bottom and the East-side of the Bay of Bengall. But on the Coast of Coromandel, which is the West-side of that Bay, the Weather is more moderate; that being an even, plain, low Coast. But on the Coast of Mallabar, which is on the West-side of that Promontory, the Land is high and mountainous, and there are violent Rains. Indeed the West-sides of any Continents are wetter than the East-sides, the Coast of Peru and Africa only excepted; in the former of which the Dryness may be occasioned (as is said before) by the Height of the Andes. And 'tis probable that the Violence of the Rains near those Mountains falls chiefly on the East-sides of them, and seldom reaches to their Tops: which yet if the Rains do, they may there be broke in pieces, and reach no further. For, among other Observations, I have taken Notice that Mountains are supplied with more Rains than low Lands, I mean the low Land bordering on the Sea. As for Instance, the South-side of Jamaica beginning at Leganea, and from thence away to the Westward, as far as Black River, including all the plain Land and Savannahs about St. Jago de la Vego, Old Harbour and Whithy-wood Savannahs. This is a plain level Country for many Miles lying near East and West, having the Sea on the South, and bounded with Mountains on the North.

Those Mountains are commonly supplied with Rain before the low Lands. I have known the Rains to have begun there three Weeks before any has fallen in the plain

Country, bordering on the Sea; yet every Day I have observed very black Clouds over the Mountains, and have heard it thunder there. And those very Clouds have seemed by their Motion to draw towards the Sea, but have been check'd in their Course, and have either returned towards the Mountains again, or else have spent themselves before they came from thence, and so have vanished away again to the great Grief of the Planters, whose Plantations and Cattle have suffered for want of a little Moisture. Nay, these Tornadoes have been so nigh, that the Sea Breeze has died away, and we have had the Wind fresh out of the Clouds, yet they have vanished, and yielded no Rain to the low parch'd Lands.

And I think that the want of seasonable Showers is one of the greatest Inconveniencies that this part of the Country suffers, for I have known in some very dry Years, that the Grass in the Savannahs has been burned and wither'd for want of Rain, and the Cattle have perished thereby for want of Food. The Plantations also have suffered very much by it; but such dry Seasons have not been known on the North-side of the Island where the Mountains are bordering on the Sea, or at least but a little Distance off it. For there they are supplied with seasonable Showers almost all the Year, and even in the dry time it self near the Full and Change of the Moon. But in the wet Season, the Rains are more violent, which is their Inconvenience.

As for the Valleys in the Country, they are not subject to such Droughts as the plain Land by the Sea, at least I have not observed it my self, nor have I heard it mentioned by others.

The Isle of Pines near Cuba is so noted a Place for Rain that the Spaniards inhabiting near it on Cuba, say that it rains more or less every day in the Year, at one Place or another. It is generally spoken also and believ'd by Privateers, for it has been oft visited by them. I have been there my self, but cannot confirm that Report. However, it is well known to be a very wet and rainy Place.

It is but a small Island of about nine or ten Leagues long, and three or four broad; and in the midst is a high peeked Mountain, which is commonly clouded; and the Privateers say that this Hill draws all the Clouds to it; for if there is not another Cloud to be seen any where else, yet this Hill is seldom or never clear.

Gorgonia in the South-Seas also has the same Report. It is much smaller than Pines. I have mentioned it in my "Voyage round the World," Chap. VII. Page 193.

This Isle lies about four Leagues from the Main: but the Isle of Pines not above two, and is a great deal bigger than it. The Main against Gorgonia is very low Land; but Cuba near Pines is pretty high, and the Mountain of Pines is much bigger and higher than the Hill of Gorgonia, which yet is of a good Height, so that it may be seen sixteen or eighteen Leagues off; and tho' I cannot say that it rains every day there, yet I know that it rains very much and extraordinary hard.

I have been at this Isle three Times; and always found it very rainy, and the Rains very violent. I remember when we touch'd there in our Return from Captain Sharp, we boiled a Kettle of Chocolate before we clean'd our Bark; and having every Man his Callabash full, we began to sup it off, standing all the Time in the Rain; but I am confident not a Man among us all did clear his Dish, for it rained so fast and such great Drops into our Callabashes, that after we had sup'd off as much Chocolate and Rain-Water together as sufficed us, our Callabashes were still above half full; and I heard some of the Men swear that they could not sup it up so fast as it rained in, at last I grew tir'd with what I had left, and threw it away: and most of the rest did so likewise.

As Clouds do usually hover over Hills and Mountains, so do they also keep near the Land. I have mentioned something of this in my "Voyage round the World," Chap. X. Page 296, where I have said, that in making Land we commonly find it cloudy over the Land, tho' 'tis clear every where beside: And this may still confirm what I have said in the foregoing Discourse, that Hills are commonly clouded; for high Land is the first discerned by us, and that, as I said before, is commonly clouded.

But now I shall speak how we find the Clouds, when we are but a little way from Land, either coasting along the Shore, or at an Anchor by it. I hope the Reader will not imagine that I am going to prove that it never rains at Sea, or but very little there; for the contrary is known to every Body, and I have already said in this Discourse of Winds in my first Chapter, That there are very frequent Tornadoes in several Seas especially near the Equator, and more particularly in the Atlantick Sea. Other Seas are not so much troubled with them; neither is the Atlantick so to the North or South of the Line; especially at any considerable Distance from the Shore, but yet 'tis very probable however, that the Sea has not so great a Portion of Tornadoes as the Land hath. For when we are near the Shore within the Torrid Zone, we often see it rain on the Land, and perceive it to be very cloudy there, when it is fair at Sea, and scarce a Cloud to be seen that way. And tho' we have the Wind from the Shore, and the Clouds seeming to be drawing off, yet they often wheel about again to the Land, as if they were magnetically drawn that way: Sometimes indeed they do come off a little; but then they usually either return again or else insensibly vanish; and that's the Reason that Seamen when they are sailing near the Shore and see a Tornado coming off, they don't much mind it, but cry, "The Land will devour it:" But however, sometimes they fly off to Sea; and 'tis very rare that Tornadoes arise from thence; for they generally rise first over the Land, and that in a very strange manner; for even from a very small Cloud arising over the top of a *Hill*, I have often seen it increase to such a Bulk, that I have known it rain for two or three Days successively. This I have observed both in the East and West-Indies, and in the South and North-Seas. And 'tis impossible for me to forget how oft I have been disturbed by such small Clouds that appeared in the Night. 'Tis usual with Seamen in those parts to sleep on the Deck, especially for Privateers; among whom I made these Observations. In Privateers, especially when we are at an Anchor, the Deck is spread with Mats to lie on each Night. Every Man has one, some two; and this with a Pillow for the Head and a Rug for a Covering, is all the Bedding that is necessary for Men of that Employ.

I have many times spread my Lodging, when the Evening has promised well, yet have been forced to withdraw before Day; and yet it was not a little Rain that would afright me then; neither at its first coming could I have thought that such a small Cloud could afford so much Rain: And oftentimes both my self and others have been so deceived by the Appearance of so small a Cloud, that thinking the Rain would soon be over, we have lain till we were dropping wet, and then have been forced to move at last. But to proceed.

I have constantly observed, than in the wet season we had more Rain in the Night than in the Day: for tho' it was fair in the Day, yet we seldom escaped having a Tornado or two in the Night. If we had one in the Day, it rose and came away presently, and it may be we had an Hour's Rain, more or less; but when it came in the Night, though there was little Appearance of Rain; yet we should have it three or four Hours together; but this has commonly been nigh the Shore; and we have seen thick Clouds over the Land, and much Thunder and Lightning, and to our Appearance, there was more Rain there than we had; and probably out farther off at Sea, there might be still less: For it was commonly pretty clear that way.

CHAP. VIII

Of Tiaes and Currents

The Difference between Tides and Currents. No Place in the Ocean without Tides. Where the Tides are greatest, and where smallest. Of the Tides in the Harbour and Lagunes of Trist; in the Bay of Campeachy. Of those between the Capes of Virginia. The Tides in the Gulph of St. Michael; and the River of Guiaquil, in the South-Sea. A mistaken Opinion of a Subterranean Communication between the North and South-Seas, under the Isthmus of Darien. Of the Tides at the Gallapagos Islands; at Guam, one of the Ladrones: About Panama; In the Gulph of Dulce and Nicoya River; on the Coast of Peru, in the West-Indies; and at Tonqueen; where, and at New-Holland, they are very irregular. A Guess at the Reason of so great an Irregularity. Of the Tides between the Cape of Good Hope and the Red-Sea. Of Currents. They are influenced by the Trade-Wind. Instances of them at Barbadoes, &c. at Cape La Vela; and Gratia de Dios. Cape Roman. Isle Trinidado, Surinam; Cape Blanco; between Africa and Brazil. Of Counter-Currents. Of Currents in the Bay of Campeachy; and of Mexico; in the Gulph of Florida. Of the Cacuses. No strange thing for the Surface of the Water to run counter to its lower Parts. Of the Currents on the Coast of Angola, East of the Cape of Good Hope: On the Coast of India, North of the Line: And in the South-Sea.

HAVING treated of the Winds and Seasons of the Year in the Torrid Zone, I now come to speak of the Tides and Currents there.

And by the way Note. That,

By Tides I mean Flowings and Ebbings of the Sea, on or off from any Coast. Which Property of the Sea seems to be universal; though not regularly alike on all Coasts, neither as to Time nor the Height of the Water.

By Currents I mean another Motion of the Sea, which is different from Tides in several Respects; both as to its Duration, and also as to its Course.

Tides may be compared to the Sea and Land-Breezes, in respect to their keeping near the Shore; tho' indeed they alternately flow and ebb twice in 24 Hours. Contrarily the Sea-Breezes blow on the Shore by Day, and the Land-Winds off from it in the Night; yet they keep this Course as duly in a manner as the Tides do. Neither are the Tides nor those Breezes far from the Land.

Currents may be compar'd to the Coasting Trade-Winds, as keeping at some farther Distance from the Shore, as the Trade-winds do; and 'tis probable they are much influenced by them.

'Tis a general Belief, especially among Seamen, That the Tides are governed by the Moon: That their Increase and Decrease, as well as their diurnal Motions, are influenced by that Planet; tho' sometimes accidental Causes in the Winds may hinder the true Regularity thereof.

We are taught, as the first Rudiments of Navigation, to shift our Tides; *i.e.* to know the time of full Sea in any Place; which indeed is very necessary to be known by all English Sailors, because the Tides are more regular in our Channel, than in other parts of the World.

But my subject being to speak of the Tides within or near the Tropick, I leave those in places nearer England, to be discoursed on by Coasters, who are the only knowing Men in this Mystery: They having by experience gained more Knowledge in it than others; and that is always the best Master.

I have not been on any Coast in the World, but where the Tides have ebb'd and flow'd, either more or less; and this I have commonly observ'd, that the greatest Indraughts of Rivers or Lagunes, have commonly the strongest Tides. Contrarily such Coasts as are least supplied with Rivers or Lakes have the weakest Tides; at least they are not so perceptible. Where there are great Indraughts either of Rivers or Lagunes, and those Rivers or Lagunes are wide, though the Tide runs very strong into the Mouths of such

Rivers or Lagunes, yet it does not flow so high, as in such Places where the Rivers or Lakes are bounded in a narrow Room, though the Tides do run of an equal strength at the Mouths or Entrances of either. Neither do the Tides flow so much on or about Islands remote from the Main Land, as they do on the Coasts of it.

I shall first give some Instances of these general Observations, and then proceed to Particulars.

The Places that I shall mention shall be such as I have been in my self, and where I have made the Observations before-mentioned; I shall begin with the Lagune of Trist, in the Bay of Campeachy.

This Place is very remarkable, in that it has two Mouths of a considerable bigness; the one is about a Mile and half wide, and about two Mile through, before you come to a Lagune, which is seven or eight Leagues long, and three wide. The other Mouth is 7 Leagues from it, and is about 2 Miles and half, or 3 Miles wide, and about 2 Miles long, before it opens into the Lagune: Besides, farther within Land there are 3 or 4 more Lagunes less than the former.

The Tides that flow or ebb in all the Lagunes pass in or out at the two Mouths before-mentioned, which makes them run very swift, insomuch that the Spaniards have named that great Lagune, Laguna Termina, or the Lake of Tides; because the Tides are so very strong in those two Mouths. Yet, though the Tides do run so swift at the Mouth of the Lagune, they do not rise in height proportionable to that swiftness; for the greatest Tides here do not rise or fall above 6 or 7 Foot, except forced by extraordinary Causes, as Storms, or the like: Of which I have spoken before.

I could also instance in the Channel, between the 2 Capes of Virginia, where the Tides do run very swift; yet the Floods and Ebbs are not proportionable to the swiftness of the Tides between the Capes. There are not indeed such Lagunes, as at Trist in the Bay of Campeachy; but there are many wide Rivers, and abundance of smaller Creeks. Besides, in some places there is low Land, which is over-flown by the Tides; so that all the Water that runs in with such swiftness within the Capes is insensibly swallowed up there.

These are instances of strong Tides, occasioned by great Indraughts; yet where there is but little rising and falling of the Water in comparison with the strength of the Tides at the Mouths of those Indraughts. I shall next give some Instances of the great Indraughts, where the Tides flow and ebb much more than in the former Places; though the Tide at the Mouths of those Indraughts does not run swifter than in those Places before-mentioned.

I shall only mention two Rivers in the South-Sea, that I have taken notice of in my "Voyage round the World," (viz.) the Gulph of St. Michael; and the River of Guiaquil.

In the Gulph of St. Michael there are many large Rivers, which all disembogue into a Lagune of 2 or 3 Leagues wide. This Lagune is barricadoed from the Sea with some small low Mangrovy Islands, and between them are Creeks and Channels, through which the Tides make their daily passes into the Lagune; and from thence into the Rivers, and so back again; many times over-flowing the said Islands, and leaving the tops of the lower Trees above Water.

The Rivers that run into this Lagune are pretty narrow, and bounded on each side with steep Banks, as high as the Floods use to rise, and but very little higher. For at High-water, and on a Spring-tide, the Water is almost, or altogether even with the Land.

The Lagune at the Mouth of the Rivers is but small, neither is there any other way for the Water to force it self into, beside the Lagune and Rivers; and therefore the Tides do rise and fall here 18 or 20 Foot.

The River of Guiaquil, in this respect, is much the same with the Gulph of St. Michael; but the Lagunes near it are larger. Here the Tide rises and falls 16 Foot perpendicular.

I don't know of any other such Places in all the South-Seas; yet there are other large Rivers on the Coast, between these Places; but none so remarkable for high Tides. The great Tides in the Gulph of St. Michael have doubtless been the occasion of that Opinion, which some hold, that there's a subterranean Communication between the N. and the South-Seas; and that the Isthmus of Darien is like an Arched Bridge, under which the Tides make their constant Courses, as duly as they do under London-Bridge. And more to confirm this Opinion some have said, that there are continual and strange Noises made by those Subterranean Fluxes and Refluxes; and that they are heard by the Inhabitants of the Isthmus; and also that Ships sailing in the Bay of Panama are toss'd to and fro at a prodigious rate: Sometimes (say they) they are by the boiling of the Water, dash'd against Islands; and in a moment left dry there, or staved in pieces; at other times they are drawn or suck'd up, as 'twere, in a Whirl-Pool and ready to be carried under Ground into the North-Seas, with all Sails standing. They have said also, that when the Tide flows, especially on a Spring, the Islands in the Bay are all overflown; nay, and even the Country for a great way together: and then nothing is to be seen, but the tops of Trees. But if this were so, 'tis much that I and those that I was with, should not have heard or seen something of it: For I pass'd the Isthmus twice and was 23 Days in the last Trip that I made over it; but yet did I never hear of any Noises under Ground there. I sailed also in the South-Seas (taking in both times that I was there) near 3 Years: and several Months of it I was in the Bay of Panama. And after I went away those of our Crew that remained there, spent a great deal more time in that Bay. Yet did they never meet with such strange Whirl-Pools, but found as pleasant sailing there, as any where in the World. Neither did I ever hear any of the Spaniards or Indians make mention of any such thing in all my Converse with them; which certainly they would have done, if they had ever experienced it, had it been only to terrifie us, and scare us away from their Coasts.

I remember indeed our Country-man Mr. Gage, gives some hints of these strange Currents in this Bay, in his

Book, called, "A New Survey of the West-Indies," from P. 538 to 440, but I am afraid he took most of it upon trust from others; or else he was Sea-sick all that little Voyage: for he gives a very imperfect and lame Account of that Business, as if he understood not what he wrote. I should dislike his whole Book for that one Story's sake, if I did not know that he has written candidly upon other Matters; but I think I have said enough of this: To proceed then.

As to the great Tides, which are reported to be in these Seas, I have given Instances of them, but they are not so great as is reported; neither do they ebb and flow so much any where as in the Gulph of St. Michael only: where indeed they flow over those small low Mangrove Islands, at the Mouth of the Lagune, and leave only the tops of the low Trees above Water; for those Islands are very low, neither do they afford any high Trees. But however, the Islands at the Mouth of the Gulph, before you come to these low ones, are near over-flown; yet are they very small and low, in comparison with other Islands in the Bay of Panama. And indeed should the Islands in that Bay be over-flown, the City of Panama would soon be many Yards under Water. But so far is this from being true, that the Pearl Islands which are very flat and low, are yet never overflown. For there the Tide riseth and falls not above 10 or 11 Foot on a Spring, at the Southermost end of them, which is almost opposite to the Gulph of St. Michael, and not above 12 or 14 Leagues distant from it. And yet there it flows more than it does at or near Panama, or any other Place in the Bay (except just at the Mouths of Rivers) by 2 or 3 Foot. Therefore all that report is wholly groundless.

But to go on.

I have also observed, that Islands lying afar off at Sea, have seldom such high Tides as those that are near the Main, or as any Places on the Main it self; as for example, at the Gallapagos Islands, which lie about 100 Leagues from the Main; the Tides don't rise and fall above a Foot and half, or two Foot, which is less than they do on the

Coast of the Main. For on most Places of the Main it rises and falls 2 or 3 Foot, more or less according as the Coast is more or less exposed to Indraughts or Rivers.

Guam, one of the Ladrone Islands, is also another instance of this. There the Tide riseth not above 2 or 3 Foot at most. In the Bay of Panama the Tides do keep a more constant and regular Course than on other Places on the Coasts of Peru and Mexico; it was for that reason I called them Currents in some Places (mentioned in my "Voyage round the World," as particularly near Guatulco, on the Mexican Continent, in Chap. IX. Page 255) but it was truly a Tide (which there I called a Current) and it sets to the Eastward as the Ebb doth to the West. The Tides there do rise and fall about 5 Foot, as they do on most part of that Coast.

At Rio Leja they rise and fall about eight or nine Foot.

At Amapalla they also rise and fall about 8 or 9 Foot, and the Flood there runs to the East, and the Ebb to the West.

In the Gulph of Dulce and Nicoya River, they rise to 10 or 11 Foot; but on the Coast of Peru they don't rise so high, especially on all the Coast between Cape St. Francis and the River Guiaquil; there the Flood runs to the South, and the Ebb to the North.

At the Island Plata the Tide rises and falls 3 or 4 Foot; but from Cape Blanco, in about 3 d. South, to 30 d. South, the Tides are smaller; there they rise and fall not above a Foot and a half, or 2 Foot. The Flood on this Coast sets to the South, and the Ebb to the North.

In all my Cruisings among the Privateers, I took notice of the Risings of the Tides; because by knowing it, I always knew where we might best haul ashore and clean our Ships: which is also greatly observed by all Privateers.

In most Places of the West-Indies, the Tide flows but little over what it does in our Channel.

In the East-Indies also the Tides are but small on most Coasts, neither are they so regular as with us.

The most irregular Tides that I did ever meet with,

are at Tonqueen in about 20 d. North Latitude, and on the Coast of New-Holland, in about 17 d. South. In both these Places, the neap Tides are scarce discernable. Those of Tonqueen are described at large by Mr. Davenport, who was imployed by Mr. James when he was Chief of the English Factors there, to observe them: And the whole Discourse is published in "The Philosophical Transactions of the Royal Society": whither I refer you.

At New-Holland I had two Months time to observe the Tides. There the Flood runs E. by N. and the Ebb W. by S. And they rise and fall about five Fathom.

In all the Springs that we lay here, the highest were three Days after the Full or Change, and that without any perceptible Cause in the Winds or Weather. I must confess we were startled at it; and though some of us had observed it in the Springs, that happened while we lay on the Sand to clean our Ship, (as I have mentioned in my former Volume, Entituled, "A new Voyage round the World," Ch. XVI. Page 457), yet in that Spring that we designed to haul off, in order to be gone from thence, we did all take more particular Notice of it than in the preceding Springs; for many had not taken notice of it before: And therefore the Major-part of the Company, supposing that it was a Mistake in us who made those former Observations, expected to haul off the Ship the third Tide after the Change; but our Ship did not float then, nor the next Tide neither, which put them all into an Amazement, and a great Consternation too: For many thought we should never have got her off at all, but by digging away the Sand; and so clearing a Passage for her into the Sea. But the sixth Tide cleared all those Doubts; for the Tide then rose so high, as to float her quite up; when being all of us ready to work, we haul'd her off; and yet the next Tide was higher than that, by which we were now all throughly satisfied, that the Tides here do not keep the same time as they do in England.

This I must also observe, That here was no River, nor Lagune, nor any other Indraught on the Land near us, that might occasion these great Tides; tho' 'tis very probable that the great Bending between New-Holland and New-Guinea, may have both Rivers and Lagunes, which may cause these great Tides; or else there may be a Passage of the Sea between both Places; as it is laid down in some Draughts: Or if neither of these, there may be at least a large and deep Sound.

This is the more probable, because of the extraordinary Flood that sets to the East-ward in all that Sea, between New-Holland, and the Islands lying North of it, which we most sensibly perceived, when we were near New-Holland: And such a Tide as this must of Necessity have a greater Indraught than barely a River or Lagune; and 'tis the more likely still, that this Tide should have a Passage through between New-Holland and New-Guinea, or at least a deep Sound there; because it keeps along by the Main, and doth not run in among the Islands to the North of it. And besides, the Northermost Promontory of New-Holland shoots down almost to the Line, which seems to be a Barrier to it on that side; therefore it may in Reason be supposed to have its Passage some other way; but of this guess, I have said enough.

In the Streights of Malacca the Flood sets to the East, and the Ebb to the West.

I have found the Tides at Malacca Town, to rise and fall about six Foot on a Spring. I had the Experience of two Spring-Tides, when I was Captain Minchin's Mate, as is before-mentioned in my Voyage from Achin to Malacca.

On the East-side of the African Coast, between the Cape of Good Hope and the Red-Sea; the Tide keeps its constant Course. The Flood runs to the Southward; the Ebb to the Northward. And at a Spring-tide in the Rivers on that Coast, the Tide rises and falls six Foot, especially in the River of Natal, in Lat. 30 d. South.

I have this Relation from Capt. Rogers, who is a very ingenious Person, and well experienced on that Coast; and is now gone Commander of a small Vessel thither to trade.

Having already largely treated of Tides, I come now to speak somewhat of Currents.

Currents and Tides differ many ways; for Tides run forward, and back again, twice every twenty four Hours: on the contrary Currents run a Day a Week, nay, sometimes more, one way: and then, it may be, run another way.

In some particular Places they run six Months one way, and six Months another.

In other Places they constantly run one way only a day or two, about full Moon, and then they run strong against the former Course; and after that, return the same way again.

In some Places they run constantly one way, and never shift at all.

The Force of Tides is generally felt near the Shore; whereas Currents are at a remote Distance; neither are the Effects of them sensibly discerned by the rising or falling away of the Water as those of the Tides are; for these commonly set along Shore.

'Tis generally observed by Seamen, that in all Places where Trade-winds blow, the Current is influenced by them, and moves the same way with the Winds; but 'tis not with a like Swiftness in all Places; neither is it always so discernable by us in the wide Ocean, as it is near to some Coast; and yet it is not so discernable neither, very near any Coast, except at Capes and Promontories, that shoot far forth out into the Sea; and about Islands also the Effects of them are felt more or less, as they lye in the way of the Trade-Winds.

I shall Instance Barbadoes for one, and all the Caribbees may as well be included.

The greater Islands, as Hispaniola, Jamaica and Cuba have only some particular Capes or Head-Lands, exposed to Currents, as Cape Tiberoon on Hispaniola, Point Pedro, and the N. E. Point of Jamaica, Cape de Cruz, Cape Corientes, and Cape Antonios on Cuba: But of all the Islands in the West-Indies there are none more sensible of Currents than Corrisao and Aruba, nor any Capes on the Continent so remarkable for Currents as Cape Roman, which shoots out against the Sea, between those two Places, as also Cape

Coquibaco and Cape La Vela to Leeward, all three on the same Head-Land, which shoots forth far, without any other Land on the Coast.

There is no such Head-Land till you come to Cape Gratia de Dios, which is about 260 Leagues to Leeward. Indeed to the Eastward there is Land that trends out almost so far, within 150 Leagues of it: (Viz.) The Island Trinidado and the Land against it; and there also are great Currents. But I shall first speak of the Currents between Cape La Vela and Cape Gratia de Dios.

The Currents at Cape La Vela do seldom shift, therefore Ships that ply to Windward to get about it, do not ply near the Shore, but stand off to Sea, till they come in Sight of Hispaniola, and then back again, till within about six or eight Leagues of the Cape, but not nearer. But in the Westerly Wind-Season, which is from October till March, Ships often meet Westerly Winds that last two or three Days with which they may run to the Eastward, without any Trouble.

Between Cape La Vela and Cape Gratia de Dios, the Currents are much different from what they are against the Cape: and this seems to proceed from the Make of the Land; for the Shore between the two Capes, runs into the Southward, making the great Bay: And this Bay affords more Varieties of Winds and Currents, than any one part of the West-Indies besides.

Here, in the Westerly Wind-Season, the Current sets to the Westward constantly; but sometimes stronger than at other times. At about four Leagues off Shore, you find it, and so it continues till you are 20——25,——or 30 Leagues off. Beyond that you meet with an Easterly Wind; and if there is any Current it runs also to the Westward: therefore Ships that are bound to the Westward, must run off to Sea thirty or forty Leagues to get a Wind, or else if they have but a little way to go, they must ply close under the Shore, that so they may anchor when they please: Otherwise they will be carried away to the Eastward, fourteen or sixteen Leagues in a Night's time;

and that too, though they have a faint Easterly Wind, as frequently they meet with, though 'tis the Westerly Wind-Season.

To the East of Cape Roman, as high as the Island Trinidado, you meet only a soaking faint Current, setting to the Westward, except only near such places as shoot out farthest into the Sea, as about the Testegos, which are small Islands lying to Wind-ward of the Island Margarita. Between those Islands and the Main, you meet with a pretty strong Current: therefore it is hard getting to the Eastward there; but on all the Coast, between Cape Roman and the Head-Land, shooting out towards the Testegos, you may ply up with the Land and Sea-Breezes.

From thence, till you come as high as the East-end of Trinidado Isle, you meet with an extraordinary strong Current.

From the East-end of Trinidado, till you come to Surinam, though you meet an Easterly Current, yet 'tis possible to beat it up with the Land and Sea-Breezes.

From Surinam also to Cape Blanco, you may turn it up, though to be sure you'll meet with Currents setting to the West; except near the Full of the Moon; and then on all the Coasts before mentioned, we commonly meet with Currents, setting to the Eastward; at least then it slackens and stands still, if it doth not run to the Eastward. But when you are come as far to the East as Cape Blanco, on the North of Brazil, you meet with a Current always against you; and so from thence Southerly, as far as Cape St. Augustine.

There is no dealing with this Promontory; for it shoots out so far into the Sea, and thereby lies so exposed to the Sea-Breezes and the Currents, that soak down between Africa and Brazil, that it is quite contrary to Reason to think there should not always be a strong Current setting to the N. W.

I have before hinted, That in all Places where the Trade blows, we find a Current setting with the Wind, which is not so perceptible in the wide Sea as nearer the Shores: yet even there the Force of the Winds constantly blowing one way, may, and probably does, move the Surface of the Water along with it.

From hence it may be inferred, that the Southerly Winds on the Coast of Africa, and the true Trade between it and Brazil, gently move the surface of the Sea with it, and the Trade being mostly at S. E. drives the Sea to the Northward, slanting in on the Coast of Brazil; which being there stopp'd by the Land, bends its Course Northerly towards Cape St. Augustine: And after it has doubled that great Promontory, it falls away more gently towards the Coast of Surinam; and from thence towards the West-Indies. For after it has doubled that Promontory, it has more room to spread it self, and thereby becomes weaker in Motion, being agitated by the Trade-winds, which to the North of the Line, we find commonly blowing at E. N. E. and this still bears the Sea slanting down along the Coast to the Westward. And probably 'tis for this Reason, that we find the Current setting strongest near those Head-Lands before-mentioned. Whereas at Barbadoes, and other of the Caribbee-Islands, we find only a soaking Current, such as seems to arise only from the Constancy of the Trade-winds blowing there, and not from an Original Current, from the South-part of the Atlantick: which, as I said before, doubles about Cape St. Augustine, and so coasts along pretty nigh the Shore.

The Currents about the Island Trinidado, and at Currisao and Aruba as also between them and Cape Roman seem to indicate as much. The Currents also between Cape Roman, and Cape La Vela indicate the same.

From Cape La Vela the Currents set still to the Westward, towards Cape Gratia de Dios; but in a direct Line, and not borrowing or slanting in towards the Shore. For, as I said before, it is a large Bay, and Currents commonly set from one Head-Land to another; so that Bays have seldom any; or if they have, they are only Counter-Currents. And these Counter-Currents too do set from one Point to another, without interfering with the little Bays between. And 'tis also very probable that these Counter-Currents, such as we meet with in this Bay, in their Seasons, after they have surrounded the Bay, and are got as far to the East as Cape La Vela, wheel off there, and turn about again with the Stream to the Westward, like an Eddy in a River.

From Cape Gratia de Dios the Current sets away N. W. towards Cape Catoch, and so passes away to the Northward, between Cape Catoch on Jucatan, and Cape Antonio on Cuba.

In the Channel between those two Capes, we commonly find a strong Current setting to the Northward: And here I have found them extraordinary strong.

On the North-side of Jucatan, as you pass into the Bay of Campeachy, you meet with a small soaking Current to the Westward, even down to the bottom of the Bay of Mexico; but on the North-side of the Bay of Mexico the Current sets to the Eastward: And 'tis probable that is the reason, that the Spaniards, coming from La Vera Cruz, keep that shore aboard. And 'tis as probable that the Current, which sets to Leeward, on all the Coast from Cape St. Augustine to Cape Catoch, never enters the Bay of Mexico; but bends still to the Northward, till 'tis check'd by the Florida shore; and then wheels about to the East, till it comes nearer the Gulph's Mouth, and there joyning with the soaking Current that draws down on the North-sides of Hispaniola and Cuba, passes altogether with great strength through the Gulph of Florida, which is the most remarkable Gulph in the World for its Currents; because it always sets very strong to the North. Yet near the shores on each side this Gulph, there are Tides, especially on the Florida shore; and Ships may pass which way they please, if they are acquainted.

It has formerly been accounted very dangerous to meet with a North in this Gulph; and for that Reason our Jamaica Ships to avoid them, have rather chosen to go to the Eastward, and pass through the Cacuses[1] in the Season that the Norths do blow. The Cacuses are Sands that lye off the N. W. end of Hispaniola. Those that went from

[1] Caicos.

Port-Royal in Jamaica had good Reason for this; for if a North took them at their going out, it would help them forward in their way, which, should they have been going towards the Gulph, it would obstruct them. Then besides, if a North take a Ship in the Gulph, the Wind blowing against the Current makes an extraordinary Sea, and so thick come the Waves one after another that a Ship can't possibly live in it; yet of late they go through at all times of the Year, and if a North takes them in the Gulph, they put away right before the Wind and Sea, with a small Head-Sail; yet the Current is then as strong or stronger then at other times; and forces them back, stern foremost against both Wind and Sea: For tho' the surface of the Sea is raised in Waves and driven violently with the Winds to the Southward, yet the Current underneath runs still to the Northward; neither is it any strange thing to see two different Currents at one place and time, the superficial Water running one way, and that underneath running a quite contrary: For sometimes at an Anchor, I have seen the Cable carryed thus by two different Streams, the under part having been doubled one way, and the upper part the contrary. But 'tis certain, in all other parts of the World, the Current shifts at certain times of the Year; As in the East-Indies they run from East to West one part of the Year, and from West to East the other part: Or as in the West-Indies and Guinea, where they shift only near a Full Moon. This is meant of parts of the Sea near any Coast; yet there are strong Currents in the wide Ocean also, setting contrary to the Rules before-going: I mean against the Trade; but 'tis not common.

On the Coast of Guinea the Current sets East, except at or near a full Moon; but to the South of the Line from Loango, to 25 or 30 d. the Current sets with the Wind from S. to N. except near the Full.

To the Eastward of the Cape of good Hope, from 30 d. South, to 24 d. South, the Currents from May till Oct. set E. N. E. and the Winds then are at W. S. W. or S. W. but from Oct. till May, when the Winds are between the E. N. E. and E. S. E. the Currents run to the West.

These Currents are thus found from 5 or 6 Leagues off the shore to about 50. Within 5 Leagues off the Shore you have the Tide, and not a Current; and being past 50 Leagues off Shore, the Current either ceaseth quite, or is imperceptible.

On the Coast of India, North of the Line, the Current sets with the Monsoon, but does not shift altogether so soon, sometimes not by 3 Weeks or more, and then never shifts again till after the Monsoon is settled in the contrary way. As for Example, the West Monsoon sets in the middle of April, but the Current does not shift till the beginning of May: So when the East Monsoon sets in about the middle of September, the Current does not shift till October.

In the South-Seas on the Coast of Peru, the Current sets from South to North, even from 30 d. to the Line, and to 3 or 4 d. North of it.

At the Gallapagos Islands we found a soaking Current, not very strong, but so strong that a Ship could get very little by turning; and 'tis probable that nearer the Main, they are stronger because of the constant Southerly Winds.

The most remarkable Places for Currents in the South-Seas; are Cape St. Francis, Cape Passao, Cape St. Laurence and Cape Blanco. This last has commonly very strong Currents setting to the N. W. which hinders Ships mightily; and the more because it is a very windy place; so that many times Ships are not able to carry their Top-sails; and then it is but bad plying to Windward against a Current. I had not so much Experience of the Mexican Coast, because we commonly kept within the Verge of the Tides. But on the Coast of Guatamala, in the Lat. of 12 d. 50 m. and 13 d. we had a Current setting S. W. and it is probable that there also the Current sets with the Winds. For, as it is before noted, the Currents on all Coasts sets as the coasting Trade does.

And thus have I finished what my own Experience, or Relations from my Friends, have furnished me with on this useful Subject of Winds, Tides, Currents, &c. which I humbly offer, not as a compleat and perfect Account, but as a rude and imperfect Beginning or Specimen of what may better be done by abler Hands hereafter. And I hope this may be useful so far as to give a few Hints to direct the more accurate Observation of others.

The following Paper, containing a short Description of a part of Africk that is not well known to Europeans, I thought would not be unacceptable to the curious Reader. I have therefore annexed it, as I received it from my ingenious Friend Capt. Rogers, who is lately gone to that Place: and hath been there several times before.

THE Country of Natal takes about 3 d. and half of Lat. from N. to S. lying between the Lat. of 31 d. 30 m. South and 28 N. 'Tis bounded on the S. by a Country inhabited by a small Nation of Savage People, called by our English, Wild-bush Men, that live in Caves and in Holes of Rocks, and have no other Houses, but such as are formed by Nature: They are of a low Stature, tauny-colour'd, with crisped Hair: They are accounted very cruel to their Enemies. Their Weapons are Bows and Poisoned Arrows. These People have for their Neighbours on the S. the Hottantots. Dellagoa is a Navigable River in Lat. 28. S. that bounds Natal on the N. The Inhabitants of this River have a Commerce with the Portuguese of Mozambique, who oft visit them in small Barks, and trade there for Elephants Teeth; which they have great Plenty. Some English too have lately been there to purchase Teeth, particularly Capt. Freak,[1] just mention'd in my former Volume, Ch. 18, P. 494, who after he had been in the River of Dellagoa, and purchased 8 or 10 Tun of Teeth, lost his Ship on a Rock near Madagascar. The Country of Natal lies open to the Indian Sea on the East, but how far back it runs to the Westward is not yet known.

That part of the Country which respects the Sea is plain Champion and woody; but within Land it appears more uneven, by reason of many Hills which rise in unequal Heights above each other. Yet it is interlaced with pleasant Valleys and large Plains, and 'tis checker'd with Natural Groves and Savannahs. Neither is there any want of Water; for every Hill affords little Brooks, which glide down several ways; some of which after several Turnings and Windings, meet by degrees and make up the River of Natal, which dischargeth it self into the East-Indian Ocean in the Lat. of 30 d. South. There it opens pretty wide and is deep enough for small Vessels. But at the Mouth of the River is a Bar which has not above ten or eleven Foot Water on it in a Spring-tide; though within there is Water enough. This River is the Principal of the Country of Natal, and has been lately frequented by some of our English Ships particularly by a small Vessel that Captain Rogers, formerly mentioned, commanded.

[1] Commander of the *Ann* of London.

There are also other Streams and Rivers, which bend their Courses Northerly, especially one of a considerable Bigness about 100 Mile within Land, and which runs due North.

The Woods are composed of divers sorts of Trees; many of which are very good Timber, and fit for any uses, they being tall and large. The Savannahs also are cloathed with kindly thick Grass.

The Land-Animals of this Country are Lyons, Tygers, Elephants, Buffaloes, Bullocks, Deer, Hogs, Conies, &c. Here are also Abundance of Sea-Horses.

Buffaloes and Bullocks only are kept tame, but the rest are all wild.

Elephants are so plenty here that they feed together in great Troops; 1000 to 1500 in a Company; Mornings and Evenings they are seen grazing in the Savannahs, but in the Heat of the Day, they retire into the Woods, and they are very peaceable if not molested.

Deer are very numerous here also. They feed quietly in the Savannahs among the tame Cattle, for they are seldom disturbed by the Natives.

Here are Fowls of divers sorts; some such as we have in England, viz. Duck and Teal, both tame and wild: and plenty of Cocks and Hens. Besides Abundance of wild Birds, wholly unknown to us.

Here are a sort of large Fowls as big as a Peacock, which have many fine coloured Feathers. They are very rare and shy.

There are others like Curlews, but bigger. The flesh of these is black, yet sweet and wholesome Meat.

The Sea and Rivers also do abound in Fish of divers Sorts; yet the Natives do but seldom endeavour to take any, except Tortoises; and that is chiefly when they come ashore in the Night to lay their Eggs. Though they have also another very odd way, which they sometimes make use of to catch Turtle or Tortoises. They take a living sucking Fish or Remora, and fastning a couple of strings to it, (one at the Head and the other at the Tail) they let the sucking Fish down into the Water on the Turtle Ground, among the half-grown or young Turtle: and when they find that the Fish hath fastned himself to the back of a Turtle, as he will soon do, they then draw him and the Turtle up together: This way of Fishing (as I have heard) is also used at Madagascar.

The Natives of this Country are but of a middle Stature, yet have very good Limbs: The Colour of their Skins is black; their Hair crisped: they are oval visaged: their Noses neither flat nor high, but very well proportioned: their Teeth are white, and their Aspect is altogether graceful.

They are nimble People, but very lazy: which probably is for want of Commerce. Their chief Employment is Husbandry. They have a great many Bulls and Cows, which they carefully look after; for every Man knows his own, though they run all promiscuously together in their Savannahs, yet they have Pens near their own Houses, where they make them gentle and bring them to the Pail. They also Plant Corn, and fence in their Fields to keep out all Cattle as well tame as wild. They have Guinea Corn, which is their Bread; and a small sort of Grain no bigger than Mustardseed, with which they make their Drink.

Here are no Arts nor Trades professed among them, but every one makes for himself such Necessaries, as Need or Ornament requires, the Men keeping to their Employment, and the Women to theirs.

The Men build Houses, Hunt, Plant, and do what is to be done abroad. And the Women Milk the Cows, dress the Victuals, &c. and manage all Matters within Doors. Their Houses are not great nor richly furnished; but they are made close and well thatched, that neither Winds nor Weather can hurt them.

They wear but few Cloaths, and those extraordinary mean. The men go in a manner naked, their common Garb being only a square piece of Cloath made with Silk-Grass, or Moho-Rind, and wrought in form of a short Apron. At the upper Corners it has two straps to tye round their Wastes; and the lower-end being finely fringed with the same hangs down to their Knees.

They have Caps made with Beef Tallow of about nine or ten Inches high. They are a great while of making these Caps; for the Tallow must be made very pure, before 'tis fit for this use. Besides they lay on but a little at a time and mix it finely among the Hair; and so it never afterwards comes off their Heads. When they go a hunting, which is but seldom, they pare off three or four Inches from the top of it, that so it may fit the snugger; but the next Day they begin to build it up again, and so they do every Day till 'tis of a decent and fashionable height.

It would be a most ridiculous thing for a Man here to be seen without a Tallow-Cap. But Boys are not suffered to wear any, till they come to Maturity; and then they begin to build upon their Heads. The Women have only short Petticoats, which reach from the Waste to the Knee. When it rains they cover their Bodies with a simple Cows-hide, thrown over their Shoulders like a Blanket.

The common Subsistence of these People is Bread made of Guinea Corn, Beef, Fish, Milk, Ducks, Hens, Eggs, &c. They also drink Milk often to quench their Thirst: and this sometimes when it is sweet, but commonly they let it be sower first.

Besides Milk, which is the common Drink, they make a better sort of the same Grain before mentioned, purposely to be merry with. And when they meet on such Occasions, the Men make themselves extraordinary fine, with Feathers stuck into their Caps very thick. They make use of the long Feathers of Cocks Tails, and none else.

Besides these Head-Ornaments they wear a piece of Cow-hide, made like a Tail, and 'tis fastened behind them as a Tail, reaching from their Waste to the Ground. This piece of Hide is about six Inches broad, and each side of it is adorned with little Iron Rings of their own making.

When they are thus attired, their Heads a little intoxicated and the Musick playing, they'll skip about merrily, and shake their Tails to some purpose; but are very innocent in their Mirth.

Every man may have as many Wives as he can purchase and maintain: And without buying here are none to be had: neither is there any other Commodity to be bought or sold but Women.

Young Virgins are disposed of by their Fathers, Brothers, or nearest Male Relations. The price is according to the Beauty of the Damsel.

They have no Money in this Country, but give Cows in exchange for Wives: And therefore he is the richest Man that has most Daughters or Sisters: for to be sure he will get Cattle enough.

They make merry when they take their Wives; but the Bride cries all her Wedding Day. They live together in small Villages, and the oldest Man governs the rest; for all that live together in one Village are a-kin, and therefore willingly submit to his Government.

They are very just and extraordinary civil to Strangers; This was remarkably experienced by two English Seamen that lived among them five Years; their Ship was cast away on the Coast, and the rest of their Consorts marched to the River of Dellagoa; but they stayed here till Captain Rogers accidentally came hither and took them away with him: They had gained the Language of the Country: and the Natives freely gave them Wives and Cows too. They were beloved by all the People, and so much reverenced that their Words were taken as Laws. And when they came away, many of the Boys cried because they would not take them with them.

FINIS

LETTERS AND PAPERS RELATING TO THE NEW HOLLAND VOYAGE

(Abridged from the Originals in the Public Record Office)

CAPTAIN DAMPIER'S PROPOSALS OF HIS PROCEEDING ON THE INTENDED VOYAGE. N. D. *Autograph.*

1. My Lord,—Your L^{d}ship has been pleased to order me to make a proposal of some voyage wherein I might be serviceable to my Nation. I know there are several places which might probably be visited with good Advantage: but as there is no larger Tract of Land hitherto undiscovered yn ye *Terra Australis* (if that vast space surrounding ye South Pole, and extend so far into ye warmer Climate be a continued Land, as a great deal of it is known to be) so 'tis reasonable to conceive yt so great a part of the World is not without very valluable commodities to incourage ye Discovery, and great variety of ym according to ye various Latitudes in wh such Countreys are seated, whether they be contenent or island; and of much ye same kindes; probably, as are produced in Countryes of *Asia, Africk,* or *America* of ye same Latitudes. An attempt upon ye unknown Tracts of yt part of ye World, has y^{e} to recommend it, yt none of our European Neighbours can think themselves injured thereby: nor shall we need to interfere with any of ym even in ye passage thither, wheather ye Discovery be made towards ye East or West of ye meridian there being a clear Ocean either way.

And for such a Discovery as this I may be more particularly qualified by reason of ye experience I have already gained in former Voyages; the Scean of which has lain much among unknown shores and savage nations. If I be pitched on for an Expedition of this kinde I would desire to have a Commission as unlimited as might be wth respect either to *Time* or *Place*: for in so long a Voyage and an attempt so full of difficulties, 'tis impossible to foresee a thousand Accidents w^{h} may require ye goeing somewhat aside from ye Principall Designe; and may at the same time offer a yet more valuable Opertunity of some Collaterall Discovery. I would desire but 2 Vessels well provided of all necessaries: and considering ye Temptations our Seamen have had of late [1] to break loose and turn pirate when they come into ye nither parts of ye World I should be glad yt some good encouragement might be proposed to those whoe should goe in this Voyage upon their return. But these things and other necessary Circumstances I

[1] Perhaps alluding to the exploits of the pirate Avery, who deposed his Captain and ran away with the ship at about this time.

would leave to yor Lordships further consideration, if in the meantime the Expedition it self be approved of: and as to yt alsoe and ye particulars relating to it I may be better able to satisfie your L^{d}ship by word of mouth. (No signature, no endorsement.)

2. My Lord,—I formerly acquainted yor L^{d}ship that the Discovery I would chuse to goe uppon should be to ye remoter part of the *East India Islands* and the neighbouring Coast of *Terra Australis*, and that for this purpose I would be furnished with two small Ships, a Commission as unlimmetted as might be, and the Seamen assured of good Incouragement upon their return etc.: I cannot expect to return to England in less than three yeares, therefore it would not only be convenient to carry out as much provision as is possible in our own Ship, but it would be well if those Ships also that are to return again after the expedition is over should carry some provision extraordinary purposely for us as much at least as would last us six monethes: there is indeed good store of Beef at *Madagascar*, if the Pirats have not made it scarce and dear, and we might expect to live on fresh meat while wee are there and salt som if we should have ocasion. And if we may be suplyed either with *English* provision out of our own Squadron or els with beef and rice from *Madagascar*. I should (runn, or range) [1] over directly from thence to the northermost part of *New Holland* where I would water if I had occasion, and from thence I would range toward *New Guinnia*. There are many islands in that sea between *New Holland* and *New Guinnia* which are not frequented by any Europeans, and it is probable that we may light upon some or other that are not without Spice; should I meet with nothing on any of these Islands I would range along the Main of *New Guinia* to see what that aforded; and from thense I would cross over to the East side of the *Island Gilolo* where I may be informed of the state of these parts by the Natives who speak the *Malaian* language: From Gilolo I would range away to the Eastward of *New Guinia* and so direct my course southerly coasting by the land, and where I found a harbour or river I would land and seek about for men and other Animals, Vigetables, Mineralls, etc., and haveing made what discovery I could I would (two words erased) return home by the way of Terra del fuego.

This is the course I would take if I can be suplyed with provision from ye Squadron or from *Madagascar*; But if I should be forced to goe to any of ye Factoryes in *India* to recruit and victuall; *Fort St. George* (Madras) is the place where we may best be provided with beef and porke, if I might touch there without any troublesome examination, and as for rice I could supply myself with that in my way. From *Fort St. George* I must pass the Streights of *Malacca* and then I would stretch to the Eastward as far as the *Bashee Islands* where I could furnish myself with pork which must be purchased with iron, from thence I would sail to the East of *Luconia* and all the *Philipine Islands* and soe to *Meangis Island*, and from thence I would bend my cours toward *New Guinnia* and *Terra Australis*, and soe home as before, this is much the longer way;

If I should happen to come where Spice is to be had it must be purchased with East India comodityes (viz.) long cloath, Chints, Ginghams

[1] Word illegible.

etc: The Europe comodityes y^{t} I should want in this voyage is chiefly iron barrs besides axes, hatchetts, knives etc. and alsoe beads, looking glasses, and such like toyes all which are coveted as well by people used to trade as by others.

(No signature. Autograph throughout. Endorsed Capt Dampier's Proposals of his Proceeding on his intended Voyage.)

On the 30th June, 1698, Dampier wrote a hurried scrawl to the Secretaries "to ye Rt hon^{ble} the Lords of the Admiralty," telling them that he had been on board the *Jolly Prize*, and had strictly surveyed her; but did not think her "any way fitt for the service intended"; adding that he meant to return to town "to give my Lords further satisfaction in this affair."

July 6, 1698. A note to the Secretary to the Lords Commissioners of the Admiralty saying that he had viewed the *Jolly Prize*, and "found her altogether unfitt," she "being so small that she cannot stow provisions enough for such number of men as will be required to navigate her, neither is their convenience in her for many Lodgings and other accommodations."

Treasury Chambers, Customs, 12, *f*. 448: *W$^{m.}$ Dampier's salary to be paid during his absence.* "After our hearty Comendacons Whereas W$^{m.}$ Dampier has Represented unto us That he is an Extraor^{dy} Land Carriage Man in ye Port of London and is Ordered to Sea upon publick Service, And therefore prayed his sallary may be continued and paid to his Wife, Which request We being willing to comply wth, These are to pray and require you to cause the Sallary of ye S^{d} W$^{m.}$ Dampier to be continued for him on ye Establishment and paid quarterly to his Assignes notwithstanding his intended absence for which this shall be your Warr^{t}.

"(Initialled) C. M. J.S. T. L.

"Cockpitt Treasy Chamb^{rs} 16th Aug '98."

August 27, 1698. A letter to the same stating that the master appointed to the *Roebuck* was "a very Old man and therefore incapable of performing so long a voyage," whereas "one Jno Knight Gun^{r} of ye *Dunwich*" would be "very fitt for ye said Employ." He asks that the said Knight may be discharged from the *Dunwich*. "The Ship (the *Roebuck*) is now almost rigged, and I expect the Carp^{rs} will have done aboard her this day, and shall be in a readiness to take in provision so soon as we have gott our Iron ballast. I have gott fourty Six men." *Letter in the clerk's hand.*

(Signed) *W$^{m.}$ Dampier.*

September 1698. A letter to the same, complaining that the complement allowed for the *Roebuck* ("being but fifty") will not be sufficient; but that "Seventy men and about twenty guns" would enable them "to make some defence in caice of any opposition." *Letter in a clerk's hand. Ink very pale.*

(Signed) *W$^{m.}$ Dampier.*

September 5, 1698. To My Lord (Orford?) Dampier has now "gott" his fifty men; but still thinks them too few, and therefore hopes his Lordship will continue his care "and order me seventy men and 20 Guns." The master he desired (John Knight) "is come to town in order to be examin'd." "The Carp[rs] have allmost done their work aboard and I hope to have in my Iron ballast and some Provision this week," at anyrate "I shall use all diligence to be goeing." *Letter in clerk's hand.*

(Signed) *W[m]. Dampier.*

September 15, 1698. "*Roebuck*" *at Deptford.* To the Secretary of the Admiralty. Dampier will observe his direction touching officers' servants. The ship still wants some iron work, and Dampier awaits instructions as to the taking in of sea provisions before dropping down the river. He has got his complement of men. *Clerk's letter.* (Signed) *W[m]. Dampier.*

September 22, 1698. "*Roebuck,*" *Deptford.* To the same. Acknowledges receipt of an order of the 16th instant, "touching Mareen Souldiers," which Dampier will "take care to comply with so soon" as he has any of them on board. He has taken in ten tunns of sea beer, most of his boatswains' and carpenter's stores, is now filling his water, and awaits the rest of his provision. "The wind is at W.S.W." *Clerk's hand. Dampier's signature.*

September 27, 1698. To the same. Reminds the Secretary how the Lords of the Admiralty had been pleased ("upon my menconing the Lowness of my present circumstances") to promise they would order him some money for the contingencies of his intended voyage. Asks that their Lordships be reminded of this, and acquainted that "a hundred pound" will be required. Is "allmost ready to fall down ye river" having all his beer and water aboard. Has been promised that by Thursday he will have "a proportion of other provision for 12 months." *Letter in clerk's hand.*

(Signed) *W[m]. Dampier.*

October 1, 1698. "*Roebuck,*" *Deptford.* To the Secretary. Acknowledges letter of the 29th inst., containing orders "for my sayling to the Hope and thence to the Downes." Will obey "so soon as the ship shall be in a condition." Has "gott aboard all the Beer and water casque and beef and pork for twelve months." Expects "the other species" daily. Can stow some eight months' more provision. Returns humble thanks to their Lordships "for their care of me in ordering the Navy Board to Imprest me an hundred pound for the contingencies on my Voyage." Hopes he will answer their Lordships' expectation. *Letter in clerk's handwriting.*

(Signed) *W[m]. Dampier.*

NOTE.—The orders "for my sayling" may be seen in Adm. Sec. Out-Letters, 25, p. 147.

October 6, 1698. "*Roebuck*" *in the Hope.* Advises the Honourable Board that this day "between eleven and twelve a clock we sett sail from Deptford" and are now got safe here. Has sent his gunner for his guns and stores, and his purser for his eight months' provision. Hopes to have all aboard in three days and will then proceed to the Downs. He has all his men aboard and sea provision for twelve months. (Signed) *Wm Dampier.*

October 12, 1698. "*Roebuck*" *in the Hope.* To the same. Has been awaiting his guns ever since his letter of the 6th; but owing to the blowing weather has only just received them. "My Gunner is getting down our Powder, etc." This evening the ship *Isabella*, "lying about half a mile above us weighed, but before she could get her anchor up, the strength of the tide forced her aboard of us. Some part of the Cuttwater, the sprit topmast and yard, and ye railes on the Quarter Deck, have been destroyed. Will repair as soon as possible. (Signed) *W^m. Dampier.*

"*Postscript.*—Will have the ship surveyed if their Lorps. think fitt."

W. D.

October 18, 1698. *In the Hope.* To the same. Asks that an allowance of Dr. Cockburn's Electuary against Dysenteries be sent to him in the Downs. Will be ready to sail to-morrow; fair frosty weather.

(Signed) *W^m. Dampier.*

October 21, 1698. "*Roebuck*" *in the Downs.* To the same. Reports safe arrival in the Downs, where he awaits further orders.

(Signed) *W^m. Dampier.*

October 29, 1698. *In the Downs.* To the same. Acknowledges promise of a supply of Dr. Cockburn's medicine, and states that the promised Carpenter has not yet arrived. His boatswain, Robert Warren, is unwilling to go on the voyage. Hopes he may have another in his stead, "for I should be very sorry to carry any with me that are not very free and willing to it." Has one man sick ashore. (Signed) *W^m. Dampier.*

A postscript notes arrival of vessels.

November 7, 1698. *In the Downs.* To the same. Sir Cloudesley Shovel's squadron sailed hence yesterday for Holland. Has hoisted the broad pendant, being the only King's ship in the Road. Hopes Sir Cloudesley "has made his report to their Lorps. of the sufficiency of ye men I have entered, and am sorry that any ill affected person should have informed their Lorps. that I had entertained any not Serviceable."

(Signed) *W^m. Dampier.*

November 13, 1698. *In the Downs.* To the same. Has taken in twelve butts of beer in lieu of that he has expended. Has endeavoured to execute a writ of State upon the body of Capt. Richard Stratton, commander of the ship *Josiah* now lying in this Road. Sent his lieutenant aboard the *Josiah*, but failed to find Capt. Stratton. Presumes that a new carpenter and boatswain will soon arrive aboard. *Clerk's hand.*

(Signed) *W^m. Dampier.*

November 17, 1698. *In the Downs.* To the same. The new carpenter has come aboard, "but no other Boatswⁿ." The present boatswain is "very negligent," and has disobeyed the lieutenant's orders. Only yesterday the yeoman of his store-room was caught selling "about seventy pound of Rope yarns" to a shore boat. "He said the Boatswⁿ had given him leave so to doe." "Boatswⁿ is now confined to his Cabbin." He hopes that the Admiralty will be pleased to rid him of this officer who, he believes, is very mutinously inclined. (Signed) *Wᵐ· Dampier.*

A postscript suggests that John Knight, chief master's mate, be appointed boatswain. "He is very well qualified for it, and a sober carefull man."

Letter enclosed from Robert Warren, the offending Boatswain. Warren admits that he has "Cometted an Earrer, and humbly Bags Captain Dampier's pardon and likewise the Leftenants. Hopes that what messe-undarstanding thare is in this Besnes he will be pleased for to Judge Charetteabell, and not wilfully go for to Reueing a famely. Remains his sarvant to Command Whills. *Robert Warren* (17 *Nov.* 1698)." He was tried aboard H.M.S. *Plymouth* on December 1, 1698, and sentenced to be dismissed his ship and "rendered uncapable of his Majᵗˢ. Service for the future." Robert Eddlington, his yeoman, was acquitted.

November 21, 1698. *In the Downs.* To the same. Acknowledges letter of the 19th. Has sent the offending boatswain (with the evidence) aboard the Commander-in-Chief in the Medway. Has had rough weather, so that the boatswain's stores have not been surveyed. "So soon as We have moderate Weather I shall over hawle them." (Signed) *Wᵐ· Dampier.*

To the Rt. Hon. the Earl of Orford, first Commissioner for executing the Office of Lord High Admiral of England. Has had a letter from Mr. Burchet asking "what I would propose to have put into my Instructions." Has answered that he had once hoped "to have been goeing out of England by ye midle of September," in which case he would have sailed round the Horn and fallen in with Terra Australis on the E. coast, and coasted northward along it till he came to New Guinea. He hints his regrets at having no more men allowed him. It is now too late in the year to go round the Horn. He will have to go round the Cape. He has desired that his Instructions may be as unlimited as possible, so that he may alter his course if need arise. He asks that he may be permitted to take aboard some natives, "in case I shall see any probability of a Comerce with them." Thinks he ought to have a supply of "Iron barrs, with some axes, hatchets, matcheats, etc., and some other trifles, as looking glasses, beads, etc., to deal with the Pore natives." He asks that if any of his hands prove mutinous he may be allowed to take in more, or exchange them with any of His Majesty's or subjects' ships. Thinks that a small gratuity, or even a "promise of somewhat at our return" would raise the spirits of his crew "to a generous resolution of hazarding their persons." Hopes their Lordships will pardon him if he has been "to bould" in his demands. He is "much a stranger to his Majesty's service," but he will comply with his Instructions "in ye strictest sense." Has had trouble with his boatswain, but expects a new man daily. *Autograph throughout.* (Signed) Your Lorps. most oblidged humble servnt, (Signed) *Wm. Dampier.*

Postscript.—I expected before this time to have presented your Lordship with the second part of my Voyages, but the gentleman that I employed to compile an Index has occasioned the delay, but I hope in ten days' time it will be finished. (Signed) *Wm. Dampier.*

A copy of this letter (wanting the postscript and other personal details) was sent by Dampier to the Secretary of the Admiralty on November 21, 1698.

Dampier's Instructions (Record Office, Adm. Sec. Out-Letters, 25) are dated November 30, 1698, and signed H. P(riestman), G. R(ussell), and J. K(endall).

They direct him to proceed to the Cape of Good Hope, "and from thence to stretch away towards New Holland, and then to New Guinea and Terra Australis." They give him permission "to steer any other Course" if he see fit; but remind him that the King has been at great charge in fitting out the expedition, and that he must "take especial care" to use his best endeavours to discover any "such things" as may tend to the good of the Nation. He is to take specimens of the produce of the lands at which he touches. He is to bring home "some of the Natives, provided they shall be willing to come along." He has been supplied with trifles with which to trade with the natives.

If any of his men should die, or prove disorderly, he is empowered to draw fresh hands from any King's ship he may meet with. Any mutinous and disorderly hands may be discharged aboard any King's ship he may meet with, and "the Comander of any such Shipp or Vessell of his Ma'y is hereby required to take them on board and give you other Men in their Roome." At the same time, he is to make it publicly known to all the officers and men of the *Roebuck* "that such of them as shall behave them-selves well, and Cheerfully performe their Duty in this Affaire, which 'tis hoped may tend to the advantage of the Nation, shall at their returne receive all fitting reward and Encouragement."

During the voyage he is to keep an "Exact Journall" of his proceedings, and of all things remarkable. At his return this journal is to be given to the honourable board "and to no other." He is to conform to the "Generall Printed Instructions annexed to his Comission, except as to what relates to the Journall as aforesaid." When he shall find that he can make no further discovery for the good of the nation, he is not to stay abroad; but to return to Plymouth for orders. If no orders lie there, he is to proceed to the Downs, from whence he shall send the Board an account of his proceedings. He is always to take especial care not to annoy the King's subjects or allies, "but rather to give them what assistance he can."

Lastly, "for the better lengthening out his Provisions, he is to put the men under his Comand (when he comes out of the Channell) to six to four Men's allowance, assureing them that they shall be punctually paid for the same at the end of the Voyage."

November 24, 1698. *In the Downs.* To the Secretary. A letter acknowledging other letters, and recapitulating former statements. The new boatswain (Norwood) has arrived aboard, and his stores are being surveyed. Two men are sick ashore, and five have gone to Robert Warren's court-martial. The wind is at W. by S., blowing weather.

(Signed) *Wm. Dampier.*

December 1. *In the Downs*. To the same. About £20 will equip him with Trifles, such as looking-glasses, beads, &c. Desires that he may have six dozen of hatchets, six dozen of axes, and eight dozen of matchetts. One man sick ashore. (Signed) *Wm. Dampier.*

December 2. *In the Downs*. To the same. Has received his sailing orders, but thinks that he cannot be required to sail without his Trifles and axes; and without the five men at the court-martial, one of whom is his lieutenant. (Signed) *Wm. Dampier.*

December 7, 1698. *In the Downs*. To the same. Acknowledges their Lordships' bounty in the matter of the trifles, hatchets, &c. With those aboard he would be ready to sail. (Signed) *Wm. Dampier.*

December 6, 1698. *In the Downs*. To the same. Has received the axes, hatchetts and macheatts and £20, with which to purchase Trifles. Has bought the latter and "now am ready to Sayle." He waits a fair wind. (Signed) *Wm. Dampier.*

December 31, 1698. *In the Downs*. To the same. Is now unmooring in order to sail; "having the wind att N.W. by N."

(Signed) *Wm. Dampier.*

January 9, 1698/9. *In the Downs*. To the same. While unmooring on the 31st last, the wind changed to S.S.W. "before we could heave up our Anchor." The wind has been westerly ever since.

(Signed) *Wm. Dampier.*

January 30, 98/9. *In St. Cruce barbour in the Island Teneriff*. To the Lords of the Admiralty. Advises the Board that on Saturday the 14th inst., he sailed from the Downs. Has had fair winds ever since. Has anchored to buy wine, but finds none fit to keep. Will sail hence to-morrow. All hands well. Sends this by "Captn. Trever of his Majtie. ship the *Experiment*, bound for Cadiz, who is now under Sayle."

(Signed) *Wm. Dampier.*

January 31, 1698/9. *In St. Cruce barbour*. To the same. A copy of the above letter "committed to the care of Mr. Hopper, an English merchant of this island, to be transmitted by the first ship bound for England." Little news here "save that several Sally rovers have lately been seen off these islands." (Signed) *Wm. Dampier.*

(Note.—He left Santa Cruz on February 4th.)

February 10, 1698, *O.S.* *At Anchor in the English roade of the Isla Maya.* To the same. Arrived here the 11th inst., for salt. Is ready to sail for St. Jago for water. Tells of the English ships in the Road, some of which sailed with him from the Downs. Sends this by Capt. Gwin. "I thank God all very healthy." (Signed) *Wm. Dampier.*

February 19, 1699, *O.S.* *Att St. Jago.* To the same. Has come hither for water. Letter a résumé of the two preceding letters. Expects to be gone hence in two days. (Signed) *Wm. Dampier.*

April 22nd, 1699, *O.S.* *In Bahia barbr. on ye Coast of Brasile.* To the same. Sailed from St. Jago on 21st February, arrived here March 25th. Has scrubbed, caulked and watered, and is now ready to sail. Discusses the quantity and condition of the provisions remaining to him, and the manner in which they have been (and will be) supplied to the crew. Has had good weather, and the crew are healthy.

"And yett all these happy circumstances were not sufficient to our ease and quiet, while I was dayly plagued by the insolence of my Lieut. Georg Fisher. At my first coming aboard, I was importuned by Lieut. Fisher to enter two little boys as officer's servants." On refusing this request (it being against their Lordship's orders) he "ceased not to importune me," and "begun to quarrell with my Purser." At the Canary Islands "he began to be more Boisterous;" and asked me "why I suffered none to goe into the Pinnace. I told him I had commanded otherwise for fear of shaking her too much, then he shaked his Fist att me, Grind in my Face, and told me that he cared not —— —— for me." However, on being threatened with confinement, he apologised in "my Cabbin," and "promised not to be guilty of the Like for the future."

Coming from St. Jago "I heard him . . . complaining in Publick of the badness of the Bread, and that itt was not fitt for men to Eate." On viewing the Bread "I . . . could not find one Bitt not fitt to Eate, att which he seemed much Displeased and Muttered his mind to some of his Accomplices. On ye 9th March Last, he sat in the Steeridge and there Exprest his grievance about the Beer . . . and Likewise said that it was not Lawfull to let them (the hands) Drink it within seven inches of the Bottom. I could not imagine that he designed less than to sett up for a Patriott amongst my men." Soon afterwards, when "I" had occasion to speak to him about the broaching of a "casque" of beer, "he grind att me after his usuall Maner and I thought he would Collar me. But his frequent affronts had so baffled my Patience, that I prevented him by striking him with my Cane, which I had then in my hands, att which he turned to me, called me Old Dog, Old Villain, and told my men Gents take care of that Old Pyrateing Dog for he designs to Run away with you and the King's Ship." "I" confined him to his cabin, and called all hands aft "to Encourage them to Obedience," but while "I" spoke, "he interrupted me by Preaching his own Doctrine . . . loading me with all the Crimes that could incense my men Against me as Piracy and Murther." He continued "railing att me Severall hours together," and behaved so outrageously that

"On the 16 I was forced to put him in Irons lest he should cause my men to mutiny." After "I" anchored here (in Bahia Bay) "his Curses and scurrilous Language" continued daily, although he was a prisoner; so that "I was oblidged either to returne home or gett rid of him." "I went to the Governor," who "had heard of my Misfortune (which any body could tell him of that had once been aboard here, such unusuall noise the L^t. made") and "he prevented my Request by proffering to secure my L^t. ashore." So "on ye 28th I sent him ashoare where he was putt in prison till this fleet sayles for Lisbon." At Lisbon, Mr. Fisher will be delivered to Mr. (Paul) Methuen, his Majesty's Envoy "to whom I writt to send him home." "I" have sent ashore four months' provision for Mr. Fisher and his servant, "because the Portuguese are loth to part with any provision." Mr. Fisher is no quieter in prison than he was aboard. He has tried "to incense some Dutch merchants against me, telling them I was a pirate, had taken a Dutch ship, tyd the men back to back and hove them overboard." [This would seem to refer to the exploit at Sierra Leone.] Since then he has been working on the Priests and Friars, and the "Ghostly Padres" have given him a writ against me. The Governor of Bahia has asked where we are bound, "so told him I was bound to Benculi on the Island Sumatra." There are three of Captain Avery's men [Avery was a pirate of some notoriety at this time] in this place. "I would have brought them away with me had it not been for these unhappy differences which made dread such infectious company." His men have made depositions against the trio "so that I hope they may be sent for Lisbon." Sends with this his officers' evidences against Fisher, "only my pursers and chirurgeons I have not sent because the Lieutenant and they were at difference, and they might be partiall." *Letter in clerk's hand.*

(Signed) *W^m. Dampier.*

June 3rd, 1699. *Off Cape Bon Esperance bearing from us N.E. by E. Distant twenty Leagues.* To the same. Having met the ship *Antelope*, thinks fit to report that he sailed from Bahia on the 23rd April last. Mentions the dispatch of the preceding letter. All aboard very healthy, and the ship in good condition. Will not touch anywhere till he comes to "ye Place I design for." *Clerk's hand.* (Signed) *W^m. Dampier.*

The following letters are to be seen in the Navy Board Papers at the Record Office (*No.* 516).

August 17th, 1699. To the Navy Board. Recommends John Knight, now gunner of the *Dunwich*, as a suitable master for the *Roebuck*, "I having known him for severall yeares to be a sober, diligent and knowing man, has been Mas^r of severall ships in ye West Indies." Does not doubt that he "will approve himself upon Examination" to be worthy this character. (Signed) *W^m. Dampier.*

October 3, 1699. To the same. Does pray that the promised "one hundred pounds for contingencies on the Service" may be paid soon. Asks also for eighteen barrecoes, or small hand casks, for filling of water while

abroad. His chirurgeon has drugs for twelve months, but the ship may be away two years, therefore hopes you will give him necessaries according.
(Signed) *Wm. Dampier.*

October 21, 1699. To the same. Reports his arrival in the Downs, and his want of a carpenter. Wind N. W. W. a fresh gale.
(Signed) *Wm. Dampier.*

December 1, 1699. To the same. On the 22nd lost "all my Oares out of my Yawle being oversett by a Ship's side in coming off from Deale beach." Cannot procure oars or any other necessary in Deal without "your Honrs orders." Desires that the Deal storekeeper may be caused to "supply his boatswain with six yawls' oars, and his Carpenter with one Iron hoop for anchor stocks, one Top maul and half a pound of Pump Nailes. One Iron pinn for the Top block." (Signed) *Wm. Dampier.*

December 15, 1699. To the same. Gives a résumé of other letters. Has cashed the bill for £20, and now waits for the hatchets.
(Signed) *Wm. Dampier.*

December 25, 1699. To the same. Has had bad weather. Asks for an order on the Deal storekeeper for a ring bolt for the stoppers, two "Ragg-bolts for ye Whelps of the Geer Capson (capstan) which were broke in heaving, and two other bolts to keep the Capsons from rising."
(Signed) *Wm. Dampier.*

Postscript.—If he may have "a dozen of Peins of glass to mend the windows in my Cabbin which are broke" he hopes to trouble them no more till his Returne. *W. D.*

December 30, 1699. To the same. Returns hearty thanks for their ready compliance with his request. (Signed) *Wm. Dampier.*

A

VOYAGE

TO

NEW-HOLLAND, &c.

In the YEAR 1699.

Wherein are defcribed,

The *Canary*-Iflands, the Ifles of *Mayo* and St. *Jago*. The Bay of *All-Saints*, with the Forts and Town of *Bahia* in *Brazil*. Cape *Salvadore*. The Winds on the *Brafilian* Coaft. *Abrohlo* Shoals. A Table of all the *Variations* obferv'd in this Voyage. Occurrences near the Cape of *Good-Hope*. The Courfe to *New-Holland*. *Shark's* Bay. The Ifles and Coaft, *&c.* of *New-Holland*.

Their Inhabitants, Manners, Cuftoms, Trade, *&c.* Their Harbours, Soil, Beafts, Birds, Fifh, *&c.* Trees, Plants, Fruits, *&c.*

Illuftrated with feveral MAPS and DRAUGHTS: Alfo divers Birds, Fifhes and Plants not found in this Part of the World, Curioufly Ingraven on Copper-Plates.

VOL. III.

By Captain WILLIAM DAMPIER.

LONDON,

Printed for JAMES *and* JOHN KNAPTON, at the *Crown* in St. *Paul's* Church-Yard.

TO THE RIGHT HONOURABLE

THOMAS

EARL OF PEMBROKE,

LORD PRESIDENT OF HER MAJESTY'S MOST HONOURABLE PRIVY-COUNCIL, &c.

MY LORD,

THE Honour I had of being employed in the Service of his late Majesty of Illustrious Memory, at the time when Your Lordship presided at the Admiralty, gives me the Boldness to ask Your Protection of the following Papers. They consist of some Remarks made upon very distant Climates, which I should have the Vanity to think altogether new, could I persuade my self they had escap'd Your Lordship's Knowledge. However I have been so cautious of publishing any thing in my whole Book that is generally known, that I have deny'd my self the Pleasure of paying the due Honours to your Lordship's Name in the Dedication. I am asham'd, my Lord, to offer You so imperfect a Present, having not time to set down all the Memoirs of my last Voyage: But as the particular Service I have now undertaken, hinders me from finishing this Volume,[1] so I hope it will give me an Opportunity of paying my Respects to Your Lordship in a new one.

The World is apt to judge of every thing by the Success; and whoever has ill Fortune will hardly be

[1] He refers to his intended cruise in command of the *St. George*, then fitting out, with the *Fame*, for a voyage to the South Seas. Both ships were of 26 guns, and 120 men. The first edition of this volume ends at or about the middle of the voyage; its 162nd page (p. 444 in this edition).

allow'd a good Name. This, my Lord, was my Unhappiness in my late Expedition in the *Roe-Buck*, which founder'd thro' perfect Age near the Island of Ascension. I suffer'd extreamly in my Reputation by that Misfortune; tho' I comfort myself with the Thoughts, that my Enemies could not charge any Neglect upon me. And since I have the Honour to be acquitted by your Lordship's Judgment, I should be very humble not to value my self upon so compleat a Vindication. This, and a World of other Favours, which I have been so happy as to receive from Your Lordship's Goodness, do engage me to be with an everlasting Respect,

My Lord,

Your Lordship's

Most Faithful and

Obedient Servant,

WILL. DAMPIER.

THE PREFACE

THE favourable Reception[1] my two former Volumes of Voyages and Descriptions have already met with in the World, gives me Reason to hope, That notwithstanding the Objections which have been raised against me by prejudiced Persons,[2] this Third Volume likewise may in some measure be acceptable to Candid and Impartial Readers, who are curious to know the Nature of the Inhabitants, Animals, Plants, Soil, &c. in those different Countries, which have either seldom or not at all been visited by any Europeans.

It has almost always been the Fate of those who have made new Discoveries, to be disesteemed and slightly spoken of, by such as either have had no true Relish and Value for the Things themselves that are discovered, or have had some Prejudice against the Persons by whom the Discoveries were made. It would be vain therefore and unreasonable in me to expect to escape the Censure of all, or to hope for better Treatment than far Worthier Persons have met with before me. But this Satisfaction I am sure of having, that the Things themselves in the Discovery of which I have been imployed, are most worthy of our diligentest Search and Inquiry; being the various and wonderful Works of God in different Parts of the World: And however unfit a Person I may be in other respects to have undertaken this Task, yet at least I have given a faithful Account, and have found some Things undiscovered by any before, and which may at least be some

[1] They had run through some three or four editions when this was written.

[2] By Lieutenant Fisher and his supporters.

Assistance and Direction to better qualified Persons who shall come after me.

It has been objected against me by some, that my Accounts and Descriptions of Things are dry and jejune, not filled with variety of pleasant Matter, to divert and gratify the Curious Reader. How far this is true, I must leave to the World to judge. But if I have been exactly and strictly careful to give only True Relations and Descriptions of Things (as I am sure I have;) and if my Descriptions be such as may be of use not only to my self (which I have already in good measure experienced) but also to others in future Voyages; and likewise to such Readers at home as are more desirous of a Plain and Just Account of the true Nature and State of the Things described, than of a Polite and Rhetorical Narrative: I hope all the Defects in my Stile, will meet with an easy and ready Pardon.

Others have taxed me with borrowing from other Men's Journals; and with Insufficiency, as if I was not myself the Author of what I write, but published Things digested and drawn up by others. As to the first Part of this Objection, I assure the Reader, I have taken nothing from any Man without mentioning his Name, except some very few Relations and particular Observations received from credible Persons who desired not to be named; and these I have always expressly distinguished in my Books, from what I relate as of my own observing. And as to the latter; I think it so far from being a Diminution to one of my Education and Employment, to have what I write, Revised and Corrected by Friends; that on the contrary, the best and most eminent Authors are not ashamed to own the same Thing, and look upon it as an Advantage.

Lastly, I know there are some who are apt to slight my Accounts and Descriptions of things, as if it was an easie Matter and of little or no Difficulty to do all that I have done, to visit little more than the Coasts of unknown Countries, and make short and imperfect Observations of Things only near the Shore. But whoever is experienced in these Matters, or considers Things impartially, will be of a very different Opinion. And any one who is sensible, how backward and refractory the Seamen are apt to be in long Voyages when they know not whither they are going, how ignorant they are of the Nature of the Winds and the shifting Seasons of the Monsoons, and how little even the Officers themselves generally are skilled in the Variation of the Needle and the Use of the Azimuth[1] Compass; besides the Hazard of all outward Accidents in strange and unknown Seas: Any one, I say, who is sensible of these Difficulties, will be much more pleased at the Discoveries and Observations I have been able to make, than displeased with me that I did not make more.

Thus much I thought necessary to premise in my own Vindication, against the Objections that have been made to my former Performances. But not to trouble the Reader any further with Matters of this Nature; what I have more to offer shall be only in relation to the following Voyage.

For the better apprehending the Course of this Voyage, and the Situation of the Places mentioned in it, I have here, as in the former Volumes, caused a Map to be Ingraven, with a prick'd Line, representing to the Eye the whole Thread of the Voyage at one View; besides Draughts and Figures of particular Places, to make the Descriptions I have given of them more intelligible and useful.

Moreover, which I had not the opportunity of doing in my former Voyages; having now had in the Ship with me a Person skill'd in Drawing,[2] I have by this means been enabled, for the greater Satisfaction of the Curious Reader, to present him with exact Cuts and Figures of several of the principal and most remarkable of those Birds, Beasts, Fishes and Plants, which are described in the following Narrative; and also of several, which not being able to give any better or so good an Account of, as by causing them to be exactly Ingraven, the Reader will not find any further Description of them, but only that they were found in such or such particular Countries. The Plants them-

[1] The azimuth compass is an instrument employed at sea to determine the amount of the magnetical variation.

[2] Perhaps James Brand, the clerk of the *Roebuck*.

selves are in the Hands of the Ingenious Dr. Woodward.[1] I could have caused many others to be drawn in like manner, but that I resolved to confine my self to such only, as had some very remarkable difference in the Shape of their principal Parts from any that are found in Europe. I have besides several Birds and Fishes ready drawn, which I could not put into the present Volume, because they were found in Countries, to the Description whereof the following Narrative does not reach. For, being obliged to prepare for another Voyage,[2] sooner than I at first expected; I have not been able to continue the ensuing Narrative any further than to my Departure from the Coast of New Holland. But, if it please God that I return again safe, the Reader may expect a Continuation of this Voyage from my departure from New Holland, till the foundring of my Ship near the Island of Ascension.

In the mean time, to make the Narrative in some measure compleat, I shall here add a Summary Abstract of that latter part of the Voyage, whereof I have not had time to draw out of my Journals a full and particular Account at large. Departing therefore from the Coast of New Holland in the beginning of September, 1699 (for the Reasons mentioned Page 444) we arrived at Timor, Sept. 15, and anchored off that Island. On the 24th we obtain'd a small Supply of fresh Water from the Governor of a Dutch Fort and Factory there; we found also there a Portuguese Settlement, and were kindly treated by them. On the 3rd of December we arrived on the Coast of New Guinea; where we found good fresh Water, and had Commerce with the Inhabitants of a certain Island call'd Pulo-Sabuti. After which, passing to the Northward, we ranged along the Coast to the Eastermost Part of New Guinea; which I found does not join to the main Land of New Guinea, but is an Island,[3] as I have described it in my Map, and call'd it New-Britain.

[1] Dr. John Woodward (1665–1728), a botanist and geologist on the Council of the Royal Society. The Herbarium of which Dampier speaks is now at Oxford.

[2] See *ante*, note to Dedication.

[3] New Pomerania. Sabuti is Dampier Island.

It is probable this Island may afford many rich Commodities, and the Natives may be easily brought to Commerce. But the many Difficulties I at this time met with, the want of Convenience to clean my Ship, the fewness of my Men, their Desire to hasten home, and the Danger of continuing in these Circumstances in Seas where the Shoals and Coasts were utterly unknown, and must be searched out with much Caution and length of Time; hindred me from prosecuting any further at present my intended Search. What I have been able to do in this Matter for the Publick Service, will, I hope, be candidly receiv'd; and no Difficulties shall discourage me from endeavouring to promote the same End, whenever I have an Opportunity put into my Hands.

May 18, in our Return, we arrived at Timor. June 21, we past by part of the Island Java. July 4, we anchored in Batavia-Road; and I went ashore, visited the Dutch General, and desired the Privilege of buying Provisions that I wanted, which was granted me. In this Road we lay till the 17th of October following; when, having fitted the Ship, recruited my self with Provisions, filled all my Water, and the Season of the Year for returning towards Europe being come; I set Sail from Batavia, and on the 19th of December made the Cape of Good Hope; whence departing Jan. 11, we made the Island of Santa Hellena on the 31st; and February the 21st, the Island of Ascension; near to which my Ship, having sprung a Leak which could not be stopped, foundered at Sea; with much difficulty we got ashore, where we liv'd on Goats and Turtle; and on the 26th of February found, to our great Comfort, on the S. E. Side of a high Mountain, about half a Mile from its Top, a Spring of fresh Water. I returned to England in the *Canterbury* East-India-Ship. For which wonderful Deliverance from so many and great Dangers, I think my self bound to return continual Thanks to Almighty God; whose Divine Providence if it shall please to bring me safe again to my Native Country from my present intended Voyage; I hope to publish a particular Account of all the material Things I observed in the several Places which I have now but barely mentioned.

THE CONTENTS

CHAP. I

CHAP. II

CHAP. III

DAMPIER'S VOYAGES

VOL. III

A VOYAGE TO TERRA AUSTRALIS

CHAP. I

The A.'s Departure from the Downs. A Caution to those who sail in the Channel. His Arrival at the Canary-Islands. Santa Cruz in Teneriffe; the Road and Town, and Spanish Wreck. Laguna T. Lake and Country; and Oratavia T. and Road. Of the Wines and other Commodities of Teneriffe, &c. and the Governours at Laguna and Santa Cruz. Of the Winds in these Seas. The A's Arrival at Mayo, one of the C. Verd Islands; its Salt-pond, compar'd with that of Salt-Tortuga; its Trade for Salt, and Frape-boats. Its Vegetables, Silk-Cotton, &c. Its Soil, and Towns, its Guinea-Hen's, and other Fowls, Beasts and Fish. Of the Sea-Turtle's (&c.) laying in the wet Season. Of the Natives, their Trade and Livelihood. The A.'s Arrival at J. St. Jago, and St. Jago Town. Of the Inhabitants, and their Commodities. Of the Custard-Apple, and the Papah. St. Jago Road, J. Fogo.

I SAIL'D from the Downs early on Saturday, Jan. 14, AN. 1699
169$\frac{8}{9}$, with a fair Wind, in his Majesty's Ship the *Roe-buck*;[1] carrying but 12 Guns in this Voyage, and 50 Men and Boys, with 20 Month's Provision. We

[1] The *Roebuck*, a ship of 290 tons. Her captain was, of course, William Dampier; her master, John Hughes; her lieutenant, George Fisher; her gunner, Philip Paine; her mates, R. Chadwick and John Knight. "The dockter and Captain's cleark were two Scotch dogs," William Borthwick and James Brand by name. She left Deptford on the 6th Oct. 1698. On the 13th, as she lay at Tilbury, the *Isabella* Pink collided with her, and damaged her head and sprit topmast. On the 22nd she anchored in the Downs, where she stayed till January 14th. Hughes (the master's) logbook has no entry after February 19, 1700.

AN. 1699 had several of the King's Ships in Company, bound for Spit-head and Plimouth; and by Noon we were off Dungeness. We parted from them that Night, and stood down the Channel, but found our selves next Morning nearer the French Coast than we expected; C. de Hague bearing S. E. and by E. 6 L. There were many other Ships, some nearer, some farther off the French Coast, who all seem'd to have gone nearer to it than they thought they should. My Master,[1] who was somewhat troubled at it at first, was not displeas'd however to find that he had Company in his Mistake: Which, as I have heard, is a very common one, and fatal to many Ships. The Occasion of it is the not allowing for the Change of the Variation since the making of the Charts; which Captain Hally[2] has observ'd to be very considerable. I shall refer the Reader to his own Account of it which he caus'd to be published in a single Sheet of Paper, purposely for a Caution to such as pass to and fro the English Channel: The Title of it is in the Margin. And my own Experience thus confirming to me the Usefulness of such a Caution, I was willing to take this Occasion of helping towards the making it the more publick.

An Advertisement necessary to be observ'd in the Navigation up and down the Channel of England.

Not to trouble the Reader with every Day's Run, nor with the Winds or Weather (but only in the remoter Parts, where it may be more particularly useful) standing away from C. la Hague, we made the Start about 5 that Afternoon; which being the last Land we saw of England, we reckon'd our Departure[3] from thence: Tho' we had rather have taken it from the Lizard, if the hazy Weather would have suffer'd us to have seen it.

The first Land we saw after we were out of the Channel was C. Finisterre, which we made on the 19th; and on the 28th made Lancerota,[4] one of the Canary Islands; of which, and of Allegrance,[5] another of them, I

[1] John Hughes.

[2] E. Halley (1656–1742), astronomer, author of the "General Chart of the Variation," published after a long cruise in command of the *Paramour* Pink.

[3] Having, until then, had the land close aboard to define their position.

[4] Lanzerote.

[5] Alegranze.

have here given the Sights,[1] as they both appeared to us at two several Bearings and Distances. AN. 1699

We were now standing away for the Island Teneriffe, where I intended to take in some Wine and Brandy for my Voyage. On Sunday, half an hour past 3 in the Afternoon, we made the Island, and crouded in with all our Sails till 5; when the N. E. Point of the Isle bore W. S. W. dist. 7 Leagues: But being then so far off that I could not expect to get in before Night, I lay by till next Morning, deliberating whether I should put in at Santa Cruz,[2] or at Oratavia,[3] the one on the E. the other on the W. side of the Island; which lies mostly North and South; and these are the principal Ports on each Side. I chose Santa Cruz as the better Harbour (especially at this Time of the Year) and as best furnish'd with that Sort of Wine which I had occasion to take in for my Voyage: So there I come to an Anchor Jan. 30th, in 33 Fathom-water, black slimy Ground; about half a Mile from the Shore; from which Distance I took the Sight of the Town.

In the Road, Ships must ride in 30, 40, or 50 Fathom-water, not above half a Mile from the Shore at farthest; And if there are many Ships, they must ride close one by another. The Shore is generally high Land, and in most Places steep too.[4] This Road lies so open to the East, that Winds from that Side make a great Swell, and very bad going ashore in Boats: The Ships that ride here are then often forced to put to Sea, and sometimes to cut or slip their Anchors, not being able to weigh them. The best and smoothest Landing is in a small sandy Cove, about a Mile to the N. E. of the Road, where there is good Water, with which Ships that lade here are supply'd; and many Times Ships that lade at Oratavia, which is the chief Port for Trade, send their Boats hither for Water. That is a worse Port for Westerly than this is for Easterly Winds; and then all Ships that are there put to Sea. Between this

[1] These have been omitted from the present edition as no longer useful.
[2] In the island of Teneriffe. There is another town of this name in the island of Palma.
[3] Orotava, a town of some importance at the foot of the Peak.
[4] Rising abruptly from the sea, with great depth of water close to the shore.

AN. 1699 Watering-place and Santa Cruz are two little Forts; which with some Batteries scatter'd along the Coast command the Road. Santa Cruz its self is a small unwalled Town fronting the Sea, guarded with two other Forts to secure the Road. There are about 200 Houses in the Town, all two Stories high, strongly built with Stone, and covered with Pantile. It hath two Convents and one Church, which are the best Buildings in the Town. The Forts here could not secure the Spanish Galleons from Admiral Blake,[1] tho' they hall'd in close under the main Fort. Many of the Inhabitants that are now living remember that Action; in which the English batter'd the Town, and did it much Damage; and the Marks of the Shot still remain in the Fort-Walls. The Wrecks of the Galleons that were burnt here, lie in 15 Fathom-water: And 'tis said that most of the Plate lies there, tho' some of it was hastily carried ashore at Blake's coming in Sight.

Soon after I had anchor'd I went ashore here to the Governour of the Town, who received me very kindly, and invited me to dine with him the next Day. I return'd on Board in the Evening, and went ashore again with two of my Officers the next Morning; hoping to get up the Hill Time enough to see Laguna, the principal Town, and to be back again to dine with the Governour of Santa Cruz; for I was told that Laguna was but 3 Miles off. The Road is all the way up a pretty steep Hill; yet not so steep but that Carts go up and down laden. There are

[1] Admiral Blake arrived off Santa Cruz on the 18th April, 1657, in search of some treasure galleons. The galleons had been hauled in "close under the main Fort," as Dampier says, while the men-of-war which convoyed them had anchored in a line outside them, so that their batteries could bear upon an enemy entering the Road. Some of the gold and silver was hastily landed; but Blake attacked before the ships were cleared. On the 20th April, Blake had a fair wind, and sailed into the Road in two divisions. One, under Captain Stayner, attacked the galleons, the other, under Blake, engaged the forts. All the Spanish ships were burnt and sunk, and, as Dampier says, "the English batter'd the Town and did it much Damage." Blake sailed from Santa Cruz that same evening, as soon as the land-breeze began to blow. The English lost some 50 killed, and about twice that number wounded. Clarendon says that "the Spaniards comforted themselves with the belief that they were Devils and not Men who had thus destroyed them."

Publick Houses scattering by the Way-side, where we got some Wine. The Land on each Side seemed to be but rocky and dry; yet in many Places we saw Spots of green flourishing Corn. At farther Distances there were small Vineyards by the Sides of the Mountains, intermixt with Abundance of waste rocky Land, unfit for Cultivation, which afforded only Dildo-bushes. It was about 7 or 8 in the Morning when we set out from Santa Cruz; and it being fair clear Weather, the Sun shone very bright and warmed us sufficiently before we got to the City Laguna; which we reached about 10 a Clock, all sweaty and tired, and were glad to refresh our selves with a little Wine in a sorry Tipling-house: But we soon found out one of the English Merchants that resided here; who entertained us handsomely at Dinner, and in the Afternoon shew'd us the Town.

AN. 1699

Laguna is a pretty large well-compacted Town, and makes a very agreeable Prospect. It stands part of it against a Hill, and part in a Level. The Houses have mostly strong Walls built with Stone and covered with Pantile. They are not uniform, yet they appear pleasant enough. There are many fair Buildings; among which are 2 Parish-Churches, 2 Nunneries, an Hospital, 4 Convents, and some Chapels; besides many Gentlemens Houses. The Convents are those of St. Austin, St. Dominick, St. Francis, and St. Diego. The two Churches have pretty high square Steeples, which top the rest of the Buildings. The Streets are not regular, yet they are mostly spacious and pretty handsome; and near the middle of the Town is a large Parade, which has good Buildings about it. There is a strong Prison on one Side of it; near which is a large Conduit of good Water, that supplies all the Town. They have many Gardens which are set round with Oranges, Limes, and other Fruits: In the middle of which are Pot-herbs, Sallading, Flowers, &c. And indeed, if the Inhabitants were curious this way, they might have very pleasant Gardens: For as the Town stands high from the Sea, on the Brow of a Plain that is all open to the East, and hath consequently the Benefit of the true

AN. 1699 Trade-wind, which blows here, and is most commonly fair; so there are seldom wanting at this Town, brisk, cooling, and refreshing Breezes all the Day.

On the Back of the Town there is a large Plain of 3 or 4 Leagues in length and 2 Miles wide, producing a thick kindly Sort of Grass, which lookt green and very pleasant when I was there, like our Meadows in England in the Spring. On the East-side of this Plain, very near the Back of the Town, there is a natural Lake or Pond of fresh Water. It is about half a Mile in Circumference; but being stagnant, 'tis only us'd for Cattle to drink of. In the Winter-time several Sorts of wild Fowl resort hither affording Plenty of Game to the Inhabitants of Laguna. This City is called Laguna from hence; for that Word in Spanish signifies a Lake or Pond. The Plain is bounded on the W. the N. W. and the S. W. with high steep Hills; as high above this Plain as this is above the Sea; and 'tis from the Foot of one of these Mountains that the Water of the Conduit which supplies the Town, is conveyed over the Plain, in Troughs of Stone rais'd upon Pillars. And, indeed, considering the Situation of the Town, its large Prospect to the East (for from hence you see the Grand Canary) its Gardens, cool Arbors, pleasant Plain, green Fields, the Pond and Aqueduct, and its refreshing Breezes; it is a very delightful Dwelling, especially for such as have not Business that calls them far and often from Home: For the Island being generally mountainous, steep and craggy, full of Risings and Fallings, 'tis very troublesome Travelling up and down in it, unless in the Cool of the Mornings and Evenings: And Mules and Asses are most us'd by them, both for Riding and Carriage, as fittest for the stony, uneven Roads.

Beyond the Mountains, on the S. W. side, still further up, you may see from the Town and Plain a small peeked Hill, overlooking the rest. This is that which is called the Pike of Teneriffe, so much noted for its Heighth:[1]

[1] The Peak is "like unto a sugar-loaf, and continually covered with snow, and placed in the middest of a goodly vallie." Its height is about 12,000 feet.

But we saw it here at so great a Disadvantage, by Reason AN. 1699
of the Nearness of the adjacent Mountains to us, that it looked inconsiderable in Respect to its Fame.

The true Malmesy Wine grows in this Island; and this here is said to be the best of its Kind in the World.[1] Here is also Canary-Wine, and Verdona, or Green-wine. The Canary grows chiefly on the West-side of the Island; and therefore is commonly sent to Oratavia; which being the chief Sea-port for Trade in the Island, the principal English Merchants reside there, with their Consul; because we have a great Trade for this Wine. I was told, that that Town is bigger than Laguna; that it has but one Church, but many Convents: That the Port is but ordinary at best, and is very bad when the N. W. Winds blow. These Norwesters give notice of their Coming, by a great Sea that tumbles in on the Shore for some Time before they come, and by a black Sky in the N. W. Upon these Signs Ships either get up their Anchors, or slip their Cables and put to Sea, and ply off and on till the Weather is over. Sometimes they are forced to do so 2 or 3 Times before they can take in their Lading; which 'tis hard to do here in the fairest Weather: And for fresh Water, they send, as I have said, to Santa Cruz. Verdona is green, strong-bodied Wine, harsher and sharper than Canary. 'Tis not so much esteemed in Europe, but is exported to the West-Indies, and will keep best in hot Countries; for which Reason I touch'd here to take in some of it for my Voyage. This Sort of Wine is made chiefly on the East-side of the Island, and shipt off at Santa Cruz.

Besides these Wines, which are yearly vended in great Plenty from the Canary Islands (chiefly from Grand Canary, Teneriffe, and Palma) here is Store of Grain, as Wheat, Barly and Maiz, which they often transport to other Places. They have also some Beans and Peas, and Coches, a Sort of Grain much like Maiz, sow'd mostly to fatten Land. They have Papah's, which I shall speak

[1] The best "Malmsey," or Madeira, came from Madeira.

AN. 1699 more of hereafter; Apples, Pears, Plumbs, Cherries, and excellent Peaches, Apricocks, Guava's, Pomegranates, Citrons, Oranges, Lemons, Limes, Pumpkins, Onions the best in the World, Cabbages, Turnips, Potato's, &c. They are also well stocked with Horses, Cows, Asses, Mules, Sheep, Goats, Hogs, Conies, and Plenty of Deer. The Lancerot Horses are said to be the most mettlesome, fleet, and loyal Horses that are. Lastly, here are many Fowls, as Cocks and Hens, Ducks, Pidgeons, Partridges, &c. with Plenty of Fish, as Mackril, &c. All the Canary Islands have of these Commodities and Provisions more or less: But as Lancerota is most fam'd for Horses, and Grand Canary, Teneriffe, and Palma for Wines, Teneriffe especially for the best Malmesy, (for which Reason these 3 Islands have the chief Trade) so is Forteventura for Dunghil-Fowls, and Gomera for Deer. Fowls and other Eatables are dear on the Trading Islands; but very plentiful and cheap on the other; and therefore 'tis best for such Ships that are going out on long Voyages, and who design to take in but little Wine, to touch rather at these last; where also they may be supply'd with Wine enough, good and cheap: And for my own Part, if I had known before I came hither, I should have gone rather to one of those Islands than to Teneriffe: But enough of this.

'Tis reported they can raise 12000 armed Men on this Island. The Governor or General (as he is call'd) of all the Canary Islands lives at Laguna: His Name is Don Pedro de Ponto. He is a Native of this Island, and was not long since President of Panama in the South Seas; who bringing some very rich Pearls from thence, which he presented to the Queen of Spain, was therefore, as 'tis said, made General of the Canary Islands. The Grand Canary is an Island much superiour to Teneriffe both in Bulk and Value; but this Gentleman chuses rather to reside in this his native Island. He has the Character of a very worthy Person; and governs with Moderation and Justice, being very well beloved.

One of his Deputies was the Governor of Santa Cruz, with whom I was to have din'd; but staying so long at

Laguna, I came but Time enough to sup with him. He is a civil, discreet Man. He resides in the main Fort close by the Sea. There is a Centinel stands at his Door; and he has a few Servants to wait on him. I was treated in a large dark lower Room, which has but one small Window. There were about 200 Muskets hung up against the Walls, and some Pikes; no Wainscot, Hangings, nor much Furniture. There was only a small old Table, a few old Chairs, and 2 or 3 pretty long Forms to sit on. Having supp'd with him, I invited him on Board, and went off in my Boat. The next Morning he came aboard with another Gentleman in his Company, attended by 2 Servants: But he was presently Sea-sick, and so much out of order, that he could scarce eat or drink any Thing, but went quickly ashore again.

AN. 1699

Having refresh'd my Men ashore, and taken in what we had occasion for, I sail'd away from Santa Cruz on Feb. 4 in the Afternoon; hastening out all I could, because the N. E. Winds growing stormy made so great Sea, that the Ship was scarce safe in the Road; and I was glad to get out, tho' we left behind several Goods we had bought and paid for: For a Boat could not go ashore; and the Stress was so great in weighing Anchor, that the Cable broke. I design'd next for the I. of Mayo, one of the C. Verd Islands; and ran away with a strong N. E. Wind, right afore it, all that Night and the next Day, at the Rate of 10 or 11 Miles an Hour; when it slackened to a more moderate Gale. The Canary Islands are, for their Latitude, within the usual Verge of the true or general Trade-Wind; which I have observ'd to be, on this Side the Equator, N. Easterly: But then lying not far from the African Shore, they are most subject to a N. Wind, which is the Coasting and constant Trade, sweeping that Coast down as low as to C. Verd; which spreading in Breadth, taking in mostly the Canary Islands; tho' it be there interrupted frequently with the true Trade-Wind, N. West-Winds, or other Shifts of Wind that Islands are subject to; especially where they lie many together. The Pike of Teneriffe, which had generally been clouded while we lay at Santa Cruz, appear'd now all

AN. 1699 white with Snow, hovering over the other Hills; but their Height made it seem the less considerable; for it looks most remarkable to Ships that are to the Westward of it. We had brisk N. N. E. and N. E. Winds from Teneriffe; and saw Flying-fish, and a great deal of Sea-thistle Weed floating. By the 9th of Feb. at Noon we were in the Lat. of 15 d. 4 m. so we steered away W. N. W. for the I. of Mayo, being by Judgment, not far to the E. of it, and at 8 a Clock in the Evening lay by till Day. The Wind was then at W. by South, and so it continued all Night, fair Weather, and a small easy Gale. All these were great Signs, that we were near some Land, after having had such constant brisk Winds before. In the Morning after Sun-rise, we saw the Island at about 4 Leagues distance. But it was so hazy over it, that we could see but a small Part of it; yet even by that Part I knew it to be the Isle of Mayo. See how it appear'd to us at several Views, as we were compassing the E. the S. E. and the S. of it, to get to the Road, on the S. W. of it, [Table omitted,] and the Road it self.

I got not in till the next Day, Feb. 11, when I come to an Anchor in the Road, which is the Lee-ward Part of the Island; for 'tis a general Rule, never to anchor to Windward of an Island between the Tropicks. We anchored at 11 a Clock in 14 Fathom clean Sand, and very smooth Water, about three quarters of a Mile from the Shore, in the same Place where I anchor'd in my Voyage round the World; and found riding here the *Newport* of London, a Merchant Man, Captain Barefoot Commander, who welcomed me with 3 Guns, and I returned one for Thanks. He came from Fayal one of the Western Islands[1]; and had Store of Wine and Brandy aboard. He was taking in Salt to carry to New-found-land, and was very glad to see one of the King's Ships, being before our coming afraid of Pyrates; which, of late Years, had much infested this and the rest of the Cape Verd Islands.[2]

I have given some Account of the Island of Mayo, and

[1] The Azores.

[2] See Johnson's "History of the Pyrates," the Life of Captain Halsey.

of other of these Islands, in my "Voyage round the World" [Vol. I. p. 99], but I shall now add some further Observations that occurr'd to me in this Voyage. The I. of Mayo is about 7 Leagues in Circumference, of a roundish Form, with many small rocky Points shooting out into the Sea a Mile, or more. Its Lat. is 15 d. N. and as you sail about the Isle, when you come pretty nigh the Shore, you will see the Water breaking off from those Points; which you must give a Birth to, and avoid them. I sail'd at this Time two Parts in three round the Island, but saw nothing dangerous besides these Points; and they all shew'd themselves by the Breaking of the Water: Yet 'tis reported, that on the N. and N. N. W. Side there are dangerous Sholes, that lye farther off at Sea; but I was not on that Side. There are 2 Hills on this Island of a considerable Heighth; one pretty bluff, the other peeked at top. The rest of the Island is pretty level, and of a good Heighth from the Sea. The Shore clear round hath sandy Bays, between the rocky Points I spake of; and the whole Island is a very dry Sort of Soil.

AN. 1699

On the West-side of the Isle where the Road for Ships is, there is a large sandy Bay, and a Sand-bank, of about 40 Paces wide within it, which runs along the Shore 2 or 3 Miles; within which there is a large Salina or Salt-pond, contained between the Sand-bank and the Hills beyond it. The whole Salina is about 2 Miles in length, and half a Mile wide; but above one half of it is commonly dry. The North End only of the Pond never wants Water, producing Salt from November till May, which is here the dry Season of the Year. The Water which yields this Salt, works in from out of the Sea through a hole in the Sand-bank before-mentioned, like a Sluce, and that only in Spring-tides; when it fills the Pond more or less, according to the Height of the Tides. If there is any Salt in the Ponds when the Flush of Water comes in, it presently dissolves: But then in 2 or 3 Days after it begins to kern; and so continues kerning till either all, or the greatest part of the Salt-water is congeal'd or kern'd; or till a fresh Supply of it comes in again from the Sea. This Water is

AN. 1699 known to come in only at that one Passage on the N. part of the Pond; where also it is deepest. It was at a Spring of the New Moon when I was there; and I was told that it comes in at no other Time but at the New Moon Spring-tides: But why that should be I can't guess. They who come hither to lade Salt rake it up as it kerns, and lay it in Heaps on the dry Land, before the Water breaks in anew: And this is observable of this Salt-Pond, that the Salt kerns only in the dry Season, contrary to the Salt-ponds in the West-Indies, particularly those of the Island Salt-Tortuga, which I have formerly mentioned [Vol. I. p. 85] for they never kern there till the Rains come in about April; and continue to do so in May, June, July, &c. while the wet Season lasts; and not without some good Shower of Rain first: But the Reason also of this Difference between the Salt-ponds of Mayo, and those of the West-Indies, why these should kern in the wet Season, and the former in the dry Season, I shall leave to Philosophers.

Our Nation drives here a great Trade for Salt, and have commonly a Man of War here for the Guard of our Ships and Barks that come to take it in; of which I have been inform'd that in some Years there have not been less than 100 in a Year. It costs nothing but Men's Labour to rake it together, and wheel it out of the Pond, except the Carriage: And that also is very cheap; the Inhabitants having Plenty of Asses, for which they have little to do besides carrying the Salt from the Ponds to the Sea-side at the Season when Ships are here. The Inhabitants lade and drive their Asses themselves, being very glad to be imployed; for they have scarce any other Trade but this to get a Penny by. The Pond is not above half a Mile from the Landing-place, so that the Asses make a great many Trips in a Day. They have a set Number of Turns to and fro both Forenoon and Afternoon, which their Owners will not exceed. At the Landing-place there lies a Frape-boat, as our Seamen call it, to take in the Salt. 'Tis made purposely for this Use, with a Deck reaching from the Stern a third Part of the Boat; where there is a kind of Bulk-head that rises, not from the Boat's Bottom, but from the Edge of the Deck, to about 2 Foot in Heighth; all calk'd very tight. The Use of it is to keep the Waves from dashing into the Boat, when it lies with its Head to the Shore, to take in Salt: For here commonly runs a great Sea; and when the Boat lies so with its Head to the Shore, the Sea breaks in over the Stern, and would soon fill it, was it not for this Bulk-head, which stops the Waves that come flowing upon the Deck, and makes them run off into the Sea on each Side. To keep the Boat thus with the Head to the Shore, and the Stern to the Sea, there are two strong Stantions set up in the Boat; the one at the Head, the other in the Middle of it, against the Bulk-head, and a Foot higher than the Bulk-head. There is a large Notch cut in the Top of each of these Stantions big enough for a small Hazer or Rope to lie in; one End of which is fasten'd to a Post ashore, and the other to a Grapling or Anchor lying a pretty way off at Sea: This Rope serveth to hale the Boat in and out, and the Stantions serve to keep her fast, so that she cannot swing to either Side when the Rope is hal'd tight: For the Sea would else fill her, or toss her ashore and stave her. The better to prevent her staving and to keep her the tighter together, there are two Sets of Ropes more: The first going athwart from Gunnal to Gunnal, which, when the Rowers Benches are laid, bind the Boats Sides so hard against the Ends of the Benches that they cannot easily fall asunder, while the Benches and Ropes mutually help each other; the Ropes keeping the Boat's Sides from flying off, and the Benches from being crush'd together inwards. Of these Ropes there are usually but two, dividing the Boat's length, as they go across the Sides, into three equal Parts. The other Set of Ropes are more in Number, and are so plac'd as to keep the Ribs and Planks of the Boat from starting off. For this Purpose there are Holes made at certain Distances through the Edge of the Keel that runs along on the Inside of the Boat; through which these Ropes passing are laid along the Ribs, so as to line them, or be themselves as Ribs upon them, being made fast to them

AN. 1699

AN. by Rattan's brought thither, or small Cords twisted close
1699 about both Ropes and Ribs, up to the Gunnal: By which Means tho' several of the Nails or Pegs of the Boat should by any Shock fall out, yet the Ropes of these two Sets might hold her together: Especially with the Help of a Rope going quite round about the Gunnal on the out-side, as our Long-boats have. And such is the Care taken to strengthen the Boats; from which girding them with Ropes, which our Seamen call Fraping,[1] they have the Name of Frape-boats. Two Men suffice to hale her in and out, and take in the Salt from Shore (which is brought in Bags) and put it out again. As soon as the Boat is brought nigh enough to the Shore, he who stands by the Bulk-head takes instantly a turn with the Hazer about the Bulk-head-Stantion; and that stops her fast before the Sea can turn her aside: And when the two Men have got in their Lading, they hale off to Sea, till they come a little without the Swell; where they remove the Salt into another Boat that carries it on board the Ship. Without such a Frape-boat here is but bad Landing at any Time: For tho' 'tis commonly very smooth in the Road, yet there falls a great Sea on the Shore, so that every Ship that comes here should have such a Boat, and bring, or make, or borrow one of other Ships that happen to be here; for the Inhabitants have none. I have been thus particular in the Description of these Frape-boats, because of the Use they may be of in any Places where a great Sea falls in upon the Shore: as it doth especially in many open Roads in the East and West-Indies; where they might therefore be very serviceable; but I never saw any of them there.

The Island Mayo is generally barren, being dry, as I said; and the best of it is but a very indifferent Soil. The sandy Bank that pens in the Salt-pond hath a Sort of Silk Cotton growing upon it, and a Plant that runs along upon the Ground, branching out like a Vine, but with thick broad Leaves. The Silk-Cotton grows on

[1] Frapping; to frap is to wrap about with rope.

tender Shrubs, 3 or 4 Foot high, in Cods as big as an Apple, but of a long Shape; which when ripe open at one End, parting leisurely into 4 Quarters; and at the first opening the Cotton breaks forth. It may be of use for stuffing of Pillows, or the like; but else is of no Value, any more than that of the great Cotton-tree. I took of these Cods before they were quite ripe, and laid them in my Chest; and in 2 or 3 Days they would open and throw out the Cotton. Others I have bound fast with Strings, so that the Cod could not open; and in a few Days after, as soon as I slackned the String never so little, the Cod would burst, and the Cotton fly out forceably, at a very little Hole, just as the Pulp out of a roasting Apple, till all has been out of the Cod. I met with this Sort of Cotton afterwards at Timor (where it was ripe in November) and no where else in all my Travels; but I found two other Sorts of Silk-cotton at Brazil, which I shall there describe. The right Cotton-shrub grows here also, but not on the Sand-bank. I saw some Bushes of it near the Shore; but the most of it is planted in the Middle of the Isle, where the Inhabitants live, Cotton-cloth being their chief Manufacture; but neither is there any great Store of this Cotton. There also are some Trees within the Island, but none to be seen near the Sea-side; nothing but a few Bushes scattering up and down against the Sides of the adjacent Hills; for, as I said before, the Land is pretty high from the Sea. The Soil is for the most part either a Sort of Sand, or loose crumbling Stone, without any fresh Water Ponds or Streams, to moisten it; but only Showers in the Wet-season, which run off as fast as they fall; except a small Spring in the Middle of the Isle, from which proceeds a little Stream of Water that runs through a Valley between the Hills. There the Inhabitants live in three small Towns, having a Church and Padre in each Town: And these Towns, as I was inform'd, are 6 or 7 Miles from the Road. Pinose is said to be the chief Town, and to have 2 Churches: St. John's the next; and the third Lagoa. The Houses are very mean; small, low

AN. 1699

AN. 1699 Things. They build with Fig-tree; here being, as I was told, no other Trees fit to build with. The Rafters are a Sort of wild Cane. The Fruits of this Isle are chiefly Figs, and Water-Melons. They have also Callavances (a Sort of Pulse like French Beans) and Pumpkins, for ordinary Food. The Fowls are Flamingo's, Great Curlews, and Guinea-Hens;[1] which the Natives of those Islands call *Gallena Pintata*, or the Painted Hen; but in Jamaica, where I have seen also those Birds in the dry Savannah's and Woods, (for they love to run about in such Places) they are call'd Guinea-Hens. They seem to be much of the Nature of Partridges. They are bigger than our Hens, have long Legs, and will run apace. They can fly too, but not far, having large heavy Bodies, and but short Wings and short Tails: As I have generally observed that Birds have seldom long Tails unless such as fly much; in which their Tails are usually serviceable to their turning about, as a Rudder to a Ship or Boat. These Birds have thick and strong, yet sharp Bills, pretty long Claws, and short Tails. They feed on the Ground, either on Worms, which they find by tearing open the Earth; or on Grashoppers, which are plentiful here. The Feathers of these Birds are speckled with dark and light Grey; the Spots so regular and uniform, that they look more beautiful than many Birds that are deck'd with gayer Feathers. Their Necks are small and long; their Heads also but little. The Cocks have a small Rising on their Crowns, like a Sort of a Comb. 'Tis of the Colour of a dry Wallnut-shell, and very hard. They have a small red Gill on each side of their Heads, like Ears, strutting out downwards; but the Hens have none. They are so strong that one cannot hold them; and very hardy. They are very good Meat, tender, and sweet; and in some the Flesh is extraordinary white; tho' some others have black Flesh: But both Sorts are very good. The Natives take them with Dogs, running them down whenever they please; for here are Abundance of them.

[1] *Numida meleagris.*

You shall see 2 or 300 in a Company. I had several brought aboard alive, where they throve very well; some of them 16 or 18 Months; when they began to pine. When they are taken young they will become tame like our Hens. The Flamingo's I have already describ'd at large [Vol. I. p. 99]. They have also many other Sort of Fowls, viz. Pidgeons and Turtle-doves; Miniota's, a Sort of Land-fowls as big as Crows, of a grey Colour, and good Food; Crusia's, another Sort of grey-colour'd Fowl almost as big as a Crow, which are only seen in the Night (probably a Sort of Owls) and are said to be good for consumptive People, but eaten by none else. Rabek's, a Sort of large grey eatable Fowls with long Necks and Legs, not unlike Herons; and many Kinds of small Birds.

Of Land-Animals, here are Goats, as I said formerly, and Asses good Store. When I was here before they were said to have had a great many Bulls and Cows: But the Pirates, who have since miserably infested all these Islands, have much lessen'd the Number of those; not having spar'd the Inhabitants themselves: for at my being there this Time the Governor of Mayo was but newly return'd from being a Prisoner among them, they having taken him away, and carried him about with them for a Year or two.

The Sea is plentifully stock'd with Fish of divers Sorts, viz. Dolphins, Boneta's, Mullets, Snappers, Silver-fish, Gar-fish, &c. and here is a good Bay to hale a Sain or Net in. I hal'd mine several Times, and to good Purpose; dragging ashore at one Time 6 Dozen of great Fish, most of them large Mullets of a Foot and a half or two Foot long. Here are also Porposes, and a small Sort of Whales, that commonly visit this Road every Day. I have already said, [Vol. I. p. 104] That the Months of May, June, July and August, (that is, the wet Season) are the Time when the green Turtle come hither, and go ashore to lay their Eggs. I look upon it as a Thing worth taking Notice of, that the Turtle should always, both in North and South Latitude, lay their Eggs in the wet Months. It might be thought, considering what great Rains there are

AN. 1699 then in some Places where these Creatures lay, that their Eggs should be spoiled by them. But the Rain, tho' violent, is soon soaked up by the Sand, wherein the Eggs are buried; and perhaps sinks not so deep into it as the Eggs are laid: And keeping down the Heat may make the Sand hotter below than it was before, like a Hot-bed. Whatever the Reason may be why Providence determines these Creatures to this Season of laying their Eggs, rather than the dry, in Fact it is so, as I have constantly observ'd; and that not only with the Sea-Turtle, but with all other Sorts of amphibious Animals that lay Eggs; as Crocodils, Alligators, Guano's, &c. The Inhabitants of this Island, even their Governour and Padre's, are all Negro's, Wool-pated like their African-Neighbours; from whom 'tis like they are descended; tho' being Subjects to the Portugueze, they have their Religion and Language. They are stout, lusty, well-limb'd People, both Men and Women, fat and fleshy; and they and their Children as round and plump as little Porposes; tho' the Island appears so barren to a Stranger as scarce to have Food for its Inhabitants. I inquired how many People there might be on the Isle; and was told by one of the Padre's that here were 230 Souls in all. The Negro-Governour has his Patent from the Portugueze Governour of St. Jago. He is a very civil and sensible poor Man; and they are generally a good Sort of People. He expects a small Present from every Commander that lades Salt here; and is glad to be invited aboard their Ships. He spends most of his Time with the English in the Salting Season, which is his Harvest; and indeed, all the Islanders are then fully employed in getting somewhat; for they have no Vessels of their own to trade with, nor do any Portugueze-Vessels come hither: scarce any but English, on whom they depend for Trade: and tho' Subjects of Portugal, have a particular Value for us. We don't pay them for their Salt, but for the Labour of themselves and their Beasts in lading it: for which we give them Victuals; some Money, and old Cloaths, viz. Hats, Shirts, and other Cloaths: By which Means many of them are indifferently well rigg'd; but some of them go almost naked. When the Turtle-season comes in they watch the Sandy-bays in the Night to turn them; and having small Huts at particular Places on the Bays to keep them from the Rain, and to sleep in: And this is another Harvest they have for Food; for by Report there come a great many Turtle to this and the rest of the Cape Verd Islands. When the Turtle Season is over they have little to do, but to hunt for Guinea-Hens, and manage their small Plantations. But by these Means they have all the Year some Employment or other; whereby they get a Subsistence, tho' but little else. When any of them are desirous to go over to St. Jago they get a Licence from the Governour, and desire Passage in any English Ship that is going thither: And indeed all Ships that lade Salt here will be obliged to touch at St. Jago for Water, for here at the Bay is none, not so much as for drinking. 'Tis true there is a small Well of brackish Water not half a Mile from the Landing-place, which the Asses that carry Salt drink at; but 'tis very bad Water. Asses themselves are a Commodity in some of these Islands, several of our Ships coming hither purposely to freight with them, and carry them to Barbadoes and our other Plantations. I stay'd at Mayo 6 Days, and got 7 or 8 Ton of Salt aboard for my Voyage: In which Time there came also into this Road several Sail of Merchants Ships for Salt; all bound with it for Newfoundland.

AN. 1699

The 19th Day of February, at about One a Clock in the Morning I weighed from Mayo-Road, in order to water at St. Jago, which was about 5 or 6 Leagues to the Westward. We coasted along the Island St. Jago, and past by the Port on the East of it, I mention'd formerly [Vol. I. p. 104] which they call Praya;[1] where some English outward-bound East-India Men still touch, but not so many of them as heretofore. We saw the Fort upon the Hill, the Houses and Coco-nut Trees: But I would not go in to anchor here, because I expected better Water on the S. W. of the Island, at St. Jago Town. By

[1] Porto Praya, "was some three leagues to the eastwards of Saint Iago." It was "placed on high, with a goodly bay." Drake sacked and burned the town in November, 1585.

AN. 1699 8 a Clock in the Morning we saw the Ships in that Road, being within 3 Leagues of it: But were forc'd to keep Turning many Hours to get in, the Flaws of Wind coming so uncertain; as they do especially to the Leeward of Islands that are high Land. At length two Portugueze Boats came off to help tow us in; and about 3 a Clock in the Afternoon we came to an Anchor; and took the Prospect of the Town. We found here, besides two Portugueze Ships bound for Brazil, whose Boats had tow'd us in, an English Pink that had taken in Asses at one of the Cape Verd Islands, and was bound to Barbadoes with them. Next Morning I went ashore with my Officers to the Governour, who treated us with Sweet-meats: I told him, the Occasion of my coming was chiefly for Water; and that I desired also to take in some Refreshments of Fowls, &c. He said I was welcome, and that he would order the Townsmen to bring their Commodities to a certain House, where I might purchase what I had occasion for: I told him I had not Money, but would exchange some of the Salt which I brought from Mayo for their Commodities. He reply'd, that Salt was indeed an acceptable Commodity with the poor People, but that if I design'd to buy any Cattle, I must give Money for them. I contented my self with taking in Dunghill Fowls: The Governour ordering a Cryer to go about the Town and give Notice to the People, that they might repair to such a Place with Fowls and Maiz for feeding them, where they might get Salt in Exchange for them: So I sent on Board for Salt, and order'd some of my Men to truck the same for the Fowls and Maiz, while the rest of them were busy in filling of Water. This is the Effect of their keeping no Boats of their own on the several Islands, that they are glad to buy even their own Salt of Foreigners, for want of being able to transport it themselves from Island to Island.

St. Jago Town[1] lies on the S. W. part of the Island, in

[1] The town of St. Iago, or Santiago, is figured in Bigges's "Summarie and True Discourse" of Sir Francis Drake's "Indies Voyage." Drake sacked and burned it November 17, 1585, it being then a fine town of 600

Lat. about 15 Deg. N. and is the seat of the General Governour, and of the Bishop of all the Cape Verd Islands. This Town stands scattering against the Sides of two Mountains, between which there is a deep Valley, which is about 200 Yards wide against the Sea; but within a quarter of a Mile it closes up so as not to be 40 Yards wide. In the Valley, by the Sea, there is a straggling Street, Houses on each Side, and a Run of Water in the Bottom, which empties it self into a fine small Cove or sandy Bay, where the Sea is commonly very smooth; so that here is good Watering and good Landing at any Time; tho' the Road be rocky and bad for Ships. Just by the Landing-place there is a small Fort, almost level with the Sea, where is always a Court of Guard kept. On the Top of the Hill, above the Town, there is another Fort; which, by the Wall that is to be seen from the Road, seems to be a large Place. They have Cannon mounted there, but how many know I not: Neither what use that Fort can be of, except it be for Salutes. The Town may consist of 2 or 300 Houses, all built of rough Stone; having also one Convent, and one Church.

AN. 1699

The People in general are black, or at least of a mixt Colour, except only some few of the better Sort, viz. the Governour, the Bishop, some Gentlemen, and some of the Padres; for some of these also are black. The People about Praya are Thievish; but these of St. Jago Town, living under their Governour's Eye, are more orderly, tho' generally poor, having little Trade: Yet besides chance Ships of other Nations, there come hither a Portugueze Ship or two every Year, in their way to Brazil. These vend among them a few European Commodities, and take of their principal Manufactures, viz. striped Cotton-cloth, which they carry with them to Brazil. Here is also another Ship comes hither from Portugal for Sugar, their other Manufacture, and returns with it directly thither: For 'tis reported that there are several small Sugar-works

or 700 houses. Drake's men found no treasure there, for "a Portingall" pirate, with a fleet of Frenchmen, had ransacked it but three years before. It was plundered again in 1596, by Sir Anthony Sherley.

AN. 1699 on this Island, from which they send home near 100 Ton every Year; and they have plenty of Cotton growing up in the Country, wherewith they cloath themselves, and send also a great deal to Brazil. They have Vines, of which they make some Wine; but the European Ships furnish them with better; tho' they drink but little of any. Their chief Fruits are, (besides Plantains in Abundance) Oranges, Lemons, Citrons, Melons, (both Musk and Water-melons) Limes, Guava's, Pomegranates, Quinces, Custard-Apples, and Papah's, &c.

The Custard-Apple[1] (as we call it) is a Fruit as big as a Pomegranate, and much of the same Colour. The outside Husk, Shell or Rind, is for Substance and Thickness between the Shell of a Pomegranate, and the Peel of a Sevil-Orange; softer than this, yet more brittle than that. The Coat or Covering is also remarkable in that it is beset round with small regular Knobs or Risings; and the Inside of the Fruit is full of a white soft Pulp, sweet and very pleasant, and most resembling a Custard of any Thing, both in Colour and Taste; from whence probably it is called a Custard-Apple by our English. It has in the Middle a few small black Stones or Kernels; but no Core, for 'tis all Pulp. The Tree that bears this Fruit is about the Bigness of a Quince-tree, with long, small, and thick-set Branches spread much abroad: At the Extremity of here and there one of which the Fruit grows upon a Stalk of its own about 9 or 10 Inches long, slender and tough, and hanging down with its own Weight. A large Tree of this Sort does not bear usually above 20 or 30 Apples; seldom more. This Fruit grows in most Countries within the Tropicks. I have seen of them (tho' I omitted the Description of them before) all over the West-Indies, both Continent and Islands; as also in Brazil, and in the East-Indies.

The Papah too is found in all these Countries, tho' I have not hitherto describ'd it. It is a Fruit about the Bigness of a Musk-Melon, hollow as that is, and much

[1] *Anona reticulata.*

resembling it in Shape and Colour, both Outside and Inside: AN.
Only in the Middle, instead of flat Kernels, which the 1699
Melons have, these have a handful of small blackish Seeds, about the Bigness of Pepper-corns; whose Taste is also hot on the Tongue somewhat like Pepper. The Fruit it self is sweet, soft and luscious, when ripe; but while green 'tis hard and unsavory: tho' even then being boiled and eaten with Salt-pork or Beef, it serves instead of Turnips, and is as much esteemed. The Papah-Tree is about 10 or 12 Foot high. The Body near the Ground may be a Foot and an half or 2 Foot Diameter; and it grows up tapering to the Top. It has no Branches at all, but only large Leaves growing immediately upon Stalks from the Body. The Leaves are of a roundish Form and jagg'd about the Edges, having their Stalks or Stumps longer or shorter as they grow near to or further from the Top. They begin to spring from out of the Body of the Tree at about 6 or 7 Foot heighth from the Ground, the Trunk being bare below: But above that the Leaves grow thicker and larger still towards its Top, where they are close and broad. The Fruit grows only among the Leaves; and thickest among the thickest of them; insomuch that towards the Top of the Tree the Papahs spring forth from its Body as thick as they can stick one by another. But then lower down, where the Leaves are thinner, the Fruit is larger, and of the Size I have describ'd: And at the Top, where they are thick, they are but small, and no bigger than ordinary Turnips; yet tasted like the rest.

Their chief Land-Animals are their Bullocks, which are said to be many; tho' they ask us 20 Dollars apiece for them; They have also Horses, Asses, and Mules, Deer, Goats, Hogs, and black-fac'd long-tail'd Monkeys. Of Fowls they have Cocks and Hens, Ducks, Guinea-Hens, both tame and wild, Parrakites, Parrots, Pidgeons, Turtle-Doves, Herons, Hawks, Crab-catchers, Galdens (a larger Sort of Crab-catchers) Curlews, &c. Their Fish is the same as at Mayo and the rest of these Islands, and for the most part these Islands have the same Beasts and Birds also; But some of the Isles have Pasturage and Employ-

AN. 1699 ment for some particular Beasts more than other; a
Birds are incourag'd, by Woods for Shelter, and Mai
Fruits for Food, to flock rather to some of the Islan
to this of St. Jago) than to others.

St. Jago Road is one of the worst that I have be
There is not clean Ground enough for above three
and those also must lye very near each other. One
of these must lye close to the Shore, with a Lan
there: And that is the best for a small Ship. I s
not have come in here if I had not been told that it
good secure Place; but I found it so much othe
that I was in Pain to be gone. Captain Barefoot
came to an Anchor while I was here, in foul Groun
quickly 2 Anchors; and I had lost a small one.
Island Fogo shews its self from this Road very pl
about 7 or 8 Leagues distance; and in the Night w
the Flames of Fire issuing from its Top.

150

noctial Line

0

Squaly Isle

Mathias I.

C. Solomaswer

Slingers Bay

NOVA

BRITTAN

NIA

5

Dampiers Passage

10

160

CHAP. II

The A.'s Deliberation on the Sequel of his Voyage, and Departure from St. Jago. His Course, and the Winds, &c. in crossing the Line. He stands away for the Bay of All-Saints in Brazil; and why. His Arrival on that Coast and in the Bay. Of the several Forts, the Road, Situation, Town, and Buildings of Bahia. Of its Governour, Ships and Merchants; and Commodities to and from Europe. Claying of Sugar. The Season for the European Ships, and Coire Cables: Of their Guinea-trade, and of the Coasting-trade, and Whale-killing. Of the Inhabitants of Bahia; their carrying in Hammocks; their Artificers, Crane for Goods, and Negro-Slaves. Of the Country about Bahia, its Soil and Product. Its Timber trees; the Sapiera, Vermiatico, Comesserie, Guitteba, Serrie, and Mangroves. The Bastard-Coco, its Nuts and Cables; and the Silk-Cotton-trees. The Brazilian Fruits, Oranges, &c. Of the Sour-sops, Cashew's, and Jennipah's. Of their peculiar Fruits, Arisah's, Mericasah's, Petango's, Petumbo's, Mungaroo's, Muckishaw's, Ingwa's, Otee's, and Musteran de ova's. Of the Palm-berries, Physick-nuts, Mendibee's, &c. and their Roots and Herbs, &c. Of their Wild-Fowl, Maccaw's, Parrots, &c. The Yemma, Carrion-crow, and Chattering-crow, Bill-bird, Curreso, Turtle-dove and Wild-pigeons; the Jenetee, Clocking-hen, Crab-catcher, Galden, and black Heron: The Ducks, Wigeon and Teal; and Ostriches to the Southward, and of the Dunghill-fowls. Of their Cattle, Horses, &c. Leopards and Tiger's. Of their Serpents; the Rattle-Snake, small Green-Snake, Amphisbæna, small black and small Grey-Snake; the great Land, and the great Water-Snake: And of the Water-dog. Of their Sea-fish and Turtle; and of St. Paul's-Town.

HAVING dispatched my small Affairs at the C. Verd Islands, I meditated on the Process of my Voyage. I thought it requisite to touch once more at a cultivated Place in these Seas, where my Men might be refresh'd, and might have a AN. 1699

AN. 1699 Market wherein to furnish themselves with Necessaries: For designing that my next Stretch should be quite to N. Holland, and knowing that after so long a Run nothing was to be expected there but fresh Water, if I could meet even with that there, I resolved upon putting in first at some Port of Brazil, and to provide my self there with whatever I might have further Occasion for. Beside the refreshing and furnishing my Men, I aim'd also at the inuring them gradually and by Intervals to the Fatigues that were to be expected in the Remainder of the Voyage, which was to be in a part of the World they were altogether Strangers to; none of them, except two young Men, having ever cross'd the Line.

With this Design I sail'd from St. Jago on the 22d of February, with the Winds at E. N. E. and N. E. fair Weather, and a brisk Gale. We steered away S. S. E. and S. S. E. half East, till in the Lat. of 7 deg. 50. min. we met with many Riplings in the Sea like a Tide or strong Current, which setting against the Wind caus'd such a Ripling. We continu'd to meet these Currents from that Lat. till we came into the Lat. of 3 deg. 22 N. when they ceased. During this Time we saw some Boneta's, and Sharks; catching one of these. We had the true general Trade-Wind blowing fresh at N. E. till in the Lat. of 4 deg. 40 min. N. when the Wind varied, and we had small Gales, with some Tornadoes. We were then to the East of St. Jago 4 deg. 54 min. when we got into Lat. 3 deg. 2 min. N. (where I said the Ripling ceas'd) and Long. to the East of St. Jago 5 deg. 2 min. we had the Wind whiffling between the S. by E. and E. by N. small Gales, frequent Calms, very black Clouds, with much Rain. In the Lat. of 3 deg. 8 min. N. and Long. E. from St. Jago 5 deg. 8 min. we had the Wind from the S. S. E. to the N. N. E. faint, and often interrupted with Calms. While we had Calms we had the Opportunity of trying the Current we had met with hitherto, and found that it set N. E. by E. half a Knot, which is 12 Mile in 24 Hours: So that here it ran at the Rate of half a Mile an Hour, and had been much stronger before. The Rains held us by Intervals till the Lat. of 1 deg. 0 min. N. with small Gales of Wind between S. S. E. and S. E. by E. and sometimes calm: Afterwards we had the Wind between the S. and S. S. E. till we cross'd the Line, small Winds, Calms, and pretty fair Weather. We saw but few Fish beside Porposes; but of them a great many, and struck one of them.

It was the 10th day of March, about the Time of the Equinox, when we cross'd the Equator, having had all along from the Lat. of 4 deg. 40 min. N. where the true Trade-wind left us, a great Swell out of the S. E. and but small uncertain Gales, mostly Southerly, so that we crept to the Southward but slowly. I kept up against these as well as I could to the Southward, and when we had now and then a Flurry of Wind at E. I still went away due South, purposely to get to the Southward as fast as I could; for while near the Line I expected to have but uncertain Winds, frequent Calms, Rains, Tornadoes, &c. which would not only retard my Course, but endanger Sickness also among my Men: especially those who were ill provided with Cloaths, or were too lazy to shift themselves when they were drench'd with the Rains. The Heat of the Weather made them careless of doing this; but taking a Dram of Brandy, which I gave them when wet, with a Charge to shift themselves, they would however lye down in their Hammocks with their wet Cloaths; so that when they turn'd out they caus'd an ill Smell where-ever they came, and their Hammocks would stink sufficiently; that I think the remedying of this is worth the Care of Commanders that cross the Line; especially when they are, it may be, a Month or more e'er they get out of the Rains, at sometimes of the Year, as in June, July, or August.

What I have here said about the Currents, Winds, Calms, &c. in this Passage, is chiefly for the farther Illustration of what I have heretofore observ'd in general about these Matters, and especially as to crossing the Line, in my "Discourse of the Winds, &c. in the Torrid Zone": [See Vol. II, Part 3. p. 235]. Which Observations I have had very much confirm'd to me in the Course of this

AN. Voyage; and I shall particularize in several of the chief
1699 of them as they come in my Way. And indeed I think I may say this of the main of the Observations in that Treatise, that the clear Satisfaction I had about them, and how much I might rely upon them, was a great Ease to my Mind during this vexatious Voyage; wherein the Ignorance, and Obstinacy withal, of some under me, occasion'd me a great deal of Trouble: Tho' they found all along, and were often forc'd to acknowledge it, that I was seldom out in my Conjectures, when I told them usually beforehand what Winds, &c. we should meet with at such or such particular Places we should come at.

Pernambuc was the Port that I designed for at my first setting out from St. Jago; it being a Place most proper for my Purpose, by Reason of its Situation, lying near the Extremity of C. St. Augustine, the Easternmost Promontory of Brazil; by which means it not only enjoys the greater Benefit of the Sea-breezes, and is consequently more healthy than other Places to the Southward, but is withal less subject to the Southerly Coasting-Trade-winds, that blow half the Year on this Shore; which were now drawing on, and might be troublesome to me: So that I might both hope to reach soonest Pernambuc, as most directly and nearest in my Run; and might thence also more easily get away to the Southward than from Bahia de Todos los Santos, or Ria Janeira.

But notwithstanding these Advantages I propos'd to my self in going to Pernambuc, I was soon put by that Design through the Refractoriness of some under me, and the Discontents and Backwardness of some of my Men. For the Calms and Shiftings of Winds which I met with, as I was to expect, in crossing the Line, made them, who were unacquainted with these Matters, almost heartless as to the Pursuit of the Voyage, as thinking we should never be able to weather Cape St. Augustine: And though I told them that by that Time we should get to about three Degrees South of the Line, we should again have a true brisk general Trade-Wind from the North-East, that would carry us to what part of Brazil we pleas'd, yet they

would not believe it till they found it so. This, with AN.
some other unforeseen Accidents, not necessary to be 1699
mention'd in this Place, meeting with the Aversion of my Men to a long unknown Voyage, made me justly apprehensive of their Revolting, and was a great Trouble and Hindrance to me. So that I was obliged partly to alter my Measures, and met with many difficulties, the Particulars of which I shall not trouble the Reader with: But I mention thus much of it in general for my own necessary Vindication, in my taking such Measures sometimes for prosecuting the Voyage as the State of my Ships Crew, rather than my own Judgment and Experience, determin'd me to. The Disorders of my Ship made me think at present that Pernambuc would not be so fit a Place for me; being told that Ships ride there 2 or 3 Leagues from the Town, under the Command of no Forts; so that whenever I should have been ashore it might have been easy for my discontented Crew to have cut or slipt their Cables, and have gone away from me: Many of them discovering already an Intention to return to England, and some of them declaring openly that they would go no further onwards than Brazil. I alter'd my Course therefore, and stood away for Bahio de todos los Santos, or the Bay of all Saints, where I hop'd to have the Governour's Help, if need should require, for securing my Ship from any such mutinous Attempt; being forced to keep my self all the way upon my Guard, and to lie with my Officers, such as I could trust, and with small Arms upon the Quarter-Deck; it scarce being safe for me to lie in my Cabbin, by Reason of the Discontents among my Men.

On the 23d of March we saw the Land of Brazil; having had thither, from the time when we came into the true Trade-wind again after crossing the Line, very fair Weather and brisk Gales, mostly at E. N. E. The Land we saw was about 20 Leagues to the North of Bahia; so I coasted along Shore to the Southward. This Coast is rather low than high, with Sandy-Bays all along by the Sea.

A little within Land are many very white Spots of

AN. 1699 Sand, appearing like Snow; and the Coast looks very pleasant, being checker'd with Woods and Savannahs. The Trees in general are not tall; but they are green and flourishing. There are many small Houses by the Sea-side, whose Inhabitants are chiefly Fishermen. They come off to Sea on Bark-logs, made of several Logs fasten'd Side to Side, that have one or two Masts with Sails to them. There are two Men in each Bark-log, one at either End, having small low Benches, raised a little above the Logs, to sit and fish on, and two Baskets hanging up at the Mast or Masts; one to put their Provisions in, the other for their Fish. Many of these were a-fishing now, and 2 of them came aboard, of whom I bought some Fish. In the Afternoon we sailed by one very remarkable Piece of Land, where, on a small pleasant Hill, there was a Church dedicated to the Virgin Mary. See a Sight of some Parts of this Coast [Table omitted] and of the Hill the Church stands on.

I coasted along till the Evening, and then brought to, and lay by till the next Morning. About 2 Hours after we were brought to, there came a Sail out of the Offin (from Seaward) and lay by about a Mile to Windward of us, and so lay all Night. In the Morning upon speaking with her, she proved to be a Portugueze Ship bound to Bahia; therefore I sent my Boat aboard and desired to have one of his Mates to Pilot me in: He answer'd, that he had not a Mate capable of it, but that he would sail in before me, and shew me the way; and that if he went into the Harbour in the Night, he would hang out a Light for me. He said we had not far in, and might reach it before Night with a tolerable Gale; but that with so small an one as now we had we could not do it: So we jogg'd on till Night, and then he accordingly hung out his Light, which we steered after, sounding as we went in. I kept all my Men on Deck, and had an Anchor ready to let go on occasion. We had the Tide of Ebb against us, so that we went in but slowly; and it was about the Middle of the Night when we anchor'd. Immediately the Portugueze Master came aboard to see me, to whom I returned Thanks for his Civilities; and indeed I found much Respect, not only from this Gentleman, but from all of that Nation both here and in other Places, who were ready to serve me on all Occasions. The Place that we anchored in was about two Miles from the Harbour where the Ships generally ride; but the Fear I had lest my People should run away with the Ship, made me hasten to get a Licence from the Governor, to run up into the Harbour, and ride among their Ships, close by one of their Forts. So on the 25th of March about 10 a Clock in the Morning, the Tide serving, I went thither, being piloted by the Super-intendant there, whose Business it is to carry up all the King of Portugal's Ships that come hither, and to see them well moored. He brought us to an Anchor right against the Town, at the outer Part of the Harbour, which was then full of Ships, within 150 Yards of a small Fort that stands on a Rock half a Mile from the Shore. See a Prospect of the Harbour and the Town, as it appear'd to us while we lay at Anchor [omitted].

AN. 1699

Bahia de todos los Santos lies in Lat. 13 deg. S. It is the most considerable Town in Brazil, whether in Respect of the Beauty of its Buildings, its Bulk, or its Trade and Revenue. It has the Convenience of a good Harbour that is capable of receiving Ships of the greatest Burthen: The Entrance of which is guarded with a strong Fort standing without the Harbour, call'd St. Antonio: A Sight of which I have given [Table omitted] as it appeared to us the Afternoon before we came in; and its Lights (which they hang out purposely for Ships) we saw the same Night. There are other smaller Forts that command the Harbour, one of which stands on a Rock in the Sea, about half a Mile from the Shore. Close by this Fort all Ships must pass that anchor here, and must ride also within half a Mile of it at farthest between this and another Fort (that stands on a Point at the inner part of the Harbour and is called the Dutch Fort) but must ride nearest to the former, all along against the Town: Where there is good holding Ground, and less exposed to the Southerly Winds that blow very hard here. They commonly set in about April,

AN. 1699 but blow hardest in May, June, July and August: But the place where the Ships ride is exposed to these Winds not above 3 Points of the Compass.

Beside these, there is another Fort fronting the Harbour, and standing on the Hill upon which the Town stands. The Town it self consists of about 2000 Houses; the major part of which cannot be seen from the Harbour; but so many as appear in Sight, with a great Mixture of Trees between them, and all placed on a rising Hill, make a very pleasant Prospect; as may be judg'd by the Draught, [Table omitted].

There are in the Town 13 Churches, Chapels, Hospitals, Convents, beside one Nunnery; viz. the Ecclesia Major or Cathedral, the Jesuits College, which are the chief, and both in Sight from the Harbour: St. Antonio, Sta. Barbara, both Parish-Churches; the Franciscans Church, and the Dominicans; and 2 Convents of Carmelites; a Chapel for Seamen close by the Sea-side, where Boats commonly land, and the Seamen go immediately to Prayers; another Chapel for poor People, at the farther End of the same Street, which runs along by the Shore; and a third Chapel for Soldiers, at the Edge of the Town remote from the Sea; and an Hospital in the Middle of the Town. The Nunnery stands at the outer-edge of the Town next the Fields, wherein by Report there are 70 Nuns. Here lives an Arch-bishop, who has a fine Palace in the Town; and the Governor's Palace is a fair Stone-building, and looks handsome to the Sea, tho' but indifferently furnish'd within: Both Spaniards and Portugueze in their Plantations abroad, as I have generally observ'd, affecting to have large Houses; but are little curious about Furniture, except Pictures some of them. The Houses of the Town are 2 or 3 Stories high, the Walls thick and strong, being built with Stone, with a Covering of Pantile; and many of them have Balconies. The principal Streets are large, and all of them pav'd or pitch'd with small Stones. There are also Parades in the most eminent Places of the Town, and many Gardens, as well within the Town as in the Out-parts of it, wherein are Fruit-trees, Herbs, Salladings and Flowers in great Variety, but order'd with no great Care nor Art. AN. 1699

The Governor who resides here is call'd Don John de Lancastrio, being descended, as they say, from our English Lancaster Family; and he has a Respect for our Nation on that Account, calling them his Country-men. I waited on him several Times, and always found him very courteous and civil. Here are about 400 Soldiers in Garrison. They commonly draw up and exercise in a large Parade before the Governour's House; and many of them attend him when he goes abroad. The Soldiers are decently clad in brown Linnen, which in these hot Countries is far better than Woollen; but I never saw any clad in Linnen but only these. Beside the Soldiers in Pay, he can soon have some Thousands of Men up in Arms on occasion. The Magazine is on the Skirts of the Town, on a small Rising between the Nunnery and the Soldiers Church. 'Tis big enough to hold 2 or 3000 Barrels of Powder; but I was told it seldom has more than 100, sometimes but 80. There are always a Band of Soldiers to guard it, and Centinels looking out both Day and Night.

A great many Merchants always reside at Bahia; for 'tis a Place of great Trade: I found here above 30 great Ships from Europe, with 2 of the King of Portugal's Ships of War for their Convoy; beside 2 Ships that traded to Africa only, either to Angola, Gamba, or other Places on the Coast of Guinea; and Abundance of small Craft, that only run to and fro on this Coast, carrying Commodities from one Part of Brazil to another.

The Merchants that live here are said to be rich, and to have many Negro-Slaves in their Houses, both of Men and Women. Themselves are chiefly Portugueze, Foreigners having but little Commerce with them; yet here was one Mr. Cock an English Merchant, a very civil Gentleman and of good Repute. He had a Patent to be our English Consul, but did not Care to take upon him any publick Character, because English Ships seldom come hither, here having been none in 11 or 12 Years before this Time. Here was also a Dane, and a French Merchant or two; but all

AN. 1699 have their Effects transported to and from Europe in Portugueze Ships, none of any other Nation being admitted to trade hither. There is a Custom-house by the Sea-side, where all Goods imported or exported are entred. And to prevent Abuses there are 5 or 6 Boats that take their Turns to row about the Harbour, searching any Boats they suspect to be running of Goods.

The chief Commodities that the European Ships bring hither, are Linnen-Cloaths, both coarse and fine; some Woollens also, as Bays, Searges, Perpetuana's, &c. Hats, Stockings, both of Silk and Thread, Bisket-bread, Wheat-flower, Wine (chiefly Port) Oil-Olive, Butter, Cheese, &c. and Salt-beef and Pork would there also be good Commodities. They bring hither also Iron, and all Sorts of Iron-Tools; Pewter-Vessels of all Sorts, as Dishes, Plates, Spoons, &c. Looking-glasses, Beads, and other Toys; and the Ships that touch at St. Jago bring thence, as I said, Cotton-Cloath, which is afterwards sent to Angola.

The European Ships carry from hence Sugar, Tobacco, either in Roll or Snuff, never in Leaf, that I know of: These are the Staple Commodities. Besides which, here are Dye-woods, as Fustick,[1] &c., with Woods for other Uses, as speckled Wood, Brazil, &c. They also carry home raw Hides, Tallow, Train-oil of Whales, &c. Here are also kept tame Monkeys, Parrots, Parrakites, &c. which the Seamen carry home.

The Sugar of this Country is much better than that which we bring home from our Plantations: For all the Sugar that is made here is clay'd, which makes it whiter and finer than our Muscovada, as we call our unrefin'd Sugar. Our Planters seldom refine any with Clay, unless sometimes a little to send Home as Presents for their Friends in England. Their way of doing it is by taking some of the whitest Clay and mixing it with Water,

[1] Bois Jaune, or Dyer's Mulberry, a tall tree with yellow wood, from which a rather sober yellow dye is obtained. The tree bears a small fruit, much sought after by birds. It is common in most tropical countries. "Speckled wood" may be the famous Brazilian rose-wood which has been exported in large quantities ever since the country was settled. "Brazil" (*Cæsalpinia Braziliensis*) is a sort of logwood used in dyeing.

till 'tis like Cream. With this they fill up the Pans of Sugar, that are sunk 2 or 3 Inches below the Brim by the draining of the Molosses out of it: First scraping off the thin hard Crust of the Sugar that lies at the Top, and would hinder the Water of the Clay from soaking through the Sugar of the Pan. The refining is made by this Percolation. For 10 or 12 Days Time that the clayish Liquor lies soaking down the Pan, the white Water whitens the Sugar as it passes thro' it; and the gross Body of the Clay it self grows hard on the Top, and may be taken off at Pleasure; when scraping off with a Knife the very upper-part of the Sugar, which will be a little sullied, that which is underneath will be white almost to the Bottom: And such as is called Brazil Sugar is thus whitened. When I was here this Sugar was sold for 50s. per 100 lb. And the Bottoms of the Pots, which is very coarse Sugar, for about 20s. per 100 lb. both Sorts being then scarce; for here was not enough to lade the Ships, and therefore some of them were to lye here till the next Season.

AN. 1699

The European Ships commonly arrive here in February or March, and they have generally quick Passages; finding at that Time of the Year brisk Gales to bring them to the Line, little Trouble, then, in crossing it, and brisk E. N. E. Winds afterwards to bring them hither. They commonly return from hence about the latter End of May, or in June. 'Twas said when I was here that the Ships would sail hence the 20th Day of May; and therefore they were all very busy, some in taking in their Goods, others in careening and making themselves ready. The Ships that come hither usually careen at their first coming; here being a Hulk belonging to the King for that Purpose. This Hulk is under the Charge of the Superintendent I spoke of, who has a certain Sum of Money for every Ship that careens by her. He also provides Firing[1] and other Necessaries for that Purpose: And the Ships do commonly hire of the Merchants here each 2 Cables to moor by all the Time they lye here, and so save their own Hempen

[1] Brushwood and the like, which, being kindled on the exposed bends of the ship, burnt off the barnacles and other accumulations.

AN. 1699 Cables; for these are made of a Sort of Hair,[1] that grows on a certain Kind of Trees, hanging down from the Top of their Bodies, and is very like the black Coyre[2] in the East-Indies, if not the same. These Cables are strong and lasting: And so much for the European Ships.

The Ships that use the Guinea-Trade are small Vessels in comparison of the former. They carry out from hence Rum, Sugar, the Cotton-cloaths of St. Jago, Beads, &c. and bring in Return, Gold, Ivory, and Slaves; making very good Returns.

The small Craft that belong to this Town are chiefly imployed in carrying European Goods from Bahia, the Center of the Brasilian Trade, to the other Places on this Coast; bringing back hither Sugar, Tobacco, &c. They are sailed chiefly with Negro-Slaves; and about Christmas these are mostly imployed in Whale-killing; For about that Time of the Year a Sort of Whales, as they call them, are very thick on this Coast. They come in also into the Harbours and inland Lakes, where the Seamen go out and kill them. The Fat of them is boiled to Oil; the Lean is eaten by the Slaves and poor People: And I was told by one that had frequently eaten of it, that the Flesh was very sweet and wholsome. These are said to be but small Whales; yet here are so many,[3] and so easily killed, that they get a great deal of Money by it. Those that strike them buy their Licence for it of the King: And I was inform'd that he receives 30000 Dollars per Annum for this Fishery. All the small Vessels that use this Coasting Traffick are built here; and so are some Men of War also for the King's Service. There was one a building when I was here, a Ship of 40 or 50 Guns: And the Timber of this Country is very good and proper for this Purpose. I was told it was very strong, and more durable than any we have in Europe; and they have enough of it. As for

[1] The Piassava palm.

[2] Coir. Piassava cables are supposed to be thrice the strength of those made of the true coir (cocoa-nut fibre) and less subject to dry-rot than cables of hemp, either Indian or Manila.

[3] This, like several other famous whale-fisheries, is now abandoned.

their Ships that use the European Trade, some of them that I saw there were English built, taken from us by the French, during the late War,[1] and sold by them to the Portugueze. AN. 1699

Besides Merchants and others that trade by Sea from this Port, here are other pretty wealthy Men, and several Artificers and Trades-men of most Sorts, who by Labour and Industry maintain themselves very well; especially such as can arrive at the Purchase of a Negro-Slave or two. And indeed, excepting people of the lowest Degree of all, here are scarce any but what keep Slaves in their Houses. The richer Sort, besides the Slaves of both Sexes whom they keep for servile Uses in their Houses, have Men Slaves who wait on them aboard, for State; either running by their Horse-sides when they ride out, or to carry them to and fro on their Shoulders in the Town when they make short Visits near Home. Every Gentleman or Merchant is provided with Things necessary for this Sort of Carriage. The main Thing is a pretty large Cotton Hammock of the West-India Fashion, but mostly dyed blue, with large Fringes of the same, hanging down on each Side. This is carried on the Negro's Shoulders by the help of a Bambo about 12 or 14 Foot long, to which the Hammock is hung; and a Covering comes over the Pole, hanging down on each Side like a Curtain: So that the Person so carry'd cannot be seen unless he pleases; but may either lye down, having Pillows for his Head; or may sit up by being a little supported with these Pillows, and by letting both his Legs hang out over one Side of the Hammock. When he hath a Mind to be seen he puts by his Curtain, and salutes every one of his Acquaintance whom he meets in the Streets; for they take a Piece of Pride in greeting one another from their Hammocks, and will hold long Conferences thus in the Street: But then their 2 Slaves who carry the Hammock have each a strong well-made Staff, with a fine Iron Fork at the upper End, and a sharp Iron below, like the Rest for a Musket, which

[1] The war of 1689–1697.

AN. 1699 they stick fast in the Ground, and let the Pole or Bambo of the Hammock rest upon them, till their Master's Business or the Complement is over. There is scarce a Man of any Fashion, especially a Woman, will pass the Streets but so carried in a Hammock. The Chief Mechanick Traders here, are Smiths, Hatters, Shoemakers, Tanners, Sawyers, Carpenters, Coopers, &c. Here are also Taylors, Butchers, &c. which last kill the Bullocks very dexterously, sticking them at one Blow with a sharp-pointed Knife in the Nape of the Neck, having first drawn them close to a Rail; but they dress them very slovenly. It being Lent when I came hither, there was no buying any Flesh till Easter-Eve, when a great Number of Bullocks were kill'd at once in the Slaughter-houses within the Town, Men, Women and Children flocking thither with great Joy to buy, and a Multitude of Dogs, almost starv'd, following them; for whom the Meat seem'd fittest, it was so lean. All these Trades-men buy Negroes, and train them up to their several Employments, which is a great Help to them; and they having so frequent Trade to Angola, and other Parts of Guinea, they have a constant Supply of Blacks both for their Plantations and Town. These Slaves are very useful in this Place for Carriage, as Porters; for as here is a great Trade by Sea, and the Landing-place is at the Foot of a Hill, too steep for drawing with Carts, so there is great need of Slaves to carry Goods up into the Town, especially for the inferiour Sort: But the Merchants have also the Convenience of a great Crane that goes with Ropes or Pullies, one End of which goes up while the other goes down. The House in which this Crane is, stands on the Brow of the Hill towards the Sea, hanging over the Precipice; and there are Planks set shelving against the Bank from thence to the Bottom, against which the Goods lean or slide as they are hoisted up or let down. The Negro-Slaves in this Town are so numerous, that they make up the greatest Part or Bulk of the Inhabitants: Every House, as I said, having some, both Men and Women, of them. Many of the Portugueze, who are Batchelors, keep of these black Women for Misses, tho' they know the Danger they are in of being poyson'd by them, if ever they give them any Occasion of Jealousy. A Gentleman of my Acquaintance, who had been familiar with his Cook-maid, lay under some such Apprehensions from her when I was there. These Slaves also of either Sex will easily be engaged to do any Sort of Mischief; even to Murder, if they are hired to do it, especially in the Night; for which Reason, I kept my Men on board as much as I could; for one of the French King's Ships being here, had several Men murther'd by them in the Night, as I was credibly inform'd.

Having given this Account of the Town of Bahia, I shall next say somewhat of the Country. There is a Salt-water Lake runs 40 Leagues, as I was told, up the Country, N. W. from the Sea, leaving the Town and Dutch Fort on the Starboard Side. The Country all around about is for the most part a pretty flat even Ground, not high, nor yet very low: It is well water'd with Rivers, Brooks and Springs; neither wants it for good Harbours, navigable Creeks, and good Bays for Ships to ride in. The Soil in general is good, naturally producing very large Trees of divers Sorts, and fit for any Uses. The Savannahs also are loaden with Grass, Herbs, and many Sorts of smaller Vegetables; and being cultivated, produce any Thing that is proper for those hot Countries, as Sugar-Canes, Cotton, Indico, Tobacco, Maiz, Fruit-Trees of several Kinds, and eatable Roots of all Sorts. Of the several Kinds of Trees that are here, I shall give an Account of some, as I had it partly from an Inhabitant of Bahia, and partly from my Knowledge of them otherwise, viz. Sapiera,[1] Vermiatico,[2] Comesserie,[3] Guitteba,[4] Serrie,[5] as they were pronounc'd to me, three Sorts of Mangrove, speckled Wood, Fustick, Cotton-Trees of 3 Sorts, &c. together with Fruit-Trees of divers Sorts that grow wild, beside such as are planted.

Of Timber-Trees, the Sapiera is said to be large and

[1] Sapupira. [2] Vinhatico de Bahia: *Plathymenicum reticulatum.*
[3] Cumesserie, *Aydendron Sp.*, a red wood used in shipbuilding.
[4] Cupiuba? [5] Sete? *Couratari rufuscens.*

AN. 1699 tall; it is very good Timber, and is made use of in building of Houses; so is the Vermiatico, a tall streight-bodied Tree, of which they make Plank 2 Foot broad; and they also make Canoa's with it. Comesserie and Guitteba are chiefly used in building Ships; these are as much esteem'd here as Oaks are in England, and they say either Sort is harder and more durable than Oak. The Serrie is a Sort of Tree much like Elm, very durable in Water. Here are also all the three Sorts of Mangrove Trees, viz. the Red, the White, and the Black, which I have described [Vol. I. p. 84]. The Bark of the Red Mangrove, is here us'd for tanning of Leather, and they have great Tan-pits for it. The black Mangrove grows larger here than in the West-Indies, and of it they make good Plank. The white Mangrove is larger and tougher than in the West-Indies; of these they make Masts and Yards for Barks.

There grow here wild or bastard Coco-Nut Trees, neither so large nor so tall as the common ones in the East or West-Indies. They bear Nuts as the others, but not a quarter so big as the right Coco-Nuts. The Shell is full of Kernel, without any hollow Place or Water in it; and the Kernel is sweet and wholsome, but very hard both for the Teeth and for Digestion. These Nuts are in much Esteem for making Beads for Pater noster's, Boles of Tobacco-Pipes, and other Toys: and every small Shop here has a great many of them to sell. At the Top of these Bastard Coco-Trees, among the Branches, there grows a Sort of long black Thread like Horse-hair, but much longer, which by the Portugueze is called Tresabo.[1] Of this they make Cables which are very serviceable, strong and lasting; for they will not rot as Cables made of Hemp, tho' they lye exposed both to Wet and Heat. These are the Cables which I said they keep in their Harbours here, to let to hire to European Ships, and resemble the Coyre-Cables.

Here are 3 Sorts of Cotton-Trees that bear Silk-Cotton. One Sort is such as I have formerly describ'd [Vol. I. p.

[1] Piaçaba.

186] by the Name of the Cotton-tree. The other 2 Sorts[1] I never saw any where but here. The Trees of these latter Sorts are but small in Comparison of the former, which are reckon'd the biggest in all the West-India Woods; yet are however of a good Bigness and Heighth. One of these last Sorts is not so full of Branches as the other of them; neither do they produce their Fruit the same Time of the Year: For one Sort had its Fruit just ripe, and was shedding its Leaves while the other Sort was yet green, and its Fruit small and growing, having but newly done blossoming; the Tree being as full of young Fruit as an Apple-Tree ordinarily in England. These last yield very large Pods, about 6 Inches long, and as big as a Man's Arm. It is ripe in September and October; then the Pod opens, and the Cotton bursts out in a great Lump as big as a Man's Head. They gather these Pods before they open; otherways it would fly all away. It opens as well after 'tis gathered; and then they take out the Cotton, and preserve it to fill Pillows and Bolsters, for which use 'tis very much esteemed: But 'tis fit for nothing else,[2] being so short that it cannot be spun. 'Tis of a tawney Colour; and the Seeds are black, very round, and as big as a white Pea. The other Sort is ripe in March or April. The Fruit or Pod is like a large Apple, and very round. The out-side Shell is as thick as the Top of one's Finger. Within this there is a very thin whitish Bag or Skin which incloseth the Cotton. When the Cotton-Apple is ripe, the outer thick green Shell splits it self into 5 equal Parts from Stemb to Tail, and drops off, leaving the Cotton hanging upon the Stemb, only pent up in its fine Bag. A Day or two afterwards the Cotton swells by the Heat of the Sun, breaks the Bag and bursts out, as big as a Man's Head: And then as the Wind blows 'tis by Degrees driven away, a little at a Time, out of the Bag that still hangs upon the Stemb, and is scatter'd about the Fields; the Bag soon following the Cotton, and the Stemb the Bag. Here is

AN. 1699

[1] The mungaba and the samauma. The sort "such as I have formerly described" is *Bombax pentandrum*, a tall, thorny tree with digitated leaves.
[2] It is sometimes used in the making of felt.

AN. 1699 also a little of the right West-India Cotton Shrub: but none of the Cotton is exported, nor do they make much Cloth of it.

This Country produces great Variety of fine Fruits, as very good Oranges of 3 or 4 Sorts; (especially one Sort of China Oranges;) Limes in Abundance, Pomegranates, Pomecitrons, Plantains, Bonano's, right Coco-Nuts, Guava's, Coco-plumbs (called here Munsheroo's), Wild-grapes, such as I have describ'd [Vol. II. Part 2, p. 151] beside such Grapes as grow in Europe. Here are also Hog-plumbs, Custard-Apples, Sour-sops,[1] Cashews,[2] Papah's[3] (called here Mamoons) Jennipah's[4] (called here Jenni-Pappah's) Manchineel-Apples and Mango's. Mango's are yet but rare here: I saw none of them but in the Jesuit's Garden, which has a great many fine Fruits, and some Cinnamon-Trees. These, both of them, were first brought from the East-Indies, and they thrive here very well: So do Pumple-musses, brought also from thence; and both China and Sevil Oranges are here very plentiful as well as good.

The Sour-sop (as we call it) is a large Fruit as big as a Man's Head, of a long or oval Shape, and of a green Colour; but one Side is yellowish when ripe. The out-side Rind or Coat is pretty thick, and very rough, with small sharp Knobs; the Inside is full of spongy Pulp, within which also are many black Seeds or Kernels, in Shape and Bigness like a Pumpkin-seed. The Pulp is very juicy, of a pleasant Taste, and wholesome. You suck the Juice out of the Pulp, and so spit it out. The Tree or Shrub that bears this Fruit grows about 10 or 12 Foot high, with a small short Body; the Branches growing pretty strait up; for I did never see any of them spread abroad. The Twigs are slender and tough; and so is the Stemb of the Fruit. This Fruit grows also both in the East and West-Indies.

The Cashew is a Fruit as big as a Pippin, pretty long, and bigger near the Stemb than at the other End, growing

[1] *Anona maxima.* [2] Acaju, or acajou (*Anacardium occidentale*).
[3] Papahs: *Papa major.*
[4] Genipapáhs: *Genipa Americana* or Surinam marmalade box.

tapering. The Rind is smooth and thin, of a red and yellow Colour. The Seed of this Fruit grows at the End of it; 'tis of an Olive Colour shaped like a Bean, and about the same Bigness, but not altogether so flat. The Tree is as big as an Apple-Tree, with Branches not thick, yet spreading off. The Boughs are gross, the Leaves broad and round, and in Substance pretty thick. This Fruit is soft and spongy when ripe, and so full of Juice that in biting it the Juice will run out on both Sides of one's Mouth. It is very pleasant, and gratefully rough on the Tongue; and is accounted a very wholesome Fruit. This grows both in the East and West-Indies, where I have seen and eaten of it.

AN. 1699

The Jennipah or Jennipapah is a Sort of Fruit of the Calabash or Gourd-kind. It is about the Bigness of a Duck-Egg, and somewhat of an Oval Shape; and is of a grey Colour. The Shell is not altogether so thick nor hard as a Calabash; 'Tis full of whitish Pulp mixt with small flat Seeds: and both Pulp and Seeds must be taken into the Mouth, where sucking out the Pulp, you spit out the Seeds. It is of a sharp and pleasing Taste, and is very innocent. The Tree that bears it is much like an Ash, streight bodied, and of a good Height; clean from Limbs till near the Top, where there Branches forth a small Head. The Rind is of a pale grey, and so is the Fruit. We us'd of this Tree to make Helves or Handles for Axes (for which it is very proper) in the Bay of Campeachy; where I have seen of them, and no where else but here.

Besides these, here are many Sorts of Fruits which I have not met with any where but here; as Arisah's, Mericasah's, Petango's, &c. Arisah's[1] are an excellent Fruit, not much bigger than a large Cherry; shaped like a Catherine-Pear, being small at the Stemb, and swelling bigger towards the End. They are of a greenish Colour, and have small Seeds as big as Mustard Seeds; they are somewhat tart, yet pleasant, and very wholsome, and may be eaten by sick People.

[1] The araça: *Psidium littorale* and *P. suaveolens*.

AN. 1699 Mericasah's,[1] are an excellent Fruit, of which there are 2 Sorts; one growing on a small Tree or Shrub, which is counted the best; the other growing on a Kind of Shrub like a Vine, which they plant about Arbours to make a Shade, having many broad Leaves. The Fruit is as big as a small Orange, round and green. When they are ripe they are soft and fit to eat; full of white Pulp mixt thick with little black Seeds, and there is no separating one from the other, till they are in your Mouth; when you suck in the white Pulp and spit out the Stones. They are tart, pleasant, and very wholesome.

Petango's,[2] are a small red Fruit, that grow also on small Trees, and are as big as Cherries, but not so globular, having one flat Side, and also 5 or 6 small protuberant Ridges. 'Tis a very pleasant tart Fruit, and has a pretty large flattish Stone in the Middle.

Petumbo's,[3] are a yellow Fruit (growing on a Shrub like a Vine) bigger than Cherries, with a pretty large Stone: These are sweet, but rough in the Mouth.

Mungaroo's,[4] are a Fruit as big as Cherries, red on one Side and white on the other Side: They are said to be full of small Seeds, which are commonly swallowed in eating them.

Muckishaw's,[5] are said to be a Fruit as big as Crab-Apples, growing on large Trees. They have also small Seeds in the Middle, and are well tasted.

Ingwa's,[6] are a Fruit like the Locust-Fruit, 4 Inches long, and one broad. They grow on high Trees.

Otee,[7] is a Fruit as big as a large Coco-Nut. It hath a Husk on the outside, and a large Stone within, and is accounted a very fine Fruit.

Musteran-de-ova's,[8] are a round Fruit as big as large Hazel-Nuts, cover'd with thin brittle Shells of a blackish Colour: They have a small Stone in the middle, inclosed within a black pulpy Substance, which is of a pleasant

[1] *Protium altissima.*
[2] Pitanga: *Myrcia rubella.*
[3] Pittombera: *Sapindus esculentus.*
[4] *Philodendron arboreum.*
[5] Macacao?
[6] Inga-louro.
[7] Oiti (*Couvepia aciva*).
[8] *Lucuma procera?*

Taste. The outside Shell is chewed with the Fruit, and spit out with the Stone, when the Pulp is suck'd from them. The Tree that bears this Fruit is tall, large, and very hard Wood. I have not seen any of these five last named Fruits, but had them thus described to me by an Irish Inhabitant of Bahia; tho' as to this last, I am apt to believe, I may have both seen and eaten of them in Achin in Sumatra. AN. 1699

Palm-berries[1] (called here Dendees) grow plentifully about Bahia; the largest are as big as Wall-nuts; they grow in Bunches on the top of the Body of the Tree, among the Roots of the Branches or Leaves, as all Fruits of the Palm-kind do. These are the same kind of Berries or Nuts as those they make the Palm-Oyl with on the Coast of Guinea, where they abound: And I was told that they make Oyl with them here also. They sometimes roast and eat them; but when I had one roasted to prove it, I did not like it.

Physick-Nuts,[2] as our Seamen call them, are called here Pineon; and Agnus Castus is called here Carrepat: These both grow here: So do Mendibees, a Fruit like Physick-Nuts. They scorch them in a Pan over the Fire before they eat them.

Here are also great plenty of Cabbage-Trees,[3] and other Fruits, which I did not get information about, and which I had not the Opportunity of seeing; because this was not the Season, it being our Spring, and consequently their Autumn, when their best Fruits were gone, tho' some were left. However I saw abundance of wild Berries in the Woods and Fields, but I could not learn their Names or Nature.

They have withal good plenty of ground Fruit, as Callavances, Pine-Apples, Pumkins, Water-Melons, Musk-Melons, Cucumbers, and Roots; as Yams, Potato's, Cassava's, &c. Garden-Herbs also good store; as Cabbages, Turnips, Onions, Leeks, and abundance of other Salading, and for the Pot. Drugs of several sorts, viz.

[1] *Carpus distichus.* [2] From the castor-oil plants.
[3] *Euterpe edulis.*

AN. 1699 Sassafras,[1] Snake-Root,[2] &c. Beside the Woods I mentioned for Dying, and other Uses, as Fustick, Speckled-wood, &c.

I brought home with me from hence a good Number of Plants, dried between the Leaves of Books; of some of the choicest of which, that are not spoil'd, I may give a Specimen at the End of the Book.

Here are said to be great plenty and variety of Wild-Fowl, viz. Yemma's, Maccaw's (which are called here Jackoo's, and a larger sort of Parrots, and scarcer) Parrots, Parakites, Flamingo's, Carrion-Crows, Chattering Crows, Cockrecoes, Bill-Birds finely painted, Corresoes, Doves, Pidgeons, Jenetees, Clocking-Hens, Crab-Catchers, Galdens, Currecoo's, Muscovy Ducks, common Ducks, Widgeons, Teal, Curlews, Men of War Birds, Booby's, Noddy's, Pelicans, &c.

The Yemma is bigger than a Swan, grey-feathered, with a long thick sharp-pointed Bill.

The Carrion-Crow and Chattering-Crows, are called here Mackeraw's, and are like those I described in the West-Indies, [Vol. II. Part II. p. 168.] The Bill of the Chattering-Crow is black, and the Upper-Bill is round, bending downwards like a Hawks-Bill, rising up in a Ridge almost Semi-circular, and very sharp, both at the Ridge or Convexity, and at the Point or Extremity: The Lower-Bill is flat and shuts even with it. I was told by a Portuguese here, that their Negro-Wenches make Love-Potions with these Birds. And the Portuguese care not to let them have any of these Birds, to keep them from that Superstition: As I found one Afternoon when I was in the Fields with a Padre and another, who shot two of them, and hid them, as they said, for that Reason. They are not good Food, but their Bills are reckoned a good Antidote against Poison.

[1] The "useful Sassafras," or sassafras laurel, a handsome aromatic tree yielding a valuable drug, and a scented wood, much used by American furniture makers.

[2] *Polygala Senega*, a drug much used at one time in gargles and emetics.

The Bill-Birds[1] are so called by the English, from their monstrous Bills, which are as big as their Bodies. I saw none of these Birds here, but saw several of the Breasts flea'd off and dried, for the Beauty of them; the Feathers were curiously colour'd with Red, Yellow, and Orange-colour. AN. 1699

The Curreso's (called here Mackeraw's[2]) are such as are in the Bay of Campeachy [Vol. II. Part 2, p. 167].

Turtle-Doves are in great plenty here; and two sorts of Wild Pidgeons; the one sort Blackish, the other a light Grey: The Blackish or dark Grey are the Bigger, being as large as our Wood-Quests, or Wood-Pidgeons in England. Both sorts are very good Meat; and are in such plenty from May till September, that a Man may shoot 8 or 10 Dozen in several Shots at one standing, in a close misty Morning, when they come to feed on Berries that grow in the Woods.

The Jenetee is a Bird as big as a Lark, with blackish Feathers, and yellow Legs and Feet. 'Tis accounted very wholesome Food.

Clocking-Hens, are much like the Crab-catchers, which I have described [Vol. II. Part 2, p. 170] but the Legs are not altogether so long. They keep always in swampy wet Places, tho' their Claws are like Land-Fowls Claws. They make a Noise or Cluck like our Brood-Hens, or Dunghil-Hens, when they have Chickens, and for that Reason they are called by the English, Clocking-Hens. There are many of them in the Bay of Campeachy (tho' I omitted to speak of them there) and elsewhere in the West-Indies. There are both here and there four sorts of these long-legg'd Fowls, near a-kin to each other, as so many Sub-Species of the same Kind; viz. Crab-catchers, Clocking-Hens, Galdens (which three are in shape and Colour like Herons in England, but less; the Galden, the biggest of the three, the Crab-catcher the smallest;) and a

[1] *Rhea Americana*, or ariel toucan. It has a golden neck, and a deep scarlet breast, with purple-black back and wings.

[2] Marecca is the Brazilian name for the wild duck. The curassow (*Mitu tuberosa*) is known as the motum.

AN. 1699 fourth sort which are Black, but shaped like the other, having long Legs and short Tails; these are about the bigness of Crab-catchers, and feed as they do.

Currecoos, are Water Fowls, as big as pretty large Chickens, of a bluish Colour, with short Legs and Tail; they feed also in swampy Ground, and are very good Meat. I have not seen of them elsewhere.

The Wild-Ducks here are said to be of two sorts, the Muscovy, and the common-Ducks. In the wet Season here are abundance of them, but in the dry Time but few. Wigeon and Teal also are said to be in great plenty here in the wet Season.

To the Southward of Bahia there are also Ostridges in great plenty, tho' 'tis said, they are not so large as those of Africa: They are found chiefly in the Southern Parts of Brazil, especially among the large Savannahs near the River of Plate; and from thence further South towards the Streights of Magellan.

As for Tame Fowl at Bahia, the chief beside their Ducks, are Dunghil-Fowls, of which they have two sorts; one sort much of the size of our Cocks and Hens; the other very large: And the Feathers of these last are a long time coming forth; so that you see them very naked when half grown; but when they are full grown and well feathered, they appear very large Fowls, as indeed they are; neither do they want for Price; for they are sold at Bahia for half a Crown or three Shillings apiece, just as they are brought first to Market out of the Country, when they are so lean as to be scarce fit to eat.

The Land Animals here are Horses, black Cattle, Sheep, Goats, Rabbits, Hogs, Leopards, Tygers, Foxes, Monkeys, Pecary (a sort of wild Hogs, called here Pica) Armadillo, Alligators, Guano's (called Quittee) Lizards, Serpents, Toads, Frogs, and a sort of amphibious Creatures called by the Portugueze *Cachora's de agua*, in English Water-Dogs.

The Leopards and Tygers of this Country are said to be large and very fierce: But here on the Coast they are either destroyed, or driven back towards the Heart of the

Country; and therefore are seldom found but in the Borders and Out-plantations, where they oftentimes do Mischief. Here are three or four sorts of Monkeys, of different Sizes and Colours. One sort is very large; and another sort is very small: These last are ugly in Shape and Feature, and have a strong Scent of Musk. AN. 1699

Here are several sorts of Serpents, many of them vastly great, and most of them very venomous: As the Rattle-snake for one: And for Venom, a small Green Snake[1] is bad enough, no bigger than the Stemb of a Tobacco-pipe, and about 18 Inches long, very common here.

They have here also the Amphisbæna,[2] or Two-headed Snake, of a grey Colour, mixed with blackish Stripes, whose Bite is reckon'd to be incurable. 'Tis said to be blind, tho' it has two small Specks in each Head like Eyes: But whether it sees or not I cannot tell. They say it lives like a Mole, mostly under Ground; and that when it is found above Ground it is easily kill'd, because it moves but slowly: Neither is its Sight (if it hath any) so good as to discern any one that comes near to kill it: as few of these Creatures fly at a Man, or hurt him but when he comes in their way. 'Tis about 14 Inches long, and about the bigness of the inner Joint of a Man's middle Finger; being of one and the same bigness from one End to the other, with a Head at each End, (as they said: for I cannot vouch it, for one I had was cut short at one End) and both alike in shape and bigness; and 'tis said to move with either Head foremost, indifferently; whence 'tis called by the Portugueze, *Cobra de dos Cabesas*, the Snake with two Heads.

The small black Snake is a very venomous Creature.

There is also a grey Snake, with red[3] and brown Spots all over its back. 'Tis as big as a Man's Arm, and about 3 Foot long, and is said to be venomous. I saw one of these.

[1] *Cobra verdas.*

[2] Amphisbœna, a sort of slow-worm, with a blunt tail. The creature sometimes wriggles backwards, which accounts for the story of the two heads. Hernandez gives a fearsome cut of the two-headed snake, in which each head has a horn between the eyes, curving outwards.

[3] The coral snake.

AN. 1699 Here are two sorts of very large Snakes or Serpents: One of 'em a Land-snake,[1] the other a Water-snake. The Land-snake is of a grey Colour, and about 18 or 20 Foot long: Not very venomous, but ravenous. I was promised the sight of one of their Skins, but wanted Opportunity.

The Water-snake[2] is said to be near 30 Foot long. These live wholly in the Water, either in large Rivers, or great Lakes, and prey upon any Creature that comes within their Reach, be it Man or Beast. They draw their Prey to them with their Tails: for when they see any thing on the Banks of the River or Lake where they lurk, they swing about their Tails 10 or 12 Foot over the Bank; and whatever stands within their Sweep is snatch'd with great Violence into the River, and drowned by them. Nay 'tis reported very credibly that if they see only a shade of any Animal at all on the Water, they will flourish their Tails to bring in the Man or Beast whose Shade they see, and are oftentimes too successful in it. Wherefore Men that have Business near any Place where these Water-Monsters are suspected to lurk, are always provided with a Gun, which they often fire, and that scares them away, or keeps them quiet. They are said to have great Heads, and strong Teeth about 6 Inches long. I was told by an Irish Man who lived here, that his Wife's Father was very near being taken by one of them about this Time of my first Arrival here, when his Father was with him up in the Country: For the Beast flourish'd his Tail for him, but came not nigh enough by a Yard or two; however it scared him sufficiently.

The amphibious Creatures here which I said are called by the Portugueze *Cachora's de Agua*, or Water-Dogs, are said to be as big as small Mastiffs, and are all hairy and shaggy from Head to Tail. They have 4 short Legs, a pretty long Head and short Tail; and are of a blackish Colour. They live in fresh Water-ponds, and oftentimes come ashore and Sun themselves; but retire to the Water

[1] The boa-constrictor.

[2] The anaconda (*Eunectes murinus*). It sometimes attains to a length of 40 feet.

if assaulted. They are eaten, and said to be good Food. AN. 1699
Several of these Creatures which I have now spoken of I have not seen, but inform'd my self about them while I was here at Bahia, from sober and sensible Persons among the Inhabitants, among whom I met with some that could speak English.

In the Sea upon this Coast there is great Store and Diversity of Fish, viz. Jew-fish, for which there is a great Market at Bahia in Lent: Tarpom's, Mullets, Groopers, Snooks, Gar-fish (called here Goolions), Gorasses, Barrama's, Coquinda's, Cavallie's, Cuchora's (or Dog-fish), Conger-Eels, Herrings (as I was told), the Serrew, the Olio de Boy (I write and spell them just as they were named to me), Whales, &c.

Here is also Shell-fish (tho' in less Plenty about Bahia than on other Parts of the Coast), viz. Lobsters, Craw-fish, Shrimps, Crabs, Oysters of the common Sort, Conchs, Wilks, Cockles, Muscles, Perriwinkles, &c. Here are three Sorts of Sea-Turtle, viz. Hawksbill, Loggerhead, and Green: But none of them are in any esteem, neither Spaniards nor Portugueze loving them: Nay they have a great Antipathy against them, and would much rather eat a Porpoise, tho' our English count the green Turtle very extraordinary Food. The Reason that is commonly given in the West-Indies for the Spaniards not caring to eat of them, is the Fear they have lest, being usually foul-bodied, and many of them pox'd (lying, as they do, so promiscuously with their Negrines and other She-Slaves) they should break out loathsomely like Lepers; which this Sort of Food, 'tis said, does much encline Men to do, searching the Body, and driving out any such gross Humours: For which Cause many of our English Valetudinarians have gone from Jamaica (tho' there they have also Turtle) to the I. Caimanes, at the Laying-time, to live wholly upon Turtle that then abound there; purposely to have their Bodies scour'd by this Food, and their Distempers driven out; and have been said to have found many of them good Success in it. But this by the way. The Hawks-bill-Turtle on this Coast of Brazil is most sought after of any,

AN. for its Shell; which by Report of those I have convers'd
1699 with at Bahia, is the clearest and best clouded Tortoise-shell in the World. I had some of it shewn me, which was indeed as good as I ever saw. They get a pretty deal of it in some Parts on this Coast; but 'tis very dear.

Beside this Port of Bahia de todos los Santos, there are 2 more principal Ports on Brazil, where European Ships Trade, viz. Pernambuc and Ria Janeira; and I was told that there go as many Ships to each of these Places as to Bahia, and 2 Men of War to each Place for their Convoys. Of the other Ports in this Country none is of greater Note than that of St. Paul's,[1] where they gather much Gold; but the Inhabitants are said to be a Sort of Banditti, or loose People that live under no Government: But their Gold brings them all Sorts of Commodities that they need, as Clothes, Arms, Ammunition, &c. The Town is said to be large and strong.

[1] Santos.

The head & greatest part of y^e neck of this bird is red. & therein differs from the Avosetta of Italy.

A Comon Noddy. P 99.

The Bill & Leggs of this Bird are of a Bright Red.

CHAP. III

The A.'s Stay and Business at Bahia: Of the Winds and Seasons of the Year there. His Departure for N. Holland. C. Salvadore. The Winds on the Brasilian Coast; and Abrohlo Shoal; Fish, and Birds: The Shear-water Bird, and Cooking of Sharks. Excessive Number of Birds about a dead Whale; of the Pintado-bird, and the Petrel, &c. Of a Bird that shews the C. of G. Hope to be near: Of the Sea-reckonings, and Variations: And a Table of all the Variations observ'd in this Voyage. Occurrences near the Cape; and the A.'s passing by it. Of the Westerly Winds beyond it: A Storm, and its Presages. The A.'s Course to N. Holland; and Signs of approaching it. Another Abrohlo Shole and Storm, and the A.'s Arrival on part of N. Holland. That part describ'd; and Shark's Bay, where he first anchors. Of the Land there, Vegetables, Birds, &c. A particular Sort of Guano; Fish, and beautiful Shells; Turtle, large Shark, and Water-Serpents. The A.'s removing to another part of N. Holland: Dolphins, Whales, and more Sea-Serpents; and of a Passage or Streight suspected here: Of the Vegetables, Birds, and Fish. He anchors on a third Part of N. Holland, and digs Wells, but brackish. Of the Inhabitants there, the great Tides, the Vegetables and Animals, &c.

MY Stay here at Bahia was about a Month; during which Time the Vice-Roy of Goa came hither from thence in a great Ship, said to be richly laden with all Sorts of India Goods; but she did not break Bulk here, being bound Home for Lisbon; only the Vice-Roy intended to refresh his Men (of whom he had lost many, and most of the rest were very sickly, having been 4 Months in their Voyage hither) and so to take in Water, and depart for Europe, in Company with the other Portugueze Ships thither bound; who had Orders to be ready to sail by the twentieth of May. He desir'd

AN. 1699

AN. 1699 me to carry a Letter for him, directed to his Successor the new Vice-Roy of Goa; which I did, sending it thither afterwards by Captain Hammond, whom I found near the Cape of Good Hope. The refreshing my Men, and taking in Water, was the main also of my Business here; beside the having the better Opportunity to compose the Disorders among my Crew; Which, as I have before related, were grown to so great a Heighth, that they could not without great Difficulty be appeased; However, finding Opportunity, during my Stay in this Place, to allay in some Measure the Ferment that had been raised among my Men, I now set my self to provide for the carrying on of my Voyage with more Heart than before, and put all Hands to work, in order to it, as fast as the Backwardness of my Men would permit; who shew'd continually their Unwillingness to proceed farther. Besides, their Heads were generally fill'd with strange Notions of Southerly Winds that were now setting in (and there had been already some Flurries of them) which, as they surmis'd, would hinder any farther Attempts of going on to the Southward, so long as they should last.

The Winds begin to shift here in April and September, and the Seasons of the Year (the Dry and the Wet) alter with them. In April the Southerly Winds make their Entrance on this Coast, bringing in the wet Season, with violent Tornado's, Thunder and Lightning, and much Rain. In September the other Coasting Trade, at East North-East comes in, and clears the Sky, bringing fair Weather. This, as to the Change of Wind, is what I have observ'd, Vol. II. Part 3. p. 244, but as to the Change of Weather accompanying it so exactly here at Bahia, this is a particular Exception to what I have experienc'd in all other Places of South Latitudes that I have been in between the Tropicks, or those I have heard of; for there the dry Season sets in, in April, and the Wet about October or November, sooner or later (as I have said that they are, in South Latitudes, the Reverse of the Seasons, or Weather, in the same Months in N. Latitudes, Vol. II. Part 3. p. 298) whereas on this Coast of Brazil, the wet Season comes in in April, at the same Time that it doth in N. Latitudes, and the dry (as I have said here) in September; the Rains here not lasting so far in the Year as in other Places; For in September the Weather is usually so fair, that in the latter part of that Month they begin to cut their Sugar-Canes here, as I was told; for I enquired particularly about the Seasons: Though this, as to the Season of cutting of Canes, which I was now assur'd to be in September, agrees not very well with what I was formerly told [Vol. II. Part 3. p. 299] that in Brazil they cut the Canes in July. And so, as to what is said a little lower in the same Page, that in managing their Canes they are not confin'd to the Seasons, this ought to have been express'd only of planting them; for they never cut them but in the dry Season. AN. 1699

But to return to the Southerly Winds, which came in (as I expected they would) while I was here: These daunted my Ship's Company very much, tho' I had told them they were to look for them: But they being ignorant as to what I told them farther, that these were only Coasting-Winds, sweeping the Shore to about 40 or 50 Leagues in Breadth from it, and imagining that they had blown so all the Sea over, between America and Africa; and being confirm'd in this their Opinion by the Portugueze Pilots of the European Ships, with whom several of my Officers conversed much, and who were themselves as ignorant that these were only Coasting Trade-Winds (themselves going away before them, in their Return homewards, till they cross the Line, and so having no Experience of the Breadth of them) being thus possess'd with a Conceit that we could not sail from hence till September; this made them still the more remiss in their Duties, and very listless to the getting Things in a Readiness for our Departure. However I was the more diligent my self to have the Ship scrubb'd, and to send my Water-Casks ashore to get them trimm'd,[1] my Beer being now out. I went also to the Governour to get my Water fill'd; for here being but one

[1] Scraped, rinsed, and burned, so that they should not impart a twang of beer to the water subsequently stored in them.

AN. 1699 Watering-place (and the Water running low, now at the End of the dry Season) it was always so crouded with the European Ships Boats, who were preparing to be gone, that my Men could seldom come nigh it, till the Governour very kindly sent an Officer to clear the Water-place for my Men, and to stay there till my Water-Casks were all full, whom I satisfied for his Pains. Here I also got aboard 9 or 10 Ton of Ballast, and made my Boatswain fit the Rigging that was amiss: And I enquired also of my particular Officers whose Business it was, whether they wanted any Stores, especially Pitch and Tar; for that here I would supply my self before I proceeded any farther; but they said they had enough, tho' it did not afterwards prove so.

I commonly went ashore every Day, either upon Business, or to recreate my self in the Fields, which were very pleasant, and the more for a Shower of Rain now and then, that ushers in the wet Season. Several Sorts of good Fruits were also still remaining, especially Oranges, which were in such Plenty, that I and all my Company stock'd our selves for our Voyage with them, and they did us a great Kindness; and we took in also a good Quantity of Rum and Sugar: But for Fowls they being here lean and dear, I was glad I had stock'd my self at St. Jago. But by the little Care my officers took for fresh Provisions, one might conclude, they did not think of going much farther. Besides, I had like to have been imbroiled with the Clergy here (of the Inquisition, as I suppose) and so my Voyage might have been hindred. What was said to them of me, by some of my Company that went ashore, I know not; but I was assured by a Merchant there, that if they got me into their Clutches (and it seems, when I was last ashore they had narrowly watch'd me) the Governor himself could not release me. Besides I might either be murther'd in the Streets, as he sent me Word, or poisoned, if I came ashore any more; and therefore he advised me to stay aboard. Indeed I had now no further Business ashore but to take leave of the Governor, and therefore took his Advice.

Our Stay here was till the 23d of April. I would have

gone before if I could sooner have fitted my self; but was now earnest to be gone, because this Harbour lies open to the S. and S. S. W. which are raging Winds here, and now was the Season for them. We had 2 or 3 Touches of them; and one pretty severe, and the Ships ride there so near each other, that if a Cable should fail, or an Anchor start, you are instantly aboard of one Ship or other: And I was more afraid of being disabled here in Harbour by these blustring Winds, than discouraged by them, as my People were, from prosecuting the Voyage; for at present I even wish'd for a brisk Southerly Wind as soon as I should be once well out of the Harbour, to set me the sooner into the true General Trade-Wind.

AN. 1699

The Tide of Flood being spent, and having a fine Land-Breeze on the 23d, in the Morning, I went away from the Anchoring place before 'twas light; and then lay by till Day-light that we might see the better how to go out of the Harbour. I had a Pilot belonging to Mr. Cock, who went out with me, to whom I gave 3 Dollars; but I found I could as well have gone out my self, by the Soundings I made at coming in. The Wind was E. by N. and fair Weather. By 10 a Clock I was got past all Danger, and then sent away my Pilot. At 12 Cape Salvadore bore N. distant 6 Leagues, and we had the Winds between the E. by N. and S. E. a considerable Time, so that we kept along near the Shore, commonly in Sight of it. The Southerly blasts had now left us again; for they come at first in short Flurries, and shift to other Points (for 10 or 12 Days sometimes) before they are quite set in: And we had uncertain Winds, between Sea and Land-Breezes, and the Coasting-Trade, which was its self unsettled.

The Easterly-Winds at present made me doubt I should not weather a great Shoal which lies in Lat. between 18 deg. and 19 deg. S. and runs a great Way into the Sea, directly from the Land, Easterly. Indeed the Weather was fair (and continued so a good while) so that I might the better avoid any Danger from it: And if the Wind came to the Southward I knew I could stretch off to Sea; so that I jogg'd on couragiously. The

AN. 1699 27th of April we saw a small Brigantine under the Shore plying to the Southward. We also saw many Men of War-birds and Boobies, and Abundance of Albicore-Fish. Having still fair Weather, small Gales, and some Calms, I had the Opportunity of trying the Current, which I found to set sometimes Northerly and sometimes Southerly: And therefore knew I was still within the Verge of the Tides. Being now in the Lat. of the Abrohlo Shoals, which I expected to meet with, I sounded, and had Water lessening from 40 to 33, and so to 25 Fathom: But then it rose again to 33, 35, 37, &c. all Coral Rocks. Whilst we were on this Shoal (which we cross'd towards the further part of it from Land, where it lay deep, and so was not dangerous) we caught a great many Fish with Hook and Line: and by evening Amplitude we had 6 deg. 38 min. East Variation. This was the 27th of April; we were then in Lat. 18 deg. 13 min. S. and East Longitude from Cape Salvadore 31 min. On the 29th, being then in Lat. 18 deg. 39 min. S. we had small Gales from the W. N. W. to the W. S. W. often shifting. The 30th we had the Winds from W. to S. S. E. Squalls and Rain: And we saw some Dolphins and other Fish about us. We were now out of Sight of Land, and had been so 4 or 5 Days: But the Winds now hanging in the South was an apparent Sign that we were still too nigh the Shore to receive the true General East-Trade; as the Easterly Winds we had before shew'd that we were too far off the Land to have the Benefit of the Coasting South-Trade: and the Faintness of both these Winds, and their often shifting from the S. S. W. to the S. E. with Squalls, Rain and small Gales, were a Confirmation of our being between the Verge of the S. Coasting-Trade, and that of the true Trade; which is here, regularly, S. E.

The 3d of May being in Lat. 20 deg. 00 min. and Merid. distance West from Cape Salvadore 234 Miles, the Variation was 7 deg. 00 min. We saw no Fowl but Shear-waters,[1] as our Sea-men call them, being a small

[1] The dusky puffin.

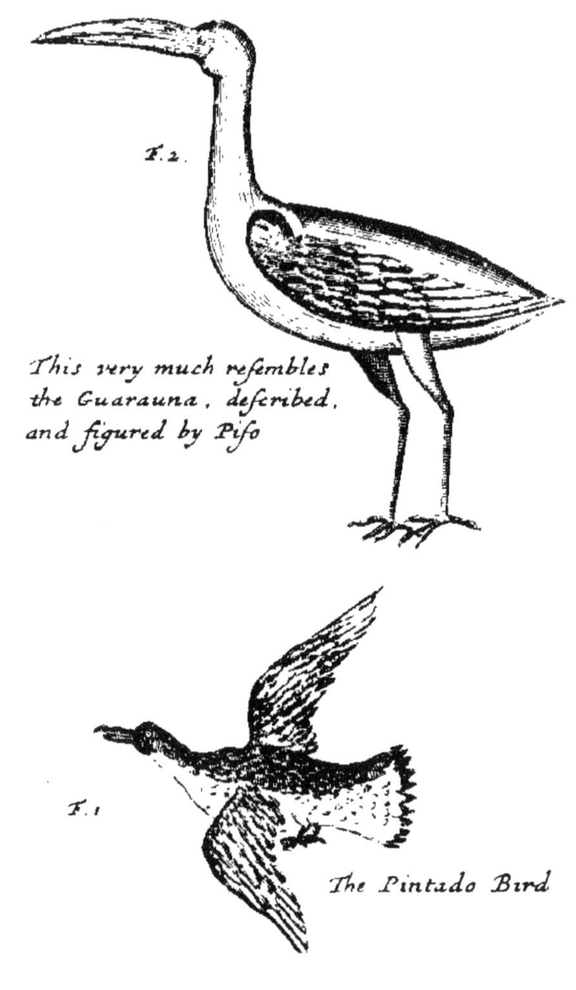

This very much resembles the Guarauna, described, and figured by Piso

The Pintado Bird

black Fowl that sweep the Water as they fly, and are much in the Seas that lie without either of the Tropicks: they are not eaten. We caught 3 small Sharks, each 6 Foot 4 Inches long; and they were very good Food for us. The next Day we caught 3 more Sharks of the same Size, and we eat them also, esteeming them as good Fish boil'd and press'd, and then stew'd with Vinegar and Pepper. AN. 1699

We had nothing of Remark from the 3d of May to the 10th, only now and then seeing a small Whale spouting up the Water. We had the Wind Easterly, and we ran with it to the Southward, running in this Time from the Lat. of 20 deg. 00 m. to 29 deg. 5 min. S. and having then 7 d. 3 m. E. Long. from C. Salvadore; the Variation increasing upon us, at present, notwithstanding we went East. We had all along a great Difference between the Morning and Evening Amplitudes; usually a Degree or two, and sometimes more. We were now in the true Trade, and therefore made good Way to the Southward, to get without the Verge of the General Trade-Wind into a Westerly Wind's way, that might carry us towards the Cape of Good Hope. By the 12th of May, being in Lat. 31 deg. 10 min. we began to meet with Westerly Winds, which freshned on us, and did not leave us till a little before we made the Cape. Sometimes it blew so hard that it put us under a Fore-course; especially in the Night; but in the Day-time we had commonly our Main Top-sail rift. We met with nothing of Moment; only we past by a dead Whale, and saw Millions (as I may say) of Sea-Fowls about the Carcass (and as far round about it as we could see) some feeding, and the rest flying about, or sitting on the Water, waiting to take their Turns. We first discovered the Whale by the Fowls; for indeed I did never see so many Fowls at once in my Life before, their Numbers being inconceivably great: They were of divers Sorts, in Bigness, Shape and Colour. Some were almost as big as Geese, of a grey Colour, with white Breasts, and with such Bills, Wings, and Tails. Some were Pintado[1]-Birds, as big as Ducks, and speckled black

[1] *Daption capensis*, or Pintado petrel.

AN. 1699 and white. Some were Shear-waters; some Petrels;[1] and there were several Sorts of large Fowls. We saw of these Birds, especially the Pintado-birds, all the Sea over from about 200 Leagues distant from the Coast of Brazil, to within much the same Distance of New-Holland. The Pintado is a Southern Bird, and of that temperate Zone; for I never saw of them much to the Northward of 30 deg. S. The Pintado-bird is as big as a Duck; but appears, as it flies, about the Bigness of a tame Pidgeon, having a short Tail, but the Wings very long, as most Sea-Fowls have; especially such as these that fly far from the Shore, and seldom come nigh it; for their Resting is sitting afloat upon the Water; but they lay, I suppose, ashore. There are three Sorts of these Birds, all of the same Make and Bigness, and are only different in Colour. The first is black all over: The second Sort are grey, with white Bellies and Breasts. The third Sort, which is the true Pintado, or Painted-bird, is curiously spotted white and black. Their Heads, and the Tips of their Wings and Tails, are black for about an Inch; and their Wings are also edg'd quite round with such a small black List; only within the black on the Tip of their Wings there is a white Spot seeming as they fly (for then their Spots are best seen) as big as a Half-crown. All this is on the Outside of the Tails and Wings; and as there is a white Spot in the black Tip of the Wings, so there is in the Middle of the Wings which is white, a black Spot; but this, towards the Back of the Bird, turns gradually to a dark grey. The Back it self, from the Head to the Tip of the Tail, and the Edge of the Wings next to the Back, are all over-spotted with fine small, round, white and black Spots, as big as a Silver Two-pence, and as close as they can stick one by another: The Belly, Thighs, Sides, and inner-part of the Wings, are of a light grey. These Birds, of all these Sorts, fly many together, never high, but almost sweeping the Water. We shot one a while after on the Water in a Calm, and a Water-

[1] *Procellaria pelagica.*

Spaniel we had with us brought it in: I have given a Picture of it [See Birds, Fig. 1] but it was so damaged, that the Picture doth not shew it to Advantage; and its Spots are best seen when the Feathers are spread as it flies. AN. 1699

The Petrel is a Bird not much unlike a Swallow, but smaller, and with a shorter Tail. 'Tis all over black, except a white Spot on the Rump. They fly sweeping like Swallows, and very near the Water. They are not so often seen in fair Weather; being Foul-weather Birds, as our Seamen call them, and presaging a Storm when they come about a Ship; who for that Reason don't love to see them. In a Storm they will hover close under the Ship's Stern, in the Wake of the Ship (as 'tis call'd) or the Smoothness which the Ship's passing has made on the Sea: And there as they fly (gently then) they pat the Water alternately with their Feet, as if they walk'd upon it; tho' still upon the Wing. And from hence the Seamen give them the Name of Petrels, in Allusion to St. Peter's walking upon the Lake of Gennesareth.

We also saw many Bunches of Sea-weeds in the Lat. of 39. 32. and by Judgment, near the Meridian of the Island Tristian d' Aconha: And then we had about 2 d. 20 min. East Variation: which was now again decreasing as we ran to the Eastward, till near the Meridian of Ascention; where we found little or no Variation: But from thence, as we ran farther to the East, our Variation increased Westerly.

Two Days before I made the Cape of G. Hope, my Variation was 7 deg. 58 min. West. I was then in 43 deg. 27 min. East Longit. from C. Salvador, being in Lat. 35 deg. 30 min. this was the first of June. The second of June I saw a large black Fowl, with a whitish flat Bill, fly by us; and took great Notice of it, because in the East-India Waggoner, or Pilot-book, there is mention made of large Fowls, as big as Ravens, with white flat Bills and black Feathers, that fly not above 30 Leagues from the Cape, and are look'd on as a Sign[1] of ones being

[1] *Cf.* the Voyage of Thomas Stevens to Goa (the Hakluyt of 1589): "As touching our first signs, the nearer we came to the people of Africa, the more strange kinds of fowls appeared. . . . Some (they call) *Velvet*

AN. 1699 near it. My Reckoning made me then think my self above 90 Leagues from the Cape, according to the Longitude which the Cape hath in the common Sea-Charts: So that I was in some doubt, whether these were the right Fowls spoken of in the Waggoner; or whether those Fowls might not fly farther off Shore than is there mentioned; or whether, as it prov'd, I might not be nearer the Cape than I reckoned my self to be; for I found, soon after, that I was not then above 25 or 30 Leagues at most from the Cape. Whether the Fault were in the Charts laying down the Cape too much to the East from Brazil, or were rather in our Reckoning, I could not tell: But our Reckonings are liable to such Uncertainties from Steerage, Log, Currents, Half-Minute-Glasses; and sometimes want of Care, as in so long a Run cause often a Difference of many Leagues in the whole Account.

Most of my Men that kept Journals imputed it to the Half-Minute Glasses: and indeed we had not a good Glass in the Ship beside the Half-watch or Two-Hour-Glasses. As for our Half-Minute-Glasses[1] we tried them all at several Times, and we found those that we had used from Brazil as much too short, as others we had used before were too long: which might well make great Errors in those several Reckonings. A Ship ought therefore to have its Glasses very exact; and besides, an extraordinary Care ought to be used in heaving the Log, for fear of giving too much Stray-Line[2] in a moderate Gale; and also to stop[3] quickly in a brisk Gale, for when a Ship runs 8, 9 or 10 Knots, half a Knot or a Knot is soon run out, and not heeded: But to prevent Danger, when a Man thinks himself near Land, the best way is to look out betimes, and lye by in the Night, for a Commander may err easily

Sleeves, because they have wings of the colour of velvet, and boweth them as a man boweth his elbow. This bird is always welcome for he appeareth nearest the Cape." The "Waggoner, or Pilot-Book," is vol. iii. of "The English Pilot."

[1] The glasses used at the heaving of the log.

[2] A few yards of log-line allowed at each heaving of the log to enable the log-ship to float clear of the "dead water" under the vessel's counter.

[3] To check the running of the log-line at the instant the sand leaves the half-minute glass.

himself; beside the Errors of those under him, tho' never so carefully eyed. AN. 1699

Another Thing that stumbled me here was the Variation, which, at this Time, by the last Amplitude I had I found to be but 7 deg. 58 min. W. whereas the Variation at the Cape (from which I found my self not 30 Leagues distant) was then computed, and truly, about 11 deg. or more: And yet a while after this, when I was got 10 Leagues to the Eastward of the Cape, I found the Variation but 10 deg. 40 min. W. whereas it should have been rather more than at the Cape. These Things, I confess, did puzzle me: Neither was I fully satisfied as to the Exactness of the taking the Variation at Sea: For in a great Sea, which we often meet with, the Compass will traverse with the Motion of the Ship; besides the Ship may and will deviate somewhat in steering, even by the best Helmsmen: And then when you come to take an Azimuth, there is often some Difference between him that looks at the Compass, and the Man that takes the Altitude heighth of the Sun; and a small Error in each, if the Error of both should be one way, will make it wide of any great Exactness. But what was most shocking to me, I found that the Variation did not always increase or decrease in Proportion to the Degrees of Longitude East or West; as I had a Notion they might do to a certain Number of Degrees of Variation East or West, at such or such particular Meridians. But finding in this Voyage that the Difference of Variation did not bear a regular Proportion to the Difference of Longitude, I was much pleas'd to see it thus observ'd in a Scheme shewn me after my Return home, wherein are represented the several Variations in the Atlantick Sea, on both Sides the Equator; and there, the Line of no Variation in that Sea is not a Meridian Line, but goes very oblique, as do those also which shew the Increase of Variation on each Side of it. In that Draught there is so large an Advance made as well towards the accounting for those seemingly irregular Increases and Decreases of Variation towards the S. E. Coast of America, as towards the fixing a general Scheme or System of the

AN. 1699 Variation every where, which would be of such great Use in Navigation, that I cannot but hope that the ingenious Author, Capt. Hally,[1] who to his profound Skill in all Theories of these kinds, hath added and is adding continually Personal Experiments, will e'er long oblige the World with a fuller Discovery of the Course of the Variation, which hath hitherto been a Secret. For my Part I profess my self unqualified for offering at any thing of a General Scheme; but since Matter of Fact, and whatever increases the History of the Variation, may be of use towards the settling or confirming the Theory of it, I shall here once for all insert a Table of all the Variations I observ'd beyond the Equator in this Voyage, both in going out, and returning back; and what Errors there may be in it, I shall leave to be corrected by the Observations of others.

A Table of Variations

1699.		D. M. S. Lat.		D. M. Longit.		D. M. Variat.	
Mar.	14	6	15	1	47 *a*	3	27 E
	21	12	45	12	9	3	27
Apr.	25	14	49	00	10 *b*	7	0
	28	18	13	00	31	6	38
	30	19	00	2	20	6	30
May.	2	19	22	3	51	8	15
	3	20	1	3	40	7	0
	5	22	47	3	48	9	40
	6	24	23	3	53	7	36
	7	25	44	3	53	10	15
	8	26	47	4	35	7	14
	9	28	9	5	50	9	45

a W. from St. Jago.
b E. from C. Salvador in Brazil.

[1] His theory of the variation of the compass was based on the supposition that there existed four magnetic poles, two of which were movable.

A TABLE OF VARIATIONS

1699.		D. M. S. Lat.		D. M. Longit.		D. M. Variat.		AN. 1699
May.	10	29	5	7	3	11	41 E	
	11	29	23	7	38	12	47	
	17	34	58	18	43	5	40	
	18	34	54	19	06	6	19	
	19	35	48	19	45	5	6	
	23	39	42	27	1	2	55	
	25	39	11	31	35	2	0	
June.	1	35	30	43	27	7	58 W	
	5	35	8	00	23 *e*	10	40	
	6	36	7	3	6	11	10	
	8	36	17	10	3	15	00	
	9	35	59	12	0	19	38	
	12	35	20	20	18	21	35	
	14	35	5	26	13	23	50	
	15	34	51	29	24	25	56	
	17	34	27	36	8	24	54	
	19	34	17	39	24	25	29	
	20	34	15	42	25	24	22	
	22	33	34	45	41	22	15	
	25	35	8	45	28	24	30	
	28	36	40	49	33	22	50	
	29	36	40	53	12	22	44	
	30	36	15	56	22	21	40	
July.	1	35	35	58	44	19	45	
	4	33	32	66	22	16	40	
	6	31	30	68	34	12	20	
	7	31	45	69	00	12	2	
	10	32	39	70	21	13	36	
	11	33	4	72	00	12	29	
	13	21	17	74	43	10	0	
	15	29	20	75	25	10	28	
	18	28	16	78	29	9	51	
	23	26	43	84	19	9	11	
	24	26	28	85	20	8	9	
	25	26	14	85	52	8	40	
	26	25	36	86	21	8	20	
	27	26	43	86	16	7	0	
	29	27	38	87	25	8	20	
	31	26	54	88	1	9	0	
Aug.	5	25	30	86	3	7	24	

e E. from C. G. Hope.

AN. 1699

1699.			D. M. S. Lat.		D. M. Longit.		D. M. Variat.	
	Aug.	15	24	41	86	2 *d*	6	6 W
		17	23	2	00	22	7	6
		20	19	37	3	00	7	00
		24	19	52	4	41	7	7
		25	19	45	5	10	6	40
		27	19	24	6	11	5	18
		28	18	38	6	57	6	12
	Sept.	6	17	16	9	18	4	3
		7	16	9	8	57	2	7
		8	15	37	9	34	2	20
		10	13	55	10	55	1	47
		11	13	12	11	42	1	47
	Dec.	29	5	1	6	34 *e*	1	2 E
1700.	*Jan.*	3	1	32	6	53	4	8
	Feb.	13	0	9	2	48 *f*	4	0
		16	0	12	7	31	6	26
		21	0	12	15	23	8	45
		23	0	43	18	00	8	45
		27	2	43	19	41	9	50
	Mar.	10	5	10	00	5 *g*	1	0
		13	5	35	00	44 *h*	9	0
		30	5	15	6	4	8	25 W
	Apr.	6	3	32	8	25	7	16
		22	1	32	00	37 *i*	3	00
	May.	1	3	00		*k*	2	15 E
		24	9	59	00	25 *l*	0	15 W
		27	14	33	3	30	1	25
	June.	2	19	44	8	7	5	38
		3	19	51	9	58	6	10
		4	19	46	11	6	6	20
		5	20	00	12	22	4	58
		6	20	00	14	17	7	20
		9	19	59	16	01	6	32
		11	9	57	17	42	8	1
		12	19	48	19	0	6	0
	Nov.	7	21	26		*m*	9	0
		14	27	1	35	35	16	50
		15	27	10	36	34	18	57
		16	27	11	37	54	17	24
		19	28	14	41	40	19	39

d E. from Sharks-Bay in N. Holland. *e* E. from Babao-Bay in J. Timor.
f E. from C. Mabu in N. Guinea.
g E. from C. St. George on I. N. Brittannia. *h* W. from ditto.
i W. from C. Mabu. *k* At Anchor off I. Ceram.
l W. from Babao-Bay. *m* W. from Princes Isle by Java-Head.

A TABLE OF VARIATIONS

AN. 1699

1700.		D. M. S. Lat.		D. M. Longit.		D. M. Variat.	
Nov.	21	29	24	44	47	20	50 W
	23	29	42	47	34	21	38
	24	30	16	49	26	26	00
	25	30	40	51	24	22	38
	27	31	51	55	5	22	40
	29	32	55	56	28	27	10
	30	31	55	57	25	27	10
Dec.	1	31	57	58	17	24	30
	2	31	57	59	33	27	57
	4	32	3	61	45	24	50
	6	32	15	66	00	23	30
	7	37	28	68	36	24	48
	8	33	49	64	38	21	53
	9	32	49	70	09	24	00
	11	32	50	71	45	21	15
	13	31	55	72	32	20	16
	14	31	35	73	39	20	00
	15	32	21	75	22	20	00
	17	33	5	79	39	18	42
	18	33	0	80	39	17	15
	21	34	39	82	46	16	41
	22	34	36	83	19	14	36
	23	34	21	83	42	14	00
	25	34	38	84	21	14	00
1701. *Jan.*	15	31	25	2	32 *n*	10	20
	16	30	5	4	42	9	36
	17	28	46	6	8	8	25
	18	27	26	7	32	7	40
	19	26	11	9	9	7	30
	20	25	00	10	49	7	9
	21	23	42	12	34	6	55
	22	22	51	14	10	5	56
	23	21	48	15	17	5	32
	24	21	24	15	51	4	56
	26	19	57	16	48	4	20
	27	19	10	17	22	3	24
	28	18	13	18	23	4	00
	29	17	22	19	29	2	00
Feb.	16	12	52	3	8 *o*	1	50
	17	11	55	4	42	1	10
	18	11	17	5	30	0	20
	19	10	22	6	32	1	10
	21	We made the I. Ascention.					

n W. from the Table Land at C. G. Hope. *o* W. from Santa Helena.

AN. 1699 But to return from this Digression: Having fair Weather, and the Winds hanging Southerly, I jog'd on to the Eastward, to make the Cape. On the third of June we saw a Sail to Leeward of us, shewing English Colours. I bore away to speak with her, and found her to be the *Antelope* of London, commanded by Captain Hammond, and bound for the Bay of Bengal in the Service of the New-East-India Company. There were many Passengers aboard, going to settle there under Sir Edward Littleton, who was going Chief thither: I went aboard, and was known by Sir Edward and Mr. Hedges, and kindly received and treated by them and the Commander; who had been afraid of us before, tho' I had sent one of my Officers aboard. They had been in at the Cape, and came from thence the Day before, having stock'd themselves with Refreshments. They told me that they were by Reckoning, 60 Miles to the West of the Cape. While I was aboard them, a fine small Westerly Wind sprang up; therefore I shortned my stay with them, because I did not design to go into the Cape. When I took leave I was presented with half a Mutton, 12 Cabbages, 12 Pumkins, 6 Pound of Butter, 6 Couple of Stock-fish, and a quantity of Parsnips; sending them some Oatmeal, which they wanted.

From my first setting out from England, I did not design to touch at the Cape; and that was one Reason why I touch'd at Brazil, that there I might refresh my Men, and prepare them for a long Run to New Holland. We had not yet seen the Land; but about 2 in the Afternoon we saw the Cape-Land bearing East, at above 16 Leagues distance; And Captain Hammond being also bound to double the Cape, we jog'd on together this Afternoon and the next Day, and had several fair Sights of it; which may be seen [Table III. omitted].

To proceed: Having still a Westerly Wind, I jog'd on in company with the *Antelope*, till Sunday June the 4th at 4 in the Afternoon, when we parted; they steering away for the East-Indies, and I keeping an E. S. E. Course, the better to make my way for New Holland: For tho'

New Holland lies North-Easterly from the Cape, yet all Ships bound towards that Coast, or the Streights of Sundy, ought to keep for a while in the same Parallel, or in a Lat. between 35 and 40, at least a little to the S. of the East, that they may continue in a variable Winds way; and not venture too soon to stand so far to the North, as to be within the Verge of the Trade-Wind, which will put them by their Easterly Course. The Wind increased upon us; but we had yet sight of the *Antelope*, and of the Land too, till Tuesday the 6th of June: And then we saw also by us an innumerable Company of Fowls of divers sorts; so that we look'd about to see if there were not another dead Whale, but saw none.

AN. 1699

The Night before, the Sun set in a black Cloud, which appeared just like Land; and the Clouds above it were gilded of a dark red Colour. And on the Tuesday, as the Sun drew near the Horizon, the Clouds were gilded very prettily to the Eye, tho' at the same time my Mind dreaded the Consequences of it. When the Sun was now not above 2 deg. high, it entered into a dark Smoaky-coloured Cloud that lay parallel with the Horizon, from whence presently seem'd to issue many dusky blackish Beams. The Sky was at this time covered with small hard Clouds (as we call such as lye scattering about, not likely to Rain) very thick one by another; and such of them as lay next to the Bank of Clouds at the Horizon, were of a pure Gold Colour to 3 or 4 deg. high above the Bank: From these to about 10 deg. high they were redder, and very bright; above them they were of a darker Colour still, to about 60 or 70 deg. high; where the Clouds began to be of their common Colour. I took the more particular Notice of all this, because I have generally observed such colour'd Clouds to appear before an approaching Storm: And this being Winter here, and the time for bad Weather, I expected and provided for a violent blast of Wind, by riffing our Topsails, and giving a strict charge to my Officers to hand them or take them in, if the Wind should grow stronger. The Wind was now at W. N. W. a very brisk Gale. About 12 a Clock at Night we had a pale whitish Glare

AN. 1699 in the N. W. which was another Sign, and intimated the Storm to be near at hand; and the Wind increasing upon it, we presently handed our Top-sails, furled the Main-sail, and went away only with our Fore-sail. Before 2 in the Morning it came on very fierce, and we kept right before Wind and Sea, the Wind still encreasing: But the Ship was very governable, and steered incomparably well. At 8 in the Morning we settled our Fore-yard, lowering it 4 or 5 Foot, and we ran very swiftly; especially when the Squalls of Rain or Hail, from a black Cloud, came over Head, for then it blew excessive hard. These, tho' they did not last long, yet came very thick and fast one after another. The Sea also ran very high; But we running so violently before Wind and Sea, we ship'd little or no Water; tho' a little wash'd into our upper Deck-Ports; and with it a Scuttle or Cuttle-Fish was cast upon the Carriage of a Gun.

The Wind blew extraordinary hard all Wednesday, the 7th of June, but abated of its fierceness before Night; Yet it continued a brisk Gale till about the 16th, and still a moderate one till the 19th Day; by which time we had run about 600 Leagues: For the most part of which time the Wind was in some point of the West, viz. from the W. N. W. to the S. by W. It blew hardest when at W. or between the W. and S. W. but after it veered more Southerly the foul Weather broke up: This I observed at other times also in these Seas, that when the Storms at West veered to the Southward they grew less; and that when the Wind came to the E. of the S. we had still smaller Gales, Calms, and fair Weather. As for the Westerly Winds on that side the Cape, we like them never the worse for being violent, for they drive us the faster to the Eastward; and are therefore the only Winds coveted by those who Sail towards such parts of the East-Indies, as lye South of the Equator; as Timor, Java, and Sumatra; and by the Ships bound for China, or any other that are to pass through the Streights of Sundy. Those Ships having once past the Cape, keep commonly pretty far Southerly, on purpose to meet with these West-winds, which in the

Winter Season of these Climates they soon meet with; for then the Winds are generally Westerly at the Cape, and especially to the Southward of it: But in their Summer Months they get to the Southward of 40 deg. usually e'er they meet with the Westerly Winds. I was not at this time in a higher Lat. than 36 deg. 40 min. and oftentimes was more Northerly, altering my Latitude often as Winds and Weather required; for in such long Runs 'tis best to shape one's Course according to the Winds. And if in steering to the East, we should be obliged to bear a little to the N. or S. of it, 'tis no great Matter; for 'tis but sailing 2 or 3 Points from the Wind, when 'tis either Northerly or Southerly; and this not only easeth the Ship from straining, but shortens the way more than if a Ship was kept close on a Wind, as some Men are fond of doing.

AN. 1699

The 19th of June, we were in Lat. 34 deg. 17 min. S. and Long. from the Cape 39 deg. 24 min. E. and had small Gales and Calms. The Winds were at N. E. by E. and continued in some Part of the E. till the 27th Day. When it having been some time at N. N. E. it came about at N. and then to the W. of the N. and continued in the West-board (between the N. N. W. and S. S. W.) till the 4th of July; in which Time we ran 782 Miles; then the Winds came about again to the East, we reckoning our selves to be in a Meridian 1100 L. East of the Cape; and having fair Weather, sounded, but had no Ground.

We met with little of Remark in this Voyage, besides being accompanied with Fowls all the way, especially Pintado-Birds, and seeing now and then a Whale: But as we drew nigher the Coast of New-Holland, we saw frequently 3 or 4 Whales together. When we were about 90 Leagues from the Land we began to see Sea-weeds, all of one Sort; and as we drew nigher the Shore we saw them more frequently. At about 30 Leagues distance we began to see some Scuttle-bones[1] floating on the Water; and drawing still nigher the Land we saw greater Quantities of them.

July 25, being in Lat. 26 deg. 14 min. S. and Longi-

[1] The white, calcareous "cuttle-bone," the dorsal piece of the common Cephalopod. It is a common object on most sea-coasts.

AN. 1699 tude E. from the C. of Good Hope 85 deg. 52 min. we saw a large Gar-fish leap 4 Times by us, which seemed to be as big as a Porpose. It was now very fair Weather, and the Sea was full of a Sort of very small Grass or Moss, which as it floated in the Water seem'd to have been some Spawn of Fish; and there was among it some small Fry. The next Day the Sea was full of small round Things like Pearl,[1] some as big as white Peas; they were very clear and transparent, and upon crushing any of them a Drop of Water would come forth: The Skin that contain'd the Water was so thin that it was but just discernable. Some Weeds swam by us, so that we did not doubt but we should quickly see Land. On the 27th also, some Weeds swam by us, and the Birds that had flown along with us all the way almost from Brazil, now left us, except only 2 or 3 Shear-waters. On the 28th we saw many Weeds swim by us, and some Whales, blowing. On the 29th we had dark cloudy Weather, with much Thunder, Lightning, and violent Rains in the Morning; but in the Evening it grew fair. We saw this Day a Scuttle-bone swim by us, and some of our young Men a Seal, as it should seem by their Description of its Head. I saw also some Boneta's, and some Skipjacks, a Fish about 8 Inches long, broad and sizeable, not much unlike a Roach; which our Seamen call so from their leaping about.

The 30th of July, being still nearer the Land, we saw Abundance of Scuttle-bones and Sea-weed, more Tokens that we were not far from it; and saw also a Sort of Fowls, the like of which we had not seen in the whole Voyage, all the other Fowls having now left us. These were as big as Lapwings; of a grey Colour, black about their Eyes, with red sharp Bills, long Wings, their Tails long and forked like Swallows; and they flew flapping their Wings like Lapwings. In the Afternoon we met with a Ripling like a Tide or Current, or the Water of some Shoal or Overfall; but were past it before we could sound. The Birds last mention'd and this were further Signs of Land. In the

[1] The minute sea-jellies and medusæ are found in great abundance in these waters.

Evening we had fair Weather, and a small Gale at West. At 8 a Clock we sounded again; but had no Ground. AN. 1699

We kept on still to the Eastward, with an easy Sail, looking out sharp: For by the many Signs we had, I did expect that we were near the Land. At 12 a Clock in the Night I sounded, and had 45 Fathom, coarse Sand and small white Shells. I presently clapt on a Wind and stood to the South, with the Wind at W. because I thought we were to the South of a Shoal call'd the Abrohles (an Appellative Name for Shoals,[1] as it seems to me) which in a Draught I had of that Coast is laid down in 27 deg. 28 min. Lat. stretching about 7 Leagues into the Sea. I was the Day before in 27 deg. 38 min. by Reckoning. And afterwards steering E. by S. purposely to avoid it, I thought I must have been to the South of it: But sounding again, at 1 a Clock in the Morning, Aug. the first, we had but 25 Fathom, Coral Rocks; and so found the Shoal was to the South of us. We presently tack'd again, and stood to the North, and then soon deepned our Water; for at 2 in the Morning we had 26 Fathom Coral still: At 3 we had 28 Coral-ground: At 4 we had 30 Fathom, coarse Sand, with some Coral: At 5 we had 45 Fathom, coarse Sand and Shells; being now off the Shoal, as appear'd by the Sand and Shells, and by having left the Coral. By all this I knew we had fallen in to the North of the Shoal, and that it was laid down wrong in my Sea-Chart: For I found it lye in about 27 deg. Lat. and by our Run in the next Day, I found that the Outward-edge of it, which I sounded on, lies 16 Leagues off Shore. When it was Day we steered in E. N. E. with a fine brisk Gale; but did not see the Land till 9 in the Morning, when we saw it from our Topmast-head, and were distant from it about 10 Leagues; having then 40 Fathom-water, and clean Sand. About 3 Hours after we saw it on our Quarter-Deck, being by Judgment about 6 Leagues off, and we had then 40 Fathom, clean Sand. As we ran in, this Day and the next, we took

[1] The Abrolhos shoal is in lat. 27° 40′ S. It is sometimes known as the Houtman Rocks, or Houtman's Abrolhos, the word "abrolhos" meaning "Look out" or "Mind yourself."

AN. 1699 several Sights of it, at different Bearings and Distances; from which it appear'd as you see in [Table IV. omitted]. And here I would note once for all, that the Latitudes mark'd in the Draughts, or Sights here given, are not the Latitude of the Land, but of the Ship when the Sight was taken. This Morning, August the first, as we were standing in we saw several large Sea-fowls, like our Gannets on the Coast of England, flying 3 or 4 together; and a Sort of white Sea-Mews, but black about the Eyes, and with forked Tails. We strove to run in near the Shore to seek for a Harbour to refresh us after our tedious Voyage; having made one continued Stretch from Brazil hither of about 114 deg. designing from hence also to begin the Discovery I had a Mind to make on N. Holland and N. Guinea. The Land was low, and appear'd even, and as we drew nearer to it, it made (as in Table IV. omitted) with some red and some white Clifts; these last in Lat. 26, 10 S. where you will find 54 Fathom, within 4 Miles of the Shore.

About the Lat. of 26 deg. S. we saw an Opening, and ran in, hoping to find a Harbour there: But when we came to its Mouth, which was about 2 Leagues wide, we saw Rocks and foul Ground within, and therefore stood out again: There we had 20 Fathom-water within 2 Mile of the Shore. The Land every where appear'd pretty low, flat and even; but with steep Cliffs to the Sea; and when we came near it there were no Trees, Shrubs or Grass to be seen. The Soundings in the Lat. of 26 deg. S. from about 8 or 9 Leagues off till you come within a League of the Shore, are generally about 40 Fathom; differing but little, seldom above 3 or 4 Fathom. But the Lead brings up very different Sorts of Sand, some coarse, some fine; and of several Colours, as Yellow, White, Grey, Brown, Blueish and Reddish.

When I saw there was no Harbour here, nor good anchoring, I stood off to Sea again, in the Evening of the second of August, fearing a Storm on a Lee-shore, in a Place where there was no Shelter, and desiring at least to have Sea-room: For the Clouds began to grow thick in the Western-board, and the Wind was already there, and began to blow fresh almost upon the Shore; which at this Place lies along N. N. W. and S. S. E. By 9 a Clock at Night we had got a pretty good Offin; but the Wind still increasing, I took in my Main Top-sail, being able to carry no more Sail than two Courses and the Mizen. At 2 in the Morning, Aug. 3, it blew very hard, and the Sea was much raised; so that I furled all my Sails but my Main-sail. Tho' the Wind blew so hard, we had pretty clear Weather till Noon: But then the whole Sky was blackned with thick Clouds, and we had some Rain, which would last a Quarter of an Hour at a Time, and then it would blow very fierce while the Squalls of Rain were over our Heads; but as soon as they were gone the Wind was by much abated, the Stress of the Storm being over. We sounded several Times, but had no Ground till 8 a Clock Aug. the 4th in the Evening; and then had 60 Fathom-water, Coral-ground. At 10 we had 56 Fathom fine Sand. At 12 we had 55 Fathom, fine Sand, of a pale blueish Colour. It was now pretty moderate Weather; yet I made no Sail till Morning; but then, the Wind veering about to the S. W. I made Sail and stood to the North: And at 11 a Clock the next Day, Aug. 5, we saw Land again, at about 10 Leagues distance. This Noon we were in Lat. 25 deg. 30 min. and in the afternoon our Cook died, an old Man, who had been sick a great while, being infirm before we came out of England.

AN. 1699

The 6th of August in the Morning we saw an Opening in the Land, and we ran into it, and anchored in 7 and a half Fathom-water, 2 Miles from the Shore, clean Sand. It was somewhat difficult getting in here, by Reason of many Shoals we met with: But I sent my Boat sounding before me. The Mouth of this Sound, which I call'd Shark's Bay,[1] lies in about 25 deg. S. Lat. and our Reckoning

[1] Sharks Bay is in lat. 25° 20′ S., long. 113° 40′ E. It retains the name Dampier gave it. He seems to have entered the Sound by the "Naturaliste Channel," with Dirk Hartog's Island on his starboard side. The berth where he anchored would seem to be Dampier Bay, to the NE. of the Peron Peninsula. Dirk Hartog's island is named after the Amsterdam skipper, who went ashore there in October, 1616.

AN. 1699 made its Longitude from the C. of Good Hope to be about 87 Degrees; which is less by 195 Leagues than is usually laid down in our common Draughts, if our Reckoning was right, and our Glasses did not deceive us. As soon as I came to anchor in this Bay (of which I have given a Plan, Table omitted) I sent my Boat ashore to seek for fresh Water: But in the Evening my Men returned, having found none. The next Morning I went ashore myself, carrying Pick-axes and Shovels with me, to dig for Water; and Axes to cut Wood. We tried in several Places for Water, but finding none after several Trials, nor in several Miles Compass, we left any farther Search for it, and spending the rest of the Day in cutting Wood, we went aboard at Night.

The Land is of an indifferent Heighth, so that it may be seen 9 or 10 Leagues off. It appears at a Distance very even; but as you come nigher you find there are many gentle Risings, tho' none steep nor high. 'Tis all a steep Shore against the open Sea: But in this Bay or Sound we were now in, the Land is low by the Sea-side, rising gradually in within the Land. The Mould is Sand by the Seaside, producing a large Sort of Sampier,[1] which bears a white Flower. Farther in, the Mould is reddish, a Sort of Sand producing some Grass, Plants, and Shrubs. The Grass grows in great Tufts, as big as a Bushel, here and there a Tuft: Being intermix'd with much Heath, much of the kind we have growing on our Commons in England. Of Trees or Shrubs here are divers Sorts; but none above 10 Foot high: Their Bodies about 3 Foot about, and 5 or 6 Foot high before you come to the Branches, which are bushy and compos'd of small Twigs there spreading abroad, tho' thick set, and full of Leaves; which were mostly long and narrow. The Colour of the Leaves was on one Side whitish, and on the other green; and the Bark of the Trees was generally of the same Colour with the Leaves, of a pale green. Some of these Trees were sweet-scented, and reddish within the Bark, like Sassafras, but redder.

[1] Samphire, the edible *Crithmum maritimum.*

Most of the Trees and Shrubs had at this Time either Blossoms or Berries on them. The Blossoms of the different Sort of Trees were of several Colours, as red, white, yellow, &c. but mostly blue: And these generally smelt very sweet and fragrant, as did some also of the rest. There were also beside some Plants, Herbs, and tall Flowers, some very small Flowers, growing on the Ground, that were sweet and beautiful, and for the most part unlike any I had seen elsewhere. AN. 1699

There were but few Land-Fowls; we saw none but Eagles, of the larger Sorts of Birds; but 5 or 6 Sorts of small Birds. The biggest Sort of these were not bigger than Larks; some no bigger than Wrens, all singing with great Variety of fine shrill Notes; and we saw some of their Nests with young Ones in them. The Water-Fowls are Ducks, (which had young Ones now, this being the Beginning of the Spring in these Parts;) Curlews, Galdens, Crab-catchers, Cormorants, Gulls, Pelicans; and some Water-Fowl, such as I have not seen any where besides. I have given the Pictures of 4 several Birds on this Coast. [See Birds: Fig. 2, 3, 4, 5.]

The Land-Animals that we saw here were only a Sort of Raccoons,[1] different from those of the West-Indies, chiefly as to their Legs; for these have very short Fore-Legs; but go jumping upon them as the others do, (and like them are very good Meat:) And a Sort of Guano's, of the same Shape and Size with other Guano's, describ'd [Vol. I. p. 87], but differing from them in 3 remarkable Particulars: For these had a larger and uglier Head, and had no Tail: And at the Rump, instead of the Tail there, they had a Stump of a Tail, which appear'd like another Head; but not really such, being without Mouth or Eyes: Yet this Creature seem'd by this Means to have a Head at each End; and, which may be reckon'd a fourth Difference, the Legs also seem'd all 4 of them to be Fore-legs, being all alike in Shape and Length, and seeming by the Joints

[1] This has been regarded as a description of the kangaroo; but it is more likely to have been the kangaroo-rat, which is fairly common in that part.

AN. and Bending to be made as if they were to go indifferently
1699 either Head or Tail foremost. They were speckled black and yellow like Toads, and had Scales or Knobs on their Backs like those of Crocodiles, plated on to the Skin, or stuck into it, as part of the Skin. They are very slow in Motion; and when a Man comes nigh them they will stand still and hiss, not endeavouring to get away. Their Livers are also spotted black and yellow: And the Body when opened hath a very unsavory Smell. I did never see such ugly Creatures any where but here. The Guano's I have observ'd to be very good Meat: And I have often eaten of them with Pleasure; but tho' I have eaten of Snakes, Crocodiles and Allegators, and many Creatures that look frightfully enough, and there are but few I should have been afraid to eat of, if prest by Hunger, yet I think my Stomach would scarce have serv'd to venture upon these N. Holland Guano's, both the Looks and the Smell of them being so offensive.

The Sea-fish that we saw here (for here was no River, Land or Pond of fresh Water to be seen) are chiefly Sharks. There are Abundance of them in this particular Sound, that I therefore give it the Name of Shark's Bay. Here are also Skates, Thornbacks, and other Fish of the Ray-kind; (one Sort especially like the Sea-Devil) and Gar-fish, Boneta's, &c. Of Shell-fish we got here Muscles, Periwinkles, Limpits, Oysters, both of the Pearl-kind and also Eating-Oysters, as well the common Sort as long Oysters; beside Cockles, &c. The Shore was lined thick with many other sorts of very strange and beautiful Shells, for variety of Colour and Shape, most finely spotted with Red, Black, or Yellow, &c. such as I have not seen any where but at this place. I brought away a great many of them; but lost all, except a very few, and those not of the best.

There are also some green Turtle weighing about 200 ℔. Of these we caught 2 which the Water Ebbing had left behind a Ledge of Rock, which they could not creep over. These served all my Company 2 Days; and

A Fish taken on the Coast of New Holland

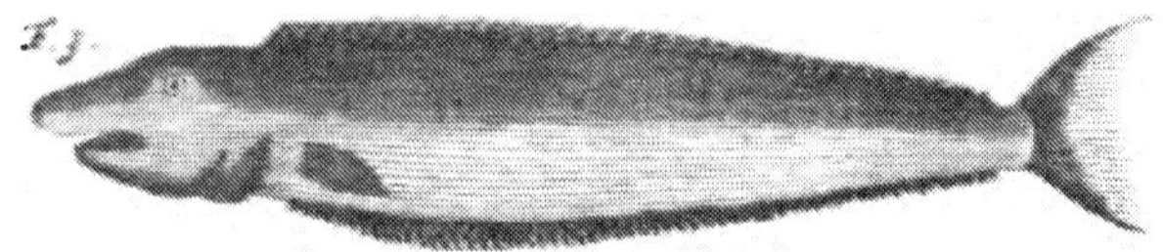

A Cuttle taken near N. Holland.

The Monk Fish.

A Remora taken sticking to Sharks backs

they were indifferent sweet Meat. Of the Sharks we caught a great many, which our Men eat very savourily. Among them we caught one which was 11 Foot long. The space between its two Eyes was 20 Inches, and 18 Inches from one Corner of his Mouth to the other. Its Maw was like a Leather Sack, very thick, and so tough that a sharp Knife could scarce cut it: In which we found the Head and Boans of a Hippopotomus; the hairy Lips of which were still sound and not putrified, and the Jaw was also firm, out of which we pluckt a great many Teeth, 2 of them 8 Inches long, and as big as a Man's Thumb, small at one end, and a little crooked; the rest not above half so long. The Maw was full of Jelly which stank extreamly: However I saved for a while the Teeth and the Sharks Jaw: The Flesh of it was divided among my Men; and they took care that no waste should be made of it.

AN. 1699

'Twas the 7th of August when we came into Shark's Bay; in which we Anchor'd at three several Places, and stay'd at the first of them (on the W. side of the Bay) till the 11th. During which time we searched about, as I said, for fresh Water, digging Wells, but to no purpose. However, we cut good store of Fire-wood at this first Anchoring-place; and my Company were all here very well refreshed with Raccoons, Turtle, Shark and other Fish, and some Fowles; so that we were now all much brisker than when we came in hither. Yet still I was for standing farther into the Bay, partly because I had a Mind to increase my stock of fresh Water, which was began to be low; and partly for the sake of Discovering this part of the Coast. I was invited to go further, by seeing from this Anchoring-place all open before me; which therefore I designed to search before I left the Bay. So on the 11th about Noon, I steer'd farther in, with an easie Sail, because we had but shallow Water: We kept therefore good looking out for fear of Sholes; sometimes shortning, sometimes deepning the Water. About 2 in the Afternoon we saw the Land a Head that makes the S. of the Bay, and before Night we had again Sholdings from that Shore:

AN. 1699 And therefore shortned Sail and stood off and on all Night, under 2 Topsails, continually sounding, having never more then 10 Fathom, and seldom less than 7. The Water deepned and sholdned so very gently, that in heaving the Lead 5 or 6 times we should scarce have a Foot difference. When we came into 7 Fathom either way, we presently went about. From this S. part of the Bay, we could not see the Land from whence we came in the Afternoon: And this Land we found to be an Island of 3 or 4 Leagues long, as is seen in the Plan, [Table omitted] but it appearing barren, I did not strive to go nearer it; and the rather because the Winds would not permit us to do it without much Trouble, and at the Openings the Water was generally Shole. I therefore made no farther attempts in this S. W. and S. part of the Bay, but steered away to the Eastward, to see if there was any Land that way, for as yet we had seen none there. On the 12th in the Morning we pass'd by the N. Point of that Land, and were confirm'd in the Persuasion of its being an Island, by seeing an Opening to the East of it, as we had done on the W. Having fair Weather, a small Gale and smooth Water, we stood further on in the Bay, to see what Land was on the E. of it. Our Soundings at first were 7 Fathom, which held so a great while, but at length it decreas'd to 6. Then we saw the Land right a-head, that in the Plan makes the E. of the Bay. We could not come near it with the Ship, having but Shole water: and it being dangerous lying there, and the Land extraordinarily low, very unlikely to have fresh Water, (though it had a few Trees on it, seemingly Mangroves) and much of it probably covered at High-water, I stood out again that Afternoon, deepning the Water, and before Night anchored in 8 Fathom, clean white Sand, about the middle of the Bay. The next day we got up our Anchor; and that Afternoon came to an Anchor once more near two Islands, and a Shole of Corral Rocks that face the Bay. Here I scrubb'd my Ship: and finding it very improbable I should get any thing further here, I made the best of my way out to Sea again, sounding all the way: but finding by the shallowness of the Water that there was no going out to Sea to the East of the two Islands that face the Bay, nor between them, I return'd to the West Entrance, going out by the same Way I came in at, only on the East instead of the West-side of the small Shole to be seen in the Plan: in which Channel we had 10, 12, and 13 Fathom-water, still deepning upon us till we were out at Sea. The day before we came out I sent a Boat ashore to the most Northerly of the Two Islands, which is the least of them, catching many small Fish in the mean while with Hook and Line. The Boat's Crew returning, told me, That the Isle produces nothing but a sort of green, short, hard, prickly Grass, affording neither Wood nor fresh Water; and that a Sea broak between the two Islands, a Sign that the Water was shallow. They saw a large Turtle, and many Skates and Thornbacks, but caught none.

It was August the 14th when I sail'd out of this Bay or Sound, the Mouth of which lies, as I said, in 25 deg. 5 min. designing to coast along to the N. E. till I might commodiously put in at some other part of N. Holland. In passing out we saw three Water-Serpents swimming about in the Sea, of a yellow Colour, spotted with dark, brown Spots. They were each about four Foot long, and about the bigness of a Man's Wrist, and were the first I saw on this Coast, which abounds with several sorts of them. We had the Winds at our first coming out at N. and the Land lying North-Easterly. We plied off and on, getting forward but little till the next day: When the Wind coming at S. S. W. and S. we began to Coast it along the Shore to the Northward, keeping at 6 or 7 Leagues off Shore; and sounding often, we had between 40 and 46 Fathom-water, brown Sand, with some white Shells. This 15th of August we were in Lat. 24 deg. 41 min. On the 16th Day at Noon we were in 23 deg. 22 min. The Wind coming at E. by N. we could not keep the Shore aboard, but were forced to go farther off, and lost sight of the Land. Then sounding we had no Ground with 80 Fathom-line; however the Wind shortly after came about again to the Southward, and then we jogg'd on again

An. 1699 to the Northward, and saw many small Dolphins and Whales, and abundance of Scuttle-shells swimming on the Sea; and some Water-snakes every day. The 17th we saw the Land again, and took a Sight of it. [Table omitted.]

The 18th in the Afternoon, being 3 or 4 Leagues off Shore, I saw a Shole-point, stretching from the Land into the Sea, a League or more. The Sea broke high on it; by which I saw plainly there was a Shole there. I stood farther off, and coasted along Shore, to about 7 or 8 Leagues distance: And at 12 a Clock at Night we sounded, and had but 20 Fathom, hard Sand. By this I found I was upon another Shoal, and so presently steered off W. half an Hour, and had then 40 Fathom. At One in the Morning of the 18th Day we had 85 Fathom: By two we could find no Ground; and then I ventur'd to steer along Shore again, due N. which is two Points wide of the Coast (that lies N. N. E.) for fear of another Shoal. I would not be too far off from the Land, being desirous to search into it where-ever I should find an Opening or any Convenience of searching about for Water, &c. When we were off the Shoal-point I mention'd, where we had but 20 Fathom-water, we had in the Night Abundance of Whales about the Ship, some a-head, others a-stern, and some on each side blowing and making a very dismal Noise; but when we came out again into deeper Water they left us. Indeed the Noise that they made by blowing and dashing of the Sea with their Tails, making it all of a Breach and Foam, was very dreadful to us, like the Breach of the Waves in very Shoal-water, or among Rocks. The Shoal these Whales were upon had Depth of Water sufficient, no less than 20 Fathom, as I said; and it lies in Lat. 22 deg. 22 min. The Shore was generally bold all along; we had met with no Shoal at Sea since the Abrohlo-shoal, when we first fell on the N. Holland Coast in the Lat. of 28, till Yesterday in the Afternoon, and this Night. This Morning also when we expected by the Draught we had with us to have been 11 Leagues off Shore, we were but 4; so that either our Draughts were faulty, which yet hitherto and

afterwards we found true enough as to the lying of the AN.
Coast, or else here was a Tide unknown to us that deceived 1699
us; tho' we had found very little of any Tide on this Coast hitherto. As to our Winds in the Coasting thus far, as we had been within the Verge of the general Trade (tho' interrupted by the Storm I mention'd) from the Lat. of 28, when we first fell in with the Coast: And by that Time we were in the Lat. of 25, we had usually the regular Trade-wind (which is here S. S. E.) when we were at any Distance from Shore: But we had often Sea and Land-Breezes, especially when near Shore, and when in Shark's-bay; and had a particular N. West Wind, or Storm, that set us in thither. On this 18th of August we coasted with a brisk Gale of the true Trade-wind at S. S. E. very fair and clear Weather; but haling off in the Evening to Sea, were next Morning out of Sight of Land; and the Land now trending away N. Easterly, and we being to the Norward of it, and the Wind also shrinking from the S. S. E. to the E. S. E. (that is, from the true Trade-Wind to the Sea-breeze, as the Land now lay) we could not get in with the Land again yet a-while, so as to see it, tho' we trim'd sharp and kept close on a Wind. We were this 19th day in Lat. 21 deg. 42 min. The 20th we were in Lat. 19 deg. 37 min. and kept close on a Wind to get Sight of the Land again, but could not yet see it. We had very fair Weather; and tho' we were so far from the Land as to be out of Sight of it, yet we had the Sea and Land-Breezes. In the Night we had the Land-Breeze at S. S. E. a small gentle Gale; which in the Morning about Sun-rising would shift about gradually (and withal increasing in Strength) till about Noon we should have it at E. S. E. which is the true Sea-breeze here. Then it would blow a brisk Gale, so that we could scarce carry our Top-sails double rift: And it would continue thus till 3 in the Afternoon, when it would decrease again. The Weather was fair all the while, not a Cloud to be seen; but very hazy, especially nigh the Horizon. We sounded several Times this 20th Day, and at first had no Ground; but had afterwards from 52 to 45 Fathom, coarse brown Sand,

AN. 1699 mixt with small brown and white Stones, with Dints besides in the Tallow.[1]

The 21st Day also we had small Land-breezes in the Night, and Sea-breezes in the Day: And as we saw some Sea-snakes every Day, so this Day we saw a great many, of two different Sorts or Shapes. One Sort was yellow, and about the Bigness of a Man's Wrist, about 4 Foot long, having a flat Tail about 4 Fingers broad. The other Sort was much smaller and shorter, round and spotted black and yellow. This Day we sounded several Times, and had 45 Fathom Sand. We did not make the Land till Noon, and then saw it first from our Topmast-head. It bore S. E. by E. about 9 Leagues distance; and it appeared like a Cape or Head of Land. The Sea-breeze this Day was not so strong as the Day before, and it veered out more; so that we had a fair Wind to run in with to the Shore, and at Sunset anchored in 20 Fathom, clean Sand, about 5 Leagues from the bluff Point; which was not a Cape (as it appear'd at a great Distance) but the Eastermost End of an Island, about 5 or 6 Leagues in length, and 1 in breadth. There were 3 or 4 Rocky Islands about a League from us between us and the bluff Point; and we saw many other Islands both to the East and West of it, as far as we could see either way from our Topmast-head: And all within them to the S. there was nothing but Islands of a pretty Heighth, that may be seen 8 or 9 Leagues off. By what we saw of them they must have been a Range of Islands of about 20 Leagues in length, stretching from E. N. E. to W. S. W. and for ought I know, as far as to those of Shark's-Bay; and to a considerable Breadth also, (for we could see 9 or 10 Leagues in among them) towards the Continent or main Land of N. Holland, if there be any such Thing hereabouts: And by the great Tides I met with a while afterwards, more to the N. East, I had a strong Suspicion that here might be a kind of Archipelago of Islands, and a Passage possibly to the S. of N. Holland and N. Guinea

[1] The tallow, or "arming," in a hole at the end of the leaden plummet used in sounding.

into the great S. Sea Eastward; which I had Thoughts also of attempting in my Return from N. Guinea (had Circumstances permitted) and told my Officers so: But I would not attempt it at this Time, because we wanted Water, and could not depend upon finding it there. This Place is in the Lat. of 20 deg. 21 min. but in the Draught that I had of this Coast, which was Tasman's,[1] it was laid down in 19 deg. 50 min. and the Shore is laid down as all along joining in one Body or Continent, with some Openings appearing like Rivers; and not like Islands, as really they are. This Place lies more Northerly by 40 min. than is laid down in Mr. Tasman's Draught: And beside its being made a firm, continued Land, only with some Openings like the Mouths of Rivers, I found the Soundings also different from what the prick'd Line of his Course shews them, and generally shallower than he makes them; which inclines me to think that he came not so near the Shore as his Line shews, and so had deeper Soundings, and could not so well distinguish the Islands. His Meridian or Difference of Longitude from Shark's-Bay agrees well enough with my Account, which is 232 Leagues, tho' we differ in Lat. And to confirm my Conjecture that the Line of his Course is made too near the Shore, at least not far to the East of this Place, the Water is there so shallow that he could not come there so nigh.

AN. 1699

But to proceed; in the Night we had a small Land-breeze, and in the Morning I weighed Anchor, designing to run in among the Islands, for they had large Channels between them, of a League wide at least, and some 2 or 3 Leagues wide. I sent in my Boat before to sound, and if they found Shoal-water to return again; but if they found Water enough, to go ashore on one of the Islands, and stay till the Ship came in: where they might in the mean Time search for Water. So we followed after with the Ship, sounding as we went in, and had 20 Fathom, till within 2 Leagues of the Bluff-head, and then we had shoal

[1] Abell Tasman. The "Draught" here mentioned was probably a copy of that in Klencke's Atlas, or in the map by Vankeulen.

AN. 1699 Water, and very uncertain Soundings: Yet we ran in still with an easy Sail, sounding and looking out well, for this was dangerous Work. When we came abreast of the Bluff-head, and about 2 Mile from it, we had but 7 Fathom: Then we edg'd away from it, but had no more Water; and running in a little farther, we had but 4 Fathoms; so we anchored immediately; and yet when we had veered out a third of a Cable we had 7 Fathom Water again; so uncertain was the Water. My Boat came immediately aboard, and told me that the Island was very rocky and dry, and they had little Hopes of finding Water there. I sent them to sound, and bad them, if they found a Channel of 8 or 10 Fathom Water, to keep on, and we would follow with the Ship. We were now about 4 Leagues within the outer small rocky Islands, but still could see nothing but Islands within us; some 5 or 6 Leagues long, others not above a Mile round. The large Islands were pretty high; but all appeared dry, and mostly rocky and barren. The Rocks look'd of a rusty yellow Colour, and therefore I despair'd of getting Water on any of them; but was in some Hopes of finding a Channel to run in beyond all these Islands, could I have spent Time here, and either get to the Main of New Holland, or find out some other Islands that might afford us Water and other Refreshments: Besides, that among so many Islands, we might have found some Sort of rich Mineral, or Ambergreece, it being a good Latitude for both these. But we had not sailed above a League farther before our Water grew shoaler again, and then we anchored in 6 Fathom hard Sand.

We were now on the inner Side of the Island, on whose out-side is the Bluff-point. We rode a League from the Island, and I presently went ashore, and carried Shovels to dig for Water, but found none. There grow here 2 or 3 Sorts of Shrubs, one just like Rosemary; and therefore I call'd this Rosemary Island. It grew in great Plenty here, but had no Smell. Some of the other Shrubs had blue and yellow Flowers; and we found 2 Sorts of Grain like Beans: The one grew on Bushes; the other on a Sort of a creeping Vine that runs along on the Ground, having very thick broad Leaves, and the Blossom like a Bean Blossom, but much larger, and of a deep red Colour, looking very beautiful. We saw here some Cormorants, Gulls, Crabcatchers, &c. a few small Land-Birds, and a Sort of white Parrots, which flew a great many together. We found some Shell-fish, viz. Limpits, Perriwinkles, and Abundance of small Oysters growing on the Rocks, which were very sweet. In the Sea we saw some green Turtle, a pretty many Sharks, and Abundance of Water-Snakes of several Sorts and Sizes. The Stones were all of rusty Colour, and ponderous.

AN. 1699

We saw a Smoak on an Island 3 or 4 Leagues off; and here also the Bushes had been burned, but we found no other Sign of Inhabitants: 'Twas probable that on the Island where the Smoak was there were Inhabitants, and fresh Water for them. In the Evening I went aboard, and consulted with my Officers whether it was best to send thither, or to search among any other of these Islands with my Boat; or else go from hence, and coast along Shore with the Ship, till we could find some better Place than this was to ride in, where we had shoal Water, and lay expos'd to Winds and Tides. They all agreed to go from hence; so I gave Orders to weigh in the Morning as soon as it should be light, and to get out with the Land-breeze.

Accordingly, August the 23d, at 5 in the Morning we ran out, having a pretty fresh Land-breeze at S. S. E. By 8 a Clock we were got out, and very seasonably; for before 9 the Sea-breeze came on us very strong, and increasing, we took in our Top-sails and stood off under 2 Courses and a Mizen, this being as much Sail as we could carry. The Sky was clear, there being not one Cloud to be seen; but the Horizon appeared very hazy, and the Sun at setting the Night before, and this Morning at rising, appeared very red. The Wind continued very strong till 12, then it began to abate: I have seldom met with a stronger Breeze. These strong Sea-Breezes lasted thus in their Turns 3 or 4 Days. They sprung up with the Sun-rise; by 9 a Clock they were very strong, and so continued till Noon, when

AN. 1699 they began to abate; and by Sun-set there was little Wind, or a Calm till the Land-breezes came; which we should certainly have in the Morning about 1 or 2 a Clock. The Land-breezes were between the S. S. W. and S. S. E. The Sea-breezes between the E. N. E. and N. N. E. In the Night while Calm, we fish'd with Hook and Line, and caught good Store of Fish, viz. Snappers, Breams, Old-Wives, and Dog-fish. When these last came we seldom caught any others; for if they did not drive away the other Fish, yet they would be sure to keep them from taking our Hooks, for they would first have them themselves, biting very greedily. We caught also a Monk-fish, of which I brought Home the Picture. See Fish, Fig. I.

On the 25th of August, we still coasted along Shore, that we might the better see any Opening; kept sounding, and had about 20 Fathom clean Sand. The 26th Day, being about 4 Leagues off Shore, the Water began gradually to sholden from 20 to 14 Fathom. I was edging in a little towards the Land, thinking to have anchored; but presently after the Water decreas'd almost at once, till we had but 5 Fathom. I durst therefore adventure no farther, but steer'd out the same way that we came in; and in a short Time had 10 Fathom (being then about 4 Leagues and a half from the Shore) and even Soundings. I steer'd away E. N. E. coasting along as the Land lies. This Day the Sea-breezes began to be very moderate again, and we made the best of our way along Shore, only in the Night edging off a little for Fear of Sholes. Ever since we left Sharks-Bay we had fair clear Weather, and so for a great while still.

The 27th Day, we had 20 Fathom Water all Night, yet we could not see Land till 1 in the Afternoon from our Topmast-head. By 3 we could just discern Land from our Quarter-deck; we had then 16 Fathom. The Wind was at N. and we steer'd E. by N. which is but one Point in on the Land; yet we decreas'd our Water very fast; for at 4 we had but 9 Fathom; the next Cast but 7, which frighted us; and we then tackt instantly and stood off: But in a short Time the Wind coming at N. W. and W. N. W. we tackt again, and steer'd N. N E and then deepned our Water again, and had all Night from 15 to 20 Fathom. AN. 1699

The 28th Day we had between 20 and 40 Fathom. We saw no Land this Day, but saw a great many Snakes and some Whales. We saw also some Boobies, and Noddy-birds; and in the Night caught one of these last. It was of another Shape and Colour than any I had seen before. It had a small long Bill, as all of them have, flat Feet like Ducks Feet; its Tail forked like a Swallow, but longer and broader, and the Fork deeper than that of the Swallow, with very long Wings; the Top or Crown of the Head of this Noddy was Coal-black, having also small black Streaks round about and close to the Eyes; and round these Streaks on each Side, a pretty broad white Circle. The Breast, Belly, and under part of the Wings of this Noddy were white; and the Back and upper part of its Wings of a faint black or smoak Colour. See a Picture of this, and of the common one, Birds, Fig. 5, 6. Noddies are seen in most Places between the Tropicks, as well in the East-Indies, and on the Coast of Brazil, as in the West-Indies. They rest ashore a Nights, and therefore we never see them far at Sea, not above 20 or 30 Leagues, unless driven off in a Storm. When they come about a Ship they commonly perch in the Night, and will sit still till they are taken by the Seamen. They build on Cliffs against the Sea, or Rocks, as I have said Vol. I. p. 83.

The 30th day, being in Lat. 18 deg. 21 min. we made the Land again, and saw many great Smokes near the Shore; and having fair Weather and moderate Breezes, I steer'd in towards it. At 4 in the Afternoon I anchor'd in 8 Fathom Water, clear Sand, about 3 Leagues and a half from the Shore. I presently sent my Boat to sound nearer in, and they found 10 Fathom about a Mile farther in; and from thence still farther in the Water decreased gradually to 9, 8, 7, and at 2 Mile distance to 6 Fathom. This Evening we saw an Eclipse of the Moon, but it was abating before the Moon appear'd to us; for the Horizon was very hazy, so that we could not see the Moon till she had been half an Hour above the Horizon: And at 2 hours, 22 min.

AN. 1699 after Sun-set, by the Reckoning of our Glasses, the Eclipse was quite gone, which was not of many Digits. The Moon's Center was then 33 deg. 40 min. high.

The 31st of August betimes in the Morning I went ashore with 10 or 11 Men to search for Water. We went armed with Muskets and Cutlasses for our defence, expecting to see people there; and carried also Shovels and Pick-axes to dig Wells. When we came near the Shore we saw 3 tall black naked Men on the sandy Bay a head of us: But as we row'd in, they went away. When we were landed, I sent the Boat with two Men in her to lie a little from the Shore at an Anchor, to prevent being seiz'd; while the rest of us went after the 3 black Men, who were now got on the top of a small Hill about a quarter of a Mile from us, with 8 or 9 Men more in their Company. They seeing us coming, ran away. When we came on the top of the Hill where they first stood, we saw a plain Savannah, about half a Mile from us, farther in from the Sea. There were several Things like Hay-cocks,[1] standing in the Savannah; which at a distance we thought were Houses, looking just like the Hottentot's Houses at the Cape of G. Hope: but we found them to be so many Rocks. We searched about these for Water, but could find none, nor any Houses; nor People, for they were all gone. Then we turned again to the Place where we landed, and there we dug for Water.

While we were at work there came 9 or 10 of the Natives to a small Hill a little way from us, and stood there menacing and threatning of us, and making a great Noise. At last one of them came towards us, and the rest followed at a distance. I went out to meet him, and came within 50 Yards of him, making to him all the Signs of Peace and Friendship I could; but then he ran away, neither would they any of them stay for us to come nigh them; for we tried two or three Times. At last I took two Men with me, and went in the Afternoon along by the Sea-side, purposely to catch one of them, if I could, of whom I might learn where they got their

[1] Flinders suggests that these were ant-hills, of the kind seen by Pelsart in 1629.

fresh Water. There were 10 or 12 of the Natives a little way off, who seeing us three going away from the rest of our Men, followed us at a distance. I thought they would follow us: But there being for a while a Sand-bank between us and them, that they could not then see us, we made a halt, and hid our selves in a bending of the Sand-bank. They knew we must be thereabouts, and being 3 or 4 times our Number, thought to seize us. So they dispers'd themselves, some going to the Sea-shore, and others beating about the Sand-hills. We knew by what Rencounter we had had with them in the Morning that we could easily out-run them. So a nimble young Man[1] that was with me, seeing some of them near, ran towards them; and they for some time, ran away before him. But he soon over-taking them, they faced about and fought him. He had a Cutlass, and they had wooden Lances; with which, being many of them, they were too hard for him. When he first ran towards them I chas'd two more that were by the Shore: But fearing how it might be with my young Man, I turn'd back quickly, and went up to the top of a Sandhill, whence I saw him near me, closely engag'd with them. Upon their seeing me, one of them threw a Lance at me, that narrowly miss'd me. I discharg'd my Gun to scare them, but avoided shooting any of them; till finding the young Man in great danger from them, and my self in some; and that tho' the Gun had a little frighted them at first, yet they had soon learnt to despise it, tossing up their Hands, and crying Pooh, Pooh, Pooh; and coming on afresh with a great Noise, I thought it high time to charge again, and shoot one of them, which I did. The rest, seeing him fall, made a stand again; and my young Man took the Opportunity to disengage himself, and come off to me; my other Man also was with me, who had done nothing all this while, having come out unarm'd; and I return'd back with my Men, designing to attempt the Natives no farther, being very sorry for what had happened already. They took up

AN. 1699

[1] The young man was Alexander Beale. Beale received a wooden lance through his chin; but "with his Cutlace did so cleave one part of his opponent's head, that he fled away."

AN. 1699 their wounded Companion; and my young Man, who had been struck through the Cheek by one of their Lances, was afraid it had been poison'd: But I did not think that likely. His Wound was very painful to him, being made with a blunt Weapon: But he soon recover'd of it.

Among the N. Hollanders, whom we were thus engag'd with, there was one who by his Appearance and Carriage, as well in the Morning as this Afternoon, seem'd to be the Chief of them, and a kind of Prince or Captain among them. He was a young brisk Man, not very tall, nor so personable as some of the rest, tho' more active and couragious: He was painted (which none of the rest were at all) with a Circle of white Paste or Pigment (a sort of Lime, as we thought) about his Eyes, and a white streak down his Nose from his Forehead to the tip of it. And his Breast and some part of his Arms were also made white with the same Paint; not for Beauty or Ornament, one would think, but as some wild Indian Warriors are said to do, he seem'd thereby to design the looking more Terrible; this his Painting adding very much to his natural Deformity; for they all of them have the most unpleasant Looks and the worst Features of any People that ever I saw, though I have seen great variety of Savages. These New-Hollanders were probably the same sort of People as those I met with on this Coast in my "Voyage round the World"; [See Vol. I. p. 453, &c.] for the Place I then touched at was not above 40 or 50 Leagues to the N. E. of this: And these were much the same blinking Creatures (here being also abundance of the same kind of Flesh-flies teizing them) and with the same black Skins, and Hair frizled, tall and thin, &c. as those were: But we had not the Opportunity to see whether these, as the former, wanted two of their Fore-Teeth.

We saw a great many places where they had made Fires; and where there were commonly 3 or 4 Boughs stuck up to Windward of them; for the Wind (which is the Sea-breeze) in the day-time blows always one way with them; and the Land-breeze is but small. By their Fire-places we should always find great heaps of Fish-shells, of several sorts; and 'tis probable that these poor Creatures here lived chiefly on the Shell-fish, as those I before describ'd did on small Fish, which they caught in Wires or Holes in the Sand at Low-water. These gather'd their Shell-fish on the Rocks at Low-water; but had no Wires (that we saw) whereby to get any other sorts of Fish: As among the former I saw not any heaps of Shells as here, though I know they also gather'd some Shell-fish. The Lances also of those were such as these had; however they being upon an Island, with their Women and Children, and all in our Power, they did not there use them against us, as here on the Continent, where we saw none but some of the Men under Head, who come out purposely to observe us. We saw no Houses at either Place; and I believe they have none, since the former People on the Island had none, tho' they had all their Families with them.

AN. 1699

Upon returning to my Men I saw that though they had dug 8 or 9 Foot deep, yet found no Water. So I returned aboard that Evening, and the next day, being September 1st, I sent my Boatswain ashore to dig deeper, and sent the Sain with him to catch Fish. While I staid aboard I observed the flowing of the Tide, which runs very swift here, so that our Nun-buoy[1] would not bear above the Water to be seen. It flows here (as on that part of N. Holland I described formerly) about 5 Fathom: And here the Flood runs S. E. by S. till the last Quarter; then it sets right in towards the Shore (which lies here S. S. W. and N. N. E.) and the Ebb runs N. W. by N. When the Tides slackned we fish'd with Hook and Line, as we had already done in several Places on this Coast; on which in this Voyage hitherto, we had found but little Tides: But by the Heighth, and Strength, and Course of them hereabouts, it should seem that if there be such a Passage or Streight going through Eastward to the Great South-Sea, as I said one might suspect, one would expect to find the

[1] The nun-buoy is a broad cylinder in its middle part and tapers to a point at each end. In the days of hemp cables such a buoy was fastened by a rope to the anchor "to determine the place where the anchor lay," that the ship might not come too near it to entangle her cable about the stock or the flukes of it.

AN. 1699 Mouth of it somewhere between this Place and Rosemary Island, which was the part of New Holland I came last from.

Next Morning my Men came aboard and brought a Rundlet of brackish Water which they got out of another Well that they dug in a Place a mile off, and about half as far from the Shore; but this Water was not fit to drink. However we all concluded that it would serve to boil our Oatmeal, for Burgoo,[1] whereby we might save the Remains of our other Water for drinking, till we should get more; and accordingly the next Day we brought aboard 4 Hogsheads of it: But while we were at work about the Well we were sadly pester'd with the Flies, which were more troublesome to us than the Sun, tho' it shone clear and strong upon us all the while, very hot. All this while we saw no more of the Natives, but saw some of the Smoaks of some of their Fires at 2 or 3 miles distance.

The Land hereabouts was much like the part of New Holland that I formerly described [Vol. I. p. 452], 'tis low, but seemingly barricado'd with a long Chain of Sandhills to the Sea, that let's nothing be seen of what is farther within Land. At high Water the Tides rising so high as they do, the Coast shews very low; but when 'tis low Water it seems to be of an indifferent heighth. At low Watermark the Shore is all Rocky, so that then there is no Landing with a Boat; but at high Water a Boat may come in over those Rocks to the Sandy Bay, which runs all along on this Coast. The Land by the Sea for about 5 or 600 yards is a dry Sandy Soil, bearing only Shrubs and Bushes of divers sorts. Some of these had them at this time of the Year, yellow Flowers or Blossoms, some blue, and some white; most of them of a very fragrant Smell. Some had Fruit like Peascods; in each of which there were just ten small Peas: I opened many of them, and found no more nor less. There are also here some of that sort of Bean which I saw at Rosemary-Island: And another sort of small, red, hard Pulse, growing in Cods also, with little black Eyes

[1] Porridge. The word is still in use at sea.

like Beans. I know not their Names, but have seen them used often in the East-Indies for weighing Gold; and they make the same use of them at Guinea, as I have heard, where the Women also make Bracelets with them to wear about their Arms. These grow on Bushes; but here are also a Fruit like Beans growing on a creeping sort of Shrub-like Vine. There was a great plenty of all these sorts of Cod-fruit growing on the Sand-hills by the Sea-side, some of them green, some ripe, and some fallen on the Ground: But I could not perceive that any of them had been gathered by the Natives; and might not probably be wholesome Food. AN. 1699

The Land farther in, that is lower than what borders on the Sea, was so much as we saw of it, very plain and even; partly Savannahs, and partly Woodland. The Savannahs bear a sort of thin coarse Grass. The Mould is also a coarser Sand than that by the Sea-side, and in some places 'tis Clay. Here are a great many Rocks in the large Savannah we were in, which are 5 or 6 Foot high, and round at top like a Hay-cock, very remarkable; some red, and some white. The Woodland lies farther in still; where there were divers sorts of small Trees, scarce any three Foot in circumference; their Bodies 12 or 14 Foot high, with a Head of small Knibs or Boughs. By the sides of the Creeks, especially nigh the Sea, there grow a few small black Mangrove-Trees.

There are but few Land-Animals. I saw some Lizards; and my Men saw two or three Beasts like hungry Wolves,[1] lean like so many Skeletons, being nothing but Skin and Bones: 'Tis probable that it was the Foot of one of those Beasts that I mention'd as seen by us in N. Holland, [Vol. I. p. 453]. We saw a Rackoon[2] or two, and one small speckled Snake.

The Land-fowls that we saw here were Crows (just such as ours in England) small Hawks, and Kites; a few of each sort: But here are plenty of small Turtle-Doves, that are plump, fat and very good Meat. Here are 2 or 3

[1] Probably dingoes.

[2] Perhaps bandicoots.

AN. 1699 sorts of smaller Birds, some as big as Larks, some less; but not many of either sort. The Sea-Fowl are Pelicans, Boobies, Noddies, Curlews, See-pies, &c. and but few of these neither.

The Sea is plentifully stock'd with the largest Whales that I ever saw; but not to compare with the vast ones of the Northern Seas. We saw also a great many Green Turtle, but caught none; here being no place to set a Turtle-Net in; here being no Channel for them, and the Tides running so strong. We saw some Sharks, and Parracoots; and with Hooks and Lines we caught some Rock-fish and Old-Wives. Of Shell-fish, here were Oysters both of the common kind for Eating, and of the Pearl kind: And also Wilks, Conchs, Muscles, Limpits, Perriwinkles, &c. and I gather'd a few strange Shells; chiefly a sort not large, and thick-set all about with Rays or Spikes growing in Rows.

And thus having ranged about, a considerable time, upon this Coast, without finding any good fresh Water, or any convenient Place to clean the Ship, as I had hop'd for: And it being moreover the heighth of the dry Season, and my Men growing Scorbutick for want of Refreshments, so that I had little incouragement to search further; I resolved to leave this Coast, and accordingly in the beginning of September set sail towards Timor.

AN ACCOUNT

OF SEVERAL

PLANTS

COLLECTED IN

BRASIL, NEW HOLLAND, TIMOR, AND NEW GUINEA, REFERRING TO THE FIGURES ENGRAVEN ON THE COPPER PLATES

TAB. 1. Fig. 1. Cotton-flower from Baya[1] in Brazil. The Flower consists of a great many Filaments, almost as small as Hairs, betwixt three and four Inches long, of a Murrey-colour;[2] on the Top of them stand small ash-colour'd Apices. The Pedicule of the Flower is inclos'd at the Bottom with 5 narrow stiff Leaves, about 6 Inches long. There is one of this Genus in Mr. Ray's Supplement, which agrees exactly with this in every Respect, only that is twice larger at the least. It was sent from Surinam by the Name of Momoo. AN. 1699

Tab. 1. Fig. 2. *Jasminum Brasilianum luteum, mali limoniæ folio nervoso, petalis crassis.*

Tab. 1. Fig. 3. *Crista Pavonis Brasiliana Bardanæ foliis.* The Leaves are very tender and like the top Leaves of *Bardana major,* both as to Shape and Texture: In the Figure they are represented too stiff and too much serrated.

Tab. 1. Fig. 4. *Filix Brasiliana Osmunaæ minori serrato folio.* This Fern is of that Kind, which bears its Seed-Vessels in Lines on the Edge of the Leaves.

[1] Bahia. [2] Of the colour of a mulberry.

AN. 1699 Tab. 2. Fig. 1. *Rapuntium Novæ Hollandiæ, flore magno coccineo.* The Perianthium compos'd of five long-pointed Parts, the Form of the Seed-Vessel and the Smallness of the Seeds, together with the irregular Shape of the Flower and Thinness of the Leaves, argue this plant to be a Rapuntium.

Tab. 2. Fig. 2. *Fucus foliis capillaceis brevissimis, vesiculis minimis donatis.* This elegant Fucus is of the *Erica Marina* or *Sargoza* kind, but has much finer Parts than that. It was collected on this Coast of New Holland.

Tab. 2. Fig. 2. *Ricinoides Novæ Hollandiæ anguloso crasso folio.* This Plant is shrubby, has thick woolly Leaves, especially on the under side. Its Fruit is tricoccous, hoary on the out-side with a Calix divided into 5 Parts. It comes near *Ricini fructu parvo frucosa Curassavica, folio Phylli, P. B. pr.*

Tab. 2. Fig. 2. *Solanum spinosum Novæ Hollandiæ Phylli foliis subrotundis.* This new Solanum bears a blueish Flower like the others of the same Tribe; the Leaves are of a whitish Colour, thick and woolly on both Sides, scarce an Inch long and near as broad. The Thorns are very sharp and thick set, of a deep Orange colour, especially towards the Points.

Tab. 3. Fig. 1. *Scabiosa (forte) Novæ Hollandiæ, statices foliis subtus argenteis.* The Flower stands on a Foot-stalk 4 Inches long, included in a rough Calix of a yellowish Colour. The Leaves are not above an Inch long, very narrow like Thrift, green on the upper and hoary on the under side, growing in Tufts. Whether this Plant be a Scabious, Thrift or Helichrysum is hard to judge from the imperfect Flower of the dry'd Specimen.

Tab. 3. Fig. 2. *Alcea Novæ Hollandiæ foliis augustis utrinque villosis.* The Leaves, Stalk, and under side of the Perianthium of this Plant are all woolly. The Petala are very tender, 5 in Number, scarce so large as the Calix: In the Middle stands a Columella thick set with thrummy apiculæ, which argue this Plant to belong to the Malvaceous Kind.

Tab. 3. Fig. 3. Of what Genus this Shrub or Tree is,

is uncertain, agreeing with none yet described, as far as can be judg'd by the State it is in. It has a very beautiful Flower, of a red Colour, as far as can be guess'd by the dry Specimen, consisting of 10 large Petala, hoary on both Sides, especially underneath; the Middle of the Flower is thick set with Stamina, which are woolly at the Bottom, the Length of the Petala, each of them crown'd with its Apex. The Calix is divided into 5 round pointed Parts. The Leaves are like those of *Amelanchier Lob.* green at Top and very woolly underneath, not running to a Point, as is common in others, but with an Indenture at the upper-end.

Tab. 3. Fig. 4. *Dammara ax Nova-Hollandia, Sanamundæ secundæ Chysii foliis.* This new Genus was first sent from Amboyna by Mr. Rumphius, by the Name of Dammara, of which he transmitted 2 Kinds; one with narrow and long stiff Leaves, the other with shorter and broader. The first of them is mention'd in Mr. Petiver's *Centuria*, p. 350. by the name of *Arbor Hortensis Javanorum foliis visce augustioribus aromaticis floribus, spicatis stamineis lutescentibus;* Mus. Pet. As also in Mr. Ráy's Supplement to his History of Plants now in the Press. This is of the same Genus with them, agreeing both in Flower and Fruit, tho' very much differing in Leaves. The Flowers are stamineous and seem to be of an herbaceous Colour, growing among the Leaves, which are short and almost round, very stiff and ribb'd on the under side, of a dark Green above, and a pale Colour underneath, thick set on by Pairs, answering one another crossways, so that they cover the Stalk. The Fruit is as big as a Pepper-corn, almost round, of a whitish Colour, dry and tough, with a Hole on the top, containing small Seeds. Any one that sees this Plant without its Seed-Vessels, would take it for an Erica or Sanamunda. The Leaves of this Plant are of a very aromatick Taste.

Tab. 4. Fig. 1. *Equisetum Novæ Hollandiæ frutesceus foliis longissimis.* 'Tis doubtful whether this be an Equisetum or not; the Textures of the Leaves agree best with that Genus of any, being articulated one within another at each Joint, which is only proper to this Tribe. The longest of them are about 9 Inches.

AN. 1699 Tab. 4. Fig. 2. *Colutea Novæ Hollandiæ floribus amplis coccineis, umbellatim dispositis macula purpurea notatis.* There being no Leaves to this Plant, 'tis hard to say what Genus it properly belongs to. The Flowers are very like to the *Colutea Barbæ Jovis folio flore coccineo Breynii;* of the same Scarlet Colour, with a large deep Purple Spot in the Vexillum, but much bigger, coming all from the same Point after the Manner of an Umbel. The Rudiment of the Pod is very woolly, and terminates in a Filament near 2 Inches long.

Tab. 4. Fig. 3. *Conyza Novæ Hollandiæ angustis Rorismarini foliis.* This Plant is very much branch'd and seems to be woody. The Flowers stand on very short Pedicules, arising from the Sinus of the Leaves, which are exactly like Rosemary, only less. It tastes very bitter now dry.

Tab. 4. Fig. 4. *Mohoh Infulæ Timor.* This is a very odd Plant, agreeing with no describ'd Genus. The Leaf is almost round, green on the upper side and whitish underneath, with several Fibres running from the Insertion of the Pedicule towards the Circumference 'tis umbilicated as *Cotyledon aquatica* and *Faba Ægyptiâ.* The Flowers are white, standing on single Foot-stalks, of the Shape of a Stramonium, but divided into 4 Points only, as is the Perianthium.

Tab. 5. Fig. 1. *Fucus ex Nova Guinea uva marina dictus, foliis variis.* This beautiful Fucus is thick set with very small short Tufts of Leaves, which by the Help of a magnifying Glass, seem to be round and articulated, as if they were Seed-Vessels; besides these, there are other broad Leaves, chiefly at the Extremity of the Branches, serrated on the Edges. The Vesiculæ are round, of the Bigness express'd in the Figure.

Tab. 5. Fig. 2. *Fucus ex Nova Guinea Fluviatilis Pisanæ J. B. foliis.* These Plants are so apt to vary in their Leaves, according to their different States, that 'tis hard to say this is distinct from the last. It has in several Places (not all express'd in the Figure) some of the small short Leaves, or Seed-Vessels mention'd in the former; which makes me apt to believe it the same, gather'd in a different State; besides the broad Leaves of that and this agree as to their Shape and Indentures.

TABLE I

TABLE II

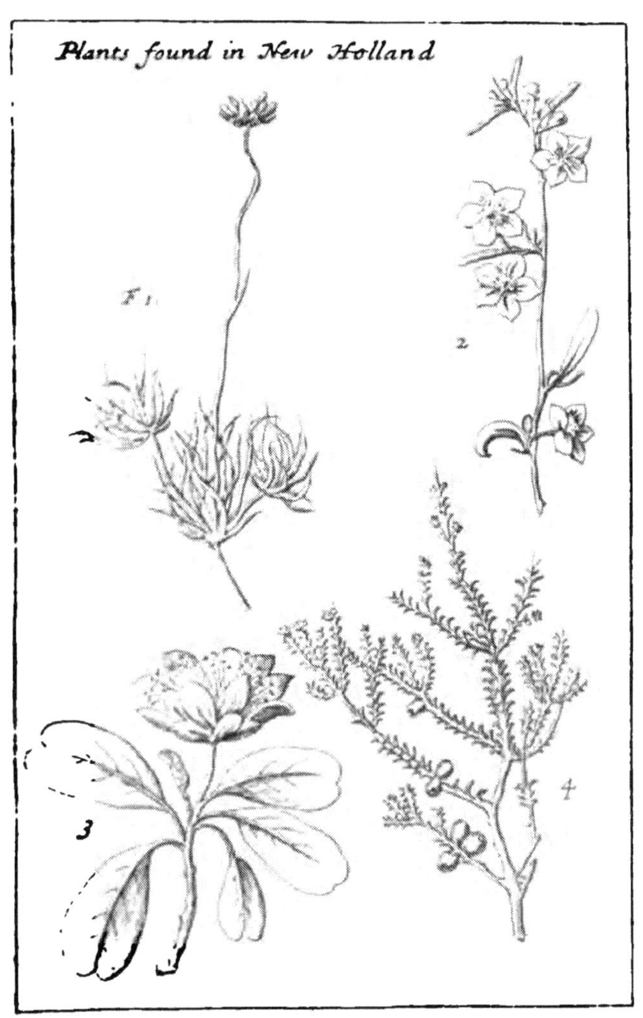
Plants found in New Holland
F 1
2
3
4

TABLE III

TABLE IV

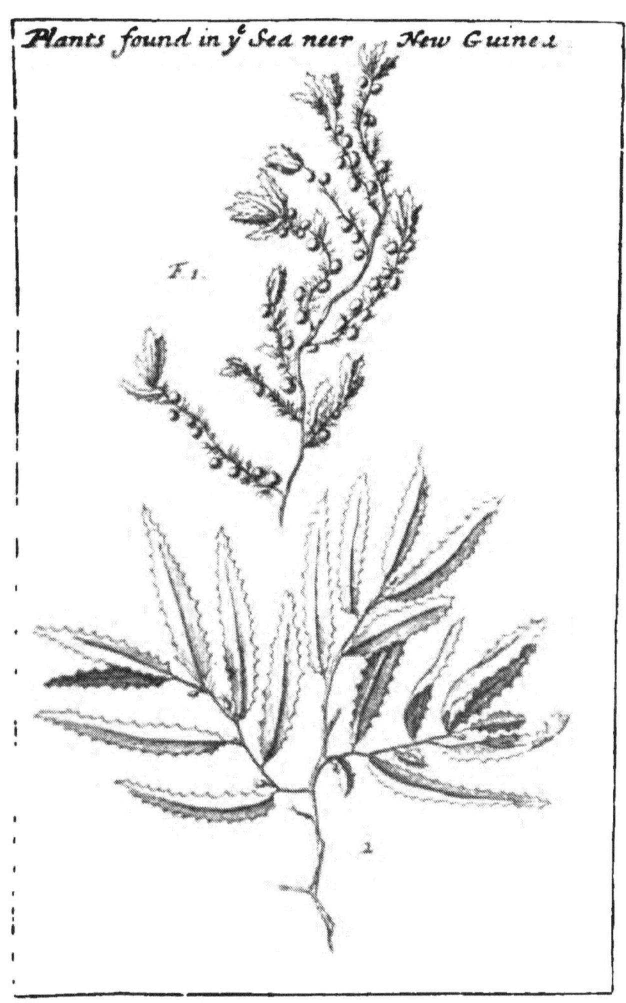
Plants found in yᵉ Sea neer New Guinea
F. 1.
2

TABLE V

The Dolphin of the Antients taken near ye Line called by our seamen a Porpus

A Dolphin as it is usually called by our seamen taken in the open Sea.

PLATE 2

A Fish of the Tunny kind taken on ye Coast of N. Holland

A Fish called by the seamen the Old Wife

PLATE 3

AN ACCOUNT OF SOME FISHES THAT ARE FIGURED IN PLATE 2 & 3.

See Plate 3, Fig. 5.

THIS is a Fish of the Tunny-kind, and agrees well enough with the Figure in Tab. 3. of the Appendix to Mr. Willughby's History of Fishes under the Name of Gurabuca; it differs something, in the Fins especially, from Piso's Figure of the Guarapucu.

See Plate 3, Fig. 4.

This resembles the Figure of the *Guaperva maxima candata* in Willughby's Ichthyol. Tab. 9, 23, and the Guaperva of Piso, but does not answer their Figures in every particular.

See Plate 2, Fig. 2.

There are 2 sorts of Porpusses: The one the long-snouted Porpuss, as the Seamen call it; and this is the Dolphin of the Greeks. The other is the Bottle-nose Porpuss, which is generally thought to be the Phæcena of Aristotle.

See Plate 2, Fig. 7.

This is the Guaracapema of Piso and Marcgrave, by others called the Dorado. 'Tis figured in Willughby's Ichthyol. Tab. O. 2. under the Name of *Delphin Belgis.*

A

CONTINUATION

OF A

VOYAGE

TO

NEW-HOLLAND, &c.

In the YEAR 1699.

Wherein are defcribed,

The Iflands *Timor*, *Rotee* and *Anabao*. A Paffage between the Iflands *Timor* and *Anabao*. *Copang* and *Laphao* Bays. The Iflands *Omba*, *Fetter*, *Bande* and *Bird*. A Defcription of the Coaft of *New-Guinea*. The Iflands *Pulo Sabuda*, *Cockle*, King *William*'s, *Providence*, *Garret Dennis*, *Ant. Cave*'s and St. *John*'s. Alfo a new Paffage between *N. Guinea* and *Nova Britannia*. The Iflands *Ceram*, *Bonao*, *Bouro*, and feveral Iflands before unknown. The Coaft of *Java*, and Streights of *Sunda*. Author's Arrival at *Batavia*, *Cape of Good Hope*, St. *Helens*, *I. Afenfion*, &c. Their Inhabitants, Cuftoms, Trade, *&c.* Harbours, Soil, Birds, Fifh, *&c.* Trees, Plants, Fruits, *&c.*

Illuftrated with MAPS and DRAUGHTS: Alfo divers Birds, Fifhes, *&c.* not found in this Part of the World, Ingraven on Eighteen Copper-Plates.

By Captain WILLIAM DAMPIER.

LONDON,

Printed for JAMES *and* JOHN KNAPTON, at the *Crown* in St. *Paul*'s Church-Yard. MDCCXXIX.

This Continuation was first published in 1709, when Dampier was at sea, on his voyage round the Horn with Woodes Rogers

THE CONTENTS

CHAP. I

CHAP. II

CHAP. III

CHAP. IV

THE CONTENTS

CHAP. V

CHAP. VI

DAMPIER'S VOYAGES

VOL. III. PART II.

CHAP. I

The A.'s Departure from the Coast of New Holland, with the Reasons of it. Water-Snakes. The A.'s Arrival at the Island Timor. Search for fresh Water on the South-side of the Island, in vain. Fault of the Charts. The Island Rotee. A Passage between the Islands Timor and Anabao. Fault of the Charts. A Dutch Fort, called Concordia. Their Suspicion of the A. The Island Anabao described. The A.'s Parly with the Governour of the Dutch Fort. They, with great Difficulty, obtain leave to water. Copang Bay. Coasting along the North-side of Timor. They find Water and an Anchoring-place. A Description of a small Island, seven Leagues East from the Watering Bay. Laphao Bay. How the A. was treated by the Portugueze there. Designs of making further Searches upon and about the Island. Port Sesial. Return to Babao in Copang Bay. The A.'s Entertainment at the Fort of Concordia. His Stay seven Weeks at Babao.

I HAD spent about 5 Weeks in ranging off and on the Coast of New-Holland, a length of about 300 Leagues: and had put in at 3 several Places, to see what there might be thereabouts worth discovering; and at the same Time to recruit my Stock of fresh Water and Provisions for the further Discoveries I purposed to attempt on the Terra Australis. This large and hitherto almost unknown Tract of Land is situated so very advantageously in the richest Climates of the World, the Torrid and Temperate Zones; having in it especially all the Advantages of the Torrid Zone, as being known to reach

AN. 1699

AN. 1699 from the Equator it self (within a Degree) to the Tropick of Capricorn, and beyond it; that in coasting round it, which I design'd by this Voyage, if possible; I could not but hope to meet with some fruitful Lands, Continent or Islands, or both, productive of any of the rich Fruits, Drugs, or Spices, (perhaps Minerals also, &c.) that are in the other Parts of the Torrid Zone, under equal Parallels of Latitude; at least a Soil and Air capable of such, upon transplanting them hither, and Cultivation. I meant, also to make as diligent a Survey as I could, of the several smaller Islands, Shores, Capes, Bays, Creeks, and Harbours, fit as well for Shelter as Defence, upon fortifying them; and of the Rocks and Shoals, the Soundings, Tides, and Currents, Winds and Weather, Variation, &c. Whatever might be beneficial for Navigation, Trade or Settlement; or be of use to any who should prosecute the same Designs hereafter; to whom it might be serviceable to have so much of their Work done to their Hands; which they might advance and perfect by their own repeated Experiences. As there is no Work of this Kind brought to Perfection at once, I intended especially to observe what Inhabitants I should meet with, and to try to win them over to somewhat of Traffick and useful Intercourse, as there might be Commodities among any of them that might be fit for Trade or Manufacture, or any found in which they might be employed. Though as to the New Hollanders hereabouts, by the Experience I had had of their Neighbours formerly, I expected no great Matters from them.

With such Views as these, I set out at first from England; and would, according to the Method I proposed formerly have gone Westward, through the Magellanick Streight, or round Terra del Fuego rather, that I might have begun my Discoveries upon the Eastern and least known Side of the Terra Australis. But that way 'twas not possible for me to go, by Reason of the Time of Year in which I came out; for I must have been compassing the South of America in a very high Latitude, in the Depth of the Winter there. I was therefore necessitated to go Eastward by the Cape of Good Hope; and when I should be past it, 'twas requisite I should keep in a pretty high Latitude, to avoid the general Trade-winds that would be against me, and to have the Benefit of the variable Winds: By all which I was in a Manner unavoidably determin'd to fall in first with those Parts of New Holland I have hitherto been describing. For should it be ask'd why at my first making that Shore, I did not coast it to the Southward, and that way try to get round to the East of New Holland and New Guinea; I confess I was not for spending my Time more than was necessary in the higher Latitudes; as knowing that the Land there could not be so well worth the discovering, as the Parts that lay nearer the Line, and more directly under the Sun. Besides, at the Time when I should come first on New Holland, which was early in the Spring, I must, had I stood Southward, have had for some Time a great deal of Winter-weather, increasing in Severity, though not in Time, and in a Place altogether unknown; which my Men, who were heartless enough to the Voyage at best, would never have born, after so long a Run as from Brazil hither.

AN. 1699

For these Reasons therefore I chose to coast along to the Northward, and so to the East, and so thought to come round by the South of Terra Australis in my Return back, which should be in the Summer-season there: And this Passage back also I now thought I might possibly be able to shorten, should it appear, at my getting to the East Coast of New Guinea, that there is a Channel there coming out into these Seas, as I now suspected near Rosemary Island: Unless the high Tides and great Indraught thereabout should be occasion'd by the Mouth of some large River; which hath often low Lands on each Side of its Outlet, and many Islands and Sholes lying at its Entrance. But I rather thought it a Channel or Streight, than a River: And I was afterwards confirmed in this Opinion, when by coasting New Guinea, I found that other Parts of this great Tract of Terra Australis, which had hitherto been represented as the Shore of a Continent, were certainly

AN. 1699 Islands; and 'tis probably the same with New Holland: Though for Reasons I shall afterwards shew, I could not return by the way I propos'd to my self, to fix the Discovery. All that I had now seen from the Latitude of 27 d. South to 25, which is Shark's Bay; and again from thence to Rosemary Islands, and about the Latitude of 20; seems to be nothing but Ranges of pretty large Islands against the Sea, whatever might be behind them to the Eastward, whether Sea or Land, Continent or Islands.

But to proceed with my Voyage. Though the Land I had seen as yet, was not very inviting, being but barren towards the Sea, and affording me neither fresh Water, nor any great Store of other Refreshments, nor so much as a fit Place for careening; yet I stood out to Sea again with Thoughts of coasting still along Shore (as near as I could) to the North Eastward, for the further Discovery of it: Perswading my self, that at least the Place I anchor'd at in my Voyage round the World, in the Latitude of 16 deg. 15 min. from which I was not now far distant, would not fail to afford me sweet Water upon digging, as it did then; for the brackish Water I had taken in here, though it serv'd tolerably well for boiling, was yet not very wholsome.

With these Intentions I put to Sea on the 5th of September 1699, with a gentle Gale, sounding all the way; but was quickly induc'd to alter my Design. For I had not been out above a Day, but I found that the Sholes among which I was engaged all the while on the Coast, and was like to be engag'd in, would make it a very tedious Thing to sail along by the Shore, or to put in where I might have occasion. I therefore edged farther off to Sea, and so deepned the Water from 11 to 32 Fathom. The next Day, being September the 6th, we could but just discern the Land, though we had then no more than about 30 Fathom, uncertain Soundings; For even while we were out of Sight of Land, we had once but 7 Fathom, and had also great and uncertain Tides whirling about, that made me afraid to go near a Coast so shallow, where we might be soon a-ground, and yet have but little Wind to bring us off: For should a Ship be near a Shoal, she might be hurl'd upon it unavoidably by a strong Tide, unless there should be a good Wind to work her and keep her off. Thus also on the 7th Day we saw no Land, though our Water decreas'd again to 26 Fathom: for we had deepned it, as I said, to 30. AN. 1699

This Day we saw two Water-snakes, different in Shape from such as we had formerly seen. The one was very small, though long; the other long and as big as a Man's Leg, having a red Head; which I never saw any have, before or since. We had this Day, Lat. 16 d. 9 m. by Observation.

I was by this Time got to the North of the Place I had thought to have put in at, where I dug Wells in my former Voyage; and though I knew by the Experience I had of it then, that there was a deep Entrance in thither from the Eastward; yet by the Shoals I had hitherto found so far stretcht on this Coast, I was afraid I should have the same Trouble to coast all along afterwards beyond that Place: And besides the Danger of running almost continually amongst Shoals on a strange Shore, and where the Tides were strong and high; I began to bethink my self, that a great Part of my Time must have been spent in being about a Shore I was already almost weary off, which I might employ with greater Satisfaction to my Mind, and better Hopes of Success in going forward to New Guinea. Add to this the particular Danger I should have been in upon a Lee-Shore, such as is here describ'd, when the North-West Monsoon should once come in; the ordinary Season of which was not now far off, though this Year it staid beyond the common Season; and it comes on storming at first, with Tornadoes, violent Gusts, &c. Wherefore quitting the Thoughts of putting in again at New Holland, I resolv'd to steer away for the Island Timor; where, besides getting fresh Water, I might probably expect to be furnished with Fruits, and other Refreshments to recruit my Men, who began to droop; some of them being already to my great Grief, afflicted with the Scurvy, which was likely to increase upon them and disable them, and was promoted by the brackish Water they took in last for

An. boiling their Oatmeal. 'Twas now also towards the latter
1699 end of the dry Season; when I might not probably have found Water so plentifully upon digging at that Part of New Holland, as when I was there before in the wet Season. And then, considering the Time also that I must necessarily spend in getting in to the Shore, through such Sholes as I expected to meet with; or in going about to avoid them; and in digging of Wells when I should come thither: I might very well hope to get to Timor, and find fresh Water there, as soon as I could expect to get it at New Holland; and with less Trouble and Danger.

On the 8th of September therefore, shaping our Course for Timor, we were in Lat. 15 d. 37 m. We had 26 Fathom, coarse Sand; and we saw one Whale. We found them lying most commonly near the Shore, or in Shoal Water. This Day we also saw some small white Clouds; the first that we had seen since we came out of Shark's Bay. This was one Sign of the Approach of the North-North-West Monsoon. Another Sign was the shifting of the Winds; for from the Time of our coming to our last Anchoring place, the Sea-Breezes which before were Easterly and very strong, had been whiffling about and changing gradually from the East to the North, and thence to the West, blowing but faintly, and now hanging mostly in some Point of the West. This Day the Winds were at South-West by West, blowing very faint; and the 9th Day we had the Wind at North-West by North, but then pretty fresh; and we saw the Clouds rising more and thicker in the North-West. This Night at 12 we lay by for a small low sandy Island, which I reckoned my self not far from. The next Morning at Sun-rising we saw it from the Top-mast-head, right a-head of us; and at Noon were up within a Mile of it: When, by a good Observation, I found it to lye in 13 d. 55 m. I have mentioned it in my first Vol. pag. 450, but my Account then made it to lye in 13 d. 50 m. We had Abundance of Boobies and Man of War Birds flying about us all the Day; especially when we came near the Island; which had also Abundance of them upon it; though it was but a little Spot of Sand, scarce a Mile round. AN. 1699

I did not anchor here, nor send my Boat ashore; there being no appearance of getting any Thing on that Spot of Sand, besides Birds that were good for little: Though had I not been in haste, I would have taken some of them. So I made the best of my way to Timor; and on the 11th in the Afternoon we saw 10 small Land-birds, about the Bigness of Larks, that flew away North West. The 13th we saw a great many Sea-snakes. One of these, of which I saw great Numbers and Variety in this Voyage, was large, and all black: I never saw such another for his Colour.

We had now had for some Days small Gales, from the South-South-West to the North-North-West, and the Sky still more cloudy especially in the Mornings and Evenings. The 14th it look'd very black in the North-West all the Day; and a little before Sun-set we saw, to our great Joy, the Tops of the high Mountains of Timor, peeping out of the Clouds, which had before covered them, as they did still the lower Parts.

We were now running directly towards the Middle of the Island, on the South-side: But I was in some doubt whether I should run down along Shore on this South-side towards the East-end; or pass about the West-end, and so range along on the North-side, and go that way towards the East-end: But as the Winds were now Westerly, I thought it best to keep on the South-side, till I should see how the Weather would prove; For, as the Island lies, if the Westerly Winds continued and grew tempestuous, I should be under the Lee of it, and have smooth Water, and so could go along Shore more safely and easily on this South-side: I could sooner also run to the East-end, where there is the best Shelter, as being still more under the Lee of the Island when those Winds blow. Or if, on the other Side, the Winds should come about again to the Eastward, I could but turn back again (as I did afterwards); and passing about the West-end, could there prosecute my Search on the North-side of the Island for Water, or Inhabitants, or a good Harbour, or whatever might be

AN. 1699 useful to me. For both Sides of the Island were hitherto alike to me, being wholly unacquainted here; only as I had seen it at a Distance in my former Voyage. [See Vol. I. pag. 450.]

I had heard also, that there were both Dutch and Portugueze Settlements on this Island; but whereabouts, I knew not: However, I was resolved to search about till I found, either one of these Settlements, or Water in some other place.

It was now almost Night, and I did not care to run near the Land in the dark, but clapt on a Wind, and stood off and on till the next Morning, being September 15th, when I steered in for the Island, which now appear'd very plain, being high, double and treble Land, very remarkable, on whatever Side you view it. A Sight of it in 2 Parts, Table V. [omitted]. At 3 in the Afternoon we anchored in 14 Fathom, soft black oasy Ground, about a Mile from the Shore. See 2 Sights more of the Coast, in Table V. [omitted], and the Island it self in the Particular Map; which I have here inserted, to shew the Course of the Voyage from hence to the Eastward; as the General Map, set before the Title Vol. III. Par. I. shews the Course of the whole Voyage. But in making the Particular Map, I chose to begin only with Timor, that I might not, by extending it too far, be forced to contract the Scale too much among the Islands, &c. of the New Guinea Coast; which I chiefly designed it for.

The Land by the Sea, on this South-side, is low and sandy, and full of tall Streight-bodied Trees like Pines, for about 200 Yards inwards from the Shore. Beyond that, further in towards the Mountains, for a Breadth of about 3 Miles more or less, there is a Tract of swampy Mangrovy Land, which runs all along between the sandy Land of the Shore on one Side of it, and the Feet of the Mountains on the other. And this low Mangrovy Land is overflown every Tide of Flood, by the Water that flows into it through several Mouths or Openings in the outer sandy Skirt against the Sea. We came to an Anchor right against one of these Openings; and presently I went in my

Boat to search for fresh Water, or get Speech of the Natives; for we saw Smoaks, Houses, and Plantations against the Sides of the Mountains, not far from us. It was ebbing Water before we got ashore, though the Water was still high enough to float us in without any great Trouble. After we were within the Mouth, we found a large Salt-Water Lake, which we hoped might bring us up through the Mangroves to the fast Land: But before we went further, I went ashore on the sandy Land by the Sea-side, and look'd about me; but saw there no Sign of fresh Water. Within the sandy Bank, the Water forms a large Lake: Going therefore into the Boat again, we rowed up the Lake towards the firm Land, where no doubt there was fresh Water, could we come at it. We found many Branches of the Lake entring within the Mangrove Land, but not beyond it. Of these we left some on the Right-hand, and some on the Left, still keeping in the biggest Channel; which still grew smaller, and at last so narrow, that we could go no farther, ending among the Swamps and Mangroves. We were then within a Mile of some Houses of the Indian Inhabitants, and the firm Land by the Sides of the Hills; But the Mangroves thus stopping our way, we return'd as we came: But it was almost dark before we reach'd the Mouth of the Creek. 'Twas with much ado that we got out of it again; for it was now low Water, and there went a rough short Sea on the Bar; which, however, we past over without any Damage, and went aboard.

AN. 1699

The next Morning at five we weighed, and stood along Shore to the Eastward, making use of the Sea and Land-Breezes. We found the Sea-Breezes here from the S. S. E. to the S. S. W. the Land-Breezes from the N. to the N. E. We coasted along about 20 Leagues, and found it all a streight, bold, even Shore, without Points, Creeks or Inlets for a Ship: And there is no anchoring till within a Mile or a Mile and an half of the Shore. We saw scarce any Opening fit for our Boats; and the fast Land was still barricado'd with Mangroves: So that here was no hope to get Water; nor was it likely that there should be here-

AN. 1699 abouts any European Settlement, since there was no Sign of a Harbour.

The Land appear'd pleasant enough to the Eye: For the Sides and Tops of the Mountains were cloath'd with Woods mix'd with Savannahs; and there was a Plantation of the Indian Natives, where we saw the Coco-Nuts growing, and could have been glad to have come at some of them. In the Draught I had with me, a Shoal was laid down hereabouts; but I saw nothing of it, going, or coming; and so have taken no Notice of it in my Map.

Weary of running thus fruitlessly along the South-side of the Island to the Eastward, I resolv'd to return the way I came; and compassing the West-end of the Island, make a search along the North-side of it. The rather, because the North-North-West Monsoon, which I had design'd to be shelter'd from by coming the way I did, did not seem to be near at Hand, as the ordinary Season of them required; but on the contrary I found the Winds returning again to the South-Eastward; and the Weather was fair, and seem'd likely to hold so; and consequently the North-North-West Monsoon was not like to come in yet. I considered therefore that by going to the North-side of the Island, I should there have the smooth Water, as being the Lee-side as the Winds now were; and hoped to have better riding at Anchor or Landing on that Side, than I could expect here, where the Shore was so lined with Mangroves.

Accordingly, the 18th about Noon I altered my Course, and steered back again towards the South-West-end of the Island. This Day we struck a Dolphin; and the next Day saw two more, but struck none: We also saw a Whale.

In the Evening we saw the Island Rotee,[1] and another Island to the South of it, not seen in my Map; both lying near the South-West-end of Timor. On both these Islands we saw Smoaks by Day, and Fires by Night, as we had seen on Timor ever since we fell in with it. I was told

[1] Rotti.

afterwards by the Portugueze, that they had Sugar-works on the Island Rotee; but I knew nothing of that now; and the Coast appearing generally dry and barren, only here and there a Spot of Trees, I did not attempt anchoring there, but stood over again to the Timor Coast. AN. 1699

September the 21st, in the Morning, being near Timor, I saw a pretty large Opening, which immediately I entered with my Ship, sounding as I went in: But had no Ground till I came within the East Point of the Mouth of the Opening, where I anchored in 9 Fathom, a League from the Shore. The distance from the East-side to the West-side of this Opening, was about 5 Leagues. But whereas I thought this was only an Inlet or large Sound that ran a great way into the Island Timor, I found afterwards that it was a Passage between the West End of Timor and another small Island called Anamabao or Anabao:[1] Into which Mistake I was led by my Sea-Chart, which represented both Sides of the Opening as Parts of the same Coast, and called all of it Timor: See all this rectified, and a View of the whole Passage, as I found it, in a small Map I have made of it. [Table omitted.]

I designed to sail into this Opening till I should come to firm Land; for the Shore was all set thick with Mangroves here by the Sea, on each Side; which were very green, as were also other Trees more within Land. We had now but little Wind; therefore I sent my Boat away, to sound, and to let me know by Signs what Depth of Water they met with, if under 8 Fathom; but if more, I order'd them to go on, and make no Signs. At 11 that Morning, having a pretty fresh Gale, I weighed, and made sail after my Boat; but edg'd over more to the West Shore, because I saw many smaller Openings there, and was in Hopes to find a good Harbour where I might secure the Ship; for then I could with more Safety send my Boats to seek for fresh Water. I had not sailed far before the Wind came to the South-East and blew so strong, that I could not with Safety venture nearer that Side, it being a

[1] Samau.

AN. 1699 Lee-shore. Besides, my Boat was on the East-side of the Timor Coast; for the other was, as I found afterwards, the Anabao Shore; and the great Opening I was now in, was the Streight between that Island and Timor; towards which I now tack'd and stood over. Taking up my Boat therefore, I ran under the Timor Side, and at 3 a Clock anchored in 29 Fathom, half a Mile from the Shore. That Part of the South-West Point of Timor, where we anchored in the Morning, bore now South by West, distance 3 Leagues: And another Point of the Island bore North-North-East, distance 2 Leagues.

Not long after, we saw a Sloop coming about the Point last mention'd, with Dutch Colours; which I found, upon sending my Boat aboard, belonged to a Dutch Fort (the only one they have in Timor) about 5 Leagues from hence, call'd Concordia. The Governour of the Fort was in the Sloop, and about 40 Soldiers with him. He appear'd to be somewhat surprised at our coming this way; which it seems is a Passage scarce known to any but themselves; as he told the Men I sent to him in my Boat. Neither did he seem willing that we should come near their Fort for Water. He said also, that he did not know of any Water on all that Part of the Island, but only at the Fort; and that the Natives would kill us, if they met us ashore. By the small Arms my Men carried with them in the Boat, they took us to be Pirates, and would not easily believe the Account my Men gave them of what we were, and whence we came. They said that about 2 Years before this, there had been a stout Ship of French Pirates here; and that after having been suffered to Water, and to refresh themselves, and been kindly used, they had on a sudden gone among the Indians, Subjects of the Fort, and plunder'd them and burnt their Houses. And the Portugueze here told us afterwards, that those Pirates, whom they also had entertain'd, had burnt their Houses, and had taken the Dutch Fort (though the Dutch car'd not to own so much), and had driven the Governour and Factory among the wild Indians their Enemies. The Dutch told my Men further, that they could not but think we had of several

Nations (as is usual with Pirate Vessels) in our Ship, and particularly some Dutch Men, though all the Discourse was in French; (for I had not one who could speak Dutch :) Or else, since the common Draughts make no Passage between Timor and Anabao, but lay down both as one Island; they said they suspected we had plundered some Dutch Ship of their particular Draughts, which they are forbid to part with. AN. 1699

With these Jealousies the Sloop returned towards their Fort, and my Boat came back with this News to me: But I was not discouraged at this News; not doubting but I should perswade them better, when I should come to talk with them. So the next Morning I weighed, and stood towards the Fort. The Winds were somewhat against us, so that we could not go very fast, being obliged to tack 2 or 3 Times. And coming near the farther End of the Passage between Timor and Anabao, we saw many Houses on each Side not far from the Sea, and several Boats lying by the Shore. The Land on both Sides was pretty high, appearing very dry and of a reddish Colour, but highest on the Timor Side. The Trees on either Side were but small, the Woods thin, and in many Places the Trees were dry and withered.

The Island Anamabao or Anabao, is not very big, not exceeding 10 Leagues in length, and 4 in Breadth; yet it has 2 Kingdoms in it, viz. that of Anamabao on the East-side towards Timor, and the North-East-end; and that of Anabao, which contains the South-West-end and the West-side of the Island; but I know not which of them is biggest. The Natives of both are of the Indian kind, of a swarthy Copper-colour, with black lank Hair. Those of Anamabao are in League with the Dutch, as these afterwards told me, and with the Natives of the Kingdom of Copang in Timor, over-against them, in which the Dutch Fort Concordia stands: But they are said to be inveterate Enemies to their Neighbours of Anabao. Those of Anabao, besides managing their small Plantations of Roots and a few Coco-nuts, do fish, strike Turtle, and hunt Buffalo's; killing them with Swords, Darts, or Lances. But I know not how they

AN. get their Iron; I suppose, by Traffick with the Dutch or
1699 Portugueze, who send now and then a Sloop and trade thither, but well-arm'd; for the Natives would kill them, could they surprize them. They go always armed themselves; And when they go a fishing or a hunting, they spend 4 or 5 Days or more in ranging about, before they return to their Habitation. We often saw them, after this, at these Employments; but they would not come near us. The Fish or Flesh that they take, besides what serves for present spending, they dry on a Barbacue or wooden Grate, standing pretty high over the Fire, and so carry it home when they return. We came sometimes afterwards to the Places where they had Meat thus a drying, but did not touch any of it.

But to proceed; I did not think to stop any where till I came near the Fort; which yet I did not see: But coming to the End of this Passage, I found that if I went any farther I should be open again to the Sea. I therefore stood in close to the Shore on the East-side, and anchored in 4 Fathom Water, sandy Ground; a Point of Land still hindring me from seeing the Fort. But I sent my Boat to look about for it; and in a short Time she returned, and my Men told me they saw the Fort, but did not go near it; and that it was not above 4 or 5 Miles from hence. It being now late, I would not send my Boat thither till the next Morning: Mean while about 2 or 300 Indians, Neighbours of the Fort, and sent probably from thence, came to the sandy Bay just against the Ship; where they staid all Night, and made good Fires. They were armed with Lances, Swords and Targets, and made a great Noise all the Night: We thought it was to scare us from landing, should we attempt it: But we took little Notice of them.

The next Morning, being September the 23d, I sent my Clerk ashore in my Pinnace to the Governour, to satisfy him that we were English Men, and in the King's Ship, and to ask Water of him; sending a young Man with him, who spake French. My Clerk was with the Governour pretty early; and in Answer to his Queries about me, and my Business in these Parts, told him that I had the King

of England's Commission, and desired to speak with him. AN. 1699
He beckned to my Clerk to come ashore; but as soon as he saw some small Arms in the Stern-Sheets of the Boat, he commanded him into the Boat again, and would have him be gone. My Clerk sollicited him that he would allow him to speak with him; and at last the Governour consented that he should come ashore; and sent his Lieutenant and 3 Merchants, with a Guard of about a hundred of the Native Indians to receive him. My Clerk said that we were in much want of Water, and hop'd they wou'd allow us to come to their Watering-place, and fill. But the Governour replied, that he had Orders not to supply any Ships but their own East-India Company; neither must they allow any Europeans to come the Way that we came; and wondred how we durst come near their Fort. My Clerk answered him, that had we been Enemies, we must have come ashore among them for Water: But, said the Governour, you are come to inspect into our Trade and Strength; and I will have you therefore be gone with all Speed. My Clerk answered him, that I had no such Design, but, without coming nearer them, would be contented if the Governour would send Water on Board where we lay, about 2 Leagues from the Fort; and that I would make any reasonable Satisfaction for it. The Governour said that we should have what Water we wanted, provided we came no nearer with the Ship: And ordered, that as soon as we pleased, we should send our Boat full of empty Casks, and come to an Anchor with it off the Fort, till he sent Slaves to bring the Casks ashore, and fill them; for that none of our Men must come ashore. The same Afternoon I sent up my Boat as he had directed, with an Officer, and a present of some Beer for the Governour; which he would not accept of; but sent me off about a Ton of Water.

On the 24th in the Morning I sent the same Officer again in my Boat; and about Noon the Boat returned again with the two principal Merchants of the Factory, and the Lieutenant of the Fort; for whole Security they had kept my Officer and one of my Boat's-crew as Hostages, confining them to the Governour's Garden all the Time:

AN. 1699 For they were very shy of trusting any of them to go into their Fort, as my Officer said: Yet afterwards they were not shy of our Company; and I found that my Officer maliciously endeavour'd to make them shy of me. In the Even I gave the Dutch Officers that came aboard, the best Entertainment I could; and bestowing some Presents on them, sent them back very well pleased; and my Officer and the other Man were returned to me. Next Morning I sent my Boat ashore again with the same Officer; who brought me word from the Governour, that we must pay 4 Spanish Dollars, for every Boat's-load of Water: But in this he spake falsly, as I understood afterwards from the Governour himself, and all his Officers, who protested to me that no such Price was demanded, but left me to give the Slaves what I pleased for their Labour: The Governour being already better satisfied about me, than when my Clerk spoke to him, or than that Officer I sent last would have caused him to be: For the Governour being a civil, genteel and sensible Man, was offended at the Officer for his being so industrious to misrepresent me. I received from the Governour a little Lamb, very fat; and I sent him 2 of the Guinea-hens that I brought from St. Jago, of which there were none here.

I had now 11 Buts of Water on Board, having taken in 7 here, which I would have paid for, but that at present I was afraid to send my Boat ashore again: For my Officer told me, among other of his Inventions, that there were more Guns mounted in the Fort, than when we first came; and that he did not see the Gentlemen that were aboard the Day before; intimating as if they were shy of us; and that the Governour was very rough with him; and I not knowing to the contrary at present, consulted with my other Officers what was best to be done; for by this the Governour should seem to design to quarrel with us. All my other Officers thought it natural to infer so much, and that it was not safe to send the Boat ashore any more, lest it should be seiz'd on; but that it was best to go away, and seek more Water where we could find it. For having now (as I said) 11 Buts aboard; and the Land being promising this way, I did not doubt finding Water in a short Time. But my Officer who occasion'd these Fears in us by his own Forgeries, was himself for going no further; having a Mind, as far as I could perceive, to make every Thing in the Voyage, to which he shew'd himself averse, seem as cross and discouraging to my Men as possible, that he might hasten our Return; being very negligent and backward in most Businesses I had occasion to employ him in; doing nothing well or willingly, though I did all I could to win him to it. He was also industrious to stir up the Sea-men to Mutiny; telling them, among other Things, that any Dutch Ship might lawfully take us in these Seas; but I knew better, and avoided every Thing that could give just Offence.

AN. 1699

The rest of my Officers therefore being resolved to go from hence, and having bought same Fish of some Anamabeans, who, seeing our Ship, came purposely to sell some, passing to and fro every Day; I sail'd away on the 26th about 5 in the Afternoon. We pass'd along between a small low sandy Island (over against the Fort), full of Bays and pretty high Trees; sounding as we went along; and had from 25 to 35 Fathom, oasy Ground. See the little Map of this Passage, Table VI. [omitted].

The 27th in the Morning we anchored in the Middle of the Bay, called Copang[1] Bay, in 12 Fathom, soft Oaze, about 4 Leagues above the Dutch Fort. Their Sloop was riding by the Fort, and in the Night fired a Gun; but for what Reason I know not: and the Governor said afterwards, 'twas the Skipper's own doing, without his Order. Presently after we had anchored, I went in the Pinnace to search about the Bay for Water, but found none. Then, returning a-board, I weighed, and ran down to the North-Entrance of the Bay, and at 7 in the Evening anchored again, in 37 Fathom, soft Oaze, close by the sandy Island, and about 4 Leagues from the Dutch Fort. The 28th I sent both my Boats ashore on the sandy Island, to cut Wood; and by Noon they both came back laden. In the

[1] Kupan.

AN. 1699 Afternoon I sent my Pinnace ashore on the North Coast or Point of Copang Bay, which is call'd Babao. Late in the Night they returned, and told me that they saw great Tracks of Buffalo's there, but none of the Buffalo's themselves; neither did they find any fresh Water. They also saw some green Turtle in the Sea, and one Alligator.

The 29th I went out of Copang Bay, designing to Coast it along Shore on the North-side of Timor to the Eastward; as well to seek for Water, as also to acquaint my self with the Island, and to search for the Portugueze Settlements; which we were informed were about forty Leagues to the Eastward of this Place.

We coasted along Shore with Land and Sea-Breezes. The Land by the Shore was of a moderate height, with high and very remarkable Hills farther within the Country; their Sides all spotted with Woods and Savannahs. But these on the Mountain Sides appeared of a rusty Colour not so pleasant and flourishing as those that we saw on the South-side of the Island; for the Trees seemed to be small and withering; and the Grass in the Savannahs also look'd dry, as if it wanted Moisture. But in the Valleys, and by the Sea-side, the Trees look'd here also more green. Yet we saw no good Anchoring-place, or Opening, that gave us any Incouragement to put in; till the 30th Day in the Afternoon.

We were then running along Shore, at about 4 Leagues distance, with a moderate Sea-breeze; when we opened a pretty deep Bay, which appeared to be a good Road to anchor in. There were two large Valleys, and one smaller one, which descending from the Mountains came all into one Valley by the Sea-side against this Bay, which was full of tall green Trees. I presently stood in with the Ship, till within two Leagues of the Shore; and then sent in my Pinnace commanded by my chief Mate, whose great Care, Fidelity, and Diligence, I was well assured of; ordering him to seek for fresh Water; and if he found any, to sound the Bay, and bring me Word what anchoring there was; and to make haste aboard.

As soon as they were gone, I stood off a little, and lay

Fishes taken on the Coast of New Guinea

This Fish fins & tail are blew on yᵉ edges & red in the middle with blew spots all over yᵉ Body, but yᵉ Belly white.

A Pike Fish Conger on yᵉ Coast of New Guinea

This Fish is a pale red with blew spots on yᵉ body the long Tail blew in yᵉ midle & white on yᵉ side.

by. The Day was now far spent; and therefore it was late before they got ashore with the Boat; so that they did not come aboard again that Night. Which I was much concern'd at; because in the Evening, when the Sea-Breeze was done and the Weather calm, I perceived the Ship to drive back again to the Westward. I was not yet acquainted with the Tides here; for I had hitherto met with no strong Tides about the Island, and scarce any running in a Stream, to set me along Shore either way. But after this Time, I had pretty much of them; and found at present the Flood set to the Eastward, and the Ebb to the Westward. The Ebb (with which I was now carried) sets very strong, and runs 8 or 9 Hours. The Flood runs but weak, and at most lasts not above 4 Hours; and this too is perceived only near the Shore; where checking the Ebb, it swells the Seas, and makes the Water rise in the Bays and Rivers 8 or 9 Foot. I was afterwards credibly informed by some Portugueze, that the Current runs always to the Westward in the Mid-Channel between this Island and those that face it in a Range to the North of it, viz. Misficomba (or Omba)[1] Pintare,[2] Laubana,[3] Ende,[4] &c.

AN. 1699

We were driven 4 Leagues back again, and took particular Notice of a Point of Land that looked like Flamborough-head, when we were either to the East or West of it; and near the Shore it appeared like an Island. Four or 5 Leagues to the East of this Point, is another very remarkable bluff Point, which is on the West-side of the Bay that my Boat was in. See two Sights of this Land, Table VI. [omitted]. We could not stem the Tide, till about 3 a Clock in the Afternoon; when the Tide running with us, we soon got abreast of the Bay, and then saw a small Island to the Eastward of us. See a Sight of it, Table VI. [omitted]. About 6 we anchored in the Bottom of the Bay, in 25 Fathom, soft Oaze, half a Mile from the Shore.

I made many false Fires in the Night, and now and then fired a Gun, that my Boat might find me; but to no

[1] Omba. [2] Pantar.
[3] Lomblem. [4] Not Andonare, but Flores.

AN. 1699 Purpose. In the Morning I found my self driven again by the Tide of Ebb 3 or 4 Leagues to the Westward of the Place where I left my Boat. I had several Men looking out for her: but could not get a Sight of her: Besides, I continued still driving to the Westward; for we had but little Wind, and that against us. But by 10 a Clock in the Morning we had the Comfort of seeing the Boat; and at 11 she came aboard, bringing 2 Barrecoes[1] of very good Water.

The Mate told me there was good Anchoring close by the Watering-place; but that there ran a strong Tide, which near the Shore made several Races; so that they found much Danger in getting ashore, and were afraid to come off again in the Night, because of the Riplings the Tide made.

We had now the Sea-breeze, and steered away for this Bay; but could hardly stemm the Tide, till about 3 in the Afternoon; when the Tide being turned with us, we went along briskly, and about 6 anchored in the Bay, in 25 Fathom, soft Oaze, half a Mile from the Shore.

The next Morning I went ashore to fill Water, and before Night sent aboard 8 Tons. We fill'd it out of a large Pond within 50 Paces of the Sea. It look'd pale, but was very good, and boiled Pease well. I saw the Tract of an Alligator here. Not far from the Pond, we found the Rudder of a Malayan Proe, 3 great Jars in a small Shed set up against a Tree, and a Barbacue whereon there had been Fish and Flesh of Buffaloes drest, the Bones lying but a little from it.

In 3 Days we fill'd about twenty six Tun of Water, and then had on Board about 30 Ton in all. The 2 following Days we spent in Fishing with the Saine, and the first Morning caught as many as served all my Ship's Company: But afterwards we had not so good Success. The rest of my Men, which could be spared from the Ship, I sent out; Some with the Carpenter's Mate, to cut Timber for my Boats, &c. These went always guarded with 3 or

[1] "Breakers" or small casks.

4 armed Men to secure them: I shewed them what Wood was fitting to cut for our Use, especially the Calabash and Maho; I shewed them also the manner of stripping the Maho-bark, and of making therewith Thread, Twine, Ropes, &c. Others were sent out a Fowling; who brought Home Pidgeons, Parrots, Cockatoos, &c. I was always with one Party or other, my self; especially with the Carpenters, to hasten them to get what they could, that we might be gone from hence. AN. 1699

Our Water being full, I sail'd from hence October the 6th about 4 in the Afternoon, designing to coast along Shore to the Eastward, till I came to the Portugueze Settlements. By the next Morning we were driven 3 or 4 Leagues to the West of the Bay; but in the Afternoon, having a faint Sea-breeze, we got again abreast of it. It was the 11th Day at Noon before we got as far as the small Island before-mentioned, which lies about 7 Leagues to the East of the Watering Bay: For what we gained in the Afternoon by the Benefit of the Sea-breezes we lost again in the Evenings and Mornings, while it was calm, in the Interval of the Breezes. But this Day the Sea-breeze blowing fresher than ordinary, we past by the Island and run before Night about 7 Leagues to the East of it.

This Island is not half a Mile long, and not above 100 Yards in breadth, and look'd just like a Barn, when we were by it: It is pretty high, and may be seen from a Ship's Topmast-head about 10 Leagues. The Top, and Part of the Sides, are covered with Trees, and it is about 3 Leagues from Timor; 'tis about Mid-way between the Watering-place and the Portugueze first and main Settlement by the Shore.

In the Night we were again driven back toward the Island, 3 Leagues: But the 12th Day, having a pretty brisk Sea-breeze, we coasted along Shore; and seeing a great many Houses by the Sea, I stood in with my Ship till I was within 2 Miles of them, and then sent in my Boat, and lay by till it returned. I sent an Officer to command the Boat; and a Portugueze Seaman that I brought from Brazil, to speak with the Men that we saw on the Bay;

AN. 1699 Harbour in the Island was at a Place called Babao, on the North side of Copang Bay; that there were no Inhabitants there, but Plenty of Buffaloes in the Woods, and Abundance of Fish in the Sea; that there was also fresh Water: That there was another Place, call'd Port Sesiall, about 20 Leagues to the Eastward of Laphao; that there was a River of fresh Water there, and Plenty of Fish, but no Inhabitants: Yet that, if I would go thither, he would send People with Hogs, Goats and Buffaloes, to truck with me for such Commodities as I had to dispose of.

I was afterwards told, that on the East-end of the Island Ende there was also a very good Harbour, and a Portugueze Town; that there was great Plenty of Refreshments for my Men, and Dammer[1] for my Ship; that the Governour or Chief of that Place, was call'd Captain More; that he was a very courteous Gentleman, and would be very glad to entertain an English Ship there; and if I design'd to go thither, I might have Pilots here that would be willing to carry me, if I could get the Lieutenant's Consent. That it was dangerous going thither without a Pilot, by Reason of the violent Tides that run between the Islands Ende and Solor. I was told also, that at the Island Solor there were a great many Dutchmen banisht from other Places for certain Crimes. I was willing enough to go thither, as well to secure my Ship in a good Harbour, where I might careen her, (there being Dammer also, which I could not get here, to make use of instead of Pitch, which I now wanted,) and where I might still be refreshing my Men and supporting them, in order to my further Discoveries; as also to inform my self more particularly concerning these Places as yet so little known to us. Accordingly I accepted the Offer of a Pilot and two Gentlemen of the Town, to go with me to Larentucka on the Island Ende: And they were to come on board my Ship the Night before I sailed. But I was hindred of this Design by some of my Officers, who had here also been very busie in doing me all the Injury they could underhand.

[1] Cat's-eye resin.

But to proceed. While I staid here, I went ashore every Day, and my Men took their Turns to go ashore and traffick for what they had Occasion for; and were now all very well again: And to keep themselves in Heart, every Man bought some Rice, more or less, to recruit them after our former Fatigues. Besides, I order'd the Purser to buy some for them, to serve them instead of Pease, which were now almost spent. I fill'd up my Water-Casks again here, and cut more Wood; and sent a Present to the Lieutenant, Alexis Mendosa, designing to be gone; for while I lay here, we had some Tornadoes and Rain, and the Sky in the North-West looked very black Mornings and Evenings, with Lightning all Night from that Quarter; which made me very uneasy and desirious to depart hence; because this Road lay expos'd to the North-North-West and North Winds, which were now daily expected, and which are commonly so violent, that 'tis impossible for any Ship to ride them out: Yet, on the other Hand, it was absolutely necessary for me to spend about 2 Months Time longer in some Place hereabouts, before I could prosecute my Voyage farther to the Eastward; for Reasons which I shall give hereafter in its proper Place in the ensuing Discourse. When therefore I sent the Present to the Governour, I desired to have a Pilot to Larentucka on the Island Ende; where I desir'd to spend the Time I had to spare. He now sent me Word that he could not well do it, but would send me a Letter to Port Sesiall for the Natives, who would come to me there and supply me with what Provision they had.

I staid 3 Days, in hopes yet to get a Pilot for Larentucka, or at least the Letter from the Governour to Port Sesiall. But seeing neither, I sail'd from hence the 22d of October, coasting to the Eastward, designing for Sesiall; and before Night, was about 10 Leagues to the East of Laphao. I kept about 3 Leagues off Shore, and my Boat ranged along close by the Shore, looking into every Bay and Cove; and at Night returned on Board. The next Morning, being 3 or 4 Leagues farther to the Eastward, I sent my Boat ashore again to find Sesiall. At

AN. 1699 Noon they returned, and told me they had been at Sesiall, as they guess'd; that there were two Portugueze Barks in the Port, who threatened to fire at them, but did not; telling them this was Porto del Roy de Portugal. They saw also another Bark, which ran and anchor'd close by the Shore; and the Men ran all away for fear: But our Men calling to them in Portugueze, they at last came to them, and told them that Sesiall was the Place which they came from, where the 2 Barks lay: Had not these Men told them, they could not have known it to be a Port, it being only a little bad Cove, lying open to the North; having 2 Ledges of Rocks at its entrance, one on each Side; and a Channel between, which was so narrow, that it would not be safe for us to go in. However I stood in with the Ship, to be better satisfied; and when I came near it, found it answer my Men's Description. I lay by a-while, to consider what I had best do; for my Design was to lye in a Place where I might get fresh Provisions if I could; For though my Men were again pretty well recruited; and those that had been sick of the Scurvy, were well again; yet I design'd, if possible, to refresh them as much and as long as I could, before I went farther. Besides, my Ship wanted cleaning; and I was resolved to clean her if possible.

At last after much Consideration, I thought it safer to go away again for Babao; and accordingly stood to the Westward. We were now about 60 Leagues to the East of Babao. The Coast is bold all the way, having no Sholes, and but one Island which I saw and describ'd coming to the Eastward. The Land in the Country is very mountainous; but there are some large Valleys towards the East-end. Both the Mountains and Valleys on this Side, are barren; some wholly so; and none of them appear so pleasant as the Place where I watered. It was the 23rd Day in the Evening when I stood back again for Babao. We had but small Sea and Land-breezes. On the 27th we came into Copang Bay; and the next Day having sounded Babao Road, I ran in and came to an Anchor there, in 20 Fathom, soft Oaze, 3 Mile from the

Shore. One Reason, as I said before, of my coming hither, was to ride secure, and to clean my Ship's Bottom; as also to endeavour by Fishing and Hunting of Buffaloes, to refresh my Men and save my salt Provision. It was like to be some Time before I could clean my Ship, because I wanted a great many Necessaries, especially a Vessel to careen by. I had a Long-Boat in a Frame, that I brought out of England, by which I might have made a Shift to do it; but my Carpenter was uncapable to set her up. Besides, by that Time the Ship's-sides were calk'd, my Pitch was almost spent; which was all owing to the Carpenter's wilful Waste and Ignorance; so that I had nothing to lay on upon the Ship's Bottom. But instead of this, I intended to make Lime here, which with Oyl would have made a good Coat for her. Indeed had it been adviseable, I would have gone in between Cross Island and Timor, and have hal'd my Ship ashore; for there was a very convenient Place to do it in; but my Ship being sharp,[1] I did not dare to do it: Besides, I must have taken every thing out of her; and I had neither Boats to get my Things ashore, nor Hands to look after them when they were there; for my Men would have been all employed; and though here are no Indians living near, yet they come hither in Companies when Ships are here, on Purpose to do any Mischief they can to them; and 'twas not above 2 Years since a Portugueze Ship riding here, and sending her Boat for Water to one of the Galleys, the Men were all killed by the Indians. But to secure my Men I never suffer'd them to go ashore unarmed; and while some were at Work, others stood to guard them.

AN. 1699

We lay in this Place from October the 28th, till December the 12th. In which Time we made very good Lime with Shells, of which here are plenty. We cut Palmeto-leaves to burn the Ship's-sides; and giving her as good a Heel as we could, we burned her Sides, and paid[2] them with Lime and Water for want of Oyl to mix

[1] As opposed to "full." So built that she could not be beached without great danger to her bends.

[2] Smeared.

AN. 1699 with it. This stuck on about 2 Months, where 'twas well burned. We did not want fresh Provisions all the Time we lay here, either of Fish or Flesh. For there were fair sandy Bays on the Point of Babao, where in 2 or 3 Hours in a Morning we used with our Sain to drag ashore as much Fish as we could eat all the Day; and for a Change of Diet, when we were weary of Fish, I sent 10 or 11 armed Men a hunting for Buffaloes; who never came empty home. They went ashore in the Evening or early in the Morning, and before Noon always returned with their Burdens of Buffalo, enough to suffice us 2 Days; by which Time we began to long for Fish again.

On the 11th of November, the Governour of Concordia[1] sent one of his Officers to us, to know who we were. For I had not sent thither, since I came to Anchor last here. When the Officer came aboard, he ask'd me why we fired so many Guns the 4th and 5th Days; (which we had done in Honour of King William, and in Memory of the Deliverance from the Powder-Plot:) I told him the occasion of it; and he replied that they were in some Fear at the Fort that we had been Portugueze, and that we were coming with Soldiers to take their Fort: He asked me also why I did not stay and fill my Water at their Fort, before I went away from thence? I told him the Reason of it, and withal offered him Money; bidding him take what he thought reasonable: He took none, and said he was sorry there had been such a Misunderstanding between us; and knew that the Governour would be much concerned at it. After a short Stay, he went ashore; and the next Morning came aboard again, and told me the Governour desired me to come ashore to the Fort and dine with him; and, if I doubted any thing, he would stay aboard till I returned. I told him I had no Reason to mistrust any thing against me, and would go ashore

[1] A sketch of Concordia, with a chart of Copang, or Kupan, Bay, appears in Dalrymple's Collection of Maps, Charts and Plans, p. 12. The fort appears to have been but a small place, as Dampier describes it. The town of Cupang lay along the beach, with tropical forest behind it. A little river supplied it with fresh water.

with him; so I took my Clerk and my Gunner, and went ashore in my Pinnace: The Gunner spoke very good French, and therefore I took him to be my Interpreter, because the Governour speaks French: He was an honest Man, and I found him always diligent and obedient. It was pretty late in the Afternoon before we came ashore; so that we had but little Time with the Governour. He seem'd to be much dissatisfied at the Report my Officer had made to me; (of which I have before given an Account;) and said it was false, neither would he now take any Money of me; but told me I was welcome; as indeed I found by what he provided. For there was plenty of very good Victuals, and well drest; and the Linnen was white and clean; and all the Dishes and Plates, of Silver or fine China. I did not meet any where with a better Entertainment, while I was abroad; nor with so much Decency and Order. Our Liquor was Wine, Beer, Toddy, or Water, which we liked best after Dinner. He shew'd me some Drawers full of Shells, which were the strangest and most curious that I had ever seen. He told me, before I went away, that he could not supply me with any Naval Stores; but if I wanted any fresh Provision, he would supply me with what I had occasion for. I thank'd him, and told him I would send my Boat for some Goats and Hogs, though afterwards on second Thoughts I did not do it: For 'twas a great way from the Place where we lay, to the Fort; and I could not tell what Mischief might befall any of my Men, when there, from the Natives; especially if incouraged by the Dutch, who are Enemies to all Europeans but such as are under their own Government. Therefore I chose rather to fish and hunt for Provisions, than to be beholden to the Dutch, and pay dearly for it too. AN. 1699

We found here, as I said before, Plenty of Game; so that all the Time we lay at this Place, we spent none or very little of our Salt-provisions; having Fish or Fresh Buffaloe every Day. We lay here 7 Weeks; and although the North-North-West Monsoon was every Day expected when I was at Laphao, yet it was not come, so that if I had

AN. 1699 prosecuted my Voyage to the Eastward without staying here, it had been but to little Advantage. For if I had gone out, and beaten against the Wind a whole Month, I should not have got far; it may be 40, 50, or 60 Leagues; which was but 24 Hours run for us with a large Wind; besides the Trouble and Discontent, which might have arisen among my Men in beating to Windward to so little Purpose, there being nothing to be got at Sea; but here we lived and did eat plentifully every Day without Trouble. The greatest Inconveniency of this Place, was want of Water; this being the latter Part of the dry Season, because the Monsoon was very late this Year. About 4 Days before we came away, we had Tornadoes, with Thunder, Lightning and Rain, and much Wind; but of no long Continuance; at which Time we filled some Water. We saw very black Clouds, and heard it thunder every Day for near a Month before, in the Mountains; and saw it rain, but none came near us: And even where we hunted, we saw great Trees torn up by the Roots, and great Havock made among the Woods by the Wind; yet none touched us.

CHAP. II

A particular Description of the Island Timor. Its Coast. The Island Anabao. Fault of the Draughts. The Channel between Timor and Anabao. Copang-bay. Fort Concordia. A particular description of the Bay. The Anchoring-place, called Babao. The Malayans here kill all the Europeans they can. Laphao, a Portugueze Settlement, described. Port Ciccale. The Hills, Water, Low-lands, Soil, Woods, Metals, in the Island Timor. Its Trees. Cana-fistula-tree described. Wild Fig-trees described. Two new sorts of Palm-trees described. The Fruits of the Island. The Herbs. Its Land-Animals. Fowls. The Ringing Bird. Its Fish. Cockle-merchants and Oysters. Cockles as big as a Man's Head. Its original Natives described. The Portugueze and Dutch Settlements. The Malayan Language generally spoken here. L'Orantua on the Island Ende. The Seasons, Winds, ana Weather at Timor.

THE Island Timor, as I have said in my "Voyage round the World," is about seventy Leagues long, and fourteen or sixteen broad. It lies nearly North-East and South-West. The Middle of it lies in about 9 d. South Lat. It has no Navigable Rivers, nor many Harbours; but abundance of Bays, for Ships to ride in at some Seasons of the Year. The Shore is very bold, free from Rocks, Shoals or Islands: excepting a few which are visible, and therefore easily avoided. On the South-side there is a Shole laid down in our Draughts, about thirty Leagues from the South-West-end;[1] I was fifteen or twenty Leagues further to the East than that distance, but saw nothing of the Shole; neither could I find any Harbour. It is a pretty even Shore, with Sandy Bays and low Land for about three or four Miles

AN. 1699

[1] The Ashmore Reef.

AN. 1699 up; and then 'tis mountainous. There is no Anchoring but within half a League or a League at farthest from the Shore; and the low Land that bounds the Sea, hath nothing but red Mangroves, even from the Foot of the Mountains till you come within a hundred and fifty or two hundred paces of the Sea: and then you have Sandbanks, cloath'd with a sort of Pine; so that there is no getting Water on this side, because of the Mangroves.

At the South-West-end of Timor, is a pretty high Island, called Anabao. It is about ten or twelve Leagues long, and about four broad; near which the Dutch are settled. It lies so near Timor, that 'tis laid down in our Draughts as part of that Island; yet we found a narrow deep Channel fit for any Ships to pass between them. This Channel is about ten Leagues long, and in some places not above a League wide. It runs North-east and South-West, so deep that there is no Anchoring but very nigh the Shore. There is but little Tide; the Flood setting North, and the Ebb to the Southward. At the North-East-end of this Channel, are two Points of Land, not above a League asunder; one on the South-side upon Timor, called Copang; the other on the North-side, upon the Island Anabao. From this last point, the Land trends away Northerly two or three Leagues, opens to the Sea, and then bends in again to the Westward.

Being past these Points, you open a Bay of about eight Leagues long, and four wide. This Bay trends in on the South-side North-East by East from the South-point before mentioned; making many small Points or little Coves. About a League to the East of the said South-point, the Dutch have a small Stone Fort, situated on a firm Rock close by the Sea: This Fort they call Concordia. On the East-side of the Fort, there is a small River of fresh Water, which has a broad boarded Bridge over it, near to the Entry into the Fort. Beyond this River is a small sandy Bay, where the Boats and Barks land and convey their Traffick in or out of the Fort. About an hundred Yards from the Sea-side, and as many from the Fort, and forty Yards from the Bridge on the East-side, the Company have a fine Garden, surrounded with a good Stone-Wall; In it is plenty of all sorts of Sallads, Cabbages, Roots for the Kitchen; in some parts of it are Fruit-trees, as Jaca's, Pumplenose, Oranges, sweet Lemons, &c. and by the Walls are Coco-nut and Toddy-trees in great plenty. Besides these, they have Musk and Water-Melons, Pine-Apples, Pomecitrons, Pomegranates, and other sorts of Fruits. Between this Garden and the River, there is a Penn for black Cattle, whereof they have plenty. Beyond the Companies Ground, the Natives have their Houses, in number about fifty or sixty. There are forty or fifty Soldiers belonging to this Fort, but I know not how many Guns they have; for I had only opportunity to see one Bastion, which had in it four Guns. Within the Walls there is a neat little Church or Chapel.

AN. 1699.

Beyond Concordia the Land runs about seven Leagues to the bottom of the Bay; then it is not above a League and a half from side to side, and the Land trends away Northerly to the North-Shore, then turns about again to the Westward, making the South-side of the Bay. About three Leagues and a half from the bottom of the Bay on this side, there is a small Island about a Musket-shot from the Shore; and a Riff of Rocks that runs from it to the Eastward about a mile. On the West-side of the Island is a Channel of three Fathom at low Water, of which depth it is also within, where Ships may haul in and careen. West from this Island the Land rounds away in a Bite or Elbow, and at last ends in a low point of Land, which shoots forth a Ledge of Rocks a mile into the Sea, which is dry at Low-Water. Just against the low Point of Land, and to the West of the Ledge of Rocks, is another pretty high and rocky, yet woody Island, about half a mile from the low Point; which Island hath a Ledge of corally Rocks running from it all along to the other small Island, only leaving one Channel between them. Many of these Rocks are to be seen at Low-Water, and there seldom is Water enough for a Boat to go over them till quarter Flood or more. Within this Ledge there is two or three Fathom Water, and without it no less than ten or twelve

AN. 1699 above nine Foot upon a Spring-tide: But it made great Riplings and a roaring Noise; whirling about like Whirlpools. We had constantly eddy Tides under the Shore, made by the Points on each side of the Bay.

When you go hence to the Eastward, you may pass between the small Island, and Timor; and when you are five or six Leagues to the Eastward of the small Island, you will see a large Valley to the Eastward of you; then running a little further, you may see Houses on the Bay: You may luff in, but anchor not till you go about the next Point. Then you will see more Houses, where you may run into twenty or thirty Fathom, and anchor right against the Houses, nearest the West-end of them. This place is called Laphao. It is a Portuguese Settlement, about sixteen Leagues from the Watering-bay.

There are in it about forty or fifty Houses, and one Church. The Houses are mean and low, the Walls generally made of Mud or watled, and their Sides made up with Boards: They are all thatch'd with Palm or Palmeto-Leaves. The Church also is very small: The East-end of it is boarded up to the Top; but the Sides and the West-end are only boarded three or four foot high; the rest is all open: There is a small Altar in it, with two Steps to go up to it, and an Image or two; but all very mean. 'Tis also thatch'd with Palm or Palmeto-Leaves. Each House has a Yard belonging to it, fenced about with wild Canes nine or ten Foot high. There is a Well in each Yard, and a little Bucket with a String to it to draw Water withal. There is a Trunk of a Tree made hollow, placed in each Well, to keep the Earth from falling in. Round the Yards there are many Fruit-trees planted; as Coco-nuts, Tamarins and Toddy-trees.

They have a small Hovel by the Sea-side, where there are six small old Iron Guns standing on a decayed Platform, in rotten Carriages. Their Vents[1] are so big, that when they are fired, the strength of the Powder flying out there, they give but a small Report, like that of a

[1] Touch-holes.

Musket. This is their Court of Guard; and here were a few armed-men watching all the time we lay here. AN. 1699

The Inhabitants of the Town, are chiefly a sort of Indians, of a Copper-colour, with black lank Hair: They speak Portugueze, and are of the Romish Religion; but they take the Liberty to eat Flesh when they please. They value themselves on the account of their Religion and descent from the Portugueze; and would be very angry, if a Man should say they are not Portugueze: Yet I saw but three White Men here, two of which were Padres. There are also a few Chinese living here. It is a place of pretty good Trade and Strength, the best on this Island, Porta-Nova excepted. They have three or four small Barks belonging to the Place; with which they trade chiefly about the Island with the Natives, for Wax, Gold, and Sandall-wood. Sometimes they go to Batavia, and fetch European Commodities, Rice, &c.

The Chinese trade hither from Macao; and I was informed that about twenty Sail of small Vessels come from thence hither every Year. They bring coarse Rice, adulterated Gold, Tea, Iron, and Iron-tools, Porcellane, Silks, &c. They take in exchange pure Gold, as 'tis gathered in the Mountains, Bees-wax, Sandall-wood, Slaves, &c. Sometimes also here comes a Ship from Goa. Ships that trade here, begin to come hither the latter-end of March; and none stay here longer than the latter-end of August. For should they be here while the North-North-West Monsoon blows, no Cables nor Anchors would hold them; but they would be driven ashore and dash'd in pieces presently. But from March till September, while the South-South-East Monsoon blows, Ships ride here very secure; For then, though the Wind often blows hard, yet 'tis off Shore; so that there is very smooth Water, and no fear of being driven ashore; And yet even then they moor with three Cables; two towards the Land, Eastward and Westward; and the third right off to Seaward.

As this is the second place of Traffick, so 'tis in Strength the second place the Portugueze have here, though

AN. 1699 Sea are overflown with Water; and then the small Drills that run into the Sea, are great Rivers; and the Gulleys, which are dry for 3 or 4 Months before, now discharge an impetuous Torrent. The low Land by the Sea-side, is for the most part friable, loose, sandy Soil; yet indifferently fertile and cloathed with Woods. The Mountains are checquered with Woods, and some Spots of Savannahs: Some of the Hills are wholly covered with tall, flourishing Trees; others but thinly; and these few Trees that are on them, look very small, rusty and withered; and the Spots of Savannahs among them, appear rocky and barren. Many of the Mountains are rich in Gold, Copper, or both: The Rains wash the Gold out of the Mountains, which the Natives pick up in the adjacent Brooks, as the Spaniards do in America: How they get the Copper, I know not.

The Trees that grow naturally here, are of divers Sorts; many of them wholly unknown to me; but such as I have seen in America or other places, and grow here likewise, are these, viz. Mangrove, white, red and black; Maho, Calabash, several Sorts of the Palm-kind: The Cotton-Trees are not large, but tougher than those in America: Here are also Locust-Trees of 2 or 3 Sorts, bearing Fruit, but not like those I have formerly seen; these bear a large white Blossom, and yield much Fruit, but it is not sweet.

Cana-fistula-trees, are very common here; the Tree is about the Bigness of our ordinary Apple-Trees; their Branches not thick, nor full of Leaves. These and the before-mentioned, blossom in October and November; the Blossoms are much like our Apple-Tree Blossoms, and about that Bigness: At first they are red; but before they fall off, when spread abroad, they are white; so that these Trees in their Season appear extraordinarily pleasant, and yield a very fragrant Smell. When the Fruit is ripe, it is round, and about the Bigness of a Man's Thumb; of a dark brown Colour, inclining to red, and about 2 Foot or 2 Foot and half long. We found many of them under the Trees, but they had no Pulp in them. The Partitions in the Middle, are much at the same Distance with those brought to England, of the same Substance, and such small flat Seed in them: But whether they be the true Canafistula or no, I cannot tell, because I found no black Pulp in them. AN. 1699

The Calabashes here are very prickly: The Trees grow tall and tapering; whereas in the West-Indies they are low and spread much abroad.

Here are also wild Tamarind-trees, not so large as the true; though much resembling them both in the Bark and Leaf.

Wild Fig-Trees here are many, but not so large as those in America. The Fruit grows, not on the Branches singly, like those in America, but in Strings and Clusters, 40 or 50 in a Cluster, about the Body and great Branches of the Tree, from the very Root up to the Top. These Figs are about the Bigness of a Crab-Apple, of a greenish Colour, and full of small white Seeds; they smell pretty well, but have no Juice or Taste; they are ripe in November.

Here likewise grows Sandal-wood, and many more Sorts of Trees fit for any Uses. The tallest among them, resemble our Pines; they are streight and clear-bodied, but not very thick; the Inside is reddish near the Heart, and hard and ponderous.

Of the Palm-kind there are 3 or 4 Sorts; two of which Kinds I have not seen any where but here. Both Sorts are very large, and tall. The first Sort had Trunks of about 7 or eight Foot in Circumference, and about 80 or 90 Foot high. These had Branches at the Top like Coco-nut Trees, and their Fruit like Coco-nuts, but smaller: The Nut was of an oval Form, and about the Bigness of a Duck's Egg: The Shell black and very hard. 'Twas almost full of Kernel, having only a small empty Space in the Middle, but no Water as Coco-nuts have. The Kernel is too hard to be eaten. The Fruit somewhat resembles that in Brazil formerly mentioned. The Husk or Outside of the Fruit, was very yellow, soft and pulpy, when ripe; and full of small Fibres; and when it fell down from the Tree, would mash and smell unsavoury.

AN. 1699 The other Sort was as big and tall as the former; the Body growing streight up without Limbs, as all Trees of the Palm-kind do: But instead of a great many long green Branches growing from the Head of the Tree, these had short Branches about the Bigness of a Man's Arm, and about a Foot long; each of which spread it self into a great many small tough Twigs, that hung full of Fruit like so many Ropes of Onions. The Fruit was as big as a large Plumb; and every Tree had several Bushels of Fruit. The Branches that bore this Fruit, sprouted out at about 50 or 60 Foot heighth from the Ground. The Trunk of the Tree was all of one Bigness, from the Ground to that Heighth; but from thence it went tapering smaller and smaller to the Top, where it was no bigger than a Man's Leg, ending in a Stump: And there was no Green about the Tree, but the Fruit; so that it appeared like a dead Trunk.

Besides Fruit-Trees, here were many Sorts of tall streight-bodied Timber-Trees; one Sort of which was like Pine. These grow plentifully all round the Island by the Sea-side, but not far within Land. 'Tis hard Wood, of a reddish Colour, and very ponderous.

The Fruits of this Island, are Guavoes, Mangoes, Jaca's, Coco-nuts, Plantains, Bonanoes, Pine-Apples, Citrons, Pomegranates, Oranges, Lemons, Limes, Musk-Melons, Water-Melons, Pumpkins, &c. Many of these have been brought hither by the Dutch and Portugueze; and most of them are ripe in September and October. There were many other excellent Fruits, but not now in Season; as I was inform'd both by Dutch and Portugueze.

Here I met with an Herb, which in the West-Indies we call Calalaloo. It grows wild here. I eat of it several Times, and found it as pleasant and wholesome as Spinage. Here are also Parsly, Sampier, &c. Indian Corn thrives very well here, and is the common Food of the Islanders; though the Portugueze and their Friends sow some Rice, but not half enough for their Subsistence.

The Land-Animals are Buffaloes, Beeves, Horses, Hogs, Goats, Sheep, Monkeys, Guanoes, Lizards, Snakes, Scorpions,

Centumpees, &c. Beside the tame Hogs and Buffaloes, there are many wild all over the Country, which any may freely kill. As for the Beeves, Horses, Goats and Sheep, it is probable they were brought in by the Portugueze or Dutch; especially the Beeves; for I saw none but at the Dutch Fort Concordia. AN. 1699

We also saw Monkeys, and some Snakes. One Sort yellow, and as big as a Man's Arm, and about 4 Foot long: Another Sort no bigger than the Stem of a Tobacco-pipe, about 5 Foot long, green all over his Body, and with a flat red Head as big as a Man's Thumb.

The Fowls are wild Cocks and Hens, Eagles, Hawks, Crows, 2 Sorts of Pidgeons, Turtle-doves, 3 or 4 Sorts of Parrots, Parrakites, Cockatoes, Black-birds; besides a Multitude of smaller Birds of divers Colours, whose charming Musick makes the Woods very pleasant. One Sort of these pretty little Birds my Men call'd the Ringing-bird; because it had 6 Notes, and always repeated all his Notes twice one after another; beginning high and shrill, and ending low. This Bird was about the Bigness of a Lark, having a small sharp black Bill and blue Wings; the Head and Breast were of a pale red, and there was a blue Streak about its Neck. Here are also Sea or Water-Fowls, as Men of War-Birds, Boobies, Fishing-hawks, Herons, Goldens, Crab-catchers, &c. The tame Fowl are Cocks, Hens, Ducks, Geese; the 2 last Sorts I only saw at the Dutch Fort; of the other Sort there are not many but among the Portugueze: The Woods abound with Bees, which make much Honey and Wax.

The Sea is very well stock'd with Fish of divers Sorts, viz. Mullets, Bass, Breames, Snooks, Mackarel, Parracoots, Gar-fish, Ten-pounders, Scuttle-fish, Sting-rays, Whip-rays, Rasperages, Cockle-merchants, or Oyster-crackers, Cavallies, Conger-Eels, Rock-fish, Dog-fish, &c. The Rays are so plentiful, that I never drew the Sain but I catch'd some of them; which we salted and dryed. I caught one whose Tail was 13 Foot long. The Cockle-Merchants are shaped like Cavallies, and about their Bigness. They feed on Shell-fish, having 2 very hard, thick, flat Bones in their Throat,

AN. 1699 with which they break in Pieces the Shells of the Fish they swallow. We always find a great many Shells in their Maws, crushed in Pieces. The Shell-fish, are Oysters of 3 Sorts, viz. Long-Oysters, Common Oysters, growing upon Rocks in great Abundance, and very flat; and another Sort of large Oysters, fat and crooked; the Shell of this, not easily to be distinguished from a Stone. Three or four of these roasted, will suffice a Man for one Meal. Cockles, as big as a Man's Head; of which 2 or 3 are enough for a Meal; they are very fat and sweet. Craw-fish, Shrimps, &c. Here are also many green Turtle, some Alligators and Grand-pisces, &c.

The Original Natives of this Island, are Indians, they are of a middle Stature, streight-bodied, slender-limb'd, long-visag'd; their Hair black and lank; their Skins very swarthy. They are very dextrous and nimble, but withal lazy in the highest Degree. They are said to be dull in every Thing but Treachery and Barbarity. Their Houses are but low and mean, their Cloathing only a small Cloath about their Middle; but some of them for Ornament have Frontlets of Mother of Pearl, or thin Pieces of Silver or Gold, made of an oval Form, of the Breadth of a Crown-piece, curiously notched round the Edges; Five of these placed one by another a little above the Eye-brows, making a sufficient Guard and Ornament for their Fore-head. They are so thin, and placed on their Fore-heads so artificially, that they seem riveted thereon: And indeed the Pearl-Oyster-shells make a more splendid Show, than either Silver or Gold. Others of them have Palmeto-caps made in divers Forms.

As to their Marriages, they take as many Wives as they can maintain; and sometimes they sell their Children to purchase more Wives. I enquir'd about their Religion, and was told they had none. Their common Subsistence is by Indian Corn, which every Man plants for himself. They take but little Pains to clear their Land; for in the dry Time they set Fire to the withered Grass and Shrubs, and that burns them out a Plantation for the next wet Season. What other Grain they have, beside Indian Corn,

This Fish is of a pale red all parts of it except ye Eye taken on ye Coast of
New Guinea
Strange & large
Batts on I Pulo Sabuda
in New Guinea described
This Birds Eye is of
a Bright red

I know not. Their Plantations are very mean; for they delight most in hunting; and here are wild Buffaloes and Hogs enough, though very shy, because of their so frequent hunting. AN. 1699

They have a few boats and some Fishermen. Their Arms are Lances, thick round short Truncheons and Targets; with these they hunt and kill their Game, and their Enemies too; for this Island is now divided into many Kingdoms, and all of different Languages; though in their Customs and manner of living, as well as Shape and Colour, they seem to be of one Stock.

The chiefest Kingdoms are Cupang, Amabie, Lortribie, Pobumbie, Namquimal; the Island also of Anamabao, or Anabao, is a Kingdom. Each of these hath a Sultan who is supreme in his Province and Kingdom, and hath under him several Raja's and other inferiour Officers. The Sultans for the most Part are Enemies to each other; which Enmities are fomented and kept up by the Dutch, whose Fort and Factory is in the Kingdom of Cupang; and therefore the Bay near which they are settled, is commonly called Cupang-Bay. They have only as much Ground as they can keep within Reach of their Guns; yet this whole Kingdom is at Peace with them; and they freely trade together; as also with the Islanders on Anabao, who are in Amity as well with the Natives of Cupang, as with the Dutch residing there; but they are implacable Enemies to those of Amabie, who are their next neighbours, and in Amity with the Portugueze: as are also the Kingdoms of Pobumbie, Namquimal and Lortribie. It is very probable, that these 2 European Settlements on this Island, are the greatest Occasion of their continued Wars. The Portugueze vaunt highly of their Strength here, and that they are able at Pleasure to rout the Dutch, if they had Authority so to do from the King of Portugal; and they have written to the Vice-roy of Goa about it: And though their Request is not yet granted, yet (as they say) they live in Expectation of it. These have no Forts, but depend on their Alliance with the Natives: And indeed they are already so mixt, that it is hard to distinguish whether they

AN. are Portugueze or Indians. Their Language is Portugueze;
1699 and the Religion they have, is Romish. They seem in Words to acknowledge the King of Portugal for their Sovereign; yet they will not accept of any Officers sent by him. They speak indifferently the Malayan and their own native Languages, as well as Portugueze; and the chiefest Officers that I saw, were of this Sort; neither did I see above 3 or 4 white Men among them; and of these, 2 were Priests. Of this mixt Breed there are some thousands; of whom some have small Arms of their own, and know how to use them. The chiefest Person (as I before said) is called Captain More or Maior: He is a white Man, sent hither by the Vice-Roy of Goa, and seems to have great Command here. I did not see him; for he seldom comes down. His Residence is at a Place called Porta Nova; which the People at Laphao told me was a great way off; but I could not get any more particular Account. Some told me that he is most commonly in the Mountains, with an Army of Indians, to guard the Passes between them and the Cupangayans, especially in the dry Times. The next Man to him is Alexis Mendosa: He is a right Indian, speaks very good Portugueze, and is of the Romish Religion. He lives 5 or 6 Miles from the Sea, and is called the Lieutenant. (This is he whom I call'd Governour, when at Laphao.) He commands next to Captain More, and hath under him another at this Fort (at the Sea-side) if it may be so called. He also is called Lieutenant, and is an Indian Portugueze.

Besides this Mungrel-Breed of Indians and Portugueze here are also some China-Men, Merchants from Maccao: They bring hither coarse Rice, Gold, Tea, Iron-work, Porcelane, and Silk both wrought and raw: They get in Exchange pure Gold as it is here gather'd, Bees-wax, Sandall-Wood, Coire, &c. It is said there are about 20 small China Vessels come hither every Year from Maccao; and commonly one Vessel a Year from Goa, which brings European Commodities and Callicoes, Muslins, &c. Here are likewise some small Barks belonging to this Place, that trade to Batavia, and bring from thence both European and

Indian Goods and Rice. The Vessels generally come here in March, and stay till September. AN. 1699

The Dutch, as I before said, are setled in the Kingdom of Cupang, where they have a small neat Stone Fort. It seems to be pretty strong; yet, as I was informed, had been taken by a French Pirate about 2 Years ago: The Dutch were used very barbarously, and ever since are very jealous of any Strangers that come this Way; which I my self experienced. These depend more on their own Strength than on the Natives their Friends; having good Guns, Powder, and Shot enough on all Occasions, and Soldiers sufficient to manage the Business here, all well disciplin'd and in good Order; which is a Thing the Portugueze their Neighbours are altogether destitute of, they having no European Soldiers, few Arms, less Ammunition, and their Fort consisting of no more than 6 bad Guns planted against the Sea, whose Touch-holes (as was before observed) are so enlarg'd by Time, that a great Part of the Strength of the Powder flies away there; and having Soldiers in pay, the Natives on all Occasions are hired; and their Government now is so loose, that they will admit of no more Officers from Portugal or Goa. They have also little or no Supply of Arms or Ammunition from thence, but buy it as often as they can, of the Dutch, Chinese, &c. So that upon the whole it seems improbable that they should ever attempt to drive out the Dutch, for fear of loosing themselves, notwithstanding their boasted Prowess and Alliance with the Natives: And indeed, as far as I could learn, they have Business enough to keep their own present Territories from the Incursions of the Cupangayans; who are Friends to the Dutch, and whom doubtless the Dutch have ways enough to preserve in their Friendship; besides that they have an inveterate Malice to their Neighbours, insomuch that they kill all they meet, and bring away their Heads in Triumph. The great Men of Cupang stick the Heads of those they have killed, on Poles; and set them on the Tops of their Houses; and these they esteem above all their other Riches. The inferiour Sort bring the Heads of those they kill, into Houses made for that Purpose;

AN. 1699 of which there was one at the Indian Village near the Fort Concordia, almost full of Heads, as I was told. I know not what Encouragement they have for their Inhumanity.

The Dutch have always 2 Sloops belonging to their Fort; in these they go about the Island, and trade with the Natives; and, as far as I could learn, they trade indifferently with them all. For though the Inland People are at war with each other, yet those by the Sea-side seem to be little concerned; and, generally speaking the Malayan Language, are very sociable and easily induced to trade with those that speak that Language; which the Dutch here always learn; Besides, being well acquainted with the Treachery of these People, they go well arm'd among them, and are very vigilant never to give them an Opportunity to hurt them; and it is very probable that they supply them with such Goods, as the Portugueze cannot.

The Malayan Language, as I have before said, is generally spoken amongst all the Islands hereabouts. The greater the Trade is, the more this Language is spoken: In some it is become their only Language; in others it is but little spoken, and that by the Sea-side only. With this Language the Mahometan Religion did spread it self, and was got hither before any European Christians came: But now, though the Language is still used, the Mahometan Religion falls, where-ever the Portugueze or Dutch are settled; unless they be very weak, as at Solor and Ende, where the chief Language is Malayan, and the Religion Mahometanism; though the Dutch are settled at Solor, and the Portugueze at the East-end of the Island Ende, at a Place called Lorantuca;[1] which, as I was informed, is a large Town, hath a pretty strong Fort and safe Harbour. The chief Man there (as at Timor) is called Captain More, and is as absolute as the other. These 2 principal Men are Enemies to each other; and by their Letters and Messages to Goa, inveigh bitterly against each

[1] Larantuka on the NE. coast of Flores.

other; and are ready to do all the ill Offices they can; yet neither of them much regards the Vice-Roy of Goa, as I was inform'd. AN. 1699

L' Orantuca is said to be more populous then any Town on Timor; the Island Ende affording greater Plenty of all manner of Fruit, and being much better supplied with all Necessaries, than Laphao; especially with Sheep, Goats, Hogs, Poultry, &c. but it is very dangerous getting into this Harbour, because of the violent Tides, between the Islands Ende and Solor. In the middle Channel between Timor and the Range of Islands to the Northward of it, whereof Ende and Solor are 2, there runs a constant Current all the Year to the Westward; though near either Shore there are Tides indeed; but the Tide of Flood, which sets West, running 8 or 9 Hours, and the Ebb not exceeding 3 or 4 Hours, the Tide in some Places riseth 9 or 10 Foot on a Spring.

The Seasons of the Year here at Timor, are much the same as in other Places in South Latitude. The fair Weather begins in April or May, and continues to October, then the Tornadoes begin to come, but no violent bad Weather till the Middle of December. Then there are violent West or North-West Winds, with Rain, till towards the Middle of February. In May the Southerly Winds set in, and blow very strong on the North-side of the Island, but fair. There is great Difference of Winds on the 2 Sides of the Island: For the Southerly Winds are but very faint on the South-side, and very hard on the North-side; and the bad Weather on the South-side comes in very violent in October, which on the North-side comes not till December. You have very good Sea and Land-breezes, when the Weather is fair; and may run indifferently to the East or West, as your Business lies. We found from September to December the Winds veering all round the Compass gradually in 24 Hours Time; but such a constant Western Current, that it's much harder getting to the East than West at or near Spring Tides: Which I have more than once made Tryal of. For weighing from Babao at 6 a Clock in the Morning on the 12th Instant, we kept

AN. 1699 By a good Observation we found that the South-East-point of Omba lies in Latitude 8 d. 25 m. In my Draughts it's laid down in 8 deg. 10 min. My true Course from Babao, is East, 25 deg. North, distance one hundred eighty three miles. We sounded several times when near Omba, but had no ground. On the North-East point of Omba we saw four or five Men, and a little further three pretty Houses on a low Point, but did not go ashore.

At five this Afternoon, we had a Tornado, which yielded much Rain, Thunder and Lightning; yet we had but little Wind. The 24th in the Morning we catched a large Shark, which gave all the Ships Company a plentiful Meal.

The 27th we saw the burning Island,[1] it lies in Latitude 6 deg. 36 min. South; it is high, and but small. It runs from the Sea a little sloaping towards the Top; which is divided in the Middle into two Peaks, between which issued out much Smoak: I have not seen more from any Vulcano. I saw no Trees; but the North-side appeared green, and the rest look'd very barren.

Having past the burning Island, I shap'd my Course for two Islands called Turtle Isles, which lye North-East by East a little Easterly, and distant about fifty Leagues from the burning Isle. I fearing the Wind might veer to the Eastward of the North, steered 20 Leagues North-East, then North-East by East. On the 28th we saw two small low Islands, called Luca-parros,[2] to the North of us. At Noon I accounted my self 20 Leagues short of the Turtle Isles.

The next Morning, being in the Latitude of the Turtle Islands, we look'd out sharp for them, but saw no appearance of any Island, till 11 a Clock; when we saw an Island at a great distance. At first we supposed it might be one of the Turtle Isles: But it was not laid down true, neither in Latitude nor Longitude from the burning Isle, nor from the Luca-parros, which last I took to be a great help to guide me, they being laid down very well from the Burning

[1] Gunong Api.

[2] Lucipara. The Turtle Islands are low sandy islets to the north of the Lucipara group, of which they are, in fact, a part.

Isle, and that likewise in true Latitude and distance from Omba: So that I could not tell what to think of the Island now in sight; we having had fair Weather, so that we could not pass by the Turtle Isles without seeing them; and This in sight was much too far off for them. We found Variation 1 deg. 2 min. East. In the Afternoon I steered North-East by East for the Islands that we saw. At 2 a Clock I went and look'd over the Fore-yard, and saw 2 Islands at much greater distance than the Turtle Islands are laid down in my Draughts; one of them was a very high peak'd Mountain, cleft at Top, and much like the burning Island that we past by, but bigger and higher; the other was a pretty long high flat Island. Now I was certain that these were not the Turtle Islands, and that they could be no other than the Bande[1]-Isles; yet we steered in to make them plainer. At 3 a Clock we discovered another small flat Island to the North-West of the others, and saw a great deal of Smoak rise from the Top of the high Island; At 4 we saw other small Islands, by which I was now assured that these were the Bande-Isles there. At 5 I altered my Course and steered East, and at 8 East-South-East; because I would not be seen by the Inhabitants of those Islands in the Morning. We had little Wind all Night; and in the Morning as soon as 'twas Light, we saw another high peak'd Island: At 8 it bore South-South-East half East, distance 8 Leagues. And this I knew to be Bird-Isle.[2] 'Tis laid down in our Draughts in Latitude 5 deg. 9 min. South, which is too far Southerly by 27 Miles according to our Observation; And the like Error in laying down the Turtle-Islands, might be the Occasion of our missing them.

AN. 1699

At night I shortned Sail, for fear of coming too nigh some Islands,[3] that stretch away bending like a half Moon from Ceram towards Timor, and which in my Course I must of necessity pass through. The next Morning betimes, I saw them; and found them to be at a farther distance from Bird-Island, than I expected. In the After-

[1] Banda. [2] Manu. [3] Serwatti Islands.

AN. 1700 Boat could come close to, and it was very easie to be fill'd; and that the Ship might anchor as near to it as I pleas'd: So I went thither. The next Morning therefore we anchor'd in 25 Fathom Water, soft oazie Ground, about a Mile from the River: We got on board 3 Tun of Water that Night; and caught 2 or 3 Pike-fish, in shape much like a Parracota, but with a longer Snout, something resembling a Garr, yet not so long. The next day I sent the Boat again for Water, and before night all my Casks were full.

Having fill'd here about 15 Tuns of Water, seeing we could catch but little Fish, and had no other Refreshments, I intended to sail next day; but finding that we wanted Wood, I sent to cut some; and going ashore to hasten it, at some distance from the place where our Men were, I found a small Cove, where I saw two Barbecues, which appear'd not to be above 2 Months standing: The Sparrs were cut with some sharp Instrument; so that, if done by the Natives, it seems that they have Iron. On the 10th, a little after 12 a-Clock, we weighed and stood over to the North-side of the Bay; and at 1 a-Clock stood out with the Wind at North and North-North-West. At 4 we past out by a White Island, which I so named from its many white Cliffs, having no name in our Draughts. It is about a League long, pretty high, and very woody: 'Tis about 5 Miles from the Main, only at the West-end it reaches within 3 Miles of it. At some distance off at Sea, the West-point appears like a Cape-land; The North-side trends away North-North-West, and the East-side East-South-East. This Island lies in Latitude 3 degrees 4 min. South; and the Meridian Distance from Bahao, 500 and 12 Miles East. After we were out to Sea, we plied to get to the Northward; but met with such a strong Current against us, that we got but little. For if the Wind favour'd us in the night, that we got 3 or 4 Leagues; we lost it again, and were driven as far astern next Morning; so that we plyed here several Days.

The 14th, being past a point of Land that we had been 3 Days getting about, we found little or no Current; so that having the Wind at North-West by West and

West-North-West, we stood to the Northward, and had several Soundings: At 3 a-Clock, 38 Fathom; the nearest part of New-Guinea being about 3 Leagues distance: At 4, 37; at 5, 36; at 6, 36; at 8, 33 Fathom; Then the Cape was about 4 Leagues distant; so that as we ran off, we found our Water shallower. We had then some Islands to the Westward of us, at about four Leagues distance. AN. 1700

A little after noon we saw Smokes on the Islands to the West of us; and having a fine Gale of Wind, I steered away for them: At 7 a-Clock in the Evening we anchored in 35 Fathom, about two Leagues from an Island, good soft oazie Ground. We lay still all night, and saw Fires ashore. In the Morning we weighed again, and ran farther in, thinking to have shallower Water; but we ran within a Mile of the Shore, and came to in 38 Fathom, good soft holding Ground. While we were under Sail, 2 Canoes came off within call of us: They spoke to us, but we did not understand their Language, nor Signs. We wav'd to them to come aboard, and I call'd to them in the Malayan Language to do the same; but they would not; yet they came so nigh us, that we could shew them such Things as we had to truck with them; Yet neither would this entice them to come aboard; but they made Signs for us to come ashore, and away they went. Then I went after them in my Pinnace, carrying with me Knives, Beads, Glasses, Hatchets, &c. When we came near the Shore, I called to them in the Malayan Language: I saw but 2 Men at first, the rest lying in Ambush behind the Bushes; but as soon as I threw ashore some Knives and other Toys, they came out, flung down their Weapons, and came into the Water by the Boat's Side, making Signs of Friendship by pouring Water on their Heads with one Hand, which they dipt into the Sea. The next Day in the Afternoon several other Canoas came aboard, and brought many Roots and Fruits, which we purchas'd.

This Island has no Name in our Draughts, but the Natives call it Pulo Sabuda.[1] It is about 3 Leagues long,

[1] It lies at the entrance to McCluer's Inlet.

AN. and 2 Miles wide, more or less. It is of a good Heighth,
1700 so as to be seen 11 or 12 Leagues. It is very Rocky; yet above the Rocks there is good yellow and black Mould; not deep, yet producing plenty of good tall Trees, and bearing any Fruits or Roots which the Inhabitants plant. I do not know all its Produce; but what we saw, were Plantains, Coco-Nuts, Pine-Apples, Oranges, Papaes, Potatoes, and other large Roots. Here are also another sort of wild Jaca's, about the bigness of a Man's two Fists, full of Stones or Kernels, which eat pleasant enough when roasted. The Libby Tree grows here in the Swampy Valleys, of which they make Sago Cakes: I did not see them make any, but was told by the Inhabitants that it was made of the Pith of the Tree, in the same Manner I have described in my "Voyage Round the World." They shew'd me the Tree whereof it was made, and I bought about 40 of the Cakes. I bought also 3 or 4 Nutmegs in their Shell, which did not seem to have been long gathered; but whether they be the Growth of this Island or not, the Natives would not tell whence they had them, and seem'd to prize them very much. What Beasts the Island affords, I know not: But here are both Sea and Land-Fowl. Of the first, Boobies and Men of War-Birds are the chief; some Goldens, and small Milk-white Crab-catchers. The Land-Fowls are Pidgeons, about the Bigness of Mountain-Pidgeons in Jamaica; and Crows about the Bigness of those in England, and much like them; but the inner Part of their Feathers are white, and the Outside black; so that they appear all black, unless you extend the Feathers. Here are large Sky-coloured Birds, such as we lately kill'd on New Guinea; and many other small Birds, unknown to us. Here are likewise Abundance of Bats,[1] as big as young Coneys; their Necks, Head, Ears and Noses, like Foxes; their Hair rough; that about their Necks, is of a whitish yellow, that on their Heads and Shoulders black; their Wings are 4 Foot over, from Tip to Tip: They smell like Foxes. The Fish are Bass,

[1] *Pteropus stramineus* (?).

This Bird was taken on the
Coast of New Guinea

A Stately Land Fowl found on the
Coast of New Guinea described
A Strange Land
Fowl found on the
Island Ceram

Rock-fish, and a Sort of Fish like Mullets, Old-wives, Whip-rays, and some other Sorts that I know not, but no great Plenty of any; for 'tis deep Water till within less than a Mile of the Shore; then there is a Bank of Coral Rocks, within which you have Shoal Water, white clean Sand: So there is no good Fishing with the Sain.

AN. 1700

This Island lies in Latitude 2 deg. 43 min. South, and Meridian distance from Port Babao on the Island Timor, 486 Miles. Besides this Island, here are 9 or 10 other small Islands, as they are laid down in the Draughts.

The Inhabitants of this Island are a Sort of very tawny Indians, with long black Hair; who in their Manners differ but little from the Mindanayans, and others of these Eastern Islands. These seem to be the chief; for besides them we saw also shock curl-pated New-Guinea Negroes; many of which are Slaves to the others, but I think not all. They are very poor, wear no Cloaths, but have a Clout about their Middle, made of the Rinds of the Tops of Palmeto Trees; but the Women had a Sort of Callicoe-Cloaths. Their chief Ornaments are Blue and Yellow-Beads, worn about their Wrists. The Men arm themselves with Bows and Arrows, Lances, broad Swords like those of Mindanao; their Lances are pointed with Bone. They strike Fish very ingeniously with wooden Fiss-gigs, and have a very ingenious way of making the Fish rise: For they have a Piece of Wood curiously carv'd and painted much like a Dolphin (and perhaps other Figures); these they let down into the Water by a Line with a small Weight to sink it; when they think it low enough, they haul the Line into their Boats very fast, and the Fish rise up after this Figure; and they stand ready to strike them when they are near the Surface of the Water. But their chief Livelihood is from their Plantations. Yet they have large Boats, and go over to New-Guinea, where they get Slaves, fine Parrots, &c. which they carry to Goram[1] and exchange for Callicoes. One Boat came from thence a little before I arriv'd here; of

[1] An island in the Ceram Laut group.

AN. 1700 whom I bought some Parrots; and would have bought a Slave, but they would not barter for any Thing but Callicoes, which I had not. Their Houses on this Side were very small, and seem'd only to be for Necessity; but on the other Side of the Island we saw good large Houses. Their Proes are narrow with Outlagers on each Side, like other Malayans. I cannot tell of what Religion these are; but I think they are not Mahometans, by their drinking Brandy out of the same Cup with us without any Scruple. At this Island we continued till the 20th Instant, having laid in Store of such Roots and Fruits as the Island afforded.

On the 20th, at half an Hour after 6 in the Morning, I weigh'd, and standing out we saw a large Boat full of Men lying at the North-point of the Island. As we passed by, they rowed towards their Habitations, where we supposed they had withdrawn themselves for fear of us (tho' we gave them no Cause of Terrour), or for some Differences among themselves.

We stood to the Northward till 7 in the Evening; then saw a Ripling; and the Water being discoloured, we sounded, and had but 22 Fathom. I went about and stood to the Westward till 2 next Morning, then tack'd again, and had these several Soundings: At 8 in the Evening, 22; at 10, 25; at 11, 27; at 12, 28 Fathom; at 2 in the Morning 26; at 4, 24; at 6, 23; at 8, 28; at 12, 22.

We passed by many small Islands, and among many dangerous Shoals, without any remarkable Occurrence, till the 4th of February, when we got within 3 Leagues of the North-West Cape of New-Guinea, called by the Dutch Cape Mabo.[1] Off this Cape there lies a small woody Island, and many Islands of different Sizes to the North and North-East of it. This Part of New Guinea is high Land, adorn'd with tall Trees that appeared very green and flourishing. The Cape it self is not very high, but ends in a low sharp Point; and on either Side there appears another such Point at equal Distances, which makes it resemble a Diamond.

[1] Cape Selee.

This only appears when you are abreast of the middle Point; and then you have no Ground within 3 Leagues of the Shore. AN. 1700

In the Afternoon we past by the Cape, and stood over for the Islands. Before it was dark, we were got within a League of the Westermost; but had no Ground with 50 Fathom of Line. However fearing to stand nearer in the dark, we tack'd and stood to the East, and plyed all Night. The next Morning we were got 5 or 6 Leagues to the Eastward of that Island; and having the Wind Easterly, we stood in to the Northward among the Islands; sounded, and had no Ground. Then I sent in my Boat to sound, and they had Ground with 50 Fathom near a Mile from the Shore. We tack'd before the Boat came aboard again, for fear of a Shoal that was about a Mile to the East of that Island the Boat went to; from whence also a Shoal-point stretched out it self till it met the other: They brought with them such a Cockle, as I have mentioned in my "Voyage round the World," found near Celebes; and they saw many more, some bigger than that which they brought aboard, as they said; and for this Reason I named it Cockle-Island. I sent them to sound again, ordering them to fire a Musquet if they found good anchoring; we were then standing to the Southward, with a fine Breeze. As soon as they fired, I tack'd and stood in: They told me they had 50 Fathom when they fired. I tack'd again, and made all the Sail I could to get out, being near some Rocky Islands and Shoals to Leeward of us. The Breeze increased, and I thought we were out of Danger; but having a Shoal just by us, and the Wind falling again, I ordered the Boat to tow us, and by their Help we got clear from it. We had a strong Tide setting to the Westward.

At 1 a-Clock, being past the Shoal, and finding the Tide setting to the Westward, I anchor'd in 35 Fathom, coarse Sand, with small Coral and Shells. Being nearest to Cockle-Island, I immediately sent both the Boats thither; one to cut Wood, and the other to fish. At 4 in the Afternoon, having a small Breeze at South-South-West, I made a Sign for my Boats to come aboard. They brought

AN. 1700 some Wood, and a few small Cockles, none of them exceeding 10 Pound weight; whereas the Shell of the great one weighed 78 Pound; but it was now high Water, and therefore they could get no bigger. They also brought on Board some Pidgeons, of which we found Plenty on all the Islands where we touch'd in these Seas. Also in many Places we saw many large Batts, but kill'd none, except those I mention'd at Pulo Sabuda. As our Boats came aboard, we weigh'd and made Sail, steering East-South-East as long as the Wind held: In the Morning we found we had got 4 or 5 Leagues to the East of the Place where we weighed. We stood to and fro till 11; and finding that we lost Ground, anchor'd in 42 Fathom, coarse gravelly Sand, with some Coral. This Morning we thought we saw a Sail.

In the Afternoon I went ashore on a small woody Island, about 2 Leagues from us. Here I found the greatest Number of Pidgeons that ever I saw either in the East or West-Indies, and small Cockles in the Sea round the Island, in such Quantities that we might have laden the Boat in an Hour's Time: These were not above 10 or 12 Pound Weight. We cut some Wood, and brought off Cockles enough for all the Ship's Company; but having no small Shot, we could kill no Pidgeons. I return'd about 4 a-Clock; and then my Gunner and both Mates went thither, and in less than 3 quarters of an Hour they kill'd and brought off 10 Pidgeons. Here is a Tide: The Flood sets West and the Ebb East; but the latter is very faint, and but of small Continuance. And so we found it ever since we came from Timor. The Winds we found Easterly, between North-East and East-South-East; so that if these continue, it is impossible to beat farther to the Eastward on this Coast against Wind and Current. These Easterly Winds encreased from the Time we were in the Latitude of about 2 deg. South; and as we drew nigher the Line, they hung more Easterly. And now being to the North of the Continent of New Guinea, where the Coast lies East and West, I find the Trade-wind here at East; which yet in higher Latitudes is usually at North-North-West and

North-West; and so I did expect them here, it being to the South of the Line. An. 1700

The 7th in the Morning I sent my Boat ashore on Pidgeon-Island, and staid till Noon. In the Afternoon my Men returned, brought 22 Pidgeons, and many Cockles, some very large, some small: They also brought one empty Shell, that weigh'd 258 Pound.

At 4 a-Clock we weigh'd, having a small Westerly Wind, and a Tide with us; at 7 in the Evening we anchor'd in 42 Fathom, near King William's Island, where I went ashore the next Morning, drank his Majesty's Health, and honour'd it with his Name. It is about 2 Leagues and a half in length, very high, and extraordinarily well cloathed with Woods. The Trees are of divers Sorts, most unknown to us, but all very green and flourishing; many of them had Flowers, some white, some purple, others yellow; all which smelt very fragrantly. The Trees are generally tall and streight-bodied, and may be fit for any Uses. I saw one of a clean Body, without Knot or Limb, 60 or 70 Foot high by Estimation. It was 3 of my Fathoms about, and kept its Bigness without any sensible Decrease even to the Top. The Mould of the Island is black, but not deep; it being very rocky. On the Sides and Top of the Island, are many Palmeto-Trees, whose Heads we could discern over all the other Trees, but their Bodies we could not see.

About 1 in the Afternoon we weighed and stood to the Eastward, between the Main and King William's Island;[1] leaving the Island on our Larboard-side, and sounding till we were past the Island; and then we had no Ground. Here we found the Flood setting East by North, and the Ebb West by South. There were Shoals and small Islands between us and the Main, which caused the Tide to set very inconstantly, and make many Whirlings in the Water; yet we did not find the Tide to set strong any way, nor the Water to rise much.

On the 9th, being to the Eastward of King William's

[1] One of the Waiang islands.

AN. 1700 Island, we plied all Day between the Main and other Islands, having Easterly Winds and fair Weather till 7 the next Morning. Then we had very hard Rain till 8, and saw many Shoals of Fish. We lay becalm'd off a pretty deep Bay on New-Guinea, about 12 or 14 Leagues wide, and 7 or 8 Leagues deep, having low Land near its Bottom, but high Land without. The Eastermost Part of New-Guinea seen, bore East by South, distant 12 Leagues: Cape Mabo West-South-West half South, distant 7 Leagues.

At 1 in the Afternoon it began to rain, and continu'd till 6 in the Evening; so that having but little Wind and most Calms, we lay still off the fore-mentioned Bay, having King William's Island still in Sight, though distant by Judgment 15 or 16 Leagues West. We saw many Shoals of small Fish, some Sharks, and 7 or 8 Dolphins; but catcht none. In the Afternoon, being about 4 Leagues from the Shore, we saw an Opening in the Land, which seem'd to afford good Harbour: In the Evening we saw a large Fire there; and I intended to go in (if Winds and Weather would permit) to get some Acquaintance with the Natives.

Since the 4th Instant that we passed Cape Mabo, to the 12th, we had small Easterly Winds and Calms, so that we anchor'd several Times; where I made my Men cut Wood, that we might have a good Stock when a Westerly Wind should present; and so we ply'd to the Eastward, as Winds and Currents would permit; having not got in all above 30 Leagues to the Eastward of Cape Mabo. But on the 12th, at 4 in the Afternoon, a small Gale sprung up at North-East by North, with Rain: At 5 it shuffled about to North-West, from thence to the South West, and continued between those 2 Points a pretty brisk Gale; so that we made Sail and steered away North-East, till the 13th in the Morning, to get about the Cape of Good Hope. When 'twas Day, we steer'd North-East half East, then North-East by East till 7 a-Clock; and being then 7 or 8 Leagues off Shore, we steer'd away East; the Shore trending East by South. We had very much Rain all Night, so that we could not carry much Sail; yet we had a very steddy Gale. At 8 this Morning the Weather clear'd up, and the Wind decreas'd to a fine Top-gallant Gale, and settled at West by South. We had more Rain these 3 Days past, than all the Voyage in so short Time. We were now about 6 Leagues from the Land of New-Guinea, which appear'd very high; and we saw 2 Headlands about 20 Leagues asunder; the one to the East, and the other to the West, which last is called the Cape of Good Hope. We found Variation East 4 deg.

The 15th in the Morning between 12 and 2 a-Clock, it blew a very brisk Gale at North-West, and look'd very black in the South-West. At 2 it flew about at once to the South-South-West, and rained very hard. The Wind settled sometime at West-South-West, and we steered East-North-East till 3 in the Morning: Then the Wind and Rain abating, we steered East half North for fear of coming near the Land. Presently after, it being a little clear, the Man at the Bowsprit end, call'd out, "Land on our Starboard Bow." We lookt out and saw it plain. I presently sounded, and had but 10 Fathom soft Ground. The Master, being somewhat scar'd, came running in haste with this News, and said it was best to anchor: I told him no, but sound again; then we had 12 Fathom; the next Cast, 13 and a half; the 4th, 17 Fathom; and then no Ground with 50 Fathom Line. However we kept off the Island, and did not go so fast but that we could see any other Danger before we came nigh it. For here might have been more Islands not laid down in my Draughts besides This. For I search'd all the Draughts I had, if perchance I might find any Island in the one, which was not in the others; but I could find none near us. When it was Day, we were about 5 Leagues off the land we saw; but, I believe, not above 5 Mile or at most 2 Leagues off it, when we first saw it in the Night.

This is a small Island,[1] but pretty high; I named it Providence. About 5 Leagues to the Southward of this, there is another Island, which is called William Scouten's

[1] Little Providence. Great Providence, a slightly larger island, lies a few miles to its SE.

AN. 1700 in our Draughts. We found Variation 9 deg. 50 min. East.

The 28th we had many violent Tornadoes, Wind, Rain, and some Spouts; and in the Tornadoes the Wind shifted. In the Night we had fair Weather, but more Lightning than we had seen at any Time this Voyage. This Morning we left a large high Island on our Larboard-side, called in the Dutch Draughts Wishart's[1] Isle, about 6 Leagues from the Main; and seeing many Smoaks upon the Main, I therefore steer'd towards it.

[1] Visscher's Island. "The Main" being New Ireland, or, as it is now called, New Mecklenburg.

CHAP. IV

The main Land of New-Guinea. Its Inhabitants. Slinger's Bay. Small Islands. Garret Dennis Isle described. Its Inhabitants. Their Proes. Anthony Cave's Island. Its Inhabitants. Trees full of Worms found in the Sea. St. John's Island. The main Land of New-Guinea. Its Inhabitants. The Coast described. Cape and Bay St. George. Cape Orford. Another Bay. The Inhabitants there. A large account of the Author's Attempts to Trade with them. He names the place Port Mountague. The Country thereabouts described, and its produce. A Burning Island described. A new passage found. Nova Britannia. Sir George Rook's Island. Long Island, and Crown Island, discovered and described. Sir R. Rich's Island. A burning Island. A strange Spout. A Conjecture concerning a new Passage Southward. King William's Island. Strange Whirlpools. Distance between Cape Mabo, and Cape St. George, computed.

THE main Land, at this place, is high and mountainous, adorn'd with tall flourishing Trees; The Sides of the Hills had many large Plantations and Patches of clear'd Land; which, together with the Smoaks we saw, were certain Signs of its being well inhabited; and I was desirous to have some Commerce with the Inhabitants. Being nigh the Shore, we saw first one Proe; a little after, 2 or 3 more; and at last a great many Boats came from all the adjacent Bays. When they were 46 in Number, they approach'd so near us, that we could see each others Signs, and hear each other speak; though we could not understand them, nor they us. They made Signs for us to go in towards the Shore, pointing that way; it was squally Weather, which at first made me cautious of going too near; but the Weather beginning to look pretty well, I endeavoured to get into a AN. 1700

AN. 1700 Bay a-head of us, which we could have got into well enough at first; but while we lay by, we were driven so far to Leeward, that now it was more difficult to get in. The Natives lay in their Proes round us; to whom I shew'd Beads, Knives, Glasses, to allure them to come nearer; but they would not come so nigh, as to receive any thing from us. Therefore I threw out some things to them, viz. a Knife fastned to a piece of Board, and a Glass-bottle corked up with some Beads in it, which they took up and seemed well pleased. They often struck their left Breast with their right hand, and as often held up a black Truncheon over their Heads, which we thought was a Token of Friendship; Wherefore we did the like. And when we stood in towards their Shore, they seem'd to rejoyce; but when we stood off, they frown'd, yet kept us Company in their Proes, still pointing to the Shore. About 5 a-Clock we got within the Mouth of the Bay, and sounded several times, but had no Ground, though within a mile of the Shore. The Bason of this Bay was above 2 Miles within us, into which we might have gone; but as I was not assured of Anchorage there, so I thought it not Prudence to run in at this time; it being near Night, and seeing a black Tornado rising in the West, which I most fear'd: Besides, we had near 200 Men in Proes close by us. And the Bays on the Shore were lined with Men from one end to the other, where there could not be less than 3 or 400 more. What Weapons they had, we know not, nor yet their Design. Therefore I had, at their first coming near us, got up all our small Arms, and made several put on Cartouch Boxes to prevent Treachery. At last I resolved to go out again: Which when the Natives in their Proes perceived, they began to fling Stones at us as fast as they could, being provided with Engines for that purpose; (wherefore I named this place Slinger's Bay:) But at the Firing of one Gun they were all amaz'd, drew off and flung no more Stones. They got together, as if consulting what to do; for they did not make in towards the Shore, but lay still, though some of them were killed or wounded; and many more of them had paid for their Boldness, but that I was unwilling to cut off any of them; which if I had done, I could not hope afterwards to bring them to treat with me. AN. 1700

The next day we sailed close by an Island,[1] where we saw many Smoaks, and Men in the Bays; out of which came 2 or 3 Canoas, taking much pains to overtake us, but they could not, though we went with an easy Sail; and I could not now stay for them. As I past by the South-East Point, I sounded several times within a Mile of the Sandy Bays, but had no Ground: About 3 Leagues to the Northward of the South-East Point, we opened a large deep Bay, secur'd from West-North-West and South-West Winds. There were 2 other Islands that lay to the North-East of it, which secur'd the Bay from North-East Winds; One was but small, yet woody; the other was a League long, inhabited and full of Coco-Nut-Trees. I endeavoured to get into this Bay: but there came such Flaws off from the high Land over it, that I could not; Besides, we had many hard Squalls, which deterr'd me from it; and Night coming on, I would not run any hazard, but bore away to the small inhabited Island, to see if we could get Anchoring on the East-side of it. When we came there, we found the Island so narrow, that there could be no Shelter; therefore I tack'd and stood toward the greater Island again: And being more than Mid-way between both, I lay by, designing to endeavour for Anchorage next Morning. Between 7 and 8 at Night, we spied a Canoa close by us; and seeing no more, suffered her to come aboard. She had 3 Men in her, who brought off 5 Coco-Nuts, for which I gave each of them a Knife and a String of Beads, to encourage them to come off again in the Morning: But before these went away, we saw two more Canoas coming; therefore we stood away to the Northward from them, and then lay by again till Day. We saw no more Boats this Night; neither design'd to suffer any to come aboard in the dark.

By nine a-Clock the next Morning, we were got within

[1] Apparently one of the Gardner islands.

AN. 1700 thinking we could run the Ship a-ground any where, as they did their Proes; for we saw neither Sail nor Anchor among any of them, though most Eastern Indians have both. These had Proes made of one Tree, well dug, with Outlagers on one side: They were but small, yet well shap'd. We endeavour'd to anchor, but found no Ground within a Mile of the Shore: We kept close along the North-side, still sounding till we came to the North-East-end, but found no Ground; the Canoas still accompanying us; and the Bays were covered with Men going along as we sailed: Many of them strove to swim off to us, but we left them astern. Being at the North-East Point, we found a strong Current setting to the North-West; so that though we had steer'd to keep under the high Island, yet we were driven towards the flat one. At this time 3 of the Natives came aboard: I gave each of them a Knife, a Looking-Glass, and a String of Beads. I shew'd them Pumpkins and Coco-nut shells, and made Signs to them to bring some aboard, and had presently 3 Coco-nuts out of one of the Canoas. I shew'd them Nut-megs, and by their Signs I guess'd they had some on the Island. I also shew'd them some Gold-Dust, which they seem'd to know, and call'd out *Manneel*, *Manneel*, and pointed towards the Land. A while after these Men were gone, 2 or 3 Canoas came from the flat Island, and by Signs invited us to their Island; at which the others seem'd displeas'd, and us'd very menacing Gestures and (I believe) Speeches to each other. Night coming on, we stood off to Sea; and having but little Wind all Night, were driven away to the North-West. We saw many great Fires on the flat Island. These last Men that came off to us, were all black, as those we had seen before, with frizled Hair: They were very tall, lusty, well-shap'd Men; They wear great things in their Noses, and paint as the others, but not much; They make the same Signs of Friendship, and their Language seems to be one: But the others had Proes, and these Canoas. On the Sides of some of these, we saw the Figures of several Fish neatly cut; and these last were not so shy as the others.

Steering away from Cave's Island South-South-East,

we found a strong Current against us, which set only in AN.
some places in Streams; and in them we saw many Trees 1700
and Logs of Wood, which drove by us. We had but little Wood aboard; wherefore I hoisted out the Pinnace, and sent her to take up some of this Drift-wood. In a little time she came aboard with a great Tree in a tow, which we could hardly hoist in with all our Tackles. We cut up the Tree and split it for Fire-wood. It was much worm-eaten, and had in it some live Worms above an Inch long, and about the bigness of a Goose-quill, and having their Heads crusted over with a thin Shell.

After this we passed by an Island, called by the Dutch St. John's Island, leaving it to the North of us. It is about 9 or 10 Leagues round, and very well adorn'd with lofty Trees. We saw many Plantations on the Sides of the Hills, and Abundance of Coco-nut-Trees about them; as also thick Groves on the Bays by the Sea-side. As we came near it, 3 Canoas came off to us, but would not come aboard. They were such as we had seen about the other Islands: They spoke the same Language, and made the same Signs of Peace; and their Canoas were such, as at Cave's Island.

We stood along by St. John's Island, till we came almost to the South-East-Point; and then seeing no more Islands to the Eastward of us, nor any likelihood of anchoring under this, I steer'd away for the Main of New-Guinea; we being now (as I suppos'd) to the East of it, on this North-side. My Design of seeing these Islands as I past along, was to get Wood and Water, but could find no Anchor-Ground, and therefore could not do as I purpos'd. Besides, these Islands are all so populous, that I dar'd not send my Boat ashore, unless I could have anchor'd pretty nigh. Wherefore I rather chose to prosecute my Design on the Main, the Season of the Year being now at hand; for I judg'd the Westerly Winds were nigh spent.

On the 8th of March, we saw some Smoaks on the Main, being distant from it 4 or 5 Leagues. 'Tis very high, woody Land, with some Spots of Savannah. About 10 in the Morning 6 or 7 Canoas came off to us: Most of them had no more than one Man in them; they were all

AN. 1700 black, with short curl'd Hair; having the same Ornaments in their Noses, and their Heads so shav'd and painted, and speaking the same Words, as the Inhabitants of Cave's Island before-mentioned.

There was a Head-land[1] to the Southward of us, beyond which seeing no Land, I supposed that from thence the Land trends away more Westerly. This Head-land lies in the Latitude of 5 deg. 2 min. South, and Meridian distance from Cape Mabo, 1290 Miles. In the Night we lay by, for fear of over-shooting this Head-land. Between which and Cape St. Maries,[2] the Land is high, Mountainous and Woody; having many Points of Land shooting out into the Sea, which make so many fine Bays. The Coast lies North-North-East and South-South-West.

The 9th in the Morning a huge black Man came off to us in a Canoa, but would not come aboard. He made the same signs of Friendship to us, as the rest we had met with; yet seem'd to differ in his Language, not using any of those Words which the others did. We saw neither Smoaks nor Plantations near this Head-land. We found here Variation 1 deg. East.

In the Afternoon, as we plied near the Shore, 3 Canoas came off to us; one had 4 Men in her, the others 2 apiece. That with the 4 Men, came pretty nigh us, and shew'd us a Coco-Nut and Water in a Bamboo, making Signs that there was enough ashore where they liv'd; they pointed to the place where they would have us go, and so went away. We saw a small round pretty high Island about a League to the North of this Head-land, within which there was a large deep Bay, whither the Canoas went; and we strove to get thither before Night, but could not; wherefore we stood off, and saw Land to the Westward of this Head-Land, bearing West by South half South, distance about 10 Leagues; and, as we thought, still more Land bearing South-West by South, distance 12 or 14 Leagues: But being clouded, it disappeared, and we thought we had been deceived. Before Night we opened the Head-Land fair,

[1] Cape St. George. [2] Cape Santa Maria, farther to the N.

and I named it Cape St. George. The Land from hence trends away West-North-West about 10 Leagues, which is as far as we could see it; and the Land that we saw to the Westward of it in the Evening, which bore West by South half South, was another Point about 10 Leagues from Cape St. George; between which there runs in a deep Bay for 20 Leagues or more. We saw some high Land in Spots like Islands, down in that Bay at a great distance; but whether they are Islands, or the Main closing there, we know not. The next Morning we saw other Land to the South-East of the Westermost Point, which till then was clouded; it was very high Land, and the same that we saw the day before, that disappear'd in a Cloud. This Cape St. George lies in the Latitude of 5 deg. 5 min. South; and Meridian distance from Cape Mabo 1290 Miles. The Island off this Cape, I called St. George's Isle;[1] and the Bay between it and the West-Point, I named St. George's Bay. Note, No Dutch Draughts go so far as this Cape, by 10 Leagues. On the 10th in the Evening, we got within a League of the Westermost Land seen, which is pretty high and very woody, but no Appearance of Anchoring. I stood off again, designing (if possible) to ply to and fro in this Bay, till I found a Conveniency to Wood and Water. We saw no more Plantations, nor Coco-nut-Trees; yet in the Night we discerned a small Fire right against us. The next Morning we saw a Burning Mountain in the Country. It was round, high, and peaked at top (as most Vulcano's are), and sent forth a great Quantity of Smoak. We took up a Log of drift Wood and split it for Firing; in which we found some small Fish.

AN. 1700

The Day after, we past by the South-West Cape of this Bay, leaving it to the North of us: When we were abreast of it, I called my Officers together, and named it Cape Orford,[2] in Honour of my noble Patron; drinking his

[1] Wallis Island. The bay is, of course, St. George's Channel.

[2] Edward Russell, Lord Orford, Admiral of the Fleet (1653-1727), a gentleman "of a sanguine complexion, inclining to fat; of a middle stature." He commanded the British fleet in the operations against the French (under the Comte de Tourville) in May, 1692. He was First Lord of the Admiralty until shortly after Dampier had sailed on this expedition.

AN. 1700 into the Inhabitants, who were very numerous, and (by what I saw now, and had formerly experienc'd), treacherous. After this I sent my Boat to sound; they had first 40, then 30, and at last 20 Fathom Water. We followed the Boat, and came to anchor about a quarter of a Mile from the Shore, in 26 Fathom Water, fine black Sand and Oaze. We rode right against the Mouth of a small River, where I hoped to find fresh Water. Some of the Natives standing on a small Point at the River's Mouth, I sent a small Shot over their Heads to fright them; which it did effectually. In the Afternoon I sent my Boat ashore to the Natives who stood upon the Point by the River's Mouth with a Present of Coco-nuts; when the Boat was come near the Shore, they came running into the Water, and put their Nuts into the Boat. Then I made a Signal for the Boat to come aboard, and sent both it and the Yawl into the River to look for fresh Water, ordering the Pinnace to lye near the River's Mouth, while the Yawl went up to search. In an Hour's time they return'd aboard with some Barrecoes full of fresh Water, which they had taken up about half a Mile up the River. After which, I sent them again with Casks; ordering one of them to fill Water, and the other to watch the Motion of the Natives, lest they should make any Opposition; but they did not, and so the Boats return'd a little before Sun-set with a Tun and half of Water; and the next Day by Noon brought aboard about 6 Tun of Water.

I sent ashore Commodities to purchase Hogs, &c. being informed that the Natives have plenty of them, as also of Yamms and other good Roots; But my Men returned without getting any thing that I sent them for; the Natives being unwilling to trade with us: Yet they admir'd our Hatchets and Axes; but would part with nothing but Coco-nuts; which they us'd to climb the Trees for; and so soon as they gave them our Men, they beckon'd to them to be gone; for they were much afraid of us.

The 18th, I sent both Boats again for Water, and before Noon they had filled all my Casks. In the Afternoon I sent them both to cut Wood; but seeing about

40 Natives standing on the Bay at a small Distance from our Men, I made a Signal for them to come aboard again; which they did, and brought me Word that the Men which we saw on the Bay were passing that way, but were afraid to come nigh them. At 4 a Clock I sent both the Boats again for more Wood, and they return'd in the Evening. Then I called my Officers to consult whether it were convenient to stay here longer, and endeavour a better Acquaintance with these People; or go to Sea. My Design of tarrying here longer, was, if possible, to get some Hogs, Goats, Yamms or other Roots; as also to get some Knowledge of the Country and its Product. My Officers unanimously gave their Opinions for staying longer here. So the next Day I sent both Boats ashore again, to fish and to cut more Wood. While they were ashore about 30 or 40 Men and Women past by them; they were a little afraid of our People at first; but upon their making signs of Friendship, they past by quietly; the Men finely bedeck'd with Feathers of divers Colours about their Heads, and Lances in their Hands; the Women had no Ornament about them, nor any Thing to cover their Nakedness, but a Bunch of small green Boughs, before and behind, stuck under a String which came round their Wastes. They carried large Baskets on their Heads, full of Yamms. And this I have observ'd amongst all the wild Natives I have known, that they make their Women carry the Burdens, while the Men walk before, without any other Load than their Arms and Ornaments. At Noon our Men came aboard with the Wood they had cut, and had catch'd but 6 Fishes at 4 or 5 Hauls of the Sain, though we saw Abundance of Fish leaping in the Bay all the Day long.

AN. 1700

In the Afternoon I sent the Boats ashore for more Wood; and some of our Men went to the Natives Houses, and found they were now more shy than they us'd to be; had taken down all the Coco-nuts from the Trees, and driven away their Hogs. Our People made Signs to them to know what was become of their Hogs, &c. The Natives pointing to some Houses in the Bottom

AN. 1700 Sorts. Many of them were now about the Houses, and none offer'd to resist our Boats landing, but on the contrary were so amicable, that one Man brought 10 or 12 Coco-nuts, left them on the Shore after he had shew'd them to our Men, and went out of Sight. Our People finding nothing but Nets and Images, brought some of them away; which 2 of my Men brought aboard in a small Canoa; and presently after, my Boats came off. I order'd the Boatswain to take care of the Nets, till we came at some place where they might be disposed of for some Refreshment for the Use of all the Company: The Images I took into my own Custody.

In the Afternoon I sent the Canoa to the Place from whence she had been brought; and in her, 2 Axes, 2 Hatchets (one of them helv'd), 6 Knives, 6 Looking-glasses, a large Bunch of Beads, and 4 Glass-bottles. Our Men drew the Canoa ashore, placed the Things to the best Advantage in her, and came off in the Pinnace which I sent to guard them. And now being well stock'd with Wood, and all my Water-casks full, I resolv'd to sail the next Morning. All the Time of our Stay here, we had very fair Weather; only sometimes in the Afternoon we had a Shower of Rain, which lasted not above an Hour at most: Also some Thunder and Lightning, with very little Wind. We had Sea and Land-breezes; the former between the South-South-East, and the latter from North-East to North-West.

This Place I named Port Mountague,[1] in Honour of my noble Patron. It lies in the Latitude of 6 deg. 10 min. South, and Meridian distance from Cape St. George, 151 Miles West. The Country hereabouts is mountainous and woody, full of rich Valleys and pleasant fresh Water-brooks. The Mould in the Valleys is deep and yellowish; that on the Sides of the Hills of a very brown Colour, and not very deep, but rocky underneath; yet excellent planting

[1] The fine bay between Cape Dampier and Roebuck Point, on the S. coast of New Britain (New Pomerania). The noble patron was Charles Montague, Earl of Halifax (1661–1715), sometime Chancellor of the Exchequer.

Land. The Trees in general are neither very streight, thick, nor tall; yet appear green and pleasant enough: Some of them bore Flowers, some Berries, and others big Fruits; but all unknown to any of us. Coco-nut-Trees thrive very well here; as well on the Bays by the Sea-side, as more remote among the Plantations. The Nuts are of an indifferent Size, the Milk and Kernel very thick and pleasant. Here is Ginger, Yamms, and other very good Roots for the Pot, that our Men saw and tasted. What other Fruits or Roots the Country affords, I know not. Here are Hogs and Dogs; other Land-Animals we saw none. The Fowls we saw and knew, were Pidgeons, Parrots, Cockadores and Crows like those in England; a Sort of Birds about the Bigness of a Black-Bird, and smaller Birds many. The Sea and Rivers have Plenty of Fish; we saw Abundance, though we catch'd but few, and these were Cavallies, Yellow-tails and Whip-rays.

AN. 1700

We departed from hence on the 22d of March, and on the 24th in the Evening we saw some high Land bearing North-West half West; to the West of which we could see no Land, though there appeared something like Land bearing West a little Southerly; but not being sure of it, I steered West-North-West all Night, and kept going on with an easy Sail, intending to coast along the Shore at a distance. At 10 a Clock I saw a great Fire bearing North-West by West, blazing up in a Pillar, sometimes very high for 3 or 4 Minutes, then falling quite down for an equal Space of Time; sometimes hardly visible, till it blazed up again. I had laid me down having been indisposed this 3 Days: But upon a Sight of this, my chief Mate called me; I got up and view'd it for about half an Hour, and knew it to be a burning Hill by its Intervals: I charg'd them to look well out, having bright Moon-light. In the Morning I found that the Fire we had seen the Night before, was a burning Island;[1] and steer'd for it. We saw many other Islands, one large high Island, and another smaller,

[1] There is a small active volcano on Ritter Island in Dampier Strait, and this may have been the one described.

AN. 1700 very well inhabited with strong well-limb'd Negroes, whom we found very daring and bold at several Places. As to the Product of it, I know no more than what I have said in my Account of Port Mountague: But it is very probable this Island may afford as many rich Commodities as any in the World; and the Natives may be easily brought to Commerce, though I could not pretend to it under my present Circumstances.

Being near the Island to the Northward of the Vulcano, I sent my Boat to sound, thinking to anchor here; but she return'd and brought me Word that they had no Ground, till they met with a Riff of Coral Rocks about a Mile from the Shore. Then I bore away to the North-side of the Island, where we found no anchoring neither. We saw several People, and some Coco-nut-Trees, but could not send ashore for want of my Pinnace which was out of order. In the Evening I stood off to Sea, to be at such a distance, that I might not be driven by any Current upon the Shoals of this Island, if it should prove calm. We had but little Wind, especially the Beginning of the Night; but in the Morning I found my self so far to the West of the Island, that the Wind being at East-South-East, I could not fetch it; wherefore I kept on to the Southward, and stemm'd with the Body of a high Island about] 11 or 12 Leagues long, lying to the Southward of that which I before designed for. I named this Island Sir George Rook's[1] Island.

We also saw some other Islands to the Westward; which may be better seen in my Draught of these Lands, than here described. But seeing a very small Island[2] lying to the North-West of the long Island which was before us, and not far from it; I steer'd away for that; hoping to find anchoring there: And having but little Wind, I sent my Boat before to sound; which, when we were about 2 Miles distance from the Shore, came on Board and brought me Word that there was good anchoring in 30 or 40

[1] Rook Island. Sir George Rooke (1650–1709) was lieutenant aboard Sir Edward Spragge's flagship, the *Royal Prince*, during Dampier's service aboard her against the Dutch, in 1673. He became one of the Lords of the Admiralty a short time before the *Roebuck* left England.

[2] A little island off Lottin Island.

Fathom Water, a Mile from the Isle, and within a Riff of the Rocks which lay in a half Moon, reaching from the North-part of the Island to the South-East; so at Noon we got in and anchored in 36 Fathom, a Mile from the Isle. AN. 1700

In the Afternoon I sent my Boat ashore to the Island, to see what Convenience there was to haul our Vessel ashore in order to be mended, and whether we could catch any Fish. My Men in the Boat rowed about the Island, but could not land by Reason of the Rocks and a great Surge running in upon the Shore. We found Variation here, 8 deg. 25 min. West.

I design'd to have stay'd among these Islands till I had got my Pinnace refitted; but having no more than one Man who had skill to work upon her, I saw she would be a long Time in Repairing; (which was one great Reason why I could not prosecute my Discoveries further:) And the Easterly Winds being set in, I found I should scarce be able to hold my Ground.

The 31st in the Forenoon we shot in between 2 Islands, lying about 4 Leagues asunder; with Intention to pass between them. The Southermost is a long Island, with a high Hill at each End; this I named Long Island. The Northermost is a round high Island towering up with several Heads or Tops, something resembling a Crown; this I named Crown-Isle, from its Form. Both these Islands appear'd very pleasant, having Spots of green Savannahs mixt among the Wood-land: The Trees appeared very green and flourishing, and some of them looked white and full of Blossoms. We past close by Crown-Isle; saw many Coco-nut-Trees on the Bays and the Sides of the Hills; and one Boat was coming off from the Shore, but return'd again. We saw no Smoaks on either of the Islands, neither did we see any Plantations; and it is probable they are not very well peopled. We saw many Shoals near Crown-Island, and Riffs of Rocks running off from the Points, a Mile or more into the Sea. My Boat was once over-board, with Design to have sent her ashore; but having little Wind, and seeing some Shoals, I hoisted her in again, and stood off out of Danger.

AN. 1700 In the Afternoon, seeing an Island bearing North-West by West, we steer'd away North-West by North, to be to the Northward of it. The next Morning, being about Mid-way from the Islands we left Yesterday, and having this to the Westward of us; the Land of the Main of New Guinea within us to the Southward, appear'd very high. When we came within 4 or 5 Leagues of this Island to the West of us, 4 Boats came off to view us; one came within call, but return'd with the other 3 without speaking to us: So we kept on for the Island; which I named Sir R. Rich's[1] Island. It was pretty high, woody, and mixt with Savannah's like those formerly mentioned. Being to the North of it, we saw an Opening between it and another Island[2] 2 Leagues to the West of it, which before appear'd all in One. The Main seemed to be high Land, trending to the Westward.

On Tuesday the 2d April, about 8 in the Morning, we discovered a high peeked Island[3] to the Westward, which seem'd to smoak at its Top. The next Day we past by the North-side of the Burning Island, and saw a Smoak again at its Top; but the Vent lying on the South-side of the Peek, we could not observe it distinctly, nor see the Fire. We afterwards opened 3 more Islands, and some Land to the Southward, which we could not well tell whether it were Islands or Part of the Main. These Islands are all high, full of fair Trees and Spots of green Savannahs; as well the Burning Isle as the rest; but the Burning Isle was more round and peek'd at Top, very fine Land near the Sea, and for two Thirds up it. We also saw another Isle sending forth a great Smoak at once; but it soon vanished, and we saw it no more. We saw also among these Islands 3 small Vessels with Sails, which the People on Nova Britannia seem wholly ignorant of.

The 11th at Noon, having a very good Observation, I

[1] After Sir Robert Rich, a Lord of the Admiralty. Sir Robert was descended from the family of Rich, earls of Warwick and Holland. The island retains its name.

[2] Probably the SE. extremity of Rich Island. The island is crescent-shaped, with a deep gut forming a harbour on the SE. side.

[3] Dampier Island.

found my self to the Northward of my Reckoning; and thence concluded that we had a Current setting North-West, or rather more Westerly, as the Land lies. From that Time to the next Morning, we had fair clear Weather, and a fine moderate Gale from South-East to East by North: But at Daybreak, the Clouds began to fly, and it lightned very much in the East, South-East, and North-East. At Sun-rising, the Sky look'd very red in the East near the Horizon; and there were many black Clouds both to the South and North of it. About a Quarter of an Hour after the Sun was up, there was a Squall to the Windward of us; when on a sudden one of our Men on the Fore-castle called out that he saw something astern, but could not tell what: I look'd out for it, and immediately saw a Spout beginning to work within a Quarter of a Mile of us, exactly in the Wind. We presently put right before it. It came very swiftly, whirling the Water up in a Pillar about 6 or 7 Yards high. As yet I could not see any pendulous Cloud, from whence it might come; and was in Hopes it would soon lose its Force. In 4 or 5 Minutes Time, it came within a Cable's Length of us, and past away to Leeward: and then I saw a long pale Stream, coming down to the whirling Water. This Stream was about the Bigness of a Rainbow: The upper End seem'd vastly high, not descending from any dark Cloud, and therefore the more strange to me; I never having seen the like before. It past about a Mile to Leeward of us, and then broke. This was but a small Spout, not strong nor lasting: yet I perceived much Wind in it, as it past by us. The Current still continued at North-West a little Westerly, which I allow'd to run a Mile per Hour. AN. 1700

By an Observation the 13th at Noon, I found my self 25 min. to the Northward of my Reckoning; whether occasion'd by bad Steerage, a bad Account, or a Current, I could not determine; but was apt to judge it might be a Complication of all; for I could not think it was wholly the Current, the Land here lying East by South, and West by North, or a little more Northerly and Southerly. We had kept so nigh as to see it, and at farthest had not been

AN. 1700 above 20 Leagues from it, but sometimes much nearer; and it is not probable that any Current should set directly off from a Land. A Tide indeed may; but then the Flood has the same Force to strike in upon the Shore, as the Ebb to strike off from it: But a Current must have set nearly along Shore, either Easterly or Westerly; and if anything Northerly or Southerly, it could be but very little in Comparison of its East or West Course, on a Coast lying as this doth; which yet we did not perceive. If therefore we were deceiv'd by a Current, it is very probable that the Land is here disjoyn'd, and that there is a Passage through to the Southward, and that the Land from King William's Cape to this Place is an Island, separated from New-Guinea by some Streight, as Nova-Britannia is by that which we came through. But this being at best but a probable Conjecture, I shall insist no farther upon it.

The 14th we passed by Scouten's Island and Providence Island, and found still a very strong Current setting to the North-West. On the 17th we saw a high Mountain on the Main, that sent forth great Quantities of Smoak from its Top: This Vulcano we did not see on our Voyage out. In the Afternoon we discovered King William's Island, and crowded all the Sail we could, to get near it before Night; thinking to lye to the Eastward of it till Day, for fear of some Shoals that lye at the West-end of it. Before Night we got within 2 Leagues of it, and having a fine Gale of Wind and a light Moon, I resolv'd to pass through in the Night; which I hop'd to do before 12 a-Clock, if the Gale continued; but when we came within 2 Miles of it, it fell calm; yet afterwards by the Help of the Current, a small Gale, and our Boat, we got through before Day. In the Night we had a very fragrant Smell from the Island. By Morning-light we were got 2 Leagues to the Westward of it; and then were becalm'd all the Morning; and met such whirling Tides, that when we came into them, the Ship turn'd quite round; and though sometimes we had a small Gale of Wind, yet she could not feel the Helm when she came into these Whirlpools: Neither could we get from amongst them, till a brisk Gale sprung up; yet we drove not much any way, but whirl'd round like a Top. And those Whirlpools were not constant in one Place, but drove about strangely; and sometimes we saw among them large Riplings of the Water, like great Over-falls, making a fearful Noise. I sent my Boat to sound, but found no Ground. AN. 1700

The 18th, Cape Mabo bore S. distance 9 Leagues. By which Account it lies in the Latitude of 50 min. South, and Meridian distance from Cape S. George 1243 Miles. S. John's Isle lies 48 Miles to the East of Cape St. George; which being added to the Distance between Cape St. George and Cape Mabo, makes 1291 Meridional Parts; which was the furthest that I was to the East. In my outward bound Voyage I made Meridian distance between Cape Mabo and Cape St. George, 1290 Miles; and now in my Return, but 1243; which is 47 short of my distance going out. This Difference may probably be occasion'd by the strong Western Current which we found in our Return, which I allowed for after I perceiv'd it; and though we did not discern any Current when we went to the Eastward, except when near the Islands; yet it is probable we had one against us, though we did not take Notice of it because of the strong Westerly Winds. King William's Island lies in the Latitude of 21 Min. South, and may be seen distinctly off of Cape Mabo.

In the Evening we past by Cape Mabo; and afterwards steer'd away South-East, half East, keeping along the Shore, which here trends South-easterly. The next Morning seeing a large Opening in the Land, with an Island near the South-side; I stood in, thinking to anchor there. When we were shot in within two Leagues of the Island, the Wind came to the West, which blows right into the Opening. I stood to the North Shore; intending, when I came pretty nigh to send my Boat into the Opening, and sound, before I would adventure in. We found several deep Bays, but no Soundings within 2 Miles of the Shore; therefore I stood off again. Then seeing a Ripling under our Lee, I sent my Boat to sound on it; which return'd in half an Hour, and brought me Word that the Ripling we saw was only a Tide, and that they had no Ground there.

CHAP. V

The A.'s return from the Coast of New-Guinea. A deep Channel. Strange Tides. The Island Ceram described. Strange Fowls. The Islands Bonao, Bouro, Misacombi, Pentare, Laubana, and Potoro. The Passage between Pentare and Laubana. The Island Timor. Babao Bay. The Island Rotte. More Islands than are commonly laid down in the Draughts. Great Currents. Whales. Coast of New-Holland. The Tryal-Rocks. The Coast of Java. Princes Isle. Streights of Sunda. Thwart-the-way Island. Indian Proes, and their Traffick. Passage through the Streight. Arrival at Batavia.

AN. 1700

THE Wind seeming to incline to East, as might be expected according to the Season of the Year; I rather chose to shape my Course as these Winds would best permit, than strive to return the same way we came; which, for many Leagues, must have been against this Monsoon: Though indeed on the other hand, the Dangers in that way, we already knew; but what might be in this, by which we now proposed to return, we could not tell.

We were now in a Channel about 8 or 9 Leagues wide, having a Range of Islands on the North-side, and another on the South-side, and very deep Water between, so that we had no Ground. The 22d of April in the Morning, I sent my Boat ashore to an Island on the North-side, and stood that way with the Ship. They found no Ground till within a Cable's length of the Shore, and then had Coral Rocks; so that they could not catch any Fish, though they saw a great many. They brought aboard a small Canoa, which they found a-drift. They met with no Game ashore, save only one party-colour'd Parrakite. The Land is of an indifferent Height; very Rocky, yet cloathed with

This Fish his fins & Taill is [illegible] Bleu, wth Bleu spots all over ye Body.

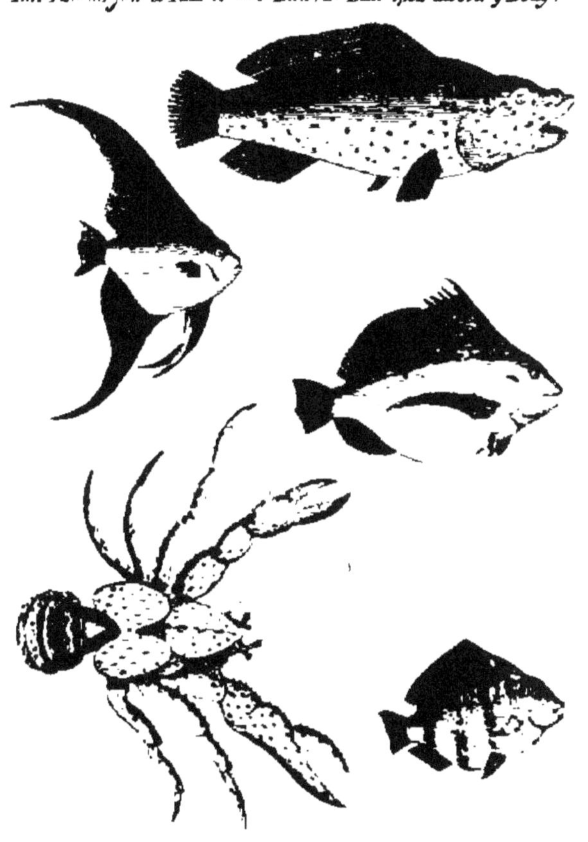

The Mountain
or as some
The Hipp

tall Trees, whose bare Roots run along upon the Rocks. Our People saw a Pond of Salt Water, but found no fresh. Near this Island we met a pretty strong Tide, but found neither Tide nor Current off at some distance.

On the 24th, being about 2 Leagues from an Island to the Southward of us, we came over a Shoal, on which we had but 5 Fathom and a half. We did not discern it, till we saw the Ground under us. In less than half an Hour before, the Boat had been sounding in discoloured Water, but had no Ground. We mann'd the Boat presently, and tow'd the Ship about; and then sounding, had 12, 15 and 17 Fathom, and then no Ground with our Hand-lead. The Shoal was rocky; but in 12 and 15 Fathom we had oozy Ground.

We found here very strange Tides, that ran in Streams, making a great Sea; and roaring so loud, that we could hear them before they came within a Mile of us. The Sea round about them seem'd all broken, and tossed the Ship so that she would not answer her Helm. These Ripplings commonly lasted 10 or 12 minutes, and then the Sea became as still and smooth as a Mill-pond. We sounded often when in the midst of them, and afterwards in the smooth Water; but found no Ground, neither could we perceive that they drove us any way.

We had in one Night several of these Tides, that came most of them from the West; and the Wind being from that Quarter, we commonly heard them a long time before they came; and sometimes lowered our Topsails, thinking it was a Gust of Wind. They were of great length from North to South, but their breadth not exceeding 200 Yards, and they drove a great pace: For though we had little Wind to move us, yet these would soon pass away, and leave the Water very smooth; and just before we encountred them, we met a great Swell, but it did not break.

The 26th we saw the Island Ceram; and still we met with Riplings, but much fainter than those we had the 2 preceeding Days. We sail'd along the Island Ceram, to the Westward, edging in withal, to see if peradventure we might find a Harbour to anchor in, where we might water, trim the Ship, and refresh our Men.

AN. 1700 In the Morning we saw a Sail to the North of us, steering in for the West-end of Ceram, as we likewise were. In the Evening, being near the Shore on the North-side of the Island, I stood off to Sea with an easy Sail; intending to stand in for the Shore in the Morning, and try to find Anchoring, to fill Water, and get a little Fish for refreshment. Accordingly in the Morning early, I stood in with the North-West point of Ceram; leaving a small Island, called Bonao,[1] to the West. The Sail we saw the Day before, was now come pretty nigh us, steering in also (as we did) between Ceram and Bonao. I shortned Sail a little for him; and when he got abreast of us, not above 2 Miles off, I sent my Boat aboard. It was a Dutch Sloop, come from Teranate,[2] and bound for Amboyna:[3] My Men whom I sent in the Boat, bought 5 Bags of new Rice, each containing about 130 pounds, for 6 Spanish Dollars. The Sloop had many rare Parrots aboard for Sale, which did not want price. A Malayan Merchant aboard, told our Men, that about 6 Months ago he was at Bencola,[4] and at that time the Governour either dyed or was kill'd, and that the Commander of an English Ship then in that Road succeeded to that Government.

In the Afternoon, having a Breeze at North and North-North-East, I sent my Boat to sound, and standing after her with the Ship, anchored in 30 Fathom Water oazy Sand, half a Mile from the Shore, right against a small River of fresh Water. The next Morning I sent both the Boats ashore to Fish; they return'd about 10 a-Clock, with a few Mullets and 3 or 4 Cavallies, and some Pan-Fish. We found Variation here, 2 deg. 15 min. East.

When the Sea was smooth by the Land-Winds, we sent our Boats ashore for Water; who, in a few Turns, filled all our Casks.

The Land here is low, swampy and woody; the Mould is a dark Grey, friable Earth. Two Rivers came out

[1] Banoa. [2] Between Celebes and Gilolo.
[3] To the SW. of Ceram.
[4] Benkulen. The governor was Dampier's old enemy, mentioned in the other volumes.

within a Bow-shot of each other, just opposite to the place where we rode: One comes right down out of the Country; and the other from the South, running along by the Shore, not Musquet-shot from the Sea-side. The Northermost River is biggest, and out of it we filled our Water; our Boats went in and out at any time of Tide. In some places the Land is overflown with fresh Water, at full Sea. The Land hereabouts is full of Trees unknown to us, but none of them very large or high; the Woods yield many wild Fruits and Berries, such as I never saw elsewhere. We met with no Land-Animals. The Fowls we found, were Pidgeons, Parrots, Cockadores, and a great number of small Birds unknown to me. One of the Master's Mates killed 2 Fowls as big as Crows; of a black Colour, excepting that the Tails were all white. Their Necks were pretty long, one of which was of a Saffron-colour, the other Black. They had very large Bills, much like a Rams-horn; their Legs were strong and Short, and their claws like a Pidgeon's; their Wings of an ordinary length: Yet they make a great Noise when they fly, which they do very heavily. They feed on Berries, and perch on the highest Trees. Their Flesh is sweet: I saw some of the same Species at New-Guinea, but no where else.

AN. 1700

May the 3d, at 6 in the Morning we weighed, intending to pass between Bonao and Ceram; but presently after we got under Sail, we saw a pretty large Proe coming about the North-West-point of Ceram. Wherefore I stood to the North to speak with her, putting abroad our Ensign. She seeing us coming that way, went into a small Creek, and skulked behind a Point a while: At last discovering her again, I sent my Boat to speak with her; but the Proe row'd away, and would not come nigh it. After this, finding I could not pass between Bonao and Ceram, as I purposed; I steer'd away to the North of it.

This Bonao is a small Island, lying about 4 Leagues from the North-West Point of Ceram. I was inform'd by the Dutch Sloop before-mentioned, that notwithstanding its smallness, it hath one fine River, and that the Dutch are there settled. Whether there be any Natives on it, or

AN. 1700 After Noon, being near the end of the Isle Pentare, which lies West from Misacomby, we saw many Houses and Plantations in the Country, and many Coco-nut-Trees growing by the Sea-side. We also saw several Boats sailing cross a Bay or Channel at the West-end of Misacomby, between it and Pentare. We had but little Wind, and that at North, which blows right in, with a Swell rowling in withal; wherefore I was afraid to venture in, though probably there might be good Anchoring, and a Commerce with the Natives. I continued steering to the West, because the Night before, at Sun-setting, I saw a small round high Island to the West of Pentare, where I expected a good Passage.

We could not that Day reach the West-end of Pentare, but saw a deep Bay to the West of us, where I thought might be a Passage through, between Pentare and Laubana. But as yet the Lands were shut one within an other, that we could not see any Passage. Therefore I ordered to sail 7 Leagues more Westerly, and lye by till next Day. In the Morning we look'd out for an Opening, but could see none; yet by the distance and bearing of a high round Island called Potoro, we were got to the West of the Opening, but not far from it. Wherefore I tack'd and stood to the East; and the rather, because I had reason to suppose this to be the Passage we came through in the *Cygnet* mentioned in my "Voyage round the World"; but I was not yet sure of it, because we had rainy Weather, so that we could not now see the Land so well as we did then. We then accidentally saw the Opening, at our first falling in with the Islands; which now was a Work of some time and difficulty to discover. However before 10 a Clock we saw the Opening plain; and I was the more confirm'd in my Knowledge of this Passage, by a Spit of Sand and 2 Islands at the North-East part of its Entrance. The Wind was at South-South-West, and we plied to get through before Night; for we found a good Tide helping us to the South. About 7 or 8 Leagues to the West of us we saw a high round piked Mountain, from whose Top a Smoak seem'd to ascend as from a Vulcano. There were 3 other very high piked Mountains, 2 on the East, and 1 on the West of that which smoaked. AN. 1700

In our plying to get through between Pentare and Laubana, we had (as I said) a good Tide or Current setting us to the Southward. And it is to be observed, that near the Shores in these Parts we commonly find a Tide setting Northwardly or Southwardly, as the Land lyes; but the Northwardly Tide sets not above 3 Hours in 12, having little strength; and sometimes it only checks the contrary Current, which runs with great Violence, especially in narrow Passes, such as this, between 2 Islands. It was 12 at Night before we got clear of 2 other small Islands, that lay on the South-side of the Passage; and there we had a very violent Tide setting us through against a brisk Gale of Wind. Notwithstanding which, I kept the Pinnace out, for fear we should be becalm'd. For this is the same place, through which I passed in the Year 1687, mentioned in my "Voyage round the World" (pag. 449). Only then we came out between the Western small Island and Laubana, and now we came through between the two small Islands. We sounded frequently, but had no Ground. I said there, that we came through between Omba and Pentare: For we did not then see the Opening between those 2 Islands; which made me take the West-side of Pentare for the West-end of Omba, and Laubana for Pentare. But now we saw the Opening between Omba and Pentare; which was so narrow, that I would not venture through: Besides, I had now discovered my Mistake, and hop'd to meet with the other Passage again, as indeed we did, and found it to be bold from Side to Side, which in the former Voyage I did not know. After we were through, we made the best of our way to Timor; and on May the 18th in the Morning, we saw it plain, and made the high Land over Laphao the Portugueze Factory, as also the high Peak over our first Watering-place, and a small round Island about mid-way between them.

We coasted along the Island Timor, intending to

AN. 1700 West of Timor; But being got so far out to Sea as we were, though there may be a very great Current, yet it does not seem probable to me that it should be of so great Strength as we now found: For both Currents and Tides lose their Force in the open Sea, where they have room to spread; and it is only in narrow Places, or near Headlands, that their Force is chiefly felt. Besides in my Opinion, it should here rather set to the West than South; being open to the narrow Sea, that divides New-Holland from the Range of Islands before-mentioned.

The 27th, we found that in the last 24 Hours we had gone 9 Miles less South than the Log gave; So that 'tis probable we were then out of the Southern Current, which we felt so much before. We saw many Tropick-Birds about us. And found Variation 1 deg. 25 min. West.

On June the 1st, we saw several Whales, the first we had at this Time seen on the Coast: But when we were here before, we saw many; at which Time we were nearer the Shore than now. The Variation now, was 5 deg. 38 min. West.

I design'd to have made New-Holland in about the Latitude of 20 deg. and steer'd Courses by Day to make it, but in the Night could not be so bold; especially since we had sounding. This afternoon I steer'd in South-West, till 6 a-Clock; then it blowing fresh, and Night coming on, I steer'd West-South-West, till we had 40 Fathom; and then stood West, which Course carries along Shore. In the Morning again from 6 to 12 I steer'd West-South-West, to have made the Land, but, not seeing it, I judged we were to the West of it. Here is very good Soundings on this Coast. When we past this way to the Eastward, we had, near this Latitude of 19 deg. 50 min. 38 Fathom, about 18 Leagues from the Land: But, this Time, we saw not the Land. The next Morning I saw a great many Scuttle-Fish-bones, which was a Sign that we were not far from the Land. Also a great many Weeds continually floating by us.

We found the Variation increase considerably as we went Westward. For on the 3d, it was 6 deg. 10 min.

West: on the 4th, 6 deg. 20 min. and on the 6th, 7 deg. 20 min. That Evening we saw some Fowls like Men of War Birds flying North-East, as I was told: for I did not see them, having been indisposed these 3 or 4 Days. AN. 1700

On the 11th we found the Variation 8 deg. 1 min. West; on the 12th, 6 deg. 0 min. I kept on my Course to the Westward till the 15th, and then altered it. My Design was to seek for the Tryal Rocks[1]; but having been sick 5 or 6 Days, without any fresh Provision or other good Nourishment aboard, and seeing no Likelihood of my Recovery, I rather chose to go to some Port in Time, than to beat here any longer; my People being very negligent, when I was not upon Deck my self: I found the Winds variable, so that I might go any way, East, West, North, or South; wherefore, its probable I might have found the said Rocks, had not Sickness prevented me; which Discovery (when ever made) will be of great use to Merchants trading to these Parts.

From hence nothing material happened, till we came upon the Coast of Java. On the 23d we saw Princes-Isle plain, and the Mouth of the Streights of Sunda. By my Computation, the Distance between Timor and Princes-Isle, is 14 deg. 22 min. The next Day in the Afternoon, being abreast of Crockadore[2] Island, I steer'd away East-North-East for an Island that lies near Mid-way between Sumatra and Java, but nearest the Java Shore; which is by English Men called Thwart-the-way. We had but small Winds till about 3 a-Clock, when it freshned, and I was in good Hopes to pass through before Day: But at 9 a Clock the Wind fell, and we got but little. I was then abreast of Thwart-the-way, which is a pretty high long Island; but before 11, the Wind turned, and presently afterward it fell calm. I was then about 2 Leagues from the said Island; and, having a strong Current against us, before Day we were driven astern 4 or 5 Leagues. In the Morning we had the Wind at North-North-West; it look'd black

[1] The Trial Rocks were said to lie in lat. 20° S. and long. (approx.) 124° 34′ E. There was some question of their existence.
[2] Krakatoa.

AN. 1700 and the Wind unsettled: So that I could not expect to get through. I therefore stood toward the Java Shore, and at 10 anchored in 24 Fathom Water, black oazy Ground, 3 Leagues from the Shore. I sounded in the Night when it was calm, and had 54 Fathom, coarse Sand and Coral.

In the Afternoon before, we had seen many Proes; but none came off to us; and in the Night we saw many Fires ashore. This Day a large Proe came aboard of us, and lay by our Side an Hour. There were only 4 Men in her, all Javians, who spoke the Malayan Language. They ask'd if we were English; I answered, we were; and presently one of them came aboard, and presented me with a small Hen, some Eggs and Coco-nuts; for which I gave some Beads and a small Looking-Glass, and some Glass-Bottles. They also gave me some Sugar-Canes, which I distributed to such of my Men as were scorbutick. They told me there were 3 English Ships at Batavia.

The 28th at 2 in the Afternoon we anchored in 26 Fathom Water; presently it fell calm and began to rain very violently, and so continued from 3 till 9 in the Evening. At 1 in the Morning we weigh'd with a fine Land-wind at South-South-East; but presently the Wind coming about at East, we anchored; for we commonly found the Current setting West. If at any Time it turn'd, it was so weak, that it did us little good; and I did not think it safe to venture through without a pretty brisk leading Gale; for the Passage is but narrow, and I knew not what Dangers might be in the way, nor how the Tide sets in the Narrow, having not been this way these 28 Years, and all my People wholly Strangers: We had the Opening fair before us.

While we lay here, 4 Malayan Proes came from the Shore, laden with Coco-nuts, Plantains, Bonanoes, Fowls, Ducks, Tobacco, Sugar, &c. These were very welcome, and we purchased much Refreshment of them. At 10 a-Clock I dismiss'd all the Boats, and weigh'd with the Wind at North-West. At half an Hour past 6 in the Evening, we anchored in 32 Fathom Water in a coarse Sort of Oaze. We were now past the Island Thwart-the-way, but had still one of the small Islands to pass. The Tide begun to run strong to the West; which obliged me to anchor while I had Soundings, for Fear of being driven back again or on some unknown Sand. I lay still all Night. At 5 a Clock the next Morning, the Tide began to slacken: At 6, I weigh'd with the Wind at South-East by East, a handsom Breeze. We just weather'd the Button,[1] and sounding several Times, had still between 30 and 40 Fathom. When we were abreast of the Button, and about 2 Leagues from the Westermost point of Java, we had 34 Fathom, small Peppery Sand. You may either come between this Island and Java, or, if the Wind is Northerly, run out between the Island Thwart-the-way and this last small Island. AN. 1700

The Wind for the most Part being at East and East by South, I was obliged to run over towards the Sumatra Shore, sounding as I went, and had from 34 to 23 Fathom. In the Evening I sounded pretty quick, being got near the Sumatra Shore; and, finding a Current setting to the West, between 8 and 9 a-Clock we anchored in 34 Fathom. The Tide set to the West from 7 in the Evening to 7 this Morning; and then, having a small Gale at West-South-West, I weigh'd and stood over to the Java Shore.

In the Evening having the Wind between East-North-East and South-East by East, we could not keep off the Java Shore. Wherefore I anchored in 27 Fathom Water, about a League and a half off Shore. At the same Time we saw a Ship at anchor near the Shore, about 2 Mile to Leeward of us. We found the Tide setting to the Westward, and presently after we anchored it fell calm. We lay still all Night, and saw many Fires ashore. At 5 the next Morning, being July the 1st, we weigh'd and stood to the North for a Sea-breeze: At 10 the Wind coming out, I tack'd and had a fine brisk Gale. The Ship we saw at anchor, weigh'd also and stood after us. While we past by Pulo Baby,[2] I kept sounding, and had no less than 14 Fathom. The other Ship coming after

[1] The Button lies a few miles beyond Thwart-the-Way Island.
[2] Babie.

AN. 1700 us with all the Sail she could make, I shortned Sail on Purpose that she might overtake us, but she did not. A little after 5, I anchored in 13 Fathom good oazy Ground. About 7 in the Evening, the Ship that followed us, past by close under our Stern; she was a Dutch Fly-boat; they told us they came directly from Holland, and had been in their Passage six Months. It was now dark, and the Dutch Ship anchored within a Mile of us. I order'd to look out sharp in the Morning; that so soon as the Dutch Man began to move, we might be ready to follow him; for I intended to make him my Pilot. In the Morning at half an hour after 5 we weigh'd, the Dutch Man being under Sail before; and we stood directly after him. At 8, having but little Wind, I sent my Boat aboard of him, to see what News he had brought from Europe. Soon after, we spied a Ship coming from the East, plying on a Wind to speak with us, and shewing English Colours. I made a Signal for my Boat, and presently bore away towards her; and being pretty nigh, the Commander and Super-cargoe came aboard, supposing we had been the Tuscany Galley, which was expected then at Batavia. This was a Country Ship, belonging to Fort St. George, having come out from Batavia the Day before, and bound to Bencola. The Commander told me that the *Fleet*-frigat was at Anchor in Batavia Road, but would not stay there long: He told me also, that his Majesty's Ships commanded by Captain Warren were still in India, but he had been a great while from the Coast and had not seen them. He gave me a Draught of these Streights, from the Button and Cap to Batavia, and shew'd me the best way in thither. At 11 a Clock, it being calm, I anchored in 14 Fathom good oazy Ground.

At 2 a Clock we weigh'd again; the Dutch Ship being under Sail before, standing close to Mansheters[1] Island; but finding he could not weather it, he tack'd and stood off a little while, and then tack'd again. In the mean Time I stood pretty nigh the said Island, sounding, but

[1] Menscheneters.

could not weather it. Then I tack'd and stood off, and the Dutch stood in towards the Island; and weathered it. I being desirous to have room enough, stood off longer, and then went about, having the Dutch Ship 4 Points under my Lee. I kept after him; but as I came nearer the Island, I found a Tide setting to the West, so that I could not weather it. Wherefore at 6 in the Evening I anchored in 7 Fathom oazy Ground, about a Mile from the Island: The Dutch Ship went about 2 Miles further, and anchored also; and we both lay still all Night. At 5 the next Morning we weigh'd again, and the Dutch Ship stood away between the Island Cambusses[1] and the Main; but I could not follow, because we had a Land-wind. Wherefore I went without the Cambusses, and by Noon we saw the Ships that lay at the careening Island near Batavia. After the Land-wind was spent, which we had at South-East and South-South-East; the Sea-breeze came up at East. Then we went about; and the Wind coming afterward at East-North-East, we had a large Wind to run us into Batavia Road: And at 4 in the Afternoon, we anchored in 6 Fathom soft Oaze.

AN. 1700

[1] Kombuys.

CHAP. VI

The A. continues in Batavia-Road, to refit, and to get Provisions. English Ships then in the Road. Departure from Batavia. Touch at the Cape of Good Hope. And at St. Helena. Arrival at the Island of Ascension. A Leak Sprung. Which being impossible to be stopped; the Ship is lost, but the Men saved. They find Water upon the Island. And are brought back to England.

AN. 1700 WE found in Batavia Road a great many Ships at anchor, most Dutch, and but one English Ship named the *Fleet*-frigat, commanded by one Merry. We rode a little without them all. Near the Shore lay a stout China Junk, and a great many small Vessels, viz. Brigantines, Sloops and Malayan Proes in abundance. As soon as I anchored, I sent my Boat aboard the *Fleet*-frigat, with orders to make them strike their Pendant, which was done soon after the Boat went aboard. Then my Clerk, whom I sent in the Boat, went for the Shore, as I had directed him; to see if the Government would answer my Salute: But it was now near Night, and he had only time to speak with the Shipbander, who told him that the Government would have answered my Salute with the same number of Guns, if I had fired as soon as I anchored; but that now it was too late. In the Evening my Boat came aboard, and the next Morning I my self went ashore, visited the Dutch General, and desir'd the Priviledge of buying such Provision and Stores, as I now wanted; which he granted me.

I lay here till the 17th of October following, all which time we had very fair Weather, some Tornadoes excepted. In the mean time I supplied the Carpenter with such Stores as were necessary for refitting the Ship; which prov'd more leaky after he had caulk'd Her, then she was before: So that I was obliged to careen her, for which purpose [illegible] Vessels to take in our Guns, Ballast, Provision and [illegible].

The English Ships that arriv'd here from England were first the *Liampo*, commanded by Captain [illegible], bound for China; next, the *Panther*, commanded by Captain Robinson; then the *Mancel-Frigat*, commanded by Captain Clerk. All these brought great Things from England. Most of them had been unfortunate in their Officers; especially Captain Robinson, who said that some of them had been conspiring to run him and his [illegible]. There came in also several English Country Vessels; first a Sloop from Ben-jarr; commanded by the [illegible]: next, the *Monsoon*, belonging to Bengale [illegible] had been at Malacca at the same time that his Majesty's Ship the *Harwich* was there: Afterwards came in also another small Ship from Bengale.

While we stay'd here, all the forenamed English Ships sailed hence; the 2 Bengale Ships excepted. Many Dutch Ships also came in here, and departed again before us. We had several Reports concerning the Men of [illegible] India, and much talk concerning [illegible] who had committed several Spoils upon the Coast, and in the Streights of Malacca. I did not hear of any Ships sent out [illegible] them. At my first coming in, I was told that 2 Ships had been sent from Amboyna in quest of me: which was after confirm'd by one of the Skippers, whom I [illegible] with here. He told me they had [illegible] against me; that they came to Pulo-Sabuda on the Coast of New-Guinea 28 Days after my departure thence, and went as far as Scouten's Island, and hearing no further News of me returned. Something likewise [illegible] Commander of the *Fleet-frigat* [illegible] here; and that the General at Batavia had a Copy of my Commission and Instructions; but I [illegible] a very improbable thing.

While we lay here, the Dutch had several Consultations about sending some Ships for Europe sooner than ordinary: At last the 16th of October was agreed upon for the Day of Sailing, which is 2 Months sooner than

AN. 1700 usual. They lay ready 2 or 3 Days before, and went out on the 10th. Their Names were, the *Ostresteen*, bound to Zealand; the *Vanheusen*, for Enchiehoust;[1] and the 3 *Crowns*, for Amsterdam, commanded by Skipper Jacob Uncright, who was Commadore over all the rest. I had by this time finished my Business here; viz. fitted the Ship, recruited my self with Provision, filled all my Water; and the time of the Year to be going for Europe being now at hand, I prepar'd to be gone also.

Accordingly on the 17th of October, at half an Hour after 6 in the Morning, I weigh'd Anchor from Batavia, having a good Land-wind at South, and fair Weather: And by the 19th at Noon, came up with the 3 Dutch Ships before-mentioned. The 29th of November in the Morning we saw a small Hawk flying about the Ship till she was quite tired. Then she rested on the Mizen-Top-Sail-Yard, where we catch'd her. It is probable she was blown off from Madagascar by the violent Northerly Winds; that being the nighest Land to us, though distance near 150 Leagues.

The 30th of December, we arrived at the Cape of Good Hope; and departed again on the 11th of January, 1701. About the end of the Month, we saw abundance of Weeds or Blubber swim by us, for I cannot determine which. It was all of one Shape and Colour. As they floated on the Water, they seem'd to be of the breadth of the Palm of a Man's Hand, spread out round into many Branches about the Bigness of a Man's Finger. They had in the middle a little Knob, no bigger than the Top of a Mans Thumb. They were of a Smoak-colour; and the Branches, by their pliantness in the Water, seem'd to be more simple than Gellies, I have not seen the like before.

The 2d of February, we anchored in St. Helena Road, and set sail again from thence on the 13th.

On the 21st we made the Island of Ascension, and stood in towards it. The 22d between 8 and 9 a-Clock, we

[1] Enkhuizen.

sprung a Leak, which increased so that the Chain-pump[1] [illegible] could not keep the Ship free. Whereupon I set the Hand-pump to work also, and by 10 a-Clock suck'd her: Then wore the Ship, and stood to the Southward, to try if that would ease her: and then the Chain-pump just kept her free. At 5 the next Morning we made Sail and stood in for the Bay; and at 9 anchored in 10 and a half Fathom, sandy Ground. The South-point bore South-South-West, distance 2 Miles, and the North-point of the Bay, North-East half North, distance 2 Miles. As soon as we anchored, I ordered the Gunner to clear his Powder-room, that we might there search for the Leak, and endeavour to stop it within board if possible; for we could not heel the Ship so low, it being within 4 Streaks of the Keel; neither was there any convenient place to haul her ashore. I ordered the Boatswain to assist the Gunner; and by [illegible] a-Clock the Powder-room was clear. The Carpenter's Mate, Gunner, and Boatswain went down: and soon after I followed them my self, and ask'd them whether they could come at the Leak: They said they believed they might, by cutting the Cieling;[2] I told the Carpenter's Mate (who was the only Person in the Ship that understood any Thing of Carpenters-work,) that if he thought he could come at the Leak by cutting the Cieling [illegible] weakening the Ship, he might do it; for he had [illegible] one Leak so before; which though not so big as [illegible] having seen them both, I thought he might as [illegible] as the other. Wherefore I left him to [illegible] The Ceiling being cut, they could not come at the Leak; for [illegible] was against one of the Foot-hook-Timbers,[3] [illegible] Carpenter's Mate said he must first cut [illegible]

[1] The chain-pump. "This is [illegible] a sufficient number of valves, a[illegible] through a wooden tube and re[illegible] other side. It is managed by a [illegible] be employed at once. The hand-pump was [illegible] hardly more powerful. The [illegible] the water in the well, and drew up a [illegible]

[2] The inside planks, or inner [illegible]

[3] Foot-hook, or futtock, timbers are [illegible] floor and the top-timbers of a [illegible]

AN. 1701 In the Afternoon, with the Help of a Sea-breeze, I ran into 7 Fathom, and anchored; then carried a small Anchor ashore, and warp'd in till I came into 3 Fathom and a half. Where having fastned her, I made a Raft to carry the Men's Chests and Bedding ashore; and, before 8 at Night, most of them, were ashore. In the Morning I ordered the Sails to be unbent, to make Tents; and then my self and Officers went ashore. I had sent ashore a Puncheon, and a 36 Gallon Cask of Water, with one Bag of Rice for our common use: But great Part of it was stolen away, before I came ashore; and many of my Books and Papers lost.

On the 26th following, we, to our great Comfort, found a Spring of fresh Water, about 8 Miles from our Tents, beyond a very high Mountain, which we must pass over: So that now we were, by God's Providence, in a Condition of subsisting some Time; having Plenty of very good Turtle by our Tents, and Water for the fetching. The next Day I went up to see the Watering-place, accompanied with most of my Officers. We lay by the way all Night, and next Morning early got thither; where we found a very fine Spring on the South-East-side of the high Mountain, about half a Mile from its Top: But the continual Fogs make it so cold here, that it is very unwholsome living by the Water. Near this Place, are Abundance of Goats and Land-crabs. About 2 Mile South-East from the Spring, we found 3 or 4 shrubby Trees, upon one of which was cut an Anchor and Cable, and the Year 1642. About half a Furlong from these, we found a convenient Place for sheltering Men in any Weather. Hither many of our Men resorted; the hollow Rocks affording convenient Lodging; the Goats, Land-crabs, Men of War Birds, and Boobies, good Food; and the Air was here exceeding wholsome.

About a Week after our coming ashore, our Men that liv'd at this new Habitation, saw 2 Ships making towards the Island. Before Night they brought me the News; and I ordered them to turn about a Score of Turtle, to be in Readiness for these Ships if they should touch here: But before Morning they were out of Sight, and the Turtle were releas'd again. Here we continued without seeing any other Ship till the second of April; when we saw 11 Sail to Windward of the Island: But they likewise past by. The Day after appear'd 4 Sail, which came to anchor in this Bay. They were his Majesty's Ships the *Anglesey*, *Hastings* and *Lizard;* and the *Canterbury* East-India Ship. I went on board the *Anglesey* with about 35 of my Men; and the rest were dispos'd of into the other 2 Men of War. AN. 1701

We sail'd from Ascension, the 8th; and continued aboard till the 8th of May: At which Time the Men of War having miss'd St. Jago, where they design'd to Water, bore away for Barbadoes: But I being desirous to get to England as soon as possible, took my Passage in the Ship *Canterbury*, accompanied with my Master, Purser, Gunner, and 3 of my superiour Officers.

CAPTAIN DAMPIER'S VOYAGES

Kinsale, 6th of August 1703.—Arrived *Cinque Ports*, galley of London, Bur. 120[ts] Charles Peckering Comander, goes in Company with Capt. W[m.] Dampier to the South Seas.

WILLIAM FUNNELL'S CHIMERICAL RELATIONS

Page 2, line 13.—But whilst we were in the *Downs*, there arising some difference between the two Captains, Captain *Pulling* in his Ship the *Fame* went away and left us; intending, as he said, to go and cruize among the *Canary Islands*; and we never saw him after.

P. 2, l. 27.—Our Proposals were to go into the River of Plate, to Buenos Ayres, to take two or three Spanish galleons which Captain Dampier gives an account are usually there: And if by that Expedition we got to the value of 600,000 Pounds then to return again without proceeding further: But if we missed of Success there, then to cruize upon the Coast of Peru, for the *Valdivia* Ships, which commonly are said to bring down store of Gold to *Lima*: But if that Design should also fail, then to attempt some rich Towns, according as Captain *Dampier* should think fit.

P. 6, l. 1.—At this place (Porto Praya) we watered our Ship and refreshed ourselves; and here being some Disagreement between our Captain and first Lieutenant, our Captain turned him ashore with his Chest and Cloaths and Servant, much against both their Wills, about twelve at Night.

P. 11, l. 32.—(Isla Grande). Here our first Lieutenant (Barnaby) (with eight of our Men) our Captain and they falling out, went ashoar with their goods and left us.

P. 13, l. 12.—Betimes in the Morning we saw the Islands of Sibbil de Wards, which are three in Number, lying in the Latitude of 51 d. 35 m. S. Longitude W. from *London*, by my account 51 d. 37 m. . . . Captain *Dampier* in his *Voyage round the World*, computes the Longitude of these Islands West from the Lizard to be 57 d. 28 m. The occasion of which difference I suppose to be his having made longer Runs in that Voyage, and so more liable to mistakes of this Nature.

P. 25, l. 16. At Sun-rise the next Morning being March the 1st, we began to engage the said Ship. . . . We fought her very close, broadside and broadside, for seven Hours; and then a small gale springing up, she shear'd off. As for our Consort, he fired about ten or twelve guns, and then fell a Stern, and never came up again during the Fight. We had nine of our Men killed in the Fight, and several wounded. We were desirous to have the other Tryal with him knowing it would be of dangerous consequence to let him go; for if we did, we were sure he would discover us to the *Spaniards*, which would be of ill consequence to our whole Proceedings: But our Captain was against it, saying, that at the worst, if the Spaniards should know of our being in those Seas, and so should hinder their Merchant-Ships from coming out, yet that he knew where to go and could not fail of taking to the value of £500,000 any Day in the Year. Upon this we lay by for our Consort, who soon came up: And it was quickly agreed between the two Captains to let her go. So the Enemy stood from us, I suppose very well satisfied that he had disappointed us both.

P. 30, l. 29.—We . . . soon descryed two Sail. We presently made a clear Ship, and gave chase, and soon came up with the stern-most; she proved to be the ship we fought with off the Island Juan Fernandos. . . . We were very eager to stop her, . . for if we could, it would hinder the *Spaniards* from having Intelligence of us. Besides, we did not question the taking of her, because now our Men were all in Health, whereas when we fought her before, we had between twenty and thirty Men very sick and weak; but being willing to show themselves, they had done what good they could. We knew also, if we took her, that she must needs prove a good Prize: And her Guns, Ammunition, and Provisions, would have been very welcome to us. So we concluded to engage her ourselves, and to send Captain Stradling after the other, which seemed not so big. But our Captain thought it not advisable to venture upon her: And whilst the matter was disputing the two Ships got into *Lima*.

P. 31, l. 32.—We saw a Sail . . . and took her. We kept her with us till March the 30th, and then having taken out a little of every thing, our Captain discharged her, alledging that, if we kept her, it would be a hindrance to his greater Designs. We were forced to be as well content as we could.

P. 33, l. 3.—On the 4th of *April* this Second Prize, after we had taken out a few odd Things, was, contrary to most of our Minds dismist; the Captain alledging, that he would not cumber up the Ship.

P. 41.—By Daylight the next Morning, as we lay at anchor, the Tide of Ebb not being done, a Canoa with five *Indians* came within call of us. They haled us and asked from whence we came. Our Indian Pilot, by the Captains Directions, made answer that we came from *Panama*. He bid them come on board, but they answered they would not: So our Captain ordered them to be fired at, which accordingly was done . . . . This was of ill consequence; for we were sure they would discover us to the Spaniards.

P. 44, l. 19.—The next Day . . . April 30th, Captain Dampier and Captain Stradling, with three Launches and the Canoa, with 87 of our men, proceeded for *Santa Maria*: . . . About Twelve this Night they returned on board, frustrated of their Design. Our men gave us an account, that they were up within a Quarter of a Mile of the Town: that they were assaulted by three Ambuscades [P. 45, l. 4], and w[d] willingly have put ashoar, but Captain Dampier advised, that since the Spaniards knew of our coming . . . it c[ld] not be doubted but they had made the best of their time . . . so it was resolved to return to Schuchadero.

P. 45, l. 25.—So scant of provisions orders given to boil 5 green Plantains for every six Men. To our great comfort, when we were almost at our Wits end, we descried a Sail who came to an Anchor close by us [P. 45, l. 25], . . . we took her without any resistance. A great ship, of about 550 Tuns, deeply laden with Flower, Sugar, Brandy, etc., etc., . . . so now we might supply ourselves with Provisions for four or five years.

P. 46, l. 25.—On the 18th a small Bark . . . coming in sight . . .

we took her. She had little in her, only a small quantity of money. This Bark Capt. Stradling kept for his own use.

P. 46, l. 31.—Here (near to the Island Tabago, in the Bay of Panama) our Captain and Captain Stradling having some disagreement, concluded to part company: [P. 47, l. 1] which accordingly they did: and the men of each Ship had their liberty to go in which Ship they thought convenient. So five of our men went to Capt. Stradling, and five of his came to us. We were told by the Prisoners, that there were 80,000 Dollars on board the Prize; that they were taken in by stealth at Lima [P. 47, l. 8], and lay at the bottom in the Run of the Ship. Our Captain did not believe this; and was unwilling to tarry longer, . . . because he thought loss of time would spoil his greater Designs.

P. 55, l. 3.—We saw a sail, . . . she proved to be a *Spanish* Man of War which was fitted out on purpose to take us. They gave us a broad-side, but we did not mind them; all our care was to get the weather-gage. In order to which, while we carried too much Sail, and the Wind blew very fresh, our fore-top Mast unfortunately came by the board. Immediately we got our Hatchets and cut all clear away, and our Captain ordered the Helm to be clapt a Weather and bore away. The Enemy . . . bore away after us with all the sail they could; . . . and doubted not but they sh[ld] take us. We . . . resolved thereupon to lie by, and fight it out. Captain Dampier's *Opinion* was, that we could sail better upon one mast than the Enemy; [P. 56] and therefore that it was best to put before the Wind. But, however, we being embayed, chose rather to fight, than to be chased ashoar. So . . . we began the fight. [L. 1].—We fired about 560 Guns, and he (Enemy) about 110 or 115. . . . At half an hour past six, it growing duskish, they left off firing, and we did the same.

P. 58, l. 13.—We anchored at *Tacames* and sent our Boat ashoar . . . hoping to get Provisions; but the Inhabitants having notice of an Enemy's being in those Seas, as soon as they saw us, drove the Cattle from the Water-side up into the Country. So our Men went into the Village, which consisted of about fifty *Indian* Houses. Here in the River we found a Bark . . . with new Plank enough by her, to build another. And we took another small Bark . . . laden with Plantains.

P. 68, l. 25.—Sep[t.] the 2nd. Our Captain and Mr. *Clippinton* the chief mate falling out; Mr. *Clippinton*, with 21 of our Men, seized upon the Bark, in which was all our Ammunition, and a great part of our Provisions; and got up her anchor, and went without the Islands. From thence he sent us word, that if any of us had a mind to go with him, we should be welcome; but however, that we might not be quite destitute, he w[ld] restore us all our Powder, Shot and Ammunition; reserving only two or three Barrels for his own use: and according to his promise he put on shore our Powder, Shot, and other Ammunition . . . and sent us word of his so doing. And we went with our Canoas and fecht it aboard.

P. 83, l. 20.—In the Morning, we saw a Sail and soon came up with her. She proved to be the *Manila*-ship. So we, being all provided, gave her several broad-sides, before she could get any of her Guns clear.

P. 84, l. 7.—Time being delayed in quarrelling, between those of us that would lay her aboard, and those that w[ld] not, the Enemy got out a tire of Guns, and then were too hard for us; so that we could not lie along her side, to do her any considerable damage. . . . So being much damaged . . . the Signal was made to stand off from the Enemy.

P. 86.—On the 6th it was concluded between Capt. *Dampier* and 30 of our Men, to continue in the South-Seas; but upon what Terms this Agreement was made, was kept secret. We who were resolved to go for India, used our endeavours to get into the Gulf of *Amapalla* (which was the place we designed to water at) with all the haste we could. Where we anchored on the 26th of January 1704. And the same day: the Provisions being equally parted according to the directions of the Owners Agent; and four great Guns, with some Small Arms, Powder and Shot, etc., being taken out for us; we (that is, 33 of us who resolved to go in the Bark for India) went on shore in order to water our Vessel for the said Voyage.

CAPTAIN DAMPIER'S VINDICATION OF HIS VOYAGE TO THE SOUTH SEAS IN THE SHIP "ST. GEORGE"

With some small Observations for the Present on Mr. Funnel's Chimerical Relation Of the Voyage Round the World; and Detected in Little, until he shall be Examin'd more at Large.

In the first place, he calls himself my Mate; He went out my Steward, and afterwards I did make a Midshipman of him: Indeed he had the Advantage of perusing Draughts and Books, of which he afterwards gave but a slender Account, for some he pretended were lost, and others the Draughts are torn out of them; Especially the Draughts of Winds, which I greatly suspect him of Doing, because he is not the first Man that has Endeavour'd to build upon another Man's Foundation.

2. In pag. 2, lin. 4, he says, that Capt. *Pullen* was going in Company with us; but while we lay at Anchor in the *Downs*, there arose a Difference between us two Captains, on which *Pullen* went away.

I wonder at his Impudence, for I was at London, when Capt. PULLEN *went away; and 'tis well known 'twas the Owner's, His, and Mine could not agree; to whom I Appeal.*

3. In p. 2, l. 27. Our Proposals, says he, were to go into the River of Plate and to Buenos Ayres to take 2 or 3 Spanish galleons which Capt. Dampier gives an Account of (I say Capt. Dampier, as he does, because I was a Foreign Gentleman that was not to return home) are usually there. I desire to know of this gentleman, when it was that I gave this Account, and to whom; I must confess there was some Discourse about it; but I never design'd to go to Buenos Ayres, for them, being such a Dangerous River to go Up: And I think Capt. Pullen talk'd something like this, and so Mr. Funnel from thence may conclude what he pleases. But in p. 3 He gives Reasons of his own; why we did not go to Buenos Ayres Indeed he has a very Productive Brain to produce Reasons!

Where Mr. Funnell says Capt. Dampier and Lieut. Huxford Disagreed

There was no such thing; for it was Mr. Morgan, Purser and Ayres, that disagreed with Lieut. Huxford, went ashore, and Fought; upon which a Portugueze, a sort of Corrigidor, Confin'd Mr. Huxford; and a day or two afterwards, he himself sent for his Chest and Cloaths, which were deliver'd. But the Day before I sail'd I sent for him Aboard, and his Chest and Cloaths actually came, so that I had no manner of Aversion to him; but Mr. Morgan swore, if Mr. Huxford sailed with us, he would not go the Voyage. And where ill Blood is, this ordinarily happens; upon which I ordered him to go on Board Capt. Pickering, whose Boat was on Board along our Side, and Lieut. Stradling in it. This will shew (until I could Reconcile these Two after a Gentleman-like manner) I did the best I could, but it happen'd otherwise, for instead of carrying him to the *Cinque-ports*, He and Huxford disagreeing when they were going from me, he set him on Board a Portuguese Merchant-Man.

4. In relation to James Barnaby, second Lieut., He says, that (upon a) Disagreement with him, the Lieut. (meaning *Barnaby*) and eight of the Men went on shore and left us, taking their Chests and Cloaths with them.

To the Contrary of this I answer: I take God to witness I never disagreed with him; but finding him a little Pert in Opinion on a Dispute between him and Mr. Morgan, I ordered him out of the Cabbin. Some little time after this, as we Rode at the Isle of Grandee, he goes on board the *Cinque Port*, sent for his Things, but I refus'd them; whereupon he comes on board after a Refractory manner, Charges me with a Promise; and he, and eight of the Men, being rather Assisted than hinder'd by the Crew (as Mr. Funnell knows) Mutiny'd, to begin their Roguery; they took my Boat and went away per Force, on a Design to board a Portugueze Bark that was lying on the other shore, nearer the Main, but that Bark and Crew was aware of them. Upon which to acquit my self Fairly to all Nations, I sent Letters to the Governor of Rio de Janeiro, to acquaint him with the Knavish Part of their Intent, and that they might have Sculk'd and Prosecuted something like the former Design; This Mr. Morgan can Testify.

In p. 13, Mr. Funnell, to settle my Mistakes, says he saw the Cibald d' Wards (Falkland Islands). But every body knows it is a greater mistake to be Positive in seeing that he never saw: For none but Mr. Morgan and my Self could know the Contrary.

In p. 14, towards the latter End, he says we saw a Land, January 11th, contrary to all Expectations.

This is a Merry way of his; for it is well known the Evening before, I told them we should see Land the next Morning, that of Terra del Fuego, the South Part of it: Now I look upon that to be a greater Mistake, to take one side of the Land for the other, than 'tis to be mistaken that we were Westward of the whole Island, and miss his Longitude, for that comes of course.

Tho' there may be more Mistakes that we pass over to abreviate this Matter, as yet, my crew not being wholly here, I mention only the two Actions of the Voyage, on which depend the Miscarriage of the whole, by the Mens Disorder.

The first of which is the French ship that we Engag'd that was coming to the Island of Juan Fernando's, to whom we gave Chace from 3 in the Afternoon, and fetch'd upon her so fast, that making of her to

Hull, I found she was an European Ship and not a Spaniard, upon which, I was not willing to pursue her any further, but the men being (as they Pretended) in a Desire of Engagement, Right or Wrong, I follow'd her, And next Morning early, we came up with her, and when I saw nothing would disengage them from an Insignificant Attempt, I encourag'd them all I could. By this time my Consort had given her a Broad side, so I ranged up her other side, and gave her a Broad-side likewise. Now to shew the Confusion they were then in, they Fir'd upon our own Consort in his falling a Stern, and Hinder'd his Help. Notwithstanding this I came up again, and Exchang'd 3 or 4 Broadsides with her, wherein Ten of my Men suffer'd, 9 kill'd and 1 wounded; which Dismay'd my Men so much, they actually run down off the Deck, and made nothing of it afterwards, so that when I could have boarded her and carried her, the Mate, Cleppington by Name, cry'd The Men are all gone; and Bellhash the Master, whose Office it was to be always upon Deck, was gone also; tho' this Gentleman is now a Valiant Talker, to my Detriment.

In p. 25, 26, Mr. Funnell says the Crew were Desirous to Fight this Ship again. Now since they made nothing of it while in my Power; What was to be done afterwards? And as to my telling them (as he says) I could get at any time £500,000, I say, so I, kept my Boats which were then lost, or would my People have been Rul'd.

In p. 32 Mr. Funnell says we took a ship of 200 Tuns, loaden with several good Commodities, as Indigo, Cochineal, &c.

Now for Cochineal, I never heard of any. Indigo there was: but the other, and the Turtleshel, he so frequently speaks of, may be gone the same way that many Rich and Valuable Goods have, by the Management of those Pyrating Fellows, rather than Sailors, the Indigo I could not take on Board; nor could I trust any of them with the Sailing such a ship, as could neither keep me Company, nor make a right Steerage-way.

In p. 33 He says truth as to Mr. Observator's Ship and the Monkey that was left in her; but as to Firing at anything but the Ship, and the whole Crew, who before we could make up to her, had made into their Boats, and nothing besides the Cargo and the Monkey were indeed on Board, which shou'd have been brought along, had we not Observators enough at Home.

The next thing they Charge me with, especially Mr. Funnell in p. 41 in the Gulph of St. Michael, says, when we were in the Barque last taken, an Indian Canoe Haled us, and that I order'd her to be Fir'd upon. The Contrary is very plain, for when I saw some of them that had Fir'd without my Orders, I was very Uneasy and Troubled at it, knowing the Consequence of it.

The Second Thing that's Matterial is, that the Ship mentioned by Mr. Funnell in p. 45, 46, where he seems to Explain $80,000 was Hid in the Run of the Ship, and I slipt the Opportunity of taking it, and turning her Adrift; So this I answer, That I had evident Proof she had Landed her Money at Truxillo; and as to Provisions, we took as much as would provide us for One Year, and much longer, if well manag'd, that was, what our Ship could well Stow, and this was the Steward and the Crew's Calculation.

Now as to a Report that they make about Town $50,000 that shou'd be offer'd for her Ransom: First I had no convenient Road to Ride in, and the strong Southerly Winds were set in, and so if I had Loyter'd for her must certainly been Imbay'd for 3 or 4 Months: Besides the Winds, thro' the Treachery of the Spaniards, I have had the Experience of it before in a like Case, Riding there for Ransom with Capt. Swan and Capt. Davis, for instead of keeping their Faith, they came off with a Fire-Ship in the Night and 14 Periagoes; and tho' we had much better Crews and Stouter men, we came narrowly off.

Now, that they are Judges in my Case and Conduct, a Parcel of Fellows who were Perpetually drunk. And very fit, you'll say, for Guarding a Ship in the Night, or being kept in any Decorum.

Again in p. 46, 47. Whereas Mr. Funnell frequently would insinuate, that I could agree with nobody; and so says that I parted this way with Capt. Stradling. I say, I Deputed Capt. Stradling; nay not only that, but at Juan de Fernando's, when all his Men left him, I reconcil'd them and him again: therefore I might expect a Reasonable Command; but never entered into a Dispute. I lent him a spare Top-Mast, his Ship's Crew being sickly, he had always my Chirurgeon, and the Mate he carried away a last, and any Kindness I could do him, I did in Heartily for the Good of his Voyage.

In p. 55, he says we met a Spanish Man of War, and after our usual manner, we got to Leeward of Her thro' their Miscarriage; and after a Broad-side or two were Given and Taken, I endeavouring to make more Sail, flung out my Flying Gib. They who were alway Doing something they should not; and did not think me worthy their Council, had sprung my Fore-Top Mast in the Night, so it immediately came by the Board. By this I was utterly deprived of means to get a windward, or anything else, I lying wholly at her Mercy: that Fighting her this way was inconsistent with Reason.

And whereas he says we Fir'd 560 Guns at her—I do verily believe not 60 ever Hit her: now to what purpose they Convict themselves, I know not. For I was forced to Command 'em to forbear Firing.

P. 58.—In our going to Tacames, he Talks of Provision, and seems to call my judgement in question about getting it, and that the People drove away the Cattle. There may be wild Hogs and Plantanes there, but nothing else, so that I suppose this is to Redicule my Great Designs. Not but that there might be 2 or 3 Cows. He makes 3 Indian Houses 50, and there they did bring off a little Boat, and told me there was a great deal of Plank ashore.

The next Morning I sent the Master, Bellhash, who is a very valiant Man now, with 20 or 30 Men and Fire-Arms with them. They were so far from bringing Plank, that upon one Shot fir'd at 'em, they all came Running Aboard frighted, lost 2 or 3 Pieces; And these are the Mighty Bravoes that are fit to set People by the Ears at Home, and make Scandal as Rife with me as 'tis with them.

What's observable, is, it is not enough to Run away with the Owner's Goods, and do what you please with Bales of Silk, small Arms, or any other Stores; and under Pretence of Shares, take away the Owner's Part, and do what else they please: offer to kill the Captain or any other Villany. This Mr. Funnell calls Falling out with the Captain; This is his frequent Dialect.

But as to Mr. Cleppington, that he mentions in p. 68, where he says he sent us word. On the contrary, he seized my Barque, therein was two quarter Deck Guns, two Pattereroes, with all my Powder and Shot. For here you may observe, that we were upon the Careen in the Gulph of Nicoya; all my Great Guns, except four, were ashore, and those 4 in my Hole: my small Arms wet, so that I had nothing to command him back.

I can't forget to tell the World these Fellows in their common Practice, Bellhash, Cleppington, and the rest, whenever they were upon Command, stript the Prisoners, Indians or Spaniards; whereas let them convict me of anything more than the most Compassionate Christian Usage to all Ranks of Men, and this I thought was the best way of Performing the Voyage. Therefore to return to Mr. Cleppington, let the World judge if these Rogues (whose Cruelty is a Mark of Cowardice) were not upon the Watch from time to time, to disappoint and overset the Voyage; For here was Bellhash the Master, Cleppington the Mate, Bath the Gunner, and about 20 Men; with the never be forgotten noble Capt. Thomas, which I will speak of hereafter. But in the Evening comes back Bath, Bellhash, Thomas, and some others, demanding their Cloaths, these I stopt. As soon as ever the Mate Cleppington was gone, then the rest of the Crew made a Demand to have the Money and Plate: and what was got shar'd amongst them, which I refus'd to do; and when I found they were in the Mutinying Vein, I produc'd the Queen's Orders, and told 'em it was out of my Power; but if at the End of the Voyage, they would carry the Ship into any Port of the West-Indies, or East, I would do Justice to my Owners and them.

Mr. Funnell forgets that he minded them of one thing that is very honest in him (which was), that all Governours of Forts were my Friends, and then they should have nothing. Now in a Ship of War this would be Mutiny, and punish'd with Death.

As to the Acapulca Ship which he mentions in p. 83. He says—when we came up with the Acapulca Ship, we gave her several Broadsides before she could get any of her Guns clear. To this I answer,

It is False Intirely so; for I no sooner Fir'd on her, but she Fir'd on me, and had her Guns out before. Again he says,

That while some of them were Quarrelling about Laying her on Board, and some Disputing the Contrary, she got out a Teer of Guns, and then was too hard for us.

Mr. Funnell might hear Disputs, as he calls it, among the Men: That was nothing to my Command. They might have taken her, would they have Obey'd my Advice, which was to Ply her with my Chace Guns, and Command her that way: For we had nothing to do along Side, and that I refer myself to all Sailors in the World, whether it was right or not. And considering the Inequality of our Numbers and Bulk of Ship.

Before the beginning of this Action, we were to the Windward of her, she standing to the Westward, and we Bearing away upon her with a Flown

Sheet I then order'd my Officers to keep enough to be sure to Windward of her: instead of this, spite of my Heart, they Edg'd away, and were so far from having the Power to Command and Board her, as I intended, that we lost the Opportunity, and were forc'd to Leward the first time; after that I Tack'd, came about, and had her under my Lee-Bow: and then I hop'd to Batter her with my Chace Guns, she having no Stern-Chace to Gall us; this I took to be the best way of Disabling her, and this way I could have made her yield. Instead of this, to shew the World how ready my Officers were to Board her, or Perform their Duty, the Master and the Mate left the Braces, and betook them to the Great Guns: so in this Confusion, neither they nor the private Men (let 'em talk what they will) ever intended Boarding her: For 'tis an Argument against all they can say, there was not a Man to be Assistant to any Purpose; No Yards brac'd not a Rope splic'd or knotted in all the Action. For the very Man at Helm contradicted my Orders, Edg'd her away to Leward once more: at which I offered to shoot him through the head. While things were at this Pass, the Boatswain being at the Braces, I ask'd him what did they intend to do? He told me to Board her. Clap her on a Wind then, said I. But for want of Wind by this time (they being Drunk and Bewitch'd) as if all things had concurr'd to our wrong, The Ship had neither way, or would she keep to. Now could I have gotten along side, they were so far from being Desirous to Board her, that the Master went about Discouraging of the Men: Not only that, but he and another came to me, shewing the Powder Barrels at the Enemy's Yard Arms. About 4 in the Afternoon, when we were a great way to the Leward, Clark the Mate, who by this time was Potent in Liquor, cry'd Board, board her.

I answer'd, to Night, 'tis Impossible, we have a fair Day to Morrow before us, and now no Wind to work the Ship. But to see the nature of these Fellows, in the Night they actually lost her in Steering directly from her; and for 3 days after this, they were frighted, and not Dissatisfied, as they call it, their Pannick Qualms, was ever Incurable, and they w^ld^ not Tack about again on any Account.

To conclude then: to engage them to cruize six weeks longer, I was forc'd to set my Hand to a Paper, that I would (after that time) make the best of my way to India. So once more we stood towards Acapulca again; and after standing Eastward for some time, we, with a Joint-Consent, went to Amapala to Water.

In p. 86.—We must not omit that Funnell says, that it was Concluded between Capt. Dampier and 30 of our Men, to continue in the South-Seas; but upon what Terms this Agreement was made, was kept a Secret.

'Tis well known I never professed anything that was otherwise than Honourable and Justifiable on our Return to England: He knows their Villany, and is really Witty in his turning Robbery and Mutiny upon me; Whereas I w^ld^ have kept all my Men, and begg'd for any little Respite, that they w^ld^ Consider the Blackness of the Action. So that where Mr. Funnell himself was chiefly an Undertaker, his Fear of being up at Home, may extort his as well as other Follies that he is Guilty of.

For when he w^ld^ Colour over the Matter, he says his Owner's Agent (Mr. *Morgan*, who is Beholden to him) appointed and shar'd the Provision:

so among be it. I was no sooner at an Anchor at Amapala, but all Hands as One Man, went to *work* in getting the Barque on Board, and took my Guns and Provision out by Force.

And that *Mr. Bellbash* by name, that all men may know him, and how far he is to be Intrusted, took me by the Throat, and Swore if I spoke a Word, they would Dash my Brains out, and the rest standing by Conniving at the Action. So that when we come to Repeat that which may be spoken of more at large, they ask'd for my Keys of the *Powder Room* and Chest of small Arms; *I deny'd 'em. Mr.* Morgan *himself said*, as to that we have Iron Crows on Board, they are as good Keys as we desire, and with that broke 'em open.

Note.—Out of 60 Hands that remain'd, they left me 72 Men after Rifling everything. Now I refer myself to all Mankind, as they made their Brags they left me but One Sailor; So they left me Life there. But they would bereave me of my Good Name here, and stab my Reputation for ever? But to make sure Play still, they turn'd my Prisoners ashore, and by this method intended to lay such a Bar in my way, That as they have reported I should never come Home; it is a Miracle in Nature how I did.

Considering the Spaniards had Notice of me before I got upon the Coast of Peru, through their Releasing the Prisoners; Now let all Mankind judge of the Miserable condition I was in, there being a Man of War that lay ready for me. So that let 'em colour one Villany on another, and excuse it as they will, I am satisfy'd the Fear of meeting the Spanish Men of War on the Coast, was the Occasion. 'Twould be tedious to insert their Impudence; But when that Buffoon *Toby Thomas* by name, said, *Poor* Dampier, thy Case is like King James, every Body has left thee: I must declare to the World then, and Always, the Doctor was the only Officer that stood by me in all my Adversities. More shall be said of Mr. Funnell hereafter, when his whole Book is more seriously consider'd.

Postscript.—Having Read Capt. Le Wright's Proposals for another Expedition into the South Seas, I do think it Proper and Advantagious, and that he was Intirely in the Right; and I am ready to Satisfy any Committee of Merchants how Practicable & Expedient it is to put it in Execution forthwith.

ANSWERS TO CAPT. DAMPIER'S VINDICATION, BY JOHN WELBE (MIDSHIPMAN ON BOARD CAPTAIN DAMPIER'S SHIP.)

Secondly.—As for what Capt. Dampier says concerning Lieutenant Huxford, it is true, Mr. Morgan and he had a small Quarrel; but it was in taking Captain Dampier's Part, who were, both after and before we left Ireland, at continual Variance. Witness the very first Night we came to Sea, they had such high Words in the Cabbin, that Capt. Dampier called to the Master, in order to put the Ship about, and stand in again for Kingsail, in order to put him ashore. Now, had he put him ashore at Ireland, I should not have blam'd him; but this last Quarrel happen'd at the Island of St. Jago, one of the Cap de Verd Islands; and Capt. Dampier order'd the Portugueze Officer to confine him. And the next Day, Mr. Huxford sent for his Chest and Cloaths, which were sent him. But the Day before we sail'd, he came on Board again, and brought his Chest and Cloaths with him; but as soon as the Capt. saw him, he order'd him to go out of the Ship. Mr. Huxford begg'd of him not to be so barbarous, as to turn him ashore amongst a Parcel of Banditties and Negro's; but desir'd him to let him lye in the Long-boat; or he w[ld] be contented to go before the mast, rather than go ashore amongst a Parcel of Heathens. But our Consort's Boat coming on Board, with Lieut. Stradling, Capt. Dampier and he contriv'd together to get Mr. Huxford into his Boat, under a Pretence of carrying him on Board of our Consort, and so to carry him on Board of one of the Portugueze Ships, that lay in the Road: but Mr. Huxford being unwilling to go out of the Ship, Capt. Dampier, with his own Hands, took hold of him, and thrust him out of the Ship into Lieut. Stradling's Boat, who put him on Board a Portugueze Ship in the Road, according to the Contrivance aforesaid; where he remain'd not long, before they turn'd him ashore, and within three months afterwards miserably ended his Days, partly with Hunger; yet I wonder not at the Captain's monstrous Barbarity, knowing the like Scene of Cruelty was acted by him, when Commander of the *Roe-Buck*.

Thirdly.—As to Mr. James Barnaby, our Second Lieutenant, he says, he never disagreed with him; which is false: For being both drunk together in the Cabbin, they quarrell'd, Mr. Morgan being ashore knew nothing of it; upon which Mr. Barnaby desir'd Capt. Dampier to give him Leave to take his Chest and Cloaths out of the Ship, and he w[ld] go ashore to the Portugueze; and Capt. Dampier told him, he might take his Things, and go where he pleas'd. Accordingly the next day he w[ld] have gone ashore; but Capt. Dampier w[ld] not let him, but took him, and ty'd his Hands behind him: But towards the Evening, one of our men cut his Hands loose; and about ten at Night, he and eight more of our men put their Chests and Cloaths in the Pinnace, and desir'd some of the Ship's Company to go in the Boat with them, to bring her back again; which accordingly they did, Capt. Dampier being in his Cabbin quite drunk.

Fourthly.—He says he mentions only the two Actions of the Voyage, on which depends the Miscarriage of the whole, by the Men's Disorder.

To which I answer, That the Miscarriage of the Voyage depends wholly on the Want of Courage and Conduct in the Commander. As for the French Ship, that we engag'd near the Island Juan de Fernando's, 'tis true, we chased her all the Afternoon, and fetch'd upon her; but taking her to be an European Ship, (as Capt. Dampier says in his own scandalous Vindication) he did not care to engage her, (he believing, that she might have Guns on Board, to which he always had a natural Aversion; and besides, not knowing how to behave himself, or work his Ship in Time of Engagement, as it plainly appear'd afterwards). Having chas'd this Ship all Night, in the Morning our Consort came first up with her, and gave her a Broadside or two; but finding her to be a Ship of greater Force than his was, he soon shear'd off, and shorten'd Sail, which was the Occasion of his falling astern: and now it being left to the courageous Capt. Dampier, to dispute the Decision of the Victory, he, as soon as we came within Gun-shot of the Enemy, thought it convenient to shorten Sail; but, by the Persuasions of the Officers, made Sail, and run along her Side, often asking his men, whether he was near enough? Capt. Dampier is pleas'd to say in his own Vindication, that after we had exchang'd several Broadsides with the enemy, wherein several of our Men was kill'd and wounded, that his Men run down off the Deck, and made nothing of it.

To this I answer, that none of our Men quitted their Posts, during the Time of Engagement, except Capt. Dampier himself, who the whole Time of Engagement, neither encourag'd his Men, nor gave any regular Command, as is usually required from a Commander at such Times; but stood upon the Quarter-Deck behind a good Barricado, which he had order'd to be made of Beds, Rugs, Pillows, Blankets, etc. to defend him from the small shot of the Enemy: where he stood with his Fusee in his Hand, and never so much as took Care to have the Quarter-Deck Guns and Pattareros fir'd. And whereas he says, he could have boarded her, and carry'd her, it is probably true; but he was so far from intending it, that he call'd out to make Sail, for Fear the Enemy should clap us on Board, and take us; which was the first Word that I heard him speak during the Engagement; and so accordingly we sheer'd off from her, and lay by, 'till our Consort came up; and then both Ships Companies would fain have attack'd her again, knowing that if we did not take her, that she w[ld] discover our being in the Seas, to the Spaniards, which w[ld] consequently frustrate our Designs on the Coast of Peru, (as accordingly it afterwards happen'd) but Capt. Dampier w[ld] not consent to it. And afterwards meeting her the second Time off Lima, all our Men being in Health, and both Ships Companies willing to fight her again, for the aforesaid Reasons, Capt. Dampier w[ld] in no wise consent to it; but calling for the Doctor, ask'd him, If he c[ld] make any more Men, in Case he should engage this Ship, and lose any? But the Doctor told him, That he c[ld] not make Men; yet he w[ld] do his Endeavour to preserve those he had, if he should have any wounded. Upon which Answer, the Capt. order'd us to stand to Sea, and w[ld] in no wise Consent to hazard his Person in a second Engagement. Upon which, one of our Men told him to his Face, he was a Coward, and ask'd him, Whether he came to those Parts of the World to fight, or not? And he reply'd, He did not come to fight; for he knew where to make a Voyage, without fighting.

Likewise Capt. Dampier says, in his own Vindication, that he could have got £500,000, if he had kept his Boats, which were then lost. This is but a very slender Excuse of Captain Dampier's; for the very next Day after that he refused to fight the French ship off of Lima, We took a Ship of 150 Tuns, which had two Boats; and six Days after, we took another Ship of 200 Tuns, which had a large Boat likewise; so that it could not be for want of Boats, that he fail'd in his Design, but only his not knowing where to light of such a considerable Sum of Money, after he was discover'd on the Coast, (which he must blame himself for.) He likewise says, that he never heard of any Cochineel, that was on Board the second Prize; which is false; for I heard several of the Ship's Company tell him of it, and was on Board the Ship myself, and saw some of the Cochineel; but I can give no Account of what Quantity there was on Board, because she was a deep loaden Ship, and we were not allow'd the Liberty to search her; so that I cannot tell what more valuable Goods she might have on Board. I w[ld] willingly know what Reasons Capt. Dampier can give for his taking of Prizes, and discharging of them, without ransoming or searching of them.

He allows some Part of the Story of the Observator's Ship and the Monkey, to be true; but says, he knew that the Ship's Company had left the Ship, which if he did, what was his Reason, as soon as we came along her Side, for hailing of her himself, when there was none but his Brother Captain (the Monkey) on Board to answer him?

Likewise he denies, that he order'd the Indian Canoe, that hailed us in the Bark, to be fir'd at, which is false: for it was by his own Order; which, together with his ill Conduct in anchoring so often, when there was no Occasion for it, and making so much Delay in that Attempt, that gave the Spaniards an Opportunity of discovering us, and so frustrated that Design.

He also pretends, that he had evident Proof, that the Ship which we took in the Bay of Panama, loaden with Flower, had landed her money at Truxillo.

To this I answer, that as soon as the Capt. of the Spanish Ship came on Board of us, being an old Commander, and well acquainted with the Ways of the Buckaneers of America, he asked Capt. Dampier, Who he was? Whether a Man of War, or a Pirate? Capt. Dampier told him, he had a Commission for what he did; and then asking, If he had any Money on Board? To which the Spanish Captain answered him, If he found any Money on Board, except what he gave him an Account of, which was but very little, he w[ld] give him leave to hang him at the Yard-Arm: for, said he, hearing of your being in the Seas, by the French Ship that you fought with near the Island of Juan de Fernando's, I put all my money ashore at Truxillo, and so put to Sea, being in hopes to miss you. This is all the evident Proof that Capt. Dampier had of their Money being landed at Truxillo; which is no Proof at all; for the Spanish Captain knew very well, that Captain Dampier having a Commission, w[ld] be oblig'd, at his Return, to give an Account of his Voyage, and had no Power to punish him, if he told him any Lies, he being a Prisoner of War: But on the contrary, if we had been Pirates, he knew he must expect no Mercy, if he gave any wrong Account. I was on Board this Prize my self several Times, and was told by some of the Prisoners, that there was $80,000 hid in the Run of the Ship; and I sent Captain Dampier Word of it: but I c[ld] not have the Liberty to search her, Capt. Dampier putting so much Confidence in the Spanish Captain's word.

The Reasons that he gives for his not taking the $50,000, that was proffer'd him for the Ransom of this Ship, are but very slender and weak. In the first Place, he says, He had no convenient Road to ride in; this is a wilful Mistake of Captain Dampier's, for there was Port Pinas, in the Latitude of 7 Degrees North, which is a very safe Port, and good Anchoring, it being a Place of no Trade; neither is there any Inhabitants, except a few Indians, it being a good Place for Ships to get Wood and Water at. When we took this Prize, we were lying at an Anchor at Point Garrachina, which lies in the Latitude of 7 Degrees and 20 Minutes North, which is but 20 Miles distant from Port Pinas. I would willingly know what Reason Captain Dampier can give for his not going to this Place?

The next Reason that he gives, is, his Fear of loytering away his

Time, and being imbayed for 3 or 4 Months. To this I answer, that had Capt. Dampier carry'd the Prize to Port Pinas, he need not have lost so much Time, as he did by tarrying where he was with her; for he kept her twelve Days in Custody, when the Spanish Captain desir'd but three Days Time to fetch the Ransom, and w[ld] have left his two Brothers as Hostages, and the Ship in our Custody, 'till his Return. We were Ships of good Force, considering where we were, having 26 Guns, and our Consort 16 Guns: besides we knew, that there was no Men of War in the Bay of Panama nor within 400 Leagues of us: and therefore consequently could not presently have Intelligence of our being in the Bay.

Likewise on the Coast of Mexico, we had an Account of four or five Ships, that were at Anchor in the Port of Guatalco, which is a place of no Force, they were laden with Silks there: yet w[ld] the Captain in no wise be persuaded to let us go in and fetch them, which we might very easily have done.

He us'd sometimes to call the Officers aft to a Council of War. Now, it is usual in a Council of War for the youngest Officer to give his Opinion first: but, to the contrary, Capt. Dampier w[ld] always give his own Opinion first: and then, if any of the Officers gave their Opinion contrary to his, he w[ld] fly out in a Passion, and say, If you know better than I do, take you Charge of the Ship. He was always a Man so much self-conceited, that he w[ld] never hear any Reason.

When we met the Spanish Man of War, we got to the Leward of her, not through our own Miscarriages (as Capt. Dampier Terms it), but through his own obstinate Humour: for the Night before we engag'd her, she was about a League and an half to the Windward of us, plying to the Windward, as we were; but however, in the Morning we were almost up with her, she, as I believe, not keeping up so close to the Wind as she might have done; for I found afterwards she held as good a Wind as we; but we had the Advantage of fore-reaching on her: We were then about three Leagues off of the Shore, she was about three Points on our Weather-Quarter, above a League distant. About 10 in the Morning Capt. Dampier order'd us to make ready to tack the Ship: Upon which I ask'd him what he design'd to do? He said, He w[ld] tack the Ship, and see what she was upon: Which I advised him not to tack the Ship, 'till we had the Advantage of the Sea-Breeze, and then we might be sure of getting to the Windward of her; but if we tack'd the Ship then, as he intended to do, we sh[ld] lose the Advantage of the Sea-Breeze, and be sure to go to the Leward of her. But he w[ld] not consent to it, but took his own Way, and immediately tack'd the Ship. And as I said, so it happen'd; for we were not able to fetch to the Windward of her. But if Capt. Dampier had taken my Advice, we had not had any Occasion to have Crowded so much, and disabled our Mast, but might easily have taken her, all our Men being in Health, and very willing to engage her.

As for Mr. Cleppington's leaving of him, it was Capt. Dampier's own Fault; for Mr. Cleppington and he, having some Words about the Ship's Bottom, she being very much worm-eaten, the Captain told him, that he, and as many as were willing to go with him, might take the Bark, and go where they pleas'd, and he w[ld] give them Arms: for, says he, if I have but

20 or 30 Men, I know where to make a Voyage: Which was like the rest of his Bravados. So that Mr. Cleppington did but as he bid him: not that I pretend to justify Mr. Cleppington in carrying away any of the Owner's Goods, but only blame the Capt. for his ill Conduct in being the Occasion of it.

November the 21st 1704, there being 10 of us on Board a small Prize, Capt. Dampier Call'd on Board of us: and told us, that he was going to Salaugua, which is about twelve Leagues to the Westward of us, to get some Water, and order'd us to come to him: After which, he made all the Sail he could from us, and soon run us out of Sight. After which, he call'd all Hands on the Deck, and told them, that we that were in the Prize, had run away with her, and so alter'd his Course, and stood to another Place. But it pleas'd God, on the 24th, we happen'd to stand a little nearer the Shore than ordinary, and saw a Ship at an Anchor: upon which, we being but ten of us, and had 8 Prisoners: and the Capt. w[ld] let us have but four Muskets to defend our selves, we having but ten Days Water on Board when the Capt. left us, and about 12 days Provision, resolv'd to go in and see what Ship she was, which accordingly we did; and, to our great Comfort, found her to be our own Ship, the Ship's Company telling us, that the Capt. did it on purpose to lose us.

Likewise he says: that when we first saw the Acapulca Ship, she was standing to the Westward: which is a very great Mistake of Capt. Dampier's; for she came from the Fillipin Islands, which lyes to the Westward, and was bound for Acapulca, which was to the Eastward of us.

Likewise he says: It was his Mens Fault, that he did not take her: Which is like the rest of his false Stories; for we were close upon a Wind, having our Larboard Tacks on Board, standing off Shore, the Wind being Easterly. She was about two Leagues a-head of us, a little on our Lebow, having her Star-board Tacks on board, standing in for the Shore; and as soon as she came right Head of us, she bore away, and stood directly to us; and a little before she came within Gun-shot of us, which was about 10 in the Morning, she hoisted her Spanish Ensign, and fir'd a Gun to the Leward, as a Friend, believing us to be a Spanish Ship. Upon which, the Officers desir'd the Capt. to hoist Spanish Colours, and answer her with a Gun to the Leward; but he w[ld] not consent to it, but immediately hoisted an English Ensign, and fir'd a Shot at her. She no soon'r perceiv'd that we were an Enemy, but immediately sprung her Luff, and hail'd close upon a Wind, and so got to the Windward of us, and got Time to heave all her Boats over Board, and her Goods from betwixt Decks, and made a clear Ship: and got a teer of Guns out from betwixt Deck, she having but two Guns upon the upper Deck, which were all the Guns that she had clear to fight, when we came first up with her. After which we tack'd, and run along her Side, the Men being resolv'd to clap her on Board; but the Capt. was so much against it, that when the Boatswain order'd the Man at the Helm to edge near her, in Order to clap her on Board, the Capt. Swore he w[ld] shoot the Man at the Helm through the Head, if he offer'd to edge near her. After which, we having receiv'd several Shot under water, one of the Men told the Captain, that our Ship was a sinking, and that now was the Time to clap her on Board. But instead of clapping her on Board, the Capt. cry'd out, Where is the Canoe?

Where is the Canoe? And was for getting into the Boat to save his Life, which shew'd what Man of Courage and Conduct he was. But we shearing off from her, the Carpenter stopp'd the Leaks. After which, the Capt. order'd us to stand off from her, which accordingly we did: all the Ship's Company being exceedingly vex'd at the Captain's ill Conduct. We stood about two Leagues off from her; and then the Captain said, Well, Gentlemen, I will not say, as Johny Armstrong said, I'se lay me down and bleed a while; but I will lay me down and sleep a while: but he forgot to wake again, 'till 7 or 8 a clock the next Morning. He never so much as left any Orders, with the Officers, what they shou'd do; but set a Centry at his Cabbin-Door, that no Body shou'd disturb him. And whereas he says, that the Men lost him in the Night, it is false; for we were in Sight of her the next Morning, and he order'd us to steer away directly from her. Now, if so be that Capt. Dampier w[ld] have done as the Officers advis'd him, which was, when we first came up with her, to have hoisted Spanish Colours, and fir'd a Gun to the Leward, as a Friend, we might have run along her Side, she not suspecting us to be an Enemy; and then hoisted our English Colours, and gave her a Broad-side, and a Volley of Small-shot; which w[ld] have been a great Surprize to them, and so clapp'd her on Board: In the Confusion, we might very easily have taken her. . . .[1]

That after having fought the Acapulco Ship, all the Ship's Company being tir'd of their bad Fortune, and the Captain's ill Management, (as they term'd it) were for staying no longer in these Seas; but, as long as they had Provisions, was for going to the East Indies, in order to get Home. But the Capt. not consenting, saying, that it was too soon for the Season, desir'd them to stay but six Weeks longer, in which Time he hop'd to get something, or, at least, a better Ship; for he protested against venturing in the *St. George*, she being so very leaky; and as for the Bark, she was too little to carry us all (as he said:) To which they consented (I mean the Crew) to stay with him, upon Condition he w[ld] stay no longer than the said 6 Weeks; which he did. After which, we made the most sail we could towards Acapulco, off of which Place we lay to see if we c[ld] meet with any Ships coming from the Coast of Peru, to trade with the Acapulco Ship, as they said was usual: but not meeting with any, we sail'd farther along the Shore, to the Eastward, in order to look into all the Harbours, as we pass'd by: But whether by our Captain's usual Fear of going too near the Shore, or other Reasons known to no Body but himself, we never look'd into any.

January the 6th, ab[t] three a Clock in the Afternoon, the Captain call'd to the Boatswain from the Quarter-Deck, to call all Hands upon Deck, when he ask'd, Who w[ld] stay with him to get Money? For his Part, he came with that Design, and did not intend to go out of them Seas, 'till he got Some. And all those that w[ld] stay with him, he had them come upon the Quarter-Deck; and those that were for going away, might go forwards, and there was a Bark for them. Mr. Morgan ask'd him, upon what Account he was going? That if he continu'd still upon the same Account he came

[1] When we went to take the town of St. Mary's, Captain Stradling would have had Captain Dampier to have given each man a Dram of brandy to encourage them. But Captain Dampier answered, If we take the town, they will get brandy enough; but if we don't take the town, I shall want it myself.

out upon, he w^ld not leave him; but otherwise he c^ld not stay. The Capt. made Answer, That then he w^ld not resolve him; but that he was going upon the Queen's Account. Mr. Morgan answer'd, That was not the Queen's, but the Owner's. No matter for that, (said he) I have a Commission. Upon which, a great many went aft to him, whose Names were taken, though he knew partly most of them before, he having one Clark, and others, who made it their Business, for some Time before, to persuade and sound those who were willing, upon condition of their sharing all that they got, and nothing for the Owners.

On the 11th December 1704, the said Clark went on Board the Bark, by the Captain's Orders, where he openly spoke to the men there, asking, Who w^ld stay with Capt. Dampier? And that they were going now no more upon the same Account that they came out upon; tho' all the World must suppose if they were, there was no need of the Captain's desiring to know then who w^ld stay with him; for if he had a Mind to stay longer than his Promise, no Body could force him, nor them that stay'd with him: on the contrary, those that came away, w^ld be more fearful of leaving him. In short, it is to be much doubted, if those that stay'd with him, whom he calls all Rogues, had not forc'd him away, when they found themselves under the Necessity of surrendering themselves Prisoners, or starving, whether ever he w^ld come for England, or not.

But to return, we continu'd sailing along the Shore, 'till the 22nd, without seeing any Thing, or looking into any Harbour where we might expect to get something, and so came to an Anchor in the Bay of Amapala. In which Time it was continually spoke by those that stay'd with him, that they w^ld take the Money Mr. Morgan had, which was shar'd for the Owners, saying—It was their free Plunder. And Capt. Dampier himself said: It not being mentioned in the Bills of Lading, it could not belong to the Owners, but that it ought to be divided amongst the Men. But several not consenting to the forcing of it from Mr. Morgan, it came to nothing; as well as several other Contests betwixt those that stay'd with him, and those that came away. Captain Dampier's usual Treatment to every Body, being Rogue, Rascal, Son of a Bitch, and other such vulgar Expressions, which was the Occasion of Mr. Bellhash's Quarrel last with him.

On the 26th, we that were for coming away, hail'd the Bark on Board, in order to take our Part of Provisions, which was equally divided, one Henry Vernon being appointed for that by Capt. Dampier, and John Dew, Cooper, for them that were going away. After which to secure the Owners Interest, and our selves from the Enemy, we took 4 Guns, and 25 or 26 small Arms, some Cases of Pistols, and a Barrel of Powder. . . .[1] our Intent was not for Robbing or Piracy, we made the best of our Way for the East-Indies, without a Boat, Rigging, Cables, or any Thing else fitting for the Sea; and by a greater Providence than what Capt. Dampier says, we got safe to Amboyna. For his Part, he was a great Pilot, and had been there before, but none of us ever had; and if he c^ld have help'd it, never should: for then he w^ld be sure none could give any Account of his Transactions and Conduct, but the World must have been amuz'd with his Stories.

More shall be said of Captain Dampier hereafter, when Occasion requires.

1 Words illegible.

The reader will do well to compare the above with the following letter, dated Augt. 10th 1722.—The humble Petition of Captain John Welbe to Lord Townshend, Principal Secretary of State.

Second Clause.—That there is another Conspiracy against Your Petitioner by Mr. Edward Morgan, a Roman Catholick liveing in Bloomsbury Square who was round the globe with Capt. Dampire, the same voyage that Your Petitioner was, and was the death of the first Lievetennant by turning him most barbarously ashore at the Island of St. Jago, where he miserably ended his days with hunger and greife, and the said Morgan was afterwards the ruin of the said expedition, and now endeavours to ruin Your Petitioner.

Augt. 22, 1722.—John Welbe to Mr. Burtt, book-keeper to Mr. Richard Cambridge.

Your Master desired them to have regard to Mr. Morgan's caractor, and not speak disrespectfully of him, etc., altho' you knew he was a Roman Catholick, and had ruind Capt. Dampire's Expedition, and was then endeavouring to ruin mine. (Signed) Jno Welbe.

EDITOR'S NOTE

The foregoing pages give the reader the statements of William Funnell, Dampier's reply to them, and John Welbe's answer to the reply. Funnell's statements have been discredited by Admiral Smyth; but I shall refrain from attacking Funnell till I have found more corroborative evidence either for or against him. Dampier's Vindication must speak for itself.

As for Welbe's evidence against Dampier, though it is plausibly put forward, and to some extent supported by what we learn of Dampier from Fisher's evidence (p. 596), it is made worthless by the statements in the above letters. One has but to compare his answer with the extracts given above from the Townshend MSS., to see that he was a man of little truth and evil temper.

COURTS-MARTIAL

August 21, 1701. *To the Secretary.* His Maj^tys^ ships the *Anglesea, Hastings* and *Lizard* having arrived with "some of my Officers and most of the *Roebuck's* men," he hopes their Lordships will order a speedy trial on the loss of the said ship. Clerk's hand. (Signed) *Wm Dampier.*

August 27, 1701. *To the Same.* Has been making enquiries, and finds that the *Roebuck's* boatswain died at Barbadoes, and that "ye Carp^r^" is not come home. Hopes their absence will not occasion "any further delay of our Trial which is frequently solicited by some of my officers and men."

(Signed) *Wm Dampier.*

Kings Street, Golden Square, September 23, 1701. *To the Same.* Returns hearty thanks for "ye hon^r^ and favour you doe me by so timely notice of my approaching triale." Has his papers ready, and will try to get all his officers and as many of his men as he can "find ready to go down." Presumes that it will be necessary to have "your Honr^rs^ Certificat of having delivered you my Journal which please to send me by the bearer my Clerk."

(Signed) *Wm Dampier.*

Postscript. Hopes that their Lordships will send down to the Court Martial such Letters and Evidences as were sent from Brazil relating to Lt Fisher, that the witnesses may be there sworn.

On September 29, 1701, a Court-Martial (held presumably at Portsmouth) enquired into the loss of the *Roebuck* at Ascension. The papers giving the finding of the Court have not been preserved; but the depositions of the Captain (Dampier), Master, Boatswain's and Carpenter's mates, and others are to be seen at the Record Office (Courts-Martial, 5262). They add nothing to the information given by Dampier in his published narrative, except that "the leak was very large," and that the *Roebuck* sank (apparently) "in ye Evining" of September 23, 1700.

Letter. To the Honb^le^ Josia Burchet Esqr, Secretary to the Admiralty.

Sir,—I make bould to trouble yo^e^ Hon^r^ with this, to informe you that I have been to enquire where I may find more of my ould crewe, that may be material witnesses for me in Mr. Fisher's tryall, Mr. Barnaby lives at the Three Tun Tavern in Holbourn, Mr Philip Pain is now in Town, and lives in London street nere Ratcliff Cross, he belongs to some ship but I know not her name, Mr. Hugh Davis belongs to a storeship, I cannot learn her name; Mr. Baptist Watson is as I am informed abord of some ship but I know not her name, Mr. John Pary belongs to Captain Haddock abord the *Reserve*, Alexander Beal I cannot here of and as I sent in my former that I desired to have besides my Officers as many of the Seamen as can be found, for every one can say somewhat in the tryall, viz., Robert Edlington, Paul Hallaway, &c: Honble Sir, I humbly desire that I may have all or most of these men and those formerly mentioned at the Tryall, I am yor Hon^{rs}

humble servant

May the 23^{d} 1702. *Wm Dampier.*

Lieutenant George Fisher, the cause of Dampier's disgrace, entered the King's employment in 1688, and did such service as a gunner at the relief of Londonderry, "on the 12th of June 1689" that he received a warrant as gunner of the Fireship *Griphon*. He took part in the engagement off Beachy Head, and served in the *Royal Oak*, the *St. Michael* and the *Albemarle*. On 26th July 1698 he was "Commissioned Lieutenant of ye *Roe-Buck*."

He brought a number of accusations against Dampier; the chief of them being that of cruelty towards himself. He also accuses Dampier of being a bad artist or navigator; of laying an abominable plot to have him (Fisher) murdered; and of excessive laxity in maintaining discipline.

Dampier's counter-charges accused Fisher (*inter alia*) of "speaking contemptuously of the Lords of the Admiralty," of "disobedience, impudence and threats;" of altering the ship's course contrary to orders; of calling his captain "old Rogue, old Dog, old Cheat"; and of "railing and incensing the men against the Captain."

INFORMATION OF LIEUTENANT FISHER AGAINST CAPTAIN DAMPIER, LATE COMMANDER OF THE "ROEBUCK"

To his Ex^{cie} Thomas Earle of Pembroke and Montgomery &^{c} Lord High Admirall of England &^{c}., is most humbly addressed, The Case of Lieut. George Fisher together with the Sufferings and Oppressions laid on him by his late Comander Capt. William Dampier in his Maties Ship *Roe-Buck*, without any Cause, save his faithfulness in Discharge of his Duty as will fully appear when it shall please your Ex^{cie} to grant him the favour of being Tryed at a Court Martiall.

1688. He went voluntarily into his Maties Service, and was made a Gunner in the Traine of Artillery in Ireland and for his great service at the Releife of London Derry on the 12th of June 1689 was Disscharged that Service, and by letters from Major Generall Kirk to the Lords of the Admiralty recomended for preferment in the Royal Navy, who were pleased upon y^{t} recomendation to warrant him Gunner of his Maties fireship *Griphon*, Captaine Chamberlaine Comander.

After Beachey head Engagement, upon Capt. Chamberlaine's Certificate of his behaviour your Ex^{cie} was pleased to appoint him in 1690 Lieutenant of the *Royall Oake*, and he there Continued during the Commands of Capt. Byng, Capt. Lee, Capt Gardner, Capt. Elves and Sr George Rooke as flagg,

Thence he was removed into the *St. Michaell* under Capt. Munden, and with him afterwards removed into the *Albemarle*, and there served dureing his and Capt. Fairbourne's Comād of her, untill the Peace dureing all which services he behaved himselfe as became his Duty without any complaint as by the Certificates of his Comanders more fully appears not only by these following but by more in this Honble office.

November 1, 1698.—Then he was Commissioned Lieutenant of ye *Roe-Buck* on Board of wch in disscharge of his Duty he lay in the Downes, Capt. Wm Dampier Comander.

Article 1.—Sr Cloudsley Shovell in the *Swiftsure* came to an Anchor in ye Downes and made a Signall for Lieutenants, Fisher being then ashoar with leave Imediately hired a Deal Boat, And went on Board ye flagg where he found his Commander on the Quarter Deck, who said he had a Secrett to tell him in private, and (having leave) they two went into the Lieutenants Cabin and being alone ye Capt. said Since you have been ashoar there was like to have been a Mutiny on Board the *Roe-Buck* for yt James Grigsen and Jn. Knight had been drinking with the Boatswaine in his Cabin and were over heard by the Master to swear that when they came to sea they would heave the Master over Board and run away with the King's Ship as the Mae Jacob Hews had acquainted him adding he did not like Mr —— our Boatswaine, and demanded Fisher's advice in the Case. Fisher answered it was proper to acquaint the flagg thereof, which the Capt. promised to do but did not, thoh Fisher Reminded him severall times thereof.

November 5*th*, (2).—At 5 at Night Capt. Jumper, Captaine Cleasbie and Sr Cloudsley's Secretary came on Board the *Roe-Buck* with an order to Examine if our Crew were *Seamen*; as they were comeing on Board, Fisher Comanded the Boatswaine to order the Pinnace a Stern out of their way, but he answered with an Oath he would not obey his Comands when the Capt. was on Board, so that the Capt. and Secretary was forced to come over the Boate to come in, before whom Fisher Complained to his Capt., who was told by them, that he ought to see that Fisher should be protected in his Commands and with all reprimanded the Boatswaine.

November 17*th*, (3).—This morning Fisher moved the Capt. to Punish James Grigsen still finding him a refractory and dangerous Fellow, ye Capt. seemed unwilling, untill Fisher told him the Lords of ye Admiralty ought to be acquainted with it; Then he ordered Fisher to see him made fast to the Gang-way which he did, and in an hour he was set Loose without any punishment, Fisher told the Capt. it would give an ill Example if he was not punished and sent ashoar;

Then the Captaine ordered him to be made fast a second time, and that Fisher should order the Boatswaine to give him 6 Blows on his back with all his Cloaths on, which was done, and the Captaine said he would turne him and John Knight on shoar just before the ship sailed, Fisher then answered he would goe on Board the Comadore to get 2 Men in their Roomes.

December 4*th*.—Sr Cloudesley Shovell came into the Downes from Holland, and Fisher moved the Captaine to Complaine of these Men to Sr Cloudesley, but he Cou'd not prevaile.

December 6*th*.—The Flagg was Struck on Board the *Swift-Sure* and the

Broad Pinnant Hoysted on Board the *Resolution*, Captaine Beaumont Commander, whither Fisher went and acquainted Lieutenant Burlington, Lieutenant Fairborne with the threatened Mutiny, desireing two men in the Room of the s[d] Grigsen and Knight, and the word being given three good men offered themselves, which Fisher acquainted the Captaine with, who Answered as before, that he would send them ashoar when the shipp was upon Saileing, and not before, to avoid a Noise; Notwithstanding which, they being his Old Acquaintance, he carried them to sea.

January 28th, 169$\frac{8}{9}$, (4).—Last Night as walking on the Deck with the Captaine and Captaines Clerk, Fisher was taken ill, and 3 Drops of Blood fell from his Nose on his hand, and fainting, went to his Cabbin, Sent for the Dr., and was Lett Blood, and putt into a Sweat, but Considering he had 2 Watches that night, sent for the Cheife Mate and askt where by his Reconing the shipp was, but he Cou'd not tell, Fisher said by his Reconing they were within 15 Leagues of Algoranca, and Wondred that neither he nor the Captaine had ordered to Look out for Land, Advising him to Shorten Saile and keep a good Look out, which he promised to do, at 6 Next Morning wee made the Island Lanceratta about 8 Leagues Bearing S.E., at which the Captaine and Master were Much Surprised, being 60 Leagues out of their Reckoning.

January 30th, (5).—They came to an Anchor in Sancta Cruz Roade, where was the *Experriment* Galley, Captaine Trevars Comander, who Came on Board and Desired a Hogshead of Small Beer, which the Captaine granted, and ordered Fisher to see it done. Fisher thereupon ordered the Cooper to Break a Butt, and as he was going to do it mett the Purser on the Deck, who Threatened to break his head if he obeyed Fishers order therein. Fisher thereupon before Captaine Trevars Complained to his Commander, desiring to bear him out in his Comands, in which Captaine Trevers seconded him, saying, if you Suffer your Lieutenant to be thus used it may be of Ill Consequence in your Voyage. Neverthelesss his Commander would not do him Justice therein, as appears by Captaine Trevors Affidavit ready to be produced.

January 31st, (6).—This Morning the Captaine, Doctor, and Purser went ashoar, and the Captaine gave Fisher Leave to go Ashoar also, who did, and Fisher Carried some Letters to Merchants to be Sent to England by the first shipp, and coming to one Mr. Hopper, Merchant, he there found his Captaine, Doctor, Purser, Capts. Clerke and James Barnaby at the said hoppers house, Fisher Delivered his Letters and was returning, but the Capt. Invited him to stay and dine with him, he accepted it, as they stayed together untill 8 at Night, and in their returne the Capt. in a very Moross Manner said to Fisher he had better kiss the Brutch of his Young Men then to Meddle with them, which Surprised Fisher, as not knowing his meaning, and asking his Meaning, he said Fisher had beaten James Barnaby then present; Fisher deneyed it, or that he ever Threatened to Beat him, and Barnaby himselfe owned the same, and that Fisher had been very kind to him. Notwithstanding which the Captaine said he would putt Fisher in Irons when he came on Board. Fisher replyed he was not soe far from the Lords of the Admiralty but they would have notice of his doings, upon this his Clerke whispered Fisher in the Ear to cane Barnaby, which if he had done, Fisher perceiving their Intent was to draw and Runn him Through in the Scuffle as afterwards appear'd; Comeing to the Waterside the Captaine went into the Castle to the Governour, and Fisher went on Board and the Clerke with him, when he Came into the Steerage he told the Officers they would see him in Irons when the Capt. Came on Board, why said they, what have you done, nothing said Fisher, the Clerke replyed, no he should not, why said Fisher, are you Captaine, gett you out of the Steerage. This Clerke was a Base Impudent fellow, and would frequently say the shipp would not goe home this 7 Yeares, and Sometime that Shee would never goe home.

February 2nd, (7).—About Noone, Fisher being Sitting on the Quarter Deck, Orders were given for two Puncheons of Beefe to be Hoysted out of the Hold and sent ashoar to Mr. Hopper, a Merchant. The Captaines Clarke came to Fisher and askt him if he did not hear the Shipp Company Complaine of their Provisions goeing a Shoar to be sold, which themselves should want, Fisher Bid him goe downe and acquaint the Captaine of it, which he did, and comeing back said, the Captaine tooke no Notice of it. Then Fisher went downe and told the Captaine, the Consequence thereof if they came to want Provisions, upon which it was Stopt. But Fisher found reason to beleive this was a Trick betwixt the Captaine and his Clarke to putt the Purser upon Selling of Provisions to Create a Differance betwixt the Purser and him for the better Carrying on his greater and most Villanous designes wth Safety.

February 3rd, (8).—This afternoon the Shipp Weighed from Sancta Cruz Road. When under Saile James Barnaby came to Fisher and told him he had saved his life; how said Fisher, Barnaby replyed, Andrew Gastier the Spanjard on Board told his Countreymen on Shoare you had beatd and used him Barbarously, and desired their Assistance to kill you when on Shoare, which they promised to do, and I understanding Spanish and hearing this, Told the Spanjards all he had said of you was false to my knowledge, but on all Occasions the contrary, upon which the Spanjards turned him out of their Company. Fisher acquainted the Captaine herewith, who made Slight of it, and Called him fooll for believing it. But this very Spanjard afterwards Leaving the Shipp at Brazille, Confisst the whole Matter, and that it was the Captaine and his Clarke who had Sett him upon it to take away Fisher's Life, and that he had done it if Barnaby had not prevented him.

February 11th.—The Shipp Anchored in the Bay of the Isle of May where they found Mr. Barfoot, Master of the *Newport* of London, to whome the Purser Sold Provisions for Wine and Brandy, and because Fisher would not take a part of it nor be concerned in it he was very much Dissturbed and Angry.

February 17th, (9).—About Noon the Shipp sailed out of May Roade for the Island of St. Iago, which is about 5 Leagues over; it being the Masters first Watch, Fisher went to Sleep, but at 3 in ye Morning, hearing the Men cry out Land, presently got up on ye Quarter Deck and Looking under the Lee of the Maine Saile Saw the wash of the Shoare and Askt the Captaine what he Designed to doe; he Answered (as if Crying) he did not know what the Master Designed; said Fisher if you Lett him do what he pleases he will Knock the Kings Shipp at head, the Master being then So Drunk he could not stand on his Leggs. The Captaine Walked off the Quarter Deck and Fisher ordered the Helm att Lee, and if the shipp had not Stayed she had run Ashoar, shee haveing all the small Sailes Sett at ye Same time.

February 23rd, (10).—Being the 2d Day of her Saileing from St. Iago in the evening the Captaine ask't Fisher to Clubb for a Bowle of Punch, to which he Consented, the Captaine . . . . Purser and Clerke only being Present; whilst drinking it the Captaine said had he Commanded one of the Kings Shipps in the Late Warr all French Men he Took in Privateers we would have Tyed back to back and Thrown over Board, adding all the King Captaines were fools, they did not do it. Fisher Replyed it was a very Cruell thought and that the French would have retaliated it, but he swore he would have done it.

The Doctor said it was barbarously Intended.

The Captaine answered it would have made a Quick End of the Warr. Fisher said it would have rather Prolonged it and Created a Irreconcileable hatred, and that if all Nations would give noe protection to Pirates, but hang them as soon as taken it would be of good service to all Traders abroad. The Captaine Demanded what he ment by Pyrates, Fisher answered such as Everye and his men were; he swore if he mett with any of them he would not hurt them, nor a haire of y^r^ heads. Fisher answered that he being now one of the Kings Captaines and had the Kings Commission ought as he Conceived wherever he found Such, to secure them and bring them to Justice. The Capt. kept his word as will appear hereafter.

February 25th, (11).—This Evening Fisher Drinking a Bowle of Punch with the Captaine in his Cabbin there was also Doctor, Purser and Clarke, the Captaine sent for James Grigson down, and said, Mr. Grigson I Beg y^r^ Pardon for Punishing you in the Downes, but it was to please one Man. Fisher having the Bowle in his hand, and much surprised and Concerned to hear his Capt. Begg so Base a fellows Pardon whome he knew to be a Mutinus Man, and as is before said himselfe Complained off to Fisher in the Downes, and Ask't his Advice what to do with him and at whose Complaint he was Punished, Sett the Bowle downe, pulled off his hatt without saying one worde, withdrew into his owne Cabbin and reflected on other things had passed perticularly what the Clerke had said, Viz^t^ That they would find Captaine Dampier another sort of a Man when he came on the other side the Equinoctall Line, That it would be a Long time before the Shipp wou'd goe home, which Fisher often told the Captaine who never would take any notice of it to his Clarke, but upheld him in it and as Fisher had reason to beleive did Send his Clerke often among the Shipps Crew, to fathom theire Inclinations and how they were Inclined to a Long Voyage and to joyne with him into any Villanous Action.

March 4th, (12).—Walking with the Captaine on the Quarter Deck, Fisher Ask't him what Place on the Coasts of Brazille he Designed to go to, to Fernambuck or Baja, he answered he had not resolved, But as a Secreet acquainted him, That Mr. Flamstod the great Mathematition told him in England that when he Came to the Coast of Brazille his men would Mutiny, Fisher Replyed he cou'd not beleeve any such thing, for by his observation all his officers and men seemed very Easie and quiett; well says he, You will see it when you come there.

March 5th, (13).—Happened some words Betwixt Fisher and the Purser concerning 1500 weight of Bread which had received wett and was ordered downe in the Powder Roome which was a Damp place, and the Gunner had spoke severall times to the Purser to remove it and spend it first, but he would not do it, upon which the Gunner had complained to Fisher and that the Bread would be Spoyled, and Fisher to the Purser, who still answered if it was spoild he would pay it. Fisher then Complained to the Captaine, the Purser present, who gave the same answer, and told Fisher it was none of his business, Railed and Called him Knave Rogue &c., The Captaine Countenanceing him therein.

March 6th, (14).—Fisher with the Doctor and Purser being of the Captaines Mess, and at Dinner, the Capt. tooke in his Clerke; whiles at Table ye Purser said the Carpenter owed him eighteen shillings which he would not pay, would therefore putt it Downe in the Shipp Booke. The Captaine not understanding the Methods of the Navie, Fisher said ye Purser ought not to do it, nor cou'd answer it, and if the Carpenter should Complaine of it at pay Table, it would ruine him, but the —— Purser and Clerke most rudely told him, he Lyed, upon which he Desired to goe out of the Captaines Mess and after shewed him his Instructions, by wch it appeared to be true as Fisher had said, The Cap^tn.^ Replyed he Could not Comply with those Instructions.

Three or 4 Day after the Gunner Complain'd to the Cap^tn.^ y^t^ the 1500 Weight of Bread was all spoild and not Eatable; then the Cap^tn.^ ordred it up and it appeared Mouldy and full of Redd Specks. The Purser then renewed his Scurrilous Language of Rogue and Villain before the Capt. to Fisher, who finding them all of a Peece and the Captaine Suffering it, was forced to take it Quietly, and the Shipps Company was putt to whole allowance of Bread and the Mould mixt amongst the good.

March 10th, (15).—The Cooke and some of the Shipps Company Complained to Fisher it was 3 in the afternoon and had no beer. The Cooper being Examined Said it was out, Fisher ask't the Cooper if ye Capt. had ordred him not to Broach any more Beer, he answered No. Then Fisher ordred him to Broach a fresh Butt for the Shipps Company which he did. After the Captaine Sent for the Cooper upon the Quarter Deck and for no other Cause but for obeying Fishers said order, in a Violent Manner Caned him, and broke his head, Then Sent for Fisher up and Demanded why he ordred a Butt of Beer to be Broacht, and before he Could answer fell on him with his Cane and Caned him to the forecastle and confined him to his Cabbin.

Betwixt the 10th and 16th of March, Fisher found the Capt. had further Villanyes to Countenance and Act against him, having held severall Private Consults in the Night w^h^ his Clerke who Fisher knew to be a great Villaine in Divers respects and therefore was jealous they intended to take away his Life, and a Note was throwne into his Cabbin by one of the Shipps Company, that he heard the Clerke sweare if he was Captaine he would hang Fisher and 2 or 3 more in two Days, and Fisher thought his Capt. was taking his Advice, for on the 16th in the Morning he ordred all hands to be Called up, and then said they had a Designe to Mutiny; all answered No, nor never thought of Such a Designe but were very willing to Serve under him; he then Said it was a Surmise of his owne, But Fisher was informed his Clerke and Grigson were his Informers; at noon the Corporall came an Tooke Fisher out of his Cabbin, putt Irons on him and then turn'd him in againe, where he Lay in Great Misery and all this without any Cause Alledged, and under it the Captaine Caned him Violently and Lockt him up Close, that with the Heat and being under the Sunn and forced to Ease Nature, there, he was almost Stiffled to Death, as no Doubt was intended he shou'd be, for he said he Cou'd hang Fisher but he beleeved this Confinement would do his business.

March 19th, (16).—Being Sunday the Captaine ordred the Boatswaine to Call up all hands and the Small Armes on the Quarter Deck Loaded, which was done, and he told them he heard some of them designed to Leave the Shipp, when they came to Brazille, to which all were Surprisely Silent; the Captaine then Called John Boate, Owen Harris and Alexander Beale, and ordred them to be made fast to the Gangway, and then Examined them if they knew anything of an Intended Mutiny; All 3 told him No, But Fisher after understood that the Captaine and Clerke would faigne have had some of the Shipps Company Swear falsely against him, but Could find none to do it but the said James Grigson, a[nd] because those 3 poor men would not swear falsely against him they were ordred into Irons, and the Boatswaine to his Cabbin because he was found a good man and would not harken to their wicked advice.

The Shipp then Steered away for Baja in the Braziles, and there arrived on the 23rd of March, when the Capt. sent one Ashoar to . . . Acquaint the Governor, that Fisher was a great Rogue and would have killed him and the Captaine. The Governor ordred Fisher should be sent Ashoar, and if the Cap[tn] had 3 Wittness to prove it or Mutiny would hang him.

March 28, 1699.—The Cap[tn] ordered the Master to Carry Fisher out of his Close Confinem[t] Ashoar Prisoner and take a Strong Guarde wth Swords and Pistolls, and in thatt Manner he was carried on Shoar in Irons and put into a Castle amongst Negroes, Molettos and condemned persons and all manner of Villanies where he Lay untill y[e] 4th of July following.

The Shipp Stayed at Baja a Month, but the Capt. never came near Fisher nor any of his Crew but by Stealth, The Capt. Commanding them to the Contrary on Severe Threats, but the Captaine himself Associated with Severall of Everiees Crew.

Here Fisher Petitioned the Governour that Capt. Dampier and himselfe might be sent for and heard before him and all the Officers in the Shipp Examined, and if it appeared he had Comitted Mutiny or any other Crime he would not Complaine if he Suffered Death, adding it was not Legally in the Captaines Power to Leave him there a Prisoner. The Governour tore the Petition and said he could not Concerne himselfe with the King of Englands officers; had only Lent the Capt. a Prison. Fisher then wrote to the Captaine if any men he had that cou'd accuse him might be sent on Shoar and make Oath before the Justice there, but he refused and kept himselfe on Board and declared he would Leave Fisher behind, and accordingly sent one Joseph Bugsby and Robt Rayns Fishers Servant ashoar and at Baja Entred 4 men more than his Complyment.

Fisher seeing he must be left behind, sent for his Cloaths Chest, Books, Goods and some Provisions to carry him his Servant and Joseph Bugsby to Lisbon; wth much Importunity he sent what of his Goods he pleased, Tore what he pleased out of his Journall, and sent 4 Month Provisions for Fisher and his Servant which the Portuguese stole from him but none for Bugsby, and sailed ye 23th of Apll for Madagascar. As Fisher beleeves sometime after Joseph Bugsby Dyed of the Country Desease at Baja, Else would have been a good Wittness for Fisher.

Soe that Fisher besides all Abuses and Wrongs on Board was kep't a Close Prisoner at Baja from the 8th of March 1699 to the 4th of July following, when he was sent Prisoner on Board a Portuguese Shipp for Lisbon, as appears under the hand of John Earle Esqre, his Maties Consull at Lisbon, readie to be produced, where he safe arrived in October, and his Case being Examined was Sett at Liberty and came home a passenger in December 1699, And hath been ever since out of his Maties Service.

George Fisher.

Examined and declared. In Cur. (1702). Jn. Bathurst and Jn. Hov.

THE INFORMATION OF CAPTAIN Wm. DAMPIER AGAINST LIEUTENANT FISHER

1. *His Contempt of ye Captn.* When the Ship lay in ye Downes Mr. Philip Pain, Gunner of the *Roebuck*, discoursing with Lt. Fisher about the Captain, the Lt. said dam him for an old Rogue he minds nothing.

2. *Speaking Contemptuously of the Lords of the Admiralty.* He the sd Lt. did often speak against the Lords of the Admiralty before Purser, Dr. and Mr. James Brands; reproved for it by the Captn.

3. *Disobedience, Impudence and threats; this was heard and seen by Barnaby and Gunner.* The 28th of January the Lt. was goeing to put his bed and bedclothes into the Pinnace that lay on the boomes, and the Boatswain tould him that the Captn. had ordered him to suffer no man to go into the Boat, nor put anything in her, the Lt. replyed; the Captn. ought to have acquainted me with it, and ordered the bed to be put into the Boat, the Captn. seeing a man and boy in the Boat, told the Lt. that he did expect it from him to show good examples, the Lt. presently bent his fist and held it to his nose and sd he did not care a —— for him, and also tould the Captn. that if ever he saw James Barnaby on the quarter-deck he would kick him off. Mr. Barnaby was a midshipman.

4. *The Lieutenant alters ye cours contrary to ye Capts. orders.* About the 8th of March the Captn. ordered to steer away south, the wind was at East; in a short time afterwards the Captn. going off the deck, Lt. Fisher altered the Cours and ordered to keep close on a wind S.S.E.; being then two degs. soth of ye Line.

5. *The Lts. meanes to insinuate himself into the favour of ye men.* (Witnesses—*Mr. Hughes etc.*) About the 8th of March there were some bags of bread brought on the deck out of the Powder room. The Lt. opened one

of the bags in the wast and peeking out a cake that was a little mouldy held it up saying gentlemen this is not fitt to eat; the Boatswain standing by him sd twas wors than damnified bread, but the Mr. turning it all out on the deck tould them that he had eaten wors bread in the Channel of England, the Captn. tould the men they should eat good bread and the damnified should bee thrown overboard.

6. *His agravations and scandalous usage of ye Captn.* The 10th of March the Captn. speaking roughly to the Lt. for broching a butt of beer in the night, he calld the Captn. names softly, and urged the Captn. to strike him, then he loudly calld him a great many ill names, as old Rogue, old Dog, old Cheat, and indeavoured to stirr up the seamen to a mutiny, by telling them that the Captn. knew not wheather he was going, that he was no artist, that he knew nothing, but was a mere theaf, and when he would not be silent, but constantly continued railing on his Captn. he was at last confined to his Cabbin.

7. *His obstinate persistence in giving scurrulous language.* The next day when he continued railing on the Captn. and calling of him as many ill names as he could invent; the Captn. sent Mr. Hughes to the Lt. to desire him to hould his tongue or else he should be forced to take other measures with him, the Lt. replyed let the old rogue —— —— —— I am a prisoner and will speak what I please, and all the time afterward as long as he was abord he constantly raild at the Captn. and call him names especially when he passed through the steerage.

8. . . . . (Witnesses—*Mr. Hughes, Barnaby, and Gunner.*) The 18th day at night many of the officers desired the Captn. to get his bedding and cloaths on to the Quarter deck and lye there being aprehensive of some design against him by Mr. Fisher's accomplices, the Captn. (tooke) their councell and ordered the gunner to secure the Gunroom dore, and the next morning all the small armes were got on the quarter deck to prevent a rising, and some men suggested and examined, wherein they tax each other, namely Baptist Watson and Alexander Beal, and searching John Boat they found a paper written against the Captn. and he said he was ordered to write it by the Lt.

9. . . . . . . He told the Master that if the Captn. d——(word illegible—? died) that he is no more but Master; and sometime after at anchor in the harbour of Bahia de Todos Santos he sent the Master to the Captn. to desire that he might be sent to Portugall in one of the Portugues men a ware, and to be sent from thense to England, the Captn. sent no answer to this, but shortly after passing through the steredg the Lt. told him that he had sent to know if he might be sent to England by the way of Portugall the Captn. told him it was time enough to think of that, which so incensed the Lt. that he calld him all the ill names that he could invent.

10. *The Lts. malisous and fals Suggestions to the Governour and Merchants of Bahia.* (Witness—*Mr. Hughes.*) The Lt. continuing railing and incensing the men against the Captn. he was forced at last to send him ashore in hopes of tameing him there, but to no purpose for he sends letters to the Governour complaining of the Captn. but is not minded, then he sends for a Danes merchant and tells him yt it was not long since the Captn. had taken a Dutch ship and barbarously used the men and desired the merchant

to acquaint the Governour of it yt the Captn. might be secured the next day; a Dutch seaman that was their interpreter came abord and told it before the Master and severall others.

11. *Indeavours to be revenged by stirring the Cleargy.* (Witness—*Mr. Brands.*) About the 10 or 12 of April when he found that the Governour would not take notice of what he sd, he struck in with the Church, but the Captn. had notice of it and forbore coming ashore. W^M· DAMPIER.

Signature in a darker ink and written with a finer pen.

MINUTES OF THE COURT-MARTIAL

At a Court Martiall held on Board her Maj^ts· ship the *Royall Souveraine* att Spithead on Munday the 8th day of June, 1702.

PRESENT

The Honble Sir George Rooke, *Vice-Admirall of England*, and *Adml. of her Majts· Fleet, etc., President;* Sir Clowd^ey Shovell, *Adml. of ye White;* Tho. Hopson, Esqr·, *Vice-Adml.;* S^r· Stafford Fairebourne, *Rere-Adml.*

Captns. Graydon, Greenway, Haddock, Turville, Jn. Leake, Edwardes, Jn. Johnson, Guy, Myngs, Tho. Robinson, Knapp, Tho. Mitchell, Wyvell, Haughton, Crowe, Jn. Mitchell, P. Arc. Hamilton, Jn. Jennings, Pedder, Smith, Bokenham, Wisheart, Cowper, Ste. Martin, Dilke, Good, Long, Howard, Maynerd, Rumsey, Foulke, Harlow.

All duely sworne pursuant to a late Act of Parliament, etc.

Enquiry was made by the Court into the Difference betwixt Captn Willm Dampier late command^r of her Maj^ts ship the *Roe-buck*, and George Fisher Lieut^nt of the same ship, and their mutuall Complaints against each other, of many Irregularities and undue Practices committed by each of them in their late Voyage to India in the years 1698 and 1699. The Court having strictly examined into all the particulars of their severall Informations: Is of opinion that it has appeared to ye Court by Evidence upon oath that Cap^tn William Dampier has been guilty of very Hard and cruell usage towards Lieutenant Fisher in beating him on Board ye sd. Ship, and confining him in Irons for a considerable Time, and afterwards Imprisoning him on shore in a strange Countrey, and itt is Resolvd that itt dos not appeare to ye Court by ye Evidence that there has been any grounds for this his ill usage of him, and that the sd. Captain Dampier falls under ye 33rd Article for these his Irregular proceedings, and the Court dos Adjudge that Hee be Fined all His Pay to ye Chest att Chatham, exclusive of about Fifty Pounds stop'd in ye Treasurer of ye Navies Hand for indemnifying the Queen as to a Bill drawn on ye Navy Board by Lt Fisher from Lisbon; and itt is farther the opinion of ye Court that the said Capt. Dampier is not a Fitt person to be Employ'd as comd^r of any of her Ma^ty ships.

And the Court is of opinion that the Informations sett forth by Captn Dampier against Lt Fisher have not been made Good, and therefore the Court dos Aquit him from that Charge.

Then the Court proceeded to enquire concerning the death of John Norwood, late Boatswain of ye *Roe-buck*, itt having bin suggested that his death had bin in a great measure occasiond by ye severity and hardship of his confinement by Captain Dampier then command^r of the sd. Ship, in their late Voyage to India. The Court having strictly enquird into that matter: Is of opinion that itt dos not appeare by ye Evidence that the sd. Jn. Norwood's confinement was the Cause of his Death, and therefore ye Court do's Acquit the sd Captn. Dampier as to the Death of Jn. Norwood, Late Boatsw^n of ye *Roe-buck*.

(*Signed by*) Rooke. Clow^d. Shovell. Tho. Hopsonn.
J. Leake. Will. Bokenham.
S. Fairborne. Fran. Wyvell.
Jno. Graydon. Chr. Myngs. J. Dilkes.
A. Hamilton. S. G. Foulke. James Greenway.
Tho. Robinson. J. Wishart. R. Edwards.
Hen. Haughton. Edwd. Good. Jn. Maynerd.
J. Jennings. Jn. Johnson. T. Harlowe.
Pr. Haddock. J. Knapp.
Jos. Crowe.
H. Cooper. Chas. Guy.
Tho. Long. Tho. Mitchell.
C. Rumsey. Jn. Mitchell.
Hen. Turvile. Geo. Smyth.
Steph. Martin.

Act in Cur.
J. Bathurst,
Jud. Advg.

(*Endorsed*) *Soveraign* at Spithead, 8 June, 1702. Court Martiall Enquiry into the difference betw. Capt. Dampier and L Fisher, and into the Death of Jn. Norwood, his late Boatsw^n.

INDEX

INDEX

INDEX

INDEX

INDEX

INDEX

INDEX

INDEX

INDEX

INDEX

INDEX TO THE APPENDICES, ETC.

INDEX TO THE APPENDICES, ETC.

INDEX TO THE APPENDICES, ETC.

THE END

Printed by BALLANTYNE, HANSON & Co.
Edinburgh & London

CPSIA information can be obtained
at www.ICGtesting.com
Printed in the USA
LVHW080530190619
621621LV00011B/137/P

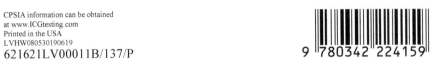